Pervasive Computing

Pervasive Computing
Next Generation Platforms for Intelligent Data Collection

Edited by

Ciprian Dobre and Fatos Xhafa

Series Editor: Fatos Xhafa

AMSTERDAM • BOSTON • HEIDELBERG • LONDON
NEW YORK • OXFORD • PARIS • SAN DIEGO
SAN FRANCISCO • SINGAPORE • SYDNEY • TOKYO

Academic Press is an imprint of Elsevier

Academic Press is an imprint of Elsevier
125 London Wall, London EC2Y 5AS, UK
525 B Street, Suite 1800, San Diego, CA 92101-4495, USA
50 Hampshire Street, 5th Floor, Cambridge, MA 02139, USA
The Boulevard, Langford Lane, Kidlington, Oxford OX5 1GB, UK

Notices
Knowledge and best practice in this field are constantly changing. As new research and experience
broaden our understanding, changes in research methods, professional practices, or medical
treatment may become necessary.

Practitioners and researchers must always rely on their own experience and knowledge in evaluating
and using any information, methods, compounds, or experiments described herein. In using such
information or methods they should be mindful of their own safety and the safety of others, including
parties for whom they have a professional responsibility.

To the fullest extent of the law, neither the Publisher nor the authors, contributors, or editors, assume
any liability for any injury and/or damage to persons or property as a matter of products liability,
negligence or otherwise, or from any use or operation of any methods, products, instructions, or
ideas contained in the material herein.

Library of Congress Cataloging-in-Publication Data
A catalog record for this book is available from the Library of Congress

British Library Cataloguing-in-Publication Data
A catalogue record for this book is available from the British Library

ISBN: 978-0-12-803663-1

For information on all Academic Press publications
visit our website at https://www.elsevier.com/

Working together
to grow libraries in
developing countries

www.elsevier.com • www.bookaid.org

The editors would like to express their outmost gratitude to all authors for their valuable and quality contributions toward making the book a comprehensive study of the area. We also want to thank the reviewers for their time and expertise, constructive comments, and valuable insight.

Contents

PART III   UBIQUITOUS SERVICES INDEPENDENT OF DEVICES/PLATFORMS

PART IV   PERVASIVE COMPUTING AND APPLICATIONS

Contributors

M. Aiash
Middlesex University, London, United Kingdom

M. Alazab
Macquarie University, Sydney, NSW, Australia

J.M. Almeida
Federal University of Minas Gerais, Belo Horizonte, MG, Brazil

L. Arantes
Sorbonne Universités, UPMC Univ Paris 06, CNRS, INRIA, LIP6, Paris, France

Y. Bocchi
HES-SO Valais, Institute of Information System, Sierre, Switzerland

G.A. Borges
Institute of Informatics, Federal University of Rio Grande do Sul, Porto Alegre, RS, Brazil

A. Bourdena
Technological Educational Institute of Crete, Crete, Greece

A. Carnielli
Middlesex University, London, United Kingdom

A. Capozzoli
Politecnico di Torino, Turin, Italy

T. Cerquitelli
Politecnico di Torino, Turin, Italy

C.S.F.S. Celes
Federal University of Minas Gerais, Belo Horizonte, MG, Brazil

M. Chinnici
ENEA, Rome, Italy

V. Cristea
University Politehnica of Bucharest, Bucharest, Romania

F.D. da Cunha
Federal University of Minas Gerais, Belo Horizonte, MG, Brazil

C. Dobre
University Politehnica of Bucharest, Bucharest, Romania

A.P.G. Ferreira
Federal University of Minas Gerais, Belo Horizonte, MG, Brazil

C.F.R. Geyer
Institute of Informatics, Federal University of Rio Grande do Sul, Porto Alegre, RS, Brazil

J. Gustedt
ICube, University of Strasbourg, Illkirch Cedex; INRIA, Le Chesnay Cedex, France

S.L. Hernane
ICube, University of Strasbourg, Illkirch Cedex, France

M. Imran
King Saud University, Almuzahmiah, Saudi Arabia

N. Javaid
COMSATS Institute of Information Technology, Islamabad, Pakistan

Z.A. Khan
Dalhousie University, Halifax, NS, Canada; Higher Colleges of Technology, Fujairah, United Arab Emirates

V. Leithardt
Institute of Informatics, Federal University of Rio Grande do Sul, Porto Alegre, RS, Brazil

A.A.F. Loureiro
Federal University of Minas Gerais, Belo Horizonte, MG, Brazil

D. Mahmood
COMSATS Institute of Information Technology, Islamabad, Pakistan

E. Markakis
Technological Educational Institute of Crete, Crete, Greece

G. Mastorakis
Technological Educational Institute of Crete, Crete, Greece

C.X. Mavromoustakis
University of Nicosia, Engomi, Nicosia, Cyprus

B.-C. Mocanu
University Politehnica of Bucharest, Bucharest, Romania

W. Moreira
COPELABS, University Lusofona, Lisbon, Portugal; PPGMO, Federal University of Goiás, Goiás, Brazil

V.F.S. Mota
Federal University of Minas Gerais, Belo Horizonte, MG, Brazil

D. Negru
University of Bordeaux I, Bordeaux, France

J.B.B. Neto
Federal University of Minas Gerais, Belo Horizonte, MG, Brazil

A.C. Olivieri
HES-SO Valais, Institute of Information System, Sierre, Switzerland

S. Pal
School of Computer Science, University of St Andrews, St Andrews, United Kingdom

E. Pallis
Technological Educational Institute of Crete, Crete, Greece

E.G. Pereira
Edge Hill University, Ormskirtk, United Kingdom

R. Pereira
Liverpool John Moores University, Liverpool, United Kingdom

M.S. Piscitelli
Politecnico di Torino, Turin, Italy

F. Pop
University Politehnica of Bucharest, Bucharest, Romania

U. Qasim
Cameron Library, University of Alberta, Edmonton, AB, Canada

A.I.J.T. Ribeiro
Federal University of Minas Gerais, Belo Horizonte, MG, Brazil

G. Rizzo
HES-SO Valais, Institute of Information System, Sierre, Switzerland

C.O. Rolim
Institute of Informatics, Federal University of Rio Grande do Sul, Porto Alegre, RS, Brazil

A.G.d.M. Rossetto
Federal Institute of Rio Grande do Sul (IFSUL), Passo Fundo, RS, Brazil

P. Sens
Sorbonne Universités, UPMC Univ Paris 06, CNRS, INRIA, LIP6, Paris, France

G. Serale
Politecnico di Torino, Turin, Italy

T.H. Silva
Federal University of Minas Gerais, Belo Horizonte, MG, Brazil; Federal University of Technology – Paraná, Curitiba, PR, Brazil

J. Sliwa
Bern University of Applied Sciences, Bern, Switzerland

P.O.S. Vaz de Melo
Federal University of Minas Gerais, Belo Horizonte, MG, Brazil

M. Zhanikeev
Kyushu Institute of Technology, Iizuka, Fukuoka Prefecture, Japan

About the Editors

Ciprian Dobre received his PhD in Computer Science in 2008 from the Computer Science Department at the University Politehnica of Bucharest (UPB), Romania. Currently, he holds a permanent position of Associate Professor at UPB, where he teaches classes on Parallel and Distributed Algorithms, Cloud Computing, and others. Ciprian Dobre has made early scientific and scholarly contributions to the field of large-scale distributed systems concerning mobile applications and smart technologies to reduce urban congestion and air pollution (coordinator of projects MobiWay and TranSys), context-aware applications (coordinator of CAPIM, projects SPRINT, ONSIDE, HYCCUPS, and others), monitoring (project MonALISA), high-speed networking (projects VINCI and FDT), and evaluation using modeling and simulation (developer of MONARC 2, coordinator of projects VNSim and Sim2Car). Such contributions have led to results that are beyond state-of-the-art. Ciprian Dobre was awarded a PhD scholarship from California Institute of Technology (Caltech, USA), and another one from Oracle. His results received one IBM Faculty Award, two CENIC Awards, and three Best Paper Awards. Dr. Dobre has published widely in peer-reviewed international journals, conferences/workshops, book chapters and edited books, and proceedings in the field: over 100 books, chapters in edited books, and articles in major international peer-reviewed journals and in well-established international conferences and workshops. Currently he is local project coordinator for national projects "CAPIM—Context-Aware Platform Using Integrated Mobile Services," and "MobiWay—Mobility beyond Individualism." Ciprian Dobre's research interests involve research subjects related to mobile wireless networks and computing applications, pervasive services, context-awareness, and people-centric or participatory sensing. He can be reached at ciprian.dobre@cs.pub.ro and more information can be found at http://cipsm.hpc.pub.ro.

Fatos Xhafa received his PhD in Computer Science in 1998 from the Department of Computer Science of the Technical University of Catalonia (UPC), Barcelona, Spain. Currently, he holds a permanent position of Professor Titular at UPC, BarcelonaTech. He was a Visiting Professor at Birkbeck College, University of London (UK) during the academic year 2009–10 and Research Associate at Drexel University, Philadelphia (USA) during academic term 2004–05. Dr. Xhafa has widely published in peer-reviewed international journals, conferences/workshops, book chapters and edited books, and proceedings in the field (http://dblp.uni-trier.de/pers/hd/x/Xhafa:Fatos). He has been awarded teaching and research merits by Spanish Ministry of Science and Education. Dr. Xhafa has an extensive editorial and reviewing service. He is editor in chief of *International Journal of Grid and Utility Computing* and *International Journal of Space-Based and Situated Computing* from Inderscience. He is actively participating in the organization of several international conferences and workshops. His research interests include parallel and distributed algorithms, optimization, networking, P2P and cloud computing, security and trustworthy computing, among others. He can be reached at fatos@cs.upc.edu and more information can be found at http://www.cs.upc.edu/ fatos/.

Foreword

A revolution is occurring today in terms of how pervasive computing hardware is designed, prototyped, and manufactured, as a broad set of researchers and users now have access to a host of digital fabrication tools and techniques that empower them to create new devices and realize new concepts more quickly, cheaply, and easily. Pervasive technologies are finding their way into every aspect of our lives. Still, many fundamental issues in pervasive computing remain open.

As technology becomes more miniaturized, and it supports mobility for novel application models where users are able to access content that is dependent on context, anywhere and anytime, *pervasive computing* (also called ubiquitous computing) is a growing trend and embedding devices into everyday objects so they can communicate information is now commonplace. As a field of research, it relies on the convergence of wireless technologies, advanced electronics and the Internet, and introduces revolutionary paradigms to the computing models of the 21st century.

Tremendous developments in such technologies as wireless communication and networking, mobile computing and handheld devices, embedded systems, wearable computers, sensors, RFID tags, smart spaces, middleware and software agents, and the like, have led to the evolution of pervasive computing platforms as a natural successor to mobile computing systems. However, being a relatively young area of research, pervasive computing still has a lot of problems that need to be overcome. In particular, the book presents advances toward the creation of *next generation platforms for smart data collection*. The type of the received sensor data can change together with the dynamics of the participating devices. Moreover the quality of the data, in terms of accuracy, latency and availability may vary with the mobility of devices, or with the dynamics of the environment. Difficulties are partly caused by a lack of sufficient, properly validated application information obtained from the raw sensed data. As a consequence, automatically deriving accurate predictions, for example, based on input from various data sources is generally lacking. This leaves the experts to rely mostly only on their experience when it comes to developing proactive solutions for pervasive data monitoring (such as in participatory sensing).

Creating a data system that deals with missing or erroneous data in an adaptive and scalable manner is another key factor in the construction of robust pervasive systems. Security and privacy of individuals also need to be ensured (eg, recording the location at any given time can go against a user's wishes). The time it takes for the data to reach its destination must be kept under minimum (data could be useful only for a few minutes or hours), as data only make sense in the context of certain events. Thus, networking technologies to support efficient and smart data collection processes need to be designed. Applications need to include the necessary levels of context-aware intelligence.

The present book provides solutions in this field that are state-of-the-art and beyond, following both theoretical and practical results. Effective pervasive computing requires appropriate ICT algorithms, architectures, and platforms, keeping in view the advances of science in this area and the development of new and innovative connected solutions (particularly in fields such as pervasive wireless and mobile networks, Big Data and Cloud Computing, Internet of Things, and Mobile Computing). The book is intended as a platform for the dissemination of research efforts and presentation of advances in pervasive computing, and constitutes a flagship driver toward presenting and supporting advance research in this area.

I would like to stress the high quality of the chapters in this book, providing views on the solutions, challenges, and research trends around three critical technical issues: location, scale, and networking. The multidisciplinary nature of this book is a valuable feature. It comprises domains such as computer science, computer engineering, applied informatics, intelligent processing systems, information systems, computational modeling, data technologies, sensorial technologies, and privacy, trust, and security. In the new era of Internet technologies, it is necessary to increase efforts and provide professionals and students with state-of-the-art knowledge on the principles and technologies for developing pervasive systems and platforms for smart data collection. This book is a valuable achievement in that direction and I would like to congratulate the editors.

I hope the readers will enjoy the book and will find it useful for their professional activity.

Professor Nicolae Ţăpuş
University Politehnica of Bucharest,
Bucharest, Romania

Nicolae Ţăpuş is a Professor of the Computer Science and Engineering Department, Head of Department, and Vice President of Politehnica University. His main fields of expertise are Distributed Systems, Local Area Networks, Computer Architecture, and Grid Computing. He is member of the board of the National Centre for Information Technology. Nicolae Ţăpuş published more than 140 articles and papers at international conferences, 7 books and 12 university textbooks. He is PhD supervisor. He was a visiting professor in European and U.S. universities. Prof. Ţăpuş was advisor for student team's winners at IEEE Annual Computer Society International Design Competition (CSIDC): first place in the world in 2002. Romanian Academy—1975 and Education Ministry—1978 awarded his activities; He is Member of Romanian Technical Science Academy (2004) and Vice President of Information Technology and Communication Academy Section. Prof. Ţăpuş is involved in FP7 research activities as responsible of Romania team of SENSEI—Integrating the Physical with the Digital World of the Network of the Future, FP7-ICT-2007-1, P2P-Next Next Generation Peer-to-Peer Content Delivery Platform, FP7-ICT-2007-1, EU-NCIT leading to EU IST Excellency, HP-SEE. He is a senior member of the IEEE and senior member of the ACM.

Preface

Starting from Mark Weiser's vision of ubiquitous computing, as technologies that disappear and weave into the fabric of everyday life until they are indistinguishable from it, the pervasive computing domain have seen a lot of progress lately. The essence of this vision is the creation of environments saturated with computing and communication capability, yet gracefully integrated with human users. Many critical elements of pervasive computing that were exotic back in Weiser's time, are now viable commercial products: wearable computers, smart mobile and wireless technologies, and devices to sense and control appliances. Pervasive computing projects have emerged at major universities and in industry, each address a different mix of issues in pervasive computing, and a different blend of near-term and far-term goals. Together, they represent a broad communal effort to make pervasive computing a reality.

For the past 20 years, the pervasive computing community has developed technology that allows sensing, computing, and wireless communication to be embedded into everyday objects, from cell phones to running shoes, enabling a range of context-aware applications. Pervasive computing is supported by technology able to acquire and make use of the ubiquitous data sensed or produced by many sensors blended into our environment, designed to make a wide range of new context-aware applications and systems available. While such applications and systems are useful, the time has come to develop the next generation of pervasive computing systems. Today, pervasive computing is all about the convergence of virtually all types of information technology: hardware (PCs, routers, switches, and wearable and mobile consumer electronics); software (operating systems, application, middleware, and network management); Internet, telcos, wireless, and other service providers (SPs); consultants, system integrators, and networking; along with broadcasters, cable TV, and content providers. Future systems will need to further support applications that have much deeper awareness of users and their activities, context, and goals. They will be able to learn and adapt continuously to users' habits, routines, and preferences. These future applications will be capable of supporting complex tasks. In the process, they will deliver far richer user experiences than the technologies of today can offer.

Researchers working in pervasive computing create smart products that communicate unobtrusively, by being connected to the Internet and generating easily available data. In pervasive computing, the world around us (eg, key chains, coffee mugs, computers, appliances, cars, homes, offices, cities, or the human body) is interconnected as a pervasive network of intelligent devices that cooperatively and autonomously collect, process and transport information that adapts to context and activity. In this field, the book presents current advances and state-of-the-art work on the methods, techniques, and algorithms designed to support the pervasive collection of data, using ubiquitous networks of devices that are able to intelligently collaborate toward common goals. The book features contributions from a selection of experts and highly visible researchers and practitioners in the field of pervasive computing.

The book's mission is to make readers familiar with the concepts and technologies that are successfully used in the implementation of pervasive systems, or have a good chance to be used in the future developments of such systems. The approach involves not separating the theoretical concepts concerning the design of such systems from their real-world implementations. For each important topic that one should master, the book plays the role of a bridge between the theory and practice and of the instrument needed by professionals in their activity. To this aim, the topics are presented in a logical sequence, and the introduction of each topic is motivated by the need to respond to claims and requirements coming from a wide range of pervasive applications. The advantages and limitations of each model or technology in terms of capabilities and areas of applicability are presented through concrete case studies for pervasive systems and applications.

The structure of the book aims to ensure a pleasant reading and has an intuitive style to guarantee the successful description of complex issues in fairly easy-to-comprehend terms. The chapters in this book present approaches, views, and discussions, and identify challenges and future research trends in the field of pervasive systems, showing success stories in the building of smart platforms for sensing, collecting, and exchanging information using the myriad devices surrounding the user's environment. The chapters of the book provide the basis for developing such platforms in the future, showing technical solutions to effectively deal with the challenges, such as quality of data, understanding and actively using context, dealing with trust and security, and many others.

ORGANIZATION OF THE BOOK

The book is organized into 14 chapters. A brief description of each chapter follows:

Chapter 1 by Carnielli et al. discusses privacy challenges in cloud-based systems, specifically presenting a qualitative analysis of the feasibility and efficiency of The Onion Router (ToR) in cloud infrastructure and the possibility of integrating ToR with cloud applications. With the ever increasing integration of mobile devices with cloud systems, as well as the increasing growth of social networking, this research and development topic is indeed very important nowadays, due to the need to support demanding requirements of security and privacy.

Chapter 2 by Mocanu et al. presents a survey of existing solutions for Peer-to-Peer (P2P) overlays. The review is split into three categories (of overlays): unstructured, structured, and bio-inspired overlays. For each overlay, the authors present the main principles and operations. For each category, authors draw conclusions and present a comprehensive discussion, showing current limitations and challenges still needing answers in the field. Such challenges include aspects related to redundancy and replication (with appropriate solutions to deal with data consistency), autonomous resource management, or security privacy aspects.

From this perspective, the chapter creates an overview for practitioners in the field of current and near-future trends.

In Chapter 3, Silva et al. present an analysis of participatory sensor networks, showing an overview of the area, and discussing both the challenges and opportunities. With the ever increasing integration of mobile devices with cloud systems, as well as high growth of social networking, this research and development topic is indeed very important nowadays. Authors show how participatory sensor networks, such as Instagram, Foursquare, and/or Waze, can be valuable sources of large-scale sensing, providing access to important characteristics of city dynamics and urban social behavior.

Olivieri et al. in Chapter 4 present an integration platform for Internet of Things (IoT) systems. They propose to surround a Publish/Subscribe framework developed within an EU project, with a layer that allows different IoT technologies to be easily interfaced with the framework (the motivating example is quite illustrative for this process). This research and development topic is very important nowadays and will be even more so in the near future. The authors discuss the issues and challenges to the integration of various protocols and technologies in IoT systems and mainstream technologies.

In Chapter 5, Markakis et al. propose a context-aware system for content delivery to support efficient resource sharing among different Home-Boxes (HBs), by exploiting P2P approaches and configurations. Instead of retrieving content from the servers solely, the HB can download content from other HBs, which are caching and forwarding/seeding the content. A HB P2P Engine module is exploited to assist the content distribution. The proposed approach brings the best of P2P content delivery mechanism, ie, being cheap and scalable, to the managed networks, instead of over-the-top delivery. Through this symbiosis, most of the P2P limitations may be overcome and some control to the SP. Via this integration, the SP is now able to control exactly who, how, when, and where the content is being accessed and distributed in the entire services delivery infrastructure. This research and development topic is very important nowadays and will be even more so in the near future. In particular, the authors discuss the issues and challenges for HBs P2P approaches, which is of extreme value to practitioners.

Hernane and Gustedt in Chapter 6 present an architecture for sharing resources transparently in large distributed systems. Their approach is based on Data Handover technique together with a P2P system. The authors discuss consistency problems and present two algorithms to address them. This research topic is very important nowadays due to ever increasing amount of data and the need to share it among large numbers of users.

Zhanikeev in Chapter 7 presents an information-centric space based on the concept of converged wireless networks (two connectivity modes—3G/LTE/WiFi and P2P WiFi) and wireless data hubs. The wireless networking inside the space converges because it uses at least two connectivity modes—3G/LTE/WiFi and P2P WiFi. This research and development topic is very important nowadays and will be even more so in the near future. The P2P WiFi functionality is an interesting and promising feature to be further explored in the area of pervasive computing.

In Chapter 8, Mahmood et al. present data fusion and data fusion algorithms for orientation sensing, considering wireless body area networks, and it compares two algorithms (ie, Kalman and Complementary data fusion techniques). The research and development topic is very important nowadays especially due to fast advances in sensor networks and applications in eHealth and monitoring-based applications.

Sliwa in Chapter 9 presents an interesting analysis of today's limitations for implementing truly reliable ambient assisted living patient-monitoring systems, making a distinction from the ideal vision being presented by so many authors before. The author advocates the use of data gathered from smart medical devices in the health system for several purposes: health support, quality assurance, and medical research. The author presents novel ideas on how to construct a vendor-independent, neutral system of quality monitoring (organizational and architectural dimensions). This research and development topic on eHealth is very important nowadays especially considering the speed at which advances in smart medical devices, applications in eHealth, and monitoring-based applications are occurring.

In Chapter 10, Chinnici et al. presents a critical analysis of existing energy, thermal, and productivity metrics for Data Centers—the study provides a methodology aimed at measuring the energy efficiency in Data Centers through a framework, and critically considering the advantages and the shortcomings of existing and emerging metrics. They present a comprehensive overview of energy, thermal, and productivity metrics for Data Centers as well as a general methodology for the measurement of the energy efficiency in Data Centers comprising a set of metrics. This research and development topic on energy consumption for Data Centers is very important nowadays especially due to the constant advances in Cloud Computing and social networking.

In Chapter 11, Capozzoli et al. present an analysis of the different platforms for buildings to exploit novel technologies based on sensor networks, smart meters, and database management systems in order to collect and store energy-related data. The authors use analytics technologies to characterize energy consumption and identify the main factors that increase energy consumption in order to improve energy efficiency. This is an interesting and up-to-date research topic, with relevant impacts on application-related to energy efficiency.

Rossetto et al. in Chapter 12 propose an unreliable failure detector for pervasive computing systems, which is based on the processes' relevance and the confidence degree in the system, for a self-healing system. Among the advantages, it offers a degree of flexibility for the user to tune it according to the needs and acceptable margin of failure for the upper-layer application. With the ever increasing spread of IoT systems, this research and development topic is indeed very important nowadays due to the need to mitigate faults in pervasive (and especially IoT) systems.

In Chapter 13, Pereira and Pereira discuss and present the IoT as a potential enabler in video streaming. It is an emerging scenario that brings substantial challenges and opportunities in video streaming field. The authors discuss important streaming technologies, such as video compression, streaming protocols, and Content Delivery Networks, together with the challenges associated and interactions between them. With the ever increasing spread of IoT systems and social networking, this research and development topic is important due to the needs to support demanding quality of service requirements.

Finally, **Pal and Moreira in Chapter 14** makes an interesting analysis of privacy and security challenges related to the adoption of mobile opportunistic (challenged) networks as a means for users to send/retrieve information in constrained locations. Authors address both the networking issues and functional challenges related to these networks. With the ever increasing integration of mobile devices with cloud systems, as well as the increasing growth of social networking, it is very important nowadays to support the demanding requirements of security and privacy.

Ciprian Dobre
University Politehnica of Bucharest, Romania
Fatos Xhafa
Universitat Politècnica de Catalunya, Spain

Acknowledgments

Ciprian Dobre's work was supported by the nationals project MobiWay: Mobility beyond Individualism (ref. PN-II-PT-PCCA-2013-4-0321) and DataWay: Real-Time Data Processing Platform for Smart Cities: Making sense of Big Data (ref. PN-II-RU-TE-2014-4-273).

Fatos Xhafa's work was supported by the Spanish Ministry for Economy and Competitiveness (MINECO) and the European Union (FEDER funds) under grant COMMAS (ref. TIN2013-46181-C2-1-R).

Automated capture of experiences with easy access

On preserving privacy in cloud computing using ToR

A. Carnielli[a], M. Aiash[a], M. Alazab[b]
Middlesex University, London, United Kingdom[a]
Macquarie University, Sydney, NSW, Australia[b]

1 INTRODUCTION

Over the past two decades, threats to users' privacy and identities have been of rising concern for Internet surfers. According to a report on anonymity, privacy, and security online (Dingledine et al., 2004), most Internet users would like to be anonymous online, at least occasionally, but many think it is not possible to be completely anonymous. The reasons behind such a belief vary from the increasing number of data leakage scandals, to the increasing demands by surfers to not be observed by specific people, organizations, or governments. The report in Dingledine et al. (2004) shows that 55% of Internet users have taken steps online to remove or mask their digital footprints and to avoid their activities being monitored and traced. Such steps range from clearing cookies to encrypting their email and using virtual networks that mask their Internet Protocol (IP) address. Such an attitude is ascribed to the fact that certain authoritative bodies and governments tend to misuse their power and spy on their own people. Several governments also filter specific websites through their border gateways in order to prevent flows of information from reaching their countries (as is the case for People's Republic of China, North Korea, Bahrain, Iran, Vietnam (Rininsland, 2012), or, most recently, Venezuela (Bajak, 2014)).

Obviously, governments justify these activities of wire-tapping and interception as measures to ensure the "National Security." Nevertheless, because of the invasive nature of such methods, Internet dwellers began to design and develop software in the forms of browsing anonymizers and communication obfuscation techniques to maintain their privacy and anonymity in the cyber world. Furthermore, considering the situation and events in some parts of the world such as "The Arab Spring" in the Middle East, hiding one's identity while browsing the Internet might be crucial for personnel safety in these oppressive countries.

This situation highlights the huge demand placed on security mechanisms for protecting users' privacy and anonymity on the Internet. An example of such a mechanism that has been made freely available to users is called The Onion Router

Pervasive Computing. http://dx.doi.org/10.1016/B978-0-12-803663-1.00001-2

(ToR) (Fang et al., 2000; Danezis et al., 2010; Michael et al., 2010). ToR has been designed to make it possible for users to surf the Internet anonymously, so that their activities and locations cannot be discovered by government agencies, corporations, or anyone else. Compared with other anonymizers such as Invisible Internet Project (I2P) (Wang et al., 2011), ToR is more popular; has more visibility in the academic and hacker communities; and benefits from formal studies of anonymity, resistance, and performance.

ToR and other anonymizers were initially conceived to run over the traditional Internet. However, the emergence and wide adoption of cloud-based services raises huge doubts about the efficiency of these anonymizers if used with these new technologies. Furthermore, customers of cloud computing have more concerns about the secrecy of their data, due to the fact that such data are being moved from the client's local devices to third party online storage. The purpose of this research is to analyze the feasibility of running the ToR network on top of an infrastructure embracing both the traditional and the cloud computing models.

The rest of the paper is organized as follows. Section 2 gives an overview of cloud computing architecture and sheds light on issues such as privacy and anonymity in cloud computing. Section 3 describes the ToR network. Our experiments to deploy ToR with cloud-based services are described in Section 4.

2 OVERVIEW OF CLOUD COMPUTING

Arguably, there is not a single, unified definition for cloud computing. Being a relatively new concept, different institutions and researchers define cloud computing in their own way; obviously, the key features of the cloud remain the same in each definition. Foster et al. (in Zhao et al., 2008) give a very deterministic and perhaps complicated delineation of this new technology. They define cloud computing as "A large-scale distributed computing paradigm that is driven by economies of scale, in which a pool of abstracted, virtualized, dynamically scalable, managed computing power, storage, platforms, and services are delivered on demand to external customers over the Internet." In this research, when referring to cloud computing, we avail ourselves of the following simpler description, given by Danish et al. (in Wang et al., 2011): "Cloud Computing technology is a new concept of providing dramatically scalable and virtualized resources, bandwidth, software and hardware on demand to consumers. Consumers can typically requests Cloud services via a web browser or web service."

The statement is self-explanatory. In simple terms, cloud computing is a revolutionary way of providing users (who may be a single person or even medium-size companies) with all the kinds of IT resources that they may need in order to fulfill their IT infrastructure requirements. In a cloud computing environment, there are two main players: the cloud provider (CP) (who owns a very huge data center and loans hardware and software resources) and the cloud consumer (who pays a fee to use

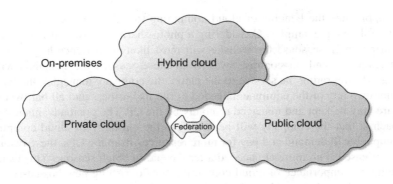

FIG. 1

Types of cloud computing.

From Ribeiro, M., 2010. Thoughts on Information Technology. https:// itechthoughts.wordpress.com/ .

such resources). Three main categories (models) exist for cloud deployment: public cloud, private cloud, and hybrid cloud as shown in Fig. 1.

When the hardware and software resources of a CPs data center are available as a pay-as-you-go service to the general public, the infrastructure is called a public cloud. When, on the other hand, the data center's resources are only available to a group of users confined within the perimeter of a company's internal network (such as its Intranet), the infrastructure is called a private cloud. A hybrid cloud forms in cases where the internal users of a big corporation or institution can afford both a public and a private cloud and are forced to utilize some of the public cloud resources in order to accomplish tasks that were meant to be executed within the private cloud environment. The latter situation can arise when the amount of tasks to be accomplished in a specific time frame is so high that the private cloud's infrastructure is not enough.

2.1 CLOUD COMPUTING REFERENCE MODEL

In cloud computing, because of the extremely high availability of hardware and software components, thanks to the improvements in virtualization techniques, resources appear infinite to the consumers, who do not have to worry about any possible under-provisioning. All resources, in fact, are being used almost ceaselessly since they are virtualized (estimates of the average server utilization in conventional data centers range from 5% to 20% according to Rivlin, 2008) and hence their throughput is maximized. Apart from under-provisioning, users do not need to worry about over-provisioning either because cloud consumers pay only for the resources they need on a very short-term basis (for certain resources, such as CPUs, the granularity is as fine as an hourly fee).

To appreciate the benefits of cloud computing to online service providers, we give the following examples. Considering a photo-sharing website: it is anticipated that during "high seasons" the website will most likely experience huge demands on its resources and, in contrast away from these seasons the demands will be minimal. By migrating the service to the cloud, the company managing the website need not own any of the equipment needed to run its business and all hardware and software may be kept and managed remotely by the CP. The great advantage of this approach is that the company will benefit from the elasticity of cloud computing; the company will demand and pay for more resources from the CPs, these resources will be released if no more are needed after the end of "high season." This example highlights the importance of cloud computing for flourishing new businesses. One major technology that enables this flexibility in cloud computing is virtualization. With virtualization, a CP uses a virtual machine monitor to manage and share the hardware resources among different virtual machines and can also seamlessly set up and run more virtual machines to accommodate customers' demands. This concept is shown in Fig. 2.

As shown in Fig. 3, cloud computing comprises the following computing services at both hardware and software levels (Aiash et al., 2015).

- **Infrastructure as a Service (IaaS)** provides the infrastructural components in terms of processing, storage, and networking. It uses virtualization techniques to provide multi-tenancy, scalability, and isolation; different virtual machines can be allocated to a single physical machine known as the host. Examples of such service are Amazon S3, EC2; Mosso and OpenNebula (Varia et al., 2014; Llorente, 2014).

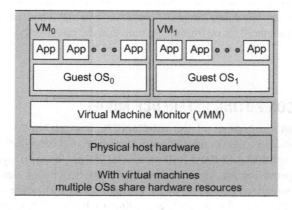

FIG. 2

VM architecture.

From Walker, G., 2012. Cloud Computing Fundamentals. https://www.ibm.com/developerworks/cloud/library/cl-cloudintro/.

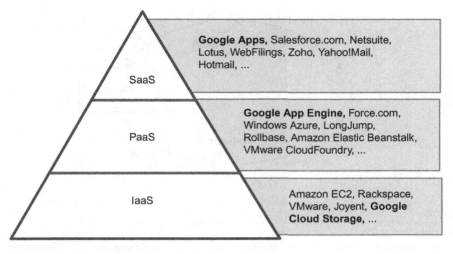

FIG. 3

Cloud computing architecture.

From Aiash, M., et al., 2015. Introducing a hybrid infrastructure and information-centric approach for secure cloud computing. In: Proceedings of IEEE 29th International Conference on Advanced Information Networking and Applications Workshops (WAINA).

- **Platform as a Service (PaaS)** provides the service of running applications without the hassle of maintaining the hardware and software infrastructure of the IaaS. Google App Engine and Microsoft Azure (Tulloch, 2013) are examples of PaaS.
- **Software as a Service (SaaS)** is a model of software deployment that enables end-users to run their software and applications on-demand. Examples of SaaS are Salesforce.com and Clarizen.com.

2.2 PRIVACY IN THE CLOUD

"A significant barrier to the adoption of Cloud services is customer fear of privacy loss in the Cloud" (Khan et al., 2012). The statement highlights one of the major problems in cloud computing. According to a statistic of the Fujitsu Research Institute (Fujitsu Research Institute, 2010), 88% of potential cloud customers are hesitating on whether to move to the cloud because of their concerns about the privacy of their data. Due to the intrinsic nature of this new technology and to the concerns shown by customers, privacy-preservability has been considered as a fundamental requirement for cloud computing. When a customer decides to entrust his or her data to a third party corporation, he or she has to be aware of the fact that the data might be physically stored together with sensitive information of other companies. This implies that an efficient access control system must be put in place

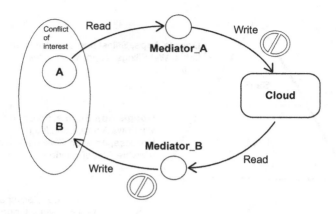

FIG. 4

Chinese wall model.

From David, F., et al., 2013. The Chinese Wall Security Policy. http://www.gammassl.co.uk/research/
chinesewall.php.

in order to avoid privacy violations. To clarify this important concept, let us provide an example. Suppose that two banks "A" and "B" rely on the same CP and use the same model (IaaS). Each bank holds very confidential information about its clients (account numbers, balance, last transactions, etc.). Due to the deployment of virtualization by the CP, the sensitive information from "A" is likely to physically reside together with other information, not pertaining to "A." Indeed, data belonging to "A" may be contiguous in the memory device to the data belonging to "B." This means that if a very efficient access control system is not in place, the two competitors may be able to access each other's data. One of the various solutions to this problem is an access control policy called the "Chinese wall model," which prevents two competitors who have a conflict of interests from accessing the information that does not belong to them. The Chinese wall model is illustrated in Fig. 4.

In simple terms, the figure shows that if bank "A" shares the same CP as bank "B," then the data from "A" will not be readable to "B" and vice versa. This is possible thanks to the property of the Chinese wall model that states that "A subject (s) is permitted write access to an object only if (s) has no read access to any object o', which is in a different company dataset and is unsanitized." In this case, (s) is the bank "B," (o') is the information from bank "A," and both "A" and "B" have two different company datasets. If "B" tries to access the information from "A," the operation will be denied. The same happens if "A" tries to access the information from "B." This example is just used for highlighting the severity of data privacy issue in cloud computing. This is a major issue and has attracted huge research efforts. Discussing these efforts is beyond the scope of this paper; nevertheless, more information about the Chinese wall model can be found in Brewer et al. (2013).

Another example that highlights the importance of privacy in a shared infrastructure such as that of a public cloud is the one of medical data. Imagine if it was possible for users of a cloud to access all the information in that cloud. More technically, imagine if a customer renting a pool of shared memory devices from a CP could access all the information on those devices (even though it did not belong to the customer). The consequences would be dramatic, especially if non-authorized users had access to medical records of the patients of a health institution.

Besides access-control mechanisms, there are other ways to enforce privacy-preservation. Confidentiality and integrity together provide a sort of data privacy. By using confidentiality, unauthorized users will not be able to understand the data. By using integrity, if any user tries to modify the data this will be detected and the data owner alerted (via checksum or Cyclic Redundancy Check or any other integrity checking algorithm). As Xiao et al. discuss in Xiao and Xiao (2013), "In some sense, privacy-preservability is a stricter form of confidentiality, due to the notion that they both prevent information leakage." We share the view that in order to enforce privacy, confidentiality is an essential factor. If data are being encrypted and the decryption key is known only to the designated parties, such data are going to be readable by but not understandable to anyone who does not have the decryption key, hence guaranteeing privacy. Providing integrity to the encrypted data further ensures that these data have not been altered and this, therefore, ensures privacy. Unfortunately, encrypting data using an algorithm that is both strong and efficient is a very expensive operation and is not yet feasible without heavily affecting performance. In an environment such as the cloud, where a tsunami of data is being processed every second, the amount of encryption/decryption operations per second would be extremely high. A solution that has been adopted by the computer experts and by the non-standard users is encryption before submission. In this procedure, data/processes are being encrypted directly by the user before submitting them to the cloud, where they are handled in an encrypted form. This solution has several positive perspectives but it has not been widely deployed yet due to the lack of knowledge of the standard user. There is another property which is necessary and is argued to enhance privacy, but which actually may undermine it: accountability. Accountability is the process of monitoring the resources used by a customer and charging him or her accordingly. This property is at the center of a battle of opinions because some researchers claim accountability and confidentiality to be in conflict due to the fact that if you avail yourself of one, you automatically renounce the other. We acknowledge that accountability and confidentiality are two distinct properties that can work very well together if the underlying system is designed and configured in an appropriate manner.

Although a full privacy-preserving solution in cloud computing has not been standardized as yet, studies and attempts have been made to integrate such a service in the cloud environment. In Craig (2009), Gentry proposed Fully Homomorphic Encryption (FHE), which appears to work well but is still too inefficient for practical use since the complexity of the involved operations is greater than the acceptable level to which average CPUs work nowadays. A possible solution to this problem might be a sort of reduced homomorphic encryption; an example is the one presented by Naehrig et al. (in Craig, 2009). Itani et al. (2009) presented Privacy-as-a-Service, which tries to exploit the power corruption-proof characteristics of cryptographic coprocessors in order to enable secure storage and data privacy. This scheme could work well if the protected environment in which the coprocessors reside within the cloud infrastructure is part of a trusted party and is constantly monitored against tampering. Pearson et al. (in Pearson et al., 2009; Miranda and Siani, 2009) discussed a privacy manager that works by using obfuscation and de-obfuscation techniques on data in order to process such data only when they are already in an encrypted form. In this case, data are obfuscated with a user-chosen key before being sent to the cloud in such a way that the cloud cannot de-obfuscate them. This guarantees absolute secrecy. Most recently, Jin Li et al. considered the challenge of data privacy in the cloud. In Li et al. (2015a), they proposed L-EncDB, a novel lightweight encryption mechanism for database, which (i) keeps the database structure and (ii) supports efficient SQL-based queries. Furthermore, in Li et al. (2015b), they considered the problem of ensuring the integrity of data storage in cloud computing. The main aim was to reduce the computational cost to the user during the integrity verification of their data, especially in the case of power/resource-constrained users. To tackle the challenge, they proposed OPoR, a new cloud storage scheme involving a cloud storage server and a cloud audit server.

2.3 ANONYMITY IN THE CLOUD

Related to the problem of data privacy is the issue of preserving users' anonymity online. Arguably, anonymity have long been considered as a complementary security feature. However, as described in Section 1, anonymity and privacy are becoming rather fundamental services that should be available to online customers.

In this regard, Jensen et al. (2010) propose a possible method to guarantee anonymity in the cloud. However, such a method cannot work properly if the resources' billing process is not flat rate. The solution proposed by them involves ring and group signatures with the constraint of the cloud customer having a flat rate billing system instead of the usual pay-as-you-go system.

- In ring signatures, the cloud customers are part of a huge group the (L) of users. The bigger the (L) group is the greater the guaranteed anonymity level. Customers willing to request a cloud resource will have to sign the request anonymously with respect to (L). The cloud (which acts as the verifier) will be able to determine that the customer pertains to (L), but will not be able to decide which member of (L) produced the signature. This way, anonymity will be guaranteed for requests. However, in the case of a two-way interaction where the customer needs an output, additional anonymity-preserving measures will have to be deployed. In addition, by using ring signatures the cloud cannot identify the source of a request and that is why this scheme works only if the users of (L) use a flat rate billing procedure, by which they pay an initial fee and then are allowed to use resources for a determined time frame. It is not possible to charge using the traditional pay-as-you-go method.

- In group signatures, on the other hand, cloud customers have to register with a group manager that provides each user with a sort of public key infrastructure (PKI) certificate. Every request from a customer will be signed with the certificate and since the group manager is supposed to be a trusted entity, the identity of the requester will not be disclosed. In case of policy violations (eg, the cloud customer uploads illegal material on a website), however, the group manager will be authorized to reveal to the authorities in charge the identity of the lawbreaker.

However, for the time being, it is not yet possible to provide a full anonymity solution unless we rely on external anonymizing platforms such as ToR, as described in the following sections.

3 AN OVERVIEW OF ToR

ToR is a low-latency, circuit-based and privacy-preserving anonymizing platform and network. It is one of several systems that have been developed to provide Internet users with a high level of privacy and anonymity in order to cope with the censorship measures taken by authorities and to protect against the constantly increasing threats to these two key security properties. ToR achieves its goals by creating an overlay network, composed of relays (nodes) that randomly forward users' data between the originator (source) and destination. ToR, therefore, operates over the traditional TCP/IP network, sets up an overlay network that hides the identity of both source and destination nodes, and preserves the confidentiality of the traversing packets. It is worth mentioning that the words node and relay will be used interchangeability throughout the rest of the paper.

3.1 THE ToR NETWORK

The ToR network is composed of the ToR-client, an entry/guard node, several relays, and the exit node.

- The ToR-client: Is a piece of software, installed on each ToR user's device. It enables the user to create a ToR anonymizing circuit and to handle all the cryptographic keys needed to communicate with all the nodes within the circuit.
- The Entry Node: Is the first node in the circuit that receives the client request and forwards it to the second relay in the network.
- The Exit Node: Is the last ToR-relay in the circuit.

Once the connection request leaves the entry node, it will be bounced among all the relays in the circuit until it reaches the exit node. The latter receives the request and relays it to the final destination.

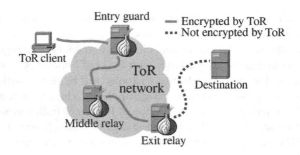

FIG. 5

The ToR network.

From ToR, 2015a. ToRChat. https://github.com/prof7bit/TorChat.

As shown in Fig. 5, the connections in the ToR network between the entry and exit nodes are encrypted using advanced encryption standard (AES). However, the connections between the exit node and the final destination are not encrypted by ToR. This implies that if the session between the client and the destination is not encrypted as part of a higher layer security protocol, such as the HTTPS, an attacker residing near the destination will be able to disclose the data.

3.2 CONNECTION/CIRCUIT SETUP IN ToR

As mentioned previously, ToR uses AES to encrypt the connections between the relays. However, AES is a symmetric encryption algorithm where the same key is used for encryption and decryption. This means that for the ToR-client to use AES, it needs to have shared encryption keys with the relaying nodes. For sharing these keys, ToR uses asymmetric encryption as part of the transport layer security (TLS) protocol.

Each connection from a ToR-relay to another within the ToR network is protected by the TLS protocol. At the moment of building the circuit, the ToR-client needs to gather all the public keys of the nodes in the circuit and has to establish a connection to each of them; these connections will be used to exchange the relevant symmetric keys. To agree on a shared key with a relay, the ToR client starts a Diffie-Hellman key exchange (Chaum, 1998). Initially, the ToR-client encrypts the Diffie-Hellman challenge with the public key of the receiver; it then encrypts the message obtained with the public key of the ToR-relay preceding the receiver in the circuit. This new message will be further encrypted with the public key of all the remaining relays in the circuit going backwards and in their order of encounter respectively. Eventually, the multi-encapsulated message is sent. This procedure is showed in Fig. 6.

When the entry node receives the message, sent from the ToR-client, it peels off the first layer of encryption using its private key and, hence, finds enclosed another encrypted message. The relay cannot decipher the enclosed message since it is encrypted with the public key of the next relay. However, within the content

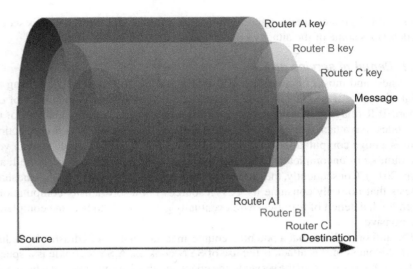

Router A key

Router B key

Router C key

Message

Router A

Router B

Router C

Source

Destination

FIG. 6

The ToR cryto-encapsulation.

From ToR, 2015b. What is the ToR Browser? https://www.torproject.org/projects/torbrowser.html.en.

that it can understand, it will receive its personal Diffie-Hellman challenge and the instruction to forward the rest of the message to the next relay. When the next relay in the circuit receives the message, it peels off another layer of the multi-encapsulated message (hence the name ToR) and similarly will not be able to understand the inner content except from the forwarding instruction and its own challenge. It is important to note that the routing information of each message is also encrypted with each relay's public key (that is why it is an encapsulation technique and not a simple encryption one). Using the multi-encapsulation guarantees that the intermediate relays are anonymized; each receiver cannot know the identity of the relay that comes after the next one in the circuit. Eventually, when the multi-decapsulated message reaches the exit relay, the latter will remove the encryption layer using its own private key and will retrieve its Diffie-Hellman challenge.

At this point, all the relays in the circuit are able to establish a secret shared with the ToR-client (by completing the challenge-response procedure), and the latter can start sending data to the final destination using symmetric encryption (which is by far less computationally expensive than the asymmetric one).

3.3 ATTACKS AGAINST ToR

Privacy mechanisms, such as SSL, ToR, and encrypting tunnels, hide the content of the data transferred, but they do not obscure the size, direction, and timing of packets transmitted between clients and remote servers. Researches have analyzed and demonstrated several flaws deriving from both conceptual and implementation issues, but the greatest attack opportunities derive from traffic analysis. This section will describes some of the attacks against ToR.

3.3.1 Denial of service attack

The easiest and most effective way to compromise the ToR system is by using the denial of service (DoS) attack. In this scenario, a malicious user is in control of one or more ToR-relays within the network and its aim is to attack the availability of the ToR nodes. An attacker exploits the fact that the establishment of TLS connections requires a huge computational power. In this attack, the malicious node starts a very large number of uncompleted TLS handshakes with the targeted node (Carnielli and Aiash, 2015). Consequently, the victim will be so overwhelmed with TLS handshake requests that not only consume its TCP resources but also drain its computational power. Such a deficit of resources will eventually get the node to become completely unresponsive.

The authors believe that a potential countermeasure that would drastically reduce the effectiveness of this attack is the use of SYN cookies. A SYN cookie is a special challenge that is sent from the server to the client and that is used to verify whether the client is actually willing to establish a connection to the server. In a scenario where SYN cookies are used, when the server, the victim of the ToR-relay in this case, receives a SYN packet from the client (the attacker), it will respond with another SYN packet which includes the cookie. If the client responds to the server with an ACK packet that includes the same cookie that was sent in the preceding message, the server will be assured that the source address of the initial SYN has not been spoofed, and hence will trust the client to complete the TLS handshake. In the case of an attack, the attacker will not respond to the SYN cookie if it has spoofed its address to launch the attack. Even if spoofing has not been used in the attack, the attacker needs to carry on with the creation of the TLS links, and responding to the SYN cookies will delay the attack and waste the attacker' processing power. ToR relays can in this way prevent fake TLS connection attempts and hence avoid the attack.

3.3.2 The timing attack

For this attack, the adversary needs to control both the entry and the exit relay of the ToR circuit. To perform the timing attack, the attacker needs to correlate the information gathered through traffic analysis at both endpoints. The attacker, in fact, attempts to detect an ongoing communication between two parties by just observing the time when packets leave the entry relay and when they reach the exit. As an outcome of a successful attack, the adversary will manage to correlate the traffic patterns on both ends of the connection and could, with high probability, guess which packet streams are related, hence breaking the anonymity property of ToR. However, despite the fact that the adversary will be able to determine (with a high percentage) the two communicating parties, it will not be able to disclose the payload of the traversing packets. The Dynamic Multipath Onion Router (MORE) has been proposed as a solution to address this attack. In the MORE scheme, the path taken by each packet traveling through the ToR network is different (Carnielli and Aiash, 2015). The first half of such a path is chosen by the initial ToR while the second half is chosen by the other endpoint. Since various packets take different circuits to reach the same destination, an adversary cannot successfully perform the timing attack. This is due to the fact that different circuits entail different traveling times. The drawback of this approach is that the initial ToR needs to know the public key of all the routers of all circuits and each time construct a new circuit with different public keys.

3.3.3 Website fingerprinting attack

In a web page fingerprinting attack, an adversary attempts to use information revealed from the ToR traffic to identify the web page a victim is visiting. This attack was initially proposed by Herrmann et al. (2009). In their research, the factors used to generate fingerprints were limited to the mere analysis of the size and timing of ToR packets. In this first version of the attack, due to the poor metrics that were used, Hermann et al. were able to detect only 3% of the websites that were visited in a browsing session. Carballuda (in Gonzalez, 2013) introduced a refined version of the attack by enhancing its metrics. In this enhanced version, extra metrics, such as the size of each packet's payload, the number of ACK packets and the number of packets between two ACK packets, are taken into consideration while performing traffic analysis. The extra metrics have produced incredibly improved results compared to the work of Hermann. This implies that website fingerprinting is an issue that should be considered carefully when using the ToR network to bypass censored sites.

3.4 ToR IN EXISTING IMPLEMENTATIONS

Although the ToR network is not as attack-resistant as it was initially believed to be, the number of ToR users is high nowadays and has been increasing over the past few years, as statistics from Sophos show (ToR, 2015b). The security properties provided by this technology attract not only the single user who wishes to remain anonymous during his or her web surfing sessions, but also entire systems that use ToR as a platform on which to rely in order to supply some services. An example of such systems is the Plug-and-Play IP Security, developed by Gilad et al. and described in Gilad and Herzberg (2013). Gilad and his research group combined ToR and the self-validated public data distribution (SvPDD) protocol (a protocol developed by them which makes it possible for two peers to exchange their public keys without the need for CAs or third party entities) to create a version of IP Sec that does not need manual configurations anymore since they become automated. Gilad et al. demonstrated how ToR can work without any issue with their PnP IP Sec model by implementing a real world scenario and by testing it. By carefully analyzing their work, it is possible to glimpse a security flaw in the SvPDD protocol; this conceptual bug, however, does not jeopardize the correct operation of ToR, which works very well as a supporting, anonymizing platform.

Other implementations of this powerful technology include the ToR Browser Bundle (ToR, 2015b) and the ToRChat (ToR, 2015a). The first one is a modified version of the Firefox browser from Mozilla, which runs on top of the ToR network in order to provide anonymity and privacy to users wishing to surf the web in a secure way. The second one is a decentralized anonymous instant messenger that runs on top of ToR. These two implementations are freely available to the public, together with their source code, in order to give the users the possibility to personalize them according to their needs.

4 ToR IN CLOUD COMPUTING

The discussion above is based on implementing ToR using the Internet in its current form. With the advent of cloud computing, users more than ever have the need for privacy and anonymity, since they entrust their data to CPs. If data are not protected properly within a cloud platform, users risk not only their confidentiality but also their anonymity (since the CP has to keep associations between users and data). Unfortunately, despite the research efforts, no authoritative body has designed or implemented a standard platform that delivers anonymity and privacy in cloud systems. In the absence of such a platform, we conducted practical research to investigate whether the existing ToR system could be merged to cloud computing ones in order to obtain a cooperation that would deliver privacy and anonymity in the cloud.

As mentioned in Section 1, few researchers have, to the best of our knowledge, investigated the feasibility of providing anonymity and privacy in the cloud using current anonymizers. Of particular interest among these are the "ToR Cloud Project" (ToR, 2013) and the "AnonymousCloud" project, led by Khan et al. (2012). In the ToR Cloud Project, the user is given the opportunity to access the IaaS cloud resources from Amazon while using the ToR. The AnonymousCloud, is a completely new and modern scheme that ensures that the customer of a cloud platform remain anonymous when using the platform itself, by making use of the ToR network. However, it is crucial to realize that the task of ensuring anonymity is particularly challenging in cloud computing since the system should guarantee accountability as well. Customers, must be able to access anonymously the cloud resources while their usage is being accounted to them at the same time.

The AnonymousCloud architecture, depicted in Fig. 7 comprises the customer (C), a manager (M) and the CP. The CP is further composed of a Master Node (MN) and multiple Slave Nodes (SNs) (hundreds of thousands). The Customer is the entity in the system requesting its data to be processed by AnonymousCloud; these can either be user data to be stored within the CP or Customer operations that should be kept private and confidential. The Manager is the system entity that authenticates customers and provides them with a list of the ToR relays, used to build a ToR circuit along with their public keys. The MN elaborates the requests made by the Customer

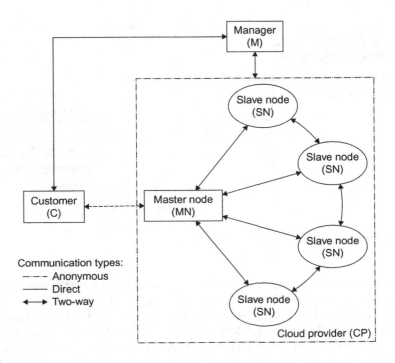

FIG. 7

The AnonymousCloud architecture.

based on information received by the Manager. Additionally, the MN manages the SNs which perform the operations requested by the Customer.

A key characteristic of the success of the AnonymousCloud is the separation between the user's data and the user's metadata. The user's data are the information that are meant to be elaborated by the SNs (eg, personal data or calculations) while the metadata contain information used to authenticate the Customer to the Manager (a token t, some credentials c, and a value k). The operation of the AnonymousCloud goes as follows: The first message sent at the beginning of a session contains t (which changes at every transaction in order to prevent replay attacks), c (known only by the Manager and the Customer and used for authentication), and k (which is a value that indicates to the Manager the number of desired relays within the ToR circuit). This whole message is encrypted with the public key of the Manager (K_M), so that only the latter can understand its content by using the private key. If the authentication procedure succeeds, the Manager sends back a list of SNs that will be used to create a ToR circuit between the Customer and the MN along with their public keys (K_{SN}), the public key of the MN (K_{MN}), and with a nonce (n) to prevent future replay attacks. On receipt of the message, the Customer builds the ToR circuit through the SNs and establishes an anonymous and private connection with the MN. Over this connection,

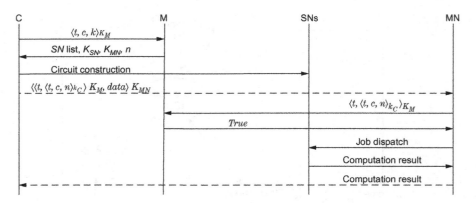

FIG. 8

The operation of AnonymousCloud architecture.

the Customer sends a multi-encrypted message that has two parts: authentication information and user data. The whole message is encrypted with (K_{MN}), as shown in Fig. 8, the enclosed authentication information are encrypted with the Manager's public key (K_M). Therefore, the MS will hold the user data part of the message and forward the authentication part to the Manager for verification. On successful authentication, the Manager will direct the MN to accept the data and to forward them to the SNs for processing. The SNs will elaborate the data and return the results to the MN which will eventually relay them via the anonymous connection to the Customer.

While this anonymizer achieves its goals, there are performance concerns in case of a large value of k. No such performance analysis has been conducted yet; however, analyzing the performance of the AnonymousCloud is beyond the scope of this paper. Furthermore, the AnonymousCloud is still at a development stage and has not been standardized yet. The authors advocate the need for a more mature privacy-preserving mechanism. Therefore, in the following section we analyze the feasibility of deploying an existent anonymizing network (ToR) to access three different cloud-based systems, namely Dropbox, Facebook, and YouTube.

4.1 OUR EXPERIMENTS

4.1.1 ToR with DropBox

When opening the ToR Browser to connect to Dropbox, it initially requires a minute to fully load; this is due to the creation of the ToR circuit, which involves public key cryptography, symmetric encryption and multiple nodes. Once the circuit is established, a connection to the Dropbox website is made, the website loads up almost as fast as if a traditional web browser was being used. At this point, the user is anonymous to Dropbox and the communication is confidential. When the credentials

FIG. 9

DropBox with ToR.

are inserted, these travel along the ToR network while being encrypted twice: first by ToR and then by the HTTPS protocol at the application layer. This ensures that the connection is fully private since not even the exit node is able to understand the content of the packets. Dropbox authenticates the client and the latter manages to access its account flawlessly, as shown in Fig. 9.

4.1.2 ToR with FaceBook

In order to perform the second experiment, an additional analysis metric is added. To effectively verify the properties that it is claimed the ToR network provides, we use Wireshark, a traffic analysis tool that captures and analyses the packets flowing from the client to the server. When connecting to the Facebook server, the page again loads quickly and without errors. Before inserting the login credentials, this time, the capture in Wireshark is started and the flow of packets is recorded. After the user logs in, the capture is stopped. Some of the output is shown in the Fig. 10.

As shown in Fig. 10, the traffic exchanged between the two IP addresses is TCP traffic. Wireshark is not able to detect which type of higher layer (application)

```
 8 1.026468000  192.168.1.8     94.242.209.120   TCP   552 45799→9001 [PSH, ACK] Seq=1847 Ack=1 Win=38283 Len=498
 9 1.071943000  94.242.209.120  192.168.1.8      TCP    60 9001→45799 [ACK] Seq=1 Ack=587 Win=501 Len=0
10 1.095729000  94.242.209.120  192.168.1.8      TCP    60 9001→45799 [ACK] Seq=1 Ack=1847 Win=501 Len=0
11 1.106349000  94.242.209.120  192.168.1.8      TCP    60 9001→45799 [ACK] Seq=1 Ack=2345 Win=501 Len=0
12 1.338663000  94.242.209.120  192.168.1.8      TCP   640 9001→45799 [PSH, ACK] Seq=1 Ack=2345 Win=501 Len=586
```

FIG. 10

Wireshark capture.

protocol is being used between the two endpoints and this is due to the onion-like encryption that ToR applies to all messages. Based on the discussion in Section 3, the client establishes a connection with the server through multiple nodes that repeatedly apply a cryptographic operation on a portion of the message. Consequently, the flow of traffic is confidential from the beginning to the end of its path. In addition to the level of encryption provided by the ToR network, the Facebook server uses TLS to secure data exchange with clients and, therefore, as with the Dropbox server, the traffic is encrypted beyond the exit relay. Furthermore, as shown in Fig. 10, it is possible to infer that the IP address of the client is 192.168.1.8 and the one of the server is 94.242.209.120. However, by reflecting on the ToR operation as described in Section 3, we anticipate that 94.242.209.120 is the IP address of the entry relay of the ToR circuit and not the Facebook server. In order for the client to remain anonymous, its packets have to be sent through several relays, starting from the entry one. The client first establishes a connection with this entry node before reaching the final destination and Wireshark is not aware of it; that is why the network analysis tool only shows the connection to the first hop and not to the rest of them. To confirm this, we avail ourselves of a free online tool to examine public IP addresses (IP address lookup) and we find out that effectively the 94.242.209.120 IP address does not pertain to the Facebook organization and it is a simple ToR relay in the Internet (located in Luxembourg precisely) as shown in Fig. 11. This test proves that we are not connected directly to the Facebook server even though the browser displays the

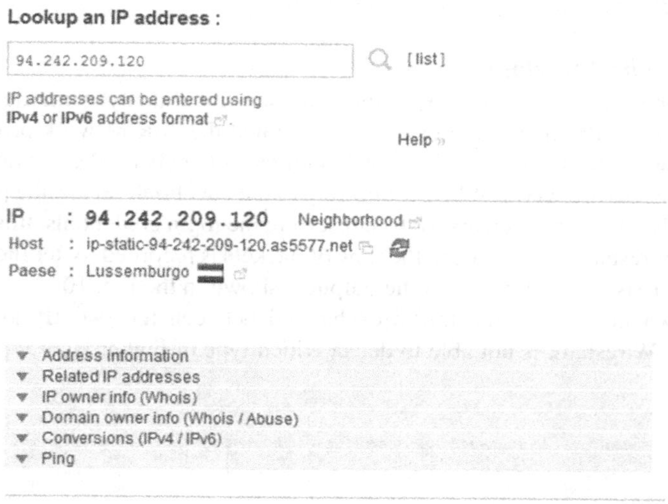

Lookup an IP address :

94.242.209.120 $\quad$ Q [list]

IP addresses can be entered using
IPv4 or IPv6 address format.

Help »

IP   : **94.242.209.120**   Neighborhood
Host   : ip-static-94-242-209-120.as5577.net
Paese : Lussemburgo

▼ Address information
▼ Related IP addresses
▼ IP owner info (Whois)
▼ Domain owner info (Whois / Abuse)
▼ Conversions (IPv4 / IPv6)
▼ Ping

FIG. 11

IP address lookup.

authentic Facebook main page. This means that the client is anonymous to the server and, therefore, ToR achieves its aims in this case as well.

4.1.3 ToR with Youtube

For the last test, the same metrics as with the previous experiments are taken into consideration. After opening the ToR Browser and waiting for it to build a circuit and load completely, the client requests a connection to the YouTube server. Similarly to with Dropbox and Facebook, the YouTube website opens quickly. In this case, before accessing the account, the language is automatically set to Polish (meaning that the ToR circuit's exit relay should be in Poland) even though the experiment is being carried out in the UK. Just before submitting the client's login credentials into the server, a new Wireshark capture is started. The client then logs into the system via ToR and the packets capture is stopped. After logging in, the site language is switched to Italian, indicating that the language is associated to the user account (Italian user account) rather than to the country where the access is made from. A part of the Wireshark capture is shown in Fig. 12.

The analysis capture file shows interesting results. As expected, all the traffic exchanged between the client and the guard node is encrypted by ToR, hence Wireshark could not detect the higher level protocol which is being used. What is particularly interesting in this last test, is that the IP address of the entry relay is the same as the one to which the client connected while requesting the Facebook web page (94.242.209.120). This contradicts the randomness of the circuit building promised by ToR. This observation could be ascribed to one of two reasons:

- The circuit construction in the ToR network is not as random as it claims to be.
- The client always connects to the same entry relay (possibly because of a caching mechanism that comes with the ToR software).

```
  8 1.122916000  192.168.1.8      94.242.209.120   TCP    640 13651-9001 [PSH, ACK] Seq=587 Ack=1 Win=64787 Len=586
  9 1.171984000  94.242.209.120   192.168.1.8      TCP     60 9001-13651 [ACK] Seq=1 Ack=1173 Win=931 Len=0
 10 1.236537000  94.242.209.120   192.168.1.8      TCP    640 9001-13651 [PSH, ACK] Seq=1 Ack=1173 Win=931 Len=586
 11 1.243788000  94.242.209.120   192.168.1.8      TCP   1314 9001-13651 [ACK] Seq=587 Ack=1173 Win=931 Len=1260
 12 1.244031000  192.168.1.8      94.242.209.120   TCP     54 13651-9001 [ACK] Seq=1173 Ack=1847 Win=64326 Len=0
 13 1.246843000  94.242.209.120   192.168.1.8      TCP   1314 9001-13651 [ACK] Seq=1847 Ack=1173 Win=931 Len=1260
 14 1.249633000  94.242.209.120   192.168.1.8      TCP   1314 9001-13651 [ACK] Seq=3107 Ack=1173 Win=931 Len=1260
 15 1.249821000  192.168.1.8      94.242.209.120   TCP     54 13651-9001 [ACK] Seq=1173 Ack=4367 Win=63696 Len=0
 16 1.252617000  94.242.209.120   192.168.1.8      TCP   1314 9001-13651 [ACK] Seq=4367 Ack=1173 Win=931 Len=1260
 17 1.255541000  94.242.209.120   192.168.1.8      TCP   1314 9001-13651 [ACK] Seq=5627 Ack=1173 Win=931 Len=1260
 18 1.255780000  192.168.1.8      94.242.209.120   TCP     54 13651-9001 [ACK] Seq=1173 Ack=6887 Win=63066 Len=0
 19 1.258835000  94.242.209.120   192.168.1.8      TCP   1314 9001-13651 [ACK] Seq=6887 Ack=1173 Win=931 Len=1260
 20 1.261666000  94.242.209.120   192.168.1.8      TCP   1314 9001-13651 [ACK] Seq=8147 Ack=1173 Win=931 Len=1260
 21 1.261823000  192.168.1.8      94.242.209.120   TCP     54 13651-9001 [ACK] Seq=1173 Ack=9407 Win=62436 Len=0
 22 1.264714000  94.242.209.120   192.168.1.8      TCP   1314 9001-13651 [ACK] Seq=9407 Ack=1173 Win=931 Len=1260
 23 1.267574000  94.242.209.120   192.168.1.8      TCP   1314 9001-13651 [ACK] Seq=10667 Ack=1173 Win=931 Len=1260
 24 1.267781000  192.168.1.8      94.242.209.120   TCP     54 13651-9001 [ACK] Seq=1173 Ack=11927 Win=61806 Len=0
 25 1.285116000  94.242.209.120   192.168.1.8      TCP   1314 9001-13651 [ACK] Seq=11927 Ack=1173 Win=931 Len=1260
 26 1.288011000  94.242.209.120   192.168.1.8      TCP   1314 9001-13651 [ACK] Seq=13187 Ack=1173 Win=931 Len=1260
 27 1.288181000  192.168.1.8      94.242.209.120   TCP     54 13651-9001 [ACK] Seq=1173 Ack=14447 Win=61176 Len=0
 28 1.290973000  94.242.209.120   192.168.1.8      TCP   1314 9001-13651 [ACK] Seq=14447 Ack=1173 Win=931 Len=1260
 29 1.294158000  94.242.209.120   192.168.1.8      TCP   1314 9001-13651 [ACK] Seq=15707 Ack=1173 Win=931 Len=1260
 30 1.294242000  192.168.1.8      94.242.209.120   TCP     54 13651-9001 [ACK] Seq=1173 Ack=16967 Win=60546 Len=0
 31 1.296726000  94.242.209.120   192.168.1.8      TCP   1314 9001-13651 [ACK] Seq=16967 Ack=1173 Win=931 Len=1260
 32 1.299614000  94.242.209.120   192.168.1.8      TCP   1314 9001-13651 [ACK] Seq=18227 Ack=1173 Win=931 Len=1260
```

FIG. 12

Wireshark capture.

We therefore investigated further the origin of the IP address and the latter reveals itself to be a "special" guard relay. According to the official documentation of the ToR Project (ToR, 2015b), a ToR client selects a limited number of guard relays each time and then connects to one of them in order to lower the possibilities for an attacker to create a definite profile of the client itself. This explains why our ToR client used the same IP address twice as the entry relay of two different circuits. To have a more clear vision of how this mechanism is being applied, we repeat the experiment from the same device but in another network. The ToR client still connects to the same guard node as before. Repeating the test one more time from a different device but in the same network, the guard relay's IP address changes, indicating that there is a caching mechanism (as it was hypothesized) in the ToR client that determines the selection of the entry node in the circuit, independently of the network address from which the request is being made. In any case, even though the ToR client caches a limited set of guard relays IP addresses, its anonymity is never compromised and the confidentiality of the information flowing is also maintained and, therefore, it is not possible to infer the two endpoints by analyzing the traffic.

5 CONCLUSION

Communicating anonymously online is popular across all age groups, and it can bring both benefits and challenges. As we share more and more information online, anonymity can be a way of protecting personal information and exploring sensitive topics, friendships and identities without the risk of these actions being linked back to their source; indeed it can also help people to escape the prejudices that can come into play. Many users also felt that being anonymous online facilitated their freedom of expression, with many people saying they feel more comfortable with expressing their views, protesting and discussing taboo subjects. This need to be anonymous has driven research in the area of data privacy and anonymity in the Internet. Consequently, a number of techniques and protocols have been developed to maintain surfers' anonymity. ToR has been the preferred anonymizer of Internet surfers. Currently, we are witnessing a wide deployment of new inter-networking trends such as the cloud computing. However, with the absence of a standardized anonymity and privacy-preserving platform for cloud computing, there is a question mark as to whether current anonymizers such as ToR will "fill the gap!" This paper attempts to answer the question by implementing ToR to access a number of cloud-based services namely, DropBox, Youtube, and Facebook. We use Wireshark to analyze the traffic between the users and these services and to verify the privacy and anonymity of users. The analysis shows that ToR meets its promises by maintaining users privacy and anonymity.

ACRONYMS

AES	advanced encryption standard
CA	certification authority
HTTPS	hyper text transfer protocol secure
IaaS	infrastructure as a service
PaaS	platform as a service
PKI	public key infrastructure
PnP IPSec	plug and play IP security
SaaS	software as a service
SSL	secure socket layer
SvPDD	self-validated public data distribution
TLS	transport layer security
TOR	The Onion Router

GLOSSARY

AES Advanced encryption standard for asymmetric encryption.
CA An entity that is responsible for managing digital certificates.
HTTPS Hyper text transfer protocol secure for secure web browsing.
IaaS A mode of cloud computing, where infrastructure components are managed by cloud providers.
PaaS A mode of cloud computing, where platforms and frameworks are offered by cloud providers.
PKI Public key infrastructure for keys management.
PnP IPSec Is new extension to the current IPSec protocol.
SaaS A mode of cloud computing, where software and applications are offered by cloud computing.
SSL Secure Socket Layer for secure communications.
SvPDD Self validated public data distribution mechanisms.
TOR An anonymity preserving mechanisms.
TLS Transport Layer Security for secure point-to-point communications.

REFERENCES

Aiash, M., et al., 2015. Introducing a hybrid infrastructure and information-centric approach for secure cloud computing. In: Proceedings of IEEE 29th International Conference on Advanced Information Networking and Applications Workshops (WAINA).
Bajak, F., 2014. Venezuela Cuts Off Internet, Blocks Communication for Protestors. http://www.huffingtonpost.com/2014/02/21/venezuela-internet-_n_4832505.html.
Brewer, F., et al., 2013. The Chinese Wall Security Policy. http://www.gammassl.co.uk/research/chwall.pdf.

Carnielli, A., Aiash, M., 2015. Will ToR achieve its goals in the future Internet? An empirical study of using ToR with cloud computing. In: Proceedings of IEEE 29th International Conference on Advanced Information Networking and Applications Workshops (WAINA).

Chaum, D., 1998. The dining cryptographers problem: unconditional sender and recipient untraceability. J. Cryptol. 1 (1), 65–75.

Craig, G., 2009. Fully homomorphic encryption using ideal lattices. In: Proceedings of Forty-First Annual ACM Symposium on Theory of Computing.

Danezis, G., et al., 2010. The application of onion routing in anonymous communication. In: Proceedings of the Second International Conference on Multimedia and Information Technology (MMIT).

Dingledine, R., et al., 2004. ToR: the second-generation onion router. In: Proceedings of the 13th USENIX Security Symposium.

Fang, Q., et al., 2000. Onion routing access configurations. In: Proceedings of the DARPA Information Survivability Conference and Exposition. DISCEX '00.

Fujitsu Research Institute, 2010. Personal Data in the Cloud: A Global Survey of Consumer Attitudes. http://www.fujitsu.com/downloads/SOL/fai/reports/fujitsu_personal-data-in-the-cloud.pdf.

Gilad, Y., Herzberg, A., 2013. Plug-and-play IP security: anonymity infrastructure instead of PKI. In: ESORICS 2013.

Gonzalez, P., 2013. Fingerprinting Tor. Inform. Manage. Comput. Secur. 21 (2), 73–90.

Herrmann, D., et al., 2009. Website fingerprinting: attacking popular privacy enhancing technologies with the multinomial naïve-bayes classifier. In: Proceedings of the ACM Workshop on Cloud Computing Security.

Itani, W., et al., 2009. Privacy as a service: privacy-aware data storage and processing in cloud computing architectures. In: Proceedings of Eighth IEEE International Conference on Dependable, Autonomic and Secure Computing.

Jensen, M., et al., 2010. Towards an anonymous access control and accountability scheme for cloud computing. In: Proceedings of IEEE 3rd International Conference on Cloud Computing (CLOUD).

Khan, S., et al., 2012. AnonymousCloud: a data ownership privacy provider framework in cloud computing. In: Proceedings of IEEE 11th IEEE International Conference on Trust, Security and Privacy in Computing and Communications.

Li, J., et al., 2015a. L-EncDB: a lightweight framework for privacy-preserving data queries in cloud computing. Knowl. Based Syst. 79 (4), 18–26.

Li, J., et al., 2015b. OPoR: enabling proof of retrievability in cloud computing with resource-constrained devices. IEEE Trans. Cloud Comput. 3 (2), 195–205.

Llorente, I., 2014. OpenNebula: Enabling Business in the Cloud. http://opennebula.org/about-how-opennebula-is-enabling-business-in-the-cloud/.

Michael, A., et al., 2010. A view of cloud computing. Commun. ACM 53 (4), 50–58.

Miranda, M., Siani, P., 2009. A client-based privacy manager for cloud computing. In: Proceedings of Fourth International ICST Conference on COMmunication System softWAre and middlewaRE.

Pearson, S., Shen, Y., Mowbray, M., 2009. A privacy manager for cloud computing. In: Proceedings of First International Conference, CloudCom.

Rininsland, A., 2012. Internet Censorship Listed: How Does Each Country Compare? http://www.theguardian.com/technology/datablog/2012/apr/16/internet-censorship-country-list.

Rivlin, G., 2008. Wallflower at the Web Party. http://www.nytimes.com/2006/10/15/business/yourmoney/15friend.html?pagewanted=all&_r=0.

ToR, 2013. ToR Bridges in the Amazon Cloud. https://cloud.torproject.org/.

ToR, 2015a. ToRChat. https://github.com/prof7bit/TorChat.

ToR, 2015b. What is the ToR Browser? https://www.torproject.org/projects/torbrowser.html.en.

Tulloch, M., 2013. Introducing Windows Azure. http://www.enpointe.com/images/pdf/Microsoft_Press_ebook_Introducing_Azure_PDF.PDF.

Varia, J., et al., 2014. Overview of Amazon Web Services. https://d36cz9buwru1tt.cloudfront.net/AWS_Overview.pdf.

Wang, J., et al., 2011. Security issues and countermeasures in cloud computing. In: Proceedings of the IEEE International Conference on Grey Systems and Intelligent Services (GSIS).

Xiao, Z., Xiao, Y., 2013. Security and privacy in cloud computing. IEEE Commun. Surv. Tutorials 15 (2), 843–859.

Zhao, Y., et al., 2008. Cloud computing and grid computing 360-degree compared. In: Proceedings of Workshop on Grid Computing Environments.

Self-adaptive overlay networks

2

B.-C. Mocanu, F. Pop, C. Dobre, V. Cristea

University Politehnica of Bucharest, Bucharest, Romania

1 INTRODUCTION

Taking in consideration the large increase in the number of interconnected intelligent devices, such sensors and mobile devices present a highly interest topic in the scientific community regarding trust and security assurance for such large-scale networks, which might be organized in different overlays with respect to different applications constraints.

Based on the recent developments in the infrastructure of the interconnected devices through Internet and the concept of the Internet of things peer-to-peer (P2P) overlay networks has shown an increasing interest in the computer science research community. The usage of P2P networks offers great advantages for classical client-server networks through their complexity, heterogeneity, mobility, and dynamicity. Considering this criteria, this paper will present the state-of-the-art approach, in a chronological manner, of the structured and unstructured P2P overlays.

Taking in to consideration the heterogeneity of mobile computing, building a P2P overlay on this kind of infrastructure presents many challenges. The most significant is the fact that mobile peers can join or leave the network any time without warning. This may be because of short battery lifetime, a weak service provider signal strength or even an intentional exit. In order to face such challenges researchers have developed a new concept of P2P overlays inspired by natural phenomena. This is called self-adaptive P2P overlays.

Another subject that will be presented in this paper is pervasive computing, also known as ubiquitous computing, which represents a challenging research field because it implies the existence of computing resources that are available anywhere and at any time in a dynamically and adaptive manner with a low cost and high level of elasticity and availability. Ubiquitous networks can be created based on a distributed network with a high degree of availability and adaptability.

On top of the solutions analyzed in this paper the coexistence of multiple P2P overlays is presented. The organization of the peers as several overlays with different structures and the collaboration between them represents a major challenge in this field of research.

Pervasive Computing. http://dx.doi.org/10.1016/B978-0-12-803663-1.00002-4

2 BACKGROUND/LITERATURE REVIEW/CONTEXT
2.1 UNSTRUCTURED PEER-TO-PEER

From the beginning of 2000 a new type of network emerged that was based on a different paradigm from the traditional client-server. The beginning of 2000 coincided with the development of a broadband Internet infrastructure, thus the Internet became widely available. As a consequence, computer networks have started to organize themselves in overlay structures in order to collect and distribute content over the Internet through TCP and HTTP protocols in a fully decentralized manner without any central server or point of failure.

In this kind of networks, the participation of any node is open and this ensures a higher degree of resilience and robustness in cases of dynamicity and node movements and failures, while at the same time there are reduced maintenance costs. On the other hand, this type of network suffers from frequently changes in architecture because peers join and leave the system without warning, thus keeping the robustness of the network is considered to be the most challenging aspect.

The performance of lookups in unstructured P2P overlays is not great because it is based on flooding the network, which creates a great overload.

Furthermore, several unstructured P2P overlays will be analyzed in chronological manner.

2.1.1 Freenet 2001

The Freenet unstructured P2P overlay was proposed in Clarke et al. (2001). This free approach has allowed peers to exchange information in an anonymous manner. Moreover, the main goals of Freenet are reliability and security. Even though, Freenet is fully decentralized, and there are no rules concerning node joining and leaving, it has a proper mechanism to facilitate information retrieval without flooding. The structure of the Freenet P2P overlay is shown in Fig. 1.

Joining, leaving, and lookup in Freenet overlay

Joining the Freenet overlay is realized by simply finding an existing peer in the network and connecting to it. When the new node has become part of the overlay it holds its own data store along with a routing table to other peers and an index of their stored resources. Each piece of resource is indexed by a unique identifier computed by all nodes with a hash function. Therefore, lookups in Freenet are realized through these unique keys. When a request for a key can be satisfied by a remote node, the data will return to the node that originally requested it along the reverse path.

Leaving the Freenet overlay is realized asynchronously, without any announcement in the network. The resources stored by the node that just left, disappear until the peer rejoins the overlay if there are no other nodes with that kind of resource.

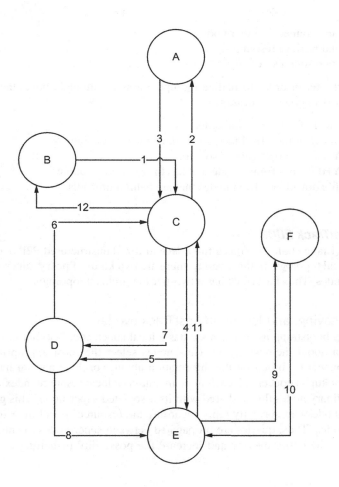

FIG. 1

Freenet unstructured peer-to-peer overlay.

2.1.2 Gnutella 2002

The most widely known unstructured P2P overlay is Gnutella (Schollmeier et al., 2003). The purpose of this overlay is to allow peers to share resources in a fully decentralized, scalable, reliable, and anonymous way.

Joining, leaving, and lookup in Gnutella overlay

Similarly to the Freenet overlay, joining in Gnutella is realized by searching for an existing node and contacting it. When a node joins Gnutella is able to realize three operations:

- Locate and connect to other nodes.
- Query and retrieve resources.
- Push data resources.

Furthermore, in order to realize the operations mentioned above, the Gnutella protocol has five types of messages:

1. PING check if a node is available.
2. PONG reply of the PING message if the node is available.
3. QUERY search a particular resource.
4. QUERYHIT reply from a node that has the queried resource.
5. PUSH file downloads from nodes that are behind firewalls.

2.1.3 FastTrack 2006

FastTrack (Liang et al., 2006) is a fully decentralized unstructured P2P overlay with a hierarchical topology. In this overlay, there are two kinds of peers: super nodes and ordinary nodes. Thus FastTrack has a two-tier hierarchical topology.

Joining, leaving, and lookup in FastTrack overlay

Concerning bootstrapping, every node has a local super-node list that also includes information about their workload. New nodes select the most appropriate super-node to connect to, based on the information about workload and on its location. As far as lookup is concerned, each node maintains a local resource index and in the case of ordinary nodes this is shared with its associated super-node. This guarantees that super-nodes can correctly reply regarding the resources of all their underlying ordinary nodes. Thus, queries are propagated between super-nodes to enhance their coverage of the entire overlay and increase the possibility of getting a successful response.

2.1.4 Other unstructured peer-to-peer overlays

BitTorrent 2003

BitTorrent (Cohen, 2003) is one of the most popular P2P file-sharing systems available nowadays with millions of active users.

Gia 2004

Gia (Chawathe et al., 2003) is an unstructured P2P overlay based on Gnutella 0.6 and implements the concept of super-node proposed by FastTrack.

UMM 2010

Unstructured multisource multicast (UMM) (Ripeanu et al., 2010) is an unstructured P2P overlay designed for group communication using multicasting.

2.2 **STRUCTURED PEER-TO-PEER**

Structured P2P overlays represent a type of network organization where data are distributed in a deterministic manner, not randomly. The access of certain data is realized in a finite number of steps based on an algorithm. The main advantage of structured P2P overlays consists of their high performance in terms of resource discovery and resource access.

Furthermore, several structured P2P overlays will be analyzed in a chronological order.

2.2.1 CAN 2001

The most mature structured P2P overlay is Content Addressable Network (CAN). CAN overlay was proposed by Ratnasamy et al. (2001a). Based of distributed hash tables (DHT) CAN overlays present the following features: self-organization, scalability, and fault tolerance. The organization of nodes in CAN overlays is in an n-dimensional coordinate space, where n represents the parameter of the CAN protocol.

In CAN overlays every node has an assigned key/value pair. Based on this fact every node has the responsibility for a certain area of the CAN space, by storing additional information regarding its neighbors, such as IP addresses or other coordinates. The key value stored by each node is generated based on a hash function, because this function has no proven collisions.

Furthermore, the fundamental operations in P2P overlays will be analyzed: joining, leaving, and lookup. The structure of the CAN P2P overlay is shown in Fig. 2.

Joining in CAN overlays

When a node joins the CAN overlay needs to follow three fundamental steps: find an existing node in the overlay, determine the zone that will be allocated to that node, and update its neighbor's sate tables. Therefore, when a node joins the overlay, it randomly picks a point in the CAN space and sends a JOIN message through a known node in the network. When the targeted node receives a JOIN message, it will begin the process of zone allocation for the new node, by splitting its zone into half and assigning it to the newly arrived node. After the zone allocation the targeted node transfers the key/value pairs to the arrived node for which it has become responsible. Finally, its neighbor's allocation tables are updated to be aware of the new peer through UPDATE messages.

Leaving in CAN overlays

A node leaving the CAN overlay deliberately occurs when the node notifies the neighbor with the smallest zone and transfers all the content in order to keep the resources available.

Another common way of departure is node failure. When this occurs the space without an owner must be taken over by an existing peer in the system. The detection of failing nodes is realized upon the update phase. When a node sends an UPDATE

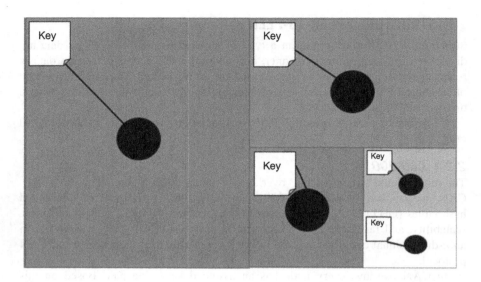

FIG. 2

CAN structured peer-to-peer overlay.

message and fails to receive an acknowledgment message from a node it triggers a self-timer and sends a TAKEOVER message. The timer for each node is dynamically allocated based on the size of their zone. If no response from the deserted node arrives, the elected node merges both zones.

Lookup in CAN overlays

Routing in CAN overlays is based on the coordinates stored by each node in its routing table. The information stored in this table consists of the IP address and the unique identifier of each neighbor. Therefore, delivering a message to its destination is realized by forwarding it to the neighbor with the coordinates nearest the destination coordinates. This procedure is realized based on the greedy mechanism. For instance, for a two-dimensional CAN space the test metric used is the Euclidian distance.

Moreover, concerning the performances of the CAN overlay, the average number of hops in an n-dimension space with m nodes is given by the following equation:

$$Hops = O \times (n \times (m^{1/n})). \tag{1}$$

Therefore, the CAN overlay can be considered reliable in respect to its construction.

Applications of CAN overlays

An interesting application based on the CAN overlay is presented by Ratnasamy et al. (2001b). The authors proposed a solution for an application-level multicast service. Their proposal has two major advantages: simplicity of the schema because of the architecture of CAN and scalability in terms of large groups without modifying the service architecture.

Another application based on CAN overlay is presented by Elmas and Ozkasap (2004). This paper presents a prototype for document sharing and text classification over CAN. The authors proposed an algorithm for classification that produces a key value for each document found in the system.

2.2.2 Kademlia 2002

Kademlia overlay was proposed by Maymounkov and Mazieres (2002). This P2P overlay is fully decentralized and structured. This overlay uses the XOR metric that measures the distance between two nodes as the result of the bit-wise exclusive OR.

In Kademlia overlay each node and resource are assigned to a 160-bit value. The distance between three nodes is given by the following equation:

$$d(a, b) = a \oplus b. \tag{2}$$

Each node in the overlay stores a table of nodes that is distanced from itself between 2^i and 2^{i+1}, where $0i < 160$. This table is called a k-bucket, with a dynamic size given by parameter k.

Joining and leaving in Kademlia overlays

Joining the Kademlia overlay practically implies that the new node will appear in a known nodes k-bucket and after that, through lookup operations, the new node populates its own list of node distances. When a new node that has not yet participated the system wants to join the overlay, it simply computes a random number that has not been used by other peers and assigns this as its ID. This value is kept by the peer until it leaves the system.

By using k-buckets, the Kademlia overlay is considered to be resistant to Denial of Service (DoS) attacks, because by its construction the k-bucket is not populated with the new node until an old node leaves the system.

Lookup in Kademlia overlays

The most advantageous feature of the Kademlia overlay is the fact that node lookup is realized in an asynchronous manner. When a node searches for another one it initiates a *FIND−NODE* request in its own k-bucket. Additional information like round trip timer is added when consulting other nodes in the system. The Kademlia architecture does not allow surpassing queries at the same time.

Concerning resource locating, these are located based on a key value generated by a hash function. These values are stored on several nodes in order to gain asynchronous access to certain data. In terms of performance, the Kademlia overlay has a value of $O \log N$ for resource discovery, where N represents the number of nodes in the overlay.

Applications of Kademlia overlays

Kademlia overlay is one of the most popular structured overlays, that has a wide applicability in open-source implementations such as BitTorrent (Pouwelse et al., 2005) or eMule (Kulbak et al., 2005).

2.2.3 Chord 2003

Even though Chord (Stoica et al., 2003) is not the most mature structured P2P overlay is considered the most popular overlay. The Chord protocol uses consistent hashing for identifying each node or resource in the system.

Moreover, based on its construction Chord is fully decentralized and distributed. Therefore, the structure of this overlay consists of a virtual ring, where every node has an identifier larger than its predecessor's one and only has knowledge of its successor neighbor. The structure of the Chord structured P2P overlay is shown in Fig. 3.

Joining and leaving Chord P2P overlays

When a new node joins the system three conditions must be satisfied:

- Every node predecessor points correctly to its first successor.
- Each key is stored in successor (k).
- For each node the finger table must be correct.

In order to fulfill the conditions mentioned above, when a node joins the following steps must have been accomplished:

1. Initialization of the new node.
2. Notification of other nodes to update their tables.
3. The new node takes over the keys from its successor.

When a node leaves the overlay, the robustness of the system is not affected because each node keeps a list of successor nodes of a fixed size. If the next immediate successor fails to respond the node can modify the entry point of the second successor and become the first one.

Lookup in Chord overlays

Data searching in Chord overlay is realized based on the successor relationships. Each node in the system stores a finger table of a maximum size of m and is constructed in such manner that every node has on its ith position in the table the pointer to the successor node of $n + 2^{i+1}$ in the Chord virtual ring. Finger tables allow a node to have information about nodes in its vicinity as well as about a few remote nodes, and a balance is possible between maintaining accurate information about a

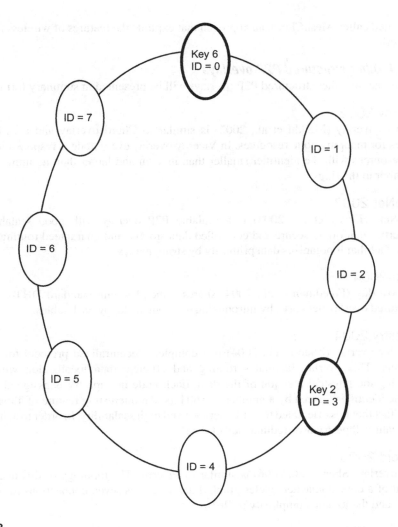

FIG. 3

Chord structured peer-to-peer overlay.

lot of nodes and only being aware of the successor in the Chord ring. Considering a stable N-node Chord overlay the number of messages needed to locate a certain resource is given by $O \log N$.

Applications of Chord overlays

Based on Chord overlay researchers have founded an interesting application for Wireless Mesh Chord (Canali et al., 2010). In this paper a new approach was presented called MeshChord, an approach that exploits the features of wireless mesh networks.

2.2.4 Other structured P2P overlays

In this section other structured P2P overlays will be presented in summary form.

Viceroy 2002

Viceroy overlay (Malkhi et al., 2002) is similar to Chord overlay and uses hash values for mapping node resources. In Viceroy overlay every node is responsible for the resources with the identifier smaller than its own and larger than its immediate neighbor in the ring.

SkipNet 2003

SkipNet (Harvey et al., 2003) is a scalable P2P overlay with good scalability properties that offers secure and controlled data storage and guaranteed routing due to the fact that it organizes data primarily by string names.

Coral 2004

This overlay (Freedman et al., 2004) shares principles with standard DHT-based, structured overlay networks by introducing distributed sloppy hash tables.

Tapestry 2004

Tapestry overlay (Zhao et al., 2004) is a complete decentralized protocol for P2P systems. This overlay facilitates routing and efficient data localization without knowing the physical location of the data. Each node in Tapestry is assigned to a unique identifier formed by a number of 160 bits. An interesting feature of Tapestry is the fact that it is orientated to fault tolerance and high scalability. In order to achieve this feature Tapestry uses redundancy of data.

Cycloid 2006

This overlay (Shen et al., 2006) is similar to Viceroy. The topology of this overlay is that of a cube connected cycles graph. Each node has seven connections to other nodes and the lookup complexity is $O(d)$.

HyPeer 2011

This approach (Serbu et al., 2011) presents an extended structured overlay of Chord based on a hypercube in order to offer flexible routing strategies due to the fact that it offers redundancy concerning the lookup paths.

---

3 SELF-ADAPTIVE OVERLAYS

3.1 BIO-INSPIRED P2P OVERLAYS

In recent years a great deal of interest has been shown by researchers in the nature-inspired design of self-adaptive P2P overlays. Modeling a natural phenomenon and implementing a distributed computing algorithm on its model is not a trivial task. Furthermore, several bio-inspired protocols for P2P systems will be presented. These models were translated from a mathematical model of a natural phenomenon into a P2P protocol with a predictable behavior.

Bio-inspired solutions have shown efficiency in the domain of computer networks. Solutions based on swarm intelligence, specifically based on the collective behavior of ant colonies or bees, have validated and guaranteed scalability due to the distributed intelligence and the reduced communication costs.

Moreover, a chronological analysis of several bio-inspired overlays will be presented.

3.1.1 Self-Chord 2010

The Self-Chord overlay was proposed in Forestiero et al. (2010) as a solution for grid and cloud computing infrastructures. The construction of this overlay is based on swarm intelligence and ant colonies, using multiple independent mobile agents.

The architecture of the overlay is based on the Chord structured overlay, thus the nodes in this P2P system are structured in a ring form. Each node is ordered according to its unique key and computed by using a hash function. The difference lies in the placement of resource identifiers. The main difference between Chord relies on the fact that resources obtain their identifiers from different namespaces and are placed on nodes based on load balancing criteria, as well as semantic ones.

Furthermore, Self-Chord is considered a good proof of concept for a successful application of bio-inspired swarm intelligence algorithms in structured P2P overlays. Self-Chord is considered to be very efficient due to the fact that it uses finger tables to provide logarithmic guarantees in locating resources. The distribution of the resourced keys is realized in such a manner that it facilitates better load balancing. Moreover, the management of the Self-Chord overlay is more efficient than the management of Chord because there is no need to re-arrange resource identifiers subject to node churn because.

3.1.2 P2PBA 2011

The Peer-to-Peer Bee Algorithm (P2PBA) (Dhurandher et al., 2011) is designed for efficient resource discovery on mobile ad hoc networks. This overlay is inspired by the foraging behavior of honey bees. Due to this fact it is very lightweight in terms of exchanged messages. The main idea of this algorithm is the fact that by reducing the search area it returns a list of zones, called patches, where high concentrations of results can be found.

3.1.3 Self-CAN 2012

This overlay (Giordanelli et al., 2012) is similar to Self-Chord. The topology of the underlay remains identical to Self-Chord, while the identifiers of the resources are rearranged by ant-inspired mobile agents to improve the performance of resource discovery. The rearrangement of resource identifiers aims to minimize the centroid value of each node, thus essentially promoting the collection of similar resources at every node and speeding up lookup operations.

Further research will consider a better understanding of the bio-inspired P2P overlays and simulate the performances of the overlays with existing tools. For example, in the next report an analysis of the Self-Chord overlay will be presented in terms of performance. Also in the next report the opportunity to improve the security of the Self-Chord overlay by adding a new layer for this purpose will be presented.

3.1.4 Honeycomb 2014

This overlay (Pop et al., 2014) is a P2P overlay that is based on the hexagons of the honeycomb. The main advantage of this structure is the minimum number of neighbors in the network is three.

3.1.5 SPIDER 2015

In a paper by Mocanu et al. (2015) a bio-inspired P2P network based in the spider web is presented. In this type of overlay each node can have a maximum of four neighbors. The structure of this overlay consists of a fixed number of chains and a variable number of rings.

3.2 MULTI-LAYER PEER-TO-PEER

In real-life situations it is more feasible to use several P2P overlays on the same hardware infrastructure due to the fact that there is no P2P overlay that satisfies all the pervasive network issues. For instance, a node can be part of several domains or applications because it can facilitate data dissemination through file-sharing or VoIP (Hsu et al., 2010).

Fig. 4 represents a multilayer P2P overlay that runs on the same physical network.

For this N layer P2P overlay the management must be realized simultaneously in order to have the same hardware infrastructure updated on each overlay. In order to realize such management the existence of a communication layer between each overlay, called overlay coexistence, is required.

Another strong point for the usage of the same hardware infrastructure on the bottom of several P2P overlays is presented in a paper by Mao et al. (2012). This aim of this paper is to create a new platform for P2P overlays called MOSAIC. Visualization, in terms of P2P overlays, can ensure easy deployment of network protocols in real life networks.

The problems encountered when using multiple P2P overlays at the same time have been presented in a paper by Jiang et al. (2005). Maniymaran et al. (2007) is also a good reference for multiple P2P overlays. This paper presents the benefits of using both structured and unstructured overlays for the same hardware infrastructure.

The most important issue in multi-layer overlays is the manner in which the resources shared by the physical nodes in the physical network are distributed

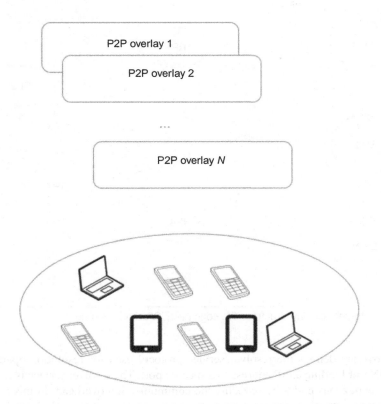

FIG. 4

Multi-layer P2P overlay with *N* overlays situated on top of a single set of hardware devices.

between the multi-layer overlays. In order to realize such coexistence a middleware layer is introduced. In a paper by Cooper (2006) a priority-based coexistence of multiple P2P overlays is presented.

4 HYBRID PEER-TO-PEER SYSTEMS

In this section two hybrid P2P overlays will be presented.

4.1 JXTA

The JXTA overlay was first presented by Barolli and Xhafa (2011). This overlay represents a building block for the development of P2P applications and services. In JXTA overlay, the nodes are self-organized in a group manner called peergroup. A peergroup is defined as a set of nodes that share common interests and respect the same politics and rules regarding look-ups, joining, leaving, and naming. The

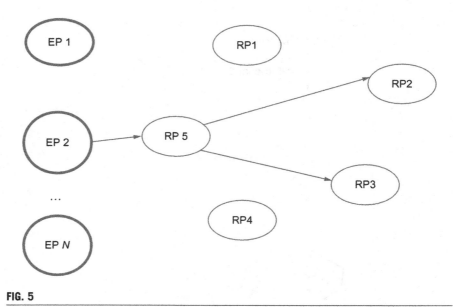

FIG. 5

JXTA peer-to-peer overlay structure. *EP*, edge peer; *RP*, rendezvou peer.

JXTA overlay defines the resolver service protocol used for resolution operations such DNS or binding an IP address to a specific port. The resolver service is realized by the rendezvous nodes by reducing the communication overhead. In this overlay there are no restrictions for any peers to become a rendezvous peer. Each rendezvous peer in the overlay stores a list of advertisement messages delivered by each peer nodes through a service called Shared Resource Distributed Index. Fig. 5 shows the structure of JXTA overlay.

4.2 MOPAR

MOPAR (Yu and Vuong, 2005) is a hybrid P2P overlay designed for Interest Management of Massively Multiplayer Online Games. This overlay is based on network virtual environment (NVE) in a fully distributed manner. This approach uses both structured P2P overlay such as DHT and unstructured P2P overlay. The architecture of this overlay is based on a hexagonal zoning approach. The main reason why the hexagonal zoning approach is used mainly in game applications is the uniformity of both the orientation and adjacency of the hexagons.

5 DISCUSSION AND CONCLUSIONS

This chapter presented a state-of-the-art survey of the existing solutions for P2P overlays. The review was split into three categories of P2P overlays: unstructured, structured, and bio-inspired overlays. For each overlay the main idea and the basic operations were presented. The conclusions drawn concerning the unstructured P2P overlays are shown in Table 1. As can be seen in terms of redundancy, Freenet offers path redundancy and FastTrack only offers resource indices replication. For the Gnutella overlay there is no redundancy support. Concerning dynamicity neither Freenet nor FastTrak overlays support any dynamical modifications on the fly. The security aspect is treated by the Freenet overlay in terms of assuring anonymity and privacy, while the Gnutella overlay assures only anonymity. In all three analyzed unstructured P2P overlays the lookup operation is realized by flooding the network; therefore, the overhead in the network is large.

Table 2 presents the taxonomy of three structured P2P overlays. As it can be seen in the table in terms of redundancy, CAN overlay supports routing redundancy and Kademlia overlay supports response replication and caching. Concerning the security issue Kademlia is the only structured P2P overlay that offers security facilities for all nodes, which are more trusted. In terms of speed both Chord and Kademlia overlays offer the same values for lookups which is faster in comparison with the CAN overlay.

Table 3 shows the taxonomy of bio-inspired P2P overlays. Therefore, redundancy is a property of the mentioned overlays only for the BlatAnt and AntOM overlays while Self-Chord does not support such property. In terms of dynamicity the same overlays that have the redundancy property are satisfying this condition.

Table 1 Taxonomy of Unstructured Peer-to-Peer Overlays

Overlay	Redundancy	Dynamicity	Security	Lookup	Queries
Freenet	Path redundancy	Distributed design	Anonymity and privacy	Constrained flooding	Any type of queries
Gnutella	No particular support	Periodic initiation of node discovery	Anonymity	Pure flooding	Any type of queries
FastTrack	Resource indices replication	No particular support	No	Flooding between super-nodes	Any type of queries

Table 2 Taxonomy of Structured Peer-to-Peer Overlays

Overlay	Redundancy	Dynamicity	Security	Lookup	Queries
CAN	Routing redundancy	No	No	$(d/4)n^{1/d}$	Standard queries
Kademlia	Resource replication and caching	Node behavior for routes longevity	Old nodes more trusted	$O(\log N)$	Standard queries
Chord	No	No	No	$O(\log N)$	Standard queries

Table 3 Taxonomy of Bio-Inspired Peer-to-Peer Overlays

Overlay	Redundancy	Dynamicity	Security	Lookup	Queries
Self-Chord	No	No	No	$O\,(\log N)$	Standard queries
BlatAnt	Yes	Yes	No	Flooding and random walks	Standard queries
AntOM	Yes	Yes	No	$O\,(\log N)$	Standard queries

Moreover, the security issue is not addressed by any of the studied bio-inspired overlays. BlatAnt is a bio-inspired overlay that has a higher overhead for lookups in comparison with the other overlays due to the fact that is uses flooding and random walks.

ACRONYMS

CAN   content addressable network
DHT   distributed hash tables
P2P   peer-to-peer
P2PBA peer-to-peer bee algorithm
UMM   unstructured multisource multicast

ACKNOWLEDGMENTS

The work has been funded by the Sectoral Operational Programme Human Resources Development 2007–2013 of the Ministry of European Funds through the Financial Agreement POSDRU/187/1.5/S/155420 (PROSCIENCE). The research presented in this paper is supported also the project *DataWay*: Real-time Data Processing Platform for Smart Cities: Making sense of Big Data, PN-II-RU-TE-2014-4-2731.

REFERENCES

Barolli, L., Xhafa, F., 2011. JXTA-overlay: a P2P platform for distributed, collaborative, and ubiquitous computing. IEEE Trans. Ind. Electron. 58 (6), 2163–2172.
Canali, C., Renda, M.E., Santi, P., Burresi, S., 2010. Enabling efficient peer-to-peer resource sharing in wireless mesh networks. IEEE Trans. Mob. Comput. 9 (3), 333–347.
Chawathe, Y., Ratnasamy, S., Breslau, L., Lanham, N., Shenker, S., 2003. Making Gnutella-like P2P systems scalable. In: Proceedings of the 2003 Conference on Applications, Technologies, Architectures, and Protocols for Computer Communications, pp. 407–418.

Clarke, I., Sandberg, O., Wiley, B., Hong, T.W., 2001. Freenet: a distributed anonymous information storage and retrieval system. In: Designing Privacy Enhancing Technologies, pp. 46–66.

Cohen, B., 2003. Incentives build robustness in BitTorrent. In: Workshop on Economics of Peer-to-Peer Systems, vol. 6, pp. 68–72.

Cooper, B.F., 2006. Trading off resources between overlapping overlays. In: Proceedings of the ACM/IFIP/USENIX 2006 International Conference on Middleware, pp. 101–120.

Dhurandher, S.K., Misra, S., Pruthi, P., Singhal, S., Aggarwal, S., Woungang, I., 2011. Using bee algorithm for peer-to-peer file searching in mobile ad hoc networks. J. Netw. Comput. Appl. 34 (5), 1498–1508.

Elmas, T., Ozkasap, O., 2004. Distributed document sharing with text classification over content-addressable network. In: Content Computing. Springer, Berlin, pp. 70–81.

Forestiero, A., Leonardi, E., Mastroianni, C., Meo, M., 2010. Self-Chord: a bio-inspired P2P framework for self-organizing distributed systems. IEEE/ACM Trans. Netw. 18 (5), 1651–1664.

Freedman, M.J., Freudenthal, E., Mazieres, D., 2004. Democratizing content publication with coral. In: Proceedings of the 1st Conference on Symposium on Networked Systems Design and Implementation (NSDI'04), vol. 1. USENIX Association, Berkeley, CA, pp. 18–18.

Ghit, B., Pop, F., Cristea, V., 2010. Epidemic-style global load monitoring in large-scale overlay networks. In: 2010 International Conference on P2P, Parallel, Grid, Cloud and Internet Computing (3PGCIC), pp. 393–398.

Giordanelli, R., Mastroianni, C., Meo, M., 2012. Bio-inspired P2P systems: the case of multidimensional overlay. ACM Trans. Auton. Adapt. Syst. 7 (4), 35.

Harvey, N.J.A., Jones, M.B., Saroiu, S., Theimer, M., Wolman, A., 2003. SkipNet: a scalable overlay network with practical locality properties. In: Proceedings of the 4th Conference on USENIX Symposium on Internet Technologies and Systems (USITS'03), vol. 4. USENIX Association, Berkeley, CA, pp. 9–9.

Hsu, C.J., Chung, W.C., Lai, K.C., Li, L.K.C., Chung, Y.C., 2010. A novel approach for cooperative overlay-maintenance in multi-overlay environments. In: 2010 IEEE Second International Conference on Cloud Computing Technology and Science (CloudCom), pp. 81–88.

Jiang, W., Chiu, D.M., Lui, J.C., 2005. On the interaction of multiple overlay routing. Perform. Eval. 62 (1), 229–246.

Khan, R., Hasan, R., 2014. SecP2PSIP: A Distributed Overlay Architecture for Secure P2PSIP. Academy of Science and Engineering (ASE), USA, ASE 2014.

Kulbak, Y., Bickson, D., et al., 2005. The eMule protocol specification. eMule project.

Liang, J., Kumar, R., Ross, K.W., 2006. The FastTrack overlay: a measurement study. Comput. Netw. 50 (6), 842–858.

Malkhi, D., Naor, M., Ratajczak, D., 2002. Viceroy: a scalable and dynamic emulation of the butterfly. In: Proceedings of the Twenty-First Annual Symposium on Principles of Distributed Computing, pp. 183–192.

Maniymaran, B., Bertier, M., Kermarrec, A.M., 2007. Build one, get one free: leveraging the coexistence of multiple P2P overlay networks. In: 27th International Conference on Distributed Computing Systems, 2007. ICDCS'07, p. 33.

Mao, Y., Loo, B.T., Ives, Z., Smith, J.M., 2012. MOSAIC: declarative platform for dynamic overlay composition. Comput. Netw. 56 (1), 64–84.

Maymounkov, P., Mazieres, D., 2002. Kademlia: a peer-to-peer information system based on the XOR metric. In: Peer-to-Peer Systems. Springer, Berlin, pp. 53–65.

Mocanu, B., Pop, F., Mihaita, A., Dobre, C., Cristea, V., 2015. SPIDER: a bio-inspired structured peer-to-peer overlay for data dissemination. In: 2014 IEEE 10th International Conference on P2P, Parallel, GRIS, CLOUD and Internet Computing (3PGCIC).

Pop, F., Citoteanu, O.M., Dobre, C., Cristea, V., 2014. Resource trust management in auto-adaptive overlay network for mobile cloud computing. In: 2014 IEEE 13th International Symposium on Parallel and Distributed Computing (ISPDC), pp. 162–169.

Pouwelse, J., Garbacki, P., Epema, D., Sips, H., 2005. The BitTorrent P2P file-sharing system: measurements and analysis. In: Peer-to-Peer Systems IV. Springer, Berlin, pp. 205–216.

Ratnasamy, S., Francis, P., Handley, M., Karp, R., Shenker, S., 2001a. A scalable content-addressable network. In: Proceedings of the 2001 Conference on Applications, Technologies, Architectures, and Protocols for Computer Communications (SIGCOMM'01). ACM, New York, NY, pp. 161–172.

Ratnasamy, S., Handley, M., Karp, R., Shenker, S., 2001b. Application-level multicast using content-addressable networks. In: Networked Group Communication. Springer, Berlin, pp. 14–29.

Ripeanu, M., Iamnitchi, A., Foster, I., Rogers, A., 2010. In search of simplicity: a self-organizing group communication overlay. Concurr. Comput. 22 (7), 788–815.

Schollmeier, R., Gruber, I., Niethammer, F., 2003. Protocol for peer-to-peer networking in mobile environments. In: Proceedings of the 12th International Conference on Computer Communications and Networks, 2003. ICCCN 2003, pp. 121–127.

Serbu, S., Felber, P., Kropf, P., 2011. HyPeer: structured overlay with flexible-choice routing. Comput. Netw. 55 (1), 300–313.

Shen, H., Xu, C.Z., Chen, G., 2006. Cycloid: a constant-degree and lookup-efficient P2P overlay network. Perform. Eval. 63 (3), 195–216.

Stoica, I., Morris, R., Liben-Nowell, D., Karger, D.R., Kaashoek, M.F., Dabek, F., Balakrishnan, H., 2003. Chord: a scalable peer-to-peer lookup protocol for internet applications. IEEE/ACM Trans. Netw. 11 (1), 17–32.

Wei, T.-T., Wang, C.-H., Chu, Y.-H., Chang, R.-I., 2012. A secure and stable multicast overlay network with load balancing for scalable IPTV services. Int. J. Digital Multimedia Broadcasting 2012, 540801:1–540801:12. http://dx.doi.org/10.1155/2012/540801.

Yu, A.P., Vuong, S.T., 2005. Mopar: a mobile peer-to-peer overlay architecture for interest management of massively multiplayer online games. In: Proceedings of the International Workshop on Network and Operating Systems Support for Digital Audio and Video, pp. 99–104.

Zhao, B.Y., Huang, L., Stribling, J., Rhea, S.C., Joseph, A.D., Kubiatowicz, J.D., 2004. Tapestry: a resilient global-scale overlay for service deployment. IEEE J. Sel. Areas Commun. 22 (1), 41–53.

Users in the urban sensing process: Challenges and research opportunities

3

T.H. Silva*,a,b, C.S.F.S. Celes[a], J.B.B. Neto[a], V.F.S. Mota[a], F.D. da Cunha[a],
A.P.G. Ferreira[a], A.I.J.T. Ribeiro[a], P.O.S. Vaz de Melo[a], J.M. Almeida[a],
A.A.F. Loureiro[a]

Federal University of Minas Gerais, Belo Horizonte, MG, Brazil[a]
Federal University of Technology – Paraná, Curitiba, PR, Brazil[b]

1 INTRODUCTION

The study of the urban data provided by users in participatory sensor networks (PSNs) is a recent research area. PSNs allow large-scale observations of people's actions in (almost) real time during long periods of the time. With that, PSNs have the potential to become a fundamental tool to better understand urban human interaction in the future. Data from PSNs can increase our knowledge of different aspects of our life in urban scenarios, which can be useful in the development of more sophisticated applications in several segments, such as, in the urban computing area (Silva et al., 2014b).

Furthermore, PSNs have the potential to complement traditional wireless sensor networks (WSNs) (Akyildiz et al., 2002) in several aspects. While WSNs are designed to sense limited size areas, such as forests and volcanoes, PSNs can reach areas of varying size and scale, such as large cities, countries, or even the planet. Additionally, a WSN is more subject to failure, since its operation depends on proper coordination of the actions of its sensor nodes that have severe power, processing, and memory constraints. On the other hand, PSNs are formed by autonomous and independent entities, ie, humans with their mobile devices. This makes the sensing task highly resilient to individual failures.

The objective of this chapter is to discuss the concept of PSNs, presenting an overview of the area, research trends and the main challenges. We aim to show that

---

*T.H. Silva is now with the Department of Informatics at Federal University of Technology, where he finished this work.

Pervasive Computing. http://dx.doi.org/10.1016/B978-0-12-803663-1.00003-6

the PSNs (eg, Instagram,[1] Foursquare,[2] and Waze[3]) can act as valuable sources for large-scale sensing, providing access to important features of city dynamics and urban social behavior quickly and comprehensively. First, we analyze the properties of PSN data studied on various systems. Next, we discuss how to work with PSN data, showing its applicability in the development of more sophisticated applications. Furthermore, we discuss several challenges and research opportunities related to PSNs.

The remainder of this chapter is organized as follows. Section 2 discusses the emerging concept of PSNs. Section 3 presents the properties of PSNs. Section 4 discusses how to work with PSN data, including how to obtain them. Section 5 presents the challenges and opportunities presented by the current research topics related to PSNs. Finally, Section 6 presents the conclusions.

2 PARTICIPATORY SENSOR NETWORKS

There are several ways to get urban data, among them we can mention the emerging PSNs (PSNs) (Burke et al., 2006; Silva et al., 2014b). Section 2.1 presents the definition of PSN; Section 2.2 discusses the functioning of PSN, while Section 2.3 illustrates examples of PSNs.

2.1 WHAT IS A PARTICIPATORY SENSOR NETWORK?

PSNs rely on the idea of participatory sensing (Burke et al., 2006), and can be defined as a system that supports a distributed process of gathering data about personal daily experiences and various aspects of the city. Such a process requires the active participation of people using portable devices to voluntarily share contextual information and/or make their sensed data available, ie, the users manually determine how, when, what, and where to share the sensed data. Thus, through PSNs we can monitor the different conditions of a variety of cities, as well as the collective behavior of people connected to the Internet in (almost) real time (Silva et al., 2014b).

PSNs have become popular thanks to the increasing use of portable devices, such as smartphones and tablets, as well as the global adoption of social media services. Therefore, a central element of a PSN is a user with a portable computing device. In this scenario, people participate as social sensors, voluntarily providing data on a particular aspect of a place that implicitly captures their experiences of daily life. These data can be obtained with the aid of sensing apparatus, for example, sensors embedded in smartphones (eg, GPS, accelerometer, microphone, and so on) or by human sensors (eg, vision). In the latter case, data are subjective observations produced by the users (Silva et al., 2014b).

---

[1] http://www.instagram.com.
[2] http://www.foursquare.com.
[3] http://www.waze.com.

PSNs provide unprecedented opportunities to access sensing data on a global scale. This large amount of data eases the gathering of information that is not otherwise available with the same global reach, and these data can be used to improve the processes of decision making regarding different entities (eg, individuals, groups, services, and applications).

It is worth mentioning that several terms defined recently, for example, *Humans as Data Sources* and *Ubiquitous Crowdsourcing* reflect the idea of PSNs (Srivastava et al., 2012; Mashhadi and Capra, 2011; Ganti et al., 2011). It is also important to mention that the term opportunist sensing (Lane et al., 2010), which is a type of sensing that also uses portable computing devices, can lead to confusion with the term participatory sensing. Participatory sensing differs from opportunistic sensing mainly in the user participation, in the latter the data collection stage is automated without user participation (Lane et al., 2008, 2010). Opportunistic sensing supports the sensing process of an application without requiring user efforts, determining automatically when the devices should be used to meet the specific demands of the applications. Thus, applications can take advantage of the sensing capabilities of all devices of users of the system without the need for human intervention (Lane et al., 2008).

2.2 THE FUNCTIONING OF PSN

Similarly to traditional WSNs, data sensed in a PSN is sent to the server, or "sink node," where the data can be accessed (using, for example, APIs, such as the API of Instagram[4]). But unlike WSNs, PSNs have the following characteristics: (a) sensor nodes are autonomous mobile entities, ie, a person with a mobile device; (b) the cost of the network is distributed among the sensors, providing a global scale; (c) the sensing depends on the willingness of people to participate in this process; and (d) sensor nodes do not have severe limitations of energy.

PSNs have the potential to complement WSNs in several aspects. Traditional WSNs are designed to sense areas of limited size, such as forests and volcanoes. In contrast, PSNs can reach areas of different sizes and scale, such as large cities, countries or even the planet (Silva et al., 2014b). Additionally, a WSN is subject to failure, since its operation depends on proper coordination of the actions of its sensor nodes, which have severe power, processing, and memory constraints. Since PSNs are formed by autonomous and independent entities, human beings, the sensing task becomes more robust to individual failures. Obviously, PSNs also bring several new challenges, for example, its success is directly linked to the popularity of smartphones and social media services.

Fig. 1 illustrates the idea of PSN consisting of users with their mobile devices sending sensed data about their locations for systems in the Internet. The figure shows sharing activities (represented by dots in the cloud) of four users in three different

---

[4]http://instagram.com/developer.

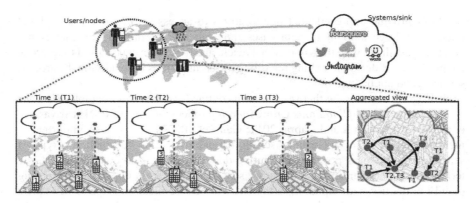

FIG. 1

Illustration of participatory sensor network.

Source: Image from: Silva, T.H., Vaz De Melo, P.O.S., Almeida, J.M., Loureiro, A.A.F., 2014b, February, Large-scale study of city dynamics and urban social behavior using participatory sensing. IEEE Wirel. Commun. 21 (1), 42–51.

moments in time, labeled as "Time 1," "Time 2," and "Time 3." Note that a user does not participate necessarily in the system at all times. After a certain time, these data can be analyzed in different ways. For example, the bottom rightmost part of the figure shows, by an aggregate view, a directed graph in which nodes/vertices represent the locations where the data have been shared, with edges connecting locations that were shared by the same user. Using this graph we can extract, for instance, the mobility patterns of users and this information can be used to perform load management more efficiently in urban infrastructure of mobile networks. In fact, knowledge gained from PSNs goes together with the use of graph/networks theory (Easley and Kleinberg, 2010; Newman, 2010, 2003).

2.3 EXAMPLES OF PSNs

The location-based social network, which is a special kind of social media that combines online social networks[5] features and the possibility of sharing data with spatial and temporal information[6] can be considered the most popular example of a PSN. It is possible to find several examples of such systems already deployed on the Internet, such as Waze, which serves to report traffic conditions in real time; Foursquare, which shares where the user is visiting; and Instagram, to send real time images to the system. In particular, Instagram can be seen as one of the most popular PSN, with 200 million users (Instagram, 2014). When considering this network, the sensed data provide a picture of a specific place. We can extract information of such

---

[5]Virtual platform that built and reflects social relations of real life among people.
[6]Data type that allows, for example, building location-based services.

data in various ways. One possibility is to visualize in real time the situation in a certain area of the city.

Note that all described systems above are composed of an online social network. However, there are several examples of PSNs that do not contain online social networks. For example, Weddar[7] to report weather conditions, NoiseTube[8] to share noise level in a given region of the city, or Colab[9] for sharing various problems of cities.

Some other types of social media, such as Twitter,[10] which allows its users to share personal updates in texts up to 140 characters, known as "tweets," may also be examples of PSNs. Twitter is considered an example of a PSN because the content shared on it may also enable the monitoring of various aspects of cities, as well as the collective behavior of people in near real time. For example, people could use their portable devices to share tweets containing real time information about demonstrations or accidents in the city. Beyond these examples, we can also mention GarbageWatch (CENS/UCLA, 2016), which monitors the garbage situation of a city. This example is particularly interesting because it illustrates that the use of the Web is not mandatory in a PSN. Sensed data can be sent to a specific application running on the Internet but outside the Web.

3 PROPERTIES OF PSN

Many questions arise from the concept of PSNs. Among them, one key question is: what are the properties of PSN? Answering this question helps us to understand, for instance, what are the limitations of PSNs and for what types of application we can use the data from PSNs.

As data provided by PSNs can be complex, a key step in any investigation is to characterize the data collected in order to understand their challenges and usefulness. Thus, in this section we study the properties of three PSNs used for location sharing, namely, Foursquare, Gowalla, and Brightkite.[11] In addition, we also study a PSN for photo sharing, particularly Instagram, as well as a PSN for traffic alert sharing (Waze).

The rest of this section is organized as follows. Section 3.1 describes the datasets of the PSNs used in this chapter. Next, Section 3.2 analyzes the coverage of these PSNs in different spatial granularity. Section 3.3 discusses the frequency with which nodes share data on individual regions of our dataset. Section 3.4 discusses the seasonality in the sensing process. Finally, Section 3.5 studies the behavior of the nodes of the PSNs.

---

[7] http://www.weddar.com.
[8] http://noisetube.net.
[9] http://www.colab.re.
[10] http://www.twitter.com.
[11] Gowalla and Brightkite are not in operation currently.

Table 1 Description of Used Datasets

Location sharing services		
System	*# check-ins*	Interval
Foursquare1	≈5 million	April 2012 (1 week)
Foursquare2	≈12 million	Feb2010–Jan2011
Foursquare3	≈4 million	May 2013 (2 weeks)
Gowalla	≈6 million	Feb2009–Oct2010
Brightkite	≈4 million	Apr2008–Oct2010
Photo sharing services		
System	*# of Photos*	Interval
Instagram1	≈2 million	Jun2012–Jul2012
Instagram2	≈2 million	May 2013 (2 weeks)
Traffic alert services		
System	*# of alerts*	Interval
Waze	+212 thousands	Dec2012–Jun2013

3.1 DATA DESCRIPTION

Table 1 displays all datasets considered in the analysis performed in this section. The data were collected through Twitter because, in addition to plain text, users can also share other types of contents, for instance, photos, check-ins, or traffic alerts, from an integration with Instagram, Foursquare, or Waze. In this case, Instagram photos, Foursquare check-ins, or Waze alerts announced on Twitter become available publicly, which by default does not happen when the data are published solely in the analyzed systems. As we can see in Table 1, the data reflect different periods. Furthermore, the datasets include a significant amount of data: Over 30 million records considering all sources.

Each sensed data (photo, check-in, or alert) consists of GPS coordinates (latitude and longitude), the data sharing time, and the id of the user who shared the data. Foursquare1 dataset has extra information about the type of place: category (eg, food) and a local unique identifier. More information about these specific datasets and how they were obtained can be found in Cheng et al. (2011) and Silva et al. (2012, 2013b,c,d). Section 4.1, however, discusses how to obtain data from PSNs.

3.2 NETWORK COVERAGE

In this section, we study the coverage of PSN at different spatial granularity, starting from the entire globe, to cities and, finally, specific areas of a city. Fig. 2 shows the global coverage in different PSNs: Foursquare (Foursquare1 dataset, Fig. 2A); Gowalla (Fig. 2B); Brightkite (Fig. 2C); Instagram (Instagram1 dataset, Fig. 2D);

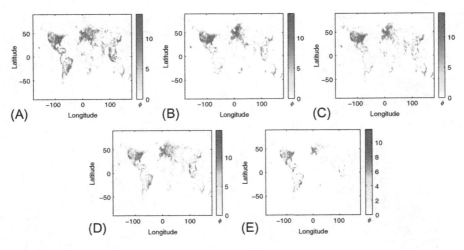

FIG. 2

Coverage of PSNs. Number of data n per pixel indicated by the value of ϕ shown
in the figure, where $n = 2^{\phi} - 1$. (A) Foursquare1; (B) Gowalla; (C) Brightkite;
(D) Instagram1; (E) Waze.

Source: Images from: Silva, T.H., Vaz de Melo, P.O.S., Almeida, J.M., Loureiro, A.A.F., 2013a, July,
Challenges and opportunities on the large scale study of city dynamics using participatory sensing. In: Proc. of
IEEE ISCC'13, Split, Croatia, pp. 528–534; Silva, T.H., Vaz de Melo, P.O.S., Viana, A., Almeida, J.M.,
Salles, J., Loureiro, A.A.F., 2013d, November, Traffic condition is more than colored lines on a map:
characterization of Waze alerts. In: Proc. of SocInfo'13, Kyoto, Japan, pp. 309–318.

and Waze (Fig. 2E). Data from these figures represent a heatmap of user participation:
darker colors represent a larger number of shared data in a given area. As we can see,
the coverage is very comprehensive and has a planetary scale.

Now we evaluate the participation of users in several large cities located in
different regions, but we will only show the results for a selection: New York, Rio
de Janeiro and Cairo. Fig. 3 shows a heatmap of sensing activity for each of these
cities. Again, darker colors represent larger numbers of data in a given area. We
observe a high coverage for some cities, as shown in Fig. 3A and D (New York).
However, as we can see in Fig. 3B and E, the sensing in Cairo, city that also has a high
number of inhabitants, is significantly lower. Such a difference in the coverage can
be explained by several factors. Besides the economic aspects, cultural differences
can have a significant impact on the adoption and use of these considered systems in
Cairo (Barth, 1969).

In addition, we can observe that the coverage in some cities, such as in Rio de
Janeiro (Fig. 3C and F), is far more heterogeneous when compared with New York.
This is probably because of particular geographical aspects, ie, large green areas

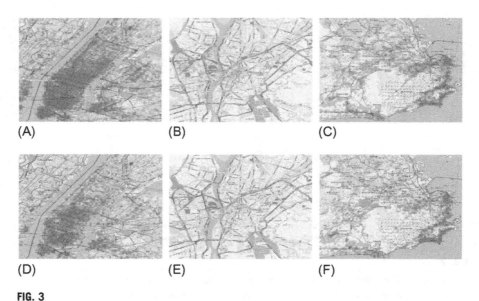

FIG. 3

Spatial coverage of Foursquare and Instagram in three populous cities around the world.
(A) New York—Foursquare; (B) Cairo—Foursquare; (C) Rio de Janeiro—Foursquare;
(D) New York—Instagram; (E) Cairo—Instagram; (F) Rio de Janeiro—Instagram.

Source: Images from: Silva, T.H., Vaz de Melo, P.O.S., Almeida, J.M., Loureiro, A.A.F., 2013a, July,
Challenges and opportunities on the large scale study of city dynamics using participatory sensing. In: Proc. of
IEEE ISCC'13, Split, Croatia, pp. 528–534; Silva, T.H., Vaz de Melo, P.O.S., Almeida, J.M., Salles, J.,
Loureiro, A.A.F., 2013b, A picture of Instagram is worth more than a thousand words: workload
characterization and application. In: Proc. of DCOSS'13, Cambridge, USA, pp. 123–132.

and large portions of water. Rio de Janeiro has the largest urban forest in the world, located in the middle of the city, and many hills with difficult access for humans. These geographical aspects limit the sensing coverage. In addition, the points of public interest, such as tourist spots and shopping centers, are unevenly distributed around the city. There are large residential areas with few points of this type, while other areas have high concentrations of these points.

The spatial coverage of data from PSNs for traffic alerts is not as comprehensive as PSNs for location and photo sharing. This can be seen in Fig. 4, which shows the number of alerts in different regions of Rio de Janeiro by using a heatmap. One factor that may help to explain this result is the population of users for the dataset of traffic alerts, which is smaller than the others studied. Another factor is that users may have fewer opportunities to share traffic alerts compared to the sharing of photos or check-ins.

As the activity of participation can be quite heterogeneous within a city, we analyze the coverage of PSN in specific areas of a city. To have an id of a specific area

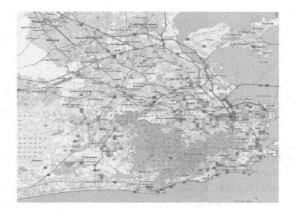

FIG. 4

Spatial coverage of PSN for traffic alerts sharing in Rio de Janeiro.

Source: Image from: Silva, T.H., Vaz de Melo, P.O.S., Viana, A., Almeida, J.M., Salles, J., Loureiro, A.A.F., 2013d, November, Traffic condition is more than colored lines on a map: characterization of Waze alerts. In: Proc. of SocInfo'13, Kyoto, Japan, pp. 309–318.

of the city for datasets of Instagram and Waze, we propose to divide the area of the cities into smaller rectangular spaces, as in a grid.[12] We call each rectangular area of a *specific area* within a city. We consider that a specific area has the following definition: $1 \cdot 10^{-4\circ}$ (latitude) $\times$ $1 \cdot 10^{-4\circ}$ (longitude). This represents an area of approximately 8×11 m in New York and 10×11 m in Rio de Janeiro. For other cities, the areas can also vary slightly, but not enough to significantly affect the analysis.

Fig. 5 shows the Complementary Cumulative Distribution Function (CCDF) of the number of shared data (check-ins, photos, or alerts) by specific area of all locations in our datasets. First, note that, in both cases, a power law[13] describes this distribution well. This implies that in most of the specific areas there are few shared data, while there are a few areas with hundreds of shared data. These results are consistent with the results presented in Noulas et al. (2011), work that studied the participation of users in location sharing systems. In the analyzed systems, it is natural that some areas have more activity than others. For example, in tourist areas the number of photos shared tends to be higher than in a supermarket, although a supermarket is usually a popular site. If a particular application requires a more comprehensive coverage, it is necessary to encourage users to participate in places they normally would not. Micro-payments or scoring systems are examples

---

[12]Note that in selected areas borders are not considered.

[13]Mathematically, a quantity x follows a power law if it can be obtained from a probability distribution $p(x) \propto x^{-\alpha}$, where α is a constant parameter known as exponent or scale parameter, and it is a value typically between $2 < \alpha < 3$ (Clauset et al., 2009).

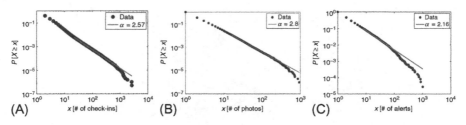

FIG. 5

Distribution of number of data in specific areas in log-log scale. (A) Foursquare;
(B) Instagram; (C) Waze.

Source: Images from: Silva, T.H., Vaz de Melo, P.O.S., Almeida, J.M., Loureiro, A.A.F., 2013a, July,
Challenges and opportunities on the large scale study of city dynamics using participatory sensing. In: Proc. of
IEEE ISCC'13, Split, Croatia, pp. 528–534; Silva, T.H., Vaz de Melo, P.O.S., Viana, A., Almeida, J.M., Salles,
J., Loureiro, A.A.F., 2013d, November, Traffic condition is more than colored lines on a map: characterization
of Waze alerts. In: Proc. of SocInfo'13, Kyoto, Japan, pp. 309–318.

of alternatives that could work in this case. We discuss these opportunities in
Section 5.3.

We show that a PSN may have a global scale coverage. However, this coverage
can be quite uneven, where large areas are practically uncovered. With that in mind,
Fig. 6 shows the percentage of different locations where users shared data in a given
time interval in Instagram and Foursquare,[14] which have 598,397 and 725,419 unique
places, respectively. The maximum percentage of distinct places that have new data
shared on it per hour is less than 3% for all systems. This indicates that the instant
coverage of these PSNs is very limited when we consider all locations that could be
sensed on the planet (considering all the locations already sensed at least once). In
other words, the probability of a random specific area being sensed at a random time
is very low.

3.3 SENSING INTERVAL

PSNs are very scalable because their nodes are autonomous, that is, users are
responsible for their own operation and functioning. As the cost of infrastructure
is distributed among the participants, this huge scalability and coverage is achieved
more easily. The success of this type of network is to have sustainable and high-
quality participation. In other words, the sensing is efficient since users are kept
motivated to often share their resources and sensed data.

This motivates the study of frequency that users perform data sharing in PSNs.
In Silva et al. (2013a,b,d) the authors show that there are times when a lot of data

---

[14]We consider the datasets Instagram2 and Foursquare3 because they represent the same time interval.

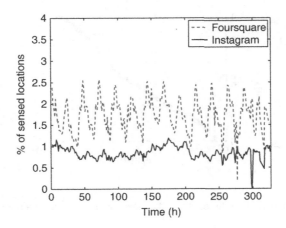

FIG. 6

Percentage of specific areas sensed over time.

Source: Image from: Silva, T.H., Vaz De Melo, P.O.S., Almeida, J.M., Loureiro, A.A.F., 2014b, February,
Large-scale study of city dynamics and urban social behavior using participatory sensing. IEEE Wirel.
Commun. 21 (1), 42–51.

are shared over intervals of a few minutes and times when there is no sharing for hours. This may indicate that the majority of data sharing occurs at specific intervals, probably related to people's routines. For example, photo sharing in restaurants tends to happen more in the lunch and dinner hours. Applications based on this type of sensing should consider that user involvement can vary significantly over time.

Fig. 7 shows the Cumulative Distribution Function (CDF) of the interval between photos shared by the same user on a popular specific area. We can see that a significant portion of users performs consecutive photos sharing over a short time interval. For example, about 20% of all observed photo sharing occurs within 10 min. This suggests that users tend to share more than one photo in the same area. Noulas et al. (2011) also noted that a significant number of check-ins on Foursquare are performed within a short time. For example, more than 10% of check-ins occur within 10 min.

3.4 ROUTINES AND DATA SHARING

We analyze now how the routine of humans affect data sharing. Fig. 8 shows the weekly data sharing pattern in all types of PSNs analyzed.[15] As expected, data shared in PSNs have a diurnal pattern, which implies that during the night the sensing activity is quite low.

---

[15]The sharing time was normalized according to the location where the data were shared, making use of geographic information of the location.

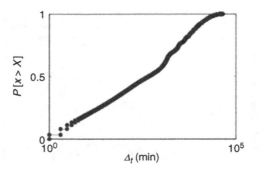

FIG. 7

Cumulative distribution of the time interval between photos shared in a popular
specific area.

Source: Image from: Silva, T.H., Vaz de Melo, P.O.S., Almeida, J.M., Salles, J., Loureiro, A.A.F., 2013b,
A picture of Instagram is worth more than a thousand words: workload characterization and application. In:
Proc. of DCOSS'13, Cambridge, USA, pp. 123–132.

Considering weekdays, we can see a slight increase in activity throughout the
week, with a few exceptions when there is a peak of activity. The study of Cheng
et al. (2011), who analyzed systems for location sharing, also observed this same
behavior without any day being an exception.

We can also note that some activity peaks vary throughout the day according to the
purpose of the PSN. As we can see in Fig. 8, in PSN for location sharing (Fig. 8A–C)
there are three peaks evident around the breakfast, lunch, and dinner time. This was
also noted by Cheng et al. (2011). In PSN for photo sharing (Fig. 8D) there are
only two obvious peaks occurring around lunch and dinner time. And in the case of
PSN for traffic alerts sharing (Fig. 8E) there are also two obvious peaks, one around
7:00am and 8:00am, and another around 6:00pm, coinciding with typical times of
highest traffic intensity.

Fig. 9 shows the temporal sharing pattern for Instagram and Foursquare considering all datasets. This figure shows the average number of data shared per hour
during weekdays (Monday to Friday) and during weekend (Saturday and Sunday).
Analyzing different patterns of behavior for weekdays and weekend we can see that
the pattern is significantly different. Note that the peaks observed on weekdays are
not evident on weekends. The lack of a well-defined routine on a weekend is one
of the possible explanations for that. Moreover, differences between the results for
weekdays and weekends are related to the type of the analyzed system. For example,
as on weekends many people do not need to drive, it is natural to expect a lower
volume of data in Waze.

Surprisingly, we see that each sharing pattern is very similar, despite the huge
gap between the samples (approximately 1 year). This happens for weekdays and
weekends, suggesting that user behavior in both systems tends to remain consistent

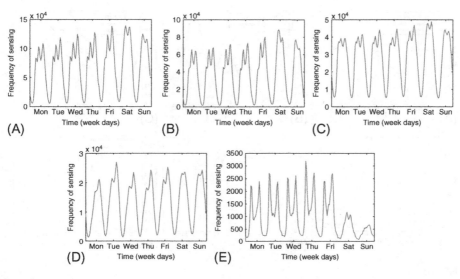

FIG. 8

Data sharing pattern during weekdays. (A) Foursquare; (B) Gowalla; (C) Brightkite;
(D) Instagram; (E) Waze.

*Source: Images from: Silva, T.H., Vaz de Melo, P.O.S., Almeida, J.M., Loureiro, A.A.F., 2013a, July, Challenges
and opportunities on the large scale study of city dynamics using participatory sensing. In: Proc. of IEEE
ISCC'13, Split, Croatia, pp. 528–534; Silva, T.H., Vaz de Melo, P.O.S., Almeida, J.M., Salles, J., Loureiro,
A.A.F., 2013b, A picture of Instagram is worth more than a thousand words: workload characterization and
application. In: Proc. of DCOSS'13, Cambridge, USA, pp. 123–132; Silva, T.H., Vaz de Melo, P.O.S., Viana,
A., Almeida, J.M., Salles, J., Loureiro, A.A.F., 2013d, November, Traffic condition is more than colored lines
on a map: characterization of Waze alerts. In: Proc. of SocInfo'13, Kyoto, Japan, pp. 309–318.*

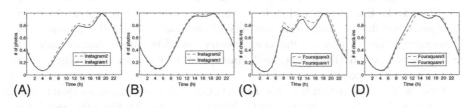

FIG. 9

Temporal sharing pattern on Instagram and Foursquare. (A) Instagram—weekday;
(B) Instagram—weekend; (C) Foursquare—weekday; (D) Foursquare—weekend.

*Source: Images from: Silva, T.H., Vaz de Melo, P.O.S., Almeida, J.M., Salles, J., Loureiro, A.A.F., 2013c,
A comparison of Foursquare and Instagram to the study of city dynamics and urban social behavior. In: Proc.
of UrbComp'13, Chicago, USA, pp. 1–8.*

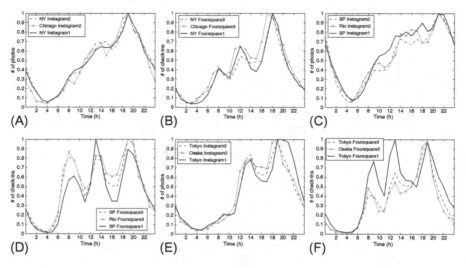

FIG. 10

Temporal sharing pattern for Instagram and Foursquare to New York, Sao Paulo, and Tokyo during weekdays. (A) New York—Instagram; (B) New York—Foursquare; (C) Sao Paulo—Instagram; (D) Sao Paulo—Foursquare; (E) Tokyo—Instagram; (F) Tokyo—Foursquare.

Source: Images from: Silva, T.H., Vaz de Melo, P.O.S., Almeida, J.M., Salles, J., Loureiro, A.A.F., 2013c, A comparison of Foursquare and Instagram to the study of city dynamics and urban social behavior. In: Proc. of UrbComp'13, Chicago, USA, pp. 1–8.

over time. This is an interesting and important result because it indicates that we can use different datasets of similar purposes.

We now show how the routines impact on the sharing behavior during the week. For this analysis, we consider the datasets of Instagram and Foursquare for New York, Sao Paulo, and Tokyo. The results are shown in Fig. 10.[16] In all figures we display data from datasets of the same period (Instagram2 and Foursquare3) for two cities in the same country, and data from a dataset referring to a previous period (Instagram1 and Foursquare1) to one of these cities, as a comparison reference.

First, note the distinction between the curves of each city in the same system (eg, in Instagram Fig. 10A, C, and E) and in different systems (eg, Fig. 10A and B for New York). Then note that the sharing pattern for each city in the same country is quite similar, which may be a consequence of the cultural patterns of inhabitants of

---

[16]Each curve is normalized by the maximum number of shared content in a specific region representing the city.

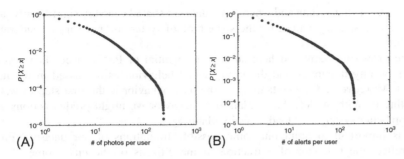

FIG. 11

Distribution of the number of data shared by users. (A) Instagram; (B) Waze.

Source: Images from: Silva, T.H., Vaz de Melo, P.O.S., Almeida, J.M., Salles, J., Loureiro, A.A.F., 2013b, A picture of Instagram is worth more than a thousand words: workload characterization and application. In: Proc. of DCOSS'13, Cambridge, USA, pp. 123–132; Silva, T.H., Vaz de Melo, P.O.S., Viana, A., Almeida, J.M., Salles, J., Loureiro, A.A.F., 2013d, November, Traffic condition is more than colored lines on a map: characterization of Waze alerts. In: Proc. of SocInfo'13, Kyoto, Japan, pp. 309–318.

those countries. That is, in some way, a signature of cultural aspects, illustrating once again the potential for this type of data for the study of city dynamics and urban social behavior.

3.5 NODE BEHAVIOR

In this section we analyze the performance of PSN nodes (ie, users) regarding data sharing. Fig. 11 shows the distribution of the data (photos and alerts) shared by each user in our database. As we can see, the distribution has a heavy tail, meaning that the participation of users can be very uneven. For example, about 40% of users contributed with only a picture during the period considered, while that 17% and 0.1% of users contributed with more than 10 and 100 pictures, respectively. It is natural that this variability occurs for several reasons. For instance, some users may give more importance to privacy questions than others. A heavy tail is also observed in the distribution of the number of check-ins, as shown by Noulas et al. (2011). About 20% of users performed only one check-in, 40% above 10, while about 10% performed more than 100 check-ins.

3.6 DISCUSSION

In this section we studied the properties of PSNs for location sharing, photo sharing, and traffic alert sharing. These PSNs have several properties in common: (i) global scale; (ii) highly unequal frequency of data sharing, both spatially and temporally, which is highly correlated with the typical routine of people; (iii) user participation in the number of shared data and where such data are shared can vary significantly; and (iv) temporal sharing pattern for the same type of system do not vary considerably over time.

The properties identified here show the potential of PSNs to conduct several studies on city dynamics and the urban social behavior, as discussed in the next section. Moreover, an understanding of the user behavior is the first step to wards modeling it. With models that explain user behavior we might predict actions and develop better systems for load capacity planning.

It is important to point out some possible limitations of our datasets. First, they reflect the behavior of a fraction of the citizens of the city. Some of our datasets are based on data shared by users of Foursquare, Instagram and Waze on Twitter. Therefore, data is skewed to the citizens that use these systems. Second, our datasets are based on a limited sample of data. This means we have just a sample of activities. External factors, such as bad weather may have affected the total number of data we collect for some places, especially in outdoor locations. Therefore, before drawing conclusions with PSN data, it is highly recommended that the results are compared with data obtained in a traditional way (offline), as done, for example, in Silva et al. (2014c).

4 WORKING WITH PSN DATA

In this section we discuss how to work with PSN data. In Section 4.1 we present how to obtain data from PSN. Next, we discuss some approaches to extract and generate contextual information from data of PSNs. These studies are grouped into two classes: Understanding city dynamics (Section 4.2); and Social, Economic, and Cultural patterns (Section 4.3).

4.1 DATA COLLECTION

In this section we introduce three main ways to collect data in PSNs: APIs, Web Crawler, and applications.

4.1.1 APIs

The web is full of sources of data, among them PSNs, representing a huge opportunity for researchers in several areas to collect large-scale data and extract information from them.

Some PSNs provide APIs that could be used to collect data. Through this process it is possible to obtain data from PSNs that can be used in other applications or in specific analysis. Several popular PSNs, such as Twitter, Instagram, and Foursquare, have APIs to access data shared by users. However, it is common to have different rules for their use.

Basically, there are two main ways of working with APIs: (1) Based on streaming; (2) Based on requests. The API based on streaming allows the collection of data in (almost) real time that they are published in a PSN. Twitter Streaming API, for instance, allows collecting in almost real time public tweets. On the other hand, an API based on requests makes data available upon request, which typically includes specifics demands, such as all the last 10 tweets from a user. Both methods can suffer limitations about the amount of data that can be provided. For example, Flickr API allows 5000 requests per hour, and the Twitter API might make approximately 1% from all the total public tweets available. This might prevent some kind of analysis that needs a large number of samples, for instance, in a 1 h period.

In fact, the use of APIs is a popular way to obtain data. Data collected from APIs, such as Twitter API, was used in many ways, ranging from the measurement of a user's influence in an network (Cha et al., 2010) to predicting earthquakes (Sakaki et al., 2010a).

An example of the use of Twitter Streaming API, written in (pseudo) Python and using TwitterAPI library,[17] is showed in Algorithm 3.1. This algorithm accesses tweets searching by keyword "foursquare." As we can see, in few lines of code it is possible to collect data from Twitter. Fig. 12 illustrates this result with two tweets: *tweet1* and *tweet2*.

ALGORITHM 1 EXAMPLE OF TWITTER DATA COLLECTION

```
 1: from TwitterAPI import TwitterAPI    ▷ Library that ease the interaction with the Twitter API
 2:
 3: twitter_api = TwitterAPI(consumer_key = 'XX',
 4: consumer_secret = 'XX',
 5: access_token_key = 'XX',
 6: access_token_secret = 'XX')        ▷ A registration in the API website provides the credentials
                                          needed
 7:
 8: filters = { 'track': ['4sq']}                ▷ Searching tweets with the keyword "foursquare"
 9: stream = twitter_api.request('statuses/filter', filters)
10:
11: for item in stream.get_iterator() do
12:     print item['text']                                        ▷ Display the tweet text
13: end for
```

Some PSNs offer APIs, but with restrict access. This is the case for Foursquare, where few data are can be collected without user agreement. Most of the data available through this API are related to places, such as: tips, location, and pictures.

These limitations encourage the collection of data using alternative ways. For instance, in Silva et al. (2014c) the authors collected data about Foursquare check-ins through public messages shared at Twitter. This is possible because Foursquare allows users to share check-ins in Twitter. This procedure is shown in Fig. 12. This picture shows a tweet that came from Foursquare and has an URL that represents a

---

[17]https://github.com/geduldig/TwitterAPI.

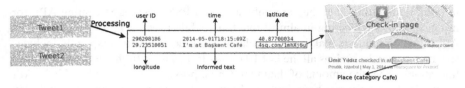

FIG. 12

Steps for Foursquare data collection through tweets.

web page with more information about the check-in announced. In the example, the page represents a check-in performed at a cafe. To obtain more data about the check-in in this page another data collection technique is used called Web Crawler, which is introduced in the next section.

4.1.2 Web crawler

Not all data sources available on the Internet provide direct access to their data through APIs. For this reason, it is necessary to use other strategies to obtain data. One of them is called Web Crawler, which are programs that analyze web pages searching for relevant data (Anbukodi and Manickam, 2011). A Web Crawler accesses some predefined web pages and retrieves data from them.

Data collection through a Web Crawler depends on the source structure for the data that we desire to obtain, and the approach chosen. The data source structure contains the data that we want in the web page. For instance, the content of some HTML tags. With this, the construction of a Web Crawler typically demands text mining for the extraction of the desired data. However, other nonconventional ways of data extraction are possible as well. For example, in Tostes et al. (2014) the authors built a Web Crawler to collect information about traffic by taking screenshots of maps, such as Bing Maps,[18] containing this information. More details about this procedure are provided in Tostes et al. (2014).

4.1.3 Applications

Another way to collect data is by creating applications in existing platforms. Some popular websites, such as Facebook[19] and Instagram allow the creation of applications inside their platforms. In this way, developers can offer services using data that are shared in those apps.

Facebook, for instance, does not allow the collection of data about their users directly by APIs or Web Crawlers. However, it is possible to create applications in the Facebook platform for this purpose. When a Facebook user installs an application and authorizes it to manipulate his/her data, the application can obtain diverse

---

[18]http://www.bing.com/maps.
[19]http://www.facebook.com.

information, such as the shared content with his/her friends. Next we illustrate some initiatives in this direction.

In Nazir et al. (2008) the authors used this approach for data collection. They created an application for Facebook specifically to collect data that allows the study of the behavior of people using this type of application. Another example was the application used in Youyou et al. (2015). The authors created an application for Facebook that obtained the last likes[20] given by the user to draw a personality profile.

It is also possible to create applications that do not depend on platforms. This is the case of the PSN NoiseTube (Maisonneuve et al., 2009). The authors created an application that enabled users to report noises levels in the city. These data allow the identification, for instance, of areas in the city with levels of noise above of the limits of the law. Another example is Colab, cited before. Besides that, there is a platform called *ohmage*[21] that eases the construction of applications to obtain data from participatory sensing.

With data from PSNs, that could be obtained using one of the approaches mentioned, we can gain knowledge using different strategies, as is discussed in the following sections.

4.2 UNDERSTANDING CITY DYNAMICS

Information obtained from PSNs has the power to change our perceived physical limits, as well as help to better understand the city dynamics. This section focuses on the presentation of studies in this direction.

Cranshaw et al. (2012) proposed a model to identify different areas of a city that reflect current patterns of collective activities, introducing new limits for neighborhoods. The idea is to expose the dynamic nature of local urban areas, considering the spatial proximity (derived from geographical coordinates) and social proximity (derived from the distribution of check-ins) locations.

For this, the authors used data from Foursquare and developed a model that groups similar places considering social and spatial characteristics. Each cluster represents different geographic boundaries of neighborhoods. The grouping method is a variation of spectral clustering proposed in Ng et al. (2002).

Fig. 13 shows two clusters (or "livehoods," name used by the authors), found in New York, represented by the numbers 1 and 2. In this figure black lines indicate the official city limits. Note that the limits of the clusters are quite different from the original limits. To try to validate these results the authors used results of interviews with residents of the city. According to the collected answers these and other clusters were expected.

In Silva et al. (2014d) the authors proposed a technique called City Image, which provides a visual summary of the city dynamics based on the movements of

---

[20] A *like* is a user interaction with Facebook in which he demonstrates that enjoyed a shared item.
[21] http://ohmage.org.

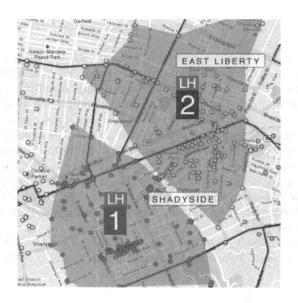

FIG. 13

"Livehoods" found in New York.

Source: Image from: Cranshaw, J., Schwartz, R., Hong, J.I., Sadeh, N., 2012. The livehoods project: utilizing social media to understand the dynamics of a city. In: Proc. of ICWSM'12, Dublin, Ireland.

people. This technique explores urban transition graphs to map the movements of users between city locations. An urban transition graph is a directed weighted graph $G(V, E)$, where a node $v_i \in V$ is the category of a specific location (for example, *food*) and a directed edge $(i, j) \in E$ marks a transition between two categories. That is, there is an edge from node v_i to the node v_j if at least one user shared data at a given place categorized by v_j after sharing data at a given place categorized by v_i. The weight $w(i, j)$ of an edge is the total number of transitions that occurred from v_i to v_j. Only consecutive data shared by the same user within 24 h starting at 5:00 are considered in calculating a transition.

City Image is a promising technique that allows a better understanding of city dynamics, helping to visualize the common routines of its citizens. Each cell in the City Image represents how favorable a transition is from a certain category in a certain place (vertical axis) to another category (horizontal axis). Red colors represent rejection, blue colors represent favorability, and white color is indifference. We exemplify the City Image technique for two cities[22]: Sao Paulo (Fig. 14A and B); and Kuwait (Fig. 14C and D). In both cases, we consider weekday during daytime,

---

[22]Using data from the dataset Foursquare1.

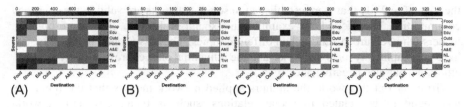

FIG. 14

Images produced with the City Image technique to Sao Paulo (SP) and Kuwait (KU) at different times. Abbreviations of category of places (names used by Foursquare): Arts & Entertainment (A&E); College & Education (Edu); Great Outdoors (Outd); Nightlife Spot (NL); Shop & Service (Shop); and Travel Spot (Trvl). (A) SP (Daytime—weekday); (B) SP (Night—weekend); (C) KU (Daytime—weekday); (D) KU (Night—weekend).

Source: Images from: Silva, T.H., Vaz De Melo, P.O.S., Almeida, J.M., Loureiro, A.A.F., 2014b, February, Large-scale study of city dynamics and urban social behavior using participatory sensing. IEEE Wirel. Commun. 21 (1), 42–51.

which is the typical period of routines, and weekend during the night, which is a representative period of leisure activities (out of routine).

First, note that transitions to *office* (workplaces) are more likely to occur on weekdays and during the day for both cities, as expected. However, note that the images of the city of Sao Paulo and Kuwait also have significant differences that reflect the cultural contrasts between the two cities. Note, for example, the image representing transitions on the weekend during the night (Fig. 14D) shows the lack of favorable transitions to the *nightlife* category in Kuwait. This is not the case for Sao Paulo (Fig. 14B), where the *food → nightlife* transition is highly favorable. This suggests that in Sao Paulo people like to go to places that involve food (*food*) before going to nightclubs (*nightlife*). In Kuwait, instead, people are probably more likely to perform the transitions *shop → food* and *food → home* in the evenings of the weekend.

Techniques to provide easy to interpret visualizations of the routines the of inhabitants of a city, such as those mentioned here, are valuable tools to help urban planners better understand the city dynamics and, therefore, make more effective decisions.

4.3 SOCIAL, ECONOMIC, AND CULTURAL PATTERNS

PSN data can also be used to study the social, economic, and cultural patterns of the inhabitants of cities. In order to better understand social patterns from PSN data, Quercia et al. (2012) studied how virtual communities, observed in the analyzed systems, resemble real-life communities. The authors tested whether sociological theories of real life that were established in social networks are valid in these virtual communities. They found, for example, that social brokers on Twitter are opinion leaders who venture "tweeting" on different topics. They also found that most users have geographically local networks, and the influential ones express not only positive emotions, but also negative ones.

To carry out this work, the authors applied network metrics that the literature has found to be related to social relations, such as reciprocity and network constraint (Quercia et al., 2012). The reciprocity r is the proportion of edges in a network that are bidirectional $L^{(-)}$ relative to the total number of edges L: $r = \frac{L^{(-)}}{L}$. Considering a social network focused on a specific node ("ego") and vertices and edges to whom the ego is directly connected, low reciprocity values could indicate, for example, a social network of a celebrity. Network constraint measures the opportunities to become influential (brokerage opportunities). A high network constraint value means fewer opportunities. In that case the authors used the Burt formulation (Burt, 1992).

In addition, by studying the social behavior of specific areas, one of the first questions that arises is: how different is one culture from other? We know that eating and drinking habits can describe strong cultural differences. Based on this, in Silva et al. (2014c) the authors propose a new methodology for identifying cultural boundaries and similarities between societies, with regard to eating and drinking habits. For this, they used check-ins from Foursquare to represent the user's preferences regarding what he/she eats and drinks locally, for example, in a particular city.

This analysis, surprisingly, says a lot about the differences and similarities between cultures. For this, the authors study the correlation between check-ins data in different types of restaurants for various cities around the world. They observed that cities of the same country, where the inhabitants are often from a similar culture, have the strongest correlations with respect to restaurant preferences. In addition to preferences for food and drink categories, it is also possible to see differences in the times that people go to restaurants and share data. These analyzes allowed the proposition of a methodology for identifying similar cultures, which can be applied in regions of varying sizes, such as countries, cities, or even neighborhoods (Silva et al., 2014c). This methodology uses a partitioning-based clustering algorithm (k-means, Hartigan and Wong, 1979), and the principal component analysis technique (Jolliffe, 2002). The results for countries and cities are illustrated in Fig. 15A and B, showing how similar cultures are well separated. These figures use the first and second principal component (P.C.) to show the results. However, to obtain the results we considered all components.

The investigation of the cultural differences between different cities and countries is valuable and can assist various applications. For example, as culture is an important aspect for economic reasons, the identification of similarities between places that are geographically separated may be required for companies with business in a country that want to assess the compatibility of preferences between different markets.

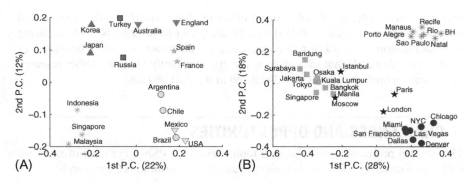

FIG. 15

Groups found using the methodology for culture separation. Each symbol reflects a group.
(A) Countries; (B) Cities.

Source: Images from: Silva, T.H., Vaz de Melo, P.O.S., Almeida, J.M., Musolesi, M., Loureiro, A.A.F., 2014c,
You are what you eat (and drink): identifying cultural boundaries by analyzing food & drink habits in
Foursquare. In: Proc. of ICWSM'14, Ann Arbor, USA.

Related to the economics of the cities, in Karamshuk et al. (2013) the authors
studied the problem of optimal allocation of retail stores in the city. They used
Foursquare data to understand how the popularity of three retail chain stores in New
York is defined in terms of number of check-ins.

The authors evaluated a diverse set of features, modeling spatial and semantic
information about the places and patterns of user movement in the area around the
analyzed site. They observed that the presence of places that attract many users
naturally, such as a train station or airport, as well as retail stores of the same
type, defining a local commercial competition area, are the strongest indicators of
popularity.

4.4 FINAL CONSIDERATIONS

PSNs provide updated information on places, as well as the opinions and preferences
of its members. Moreover, they have the potential of accessing the above data in
(almost) real time, reaching a large number of regions throughout the globe. This
section discussed several studies that serve as examples of how to work with PSN
data. The information obtained by these studies can be useful for the development of
more intelligent services and applications related to the study of city dynamics and
urban social behavior.

For example, understanding the pattern of behavior in certain places in the
city, as well as the identification of behaviors outside the expected pattern, can be

useful for load capacity planning of an urban mobile network. Studies that aim to provide solutions to ease mobile data offloading can have great benefits by using this information as a tool to reduce surprises at alterations in current demands, as well as new demands that may arise as the city constantly changes. Other research opportunities (and challenges) are discussed in the next section.

5 CHALLENGES AND OPPORTUNITIES

This section presents current research topics related to PSNs. For each of them we will also discuss the associated challenges and the opportunities for research.

5.1 SENSING LAYERS

5.1.1 Preliminaries

A sensing layer consists of data describing specific aspects of a geographic location. The concept of a sensing layer is quite broad: it represents data, with its attributes, from a particular data source, for example, a particular PSN. Each PSN provides access to data related to a certain aspect of a predefined geographic region (for instance, traffic conditions, pictures of places, etc.), and thus each single PSN can be represented as a sensing layer (Silva et al., 2014a).

In addition to PSNs, other source examples are: data available on the web not generated by users, for example, weather conditions provided by the company The Weather Channel[23] or data from traditional WSNs. We discuss here the concept of sensing layers to PSNs. However, all concepts discussed can be used for other data sources associated with predefined geographical regions, with necessary adaptations.

Fig. 16 illustrates the concept of sensing layers. This figure shows data shared in three different PSNs (p1, p2, and p3) by four different users in different time instants. As discussed in Section 2, these data should be collected (for example, using an API) and processed, using steps that include analysis and data standardization. Each plane in the figure represents a sensing layer of a specific region, for example, Manhattan in New York, with data from three different sources. Thus, the illustrated sensing layers are: check-ins (r1), from, for instance, Foursquare; traffic alerts (r2) from, for example, Waze; and pictures of places (r3), from Instagram, for example.

In one layer each item from the data has the following attributes: instant t when the data were shared; location a where the data were shared; specialty s of the layer (eg, a picture or a alert about traffic); and the id u of the user who shared the data.

5.1.2 Framework for the integration of multiple layers

In this section we present the general idea of a framework to work with multiple sensing layers defined in Silva et al. (2014a). Each user u can share unlimited data in any PSN p. Each jth data d_j shared in a PSN p_k has the form $d_j^{p_k} = \langle t, m \rangle$, where

---

[23]http://www.weather.com.

FIG. 16

Data sharing illustration in three PSNs over time, resulting in sensing layers.

Source: Image from: Silva, T.H., Vaz de Melo, P., Almeida, J., Viana, A., Salles, J., Loureiro, A., 2014a, Participatory sensor networks as sensing layers. In: Proc. of SocialCom'14, Sydney, Australia.

t refers to the moment when the user u shared data in p_k and m is a tuple containing the attributes of these data, ie, $m = (a, u, s)$, as described above.

Data shared in a PSN can be seen as a data stream B. The authors defined that a data stream B^{p_k} consists of all data shared by users in a PSN p_k in a given time interval. Thus, B^{p_k} is used to represent a sensing layer r_{p_k}. Table 2 shows the data of the sensing layers that have been shared in the three PSNs considered in Fig. 16.

Table 2 Data Stream Describing Users' Activities in Three Different PSNs: Foursquare, Waze, and Instagram

Timestamp (t)	Attributes (m)		
	Area (a)	User (u)	Specialty data (s)
(a) Foursquare PSN			
T1	a_1	1	"Times square"
T1	a_1	2	"Times square"
T2	a_2	1	"Fifth Av."
T3	a_4	1	"Statue of Liberty"
(b) Waze PSN			
T1	a_1	3	"Traffic Jam"
T2	a_2	2	"Accident"
T2	a_3	3	"Police control"
(c) Instagram PSN			
T1	a_1	3	"photo data"
T3	a_4	1	"photo data"

Source: Silva, T.H., Vaz de Melo, P., Almeida, J., Viana, A., Salles, J., Loureiro, A., 2014a, Participatory sensor networks as sensing layers. In: Proc. of SocialCom'14, Sydney, Australia.

To work with layers we need to represent them in a *work plan*, which contains one or more layers. This work plan is a combination of data from the layers that we want to work with. Making this combination of data depends on the layer functionality: what it captures. Various structures can be used for this task, in Silva et al. (2014a) the authors used a data dictionary, chosen for its simplicity which facilitates the understanding of the concepts.

5.1.3 Challenges and opportunities

There are several challenges to handling data from multiple layers simultaneously, some of the main ones are described below.

1. **Data combination:** In order to combine data we have to ensure that they are consistent across all layers. This is a mandatory condition for the correct extraction of information. For example, to combine data shared by the same user on different layers can be a problem in PSNs, because the same user may participate in different layers with different IDs. Let us assume we want to combine data from a single user that contributed in the check-ins layer and in the picture of places layer. Since the data of these layers are from independent systems, users have different IDs. One way to try to get around this problem is to check other systems in order to map the user ID of a layer in another. We know, for example, that users of Foursquare and Instagram tend also to be Twitter users. Thus, the combination process could use the identification used on Twitter. Without data management techniques that allow developers to combine data from multiple heterogeneous sensing layers, it becomes very hard to meet important requirements for urban computing applications, such as quickly responding to user queries about real time traffic conditions.

2. **Validity of the data:** Different layers can refer to data that are valid for different time intervals. This is natural because some data sources provide data in (almost) real time, while others do not. For example, an alert shared in Waze may refer to a traffic situation that may not exist 5 min later. However, census data are generally valid for a long time, months or years, until the next census is published. We have to be aware of all these issues when designing new applications.

3. **Modeling:** There are also opportunities regarding the modeling of sensing layers because in the same layer the entities can have different relationships between them. To illustrate this opportunity, consider the check-ins layer. As illustrated above, this layer may be used to represent urban mobility considering the relationship between places and people, being useful for understanding, for example, the frequency of transition between different places. Another possibility is to modify the problem modeling, for example, to study the preferences of individuals. In this case, the entity to be analyzed becomes the user. Note that data from the same layer can be modeled in different ways to answer different questions. The framework presented briefly here (discussed in more detail in Silva et al., 2014a), provides basic support for this issue. However, there are several opportunities for extending that framework to offer more sophisticated services.

5.2 TEMPORAL DYNAMICS OF PSNs

5.2.1 Preliminaries

The study of PSN data emerges as a powerful resource for understanding city dynamics (Silva et al., 2014b). Most of the studies found in the literature represent data shared in PSNs as static structures, disregarding the temporal dynamics. Despite being an acceptable strategy this procedure may result, in many cases, in loss of important information in some scenarios.

To better illustrate this problem, consider the graph presented in Fig. 17. This figure represents a static graph resulting of aggregated data from a certain day, where each vertex represents a Point of Interest (PoI) and the weighted edges represent the number of times people moved from one PoI to another (in any order). From this, note that the top three most popular transitions are A–C, D–E, and A–B. However, this observed information might present differences when a temporal perspective is considered.

When we partition the same dataset in three different intervals, as shown by Fig. 18, we can see that the graph topology, as well as the weights of the edges, change considerably throughout the time. Note first that in the second time interval we observe a disconnected graph, ie, transitions B–D, C–D, and C–F do not occur. This information could not be obtained using the static graph (Fig. 17). Furthermore, note also that the weights of the edges change over time in the dynamic model. Observe in the first time interval that the top three most popular transitions are D–E, D–F, and E–F, while in the third time interval the top three most transitions are A–B, A–C, and B–C, information significantly different from the one obtained with a static model. This type of analysis can be useful to extract more precise information on human behavior in the cities (Holme and Saramki, 2012). In this regard, the

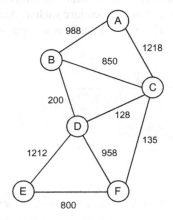

FIG. 17

Example of static graph representation.

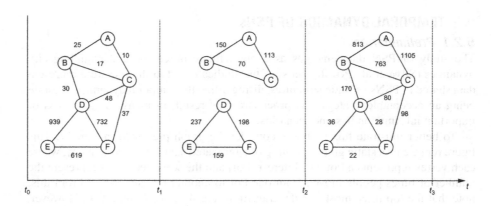

FIG. 18

Example of graphs in different periods of time.

following are some efforts that try to exploit the temporal dimension in data analysis from PSNs.

Bannur and Alonso (2014) have analyzed data from Facebook check-ins to understand the temporal user participation in various categories of places (eg, restaurants, cinemas, and get-away). The authors have defined a metric, called polarity, which represents the relationship between the number of check-ins for a category in a given region and season, and the total number of check-ins in the same region during the entire year. Fig. 19 shows the change in polarity of the category get-away among USA states throughout the four seasons. The polarity is represented by a heat map. The intensity ranges from low (light color) to high polarity (dark color). As we can see, during winter and spring, states with high temperatures have a much higher polarity compared to those with low temperature. On the other hand, during the summer, states with low temperature such as Alaska and Montana appear as states with high polarity. This type of analysis is interesting and helps to explain

Winter	Spring	Summer	Fall

FIG. 19

Visualization of check-ins for get-away category in every USA state over the four seasons.

Source: Image from: Bannur, S., Alonso, O., 2014. Analyzing temporal characteristics of check-in data. In: Proc. of WWW Companion '14, Seoul, Korea, pp. 827–832. http://dx.doi.org/10.1145/2567948.2579041.

certain human behaviors based on seasonal phenomena. For example, in the fall, Nebraska has a high polarity. Nebraska is subject to tornadoes and thunderstorms during the summer and spring, whereas in winter it suffer from ice storms, thereby influencing human behavior in the category of get-aways.

Zhang et al. (2013) have analyzed urban activities from Foursquare data considering temporal dynamics. For this, they studied activities of groups of users with similar characteristics, considering the categories of places visited by them. Considering first the whole dataset without any separation of periods of the day, ie, aggregated data, activities on the food category of places are prevailing. However, analyzing the same dataset partitioned in different periods of the day (morning, afternoon, and evening), there is a greater distinction between the prevailing activities. For instance, activities in food places in the afternoon are not as popular as in the morning and evening. In the aggregated view they do not notice this difference. This approach is interesting and shows that certain activities may be performed only at a certain time of day, but when they are analyzed disregarding the temporal aspect, important insights about users' behaviors may be missed.

The City Image technique, presented in Section 4.2, is another initiative that exploits the temporal dimension. This dimension is applied for partitioning the data on weekdays/weekend into different periods of the day; from that the authors performed analysis on the partitioned data. With the help of this technique it is possible to see that there is significant variation in the popular types of activities at different periods of the day. Moreover, the results from applying this technique without considering the time dimension are quite different from those when considering it (Silva et al., 2012).

5.2.2 Challenges and opportunities

The related work described above provides evidence of the advantages of using temporal information for the data obtained from PSNs. However, if on one hand the investigation of temporal dynamics of PSNs is an opportunity to obtain information closer to the real network behavior, on the other hand, new challenges arise when we consider the temporal dimension of a study, as described below:

1. **Temporal information:** An initial issue is how to represent and store temporal information. Since data can be derived from many sources, we face problems related to inconsistency, redundancy, and granularity when extracting the relevant temporal information. In addition, there are questions as to the validity of the information obtained. For instance, how long will the information be useful or how often should the information be updated?

2. **Time windows:** Studies that analyze the temporal aspect often partition the data into time intervals called time windows, eg, morning, afternoon, and evening. However, the proper definition of the time window size is a problem, it is necessary to define a window size that captures relevant dynamics. In this case, there are many opportunities for new approaches that consider time windows with flexible and dynamic sizes;

3. **Dynamic participation:** Since the structure of a PSN is composed of autonomous nodes (people), it is sensitive to the participation of these nodes over time. This brings with it a range of challenges related to the evolution of user participation in these networks, some examples are: identification of periodic behavior, detection of outliers, and activity tracking. In this direction there are several opportunities for the development of new techniques/approaches;

4. **Modeling:** Typically, data from PSNs are represented as a set of entities, for example, users or points of interest, and their relationships, eg, transitions or communication. As the contribution of these data can vary greatly over time, a model based on static graphs may not be enough to capture this dynamism. For example, data from Foursquare uses spatiotemporal information, such as the positioning of users and the moments of interaction. Therefore, a challenge is to model spatiotemporal dynamics in order to better understand, for example, user participation. In this direction, temporal graphs (Kostakos, 2009) appears as a promising alternative that can be used to understand spatiotemporal dynamics. In a temporal graph, relations between entities can be modeled as edges that can be created and destroyed over time. This is useful, for instance, to understand the temporal aspects of interactions between users with certain places in the city.

5. **Data visualization:** The use of visualization techniques that help in the understanding of network behavior is fundamental to assist in decision making. Thus, visualizations that explore the temporal dynamics of PSNs are of paramount importance. For example, a proper visualization of the transitions of users in the city over time is useful to planners and other professionals who need to make decisions related to urban planning.

5.3 INCENTIVE MECHANISM FOR PSN

5.3.1 Preliminaries

The selfish, altruistic, and cooperative behavior of human beings has been extensively studied in philosophy, psychology, economics, and, recently, in the context of computer science (Miao et al., 2013). Selfishness can be defined as the act that benefits oneself instead of another. On the other hand, altruism favors others instead of oneself (Levine, 1998). Incentive mechanisms aim to encourage users to cooperate with others. Cooperation occurs when an individual devotes an effort that implies a cost to some collective activity and expects some benefit. Unlike altruism, in cooperation the individual expects a benefit that is greater than the costs (Bowles and Gintis, 2003).

Cooperation is a key point for PSN since it relies on users' willingness to collect, process, and transmit the sensed data (Lee and Hoh, 2010). The cooperation among PSN participants reflects directly on the quality and quantity of the sensed data, and hence in improving services offered by PSNs.

However, as PSNs consume the resources of devices, the users may be reluctant to contribute to the network. There are several reasons why a user may not collaborate with PSNs, despite the potential benefit, such as to save battery power, data transmission costs, or even privacy issues (Lee and Hoh, 2010).

Thus, incentive mechanisms aim to encourage users to with the PSNs. In recent years, academia and industry have proposed dozens of incentive mechanisms (Gao et al., 2015). The motivation for cooperation can be extrinsic, in which participants receive a direct reward for participating, or intrinsic, in which participants must be satisfied psychologically (Kaufmann et al., 2011).

As extrinsic mechanisms reward participants through payments, real or virtual, we will refer to these mechanisms as *Reward-based*. Intrinsic mechanisms are based on transforming the sensing task into a more enjoyable and challenging one for the user by adding common game elements, such as a contest among users, badges, and trophies. Therefore, we will address these mechanisms as *Gamification-based*.[24]

5.3.2 User cooperation

Cooperation in the context of PSNs depends on the relationship between the cost and benefit to participate on them. Fitzek et al. (2013) claim that cooperation will occur whenever a participant of the network has the feeling that the benefit is higher than the cost of collaborating. This benefit could be one of many things, for example, the quality of the information that a PSN can offer.

Fig. 20 illustrates important aspects about user cooperation in a PSN. A user requests information from a PSN using a mobile network (eg, 3G), while obtaining his or her location using a GPS network and collecting the new information using sensors from a portable device. Next, the user transmits the sensed data to the PSN. The costs for accomplishing this task can be listed as: power consumption; data transmission over the mobile network; and the effort to perform the sensing task. Meanwhile, the user obtains as benefits: updated real-time information; and the feeling of helping other participants in the network (for altruistic users). Note that,

FIG. 20

Important aspects about user cooperation in an PSN.

---

[24]The use of game features as incentive mechanisms to perform tasks is known in the literature as *gamification*.

a user with resource constraints or a selfish user could obtain information from the PSN without contributing new data to it.

There are also situations in which the benefit for cooperative behavior is unclear. For instance, PSNs that aim to gather information about pollution or the health of the individual (Burke et al., 2006). In these examples, participants may not have access to real-time information and the beneficiaries of the information gathered would be public authorities and health centers. In these situations, incentive mechanisms act as a "driving force" to encourage user cooperation.

5.3.3 Reward-based incentive mechanisms

Reward-based incentive mechanisms rely on the assumption that participants will not contribute or will contribute only for a short period to the PSN if the benefits are less than their expectations (Lee and Hoh, 2010).

In some mechanisms, users negotiate with the PSN platforms regarding how much they will receive for the sensed data before sending them, in others the platform decides how much is going to be paid for data sent by the users. In any case, these mechanisms aim to improve the quality of data and minimize sensing costs.

Yang et al. (2012) proposed two incentive mechanisms: *MSensing Platform-Centric* and *MSensing Auction*. In the *MSensing Platform-Centric*, PSNs have a limited budget to spend with sensing tasks. The PSN announces the reward for a certain task and each participant receives a reward proportional to the time dedicated to the task. One problem with this model is that if the number of active participants increases, the reward for each participant decreases.

In the *MSensing Auction*, the PSN platform announces a set of tasks and each user chooses a subset. For each task chosen, users must submit a tuple, *task-bid*, to the platform, where the "bid" is the value of reward he/she wants to receive to perform the task. After receiving the offers from the users, the PSN platform selects a set of users as the winners of the auction, and these users will perform the tasks. A problem encountered in this type of mechanism is the explosion of the incentive costs (Lee and Hoh, 2010). This problem can derail the mechanism due the high cost that might be incurred by the platform. In addition, if the winner is always the user that offers the lowest price, this user may be discouraged from continuing to sense data for the PSN, due to the low values received. Incentive mechanisms based on game theory attempt to overcome the issues above by aiming to achieve the equilibrium of the system, ie, maximize the gain for the user, while minimizing the costs for the platform (Xie et al., 2009; Lee and Hoh, 2010; Yang et al., 2012).

Reddy et al. performed small-scale experiments to evaluate the effect of payments for cooperation in participatory sensing (Reddy et al., 2010a). The authors concluded that incentives work better when micro payments are combined with other factors, such as user altruism and competition. In addition, they showed that a fair payment for all participants kept them motivated for a longer time than low payments.

Indeed, payments can be counterproductive in some cases, as shown by Kamenica in Kamenica (2012). After reviewing several studies in psychology and economics on the effect of payment as an incentive mechanism, the author concluded that, in many cases, paying a high or too low value proved to be counterproductive when it came to inducing participants into collaborative behavior.

5.3.4 Gamification-based incentive mechanism

Gamification can be defined as the use of elements (and design) of games in non-related game contexts (Deterding et al., 2011). Examples of such elements are: score tables; trophies or medals to reward users who perform a given task; challenges; avatars; difficulty levels; and social networks to check on the performance of "friends" in the task development, with those who performed more tasks, for instance, having a higher ranking.

Unlike traditional games, gamification uses game elements with the purpose of encouraging users to perform tasks not related to a game (Werbach and Hunter, 2012). These tasks may linked to, for instance, improving a skill, encouraging fitness, or, in the context of PSNs, engaging users to contribute sensed data for a long period.

As an example of a PSN that uses a gamification-based mechanism, we can mention Waze. In order to keep information up to date, Waze requires the active participation of users, ie, participants must manually report observed situations, such as car accidents. In Waze, game elements are represented by the use of avatars and a score system. In this case, more cooperative users achieve special avatar or badges. As a result, Waze helps to raise the volume of shared data, and the quality of traffic information for all users. The incentives that lead a user to cooperate with Waze can range from simple altruistic motivation to the social rewards (score and badges) given by gamification.

5.3.5 Challenges and opportunities

An incentive mechanism is efficient if it recruits more participants to a PSN and keeps them active in the network. In order to encourage users to become active participants a PSN also faces social and psychological challenges. In this section, we present some of the main challenges for the proposition of incentive mechanisms for PSNs:

1. **Costs of incentive mechanisms based on monetary reward:** For monetary incentive mechanisms to be successful the costs for PSN platforms, as well as the earnings for participants must be considered. PSN platforms can limit these costs by defining a maximum value to be paid to the active network participants. However, finding and deciding a value that minimizes the cost to the platform and, at the same time, motivates the users requires further investigation (Gao et al., 2015).
2. **Combination of different strategies:** The majority of the proposals to encourage cooperation in PSNs focuses on only one strategy. However, as observed by Reddy et al., a combination of more than one incentive mechanism simultaneously may achieve better results (Reddy et al., 2010a).
3. **Proposal validation:** Authors commonly validate their proposals of incentive mechanisms using a theoretical approach or small controlled experiments.

However, these strategies may not be able to predict with high accuracy the participation of users over time on the platform. Although there are already successfully PSNs on the market using gamification as an incentive mechanism, there is no guarantee that this technique would work on other PSNs. Which elements work (or not work) for certain types of PSNs requires further investigation.

5.4 QUALITY OF DATA FROM PSN

5.4.1 Preliminaries

The quality of data is a topic widely studied by the scientific community, and the topics range from the definition of the metrics to qualitatively assess a given piece of data to solutions that ensure the generation and recovery of quality data.

According to the dictionaries, the term *quality*, by itself, can be used to express both a characteristic possessed by someone or something, or a degree of excellence in a given subject. Adapting this to our context, we need to think of quality as the property that a given piece of data, originated from a PSN, has or has not, and also as a way to evaluate the degree of confidence we can have in this piece of data.

This means that we need to represent quality in a more technical way. From a computer perspective, quality refers to the correct compliance with the requirements for a system. Therefore, to evaluate if these requirements are met, some metrics that summarize the main characteristics of such system have to be defined.

Generally, data collected from the PSNs, after processing, are used to extract contextual information, which is essential to the context aware systems (Dey and Abowd, 2000). Thus, one way to evaluate the quality of data from a PSN is by the expected quality of contextual information they provide, which can be defined by the concept of Quality of Context (QoC) (Buchholz and Schiffers, 2003).

Buchholz and Schiffers (2003) define QoC as any information that describes the quality of the inferred context, which is consistent with our needs. The authors also outline the differences between QoC and Quality of Service (QoS) and Quality of Device (QoD) concepts. QoS refers to any information that describes how well a service operates, and QoD is related to any information about the technical properties and capabilities of a given device. Thus, the authors propose the following QoC metrics to measure quality: *precision*, *probability of correctness*, *trust-worthiness*, *resolution*, and *up-to-dateness*.

Contextualizing these metrics to a PSN scenario, *precision* of the data is related to how well it reflects the current state of a specific phenomenon or locality. *The probability of correctness* denotes the probability that a given piece of data is correct, this metric can be seen as a statistic that reflects an *a priori* knowledge of the data or the user that generated it. *Trust-worthiness* is similar to the probability of correctness, but it is used to classify the quality of the user that generated the data. *Resolution* denotes the granularity of the information, that, as discussed in Section 3, may represent the details of coverage of a particular region. Finally, *up-to-dateness* describes the age of the data, being essential to assess its validity when there are real-time requirements.

In the same direction, Li et al. (2012) extended this QoC definition to evaluate the quality of the data from pervasive environments. By investigating the challenges of providing data with quality in such environments, they proposed three additional metrics to assess the source of these data: *currency*, *availability*, and *validity*. *Currency* is related to the previously discussed up-to-dateness, it represents the temporal utility of the data, from the moment it is created until it becomes worthless. *Availability* measures the capability of an entity to provide data when the information about a region is needed. In the context of PSNs, this can be expressed as the expectation that the data are generated by a user. *Validity* is defined as a set of rules that can be used to validate the generated data, according to previous knowledge about the type of the data and the behavioral pattern of the users.

With the computational representation of quality, we can describe some challenges and opportunities when dealing with the quality of data from PSNs.

5.4.2 Challenges

Following the aforementioned discussion, we can summarize the main expected requirements for data generated by PSNs in two aspects: (i) data reliability; and (ii) users' credibility. Data reliability means the confidence we can assign to the data we have. The credibility of the users generating these data is another important aspect of quality of data. Thus, some of the main challenges that may affect quality of data in PSNs, impacting on the metrics previously presented, are:

1. **Sample representativeness:** This challenge is related to how representative a sample is about a specific phenomenon, based on the amount of collected data. Due to its high relevance, this is a widely discussed aspect in several studies that deal with data sampling. From the PSN point of view, as discussed in Section 3, the collected data may represent a portion of the population of a city and the extracted information is based on this sample. Depending on the sampling, it is possible that the inferred information does not correctly represent the analyzed phenomenon. Then, as previously mentioned, before inferring conclusions from the data sampled from PSNs, it is necessary to compare them with other sources, for instance with data collected in offline mode.
2. **Sensing errors:** Another challenge that might affect the precision of PSN data is the occurrence of possible sensing errors in the user's portable device. For instance, a Global Positioning System (GPS) might be poorly calibrated, generating data whose accuracy is beyond the acceptable range for this type of data. Although some errors may seem totally tolerable, depending on the application it is possible that it demands a high precision for its correct functioning.
3. **Subjectivity of interpretation:** This challenge concerns the different meanings the data may have, one for the user that generated it and another for whoever will use it. For example, it is possible to find data that were misclassified and shared in a PSN. Foursquare, for instance, allows the definition of a category to

be added to a new place, even if this definition is not the most appropriated, and the system must correct it subsequently. Another example is the Weddar system, which allows its users to share their interpretations of current weather conditions. While a user may interpret a shared temperature as the temperature inside his house, another user may interpret it as the temperature in a park in the same region. In this case, the interpretation of these two users may be quite different.

4. **Absence of structure:** Data shared in PSNs, in some cases, are composed by free text, without a semantic structure or encoding. This freedom given to users allows them to post whatever they want, even wrong information, and in different formats. For instance, a user could describe a traffic accident in a foreign language or by using slang through a microblog like Twitter. Thus, the processing of these data is complex and prone to errors, since there is the possibility, for example, of data duplicity, ie, the same data being identified as distinct, or distinct data interpreted as the same due to differences in filled fields.

5. **Pollution of data:** Pollution of data is related to the possibility of data being incorrect due to the user's malicious behavior (Coen-Porisini and Sicari, 2012; Mashhadi and Capra, 2011). We can find this malicious behavior in several social activities, and the same can also occur in PSNs. As an example, users in PSNs for traffic alert sharing like Waze can generate false alerts for traffic jams or accidents in order to discourage other users from using certain streets on his/her route. Malicious behavior may result in false positives on the detection of social patterns or events.

5.4.3 Opportunities

An important research topic that is affected by the quality of data in PSNs is the one related to the techniques of processing and knowledge extraction. One possible approach to the handling of this problem is to model the data as a time series and extract knowledge using signal processing techniques (Lathi and Green, 2014). However, in some cases, data from PSNs may not follow a constant pattern in order to ease this processing. As previously mentioned, data from PSNs are subject to problems of subjectivity in interpretation and an absence of structure, which may result in errors during the learning of the pattern and other properties of a certain phenomenon.

An interesting approach to solving these problems in interpretation is given by Georgescu et al. (2014). The authors improved some data classification algorithms by using Mechanical Turk (Mturk).[25] In this service users are financially rewarded for completed tasks, eg, solving issues raised by classification algorithms. The combination of computational processing and human intelligence offers important research opportunities regarding the participatory sensing scenarios.

Another opportunity is to evaluate the reliability of a given user in a PSN, since data generated by reliable users probably also will be more reliable. One possible

---

[25] http://www.mturk.com.

direction in this sense is related to the identification of the behavioral patterns of users in the PSN. As shown in Fig. 8, when a sufficient amount of data are aggregated, it is clearly possible to identify these patterns in the shared data for different week days. Assuming this previous knowledge as a reference of the expected pattern by users in a given PSN, one possibility would be to compare the behavior of a suspected user with this reference pattern. For instance, users with a sharing pattern quite different from the majority may represent an unreliable user (eg, a malicious robot).

That approach can be characterized as a kind of collaborative filtering technique (Adomavicius and Tuzhilin, 2005). This is a strategy used by recommending systems when there is no previous knowledge available regarding the user for whom it should recommend an item. For instance, by using the preferences of other similar users, assuming that their preferences are also similar.

Other alternatives to assess the quality of data in PSNs are based on the analysis of the reputation of the users generating it, aiming to increase the credibility with their good behavior. Huang et al. (2010) propose the computation of a user reputation score, which is related to the trustworthiness of his contributed data. They compute this score for each user based on an outlier detection algorithm, that uses a consensus-based technique to identify the users that deviate most from the consensus data of all users.

Mashhadi and Capra (2011) propose an extension to the previous work of Huang et al. (2010) to estimate the quality of users' contributions considering their credibility. They consider the contribution of points of interest by users and define regularity functions with respect to the mobility pattern of these users, and a reputation function considering their reliability based on previous contributions with the system. The feasibility of this proposal is based on studies demonstrating that urban users exhibit a high level of regularity in their daily activities. This regularity, represented as the frequency of repetitions of locations, is the pattern that helps in the identification of the credibility of a user.

Several strategies discussed here point towards solutions to the two mentioned requirements of PSNs, ie, reliability of data and credibility of the users. However, an important point emphasized by Flanagin and Metzger (2008) is that such aspects are less related to the precision of the data itself and more to what information, or perspective, their users hold regarding those data. In other words, there is still a lot of subjectivity about the notion of the quality of data shared in PSNs. Thus, a strategy that focuses on dealing with the quality of these data must consider the needs of each application and try to attend their requirements specifically.

5.5 PSNs AND VEHICULAR NETWORKS

5.5.1 Preliminaries

Vehicular Networks (VANETs) offer a range of opportunities for urban monitoring and data sharing on various aspects of the traffic. Vehicular networks do not have common constraints of WSNs, such as energy, bandwidth, and memory constraints, which allows for more accurate sensing and a larger amount of data to be collected.

Furthermore, vehicles can contain sensors that are not commonly available in portable devices used in PSNs.

Another important aspect of VANETs is the coverage. Vehicles move through the whole city using streets and avenues. Because of this spread of mobility, vehicular networks can capture the details for several cities. All these features make VANETs an important data source that can complement data gained from PSNs, in order to better understand the urban phenomena.

Vehicular applications can be used in numerous scenarios. For instance, in VANETs there are diverse situations to be monitored, such as potholes, traffic jams, car accidents, and the presence of animals on the road. Thus, in this section, we present studies that focus on three main issues: monitoring general traffic events; the use of data of VANETs to study people's routines; and the study of traffic jams. We also discuss various challenges associated with these issues.

5.5.2 Monitoring events

In VANETs vehicles can cooperate in the collection of data, which enables the identification of events, and propagate them to the interested parties. Thus, these data can directly influence the vehicle routes, making drivers, in many cases, redefine their trajectories. da Cunha et al. (2014a) presented a service for event monitoring and data dissemination, which considers vehicle mobility patterns. Thus, when a vehicle detects an event in its region, it propagates this information to other vehicles, warning of danger ahead. In addition, this broadcast takes into account the interactions between vehicles, selecting those that guarantee greater coverage in the data dissemination.

Another possible method used to sense events within the vehicular networks is presented by Lee et al. (2006b), known as MobEyes. The goal of this solution is the use of vehicles equipped with sensors to collect data about roads and other vehicles nearby. However, due to the amount of data generated, we can associate some data filters, and, thus, only the most relevant data will be stored and forwarded to the sink. In this scenario, algorithms that control collection and data delivery to the sink should take account of the peculiarities and restrictions of VANETs.

With the aim of achieving different goals, Lee et al. (2006a) presented FleaNet, a platform for submitting queries regarding vehicular networks. Vehicles receive and submit queries about various traffic issues. For example, a mobile user detects an accident and shares a picture with the next vehicle. Alternatively, a market or a store can disseminate alerts offering promotions to nearby users in vehicles. In addition, a user can submit queries to the network, looking for nearby type places or attractions.

5.5.3 Routines and behaviors

Considering the mobility of vehicles and their daily routes, it is possible to extract several cultural features of the users' routines, such as their interests and the most popular places in the city. Based on this, the study proposed by da Cunha et al. (2014b) presents an analysis of GPS traces describing the mobility of vehicles in the city. From the traces, it is possible to identify similar behavioral patterns on the network and better understand the routines followed in the cities. The greater the number of records about vehicles, the better the quality of the characterized data. However, obtaining these data is not a trivial matter, because users must allow the monitoring of their vehicles.

Fiore et al. (2014) presents an analysis of vehicle mobility in order to characterize the traffic in a city through the understanding of flows and places visited. Based on the analysis of a trace of mobility, the authors demonstrate how the use of a real information about the mobility of vehicles[26] can help in the evaluation of the performance of protocols for VANETs. From the analysis, they showed that it is possible to improve the performance of protocols and better understand the traffic distribution in the city.

5.5.4 Traffic management

The literature presents several models that deal with traffic jams. Some of them only detect traffic jams (eg, Jain and Sethi, 2012; Wisitpongphan et al., 2012), others make traffic jam predictions (eg, Kong et al., 2013; Kurihara, 2013), and others do both (eg, Horvitz, 2015; Marfia and Roccetti, 2011). They are different mainly due to the following aspects: (i) time horizon to predict future jams; (ii) techniques used in the model; (iii) data sources that have been used.

Regarding the time horizon, we have the following two categories: (i) models for *Short-term traffic flow forecasting (STFF)*, which predict the traffic behavior from the next 5 min to 1 h (Sun et al., 2004); (ii) jam prediction for the next 1 hour (at least) are named *Long-term traffic flow forecasting (LTFF)*. Models that predict traffic jams for the next 15 or 30 min are much more interesting and useful than the others, since this is a reasonable time interval that can be used in making a decision. Despite having several STFF and LTFF prediction models, the usage of PSNs can improve the models' accuracy depending on which social variables have been used. Since PSN data are associated with habits and routines of users, the challenge is how to obtain and how to use such data in real time, mainly for STFF.

The most used techniques for traffic jam prediction are: Seasonal AutoRegressive Integrated Moving Average (SARIMA), multi-variate AutoRegressive Integrated Moving Average (ARIMA), Bayesian networks, *fuzzy* clustering, identification of traffic patterns, genetic algorithms, neural networks, Support Vector Machines (SVM), historical average, non-parametric regression, Kalman filter, and ant colony.

Such approaches differ in terms of the data source used to detect or to predict future jams, such as: GPS traces, tracking smartphones movements, online maps, data from sensors on roads, weather, seasons, traffic incidents, and social sensing. Sensed data on roads are most often used by these models, followed by information regarding GPS traces, weather, and seasons. For instance, the Clearflow project from Microsoft Research, described in Horvitz (2015), uses practically all the above

---

[26]The authors use the Cologne trace: http://kolntrace.project.citi-lab.fr.

mentioned sources. In the product offered by Intellione company,[27] only the data about smartphones movements in mobile networks are used to detect traffic jams (no prediction is done). In order to make traffic prediction, Yuecong et al. (2007) use a combination of several simple predictors through a genetic algorithm, achieving a forecast with a higher accuracy.

5.5.5 Challenges and opportunities

Vehicular networks and PSNs have several possibilities of integration, which presents several challenges and opportunities that we describe next.

1. **Event tracking:** There are several initiatives that use PSN data to detect events (Sakaki et al., 2010b; Lee and Sumiya, 2010; Bollen et al., 2011), and the area of event tracking in vehicular networks may benefit from some of these initiatives. Furthermore, there are events hard to be identified in a vehicular network that could be reported in PSNs, as we discussed in Section 5.1. Note also that we could suggest routes in order to avoid events in the city, or even to promote the most visited spots.

2. **Data availability:** As we discussed above, particularly in Section 4, PSNs data can be very useful for the study of the habits and routines of a city's inhabitants. This is important information for vehicular networks, as mentioned in Section 5.5.3. However, users in vehicular networks may not provide the information of the visited places, a problem that can also occur in PSNs. We can minimize this problem by stimulating the contribution of users. Another way to minimize this problem is to use data available from PSNs and vehicle networks together, which serves as a way to complement the information on the movement of users.

   Regarding to traffic jam problem, generally, the more data sources used in a model the better the performance, because more information will be used to improve its inferences. The problem is that not all data sources are correlated and relevant to the prediction of congestion. Thus, the inclusion of a new data source requires a characterization with respect to traffic performance. Moreover, as mentioned in Section 3, the data input can be inconsistent over the different areas of a city. If we do not have enough data in all regions, which regions will benefit from this information?

3. **Detection/prediction of traffic jam:** Generally, PSN data are underexploited in traffic-jam detection/forecasting models. Some of the studies in this direction are: Silva et al. (2013d) and Tostes et al. (2014). Tostes et al. have analyzed traffic conditions using two types of PSN data, from Foursquare and Instagram. As we mentioned in Section 3, PSN data provide valuable information to better understand city dynamics. For instance, a geolocated message, whether on Foursquare, Instagram or Twitter, can be used to better understand traffic conditions. In fact, Tostes et al. (2014) observed that check-ins (from

---

[27]http://www.intellione.com.

Foursquare) or photos (from Instagram) are well correlated with intense traffic conditions and can be used to design more efficient traffic prediction models. Besides that, imagine that a user shares data at home and then commutes to work and, for some reason, he/she shares another piece of geolocated data. Regardless of whether it was the same social network or not, there is intrinsic information in the time interval between the sharing of these data that may be related to traffic behavior. If the traffic is more congested, this interval between the times of the data sharing may be longer than the travel time without traffic jams, which is easily calculated by the distance and maximum speed on roads. When analyzing many users for this information, the results could provide powerful hints as to the traffic conditions. The authors have raised several questions in this regard, such as: (i) how is data to be collected from online maps in real time? (ii) is it possible to use PSN data as a predictor characteristic for intense traffic jam?

5.6 OTHER CHALLENGES AND OPPORTUNITIES RELATED TO PSNs

5.6.1 Data sampling

It is important to point out some of the challenges regarding the data sampling. PSN data are biased towards the citizens who use them. For example, the dataset discussed on Section 3 is based on data shared by users of Foursquare, Instagram, and Waze on Twitter. Therefore, it is biased towards the citizens who use those systems, who are likely to be under 50 years old; most likely between 18 and 29 years old, owners of smartphones, and there are fewer data available regarding urban dwellers (Brenner and Smith, 2013; Duggan and Smith, 2014). Consequently, urban areas with older and poorer populations.

There are some initiatives in the literature regarding methods and techniques to identify and recruit suitable candidates for data collection, most of them focusing on the selection of participants with a view to minimizing cost. For instance, Reddy et al. (2010b) developed a framework to help to identify well-suited participants for data collections based on geographic and temporal availability as well as participation habits. In a similar direction, Hachem et al. (2013) use a mobility model to predict users' future locations. Based on the predicted results they aim to select a minimal number of mobile users, expecting to cover a certain percentage of the target area. However, despite those efforts, there are still open challenges. For example, there is a lack of mechanisms for considering users with specific characteristics, such as regarding certain age, gender, or race. This type of selection is important, for instance, to the study of urban social behavior.

Another challenge related to data sampling in PSNs is that users might not share data for their destinations at all, for instance in love hotels and strip clubs. Thus, datasets from PSNs might offer a partial view of citizens' habits. Besides that, external factors, such as bad weather conditions, might affect the total amount of data collected from some places, especially outdoor locations. This means that we might only have access to a sample of data that could be shared under regular conditions. New mechanisms designed to deal with this type of situation have to be developed.

5.6.2 Large volume of data

Another important issue is to deal with a large volume of data that PSNs can offer, imposing challenges for storage, processing, and indexing in real time using tools of traditional database management and data processing applications. Fortunately, research on the challenges imposed by this huge amount of data (also known as big data) is very active, and recently, in conjunction with cloud computing solutions, advanced considerably (Jagadish et al., 2014; Reed and Dongarra, 2015).

PSNs may offer large amounts of data that grows quickly. For this reason, storage platforms have to be distributed, scalable, secure, consistent, and fault-tolerance (Hashem et al., 2015). Recently, some services were proposed to store and manage large amounts of data covering some of these requirements. For instance, Amazon Simple Storage and Service (Amazon S3)[28] and Microsoft Azure Storage[29] provide solutions to store and retrieve large amounts of data, where files can be replicated across multiple geographical sites to improve redundancy and availability. These services rely on available technologies, such as Google File System (GFS) and Hadoop Distributed File System (HDFS), to store a large volume of data across multiple machines.

Besides that, data from PSNs may have different formats (ie, structured, semi-structured, and unstructured). Consider an application for transit monitoring, like Waze. In this type of PSN, users can share observations about accidents or potholes. Since users use an application designed for a specific purpose, the sensed data are structured. Instead, if a user uses a microblog (eg, Twitter), the sensed data would be unstructured (eg, message sent by user X: "traffic now is very slow near the main entrance of campus"). With that, data modeling using the traditional relational model may be hard. This motivates the adoption of new alternatives, such as NoSQL databases, which allows the storing and retrieval of large volumes of distributed data (Cattell, 2011). NoSQL databases are non-relational, highly distributable, and schema-free, meaning that they are being increasingly used in big data and real time web applications, such as PSNs (Andlinger, 2013).

Another issue when working with PSN is the processing of a large volume of data in real time. For this task, one important aspect is how to distribute computation. MapReduce model is the first major contribution to data-processing for a parallel, distributed algorithm on a cluster (Dean and Ghemawat, 2008). Currently, this model in combination with HDFS from the Hadoop core. Hadoop[30] is a project that allows the distributed processing of large datasets across clusters of computers. Alternatively, Apache Spark[31] is a fast and general engine for large-scale data processing, and it is appropriated to applications that reuse a working dataset across multiple parallel operations, such as iterative machine learning algorithms and interactive data analysis

---

[28] http://aws.amazon.com/s3.
[29] https://azure.microsoft.com/en-us/services/storage.
[30] https://hadoop.apache.org.
[31] http://spark.apache.org.

tools (Zaharia et al., 2010). With that, new algorithmic paradigms for processing, based, for example, on the mentioned parallel platforms, should be designed and specific data mining techniques should be created accordingly to manipulate, for instance, large urban transition graphs (as those mentioned in Section 4.2), with millions or billions of nodes/edges (Giannotti et al., 2012).

5.6.3 Privacy

Working with data from PSNs may present threats to users' privacy. For instance, these data could be used to infer a users' personal behavior and preferences, such as commonly visited locations, lifestyle, and health condition, thus, not ensuring freedom from the intrusion of others in their private life or affairs (Li and Cao, 2015). An important challenge, therefore, is to guarantee user privacy while working on potentially sensitive data from PSNs.

Data privacy has been discussed in several studies, the subjects of which rang from methods that allow participants to control their privacy preferences to anonymization techniques for data privacy-preserving (Brush et al., 2010; Evdokimov and Gunther, 2007; Li et al., 2015; Li and Cao, 2015; Pontes et al., 2012; Shen and Yu, 2013; Toch et al., 2010; Wang et al., 2011; Wu et al., 2012). These anonymization techniques, in particular, aim to protect privacy by anonymizing data fields such that sensitive information cannot be pinpointed to an individual record (Cormode and Srivastava, 2010). Anonymization can be achieved through several ways by: creating an alias that avoids user identification; aggregating data from several users, thus making it hard to identify an individual user; hiding sensitive locations; and injecting randomness into the data to create data perturbation (Christin et al., 2011). The challenge related to this last approach has been to design special data mining methods to derive knowledge from anonymized data (Wu et al., 2014). Furthermore, the development of anonymization mechanisms has to consider the tradeoff between anonymity and data fidelity.

As mentioned previously, a dataset from a PSN might be used to create an urban transition graph representing users' trajectories over a given period of time. Therefore, another challenge is how to prevent leakage of private information for individuals, while mining and releasing frequent patterns of these graphs. There are some initiatives to deal with this sort of problem. For example, Shen and Yu (2013) propose an algorithm for privacy-preserving mining of frequent graph patterns.

Another important aspect of protecting data privacy in PSNs is the consideration of security issues in the data transmission. Sensitive data have to be encrypted before they are shared by users, preventing a malicious user from obtaining this sensitive data. Although data encryption helps to protect data privacy, it also obsoletes the traditional data utilization service based on plain text keyword search. A number of studies were proposed for privacy preserving database encryption while enabling some traditional functions, for instance, query using SQL (Li et al., 2015; Wu et al., 2012; Evdokimov and Gunther, 2007; Wang et al., 2011). However, despite these efforts, this challenge is still to be met and further research needs to be conducted to make the proposed approaches more practically feasible. As an example,

Li et al. (2015) intends to research a way of providing some practical data publishing methods that are suitable for their proposed framework, which is to deal with privacy-preserving data queries. Another approach would be to improve the performance of the proposed approach for certain situations.

6 CONCLUSION

In this chapter, we show that PSNs provide unprecedented opportunities to access sensing data on a global scale. In this sense, we present a detailed view of the properties of these data, as well as their usefulness in developing smarter services that will people's needs in several areas. In addition, we discuss some of the key challenges related to PSNs, ranging from incentive mechanisms for users of PSNs, to the use of PSN data for the development of more sophisticated applications. We also highlight several opportunities related to the use of PSN data, for example, when considering the temporal dynamics of the data.

ACRONYMS

ARIMA	AutoRegressive Integrated Moving Average
CCDF	Complementary Cumulative Distribution Function
CDF	Cumulative Distribution Function
GFS	Google File System
GPS	Global Positioning System
HDFS	Hadoop Distributed File System
LTFF	long-term traffic flow forecasting
P.C.	principal component
PoI	Point of Interest
PSNs	participatory sensor networks
QoC	Quality of Context
QoD	Quality of Device
QoS	Quality of Service
SARIMA	Seasonal AutoRegressive Integrated Moving Average
STFF	short-term traffic flow forecasting
VANETs	vehicular networks
WSNs	wireless sensor networks

GLOSSARY

Altruism It is the act of favoring others instead of oneself.
Availability Measures the capability of an entity to provide data when the information about a region is needed.

City Image Technique that provides a visual summary of the city dynamics based on the movements of people.

Cooperation Occurs when an individual devotes an effort that implies a cost in some collective activity expecting some benefit.

Currency Represents the temporal utility of the data, from the moment it is created until it becomes worthless.

Gamification The use of game features as incentive mechanisms to perform tasks.

Precision Defines how well certain data reflects the current state of a specific phenomenon or locality.

Probability of correctness Denotes the probability that a given data is correct.

PSN Participatory sensor networks rely on the idea of participatory sensing, and can be defined as a system that supports a distributed process of gathering data about personal daily experiences and various aspects of the city. Such a process requires the active participation of people using portable devices to voluntarily share contextual information and/or make their sensed data available, ie, the users manually determine how, when, what, and where to share the sensed data. Thus, through PSNs we can monitor different conditions of cities, as well as the collective behavior of people connected to the Internet in (almost) real time.

QoC Any information that describes the quality of the inferred context, which is consistent with our needs.

QoD Any information about the technical properties and capabilities of a given device.

QoS Any information that describes how well a service operates.

Resolution Denotes the granularity of the information.

Selfishness It is the act of benefiting oneself instead of another.

Sensing layer It represents data, with its attributes, from a particular data source, for example, a particular PSN.

Trust-worthiness It is similar to the probability of correctness, but it is used to classify the quality of the user that generated the data.

tweets Personal updates in texts up to 140 characters shared on Twitter.

up-to-dateness Describes the age of the data.

Validity It is defined as a set of rules that can be used to validate the generated data, according to a previous knowledge about the type of the data and the behavioral pattern of the users.

REFERENCES

Adomavicius, G., Tuzhilin, A., 2005. Toward the next generation of recommender systems: a survey of the state-of-the-art and possible extensions. IEEE Trans. Knowl. Data Eng. 17 (6), 734–749. ISSN 1041-4347. doi:10.1109/TKDE.2005.99.

Akyildiz, I.F., Su, W., Sankarasubramaniam, Y., Cayirci, E., 2002. Wireless sensor networks: a survey. Comput. Netw. 38 (4), 393–422. ISSN 1389-1286.

Anbukodi, S., Manickam, K.M., 2011, March. Reducing web crawler overhead using mobile crawler. In: Proc. of ICETECT'11, Nagercoil, India, pp. 926–932.

Andlinger, P., 2013, November. RDBMS dominate the database market, but NoSQL systems are catching up. DB-Engines. http://db-engines.com/en/blog_post/23.

Bannur, S., Alonso, O., 2014. Analyzing temporal characteristics of check-in data. In: Proc. of WWW Companion '14, Seoul, Korea, pp. 827–832. http://dx.doi.org/10.1145/2567948.2579041.

Barth, F., 1969. Ethnic Groups and Boundaries: The Social Organization of Culture Difference. Little, Brown and Company, Boston, MA.

Bollen, J., Mao, H., Zeng, X., 2011. Twitter mood predicts the stock market. J. Comput. Sci. 2 (1), 1–8.

Bowles, S., Gintis, H., 2003. Origins of human cooperation. In: Genetic and Cultural Evolution of Cooperation. MIT Press, Cambridge, MA.

Brenner, J., Smith, A., 2013, August. 72% of online adults are social networking site users. http://goo.gl/HTgNy3.

Brush, A.J.B., Krumm, J., Scott, J., 2010. Exploring end user preferences for location obfuscation, location-based services, and the value of location. In: Proc. of Ubicomp '10, Copenhagen, Denmark. ACM, New York, NY, USA, pp. 95–104. http://doi.acm.org/10.1145/1864349.1864381.

Buchholz, T., Schiffers, M., 2003. Quality of context: what it is and why we need it. In: Proc. of OVUA'03, Geneva, Switzerland.

Burke, J., Estrin, D., Hansen, M., Parker, A., Ramanathan, N., Reddy, S., Srivastava, M.B., 2006. Participatory sensing. In: Proc. of Workshop on World-Sensor-Web (WSW'06), Boulder, USA, pp. 117–134.

Burt, R.S., 1992. Structural Holes: The Social Structure of Competition. Harvard University Press, Cambridge, MA.

Cattell, R., 2011, May. Scalable SQL and NoSQL data stores. SIGMOD Rec. 39 (4), 12–27. ISSN 0163-5808. doi:10.1145/1978915.1978919.

CENS/UCLA, link last visited in February 2016. Participatory Sensing/Urban Sensing Projects. http://research.cens.ucla.edu/.

Cha, M., Haddadi, H., Benevenuto, F., Gummadi, K.P., 2010. Measuring user influence in Twitter: the million follower fallacy. In: Proc. of ICWSM'10, Washington, USA.

Cheng, Z., Caverlee, J., Lee, K., Sui, D.Z., 2011. Exploring millions of footprints in location sharing services. In: Proc. of ICWSM'11, Barcelona, Spain.

Christin, D., Reinhardt, A., Kanhere, S.S., Hollick, M., 2011. A survey on privacy in mobile participatory sensing applications. J. Syst. Softw. 84 (11), 1928–1946. doi:10.1016/j.jss.2011.06.073.

Clauset, A., Shalizi, C.R., Newman, M.E.J., 2009, November. Power-law distributions in empirical data. SIAM Rev. 51 (4), 661–703. ISSN 0036-1445. doi:10.1137/070710111.

Coen-Porisini, A., Sicari, S., 2012, November. Improving data quality using a cross layer protocol in wireless sensor networks. Comput. Netw. 56 (17), 3655–3665. ISSN 1389-1286. doi:10.1016/j.comnet.2012.08.001.

Cormode, G., Srivastava, D., 2010, March. Anonymized data: generation, models, usage. In: IEEE 26th International Conference on Data Engineering (ICDE), 2010, pp. 1211–1212.

Cranshaw, J., Schwartz, R., Hong, J.I., Sadeh, N., 2012. The livehoods project: utilizing social media to understand the dynamics of a city. In: Proc. of ICWSM'12, Dublin, Ireland.

da Cunha, F.D., Maia, G., Viana, A.C., Mini, R.A.F., Villas, L.A., Loureiro, A.A.F., 2014a. Socially inspired data dissemination for vehicular ad hoc networks. In: Proc. of MSWiM'14, Montreal, Canada, pp. 81–85.

da Cunha, F.D., Viana, A., de Oliveira Rodrigues, T.A., Mini, R., Loureiro, A.A.F., 2014b. Extracao de propriedades sociais em redes veiculares. In: Proc. of SBRC 2014—WP2P+, Florianopolis, Brazil.

Dean, J., Ghemawat, S., 2008, January. MapReduce: simplified data processing on large clusters. Commun. ACM 51 (1), 107–113. ISSN 0001-0782. doi:10.1145/1327452.1327492.

Deterding, S., Dixon, D., Khaled, R., Nacke, L., 2011. From game design elements to gamefulness: defining gamification. In: International Academic MindTrek Conference: Envisioning Future Media Environments. ACM, New York, NY, USA, pp. 9–15.

Dey, A.K., Abowd, G.D., 2000. Towards a better understanding of context and context-awareness. In: Proc. of CHI 2000 Workshops, The Hague, The Netherlands.

Duggan, M., Smith, A., 2014, January. Social media update 2013. http://goo.gl/JhuiOG.

Easley, D., Kleinberg, J., 2010. Networks, crowds, and markets: reasoning about a highly connected world. Cambridge University Press, Cambridge.

Evdokimov, S., Gunther, O., 2007. Encryption techniques for secure database outsourcing. In: Biskup, J., Lopez, J. (Eds.), Computer Security—ESORICS 2007, Lecture Notes in Computer Science, vol. 4734. Springer, Berlin/Heidelberg, pp. 327–342.

Fiore, M., Barcelo-Ordinas, J.M., Trullols-Cruces, O., Uppoor, S., 2014. Generation and analysis of a large-scale urban vehicular mobility dataset. IEEE Trans. Mobile Comput. 13 (5), 1. ISSN 1536-1233. http://doi.ieeecomputersociety.org/10.1109/TMC.2013.27.

Fitzek, F.H., Heide, J., Pedersen, M.V., Katz, M., 2013. Implementation of network coding for social mobile clouds [applications corner]. IEEE Signal Process. Mag. 30 (1), 159–164.

Flanagin, A.J., Metzger, M.J., 2008, August. The credibility of volunteered geographic information. GeoJournal 72 (3–4), 137–148. ISSN 0343-2521. doi:10.1007/s10708-008-9188-y.

Ganti, R.K., Ye, F., Lei, H., 2011, November. Mobile crowdsensing: current state and future challenges. IEEE Commun. Mag. 49 (11), 32–39. ISSN 0163-6804. doi:10.1109/MCOM. 2011.6069707.

Gao, H., Liu, C., Wang, W., Zhao, J., Song, Z., Su, X., Crowcroft, J., Leung, K., 2015. A survey of incentive mechanisms for participatory sensing. IEEE Commun. Surv. Tutorials 17 (2), 918–943. ISSN 1553-877X. doi:10.1109/COMST.2014.2387836.

Georgescu, M., Pham, D.D., Firan, C.S., Gadiraju, U., Nejdl, W., 2014. When in doubt ask the crowd: employing crowdsourcing for active learning. In: Proc. of WIMS'14, Thessaloniki, Greece. ACM, New York, NY, USA, pp. 12:1–12:12.

Giannotti, F., Pedreschi, D., Pentland, A., Lukowicz, P., Kossmann, D., Crowley, J., Helbing, D., 2012. A planetary nervous system for social mining and collective awareness. Eur. Phys. J. Spec. Top. 214 (1), 49–75.

Hachem, S., Pathak, A., Issarny, V., 2013, March. Probabilistic registration for large-scale mobile participatory sensing. In: PerCom 2013—IEEE International Conference on Pervasive Computing. Elsevier, California, USA. https://hal.inria.fr/hal-00769087.

Hartigan, J.A., Wong, M.A., 1979. Algorithm AS 136: a k-means clustering algorithm. Appl. Stat. 100–108.

Hashem, I.A.T., Yaqoob, I., Anuar, N.B., Mokhtar, S., Gani, A., Khan, S.U., 2015. The rise of big data on cloud computing: review and open research issues. Inf. Syst. 47, 98–115. ISSN 0306-4379. doi:10.1016/j.is.2014.07.006. http://www.sciencedirect.com/science/article/pii/S0306437914001288.

Holme, P., Saramki, J., 2012. Temporal networks. Phys. Rep. 519 (3), 97–125. ISSN 0370-1573. doi:10.1016/j.physrep.2012.03.001. http://www.sciencedirect.com/science/article/pii/S0370157312000841.

Horvitz, E., 2015. Predictive Analytics for Traffic. http://research.microsoft.com/en-us/projects/clearflow/.

Huang, K.L., Kanhere, S.S., Hu, W., 2010. Are you contributing trustworthy data? The case for a reputation system in participatory sensing. In: Proceedings of the 13th ACM International Conference on Modeling, Analysis, and Simulation of Wireless and Mobile Systems—MSWIM '10. ACM Press, New York, NY, USA, pp. 14—22. http://portal.acm.org/citation.cfm?doid=1868521.1868526.

Instagram, 2014, April. Instagram Today: 200 Million Strong. http://blog.instagram.com/post/ 80721172292/200m.

Jagadish, H.V., Gehrke, J., Labrinidis, A., Papakonstantinou, Y., Patel, J.M., Ramakrishnan, R., Shahabi, C., 2014, July. Big data and its technical challenges. Commun. ACM 57 (7), 86–94. ISSN 0001-0782. doi:10.1145/2611567.

Jain, P., Sethi, M., 2012, January. Fuzzy based real time traffic signal controller to optimize congestion delays. In: Proc. of ACCT'12, pp. 204–207.

Jolliffe, I.T., 2002. Principal Component Analysis, second ed. Springer, Berlin.

Kamenica, E., 2012. Behavioral economics and psychology of incentives. Annu. Rev. Econ. 4 (1), 427–452.

Karamshuk, D., Noulas, A., Scellato, S., Nicosia, V., Mascolo, C., 2013. Geo-spotting: mining online location-based services for optimal retail store placement. In: Proc. of KDD '13, Chicago, IL, USA. ACM, New York, NY, USA, pp. 793–801.

Kaufmann, N., Schulze, T., Veit, D., 2011. More than fun and money. Worker motivation in crowdsourcing—a study on mechanical turk. In: Proc. of Americas Conference on Information Systems.

Kong, Q.J., Xu, Y., Lin, S., Wen, D., Zhu, F., Liu, Y., 2013, September. UTN-model-based traffic flow prediction for parallel-transportation management systems. IEEE Trans. Intell. Transp. Syst. 14 (3), 1541–1547. ISSN 1524-9050. doi:10.1109/TITS.2013.2252463.

Kostakos, V., 2009. Temporal graphs. Phys. A: Stat. Mech. Appl. 388 (6), 1007–1023.

Kurihara, S., 2013. Traffic-congestion forecasting algorithm based on pheromone communication model. In: Ant Colony Optimization—Techniques and Applications. InTech, Rijeka, Croatia.

Lane, N.D., Eisenman, S.B., Musolesi, M., Miluzzo, E., Campbell, A.T., 2008. Urban sensing systems: opportunistic or participatory? In: Proc. of HotMobile '08, Napa Valley, CA. ACM, New York, NY, USA, pp. 11–16.

Lane, N.D., Miluzzo, E., Lu, H., Peebles, D., Choudhury, T., Campbell, A.T., 2010, September. A survey of mobile phone sensing. IEEE Commun. Mag. 48 (9), 140–150. ISSN 0163-6804. doi:10.1109/MCOM.2010.5560598.

Lathi, B.P., Green, R., 2014. Essentials of digital signal processing. Cambridge University Press, Cambridge, UK. ISBN 978-1107059320.

Lee, J.S., Hoh, B., 2010. Dynamic pricing incentive for participatory sensing. Pervasive Mob. Comput. 6 (6), 693–708.

Lee, R., Sumiya, K., 2010. Measuring geographical regularities of crowd behaviors for Twitter-based geo-social event detection. In: Proceedings of the 2nd ACM SIGSPATIAL International Workshop on Location Based Social Networks, San Jose, USA, pp. 1–10.

Lee, U., Park, J.S., Amir, E., Gerla, M., 2006a, FleaNet: a virtual market place on vehicular networks. In: Proc. of Mobiquitous'06—Workshops, San Jose, USA, pp. 1–8.

Lee, U., Zhou, B., Gerla, M., Magistretti, E., Bellavista, P., Corradi, A., 2006b. Mobeyes: smart mobs for urban monitoring with a vehicular sensor network. IEEE Wirel. Commun. 13 (5), 52–57. doi:10.1109/WC-M.2006.250358.

Levine, D.K., 1998. Modeling altruism and spitefulness in experiments. Rev. Econ. Dyn. 1 (3), 593–622.

Li, F., Nastic, S., Dustdar, S., 2012, December. Data quality observation in pervasive environments. In: Proc. of IEEE CSE'12, Nicosia, Cyprus, pp. 602–609.

Li, J., Liu, Z., Chen, X., Xhafa, F., Tan, X., Wong, D.S., 2015. L-EncDB: a lightweight framework for privacy-preserving data queries in cloud computing. Knowl.-Based Syst. 79, 18–26. ISSN 0950-7051. doi:10.1016/j.knosys.2014.04.010. http://www.sciencedirect.com/science/article/pii/S0950705114001324.

Li, Q., Cao, G., 2015. Privacy-preserving participatory sensing. IEEE Commun. Mag. 53 (8), 68–74. ISSN 0163-6804. doi:10.1109/MCOM.2015.7180510.

Maisonneuve, N., Stevens, M., Niessen, M.E., Steels, L., 2009. NoiseTube: measuring and mapping noise pollution with mobile phones. In: Information Technologies in Environmental Engineering. Springer, Berlin, pp. 215–228.

Marfia, G., Roccetti, M., 2011, September. Vehicular congestion detection and short-term forecasting: a new model with results. IEEE Trans. Veh. Technol. 60 (7), 2936–2948. ISSN 0018-9545. doi:10.1109/TVT.2011.2158866.

Mashhadi, A.J., Capra, L., 2011. Quality control for real-time ubiquitous crowdsourcing. In: Proc. of UbiCrowd'11, Beijing, China, pp. 5–8.

Miao, J., Hasan, O., Mokhtar, S.B., Brunie, L., Yim, K., 2013. An investigation on the unwillingness of nodes to participate in mobile delay tolerant network routing. Int. J. Inf. Manag. 33 (2), 252–262. ISSN 02684012. doi:10.1016/j.ijinfomgt.2012.11.001. http://linkinghub.elsevier.com/retrieve/pii/S0268401212001338.

Nazir, A., Raza, S., Chuah, C.N., 2008. Unveiling Facebook: a measurement study of social network based applications. In: Proc. of IMC '08, Vouliagmeni, Greece, pp. 43–56.

Newman, M., 2010. Networks: An Introduction. Oxford University Press, Inc., Oxford.

Newman, M.E.J., 2003. The structure and function of complex networks. SIAM Rev. 45 (2), 167–256.

Ng, A.Y., Jordan, M.I., Weiss, Y., et al., 2002. On spectral clustering: analysis and an algorithm. Adv. Neural Inform. Process. Syst. 2, 849–856.

Noulas, A., Scellato, S., Mascolo, C., Pontil, M., 2011. An empirical study of geographic user activity patterns in Foursquare. In: Proc. of ICWSM'11, Barcelona, Spain.

Pontes, T., Magno, G., Vasconcelos, M., Gupta, A., Almeida, J., Kumaraguru, P., Almeida, V., 2012. Beware of what you share: inferring home location in social networks. In: Proc. of ICDMW, Brussels, Belgium, pp. 571–578.

Quercia, D., Capra, L., Crowcroft, J., 2012. The social world of Twitter: topics, geography, and emotions. In: Proc. of ICWSM'12, Dublin, Ireland.

Reddy, S., Estrin, D., Hansen, M., Srivastava, M., 2010a, Examining micro-payments for participatory sensing data collections. In: Proc. of Ubicomp '10, Copenhagen, Denmark. ACM, New York, NY, USA, pp. 33–36.

Reddy, S., Estrin, D., Srivastava, M., 2010b, Recruitment framework for participatory sensing data collections. In: Proceedings of the 8th International Conference on Pervasive Computing, Pervasive'10. Springer-Verlag, Berlin, Heidelberg, pp. 138–155.

Reed, D.A., Dongarra, J., 2015, June. Exascale computing and big data. Commun. ACM 58 (7), 56–68. ISSN 0001-0782. doi:10.1145/2699414.

Sakaki, T., Okazaki, M., Matsuo, Y., 2010a, Earthquake shakes Twitter users: real-time event detection by social sensors. In: Proc. of WWW'10, Raleigh, USA, pp. 851–860.

Sakaki, T., Okazaki, M., Matsuo, Y., 2010b, Earthquake shakes Twitter users: real-time event detection by social sensors. In: Proc. of WWW'10, Raleigh, USA. IW3C2, pp. 851–860.

Shen, E., Yu, T., 2013. Mining frequent graph patterns with differential privacy. In: Proceedings of the 19th ACM SIGKDD International Conference on Knowledge Discovery and Data Mining, KDD '13, New York, NY, USA. ACM, New York, NY, USA, pp. 545–553.

Silva, T.H., Vaz de Melo, P., Almeida, J., Viana, A., Salles, J., Loureiro, A., 2014a, Participatory sensor networks as sensing layers. In: Proc. of SocialCom'14, Sydney, Australia.

Silva, T.H., Vaz de Melo, P.O.S., Almeida, J.M., Loureiro, A.A.F., 2012. Visualizing the invisible image of cities. In: Proc. IEEE CPScom'12, Besancon, France, pp. 382–389.

Silva, T.H., Vaz de Melo, P.O.S., Almeida, J.M., Loureiro, A.A.F., 2013a, July, Challenges and opportunities on the large scale study of city dynamics using participatory sensing. In: Proc. of IEEE ISCC'13, Split, Croatia, pp. 528–534.

Silva, T.H., Vaz De Melo, P.O.S., Almeida, J.M., Loureiro, A.A.F., 2014b, February, Large-scale study of city dynamics and urban social behavior using participatory sensing. IEEE Wirel. Commun. 21 (1), 42–51.

Silva, T.H., Vaz de Melo, P.O.S., Almeida, J.M., Musolesi, M., Loureiro, A.A.F., 2014c, You are what you eat (and drink): identifying cultural boundaries by analyzing food & drink habits in Foursquare. In: Proc. of ICWSM'14, Ann Arbor, USA.

Silva, T.H., Vaz de Melo, P.O.S., Almeida, J.M., Salles, J., Loureiro, A.A.F., 2013b, A picture of Instagram is worth more than a thousand words: workload characterization and application. In: Proc. of DCOSS'13, Cambridge, USA, pp. 123–132.

Silva, T.H., Vaz de Melo, P.O.S., Almeida, J.M., Salles, J., Loureiro, A.A.F., 2013c, A comparison of Foursquare and Instagram to the study of city dynamics and urban social behavior. In: Proc. of UrbComp'13, Chicago, USA, pp. 1–8.

Silva, T.H., Vaz de Melo, P.O.S., Almeida, J.M., Salles, J., Loureiro, A.A.F., 2014d, December, Revealing the city that we cannot see. ACM Trans. Internet Technol. 14 (4), 26:1–26:23. ISSN 1533-5399. doi:10.1145/2677208.

Silva, T.H., Vaz de Melo, P.O.S., Viana, A., Almeida, J.M., Salles, J., Loureiro, A.A.F., 2013d, November, Traffic condition is more than colored lines on a map: characterization of Waze alerts. In: Proc. of SocInfo'13, Kyoto, Japan, pp. 309–318.

Srivastava, M., Abdelzaher, T., Szymanski, B., 2012. Human-centric sensing. Philos. Trans. R. Soc. A: Math. Phys. Eng. Sci. 370 (1958), 176–197. ISSN 1471-2962. doi:10.1098/rsta. 2011.0244.

Sun, S., Yu, G., Zhang, C., 2004, June. Short-term traffic flow forecasting using Sampling Markov Chain method with incomplete data. In: Proc. of Intelligent Vehicles Symposium, pp. 437–441.

Toch, E., Cranshaw, J., Drielsma, P.H., Tsai, J.Y., Kelley, P.G., Springfield, J., Cranor, L., Hong, J., Sadeh, N., 2010. Empirical models of privacy in location sharing. In: Proc. of Ubicomp'10, Copenhagen, Denmark. ACM, New York, NY, USA, pp. 129–138.

Tostes, A.I.J., Silva, T.H., Duarte-FIgueiredo, F., Loureiro, A.A.F., 2014. Studying traffic conditions by analyzing Foursquare and Instagram data. In: Proc. of ACM PE-WASUN'14, Montreal, Canada.

Wang, C., Wang, Q., Ren, K., 2011, June. Towards secure and effective utilization over encrypted cloud data. In: 31st International Conference on Distributed Computing Systems Workshops (ICDCSW), 2011, pp. 282–286.

Werbach, K., Hunter, D., 2012. For the Win: How Game Thinking can Revolutionize Your Business. Wharton Digital Press, Philadelphia.

Wisitpongphan, N., Jitsakul, W., Jieamumporn, D., 2012, July. Travel time prediction using multi-layer feed forward artificial neural network. In: Proc. of CICSyN'12, Phuket, Thailand, pp. 326–330.

Wu, X., Zhu, X., Wu, G.Q., Ding, W., 2014. Data mining with big data. IEEE Trans. Knowl. Data Eng. 26 (1), 97–107.

Wu, Z., Xu, G., Yu, Z., Yi, X., Chen, E., Zhang, Y., 2012. Executing {SQL} queries over encrypted character strings in the Database-As-Service model. Knowl.-Based Syst. 35, 332–348. ISSN 0950-7051. doi:10.1016/j.knosys.2012.05.009. http://www.sciencedirect.com/science/article/pii/S0950705112001530.

Xie, X., Chen, H., Wu, H., 2009. Bargain-based stimulation mechanism for selfish mobile nodes in participatory sensing network. In: Proc. of IEEE SECON'09, New Orleans, USA, pp. 1–9.

Yang, D., Xue, G., Fang, X., Tang, J., 2012. Crowdsourcing to smartphones: incentive mechanism design for mobile phone sensing. In: Proc. of Mobicom'12, Istanbul, Turkey, pp. 173–184.

Youyou, W., Kosinski, M., Stillwell, D., 2015. Computer-based personality judgments are more accurate than those made by humans. Proc. Natl. Acad. Sci. U. S. A. 112 (4), 1036–1040.

Yuecong, S., Wei, H., Guotang, B., 2007, August. Combined prediction research of city traffic flow based on genetic algorithm. In: Proc. of ICEMI'07, pp. 3-862–3-865.

Zaharia, M., Chowdhury, M., Franklin, M.J., Shenker, S., Stoica, I., 2010. Spark: cluster computing with working sets. In: Proceedings of the 2nd USENIX Conference on Hot Topics in Cloud Computing, HotCloud'10. USENIX Association, Berkeley, CA, USA, pp. 10. http://dl.acm.org/citation.cfm?id=1863103.1863113.

Zhang, K., Jin, Q., Pelechrinis, K., Lappas, T., 2013. On the importance of temporal dynamics in modeling urban activity. In: Proc. of UrbComp'13, Chicago, Illinois, pp. 7:1–7:8.

Integration in the Internet of Things: A semantic middleware approach to seamless integration of heterogeneous technologies

4

A.C. Olivieri, Y. Bocchi, G. Rizzo

HES-SO Valais, Institute of Information System, Sierre, Switzerland

1 INTRODUCTION

The integration of different technologies has always created great possibilities for the implementation of novel services and the creation of new interesting scenarios. In cyber-physical systems for example, the integration of more and more heterogeneous technologies means an increase in the set of available options for their design and implementation. It brings about the possibility for exploitation of the advantages of each technology while offering new options for overcoming their limitations. This perspective is even more fascinating nowadays with the advent of the Internet of Things (IoT), which extends the set of available interacting technologies to devices with low computational power.

The evolution of the integration techniques goes from the *N-to-N* approach, where the connections are point-to-point (adopted in pure Machine-to-Machine (M2M) settings, usually with little technological heterogeneity), to the *N-to-1* approach, which typically relies on some form of middleware for the management of all communications.

A predominant type of framework employed in this latter approach is based on the publish/subscribe (P/S) design pattern. Such design pattern adopts *decoupling* as fundamental paradigm when interconnecting interacting entities. This decoupling feature allows the framework to create the interconnection of entities based on the data they want to exchange rather than on direct point-to-point interconnection of those entities. These frameworks enable the integration of a large number of different technologies, and they provide good scalability features in context where the load of communications is not too heavy and some latency is accepted. Examples of these situations are web feed systems such as RSS and Atom (Liu et al., 2005).

Pervasive Computing. http://dx.doi.org/10.1016/B978-0-12-803663-1.00004-8

However, the P/S suitability described above can drop in the presence of systems that demand exceptional data loading or real-time systems that demand zero-latency. Advanced P/S architectures that address the limitations of typical P/S systems can be used to deal with such conditions (Schmidt and O'Ryan, 2003). For example, Data Distribution Service (DDS) (Pardo-Castellote, 2003)[1] is a standard that aims to enable scalable, real-time, dependable, high-performance, and interoperable data exchanges between publishers and subscribers. To overcome these limitations these P/S systems employ P2P communication models (Li et al., 2003). DDS addresses the needs of applications like financial trading, air-traffic control, smart grid management, and other big data applications.

The presence of research aiming to create new solutions based on the P/S paradigm for the IoT, such as MQTT protocol (Hunkeler et al., 2008), reinforces our idea that this type of framework is suitable for the IoT domain (Sanchez, 2012).

Even though frameworks based on the P/S design pattern, both industrial solutions, such as Xively,[2] and academic solutions, such as OpenIoT (Soldatos et al., 2015), show appreciable features for specific domains focused mainly on low computational power devices, they still have two remarkable limitations when dealing with technologies that are usually employed outside those domains. The first one concerns the inability to easily interconnect the entities with the chosen framework. This is due to the absence of standards that define how these interconnections should be designed. This situation leads to the creation of an ad hoc integration each time the need to interconnect a new entity arises. The second one comes as a consequence of the former, and it concerns the limitations of these frameworks in terms of addressing the reconfiguration and adaptation of the system when changes on scenarios happen at runtime. The capability of the system to adapt itself to changes is important in the IoT domain, because dynamism and variability are its inner features. Addressing these issues would help provide middleware for the development and management of many of the complex scenarios arising in the IoT.

In this work, we propose a stack composed by de facto standard solutions as a layer which surrounds a selected P/S framework. This layer greatly facilitates the interconnection of different entities through the framework, regardless of the technology they employ. Moreover, we modeled and deployed the system in such a way that allows the scenarios to be reconfigured at runtime creating the possibility for the system to adapt to different situations over time. We present a sample implementation of our solution, and assess it in a motivating scenario.

This work is organized as follows: Section 2 introduces a motivating scenario that shows the need for integration, and to which we will refer throughout the article; Section 3 provides the state of the art for the approaches to integration, explaining how the main integration challenges have been addressed over time, and highlighting the main open issues. Section 4 presents the main components of our integration layer

---

[1]http://www.omg.org/spec/DDS/1.4/PDF/.
[2]https://xively.com/.

and the structure of the selected P/S framework. Section 5 explains how to develop and deploy the adapters needed to connect the technologies to that framework and it shows how our system supports the configuration of new scenarios easily. Finally, Section 6 concludes the chapter recalling the contributions of our approach and pointing out some open issues that require further investigation.

2 MOTIVATING SCENARIO

In this section we introduce a futuristic example where heterogeneous technologies can be connected together effortlessly in order to perform an interesting scenario. This example will be recalled throughout the work and will be used to make the reader comfortable with the concepts explained.

Jack and John are two friends spending an afternoon together studying at Jack's place. Not really feeling motivated to study, they decide to play their favorite sports videogame, American Football (NFL), with the Playstation.[3] Given their passion for this sport, they decide to simulate, within the living room, the real conditions (climatic, environmental, etc.) of every game they will play. To do so they connect the Playstation to the air conditioning system and to the humidifier present in the living room. This connection will allow the air conditioning and the humidifier to receive the needed pieces of information from the Playstation in order to adapt the living room's environment to the conditions of the game. Since John is a fan of the Green Bay Packers (a team based in Wisconsin), and he chooses them as his team, the home games could be really cold. For this reason they decide that it would be a good idea to have hot tea when half time comes. To do so they connect the kettle and the Playstation, so that the Playstation will update the kettle according to the timing of the game, allowing it to be switched on 2 min before the pause in order to boil water for the tea. Since Jack's girlfriend Lisa is having an interview for an important job and she said that she would phone him once she had finished, Jack decides to connect his smart phone with the Playstation in order to pause the game automatically in case Lisa calls.

Now that everything seems well planned, the two friends start the first match. Suddenly, however, they realize that Jack's mother, Marta, is in the basement doing her home chores, and that she would get really upset if she caught them playing. So they decide to place a Kinect device[4] in the corridor just outside the basement in order to detect Marta if she approaches. They connect the Kinect to the Playstation and the TV in order to switch them off in case Marta shows up. At last, they feel free to start playing. Fig. 1 resumes all the connections established for the motivating scenario.

---

[3]https://www.playstation.com/en-us/.
[4]https://www.microsoft.com/en-us/kinectforwindows/.

FIG. 1

Motivating scenario.

After some hours they finish playing, and even though one of them—the loser—is not all that happy, they have really enjoyed their afternoon. The games the two friends played were joyful because they planned everything in order to being able to focus all their attention on their hobby. This was only possible because Jack's house is equipped with the necessary technological devices and due to the possibility of establishing, almost effortlessly, the interactions between all the devices employed in the scenario. In this scenario, in order to implement the desired interactions, the user just needs to wire one device with another to create the desired interconnection, treating every entity like a black box.

Nevertheless, nowadays the implementation of such a system, composed of such diverse technologies, and capable of changing configuration at runtime are very challenging. Even to an inexperienced person in the integration domain it is clear that there are some challenges to be faced. For example to connect two technologies means creating a sort of bridge between them in order to make them interoperable, and this work requires a profound knowledge of all the technologies employed. Moreover, to establish every point-to-point connection requires time and the appropriate tools, besides an understanding of what information should be exchanged in order to design the scenario. These issues make difficult to model scenarios that really focus on what matters—the business logic of the use case the user is interested in. For business logic we intend all events and actions that can occur during the scenario's execution.

We assume that once the technologies are connected and they can communicate, they are able to perform the business logic designed for the scenario automatically.

3 CURRENT APPROACHES TO INTEGRATION IN IoT

In this section we analyze in detail the motivating scenario in order to discover and formally define the challenges that the integration poses in the IoT domain. Then we describe the main approaches through which some of these challenges have been addressed, starting from the M2M approaches and finishing with the novel approaches based on frameworks. Finally, we describe in detail the frameworks based on the P/S design pattern approach, describing all of the aspects which make them particularly suitable for addressing the main challenges of IoT integration in comparison with the other integration solutions proposed for the same domain.

3.1 UNDERSTANDING THE INTEGRATION ISSUES

Integration in information systems is a "process or phase concerned with joining different subsystems or components as one large system. It ensures that each integrated subsystem functions as required. System integration (SI) is also used to add value to a system through new functionalities provided by connecting functions of different systems."[5]

In this section we analyze the integration problem and we understand the main challenges it brings to the IoT domain. To integrate heterogeneous technologies is a problematic task, and to achieve a solution it requires an understanding of the main chunks of which it is composed. To this end, we point out the processes the motivating scenario prompts and then we apply software engineering techniques to define and analyze the functionalities those chunks imply and then we analyze them.

Firstly, let us define Jack's house as our *ecosystem*. This ecosystem is composed of all the technologies and actors that compose our motivating scenario. The motivating scenario shows that to perform the desired activities we must connect the devices that will communicate between them. Each device can communicate with one or more devices at a time. As a consequence, the number of connections it can be subjected to range from one to an undefined value. The motivating scenario also shows that sometimes there is the need or wish to configure some changes to the scenario at runtime.

---

[5]http://www.techopedia.com/definition/9614/system-integration-si.

If we follow the software engineering theory (Lee, 2013) and we compare the above description to the *requirement's specification*, we can apply a tactic that is used to model a component diagram starting with the *nouns* and the *verbs* present in the specification. For the requirement's specification we can highlight the following four meaningful verbs, and deliberate that they are the main challenges that we must face if we want to be able to perform the motivating scenario.

- To Connect
- To Communicate
- To Range
- To Configure

These challenges pose issues that we must address if we want to obtain the integration we need in order to perform not only the use case proposed in the motivating scenario, but even more complex use cases which can be performed in various situations. In the following sections we analyze such issues in detail.

3.1.1 To connect: The connection problem
In the motivating scenario we often say that Jack and John connect a device to another device; but what does "connect" exactly mean to us? When we say connect we refer to the capability of a device to send something to another device. For the moment we are not interested in what is sent, we just want the devices, once connected, to be capable of reaching each other in order to eventually send something.

3.1.2 To communicate: The understanding problem
To establish connections between devices is only the first step. What utility has a connection if what one device sends is alien to the device that receives it? The understanding problem refers to the issue of a mutual understanding regarding what is being exchanged. The receiving device must be able to interpret what the sending device provides.

3.1.3 To range: The scalability problem
The motivating scenario contains some devices that are connected only with one other device, and some that are connected with several. This indicates that it is not possible to know in advance how many devices each device will be connected to. As a consequence we can assert that every device must be capable, at least in theory, of connecting to a range of others, with no predefined lower or upper bound.

3.1.4 To configure: The adaptation problem
The motivating scenario shows marginally that sometimes there can be a need for changes at runtime. For example, Jack and John decide to use the Kinect to control Jack's mother movements only at a late stage in the planning. If it was not possible to reconfigure and to adapt the scenario afterwards, it would be impossible to satisfy all the requirements that may present a later stage. Furthermore, if those changes cannot

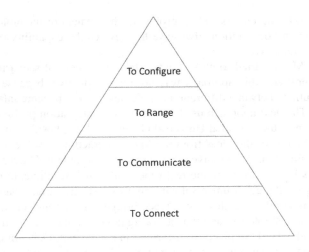

FIG. 2

Integration pyramid.

be configured at runtime, the system would need to be stopped every time a change is requested in order to reconfigure and to allow it to manage new situations.

The issues just explained are interrelated, and the order in which they are listed is not random. Without solving a previous issue, a solution for the one following cannot be achieved. Fig. 2 highlights this concept by showing that before solving the upper layer of the integration pyramid the lower layers on which it relies need to be built.

Now that we have clearly defined the set of challenges that integration brings and we have described the correlations between the different aspects of these challenges, in the next sections we will unfold the approaches that have been used to address the integration so far. We will describe which challenges are solved by each approach and we will indicate which challenges still remain unsolved.

3.2 APPROACHES FOR INTEGRATION: THE HISTORY

To integrate heterogeneous technologies has always been a complex task due to the differences that the protocols present at different levels (Zorzi et al., 2010). The recent past has seen different approaches proposed to address this issue. These approaches were designed for specific application domains, and their features were dependent on the specific domain.

One of the first domains where the integration was faced and addressed was the M2M domain. M2M interaction (Watson et al., 2004) refers to the information exchange among devices without human assistance. Formerly in the M2M domain the habit was to employ devices belonging to only one technology. In this case the challenges to be faced were mainly related to the connection problem and in a small portion to the understanding problem. The owners of technologies usually provided some ad hoc solutions that gave the devices the capability of connecting and communicating.

When the M2M started to move toward the deployment of scenarios composed of more technologies this approach was no longer effective, because the creation of ad hoc solutions between different technologies quickly became infeasible (Jung et al., 2012). The next approach used to address the integration problem was based on the adoption of the so-called Universal Gateways (Latvakoski et al., 2014). This approach uses some of the ideas from the M2M interaction to solve the connection problem, and aimed mainly to solve the understanding problem. The reason for using such gateways is to address the ineffectiveness of ad hoc solutions in resolving the understanding challenge. A universal gateway is a software or hardware component that provides internal semantics that act as a bridge between the semantics adopted by the different technologies and thus allowing devices connected to it to exchange data and to understand the pieces of information exchanged. Depending on the real implementation, some gateways can even provide features that address some aspects of the scalability and configuration problem, but only in a context for which they were designed.

The advent of the IoT brought the need of integration to a new level (Vermesan and Friess, 2013). If we consider everything as a machine, starting from simple building automation system (BAS) devices arriving to the applications running on personal computers (PC), from an integration point of view the IoT can be seen as an extension of the M2M concept. The absence of standardized M2M platforms that would enabled interconnection of heterogeneous technologies (Wu et al., 2011) and the fact that the small devices (*things*) still remain as the majority of the things involved in the IoT paradigm, led to the need for finding appropriate solutions to the interoperability. The IoT changed the world of the M2M paradigm. Indeed, through it, it is now possible to compare the set of all devices interconnected through the Internet to a system of parts, which coordinate and cooperate without human intervention. To fulfill the integration demanded by this new M2M over IoT paradigm the efforts have been directed toward the identification of an architecture for IoT integration, which is specific to some application domains.[6] These architectures aim to provide platforms that allow components to interact in order to take part in scenarios. The integration provided by these solutions is based on two approaches: *N*-to-*N* approach and *N*-to-1 approach (Rao, 2013). The *N*-to-*N* approach consists of creating a sort of bidirectional interpreter between each pairing of technologies in order to make the exchange of information possible. The *N*-to-1 approach instead is based on the idea of providing a framework (1-component) that acts as integrator for the various technologies that take part in the system (*N*-components); the components need to be able to communicate with the common framework.

---

[6]http://www.iot-a.eu/public and http://vital-iot.eu/.

The *N*-to-*N* approach has been shown to be inappropriate for the IoT domain because it is only suitable for scenarios that comprehend a small amount of heterogeneous technologies (Olivieri and Rizzo, 2015). IoT itself aims to use all possible technologies, but this implies that it has a grand heterogeneity; therefore, it does not address the scalability problem. Conversely the *N*-to-1 approach (Isenor and Spears, 2007) seems to be the correct solution because it provides all of the features needed to comply with the scalability property and heterogeneity variety the IoT domain requires.

However, problems arise when the scenarios involve a big number of different technologies and they demand high dynamism. This is due to the fact that the current solutions based on the *N*-to-1 approach do not provide the capabilities to easily design scenarios, and even if they tend to ensure the communications, they do not provide the quality of service some interesting scenarios require. Moreover, they leave the adaptation problem as a challenge still to be addressed.

Different paradigms stand behind the frameworks that act as 1-component in the *N*-to-1 approaches. For the features proposed by each of these paradigms we believe that the approaches based on the P/S design pattern overcome the others. The reason for our assumption is dictated by the manner in which its design addresses the connection problem. The connections are based on the data exchanged rather than on the instantiation of point-to-point connections between interacting components. In the next section we detail why we hold this opinion.

3.3 FRAMEWORKS BASED ON PUBLISH/SUBSCRIBE

The P/S framework is based on the homonymous design pattern and it defines a messaging strategy where the senders of messages (the publishers) do not define directly to which receivers (subscribers) will be sent the messages. This strategy is incorporated within a middleware that also provides the features to manage the communications (Eugster et al., 2003). In order to communicate, the interacting entities (publishers and subscribers) must be able to connect themselves to the P/S framework and then to express what information they provide (publishers) or require (subscribers). The information exchange starts when the coupling between sources and destinations of data is established. To do so the framework couples the pieces of information made available by the publisher with the pieces of information requested by subscribers.

To establish the couplings two main matching strategies exist: topic-based and context-based. In the topic-based strategy, messages are published to "topics" or named logical channels. Subscribers in a topic-based system will receive all messages published about the topics to which they subscribed, and all subscribers of a certain topic will receive the same messages. The publisher is responsible for defining the topics of messages to which subscribers can subscribe. In the content-based strategy, messages are only delivered to a subscriber if the attributes or content of those messages match constraints defined by the subscriber. The subscriber is responsible for classifying the messages. Some systems support a hybrid of the two strategies; publishers postmessages to a topic while subscribers register content-based subscriptions to one or more topics.

The P/S paradigm provides features that fit interaction schemes with large-scale settings, where strong and loose decoupling is required, by abstracting the interacting entities from communication issues. It provides three different kinds of decoupling:

- Space decoupling: The interacting entities do not need to know the spatial position of the entities they will interact with.
- Time decoupling: The interacting entities do not need to be actively participating in the interactions at the same time (ie, if the subscriber entities are off-line when some interesting data are provided, they will receive them anyway when they will be on-line again).
- Synchronization decoupling: Publishers are not kept waiting while they are producing events and subscribers can be asynchronously notified of the occurrence of an event while they are performing some concurrent activities.

We believe that the P/S design pattern addresses the challenges express in Section 3.1 in a quite exhaustive manner. In fact it defines how the interacting entities can be connected through a P/S framework and thanks to the time decoupling the publishers do not have to worry about the presence of the subscribers when they publish new contents. Moreover, it defines how the communications happen once the entities are connected to the framework, because both publishers and subscribers must be able to understand the semantics adopted by the framework. Furthermore, it allows the system to range thanks to the space decoupling that hides the addressing information details of the subscribers to the publishers. Further, the three features mentioned above, together with the focus of the framework on data rather than on communications, address a part of the adaptation challenge because they let publishers and subscribers free to enter and exit the scenario.

The previous reasons contributed to our decision of adopting a framework based on the P/S paradigm when we were requested from the committee of the European Project IoT6[7] to find a solution to integrate, within the context of IoT, BAS devices, and mainstream technologies. For mainstream technologies we intend technologies of disparate categories but large usage, such as PC, Playstation, mobile phones, etc. The framework that we selected is called *P/S Context Broker—Orion Context Broker* (Orion Context Broker)[8] developed for the FI-WARE European project.[9]

3.3.1 Challenges and open issues
The P/S frameworks properly address some part of the challenges envisaged, as described in Section 3.3; however, they do not achieve a full integration. As Oracle

---

[7]http://iot6.eu/.

[8]http://catalogue.fiware.org/enablers/publishsubscribe-context-broker-orion-context-broker.
[9]https://www.fiware.org/.

explains in its white paper *A Brave New Integration World*,[10] it is important especially now that we move more and more toward a mobile world, to create solution based on Service Oriented Architecture (SOA) paradigm in order to make systems independent from any vendor or technologies. SOA (Wiederhold, 1992) is an architecture for building business applications as a set of loosely coupled black-box components orchestrated to deliver a well-defined level of service by linking together business processes. To obtain this independence, which would mean reaching the integration level desired, the P/S framework should be surrounded by a adaptation layer to provide a standardized access. By standardized we mean a layer composed by technologies and/or methodologies that are of common usage nowadays and that can be seen as standard de facto.

If we recall the motivating scenario, there are devices from different technologies that play different roles. If the framework that Jack decides to use in his house does not use standardized solutions, each vendor needs to learn how to interface its devices to the framework, or hope that some developers will create some piece of code needed to integrate such devices to the framework. If a framework does not provide open and standard interfaces to external systems a two-sided problem is born: mainstream technologies vendors (such as Sony) are not interested in interfacing their products to close environments; and developers find no interest in learning how to interconnect a device to a close environment. Having said this, if the framework Jack uses is a close framework, he could have any technologies he wants, but he will never be able to model the scenario he has in mind. Therefore it is indispensable to equip the frameworks (in our case a P/S framework) with the interfaces needed to easily exploit their features.

Moreover, what if the framework does not allow runtime reconfiguration of the system? This situation would oblige the users to stop it every time a scenario requires changes. As a consequence there will be a pause in the information exchange that may be acceptable for some scenarios, but not for others, making it inappropriate for these latter scenarios. In the next section we will describe how we modeled the integration layer and how we connected it to the chosen P/S framework in order to provide standard and user-friendly interfaces for external systems.

4 DESIGN OF AN INTEGRATION LAYER FOR P/S FRAMEWORKS

In Section 3.3 we mentioned the need for solutions, based on standard and user-friendly interfaces, to address the integration problem in heterogeneous environments. This is a real motivation due to the desire to make frameworks available to different vendors efficiently and with little effort. In order to fulfill this guidance we defined an integration layer that surrounds the Orion Context Broker. The aim is to

---

[10]http://www.oracle.com/us/products/middleware/soa/soa-simplify-enterprise-integration-2209678.pdf.

provide interfaces to the external systems, and by doing so to allow them to exploit the features of the framework. In this section we move from an understanding of the integration problem to a solution that addresses it. We introduce the integration layer that performs the interfacing task, we explain how we designed it and what we implemented and deployed in order to connect it to the framework and to make it suitable for the external systems.

4.1 INTEGRATION LAYER

The layer we will describe is part of a bigger piece of work named *IoT6 Stack* that was developed for the IoT6 European Project.[11] The IoT6 Stack is the common communication interface for all systems present within the IoT6 project. The core elements of the IoT6 Stack are IPv6 as Internet Protocol, Web services based on CoAP[12] as service layer, the OASIS Open Building Information Exchange standard (oBIX)[13] as object model, and JSON[14] as message encoding.

Fig. 3 shows how the integration is obtained amid the systems operating within the IoT6 project. The IoT6 stack offers integration functionalities that allow the

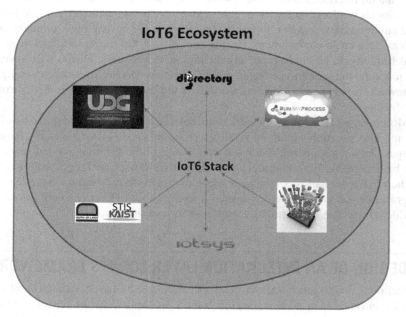

FIG. 3

IoT6 ecosystem.

[11] http://iot6.eu/.
[12] http://tools.ietf.org/html/draft-ietf-core-coap-09.
[13] https://www.oasis-open.org/committees/download.php/38212/oBIX-1-1-spec-wd06.pdf.
[14] http://www.json.org/.

interconnection of all components under a common communication environment. Each interacting system is connected to the IoT6 Ecosystem through a sort of connector that is based on the IoT6 stack, and which defines the integration between the semantic of the single component and the semantic defined in the IoT6 Ecosystem.

This integration layer was developed mainly for the IoT6 project context, but our purpose is to refine it and to make it useful even outside the IoT6 Ecosystem. For this reason we defined a subscheme of the IoT6 stack where we ignore oBIX, we replace CoAP with RESTful Web Services,[15] we make use of both IPv6 and IPv4 and we preserve JSON.

4.2 ADAPTERS DESIGN

To create the desired integration we decided to equip P/S framework with an integration layer. By definition, in computer programming, frameworks are abstractions in which software providing generic functionalities can be selectively changed by additional user-written code, thus providing application-specific software.[16] What we have to define in this phase is a way of providing some tools to the interacting systems that allow for the exploitation of functionalities provided by the selected framework.

We chose a framework based on the P/S design pattern called Orion Context Broker that provides various functionalities called primitives (TELEFONICA I+D S.A.U., 2014a,b), which allow external systems to interact with the framework through HTTP POST methods.[17] In order to attain the integration task and to create our prototype we evaluated that we needed only a subset of those functionalities. Table 1 shows the functionalities that we use for our purpose and that are made available to the interacting systems.

Table 1 Orion Context Broker Functionalities: Subset of Interest

Resource	Base URI	HTTP Verbs
		POST
Subscribe context resource	/subscribeContext	It allows systems to subscribe to Context information when something happens
Unsubscribe context resource	/unsubscribeContext	It allows systems to unsubscribe to Context information we were subscribed to
Update context resource	/updateContext	It allows systems to create (using APPEND as type action) or to update (using UPDATE as type action) a piece of information

[15]https://docs.oracle.com/javaee/6/tutorial/doc/gijqy.html.
[16]https://en.wikipedia.org/wiki/Software_framework.
[17]http://www.w3.org/Protocols/HTTP/Methods/Post.html.

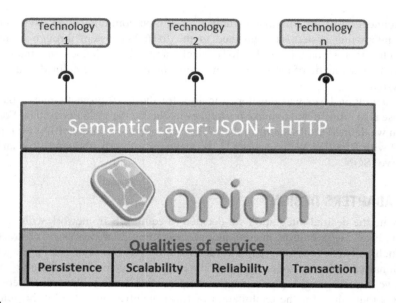

FIG. 4

Orion context broker with integration layer.

The idea is to create adapters that use these primitives to provide easy access to the framework. Fig. 4 shows how the integration layer is connected to the Orion Context Broker in order to integrate among them technologies. This layer provides interfaces that the systems must implement in order to participate in scenarios managed by the Orion Context Broker. Our aim is to create standardized self-contained adapters that the systems can use to interact through the exploitation of the Orion Context Broker.

In order to design these adapters, we decided to adopt the Software Engineering guidelines proposed in Antonio, N. and Ambra, M. (2012) and we started by defining the primary use cases that each interacting entity should pass through in order to exchange pieces of information using the framework. Fig. 5 shows the use cases (labeled as UC01, UC02, UC03, UC04) that an entity will encounter in performing the information exchange and Table 2 explain the use cases in detail.

The use cases highlight some nouns and verbs that helped us to define a first version of the Domain Model, where we defined all components and interactions needed to connect the entities to the Orion Context Broker in order to obtain the integration required. Fig. 6 shows the first version of the domain model that was used as groundwork for the system development.

Once we had defined the primary use cases needed to integrate the entities and we had modeled the domain model, we decomposed our model into the three dimensions of software (Antonio, N. and Ambra, M., 2012) to properly design our system: structure, interaction, and behavior.

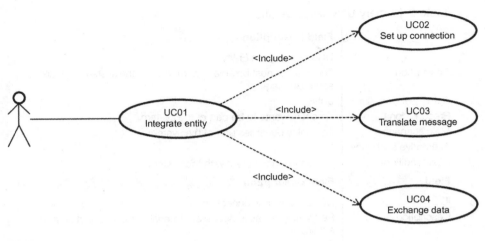

FIG. 5

Primary use cases.

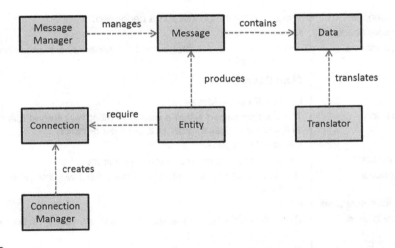

FIG. 6

Domain model.

4.2.1 Structure dimension

To structure our system we started by dividing the components present in the Domain Model into three groups that represent different vertical dimensions as described in Jacobson (1992). These dimensions are named: entity, boundary, and control.

Table 2 Primary Use Cases Details

Field	Field Description
ID	UC01—Integrate Entity
Description	The entities must be able to participate in the system and talk the same language
Actor	Entity
Preconditions	An entity wants to be part of the system
Main scenario	The entity becomes part of the system
Alternative scenarios	No
Postconditions	The entity can interact with the system

Field	Field Description
ID	UC02—Set Up Connection
Description	Performing all tasks necessary to enable the connection among entities
Actor	ConnectionManager
Preconditions	a) The entities involved are on-line when the connection establishment attempt is performed b) There is at least one entity that wants to communicate with the sender
Main scenario	The set up for the connection is performed.
Alternative scenarios	None
Postconditions	The connection is established and the sender and the receivers can communicate

Field	Field Description
ID	UC03—Translate Message
Description	The data contained within a message must be interpretable by all the other entities in order to allow the integration
Actor	MessageManager
Preconditions	The presence of a message sent by an entity
Main scenario	The data written by an entity are translated in a way interpretable by all entities
Alternative scenarios	None
Postconditions	The date contained inside the message are ready to be exchanged

Field	Field Description
ID	UC04—Exchange Date
Description	Exchanging data among sender and receiver entities
Actor	Sender entity
Preconditions	Connection between sender and receiver already set up
Main scenario	The sender sends a message containing data to a receiver. The message arrives to the receiver and it can understand the data contained
Alternative scenarios	The receiver is not on-line: in this case, the re-submission of the message must be managed
Postconditions	The receiver extracts the data from the message and performs some actions depending on its own internal logic

(a) Entity: This contains the concrete components that will be used by other components and it is considered as the central point of the project. The following list itemizes the components belonging to the entity dimension:

- Message
- Data
- Connection

(b) Boundary: This contains the components that encapsulate the interfaces of the system toward the external world. The following list itemizes the only component belonging to the boundary dimension:

- Entity

(c) Control: This is the principal group, and contains the components that mediate between the Boundary and Entity in order to perform the business logic of our system. The following list itemizes the components belonging to the control dimension:

- ConnectionManager
- Translator
- MessageManager

4.2.2 Interaction dimension

The division of the components performed in the structure dimension gave us the possibility of binding each component with the correlated use cases in order to discover all interactions present within our integration system. Fig. 7 represents the Logical Architecture of the integration layer, and it shows how the components are correlated with the use cases (solid arrows) and the dependencies between components (dashed arrows).

The dashed arrows in Fig. 7 highlight the dependencies that are envisaged among the components present in our architecture. The following list itemizes the relevant dependencies needed to accomplish the business logic of the system (some dependencies have been taken out of the list because they are not meaningful within the context of the business logic model):

- Entity—ConnectionManager
- Entity—MessageManager
- MessageManager—Translator

Once the relevant dependencies have been identified, the nature of the system must be decided. This implies determining whether the system should be either a full local one, have only some components distributed, or be fully distributed. The environment in which the system will be applied leans toward a distributed direction because it is composed of distributed heterogeneous external systems that want to use a middleware in order to exchange data. The solution chosen was one in which

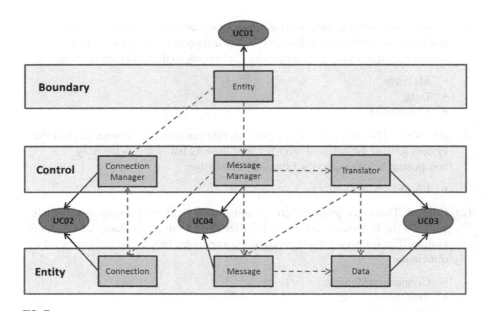

FIG. 7

Logical architecture of the integration layer.

a central framework will simulate a fully distributed environment providing a set of interfaces that will be replicated on all nodes that represent external entities. Those interfaces will allow the entities to be part of the system and communicate among them seamlessly. Below we analyze these dependencies in a more detailed manner.

Entity (E)—ConnectionManager (CM). An E depends on a CM in order to be connected to the system and to exchange information with other Es. Therefore, this interaction starts from E and goes toward CM. This leads to the following Producer-Consumer decision:

- Producer: Entity
- Consumer: ConnectionManager

Since E has to be certain that the CM has built the requested connection, a Request/Response (Antonio, N. and Ambra, M., 2012) is chosen as the communication mode. This functionality, which we called *connectEntity( )*, is provided by
the CM.

Entity (E)—MessageManager (MM). An E depends on an MM to send the information it possesses to other Es, and to do so it needs the MM as the component that takes care of the information flow. Therefore, the communication starts from *E* and goes to the *MM*, leading to the following Producer-Consumer decision:

- Producer: Entity
- Consumer: MessageManager

Since *E* assumes that the *MM* will perform its behavior properly, a response is not needed, hence a Dispatch (Antonio, N. and Ambra, M., 2012) is chosen as the communication mode between them. This functionality, which we called *dispatchInformation()* is provided by the *MM*.

MessageManager (*MM*)—Translator (*T*). An *MM* depends on a *T* because of the heterogeneity of the entities that will use the final system. Every *E* will produce pieces of information in its own way, and those pieces of information must be adapted to the common semantics in order to create messages that contain data interpretable by all other entities. Therefore, an *MM*, once it gets the information to be forwarded to others, has to ask for an interpretable representation of that information before dispatching it—this task is performed by *T*. This leads to the following Producer-Consumer decision:

- Producer: MessageManager
- Consumer: Translator

Since the *MM* wants the *T* to return the information in an interpretable format, a Request/Response as communication mode is defined between them. This functionality, which we called *produceInterpretableMessage()*, is provided by the *T* as defined.

4.2.3 Behavior dimension

In this section, the attention is focused on the business logic. Since the analysis is still being performed, we cannot dig deeply into the internal entities' behavior; therefore, the best approach is to define the behavior looking at the components as black boxes, by understanding what they perform, and evaluating eventual inputs and outputs. By doing so, the designer will be free to model all components as he wishes. The components of interest are those belonging to the control group defined in the following sections.

ConnectionManager (*CM*). The *CM*'s main task is to connect the applicant *E* into the system and to provide it with the capability to communicate with the other entities. When the system calls into action the *CM*, it wants it to perform all the steps needed to allow an *E* to be connected to the system. The *E* will have to provide some information necessary to join the system. By doing so, the system will send back all pieces of information *E* needs to participate in the system and to be attainable for external communications.

MessageManager (*MM*). The *MM*'s main task is to send the Message containing the information provided by the sender *E* to the interested *E*s. The

MM is called into action when an *E* wants to send pieces of information to other *E*s.

Translator (*T*). The *T*'s main task is to format information in an interpretable way and put them into a message. When the system calls into action the *T*, it is because information has to be formatted in order to be interpretable. The *MM* will have to pass the information to the *T*, so that it can send back a message that contains information formatted in an interpretable way.

4.3 ADAPTERS IMPLEMENTATION AND DEPLOYMENT

The introduction of the Orion Context Broker within the Logical Architecture previously described brings some constraints related to the technologies to be used. These constraints limit the freedom of the modeling phase for interactions and architecture details. The Orion Context Broker is the software framework used in this system to dispatch the information among *E*s, as previously described. It is based on RESTful web services, so the first constraint is that entities are forced to communicate with the framework through RESTful APIs. As a consequence, we must equip *E*s with web interfaces that use HTTP methods. A second constraint is the data format exchanged among the web interfaces and the Orion Context Broker. The Orion Context Broker allows two data formats: XML and JSON—we chose to employ JSON as a data format. The Orion Context Broker manages the dispatch of information to the publisher *E*s through the HTTP POST method. This feature constrains the Subscriber *E*s of being equipped with a web service interface in order to receive the information that the Orion Context Broker will dispatch to them.

4.3.1 Boundary layer

We will now clarify how the *E*s are involved in the three dimensions previously defined:

- Structure: *E*s play a role in interfacing the system with the external world. The external world refers to the real technologies used in this project.
- Interaction: *E*s interact directly with two components of the system—the *CM* through a Request interaction and the *MM* through a Dispatch interaction.
- Behavior: The behavior of *E*s changes depending on whether they act as a publisher or a subscriber. In the case where an *E* acts as a publisher, it will act as a Web Client that will communicate with the Orion Context Broker. However, if an *E* acts as a subscriber, it will act both as a Web Client of the Orion Context Broker and as a Web Service that waits for incoming communications from the Orion Context Broker.

Led by the aforementioned clarifications, we decided to model the publisher and subscriber *E*s using an Abstract class, followed by the concrete classes that extend it (Publisher and Subscriber Es). The action of performing the connection to the System is common to all Es, and this is the reason why it will be performed by the Abstract class.

4.3.2 Control layer

Previously we identified the CM as the component that allows Es to establish the connection with the Orion Context Broker. To have a connection established both the publisher and the subscriber Es need a Web Resource that allows them to join the Orion Context Broker. Since the communication between Es and the CM is defined as a Request/Response interaction, when an entity contacts the CM, it will respond with a WebResource that is necessary to join the Orion Context Broker.

Once the CM is obtained, we need the MM to manage the creation of interpretable messages exchanged between the Es and to dispatch those messages from publishers to subscribers. The integration of the Orion Context Broker brings a modification to this procedure, whereby the dispatching is not direct, but it is managed by the Orion Context Broker. Therefore, the MM provides a publish interface that allows the Es to insert information in the Orion Context Broker. In regard to the creation of interpretable messages, nothing changes. The MM provides the interfaces needed by Es to have some well-formatted information ready to be sent. The Orion Context Broker requires a payload as argument of the HTTP POST method. These payloads can be seen as data that Es send to the framework. The payload required by HTTP POST methods will create some consequences when the Data (D) component will be modeled.

The messages, for being well-formatted, need the T to create interpretable messages. It provides interfaces to allow the MM to request the creation of messages containing a JSON Object as D. This is requested in order to be compatible with the Orion Context Broker, and to allow the interpretation of the messages everywhere within the system.

Fig. 8 shows the Final Logical Architecture containing all the components and the relationships between them.

4.3.3 Entity layer

The Message (M) is the real content of the pieces of information exchanged. We decided to use JSON as data format, and by doing so an M conveys a JSON Object that can be coherently exchanged among all entities via the Orion Context Broker.

D is the actual content of the Ms that go from the entities to the Orion Context Broker and from the Orion Context Broker to the Es. Those Ms are needed for various purposes: to publish context information, to subscribe Es to context information, and to unsubscribe Es from context information. The D is the full content of the payload inserted inside an M.

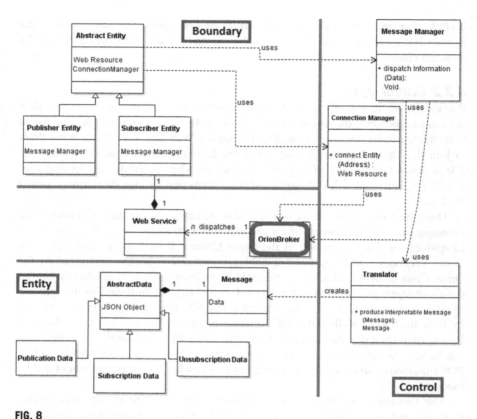

FIG. 8

Final logical architecture.

In the next section we show examples of adapters implementations and we describe how to deploy the entities in our system.

5 EXAMPLE OF ADAPTERS IMPLEMENTATION AND SYSTEM DEPLOYMENT

In this section we describe how we can configure the system to manage the motivating scenario. We also show how easy it is to change the characteristics of the scenario, demonstrating how it is possible to mutate totally its configuration in order to support different scenarios.

By recalling the motivating scenario, we can identify all interactions that the external systems have with the Orion Context Broker. Below we itemize the interactions in which each external system participates and we detail whether a piece of information acts as publisher or subscriber.

(a) Environment Condition: This information describes the climatic condition related to the game.
- Publisher: Playstation
- Subscriber: Humidifier, Air Conditioning System

(b) Time of the match: This information describes the current time of the match.
- Publisher: Playstation
- Subscriber: Kettle

(c) Call Notification: This information describes Lisa's phone call.
- Publisher: Mobile Phone
- Subscriber: Playstation

(d) Mother Movement: This information describes that Marta is leaving the basement.
- Publisher: Kinect
- Subscriber: Playstation, TV

Fig. 9 synthesizes the interactions by highlighting the directions of the information flow and the role that each system plays in the motivating scenario. Solid

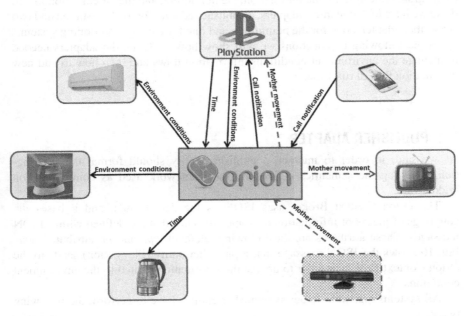

FIG. 9

System and interactions.

arrows indicate information flows established at configuration time while dashed arrows indicate information flows established at runtime through adaptations in the scenario.

As explained at the beginning, we want the interactions to be based on the data exchanged rather than on the establishment of direct communications between communicating systems. When we decide to subscribe one or more system to some data we do not have to explicitly indicate the publishers of those data. The only task we must perform is to create subscriptions for those data, without having any information about the providers of those data. This means that we have to create the right adapters for the publisher system and the subscriber(s) system(s) to let them interoperate correctly with the Orion Context Broker framework. We defined templates for the publisher and subscriber adapters based on the Logical Architecture shown in Fig. 8, and below we show some snippets of code that illustrate how these templates must be adapted to interconnect two systems. The aim here is to show how to connect systems, abstracting from their inner business logic—the business logic is outside of our area of interest. We will show a few snippets of code to let the user understand how to develop adapters and deploy them in order to integrate external systems. Everything could be done without directly implementing the adapters by hand—we provide special graphical user interfaces to perform these tasks.

Let us take as an example the environment conditions information. Here we want to integrate three system: the Playstation, the humidifier, and the air conditioning. To do so we have to define three adapters, a publisher adapter for the Playstation and two subscriber adapters, one for the humidifier, and one for the air conditioning system.

In the following two sections we will show how to define the adapters needed to manage the environment-conditions information flows and then how to add new information flow at run-time.

5.1 PUBLISHER ADAPTER

As we said, in order to interact, a publisher entity should format the information following the semantics defined by the framework used as communication middleware.

The Orion Context Broker uses JSON as the data format, and it bases the couplings of pieces of information on some attributes that are defined within JSON messages. These attributes are the following: element *type* and *id*, attribute *name*. Fig. 10 shows the JSON message that a publisher entity (Playstation) sends to the Orion Context Broker in order to update the information related to the environment conditions.

All systems that want to act as publisher entities have to perform the following two tasks:

```json
{
    "contextElements":{
        "contextElement":{
            "type":"EnvironmentCondition",
            "isPattern":false,
            "id":"FootballMatch",
            "attributes":[
                {
                    "name":"Temperature",
                    "value":"true",
                    "type":"15"
                }
{
                    "name":"Humidity",
                    "value":"true",
                    "type":"70"
                }
            ]
        }
    },
    "updateAction":"APPEND"
}
```

FIG. 10

JSON publisher message.

(a) To create a *PublisherEntity* that will allow it to work as Web Client:

```
PublisherEntity publisherEntity = new PublisherEntity();
```

(b) To connect themselves to the Orion Context Broker, by creating a WebResource as reference for that connection:

```
WebResource webResource = publisherEntity.connectEntity(url);
```

Once these two tasks are performed they can publish pieces of information into the Orion Context Broker following this three-step procedure:

(a) To create the pieces of information it wants to publish:

```
PublicationData publishData = new PublicationData();
publishData.setElement("EnvironmentCondition", "FootballMatch");
publishData.setAttribute("Temperature", "15", "true");
publishData.setAttribute("Humidity", "70", "true");
publishData.setAction("APPEND");
```

(b) To create a JSON object given the information just created:

```
JSONObject contextPayload = publishData.getData();
```

(c) To publish that information—its JSON representation—into the Orion Context Broker using the WebResource:

```
publisherEntity.publish(webResource, "updateContext",
contextPayload);
```

With this simple piece of code the publisher adapter is now created and the information concerning the environment variable is available for all systems that desire it. The updating interval is decided by the publisher entity depending on its business logic.

5.2 SUBSCRIBER ADAPTER

Like publisher entities, subscriber entities should format pieces of information as JSON.

The important attributes that should be declared in a subscriber adapter are the following: entities *type* and *id*, *attributes*, *reference*, and *notifyContitions*. Fig. 11 shows the JSON message that a subscriber entity (Air Conditioning System) sends

```
{
    "entities": [
        {
            "type": " EnvironmentCondition",
            "isPattern": "false",
            "id": " FootballMatch"
        }
    ],
    "attributes": [
        "Temperature"
    ],
    "reference": "http://ec2-54-247-170-111.eu-west-
                        1.compute.amazonaws.com/rest/notificationManager/",
    "duration": "P1M",
    "notifyConditions": [
        {
            "type": "ONCHANGE",
            "condValues": [
                "Temperature"
            ]
        }
    ],
    "throttling": "PT5S"
}
```

FIG. 11

JSON subscriber—temperature.

to the Orion Context Broker to request pieces of information about environment conditions.

To become a subscriber entity, a system has to pass through two different phases:

- Web Client phase: This phase is essential to becoming a member of the system and to express the desire of receiving notifications. It is created through a five-step procedure similar to the one described for publisher entities:

  (a) To create a Subscriber Entity that will allow it to work as the Web Client:

  ```
  SubscriberEntity subscriberEntity = new SubscriberEntity();
  ```

  (b) To connect itself to the Orion Context Broker, creating a WebResource as reference for that connection:

  ```
  WebResource webResource = subscriberEntity.connectEntity(url);
  ```

  (c) To create the pieces of information it needs in order to do the subscription:

  ```
  SubscriptionData subscribeData = new SubscriptionData ()
  subscribeData.setAttribute("Temperature");
  subscribeData.setEntity("EnvironmentCondition","FootballMatch");
  subscribeData.setDuration(1);
  subscribeData.setReference(yourWebServiceURL);
  subscribeData.setNotifyCondition("ONCHANGE", "Temperature");
  ```

  In order to subscribe to pieces of information, a Subscriber Entity has to specify the URL where it will deploy a Web Service that will manage the notifications. This is specified in the variable *yourWebServiceURL*.

  (d) To create the JSON object given the information just created:

  ```
  JSONObject contextPayload = subscribeData.getData();
  ```

  A Subscriber Entity that publishes this object intends to retrieve information that has *EnvironmentCondition* as the context type, *FootballMatch* as id, and *Temperature* as condition for the notifications. The Web Service will be listening to the referenced URL and it will receive notification when the value of the attribute changes.

  (e) To subscribe to that information—its JSON representation—in the Orion Context Broker using the WebResource:

  ```
  subscriberEntity.subscribe(webResource,"subscribeContext",
  contextPayload);
  ```

- Web Service phase: This phase is needed to create a RESTful web service that manages the notifications and make the data carried inside pieces of information available for external systems. Subscribers' adapters also contain a Web Service skeleton that users can use as a starting point for making their own web services. This skeleton provides the REST methods with the right *Headers* for communicating with the Orion Context Broker, abstracting the users from the framework details. The skeleton is made in a way that users can use it directly in their projects. Users just need to replace the italic part of the following URL (present also in Fig. 11) with their Servlet URL *http://ec2-54-247-170-110.eu-west-1.compute.amazonaws.com/*rest/**notificationManager/**. The access point of the code should be in the web path highlighted in bold. If users already have their own web service and they want to add another web resource, they can replace the web path with their new web resource path. Within the *notificationManager* access point, users should define the business logic that their systems will perform once the web service receives information from notifications.

5.3 RUN-TIME MODIFICATIONS

Fig. 9 also contains some interactions that are added at runtime (dashed arrows). These interactions are the ones that are added not at planning time, but during the game, and they are used in order to manage the situation on which Marta leaves the basement. We use them to illustrate how our solution provides support to modify the scenario at run-time. Thanks to our solution to modify a scenario at run-time it is easy and does not require any change to the already interacting systems. To modify it, users must only define/modify the adapters following the procedures showed in Sections 5.1 and 5.2. Sticking with our motivating example, a publisher adapter for the Kinect has to be defined in order to send information concerning the *MotherMovement*, and two subscriber adapters have to be defined in order to receive notifications about this piece of information. Nothing more is needed and the new interactions of a system do not influence the already existing ones.

This approach gives the framework the capability of adapting existing scenarios at runtime and to create new ones when desired providing a great flexibility really necessary in the IoT domain.

6 CONCLUSIONS AND FUTURE WORK

The development of our solution for integrating heterogeneous technologies within the IoT domain follows an approach that tries to address all the challenges the integration brings. In this work we analyzed these challenges in the context of the IoT and we described a general approach to such integration problem.

The approach behind our solution uses some ideas from leading solutions (eg, the abstraction of real devices with the concept of virtualization (Spiess et al., 2009)) and it refines them to address a more generic integration domain.

We applied our solution to a real scenario that comprehends all envisaged challenges and we described why it provides good support for integrating heterogeneous technologies in IoT.

Nevertheless we think that our solution can be improved and we hope this article paves the way for future work. We mention here a challenge that we faced during the implementation of our system that we believe should be the first problem to be addressed. P/S frameworks couple the pieces of information using approaches based on topic matching or context matching. These approaches work well as long as the interacting entities have knowledge about how to identify those pieces of information, but they can fail in absence of enough knowledge. However, in the IoT domain, it is unthinkable to presume that a system that wants to participate in a scenario knows in advance how the pieces of information it is interested about are labeled.

Some studies have already started to address such a problem (Zhang et al., 2008; Liu and Jacobsen, 2004), but they did not solved it completely, leaving open some interesting research directions.

ACRONYMS

BAS   building automation system
CM   connection manager
CoAP   constrained application protocol
DDS   data-distribution service for real-time systems
E   entity
HTTP   hypertext transfer protocol
IoT   Internet of Things
IoT6   researching IPv6 potential for the Internet of Things
IPv6   Internet protocol version 6
JSON   JavaScript Object Notation
M2M   machine-to-machine
MM   message manager
MQTT   MQ telemetry transport
oBIX   open building information Xchange
P/S   publish/subscribe
RESTful representational state transfer
T   translator
UC   use case

GLOSSARY

Actuator Device that receives data and subsequently acts properly on a mechanism or system.
Ad hoc solution Solution designed for a specific task and it is nongeneralizable or adaptable to other purposes.
Business logic Set of events and actions that models the functionalities that a system provides.
Cyber-physical system System of collaborating computational elements controlling physical entities.

Decoupling The separation of previously linked systems so that they may operate independently.

Design pattern General reusable solution to a commonly occurring problem within a given context in software design.

Ecosystem Platform defined by more components that can interact together.

Entity Component that interact with a system.

Framework Abstraction in which software providing generic functionality can be selectively changed by additional user-written code, thus providing application-specific software.

Information system Organized system for the collection, organization, storage, and communication of information.

Internet of Things The network of physical objects or "things" embedded with electronics, software, sensors, and network connectivity, which enables these objects to collect and exchange data.

Latency Time interval between the stimulation and response.

Mainstream technology Technology belonging to various categories subjected to large usage.

Middleware Computer software that provides services to software applications beyond those available from the operating system.

Paradigm Distinct set of concepts or thought patterns, including theories, research methods, postulates, and standards for what constitutes legitimate contributions to a field.

Point-to-point connection Dedicated connection link between two systems or processes that directly connects two systems.

Real-time system System that must process information and produce a response within a specified time, else risk severe consequences, including failure.

Requirements specification Description of a software system to be developed, laying out functional and nonfunctional requirements.

Scalability Capability of a system to handle a growing amount of work, or its potential to be enlarged in order to accommodate that growth.

Scenario The set of interactions that take part in accomplishing a task.

Sensor Device that detects events and sends data about the events to a system.

ACKNOWLEDGMENTS

Thanks to Milene Fauquex for helping with the images, to Michael Barry for his help, and to the University of Applied Sciences and Arts Western Switzerland Valais (HES-SO Valais-Wallis), especially the Institute Information Systems in Sierre for their financial and scientific support.

REFERENCES

Antonio, N., Ambra, M., 2012. Costruire sistemi software. Dai modelli al codice. Esculapio (Italy). ISBN 978-8874883349. http://www.amazon.it/Costruire-sistemi-software-modelli-codice/dp/887488334X.

Eugster, P.T., Felber, P.A., Guerraoui, R., Kermarrec, A.M., 2003. The many faces of publish/subscribe. ACM Comput. Surv. 35 (2), 114–131.

Hunkeler, U., Truong, H.L., Stanford-Clark, A., 2008. MQTT-S #x2014; a publish/subscribe protocol for wireless sensor networks. In: 3rd International Conference on Communication Systems Software and Middleware and Workshops, 2008. COMSWARE 2008, pp. 791–798.

Isenor, A., Spears, T.W., 2007. A conceptual model for service-oriented discovery of marine metadata descriptions. CMOS Bull. SCMO 35 (3), 85–91.

Jacobson, I., 1992. Object Oriented Software Engineering: A Use Case Driven Approach. Addison-Wesley Professional.

Jung, M., Weidinger, J., Reinisch, C., Kastner, W., Crettaz, C., Olivieri, A., Bocchi, Y., 2012. A transparent IPv6 multi-protocol gateway to integrate building automation systems in the Internet of Things. In: 2012 IEEE International Conference on Green Computing and Communications (GreenCom), pp. 225–233.

Latvakoski, J., Alaya, M.B., Ganem, H., Jubeh, B., Iivari, A., Leguay, J., Bosch, J.M., Granqvist, N., 2014. Towards horizontal architecture for autonomic M2M service networks. Future Internet 6 (2), 261–301. ISSN 1999-5903. doi:10.3390/fi6020261. http://www.mdpi.com/1999-5903/6/2/261.

Lee, R., 2013. Software Engineering: A Hands-On Approach. Atlantis Press, Bücher. ISBN 9789462390065. https://books.google.ch/books?id=zdBEAAAAQBAJ.

Li, J., Yu, K., Wang, K., Li, Y., Li, S., 2003. Peer-to-Peer (P2P) communication system. Google Patents. http://www.google.com/patents/US20030182428.

Liu, H., Jacobsen, H.A., 2004. A-ToPSS: A Publish/Subscribe System Supporting Imperfect Information Processing. University of Toronto, pp. 1107–1110.

Liu, H., Ramasubramanian, V., Sirer, E.G., 2005. Client behavior and feed characteristics of RSS, a publish-subscribe system for web micronews. In: Proceedings of the 5th ACM SIGCOMM Conference on Internet Measurement, IMC '05. USENIX Association, Berkeley, CA, USA, pp. 3–3. http://dl.acm.org/citation.cfm?id=1251086.1251089.

Olivieri, A.C., Rizzo, G., 2015. Scalable approaches to integration in heterogeneous IoT and M2M scenarios. In: 2015 9th International Conference on Innovative Mobile and Internet Services in Ubiquitous Computing (IMIS), pp. 358–363.

Pardo-Castellote, G., 2003. OMG data-distribution service: architectural overview. In: 23rd International Conference on Distributed Computing Systems Workshops, 2003. Proceedings, pp. 200–206.

Rao, P., 2013. Communication Systems. McGraw Hill Education (India). ISBN 9781259006852. https://books.google.ch/books?id=tRB_AgAAQBAJ.

Sanchez, L., 2012. Pub/Sub, the Internet of Things, and 6LoWPAN connectivity. http://www.embedded.com/electronics-blogs/cole-bin/4371184/Pub-sub-the-Internet-of-Things-and-6LoWPAN-connectivity (accessed October 13, 2015).

Schmidt, D.C., O'Ryan, C., 2003. Patterns and performance of distributed real-time and embedded publisher/subscriber architectures. J. Syst. Softw. 66 (3), 213–223. ISSN 0164-1212. doi:10.1016/S0164-1212(02)00078-X. http://www.sciencedirect.com/science/article/pii/S016412120200078X.

Soldatos, J., Kefalakis, N., Hauswirth, M., Serrano, M., Calbimonte, J.P., Riahi, M., Aberer, K., Jayaraman, P., Zaslavsky, A., Arko, I., Skorin-Kapov, L., Herzog, R., 2015. OpenIoT: open source internet-of-things in the cloud. In: Arko, I.P., Pripui, K., Serrano, M. (Eds.), Interoperability and Open-Source Solutions for the Internet of Things, Lecture Notes in Computer Science, vol. 9001. Springer International Publishing, pp. 13–25. http://dx.doi.org/10.1007/978-3-319-16546-2_3.

Spiess, P., Karnouskos, S., Guinard, D., Savio, D., Baecker, O., Souza, L., Trifa, V., 2009. SOA-based integration of the Internet of Things in enterprise services. In: IEEE International Conference on Web Services, 2009. ICWS 2009, pp. 968–975.

TELEFONICA I+D S.A.U., 2014a. FI-WARE NGSI-9 Open RESTful API Specification.

TELEFONICA I+D S.A.U., 2014b. FI-WARE NGSI-10 Open RESTful API Specification.

Vermesan, O., Friess, P. (Eds.) 2013. Internet of Things: Converging Technologies for Smart Environments and Integrated Ecosystems, River Publishers Series in Communication. River, Aalborg. ISBN 978-87-92982-73-5. http://www.internet-of-things-research.eu/pdf/Converging_Technologies_for_Smart_Environments_and_Integrated_Ecosystems_IERC_Book_Open_Access_2013.pdf.

Watson, D.S., Piette, M.A., Sezgen, O., Motegi, N., 2004. Machine to machine (M2M) technology in demand responsive commercial buildings. In: 2004 ACEEE Summer Study on Energy Efficiency in Buildings, Pacific Grove, CA.

Wiederhold, G., 1992. Mediators in the architecture of future information systems. IEEE Computer 25 (3), 38–49.

Wu, G., Talwar, S., Johnsson, K., Himayat, N., Johnson, K., 2011. M2M: from mobile to embedded Internet. IEEE Commun. Mag. 49 (4), 36–43. ISSN 0163-6804. doi:10.1109/MCOM.2011.5741144.

Zhang, W., Ma, J., Ye, D., 2008. FOMatch: a fuzzy ontology-based semantic matching algorithm of publish/subscribe systems. In: Mohammadian, M. (Ed.), CIMCA/IAWTIC/ISE. IEEE Computer Society, pp. 111–117, http://dblp.uni-trier.de/db/conf/cimca/cimca2008.html#ZhangMY08.

Zorzi, M., Gluhak, A., Lange, S., Bassi, A., 2010. From today's INTRAnet of things to a future INTERnet of things: a wireless-and mobility-related view. IEEE Wirel. Commun. 17 (6), 44–51. ISSN 1536-1284. doi:10.1109/MWC.2010.5675777.

Context-aware/ sensitive interactions and applications

II

A context-aware system for efficient peer-to-peer content provision

E. Markakis[a], G. Mastorakis[a], D. Negru[b], E. Pallis[a], C.X. Mavromoustakis[c], A. Bourdena[a]

Technological Educational Institute of Crete, Crete, Greece[a]
University of Bordeaux I, Bordeaux, France[b]
University of Nicosia, Engomi, Nicosia, Cyprus[c]

1 INTRODUCTION

A home-box (HB) is a central element in the service distribution chain aimed at enhancing today's home-gateways by incorporating into the existing network functionalities user-generated media processing and distribution. A given end-user is capable of locating, adapting, and consuming services/content in an efficient way, taking into account context-related issues, such as device capability. Additionally, the HB provides the means for efficient content sharing among other end-users and efficient content exchange mechanisms, based to multicast, unicast DASH HTTP streaming or peer-to-peer (P2P) methods. Most of these features and functionalities rely on the content, the context, and the network information gathered in several layers, by a cross-layer monitoring system. In order to efficiently distribute services and content within emerging network architectures, a logical interconnection of deployed HBs can be exploited to establish an overlay network. It empowers a system with different modes of media distribution and delivery, including traditional client/server mode, multicast mode, and P2P mode. Additionally, the HB has local storage capabilities, which allow for content caching and forwarding, as well as the reception of pushed content from the service providers (SP), so that an HB virtual overlay can assist the current content distribution networks (HB-assisted CDNs). The HB takes advantage of such distribution mechanisms and content caching functionalities to overcome some of the common issues that arise, when live content is being distributed to many consumers (by employing multicast), when a new high-popularity video on demand (VoD) is ingested into the system (pushed content to the HB caches and using DASH) and in those new scenarios, in which the end-user also plays the role of producer (distributing the content via P2P).

Pervasive Computing. http://dx.doi.org/10.1016/B978-0-12-803663-1.00005-X

Since HB is a central element in a future network architecture for multimedia content provision, through which a given end-user is capable of locating and consuming services/content in an efficient way, and having them adapted according to the consumption context, the functions it executes at the service level must be specified in detail. Through the HB service layer (SL), the HB layer is established: the end-user is able (i) to search and discover already published services at the SP, (ii) to upload and consume local stored content and access the service composition tools provided by the SP, as well as compose new services, which are then published at SP, (iii) to act as a content provider (CP) from the point of view of other end-users, and (iv) to consume services/content and adapt it according to the end-user context and network conditions.

The HB architecture, and in particular its SL, must provide efficient methods to overcome some of the most common issues related to the relevant scenarios that this chapter intends to cover, such as live TV content distribution, access of high-popularity VoD assets and user-generated content distribution among other users. In this sense, the HB takes advantage of distribution mechanisms and content caching functionalities, such as multicast content distribution, DASH streaming, P2P networks, as well as local and distributed caching strategies, in order to overcome some of the common issues. For example, when live TV content is being distributed to many consumers, the HB employs multicast, so the system is scalable with little effort compared with other methods. When high levels of VoD accessing is expected, the SP may predict it in advance and decide to ingest it into the system at special caching nodes (HBs), reducing the load of CP central servers. In scenarios, in which the end-user also plays the role of producer, the SL may decide to establish the HB layer in P2P fashion and efficiently distribute the content among HBs. The HB offers other features, such as support for service management, user mobility, and security.

In this context, this chapter proposes a context-aware system to support efficient resource sharing, by exploiting P2P approaches. P2P is considered to be a scalable and cost-effective solution for content distribution and is becoming widely deployed over the current Internet infrastructure. Several commercial deployments already exist, providing VoD services and IPTV to their customers. Even companies such as Skype, which has its P2P approach for distributed VoIP calling online, are supposedly developing a P2P IPTV service with the intention of distributing video online in the same way. When compared with CDN-assisted distributed content, or other managed network-based solution, over-the-top P2P is a very attractive solution, as some studies indicate. Taking into consideration that an HB entity has built-in storage, stable presence, monitoring capability, and management interface, it makes it a good candidate for participating in P2P networks. In this framework, an HB P2P Engine module is used to assist the content distribution. Instead of retrieving content solely from the servers, the HB can download content from other HBs, which are caching and forwarding/seeding the content.

2 RELATED WORK AND RESEARCH MOTIVATION
2.1 EFFECTIVE CONTENT DISTRIBUTION MECHANISMS

Regarding the effective content distribution technologies, it is known that current system architectures, which are based on huge data centers and content delivery networks (CDN), suffer from several problems (Koletsou and Voelker, 2001; Krishnamurthy et al., 2001). SPs are always looking for new ways to deliver their contents and services, with preference for decentralized systems, and therefore, without some of the issues encountered in centralized architectures (Aggarwal et al., 2007; Karagiannis et al., 2005). This is particular evident for VoD SPs that, as shown in some studies, are looking for alternatives, in which dedicated end-users' pieces of equipment, such as set top boxes (STB), are employed to assist the service distribution and consumption (Janardhan and Schulzrinne, 2007). In some cases, these new ways to distribute and deliver content do make use of edge technologies, like HTTP streaming (Liu et al., 2011). This is the case of proprietary IPTV platforms, for example, Microsoft Mediaroom (Microsoft, 2016). In other cases, STB-assisted CDN technologies (Tran and Tavanapong, 2005; Yin et al., 2010; Chellouche et al., 2012), P2P networks (where the STBs are interconnected, in order to have a mesh network of end-users providing and consuming similar contents) or even STBs, which are interconnected through a P2P overlay network (Aggarwal et al., 2007; Birke et al., 2011) and that take advantage of some cooperation with existing CDN to achieve cost-effective and scalable distribution, are also taking into consideration alternatives for effective content distribution. No matter what type of technology is in use, however, in every managed network it is important to guarantee that the SP retains total control of the services being delivered, as it is the entity that ultimately needs to provide means and resources, and to create the conditions for this to happen (Acemoglu and Ozdaglar, 2004). In this sense, the SP should have the final decision as to the content distribution mechanism to be used, to determine, in which conditions each distribution mechanism could eventually be employed (perhaps some of them will only be available to premium subscribers) and also when and who eventually distributes/consumes content/services using them (Arnab and Hutchison, 2004). The principle stated above is in consonance with the trend of having a rising number of SPs providing services, which once used to be free of change, with the same or better quality but with greater availability to the end-user and for a small fee (Giletti, 2012).

This trend is making new requirements of the network infrastructures and the service provisioning level, and the necessity for knowing exactly what is being exchanged among end-users and how it can be controlled. Moreover, the SPs need to have confidence that nonpremium network traffic does not, and will not, influence or deteriorate existing and forecast premium services. This means that it is now important to know what kind of services/content is being routed, the way these content/services are being distributed and how a contention mechanism may be employed; all of this information must be as much transparent as possible, from the end-user's perspective. In this sense, SPs are now looking for more efficient ways to deliver their services/content without having to invest huge amounts of money into new infrastructures (Poese et al., 2010), over-provision existing or future infrastructures, or rent new infrastructures from NP. Instead, they are looking for ways to improve the performance of already deployed systems. Special care must be taken, when dealing with multiple and simultaneous end-users, which may be accessing a given content. This is particularly true in cases where the type of access is on-demand, and for that reason, multicast content delivery methods cannot be employed. Promising technologies, such as multicast traffic and P2PTV systems (Eittenberger et al., 2010), provide the means to efficiently distribute content to a large amount of end-users that are accessing it in real time, while at the same time keeping the infrastructure costs very low and efficiency high at the network resources level. Typically this is the case for live IPTV services. Although P2PTV is being considered as an emerging content distribution technology for live IPTV with lots of potential, since it is usually much cheaper than the alternatives, it is still a P2P-based system that suffers from some typical problems, such as (1) no guarantees for reliable streams and, therefore no quality of service (QoS) compared with other content delivery mechanisms; and (2) less control from SP in terms of establishing access limits for the content based on regions, behavior viewing, trends, and viewing time, compared with a traditional delivery solutions.

The proposed approach in this chapter considers that live IPTV distribution is crucial in the scenario of future Internet architectures and, for that reason, the multicast distribution mode is seen as the most reliable technology to overcome the scalability issue encountered in alternative methodologies based in unicast connections or P2P. An HB layer is provided that can be established using multicast mode. So, in order to have an effective and efficient live IPTV distribution platform, a virtual HB overlay layer is achieved, in which multicast groups are used to distribute SVC content between the participants. In terms of UGC delivery, commercial solutions have proved that P2P possesses some advantages over other centralized solutions (Parameswaran et al., 2001), even with the help of CDNs providers (higher costs), for the distribution of this kind of content, without the need for special requirements from the SP infrastructures and at reasonable budgets. Most of today's solutions that are employing P2P technologies are achieving the content delivery using over-the-top services. The approach of this chapter brings the best of P2P content delivery mechanisms, that is, being cheap and scalable, to the managed networks, instead of over-the-top delivery. Through this symbiosis, most of the P2P limitations may be overcome (Karagiannis et al., 2004) and some control restored to the SP. Via this integration, the SP is now able to control exactly who, how, when, and where the content is being accessed and distributed in his infrastructure. Since P2P has some issues regarding reliability and QoS, a distribution mode for UGC is introduced, as it is typically a nonpremium service, when comparing with VoD or live IPTV services. Regarding VoD services, it is known that these kinds of services are accessed in a one-to-one fashion, which means that individualized streams must be provided from the content servers toward each consumer (HB). There are, however, other, similar, but not exactly equal, services like near video-on-demand (NVoD), which are used by cable operators for delivering content to multiple consumers without having to deal with individual streams. This kind of solution does not make sense in case of the one proposed, as it would be easily implemented over a multicast distribution mode.

For those real VoD services individual streams, per consumer, are necessary. In a usual VoD solution, in order to partially alleviate the load from central servers, distributed caching mechanisms, edge servers, and other techniques are put in place. However, this brings new issues such as content replication policies, rights management, and content access control. Besides that, it is common that the same content is being replicated through all the VoD content servers, to which all consumers have access. For that reason, it is not easy to implement content adaptation and target advertisement in such solutions. In this context, this chapter proposes to solve most of these issues by employing MPEG-DASH as the distribution mechanism in the case of VoD (Lederer et al., 2012) and to establish the HB overlay network in such a way that any HB may act as a consumer (from the central VoD content servers) or as a content server itself to the remaining HBs. This solution is both flexible, in terms of content adaptation, as it permits adaptation at the content server and at the HB, and scalable since any HB can also become a VoD content server, by employing caching strategies.

2.2 SERVICE PUBLICATION/MANAGEMENT

Service publication is the act of logging service descriptions onto a registry, in order to facilitate service descriptions and to support interaction among services. Registries are searchable directories, where service descriptions can be published. Such descriptions must provide to service requesters all the data needed to locate, contact and bind to the corresponding service. This description contains information that is valued concerning the identity of the organization and, most of the times, the interface associated to the service itself, including the operations signatures that may be invoked on the service. Indeed, some other data that can be relevant as well, include behavior, QoS attributes, information about the trustworthiness of the services, and test cases applied to the service. This section will try to focus on widely recognized initiatives for service publication—ie, the "Universal Description, Discovery and Integration" (UDDI) and the "Web Services Discovery Architecture" (WSDA). UDDI (n.d.) allows a provider to register information about itself, as well as the services it provides. This information can include service name, service information, and description. When service information is published in a UDDI registry, the publisher should tell potential customers how they might get in touch with a service (binding). The WSDA (Hoschek, 2002) provides a web services discovery layer on top of a grid-based architecture. The discovery layer defines proper interfaces for publishing and querying (Presenter, Consumer, MinQuery, and XQuery), along with a tuple-based universal data model, which allows for the storage of arbitrary content. Despite all the existing technologies and products available for service deployment, there are still a number of short comings which make deploying and managing services expensive and littered with manual steps. The primary challenges and areas for improvement in deployment and configuration are the creation of an automatic configuration based on dynamic service switching and feedback from monitoring. The discovery of the service is a complex issue that not only takes into account the traditional service discovery techniques but also proposes a better and clearer service selection function. Specifically, in traditional architectures, the service discovery is an issue that only takes in consideration the SP (Deora et al., 2004), which does not take into account, network, or user profile characteristics (Ververidis and Polyzos, 2008). In this context, a key innovation in the proposed system is that the separation between service discovery (selected by the EU) and end-point discovery (selected by the HB on the basis of SP selection) allows for a better selection of the delivery end-point, since the system takes decisions based on passive network measurements (ie, measurements obtained without invasive network probing), end-point load (HB distance), and user profile characteristics. Summarily, this two-level filtering approach that the proposed system is suggesting provides a better discovery and selection of filtered content to the end-user.

2.3 PEER-TO-PEER NETWORK INSTANTIATION INSIDE THE HOME BOX

The general overview of the different modules and groups of interfaces that exist at the HB SL are shown in Fig. 1. The main objective of the HB SL is to facilitate the interaction between SP and EU, such as service discovery, request, publishing, management, and delivery. On one side, HB SL retrieves service information and data from SP. On the other side, it receives the EU requests and answers with relevant data.

P2P is considered to be a scalable and cost-effective solution for content distribution and is becoming widely deployed over the current Internet. Some commercial deployments already exist, providing most of them VoD services and IPTV to their customers. Even companies such as Skype, which exploit a P2P approach for distributed VoIP calling online, are supposedly developing a P2P IPTV service with the intention of distributing video online in the same way. The major reason of this is cost-effectiveness. When compared with CDN-assisted distributed content, or other managed network-based solution, over-the-top P2P is a very attractive solution, as some studies indicate (Chen et al., 2007). Taking into consideration that the HB entity has built-in storage, stable presence, monitoring capability, and management interface, it makes the HB a good candidate for participating in P2P networks. The HB P2P Engine module is used by the SP to assist the content distribution. Instead of retrieving content from the SP/CP servers solely, the HB can download content from other HBs, which are caching and forwarding/seeding the content. This approach alleviates the load at the SP/CP servers and simultaneously the costs involved in maintain and deploy the infrastructure to achieve this goal. The P2P Engine, being part of the Connectivity Engine module, provides the necessary functionalities in order to support all aspects of the HB connectivity over the P2P network. Putting it simply, the P2P Engine is the module that is responsible for content retrieval and

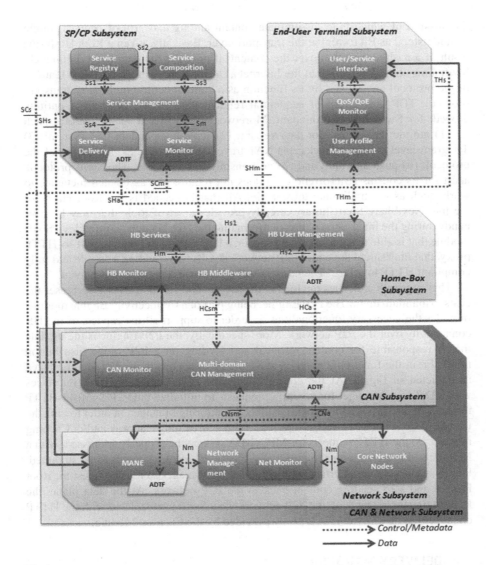

FIG. 1

HB services and its interfaces.

seeding on P2P distribution mode. The approach of this chapter is based on the integration of a new and very promising P2P protocol, called Swift, that has been specified as an Internet-Draft P2P Streaming Peer Protocol. The Swift protocol is designed to be capable of being integrated into browsers or operating systems and serve almost all the current Internet traffic. Swift is a multiparty transport protocol, the mission of which is to disseminate content among a swarm of peers. It might be understood as BitTorrent at the transport layer. Basically, given a Root Hash (the result of a hashing function over the content) it provides the data for it. Ultimately Swift aims at the abstraction of the Internet as a single big data cloud. Most features of the protocol are defined by its function as a content-centric multiparty transport protocol. TCP abstraction of sequential reliable data stream delivery is entirely droped: for Swift this is redundant. Moreover, it provides a set of features such as: (1) atomic datagrams, not data stream; (2) scale-independent unit system; (3) datagram-level integrity checks; (4) NAT traversal by design; (5) subsetting of the protocol; (6) push and pull; and (7) no transmission metadata. The Swift protocol, apart for its cousins (BitTorrent, etc.) does not require any associated metadata to work, such as the traditional torrent file. All that is needed is the Root Hash for the file. NextShare Swift library already provides a set of tools that may be very handy during the integration of this platform into the HB. Namely, it provides a Swift module that is able to act as a content seeder, a P2P tracker or both; a Swift-to-HTTP proxy, that may shield the entire P2P network details by providing a simple and fully compliant HTTP interface. The latest is still under experimental development.

This approach alleviates the load at the servers and simultaneously decreases the costs to maintain them. The P2P Engine, being part of a Connectivity Engine module, provides the necessary functionalities, in order to support all the aspects of the HB connectivity over the P2P network. More specifically, the P2P Engine is the module that is responsible for content retrieval and seeding on a P2P mode distribution mode. From the functional point of view, the modules inside the HB are organized as depicted in Fig. 2. At the control plane, the P2P Engine provides interfaces with a Delivery Manager for accepting requests to initialize the P2P Swift-to-HTTP modules. It also provides interfaces with the Monitoring Manager, in order to rank the list of available peers, as well as interfaces with a Streaming Gateway and/or Caching module. So the HTTP requests for MPEG-DASH may be properly addressed, with a Resource Manager in order to physically access the local resources to be streamed. Finally, it provides an interface with a Publishing Manager so it can request for Root Hashes and start seeding content back to the P2P network. At the data plane, the P2P Engine interfaces with the P2P network via a Swift protocol and with the HTTP client/server, or with the HTTP proxy provided by the Caching Module.

2.4 DELIVERY MANAGER

The HB plays the role of a proxy-receiver, on behalf of the EUT. This means the EUT cannot reach the SP subsystem or other HB directly, but through the HB only. The media flows established between the EUT and their respective HB are always delivered in unicast. However, the media flows at the core are transmitted over multicast, unicast, or P2P modes, depending on the distribution mode imposed by the SP for this particular service. Thus, the session establishment and media flow control protocols would be always the same in the link between the EUT and the HB (MPEG-DASH and/or SIP), independently of the distribution mode defined

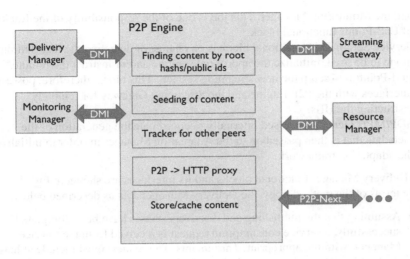

FIG. 2

Internal block of P2P Engine.

by the SP, but they may differ in the core network (according to the distribution mode and service type). The Delivery Manager is the HB module that is responsible for media service delivery coordination between the HB and end-users and for the establishment of HBs' connections with other HB(s) or the SP content servers, so the content may be efficiently distributed. Besides, it also manages the service delivery process when the related media content is locally stored. In cases of remote media content, the Delivery Manager instructs the Streaming Gateway component to initialize the streaming process with remote media content. There can be several sources for the requested media content, some of them are SP/CP Content Servers controlled by the SP, while others are remote HBs. The Delivery Manager module is the key module that executes the service consumption requests, already admitted by the Service Manager, and for that it provides the following functional blocks:

- Service request handling: This module provides an interface with the Service Manager, which is used to request a given service for consumption. A subset of the UP information is required at this point. The UP is passed on to the SP during further requests so it can filter the list of End-Points according to the End-User preferences, rights.
- Find service End-Points: This functionality is needed in order to retrieve from the Service Registry (SR), at the SP, valid End-Points that are currently providing the service, the distribution mode of that particular service and also service metadata (MPD).
- Ranking of End-Points: The list of possible End-Points received from the SP is then ranked by their HB distances, with the help of the Arrangement Manager

and the Monitoring Manager. This job is one of the responsibility of the Ranking of End-Points functional block.
- Service Setup: This functional block is on change of detecting the distribution mode to be used, initialize the appropriate engine and/or instruct the remote End-Point(s) to setup the new streaming session. This block, therefore, possesses interfaces with the P2P Engine and the Streaming Gateway for remotely instructing the HBs.
- SDP/MPD Generation: Used internally to coordinate the generation of the metadata that is then passed on to the Adaptation Manager in order to initialize the adaptation framework.

The Delivery Manager functional blocks and its interfaces are shown in Fig. 3.
In terms of the methodology, the Delivery Manager acts as described below:

(1) Assuming that the publishing and discovery phases have been completed successfully, a service consumption request is received from the Service Manager, with the appropriated arguments. The request must include at least the Service ID, used to uniquely identify the service that the end-user is interested in, a subset of the UP and some context information.

(2) The Delivery Manager tries to obtain valid End-Points and other metadata for the requested service from the SP. For that it invokes a request End-Points method via Streaming Gateway. During this call, the Delivery Manager passes on the Service ID and the subset of the UP.

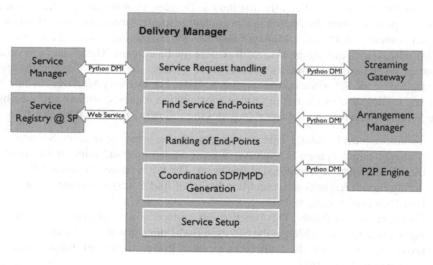

FIG. 3

The functional blocks of the Delivery Manager.

(3) The Streaming Gateway contacts the Security Manager, in order to obtain the necessary credentials to access the SP subsystem and makes the request to the SP.

(4) At the SP side, a query to the SR is performed and the result is then filtered out taking into account the subset of UP and internal police rules. The filtered list of possible End-Points is finally returned to the Delivery Manager via Streaming Gateway. Besides the End-Points information, the SP returns details of the distribution mode in which this service will be delivered and some metadata (that in the case of P2P includes the MPD).

(5) The Delivery Manager determines the distribution mode in which the service must be delivered.

(6) The Delivery Manager ranks the list of received End-Points, according to its HB distance. To achieve this, the Delivery Manager requests a ranked list from the Arrangement Manager that is then using the Monitoring Manager information to provide the ranked list.

(7) The Delivery Manager initializes the appropriate engine that in the case of P2P is the P2P Engine. In the case of a multicast delivery, the joining (and leaving previous joined) multicast groups is coordinated here. For the unicast distribution mode (MPEG-DASH), the remote End-Point (the topmost preferably) is contacted so it can initialize the streaming process.

(8) During this phase, and in the case of P2P, the P2P Engine internally initializes the appropriate Swift modules and starts the handshake with the tracker/seeder(s).

(9) The service metadata is generated (MPD is grabbed from the SP, the SDP from the remote End-Point) both for the connection between the EUT and HB, and between the HB and the remote End-Point.

(10) The Adaptation framework is initialized with the appropriated information (MPD or SDP).

(11) The CATI information along with the remote and local service metadata (MPD or SDP) is returned to the Service Manager and then to the Session Manager and to the EUT.

(12) The EUT makes requests for MPEG-DASH segments and forwards them to the HB, which will intercept them (via Streaming Gateway and Caching modules).

(13) In case of P2P those requests are chained with the P2P Engine internal module Swift-to-HTTP proxy, that will make a protocol translation to Swift messages.

This process is shown in Fig. 4.

2.5 PUBLISHING MANAGER

Service publication is the act of registering service descriptions into a registry in order to facilitate service descriptions and to support interaction among services. Taking this into account, the Publishing Manager is the HB SL module that is

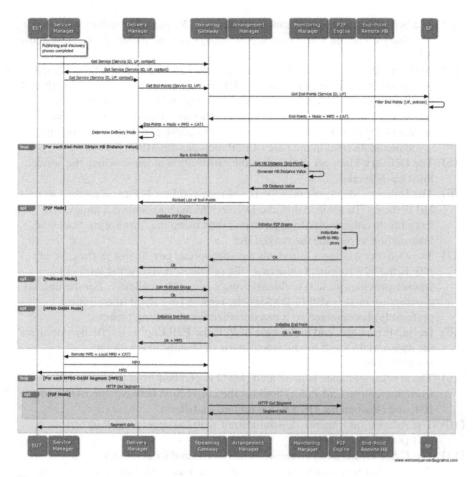

FIG. 4

High-level sequence diagram with the Delivery Manager interactions.

responsible for all functions related to content/service publication in every part of the procedure. The main responsibility of the Publishing Manager module is to create all the functionality needed for a service stemming from the end-user to be published inside the SR at the SP. The Publishing Manager component is the logical signaling and communication/call handling entity that, after receiving a publishing request, can reformulate it and send it out as a new request to the SR at the SP. Responses to the requests can also be reformulated and sent back in the opposite direction. Thus, the Publishing Manager creates the mixed push/pull scenario indicated by the design decision. More specifically, the pull function stemming from the end-user is received by the HB Publishing Manager. The Publishing Manager will push the

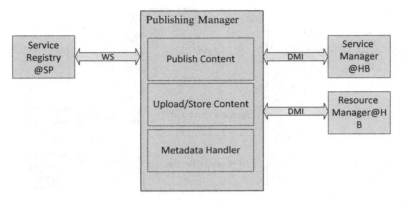

FIG. 5

The main internal blocks of the Publishing Manager.

service to the end-user after he has pulled the request to the SR at the SP. Another functionality stemming from the requirements mentioned above is that the Publishing Manager will create a metadata profile of the service that the end-user is creating. The Publishing Manager module is the module that executes the service publication requests, already admitted by the end-user, and for that it provides the following functional blocks:

- Publish Functional block: It allows a given User (through his own HB) to Publish content to the SR at the SP and at the HB Storage.
- Upload Functional block: It allows a terminal device to upload its content to the HB.
- Metadata Functional block: It allows a given User (through his own HB) to register full content description.

The Publishing Manager functional blocks and its interfaces are shown in Fig. 5.

2.6 DISCOVERY MANAGER

The Discovery of the service inside the proposed architecture is a complex issue that takes into account not only the traditional service discovery techniques but also a way to provide a better and clearer service selection function. The Discovery Manager component is the logical signaling and communication/call handling entity that, after receiving a Search Content/Service Request, will communicate with the SR in order to search for services based on EU query parameters, EU context and EU preferences. The results stems from the SR after a second filtering/taxonomy has been performed using the User profile characteristics received from the Arrangement Manager. The Discovery Manager is the module that executes the Search Service/Content Requests,

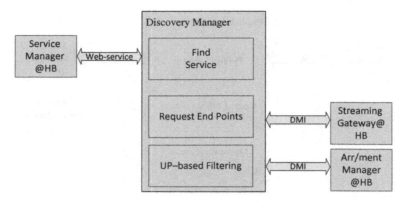

FIG. 6

The main internal blocks of the Discovery Manager.

stemming from the End-User, and for that it provides the following functional blocks (Fig. 6):

- Find Services Functional block: This is used when the Service Manager of the HB communicates with the Discovery Manager in order to ask for Searching Results from the SR at the SP.
- UP-Based Filtering Functional block: This is used in order to perform a second filtering/taxonomy on the Service List requested from the SR through the Streaming Gateway using the User profile characteristics received from the Arrangement Manager.
- Request End-Point Functional block: It is used in order to contact the Service Manager at the SP for finding the final End-Points for the particular requested service. This functional block will return also all possible URLs for the requested search.

2.7 STREAMING GATEWAY

The Streaming Gateway component within the SL of a given HB acts as the message (and even data) translation point between the EUTs located at the Home LAN side and the SP/CP (including remote HBs) entities located at the WAN side of this HB. The Streaming Gateway component is the logical signaling and communication/call handling entity that, after receiving a HTTP-, SIP-, or RTSP-based request, can reformulate it and send it out as a new request. Responses to the requests can also be reformulated and sent back in the opposite direction. Thus, the Streaming Gateway may create the illusion of one direct end-to-end communication (between a EUT and a remote SP/CP entity) by coupling two elementary communications (one between the EUT and its HB, and another between the HB and the remote SP/CP entity). It then forwards messages transparently, but always terminates elementary communications between involved communication agents (SIP UAs, HTTP/WS and RTSP, Clients, and Servers). The main advantage of the Streaming Gateway is its capacity to manage and monitor the entire communication and related parameters. It has not only full control over all parameters and headers of HTTP, RTSP, and SIP messages, but also it can process the body of these messages. Thus, the Streaming Gateway is in charge of:

- Monitoring of the state and parameters of all HTTP, RTSP, and SIP messages between the LAN and WAN sides. For instance, the Streaming Gateway can collect from the MPD or SDP payload the codecs, URL, or ports information for media traffic adaptation, message translation purposes. Note that the message translation includes new local MPD or SDP generation from the one received from the remote End-Point.
- Interacting with the Delivery Manager and the Adaptation Manager, in order to ensure the context-awareness, for example, to ensure the QoS/QoE-enabled communication viability with regard to the User Profile data and the HB status (EUT capabilities, User preferences, and HB resources requirements). This context-awareness support is one of the key progressions beyond the other gateway entities, such as the SIP-based Back-to-Back user Agent (B2BUA) of the IMS Interworking block defined in the HGI IMS-enabled Home-Gateway specification (Home Gateway Initiative, 2009).
- Creating or reformulating requests/responses and sending them out via (a) HTTP/WS, SIP, and RTSP communication agents, or (b) HB Caching/P2P Engine components, as new requests/responses (URLs, IP addresses, or port numbers changing in order to provide required interoperability between the EUTs and the SP/CP entities). The Streaming Gateway then can implement a routing behavior of a HTTP/WS, RTSP, or SIP Proxy.
- Retrieving the End-Point location information from the SP in order to support their ranking and selection before the beginning of an effective service delivery.
- Retrieving the security information (eg, HB security token) from the Security Manager in order to allow the message authentication.

   To achieve the above-mentioned functions, as shown in Fig. 7, the Streaming Gateway will include the following functional blocks:

- The HTTP Gateway, including the HTTP/WS/DASH Proxy and the HTTP to P2P Proxy. The HTTP/WS/DASH Proxy is responsible for translating not only common HTTP and WS requests/responses, but also the MPEG DASH HTTP streaming messages. The HTTP to P2P Proxy is responsible for message translations between LAN side HTTP messages and the WAN side P2P world.
- The SIP Gateway, including the SIP/RTSP to SIP/IMS/RTSP Proxy and the SIP to Multicast Proxy. The SIP/RTSP to SIP/IMS/RTSP Proxy is responsible for translating both SIP/RTSP to SIP/RTSP (ALICANTE) and SIP/RTSP to SIP/IMS/RTSP (IMS context) messages. Note that SIP is used for the main signaling (INVITE, BYE, etc.), while RTSP is used for media session tricking

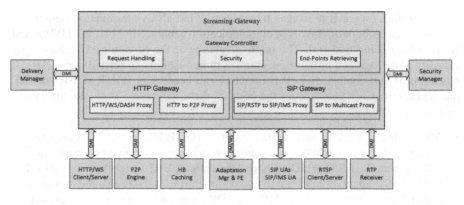

FIG. 7

The main internal blocks of the Streaming Gateway.

purposes. The SIP to Multicast Proxy is responsible for LAN side SIP message translation to WAN side IGMP join/leave multicast message through the HB RTP Receiver connectivity component.
- The Gateway Controller, including modules for requests and security handling, and for End-Points location information retrieving from the SP on request of the Delivery Manager. This block supports the two above-mentioned modules (eg, for security aspects).

2.8 HTTP GATEWAY

The SIP Gateway block of the HB Streaming Gateway includes the HTTP to P2P and the HTTP/WS/DASH Proxies. In the HTTP-based MPEG-DASH service delivery scenario the HTTP/WS/DASH Proxy interfaces via a HTTP Client toward the remote DASH End-Points (WAN side) and via a HTTP Server toward the EUTs (LAN side). The HTTP/WS/DASH Proxy then enables the context-aware interworking between both sides by performing not only the signaling translation (messages translation, local MPD generation) but also the payload data (DASH chunks) adaptation. To achieve this, it is supported by the Gateway Controller which retrieves and keeps track of related user context and security information (eg, UP data and HB security token). In the case of regular (not streaming based) HTTP/WS communications, the HTTP/WS/DASH Proxy translates mainly the signaling messages. Note that if the caching mode is enabled in HB, the WAN side communication will pass through the HB Caching component and then the HTTP/WS/DASH Proxy will then interface with the caching component, as shown in Fig. 8.

In the P2P service delivery scenario, the HTTP to P2P Proxy interfaces via the P2P Engine toward the remote peers (WAN side) and uses the HTTP/WS/DASH Proxy toward the EUTs (LAN side). The HTTP to P2P Proxy then permits a HTTP-based DASH client to consume/request content from the P2P network. It

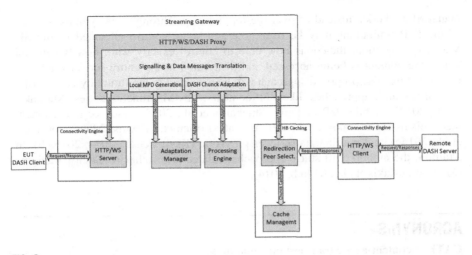

FIG. 8

HTTP/ WS/ DASH Proxy internal module in Streaming Gateway.

performs a protocol adaptation between the P2P and the HTTP worlds. In the HB architecture, the Swift-to-HTTP proxy module plays the role of the HTTP to P2P Proxy. The Swift-to-HTTP proxy is an experimental proxy that may be used to abstract and shield the entire P2P network from the rest of the system, which will recognize the Swift library as any regular HTTP server. Conceptually, the Swift-to-HTTP proxy is then a subcomponent of the Streaming Gateway. However, for implementation purposes only, since it is an autonomous module developed in the context of P2P, in the next project, it will be integrated with the P2P Engine for simplicity.

2.9 CONCLUSION

This chapter considers that live IPTV distribution is crucial in the scenario of Future Internet architectures and, for that reason, the multicast distribution mode is seen as the most reliable technology to overcome the scalability issues encountered in alternative methodologies based in unicast connections or P2P. An HB layer is provided that can be established using multicast mode. So, in order to have an effective and efficient live IPTV distribution platform, a virtual HB overlay layer is achieved, in which multicast groups are used to distribute SVC content between the participants. In terms of UGC delivery, commercial solutions have proved that for the distribution of this kind of content P2P, without special requirements from the SP infrastructures and at reasonable budgets, possesses some advantages over the other centralized solutions, even with the help of CDNs providers (higher costs). Most of today's solutions that are employing P2P technologies are achieving the content delivery using over-the-top services. The approach of this chapter brings the best of P2P content delivery mechanism (ie, being cheap and scalable), to the managed networks, instead of over-the-top delivery. Through this symbiosis, most of the P2P limitations may be overcome and some control allocated to the SP. Via this integration, the SP is now able to control exactly who, how, when and where the content is being accessed and distributed in the entire services delivery infrastructure. The proposed approach will be extended in the future by considering several research approaches, like P2P context with IMS functionalities (Markakis et al., 2014), mobile P2P systems (Shiakallis et al., 2015), resource management mechanisms (Mastorakis et al., 2014), context-oriented systems (Mavromoustakis et al., 2014c), and multimedia services provision (Kryftis et al., 2014, 2015a,b). In addition, the authors will study approaches related with other research paradigms (Mavromoustakis et al., 2014a,b, 2014).

ACRONYMS

CATI	content-aware transport information
CDN	content distribution network
CP	content provider
DASH	dynamic adaptive streaming over HTTP
EU	end-user
EUT	end-user terminal
HB	home-box
HTTP	hypertext transfer protocol
IP	Internet protocol
IPTV	Internet protocol television
JSON	JavaScript object notation
MPEG	moving picture experts group
NP	network provider
P2P	peer-to-peer
QoE	quality of experience
QoS	quality of service
RTP	real-time transport protocol
RTSP	real-time streaming protocol
SDP	session description protocol
SIP	session initiation protocol
SP	service provider
SR	service registry
STB	set-top box
SVC	scalable video coding
TCP	transmission control protocol
UGC	user-generated content
UP	user profile
URL	uniform resource locator
VoD	video on demand
WS	web service

GLOSSARY

CAN provider (CANP) is a business entity, actually being an enhanced NP (the additional CAN functions are performed by network nodes and therefore they are executed by the Network Provider). It offers content-aware network services to the upper layer entities.

Content aware network (CAN) is an emerging concept but is currently not sufficiently developed neither in terms of architectural complete specifications nor in real deployment.

Content consumer (CC) or end-user (U) is an entity (human plus a terminal or a process), which establishes a contract with a service provider for service/content delivery. These users are the final target recipients of services.

Content provider (CP) gathers/creates, maintains, and distributes digital information. The CP owns/operates network hosts that are the source of downloadable content but it might not own any networking infrastructure to deliver the content.

Context awareness is a property of mobile devices that is defined complementarily to location awareness. Whereas location may determine how certain processes in a device operate, context may be applied more flexibly with mobile users, especially with users of smart phones.

Home-box (HB) is a business entity, which can be partially managed by the SP, the NP, and the end-user. The HBs can cooperate with SPs in order to distribute multimedia services (eg, IPTV) in different modes (eg, P2P).

Network provider (NP) traditionally offers connectivity providing reachability between network domains/hosts. NPs own and administer IP connectivity infrastructures. They interact with each other for the purpose of expanding the geographical span of the offered connectivity services.

Peer-to-peer (P2P) is a distributed application architecture that partitions tasks or work loads between peers. Peers are equally privileged, equipotent participants in the application. They are said to form a P2P network of nodes.

Service environment (SE) is in charge of assuring the composition of services and the delivery of content to End-Users throughout the network.

Service provider (SP) delivers services and aggregates content from multiple CPs for offering/delivering it to CCs. SPs may not necessarily own a transport infrastructure, but rely on the connectivity services offered by network providers (NPs).

SLA/SLS are important concepts helping to control the business actors and/or layers commitments in satisfying requests of other entities. SLA/SLS definitions and usage especially in a dynamic environment by using negotiation protocols is still open issue. SLA/SLS have been insufficiently studied and used in a P2P context.

User environment (UE) is in direct relation with the End-User knowing his characteristics and interacting with the Service Environment for an efficient service provision.

User/service interface is a graphical user interface of the services accessible to the End-User.

User profile is a collection of data that characterizes both the user and his operational context, thus both static and dynamic information.

Virtual content-aware network (VCAN) support a layer, offering enhanced support for packet payload inspection, processing and caching in network equipment. It improves data delivery via classifying and controlling messages in terms of content, application, and individual subscribers, assure QoS and improve network security via content-based monitoring and filtering.

ACKNOWLEDGMENTS

The work presented in this chapter is supported by the national funding for the project "Media Ecosystem Deployment Through Ubiquitous Content-Aware Network Environments, FP7-ICT-2009-4-248652" of the General Secretariat for Research and Technology, Greece.

REFERENCES

Acemoglu, D., Ozdaglar, A., 2004. Flow control, routing, and performance from service provider viewpoint. LIDS Report.

Aggarwal, V., Feldmann, A., Scheideler, C., 2007. Can ISPS and P2P users cooperate for improved performance? ACM SIGCOMM Comput. Commun. Rev. 37 (3), 29–40.

Arnab, A., Hutchison, A., 2004. Digital rights management—an overview of current challenges and solutions. In: Proceedings of Information Security South Africa (ISSA) Conference. Citeseer.

Birke, R., Leonardi, E., Mellia, M., Bakay, A., Szemethy, T., Kiraly, C., Cigno, R.L., Mathieu, F., Muscariello, L., Niccolini, S., Seedorf, J., 2011. Architecture of a network-aware P2P-TV application: the NAPA-WINE approach. Communications Magazine, IEEE, 49 (6), 154–163.

Chellouche, S.A., Négru, D., Chen, Y., Sidibe, M., 2012. Home-box-assisted content delivery network for Internet video-on-demand services. In: 2012 IEEE Symposium on Computers and Communications (ISCC). IEEE.

Chen, Y.F., Huang, Y., Jana, R., Jiang, H., Rabinovich, M., Wei, B., Xiao, Z., 2007. When is P2P technology beneficial for IPTV services. In: Proceedings of the 17th International Workshop on Network and Operating System Support for Digital Audio and Video.

Deora, V., Shao, J., Shercliff, G., Stockreisser, P.J., Gray, W.A., Fiddian, N.J., 2004. Incorporating QoS Specifications in Service Discovery. Springer, Berlin, Heidelberg.

Eittenberger, P., Krieger, U., Markovich, N., 2010. Measurement and analysis of live-streamed P2P TV traffic. In: Czachórski, T. (Ed.), Performance Modelling and Evaluation of Heterogeneous Networks, Proc. HET-NETs 2010, Zakopane, Poland, January.

Giletti, T., 2012. Why pay if it's free? In: Streaming, Downloading and Digital.

Home Gateway Initiative, 2009. "IMS Enabled HG", HGI-GD006-R2. http://www.homegatewayinitiative.org/documents/release_2.asp.

Hoschek, W., 2002. The web service discovery architecture. In: Supercomputing, ACM/IEEE 2002 Conference, IEEE, pp. 38–38.

Janardhan, V., Schulzrinne, H., 2007. Peer assisted VoD for set-top box based IP network. In: Proceedings of the 2007 Workshop on Peer-to-Peer Streaming and IP-TV. ACM.

Karagiannis, T., Broido, A., Brownlee, N., Claffy, K.C., Faloutsos, M., 2004. Is P2P dying or just hiding? [P2P traffic measurement]. In: IEEE Global Telecommunications Conference, 2004. GLOBECOM'04, vol. 3. IEEE.

Karagiannis, T., Rodriguez, P., Papagiannaki, K., 2005. Should Internet service providers fear peer-assisted content distribution? In: Proceedings of the 5th ACM SIGCOMM Conference on Internet Measurement. USENIX Association.

Koletsou, M., Voelker, G., 2001. The Medusa Proxy: a tool for exploring userperceived web performance. In: Web Caching and Content Delivery, p. 281.

Krishnamurthy, B., Wills, C., Zhang, Y., 2001. On the use and performance of content distribution networks. In: Proceedings of the 1st ACM SIGCOMM Workshop on Internet Measurement. ACM, pp. 169–182.

Kryftis, Y., Mavromoustakis, C.X., Batalla, J.M., Mastorakis, G., Pallis, E., Skourletopoulos, G., 2014. Resource usage prediction for optimal and balanced provision of multimedia services. In: 2014 IEEE 19th International Workshop on Computer Aided Modeling and Design of Communication Links and Networks (CAMAD). IEEE, pp. 255–259.

Kryftis, Y., Batalla, G., Pallis, E., 2015a. A resource prediction engine for efficient multimedia services provision. In: Resource Management of Mobile Cloud Computing Networks and Environments, p. 361.

Kryftis, Y., Mavromoustakis, C., Mastorakis, G., Pallis, E., Batalla, J., Rodrigues, J., Dobre, C., Kormentzas, G., 2015b. Resource usage prediction algorithms for optimal selection of multimedia content delivery methods. In: Proc. of IEEE International Conference on Communications.

Lederer, S., Müller, C., Timmerer, C., 2012. Towards peer-assisted dynamic adaptive streaming over HTTP. In: 2012 19th International Packet Video Workshop (PV), IEEE, pp. 161–166.

Liu, C., Bouazizi, I., Gabbouj, M., 2011. Rate adaptation for adaptive http streaming. In: Proceedings of the Second Annual ACM Conference on Multimedia Systems. ACM.

Markakis, E., Skianis, C., Pallis, E., Mastorakis, G., Mavromoustakis, C.X., Antonas, A., 2014. Peer-to-peer constellations in an IMS-enabled network architecture based on interactive broadcasting. In: Resource Management in Mobile Computing Environments. Springer International Publishing.

Mastorakis, G., Pallis, E., Mavromoustakis, C.X., Bourdena, A., 2014. Efficient resource management utilizing content-aware multipath routing. In: Resource Management in Mobile Computing Environments. Springer International Publishing, pp. 389–395.

Mavromoustakis, C.X., Mastorakis, G., Bourdena, A., Pallis, E., 2014. Efficient Multimedia Services Provision over Cognitive Radio Networks using a Traffic-oriented Routing Scheme. Multimedia over Cognitive Radio Networks, pp. 119–148.

Mavromoustakis, C., Mastorakis, G., Bourdena, A., Pallis, E., 2014a. Energy efficient resource sharing using a traffic-oriented routing scheme for cognitive radio networks. IET Netw. 3 (1), 54–63.

Mavromoustakis, C., Pallis, E., Mastorakis, G., 2014b. Resource Management in Mobile Computing Environments, vol. 3. Springer, Berlin.

Mavromoustakis, C.X., Kormentzas, G., Mastorakis, G., Bourdena, A., Pallis, E., Rodrigues, J., 2014c. Context-oriented opportunistic cloud offload processing for energy conservation in wireless devices. In: Globecom Workshops (GC Wkshps). IEEE, pp. 24–30.

Microsoft, 2016. Microsoft Mediaroom IPTV solution. http://www.microsoft.com/mediaroom/.

Parameswaran, M., Susarla, A., Whinston, A., 2001. P2P networking: an information-sharing alternative. Computer 7, 31–38.

Poese, I., Frank, B., Ager, B., Smaragdakis, G., Feldmann, A., 2010. Improving content delivery using provider-aided distance information. In: Proceedings of the 10th ACM SIGCOMM Conference on Internet Measurement. ACM, pp. 22–34.

Shiakallis, O., Mavromoustakis, C., Mastorakis, G., Bourdena, A., Pallis, E., 2015. Traffic-based S-MAC: a novel scheduling mechanism for optimized throughput in mobile peer-to-peer systems. Int. J. Wirel. Netw. Broadband Technol. 4 (1), 62–80.

Tran, M., Tavanapong, W., 2005. Peers-assisted dynamic content distribution networks. In: 30th Anniversary. The IEEE Conference on Local Computer Networks. IEEE, pp. 123–131.

Universal Description, Discovery, and Integration (UDDI), n.d. http://uddi.XML.org/uddi-org.

Ververidis, C., Polyzos, G., 2008. Service discovery for mobile ad hoc networks: a survey of issues and techniques. IEEE Commun. Surv. Tutorials 10 (3), 30–45.

Yin, H., Liu, X., Zhan, T., Sekar, V., Qiu, F., Lin, C., Li, B., 2010. Livesky: enhancing CDN with P2P. ACM Trans. Multim. Comput. Commun. Appl. 6 (3), 16.

Transparent distributed data management in large scale distributed systems

6

S.L. Hernane[a], J. Gustedt[a,b]

ICube, University of Strasbourg, Illkirch Cedex, France[a]
INRIA, Le Chesnay Cedex, France[b]

1 INTRODUCTION AND OVERVIEW

Mobile computing, fault tolerance, high availability, and remote information access are some examples of research fields that have emerged and led to ubiquitous and pervasive computing. In pervasive computing, the connectivity of devices is always ensured and provided by the underlying technologies including Internet, middlewares, operating systems, and interfaces (Satyanarayanan, 2001). Devices should be completely hidden from users. Mostly, they are embedded in the upper software environment.

We are witnessing an increasing need to request large scale distributed resources (CPU, storage, data, etc.) while providing responses in a reasonable time-frame. These additional needs increase the complexity of the design and confront us with new challenges. The emphasis of this research is on *data resources*; we aim to provide ubiquitous access to such resources for resource-intensive applications.

Consistency, *availability*, and *fault tolerance* issues are often raised in distributed settings. It is difficult to ensure for shared resources in dynamic large-scale environments, especially when resources are not hosted at fixed locations. Trade-offs must be made to ensure at least two properties in highly scalable systems.

The famous CAP principle of Fox and Brewer (1999) states that any shared-data system can have at most two of three desirable properties:

Consistency (C) At any time, every node sees the same information
High availability (A) All requests receive a response
Tolerance to network partitions (P) No two subsets of nodes may evolve separately.

Based on the work of Brewer (2000) at PODC, Gilbert and Lynch (2002) proved this principle and presented the CAP theorem.

Usually, data consistency in distributed systems provide guarantees between the set of items comprising the system. Here, items can be a set of replicated data on one

Pervasive Computing. http://dx.doi.org/10.1016/B978-0-12-803663-1.00006-1

site and the users on the other. Consistency constraints include, for example, ordering requirements or global visibility of data existing as multiple copies. Xhafa et al. (2015) proposed a suitable replication system for XML files with fast consistency for *peers* joining last. For databases, usually the ACID properties (Atomicity, Consistency, Isolation, Durability) are considered. They prioritize consistency and partition-tolerance at the cost of potentially lower availability.

Several consistency models for parallel and distributed machines have been discussed in the literature. We mention a few of them: *strict* consistency assumes a shared clock between the processes and ensures that a value that is read is always the value that was written by the most recent write operation. For the *sequential* consistency model, all processes see the same order of all access operations, while for *Fifo* (also known as *PRAM*) consistency, writes are seen by all other processes in the same order in which they were issued.

The *release* consistency model relaxes sequencing requirements and only imposes synchronizations between processes by attributing *acquire* and *release* properties to read and write operations that are issued for the same specific data. Operations on different data then may follow different causal relations and other sequencing. As a consequence, such a system does not as a whole need to implement a common event ordering for all read and write events; it only has to guarantee that the causal relationship between these events is respected transitively for each node and data.

All these models provide *implicit* consistency, that is they do not require additional operations other than reads or writes. They are more suited for small data on shared memory systems. Nowadays some variants of these are implemented as *atomic instructions* for word-sized data on all commonly used CPUs and corresponding operations and consistency models have been added to major programming languages such as C and C++. In contrast, these models do not upscale well for large data or for large distributed environments.

In the present chapter we will explore a different type of consistency, namely *explicit consistency*, where read and write operations to shared data must be *requested* beforehand, can only be effected if such a request has been *acquired* and must be *released* at the end to the other hosts. Usual lock-based strategies such as mutexes or condition variables are well-known simple examples for such a consistency model, which in fact combine request and acquire into a single operation, a *lock*.

The resulting consistency model that we will discuss is in fact an *explicit acquire-release* consistency model with *high availability*, but here availability is only ensured if the data had been requested beforehand. We are targeting applications with needs of intensive computing on remote data. We offer two access modes: exclusive, for read-write, or shared, for reading only.

The system as a whole provides no partition tolerance. However, it enables voluntary arrivals and departures of *peers*. For the convenience of users such changes should be *transparent* and *easy-to-use*. Data's access between concurrent *peers* is fair, regulated by a first-come first-serve policy.

We are looking for a *service* and for a whole architecture which ensures simplicity of data access for users at application level, while the *peers* who host the resources are dynamically assigned. We do that by designing an API and an underlying programming model that allows applications to manage computations while transferring large amounts of data simultaneously. The target public are users that should just be familiar with the C programming language and with some commonly used tools for parallel or distributed computing. Their only role should be to handle computational tasks by inserting the set of proposed functions for claiming resources in existing applications.

1.1 MAIN OBJECTIVES

More specifically, our objectives are on two levels: system design and user environment, that is the application level. Our challenge is to reach the transparency and the simplicity needed for users at application level, while hiding all complex features of the underlying structure. Regarding the system design level, the aims are summarized as follows:

1. Provide a set of *peers* hosting data resources and an API that can be used in applications written in C or in C++ by inserting function calls.
2. Ensure scalability of the system such that the population of *peers* may vary.
3. Ensure *data consistency* and *data availability* despite the volatility of *peers*.
4. Allow the overlapping of tasks: simultaneously, the system has to deal with data requests while *peers* are joining and exiting.

The user environment that mediates between users and the proposed architecture should satisfy the following properties:

- *Simplicity* and *transparency* of access: users should care neither about the current locations of data resources nor about the details of the underlying *peer* structure. The name of the data must be sufficient to retrieve it. The library has to be easy to implement on top of existing applications.
- *Interoperability*: the API has to be as close as possible to known standards and to existing operating systems.
- *Independence* between computation and data transfer: following a data request, an application can continue computations for some time while the data acquisition is processed in the background. In other words, the API should provide *non-blocking* functions.

1.2 CONTRIBUTIONS

In order to meet the requirements described above, we propose a complete architecture consisting of an API and a grid service for shared resources in large distributed systems. In summary:

- We develop a library interface called Data Handover (DHO) (Gustedt, 2006) with a set of functions that can be included in existing applications. It overcomes the short-comings of message passing interfaces (see, eg, mpi-2, 2016) and shared memory paradigms. **DHO**, see Gustedt (2006), combines the control simplicity of MPI with the random access of memory. It introduces an abstraction level between memory and data through objects we call *handles*. An experimental study has already been given for the *client-server* paradigm, see Hernane et al. (2011).

- We propose a grid service that is modeled using a three-level architecture. It guarantees responses to all the data requests of users on the higher level (the third level) through **DHO** routines. With two processes (the Resource manager and the Lock manager) that interact with a data *handle*, the grid service transparently achieves the desired activities related to data acquisition.

- We propose the Exclusive Locks with Mobile Processes (ELMP) algorithm which is an extension of the distributed mutual exclusion algorithm of Naimi and Tréhel (1988). **ELMP** is then used by the *lock manager* on the lower level of the grid service such that we can condition the resource acquisition to the entrance of the **critical section**. **ELMP** ensures consistency for exclusive access. Then we extend the capabilities of **ELMP** to allow shared and exclusive locks, resulting in the *Read-Write Locks with Mobile Processes* algorithm (**RW-LMP**).[1] Both algorithms exhibit a $O(\log n)$ complexity in terms of messages per request. Proofs of *Safety* and *Liveness* properties are also provided. The potential flooding caused by too many new arriving *peers* can be addressed by known strategies such as Jagadish et al. (2005, 2006), Galperin and Rivest (1993), and Andersson (1999).

- We integrate these tools into a three-level *peer-to-peer* (p2p) architecture. We then introduce the notion of **critical resource** and a *state* concept for each process (*manager*).

- We present performance analysis of our architecture by a variety of benchmarks and experiments that were carried out on a real grid platform.

Through the proposal architecture, this chapter presents an appropriate methodology of sharing remote critical resources between users who are unaware of their localization. We describe all phases through which a given request of a resource passes, from its insertion until its release. However, to ease the description we start from the lowest to the highest level. This is why we first emphasize the distributed mutual exclusion algorithms in Section 2.

After giving the basic definitions of the mutual exclusion concept, we describe the Naimi and Tréhel algorithm. Then we outline the problems which may arise in the presence of concurrent requests and the reasons that led us to extend the original algorithm to ELMP we present in Section 3.

Our system is designed to offer two modes of data access. Depending on the nature of the application, the data may be accessed concurrently for reading

---

[1] We have briefly introduced this approach in Hernane et al. (2012).

or exclusively for writing: several *peers* may simultaneously read data without modifying it, but access to modify the data must be restricted to one *peer* at a time. This is why, in Section 4 we extend the capabilities of **ELMP** to allow both exclusive and shared accesses. We then present the RW-LMP algorithm. Previously, we briefly introduced this approach in Hernane et al. (2012). Both algorithms exhibit a $O(\log n)$ complexity in terms of messages. Proofs of *Safety* and *Liveness* properties are also provided.

The potential imbalance of the underlying structure is addressed by both algorithms through well-known strategies. We suggest choices in Section 3.4 and explain their possible integration into our algorithms.

We then give a modeling of the entire three-level architecture (with **DHO** API) in Section 5 which leads to a p2p system. As a main ingredient, it adds a concept of *states* for all processes comprising the system.

Section 6 gives a performance analysis of our proposed **DHO** p2p system. We discuss a variety of benchmarks and present some experiments carried out on a real grid platform before concluding in Section 8.

2 MUTUAL EXCLUSION

When concurrent processes share a file or a data resource, it is often necessary to ensure exclusiveness of access to it at a given time. In concurrent programming, a **critical section** is part of a multi-process program that cannot be executed simultaneously by more than one process. Typically, a **critical section** protects a shared data resource that should be updated by exactly one process. In other words, mutual exclusion algorithms are designed to protect one or several sections of the code that are critical. Usually, they are identified by the following requirements:

- At a given time t, one process at most may be inside the **critical section**.
- A process that requests access to a **critical section** should succeed within a finite time.
- For most of mutual exclusion algorithms, the fairness between processes is ensured. They assume that they have the same opportunity to succeed. They do not imply any order of priority between processes that want simultaneous access to the **critical section**. Many API implement it that way.

Concurrent programming control was first introduced by Dijkstra (1965). This led to the emergence of the discipline of concurrent and distributed algorithms that implement mutual exclusion. They fit into two types of architectures. In shared memory environments, data control is ensured by synchronization mechanisms between processes or threads. In distributed environments, processes communicate by asynchronous message passing. Provided that no process stays forever inside the **critical section**, a mutual exclusion algorithm must ensure the two following properties:

Liveness: A process requesting access to a **critical section** will eventually obtain it.

Safety: At any given time, at most one process is inside the **critical section**.

In other words, liveness prevents starvation of processes, while safety guarantees the integrity of concurrent processes.

2.1 DISTRIBUTED MUTUAL EXCLUSION ALGORITHMS

Several distributed algorithms have been proposed over the years. Depending on the technique that is used, these algorithms have been classified as permission-based (Lamport, 1978; Maekawa, 1985; Ricart and Agrawala, 1981) and token-based algorithms (Naimi and Tréhel, 1988; Raymond, 1989).

For the first, the process only enters a **critical section** after having received the permission from all the other processes. For the second, the entrance into a **critical section** is conditioned by the possession of a token which is passed between processes. We focus on this class of algorithms for the sake of the message complexity; the distributed algorithm of Naimi and Tréhel (1988) based on path reversal is *the* benchmark for mutual exclusion in this class. It exhibits a $O(\log n)$ complexity in terms of the number of messages per request. We will merely refer to it in the version of Naimi et al. (1996), that additionally provides the proof for the properties that we will use.

Section 2.2 gives a full description of the algorithm. Many extensions of this algorithm have already been proposed in the literature. We mention a few of them. A fault-tolerant, token-based, mutual-exclusion algorithm using a dynamic tree was presented by Sopena et al. (2005). Wagner and Mueller (2000) have proposed token-based, read-write locks for distributed mutual exclusion. Quinson and Vernier (2009) provide a byte range asynchronous locking of the Naimi-Trehel algorithm based on sub-queues when partial locks are requested. Courtois et al. (1971) extend the algorithm to *Readers/Writers* in distributed systems. However, they assume two distinct classes of processes (a reader class and a writer class) where the process cannot switch from one class to another. Lejeune et al. (2013) have presented a new priority-based mutual exclusion algorithm for situations where high-priority processes are allowed to overtake low-priority processes that are waiting for the resource. That approach is complementary to ours, where we need a strict FIFO policy for lock acquisition.

2.2 THE NAIMI AND TRÉHEL ALGORITHM

The Naimi and Tréhel algorithm is based on a distributed queue along which a token circulates which represents the protected resource. Queries are handled through a second structure, a distributed tree. The query tree is rooted at the tail of the queue to allow the appending of new requests to the queue at any moment.

The basics of the algorithm are summarized following (Naimi et al., 1996):

1. There is a logical dynamic tree structure. The *root* of the tree is always the process that requested the token last. In that tree, each process points towards a **Parent**. Requests are propagated along the tree until the *root* is reached. Initially, all processes point to the same **Parent** which is the *root* that initially holds the token.
2. There is a distributed FIFO queue which holds (in insertion order) the requests that have not yet been satisfied. Each process ρ that requested the token points to the **Next** requester of the token. This identifies the process for which access permission is to be forwarded after process ρ releases its lock.
3. As soon as a process ρ wants to reclaim the lock, it sends a request to its **Parent**, waits for the token and becomes the new *root* of the tree. If it is not the current *root*, ρs **Parent** σ forwards the request to it's **Parent** and then updates its **Parent**'s variable to ρ. If σ is the *root* of the tree and does not detain the lock, it releases the token to ρ. If it still holds the lock or waits for the token to obtain the lock, it points its **Next** to ρ.

Each process maintains local variables that it updates while the algorithm evolves:

Token_present: A Boolean set to *true* if the process owns the token, *false* otherwise.
Requesting_cs: A Boolean set to *true* if the process has claimed the lock.
Next: The **Next** process that will hold the token, *null* otherwise. Initially set to *null*. This might only be set while the process has claimed the token and a non-satisfied request has to be served after the own request.
Parent: Initially, it is the same for all processes but for the initial *root*, it is set to *null*.

Processes send two kind of messages:

Request(ρ): sent by the process ρ to its **Parent**.
Token: sent by a process ρ to its **Next**.

we have the following invariant:

Invariant 1. *At the end of request processing, the* root *of the **Parent** tree is the tail of the* **Next** *chain.*

The Naimi and Tréhel algorithm provides a distributed model that guarantees the uniqueness of the token while ensuring properties of *Safety* and *Liveness* the proof of which was given in Naimi et al. (1996)

An example of the execution of the algorithm is shown in Fig. 1. Gray circles denote processes with requests, while the black circle is one that holds the token. Initially, process ❶ holds the token, Fig. 1A. It is the **Parent** of the remaining processes and the *root*, R of the **Parent** tree. Process ② asks the token from its **Parent**, Fig. 1B. Thus, ❶ points towards ② and updates its **Next** variable to the same process. Afterwards, ③ requests the token, Fig. 1C. ❶ then forwards the request to its new **Parent**, process ② which updates in turn its variables, **Parent** and **Next** to ③.

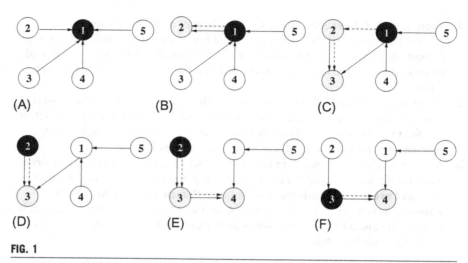

FIG. 1

Example of the execution of Naimi and Tréhel's Algorithm. (A) Initial state, **①** is *R*. (B) ②
requests the token. (C) ③ requests the token. (D) ① releases the token. (E) ④ requests
the token. (F) ② releases the token.

In Fig. 1D, ① releases the lock, while **②** obtains it and then ④ in turn, requests the
critical section, Fig. 1E. Thus, processes ① and ③ point their **Parent** variables to ④.
Obviously, the latter updates its **Next** to process ④. Finally **③** gets the lock, Fig. 1F.

2.3 SIMULTANEOUS REQUESTS

To be able to handle simultaneous requests by the same process we made an extension
to the original structure.

During the course of the original algorithm, a given **Parent** can be queried
simultaneously by different processes, see Fig. 2. This example is taken from Naimi
and Tréhel (1988) where it is presented in the context of node failures.

Initially (Fig. 2A), process **①** holds the token and ③ claims the **critical section**
by sending a request to its **Parent**. In turn, **①** updates its **Parent** and its **Next** to ③,
Fig. 2B. Then, processes ② and ⑤ claim the **critical section**. They send request to
① and set forthwith their **Parent** to *null*. So, **①** points towards ② and forwards the
request to ③, Fig. 2C. Meanwhile, process ⑤ waits and is disconnected from the tree.
Once **①** sent the request of ② to ③, it switches to ⑤'s request. Thus, it forwards the
request to ② and sets its **Parent** to ⑤. Meanwhile, ② is cut from the tree, Fig. 2D.
In Fig. 2E, request of process ② is achieved and that of ⑤ ends in Fig. 2F.

We notice that processes set their **Parent** variable to *null* as soon as they forward
the request. Thus, as long as they haven't arrived at the new *root* they disconnect
from the tree.

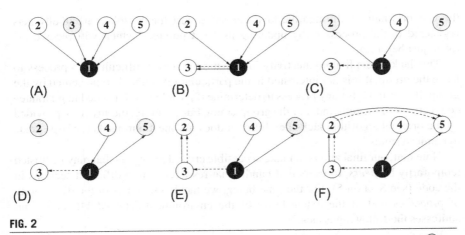

FIG. 2

Example of concurrent requests in Naimi and Tréhel's Algorithm. (A) Initial state. (B) ③ requests the token. (C) ② and ⑤ request the token. (D) ② and ⑤ in transit. (E) ⑤ in transit. (F) completion of requests.

Within a system of n processes, $n - 1$ processes could request the token concurrently. This will generate n disjoint components, the **Parent** relation then is not a tree but only a forest.

To avoid that, we amend the original algorithm by requiring that processes never be cut from the **Parent** tree. This will help us to keep all links of the data structures alive if a given process leaves the system. We assume that a process does not accept a new request before the previous one is completed.

In the following sections, we provide two extensions of the algorithm. For the first, we allow processes to enter or to leave the system. If one of them wants to enter the group, it just has to choose a relative **Parent** and to join the tree and be connected to the system. The difficulty in node dynamicity lies in the departure of processes, onto which we will thus focus. The second extension provides two ways to enter a **critical section**; either in exclusive mode or shared.

The term of **critical section** that refers to an abstract concept will be used recurrently in our extended algorithms. However, it will refer later to a concrete realization with remote **critical resources**.

3 ALGORITHM FOR EXCLUSIVE LOCKS WITH MOBILE PROCESSES (ELMP)

As we have seen in the discussion above, in the original version of the Naimi and Tréhel algorithm the **Parent** relation becomes disconnected, as soon as a process ρ requests the token. The connectivity information is only maintained implicitly in the network, namely through the fact that ρs request for the token eventually gets registered in the process r (by updating its **Next** pointer), which will receive the token just before ρ.

This lack of explicit connectivity information makes it difficult for a process to leave the group, if it is not interested in the particular token that is represented by the group. It is difficult for any process to determine if its help is still needed to guarantee connectivity of the remainder of the group or not. Furthermore, the structure provided by the original algorithm lacks flexibility, it does not meet our needs for large-scale dynamic systems.

Note that, our final aim is to make accessible critical resources that may be hosted temporarily by *peers*, to users that handle that resource within different sections in the code (see Section 5). For the time being, we tackle the issues of the dynamicity of processes and of the extensibility of the environment. The **ELMP** algorithm addresses the following issues:

1. It maintains the connectivity such that any process is able to leave the group within a reasonable time-frame; reasonable here basically is the time that is needed to forward information to the other processes.
2. It allows new processes to join the system whenever possible.
3. It keeps control of the shape of the tree in order to meet the balancing requirement, such that all operations within the system have a complexity of $O(\log n)$.

For this purpose, we reinforce processes with additional information. First, unlike the original algorithm, initially we assume that processes are arranged in a balanced tree-structure such that all links point towards the direction of the *root* that holds the token. Then, each process σ handles additional variables that we will introduce gradually in the following sections.

3.1 THE DATA STRUCTURE

With the aim of maintaining the connectivity of the parental structure as well as of the linked list, we add the following variables to the internal structure of each process σ, see Section 2.2.

Predecessor: σ knows who will hold the token before him. It is easily updated simultaneously as **Next**. Instead of a distributed queue, the **Next** and the **Predecessor** form a doubly linked list. Once a process r passes the token to its **Next** σ, rs **Next** and σs **Predecessor** are set to NULL.

children: The list of processes that are children of σ. Henceforth, σ knows its **Parent** and its **children**.

blocked: A list of processes that are **Blocked** (by σ). The **Blocked** list guarantees an atomicity on the path by a task undertaken by σ.

ID We introduce a new variable **ID** that holds a number that will be used as a tie breaker during departure, see Section 3.2. The current *root* of the tree will maintain a global value that is the maximum of all these **ID**. Since new processes must first reach the *root* such a value can easily be maintained by that *root* and propagated along if the *root* changes.

3.2 ATOMIC OPERATIONS

Our aim is to avoid the overlapping of requests, so any process σ will not handle several requests at once. Before accepting to receive a new request, σ must have completed all previous processing.

The **State** variable we introduce below, manages the atomicity of that approach. It may have different values that indicate the specific task the process is currently completing. Fig. 3 exemplifies our approach and emphasizes on the state concept.

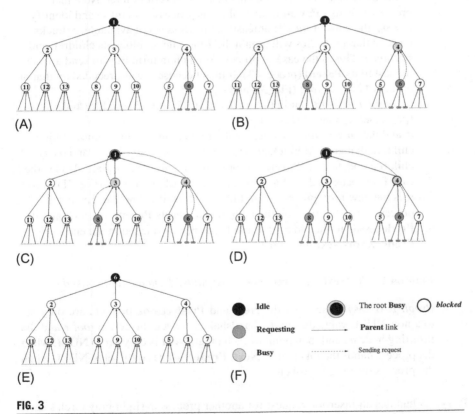

FIG. 3

Handling concurrent requests in the **ELMP** algorithm. (A) 12 requests the token, it blocks its children. (B) 8 requests the token, it blocks its children. (C) 12's request reaches first the *root*. (D) The *root* blocks its children, 8's request fails. (E) Swapping between 1 and 12. (F) Legend.

Idle: In this state, σ is not involved in any processing, whether for himself or for others. However, it may hold the token. Its corresponding list **blocked** is *empty*. From this state, σ can switch to any other state. Besides process 1 that holds the token, in Fig. 3, all white circles denote *Idle* processes.

Requesting: σ has started an insertion into the queue for requesting the token but that request is not yet completed (such as process 12 in Fig. 3A and B). It is not ready to receive any request as long as it is in this state. Dark gray circles denote the **Requesting** processes. The **blocked** list will include all corresponding children (bold circles, see Section 3f). Once in this state, σ operates in phases:

1. First it walks up the tree, if available (**Idle** state) notifies processes $p_2, \ldots, p_n$ on the path about the insertion operation. They will all switch to the **Busy** state, but will not change their **Parent** pointer. Note that processes form a **Parent** branch of σ (as processes 4 and 1) and identify $r = p_n$, the current *root*. If at least one process is not available, σ tracks back so that processes will regain the **Idle** state, unblock its children and start over. This is the case of process 8 which in turn, tries to send a request to its **Parent** (process 3). It fails because it was preceded by that of process 12 at the *root* (Fig. 3B and C).
   Once the *root* is *Idle*, it in turn includes its children in the **blocked** list (processes 2, 3 and 4 (Fig. 3D)).
2. σ and the current *root* r exchange their positions and then those of their children that are still **blocked**. Thus, r, that is no longer *root*, and its children update their **Parent**, before returning to the *Idle* state. This is the case for processes 2, 3, 4 as it is for children of process 12 (Fig. 3D).
3. σ is the new *root*, process 12 in Fig. 3E. It sends acknowledgments to processes $p_2, \ldots, p_{n-1}$ on the path. It changes its **Parent** to empty and its **Predecessor** to the old *root*. From here on, σ is queued in the end of the **Predecessor-Next** linked list.

Lemma 1. *The* **Next** *and* **Predecessor** *variables form a doubly linked list.*

Proof. It is easy to see that the **Next** and **Predecessor** pointers are only set to a non-NULL value during the handshake between the actual *root* r and the inserting node σ, and then point to each other. **Next** is only set to NULL when the process hands the token to its **Next**; **Predecessor** is only set to NULL when the process receives the token. □

Busy: ρ handles an insertion request for another process σ (light gray circles such as processes 4, 3 and the current *root* 1 in Fig. 3). It is not ready to forward other insertion requests yet (such as process 3 that rejects 8's request), neither to be involved for the departure of another process. If **Parent** is **empty** (ρ is the actual *root*), it exchanges its position with σ (the new *root*). It also sets its **Next** variable to that process and updates its list of children (process 1). From there, ρ switches back to the **Idle** state. It may request the token for itself, as it may be called again for further operations.

Lemma 2. *As soon as a request of σ reaches a tree-node ρ no other request of a process below ρ can overtake it.*

Proof. As soon as σ succeeds to notifying all processes on the path to the *root*, its **Parent** and whole parental structure switch to the **Busy** state. Thus, even if a request of another process σ' that is launched after that of σ may go up some path in the tree, it will meet a **Busy** process. The request of σ' cannot be undertaken before σ, the new *root* returns to the *Idle* state. □

Exiting: The **Exiting** state denotes the disconnecting activity for σ. When in that state, σ negotiates with some other processes (see below) and must wait in case these are in the middle of requesting the token or themselves leaving the system, or involved in the tree-restructuring for example.

Blocked: Closely tied to **Exiting** is the **Blocked** state. There are two possible scenarios:

- Another process ρ is disconnecting. In fact, ρ will promote its children to the **Blocked** state, such that they hold back any requests that might be pending in their subtrees, eg, processes 12 and 1 in the example (Fig. 3). Among these blocked neighbors, σ will choose another process ρ that will inherit all information that σ held for the system. Namely, the children of σ will become children of ρ and if σ held the token previously to its departure, ρ will do so thereafter.
- σ is part of an unbalanced branch of the tree. Thus, it will be blocked for a further positioning in the tree. In Section 3.7, we present possible strategies for maintaining the tree as balanced in case of departure.

In fact, a process σ does not disconnect from the **Parent** tree and from the linked list **Next-Predecessor** without precaution. It has to satisfy a number of constraints such that the disconnection will never compromise the consistency of the algorithm as a whole, nor the connectivity of the **Parent** tree and that of the linked list **Next-Predecessor**, in particular. σ cannot break away from its **Parent** nor from its children suddenly. It should rather find a successor.

Maintaining the fact that σ chooses another **Parent** would be more difficult. Therefore we adopt a *lazy* deletion property: any list item that is accessed by process ρ will first be checked for its validity. If the process σ in question is still accessible and its **Parent** points to ρ, σ is still a child of ρ. Otherwise, the list entry is invalid and dropped from the list.

To be able to switch to the **Exiting** state:

- The process σ must be **Idle**.
- It must not have requested the token.

The fact that σ must not have requested the token does not mean, that it cannot actually *possess* it. The following lemma is immediate.

Lemma 3. *Let σ be a process that is **Idle** and that has not requested the token.*

1. σ *possesses the token iff it is the* root *of the **Parent** tree.*
2. *If σ is the* root *of the **Parent** tree no other process has successfully inserted a token request.*

The following operations that are chronologically carried out by σ, summarize the effective departure form the system. During this departure σ will contact all its *neighbors* in the **Parent** tree, that is its children and its **Parent**, if it has any.

1. σ verifies that it is **Idle** and that it has not requested the token.
2. σ switches from the **Idle** to the **Exiting** state.
3. For all its neighbors η, **Parent** last and children, σ initializes a handshake with process η:

    - If η is already **Blocked** (by σ), we encountered a duplicate entry in the **children** list. η is already in **blocked** and the entry in **children** is simply discarded.
    - If η is **Idle**, it switches to **Blocked** (by σ). σ moves η from its **children** to its **blocked** list.
    - If η is not **Idle**, σ waits until it is contacted by η at the same point of its exit procedure.
      Once σ and η meet on their departure request, the one of them with lower ID has a priority for that request. The one with the higher ID switches to **Blocked** (by the other), and updates its lists analogous to the previous point.
    - In all other cases, σ switches back to **Idle** and restarts at 3.2.

4. Now all neighbors of σ are **Blocked** (by σ) and thus no **children** and all neighbors are listed in **blocked**. If σ is not the *root* of the tree, it chooses $\rho =$ **Parent**, otherwise it is in the situation of Lemma 3 and chooses ρ among its children.[2]
5. σ sends ρ to all its neighbors. ρ itself will discover by that message, that it has been chosen and if it will be the new *root* of the tree.
6. σ sends its **blocked** list (excluding ρ) to ρ.

---

[2]If it has neither **Parent** nor children, the system consists only of σ.

7. σ waits for an acknowledgment from ρ that it has integrated the list into the list of its children.

8. Finally, σ informs all its neighbors that it has completed the departure process.

Lemma 4 (departure). *A process σ that want to leave the system can do so within a finite time.*

Proof. First consider a departing node σ that is not the *root* of the tree and that is the only process in the system that is departing. Any child η of σ will either be **Idle** (and switch to **Blocked**) or be requesting the token for itself or some descendant process. For the latter, at the end of processing the request ηs **Parent** will point to the actual *root* of the tree, and thus not be a child of σ anymore. A similar argument holds for σs **Parent**: it may be in an non-**Idle** state for some time, but finally as it has processed token request from all its children, it will become **Idle** again. Thus, after a finite time, all neighbors of σ will be **Blocked**, and σ may leave the system.

Now suppose in addition, that there are other departing processes. A neighbor η_0 could eventually be **Blocked** (by η_1), η_1 **Blocked** (by η_2), etc., but since our system is finite, such a blocking chain leads to an unblocked vertex η_k that is departing and that has no departing neighbors. Thus, the departure of η_k will eventually be performed, and so the departures of all $\eta_{k-1}, \ldots, \eta_1$. Thus η_0 will eventually return to **Idle** and then either leave itself or be switched to **Blocked** (by σ).

Observe that if η_0 is **Parent** of σ and has an **ID** that is lower than the one of σ, it will leave the system before σ and σ may eventually become *root*.

Now, if σ also is the *root*, we have three possibilities:

- Another process requests the token eventually and σ will cease to be *root*.
- Another process ρ inserts itself into the system. σ will cease to be *root*.
- Any child η of σ in **children** will either depart from the system or will eventually become **Idle**. Then σ will be able to enter in a handshake with η and switch it to **Blocked**. Since **children** is finite and no new processes are added to it, eventually all children of σ will be **Blocked** and listed in **Blocked**.

Finally observe that only a finite number of processes can have an **ID** that is smaller than the one of σ. Thus σ while waiting for its departure, it can become *root* at most **ID** $- 1$ time. $\qquad\square$

Lemma 5. *The **Parent** tree as well as the doubly linked list are never disconnected.*

Proof. As long as there are no disconnections from the system (**Blocked** state and Lemma 5), the **Parent** tree and the doubly linked list remain connected in the **ELMP** algorithm.

In case of departure of a given process σ, the **Parent** tree also remains connected since during the effective departure of that process all neighbors are **Blocked** until they receive a new **Parent** (Steps from 3.2 to the 3.2) of the Exit atomic operation 3.2.

□

3.3 CONNECTING TO THE SYSTEM

There is no specific state for processes attempting a new connection. The connecting process is relatively straightforward. However, certain steps should be performed beforehand.

In fact, the placement of σ is closely linked to the adopted balancing strategy (Section 3.4) of the shape of the tree. If σ wants to join, first, it has to know a given process η in the tree. If η is not *Idle* or, if it has less than m authorized children, it may accept σ otherwise, it forwards σs request to its **Parent** or to one of its children. If this is the case, σs request is studied again. The process starts over again, probably down the tree, until σ finds an appropriate **Parent**.

From this point, the new connection is gradually announced along the **Parent** branch to the *root*. Once informed of the new connection, the *root* assigns an ID to σ by the same path. At the end of the insertion process, σ becomes *Idle*.

3.4 BALANCING STRATEGIES

The competitive system in which the algorithms evolve should be as extensible as possible. However, we aim to control the shape of the tree in order to ensure a logarithmic complexity.

Many approaches have been proposed in the literature in order to achieve efficient maintenance for the tree, mainly if they are binary, with the aim of finding a balance criteria that ensures a logarithmic height of the tree. We outline two approaches:

The first is to restrict the shape of the tree that should always be of order m. Jagadish et al. (2005, 2006) proposed a balanced tree structure to overlay on a p2p network. It is based on a binary balanced tree (BATON) and generalized to m-order trees (BATON*). They support the joining and departure of nodes and take no more than $O(\log n)$ steps. To ensure a balanced growth of the tree, new nodes are assigned to previously empty leaf positions. For departures, the authors propose replacement of *non-leaf* nodes by *leaf-nodes*.

Interesting for us in this schema are the additional links between siblings and adjacent nodes. These allow to reach the tree rapidly from each other node in the tree. This is particularly interesting for new processes that attempt to get their **ID** from the *root*. The cost of all atomic operations handled by our structure will then be significantly reduced since the height of the tree is controlled.

Thus, if we opt for this schema, we should review the progress of events that make changes in the shape of the **Parent** tree (see below).

The second one is a "lazy" mode. The balancing processing is not made until it is really needed. In this approach, no shape restriction is given as long as the height of the tree does not exceed some value defined by a balance criteria, see Galperin and Rivest (1993).

Andersson (1999) uses the concept of general balanced trees. So, as long as the height of the tree does not exceed $\alpha \cdot \log |T|$ for some constant $\alpha > 1$ where T is the size of the tree, nothing is done. Otherwise, we walk back up the tree, following a process insertion for example, until a node σ (usually called a *scapegoat*) where $height(\sigma) > \alpha \cdot \log |weight(\sigma)|$, is observed. Thus, a partial rebuild of the sub-tree starting from the scapegoat node is made. Many partial rebuilding techniques can be found in the literature as in Galperin and Rivest (1993).

Whatever the policy, we should add the following variables to the previous data structure (Section 3.1):

height(σ) The height of the sub-tree rooted at a process σ, that is the longest distance in terms of edges from σ to some leaf.

weight(σ): The weight of σ, ie, the number of leafs belonging to the subtree of σ.

These variables are used for decisions concerning the restructuring of the tree, for example to find a position for a new arrival. They are updated whenever necessary. Note that such operations require no more than $O(\log n)$ messages since the tree is consistently kept balanced.

Based on these balancing policies, in the following we describe how to keep our **Parent** tree balanced after the achievement of atomic operations handled by processes in the proposed algorithms (see Sections 3 and 4).

3.5 BALANCING FOLLOWING NEW INSERTIONS

Our model channels new insertions in a way to avoid the *root* to be flooded by new processes, which could inhibit handling other requests. The following steps that are carried out by a new process σ, summarizes the processing of insertion into the system.

1. σ first has to know some ρ, one of the other participants. With that information, it searches bottom up in the **Parent** tree to find the actual *root r*. Note that the *root* can be reached fast if we add adjacent links as in the BATON structure, see Jagadish et al. (2005, 2006).
2. σ tries to include η, a process on the path to its **blocked** list.
3. If η is in a *non-Idle* state, σ restarts with a certain delay at Step 3.5 and requests the same process ρ or another for the insertion issue. Note that η allows a limited amount of insertion requests per unit of time.
4. Once σ reaches the current *root r* that is *Idle*, *r* moves to another state, *Busy* for example and then:

(a) It assigns an **ID** to σ with the highest value. It can be used if conflict arises with another process, as in the case of departure (see **Exiting** and **Blocked** states in Section 3.2).

(b) If we make a shape restriction of the tree, r tries to find a **Parent** for σ, probably down the tree, at a second-last node, that has less than m children, see Jagadish et al. (2006).

In case of lazy mode, instead of finding a second-last node, σ simply (after receiving the **ID**) inserts itself into ρ, the found process.

Afterwards, we back up along the path until a possible scapegoat node. Note that this can easily be done since *height* and *weight* variables give appropriate information (for σ that is on the top) of the sub-tree. If this is the case, a partial rebuilding is made as in scapegoat trees. Note that processes on the path of σ remain **blocked** until the sub-tree is stated as balanced.

3.6 BALANCING FOLLOWING A TOKEN REQUEST

The requesting processing we have presented in Section 3.2 does not affect the shape of the tree. Indeed, at the end of a sending request, two processes (σ and the old *root*) exchange their positions. Thus, the tree remains unchanged.

3.7 BALANCING FOLLOWING DEPARTURE

The Exit strategy presented in Section 3.2 will be slightly modified if we want to keep the tree at an order m. σ that is **Exiting** will simply find another leaf process as a replacement that inherits all the needed information, rather than making a connection between **Parent** and children, neither a new **Parent** among the list of children.

In case of lazy mode, assume σ that has not yet completed its departure becomes on the path of a partial balanced restructuring. Based on this information, the **Parent** and sub-trees on the top compute again their *height* and *weight* variables and seek again a possible scapegoat process.

3.8 THE PROOF OF THE ELMP ALGORITHM

We have shown in previous sections how to deal with concurrent requests, where processes are initially arranged in a balanced tree of *order* m.

Both balancing approaches cited in Section 3.4 provide flexibility and elasticity in the structure, such that the tree can be enlarged by new processes or reduced by the current ones. The following lemma strengthens Lemma 2 when processes trigger the movements other than requests of token.

Lemma 6. *No other request of a process σ' arrived later (at the* root) *can be completed before the request for σ.*

Proof. Since no other request of a given process σ' can be completed before the previous inserted request of σ (Lemma 2), we show that it is also the case during:

1. The departure of the **Parent** of a process σ.
2. Insertion of new processes to the actual *root*.
3. Restructuring processing.

For (1), the **Parent** of a given process σ can not leave the system outside of the *Idle* state Since it is *Idle* before switching to *Exiting*, there is no request of a given process σ' on the path of σ in progress.

Furthermore, the **Blocked** state assigned to the neighbors ensures that all needed information related to any operation triggered by processes of this branch of the tree is kept. Moreover, on completion of departure, there is always a process that inherits all necessary information held by the outbound process (Step 3.2) of Section 3.2, Lemma 3 and Section 3.7.

For (2), new insertions never compromise the order of requests at the *root*, whatever the number of processes. Indeed, a process that wants to insert itself into the system first checks the availability of processes on its path to the *root* (Section 3.5). Otherwise, σ backtracks. Thus, there is no request in progress which cannot be achieved.

For (3), whichever strategy is adopted for the tree-balancing, the **blocked** state avoids any overlap between operations handled by our algorithms. □

Theorem 1 (Liveness). *A process σ that claims a **critical section** obtains it within a finite time.*

Proof. We know that the waiting time for the completion of a request is finite, and that the **Parent** tree as well as the doubly linked list are never disconnected (Lemma 5). Also, **ELMP** guarantees that requests are treated in the same chronological order as their reception at the active *root*. This even holds in case of departures or insertions (Lemma 6). Thus, a **critical section** can be accessed after all previous requests have been handled. Since the handling of each of these is finite, the overall access time is finite. □

Theorem 2 (Safety). *At any given time there is exactly one token in the system.*

In other words, the system guarantees that at most one process is inside a **critical section** and, additionally, that the token never gets lost.

Proof. Initially, there is one token in the system, it is held by the *root*. As the **ELMP** algorithm evolves, the token is passed from one process to another across the linked list **Next-Predecessor**. Whence no process has claimed the token, it remains at the current *root* of the **Parent** tree.

A process σ only leaves the system if it has not requested the token. If it holds the token without having requested it, we are in the situation of Lemma 3, that is σ is the *root* of the tree and no other process has requested the token. In such a case, the token is passed to the new *root* of the tree. □

The **ELMP** algorithm presented in this section implements exclusive sharing of the token between processes distributed over a tree. It features the voluntary departure of these processes. It also enables connection to new arriving processes. This offers the degree of elasticity that we need for the whole system we propose, see Section 5.

4 READ WRITE LOCKS FOR MOBILE PROCESSES (RW-LMP) ALGORITHM

As we have already mentioned, we aim to provide two ways to access the **critical section**, exclusively for writing by a single process or concurrently for reading by many. Therefore we provide an extension to the **ELMP** algorithm such that several processes may share access to a **critical section** without compromising the consistency of the data.

The **RW-LMP** algorithm we propose inherits all properties of **ELMP**'s principal operations that are involved in the **Parent** tree and the balancing strategies. It differs, however, in handling the entry to the **critical section**, namely by amending the FIFO data structure. In **ELMP**, the token is simply forwarded from one process σ to its **Next**, and σ just short-cuts between its **Predecessor** to its **Next** in case of departure. To be able to handle (read/shared—write/exclusive) locks we introduce a manager of readers in the **Next-Predecessor** structure. First, **Next** and **Predecessor** store the type (r or w) of the next or previous request in addition to the link itself. Then, we also maintain a pair (Read manager, *reader number*), referring to the first process that requests a shared token after an exclusive one, called a *read manager* and a counter of the number of ongoing read accesses that follow this *read manager* in the FIFO. Both are supposed to be properly initialized.

4.1 HANDLING REQUESTS IN THE LINKED-LIST

Several cases may occur when the request for a new process σ is appended to the FIFO:

If σ is a reader and its **Predecessor** is a writer, σ becomes *read manager*. It sets its own *read manager* variable to itself and starts counting the next possible readers. All readers that are inserted after σ in the FIFO will point towards σ which becomes their **Predecessor**, thereby forming a group that ends at the next **Next** with exclusive request, if any. Only σ links to this **Next** to whom it

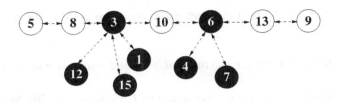

FIG. 4

A doubly linked list with two *read managers*.

will pass the token (processes 3 and 6 in Fig. 4) once the whole group of read accesses is terminated.

If both σ and its **Predecessor** are readers, σ is now the last reader of the group. It obtains the name of the *read manager* from its **Predecessor**. Then, σ informs the *read manager* that it is joining the group and the later increments the counter.

If σs request type is w, σ just links to its **Predecessor** by updating its variables and waits for the token. Likewise, **Next** is updated as soon as a new request is inserted after that of σ.

In Fig. 4 white circles denote exclusive requests. ❸ and ❻ handle groups of readers with 4 and 3 processes, respectively.

4.2 ENTERING THE CRITICAL SECTION

As soon as a process receives the token from its **Predecessor**, it enters the **critical section** and accomplishes some operations depending on its position in the linked list. In the case of an exclusive write access, the process is just removed from the FIFO. Otherwise, it is a *read manager*: it invites the members of its group to enter the **critical section**. On entry, each of these processes of the reader group sends a message to the *read manager* which in turn increments the *reader number*.

4.3 LEAVING THE CRITICAL SECTION

If the access was exclusive, the process just releases the **critical section** and passes the token to its **Next**. Otherwise, it sends a message to its *read manager*, which decrements the *reader number*. The *read manager* only releases the token to its **Next** (which is a writer) once the *reader number* is zero.

Invariant 2. The read manager *does not release the token to the first process requesting an exclusive token following the reader group, until the reader number is zero.*

Lemma 7. *Once the* read manager *enters a **critical section**, the reader group follows.*

Lemma 8. *The **Parent** tree and the doubly linked list are never disconnected.*

Proof. As long as there are no disconnections from the system (**blocked** state and Lemma 2), the statement is obvious.

In case of departure of a given process σ, the **Parent** tree also remains connected since during the effective departure of that process all neighbors are **Blocked** until they receive a new **Parent** (Steps from 3.2 to 3.2 of the Exit atomic operation 3.2). Likewise, σ links its **Predecessor** to its **Next** in the doubly linked list before exiting   □

Lemma 9. *A process with an exclusive request never shares a **critical section** with another process.*

Proof. Let σ be a process with an exclusive request. Let σ be followed in the **Predecessor**-**Next**-list of processes by processes $\{p_1 \ldots p_{j-1}, p_j, p_{j+1} \ldots p_n\}$ that together form a reader group such that p_1 is the *read manager*. Assume that the reader group is followed by a process p_{n+1} with a pending write request.

First, assume that σ holds an exclusive token. σ never shares the **critical section** with p_1 since it always forwards the token to its **Next** after releasing.

Then, according to Invariant 2, the *read manager* keeps the token while the *reader number* > 0. Therefore, p_1 never forwards the token to its **Next**, p_{n+1}, while at least one reader remains in the **critical section**.   □

4.4 LEAVING THE SYSTEM

Readers that want to leave the system that are not *read managers* of their group may do so by simply notifying the *read manager*.

Now, another process σ that wants to leave the system while it has already obtained the token (either an exclusive or a shared one), has to ensure that its **Next** is not **Exiting** itself. Once it has ensured that, it blocks its **Next** until its own **critical section** (and eventually the one of all readers in the group) is finished. It then forwards the token and unblocks **Next**.

If σ does not hold the token while it is leaving, different cases may arise depending on the request type of σ and that of its **Next** and its **Predecessor**. If σ is itself a writer or single reader between two other writers or a writer between a writer and a reader group it links its **Next** to its **Predecessor** and leaves.

If σ is a writer between two reader groups (❿ in Fig. 5A), the two groups have to merge (Fig. 5B). The second *read manager* (process ❻) will no longer be a

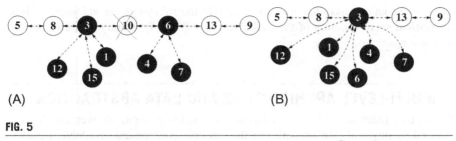

FIG. 5

Union of two readers groups following the departure of a writer. (A) ⑩ leaves the system. (B) ❸ includes ❻ in its own group.

read manager. However, it forwards the information about its group to the first *read manager*.

The remaining case is that of a *read manager* that has other readers in its group. σ waits as long as other readers in the same group are **Exiting**. Then, it chooses a member of its group, elects it as new *read manager*, notifies all members about that fact, and updates the FIFO to that new situation.

4.5 THE PROOF OF THE RW-LMP ALGORITHM

In this section we prove *Safety* and *Liveness* properties.

Theorem 3 (Liveness). *A process σ that claims a **critical section** obtains it within a finite time.*

Proof. We know that the waiting time for the completion of a request is finite, and the **Parent** tree as well as the doubly linked list are never disconnected (Lemma 8). Based on Lemma 4 and Invariant 1, **RW-LMP** guarantees that requests are treated in the same chronological order as their reception at the current *root*, even in cases of departures and mixed read-write requests. Thus, we conclude that a **critical section** is obtained within a finite time.   □

Theorem 4 (Safety). *At any time the set of processes inside a **critical section** is either empty, consists of one process that has an exclusive request, or consists only of processes with read request.*

Proof. A process with an exclusive token never shares a **critical section** with a shared one and vice versa. This results directly from Lemma 9.   □

At this point of the theoretical study, the **critical section** remains an abstract entity that is accessed consistently by one or many processes for a finite amount of time.

Consistency and *availability* are guaranteed. In the following, we are going to link the **critical section** notion of the *ELMP* and *RW-LMP* algorithms with concepts of data and resources.

5 MULTI-LEVEL ARCHITECTURE AND DATA ABSTRACTION

The locking mechanism that locks data will inevitably generate an overhead. This is induced by physical characteristics of the runtime environment (available memory, CPU time, resource size).

The memory space allocated for locks and the time that is required for lock acquisition define the lock overhead. For example, fine granularity of data locks with small sizes will increase the relative lock overhead and worsen the performance. Contrariwise, locking resources with large sizes result in costs for acquiring and releasing locks that are negligible compared to the cost of the rest of the computation.

Although the lock time itself might be negligible, transferring large shared resources is not, and delays that are related to the available bandwidth are unavoidable. Our aim is to hide the acquire and release delays between two *peers* in that unavoidable time of data transfer. A full experimental analysis of the proposed architecture will include variation in data size and lock times, Section 6.

In the following, we assume a set of *peers* distributed over a reliable network which communicate by exchanging messages and such that each *peer* has some autonomy.

The multi-level architecture we present provides and manages concurrent access to remote resources. It ensures consistency and availability of critical resources distributed over *peers* that may appear and disappear. We strongly rely on the cooperation of the different processes that are implied. To achieve these objectives, we use an API called **DHO**. It is implemented with a p2p architecture that includes our mutual exclusion algorithms **ELMP** and **RW-LMP** underneath.

DHO initially described by Gustedt (2006), is an application API that combines global addressing, read-write locking, mapping and data forwarding. It has the following goals:

- Make remote data available locally for shared reading or for exclusive writing.
- Implement a strict and predictable FIFO policy for the access.
- Allow *peers* that compose the system to join and to leave while the system as a whole continues to handle requests.

5.1 THE BASIC MODEL OF THE DHO API

With a set of **DHO** functions, applications evolve on the top of a multi-level architecture that is hidden to the user.

An application process (*peer*) attempts to gain access to a specific data **critical resource** without knowing if that resource is already present locally or on a remote machine. The first operation has always to be the `dho_create` function. It has to wait for a reply from the *peer* that holds the resource.

```
dho_create(DHO_t* h, char const* name)
```

This function initiates a so-called *handle* for data encapsulation. The argument h, a *handle*, encapsulates all the necessary information about the remote access to **critical resource**, where the `name` function links the application to that resource. All remaining functions then only use that *handle* to specify the resource. As an example, the function `dho_ew_request(DHO_t* h)` requests the future exclusive-write access to a **critical resource** that is already linked with the *handle* h.

Applications using **DHO** routines need at least one *handle* per resource, but may even use several *handles* for the same. Thereby, a process may announce that it will need to access the same resource several times, eventually interleaved with the access by other processes.

The `dho_destroy` function unlinks the corresponding data resource from the user application.

Our **DHO** implementation uses two asynchronous processes per data resource and *peer*, the *resource manager* and the *lock manager*. Once a **DHO** request is inserted by the user, the *resource manager*, a local process, takes control of that request and forwards it to the *lock manager*. It is also responsible to map the data in the local address space of the requester, and, to transfer an updated copy of the data to the next *peer* after release.

Fig. 6 shows the different states of knowledge about an acquisition that a *peer* has, while Fig. 10 gives more details (at a lower level) of the life cycle of a request by the states of the *resource manager*. We will detail these states later (Section 5.2).

Note that the states that we have assigned to the second asynchronous process *lock manager* (see Section 3.2) refer to the completion of inserting a request and not to the acquisition of the data.

To acquire the **critical resource**, the *resource manager* forwards the *locking* request to the *lock manager* which negotiates the *locking* remotely with others *lock managers* through message passing.

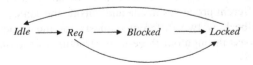

FIG. 6

DHO life cycle at the *peer* level.

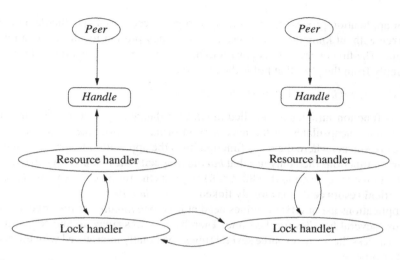

FIG. 7

Hierarchical order of processes.

As a whole, the *lock managers* of all *peers* ensure the overall consistency of the data by using **ELMP** and **RW-LMP** (Sections 3 and 4) as a locking protocol. The *lock manager* plays the role of σ in these algorithms.

The *peer* (represented by **DHO** functions), the *resource manager* and the *lock manager* form a three-level hierarchical architecture, where the *lock manager* carries out instructions of mutual exclusion algorithms at lowest level. The access is granted according to a FIFO *access control policy* and the data are then presented to the application inside its local address space.

A request for a **critical resource** triggers events at the *resource manager* and crosses various states from request insertion until resource release.

5.1.1 DHO cooperation model

Here, we present the design of a **DHO** architecture to model cooperation between *peers*. Fig. 7 illustrates the cooperation between processes in the same *peer*, the *resource manager* and the *lock manager*, as well as the relationship between *lock managers* of different *peers*. Fig. 8 shows more details and outlines the path of requests through different processes inside and outside the same *peer*.

Now, we describe how two different requests for the same resource by two neighboring *peers* pass through our three-level structure (write on the left and read on the right of Fig. 8).

- Initially, the application just needs to link to the claimed data named A by calling dho_create (level ①). The application claims the **critical resource** and the system guarantees its combined *locking* and *mapping* within a finite time.

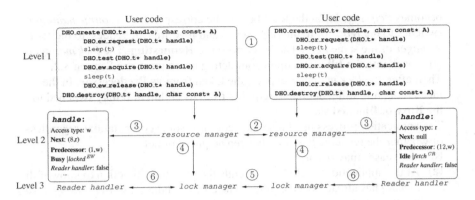

FIG. 8

Handling requests between two neighboring *peers*.

- Each *peer* runs two managers (*resource manager* and *lock manager*) that interact for acquisition and negotiation phases with each other ④ and with external managers ②.
- A negotiation phase consists of requesting, acquiring and forwarding the resource. During such a phase the *resource manager* and the *lock manager* keep information about their current activities by means of assigned states, that are saved in the *handle* by the *peer* and the *resource manager* (Fig. 7).
- Inside the same *peer*, the *resource manager* and the *lock manager* cooperate for *locking/mapping* the resource locally. The *resource manager* acts as an intermediate owner and is responsible for the *mapping* of the resource into local memory. It forwards the request to the lowest level, namely to the *lock manager* in the same *peer*, ④. In the mean time, the application may continue doing unrelated computations.
- The *lock manager* remotely negotiates the *locking* with other *lock managers* in the network, ⑤, whereas the *resource manager* is involved in transferring the data to its **Next**.
- Some *peers* may further take the additional role of *read manager* if they are the first of a number of successive readers, see Section 4.2.

Once the **critical resource** is linked to the *handle*, the request process may start. Level ① of Fig. 8 shows a code prototype of a simple call for a data resource, named *A*.

The phases of a request that passes through the multi-level architecture are described by the following sections.

5.1.2 The path of a DHO request

1. The application issues *non-blocking* requests (`dho_ew_request` or `dho_cr_request`) for future acquisition of the data resource. The *peer*'s state

becomes *Req* (Fig. 6). In the level below, the corresponding *resource manager* switches to the req^{ew} or to the req^{cr} state[3] and forwards the request to the *lock manager* of the same *peer*. The latter becomes **Requesting**. The *lock manager* goes back into the **Idle** state upon completing the request, see Section 3.2. Thereafter, the *lock manager* expects the token from its **Predecessor**. In the mean time, it is still listening to requests from its children. It may switched to the **Busy** or **Blocked** states.

The application process itself also may continue some computations regardless of whether the resource has already been acquired or not.

Now two cases may occur:

(a) At the application level, the *peer* calls the `dho_test` function to know if the *locking* has already been granted. The corresponding *resource manager* asks the *lock manager* if it has already got the token. In that case, the *resource manager* assigns the $grant^{ew|cr}$ state to the *handle*. In the sequel, we will denote the time to achieve this state by $T_{WaitGrant}$.

(b) Otherwise, the *peer* calls the `dho_ew_acquire|dho_cr_acquire` function. It is then put into the *Blocked* state until the data are mapped into its address space. This is done by the *lock manager* that informs its corresponding *resource manager*, ④, which realizes the *mapping*, ②. Likewise, the *resource manager* updates the *handle* to the $blocked^{ew|cr}$ value. The time that the *peer* waits until that is denoted by $T_{Wblocked}$.

2. After the **Predecessor** has released the resource, it forwards the token to the *lock manager* (which is its **Next**). Once the token is acquired, the *lock manager* immediately informs the *resource manager* that updates the *handle*'s state. It will then enter the $grant^{ew|cr}$ state.

3. At that point, the *resource manager* fetches the data (within a time T_{fetch}) from its **Predecessor** and becomes $fetch^{ew|cr}$. It then *maps* the resource into the address space of the *handle*.

4. Once the *mapping* is done, the *resource manager* and the *peer* become the states $locked^{ew|cr}$ and *Locked*, respectively.

5. *Unlock* is an intermediate state assigned to the *resource manager* during which the *peer* has already released the resource (through the call of the `dho_ew_release|dho_cr_release` function), although the corresponding *lock manager* still holds the token and is ready to forward it to a possible **Next**. After that, the *handle* will be *valid* again.

With this approach, the two managers simultaneously may accomplish different tasks. For example, the combined state **Busy**|$locked^{ew}$ (level 2 of Fig. 8) of the *peer* on the left shows that the same *peer* is handling another request while the application code is inside a **critical section**. The second state $locked^{ew}$ is related to the *resource manager*, see Section 5.2.

---

[3]These symbols define the type of request: **ew** refers to write exclusive request, while **cr** denotes a concurrent shared read request.

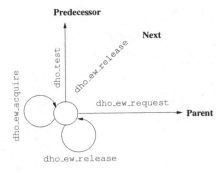

FIG. 9

peers involved in *Data Handover* functions.

On the right side, the combined state **Idle**|*fetch*^{cr} means that the corresponding *peer* is currently forwarding the resource to another *peer*. The **Idle** state assigned to the *lock manager* of that *peer* denotes that it has finished sending request.

The *read manager* interacts locally with the *lock manager* ⑥. Fig. 9 shows that the *peer* deals with three separate *peers* when it claims the resource, achieves the *locking/mapping* or grants access.

5.2 MODELING OF DHO LIFE CYCLE

For a given *peer*, a resource request triggers events at the *resource manager* and for the *lock manager*; it crosses various states from request insertion until resource release, forming a typical **DHO** life cycle. Fig. 10 shows the different states the *resource manager* can take during the **DHO** cycle. The scheme is composed of two nearly symmetric sub-cycles, the shared cycle on the left and the exclusive one on the right. Table 1 presents the hierarchical order of possible states caused by successive events triggered from the three levels.

Note that the **DHO** cycle may or may not go through a *blocked* phase. For example, in

$$\{req^{cr} \rightarrow grant^{cr} \rightarrow fetch^{cr} \rightarrow locked^{cr} \rightarrow valid\}$$

the shared access to the **critical resource** is acquired immediately just after the call of the `dho_cr_acquire` function. Whereas, the following is exclusive with a *blocked* phase.

$$\{req^{ew} \rightarrow blocked^{ew} \rightarrow fetch^{ew} \rightarrow lock^{ew} \rightarrow valid\}$$

DHO `request` and `test` functions are *non-blocking*. Thereby, the **DHO** API allows an application to continue execution regardless of the state of inserted requests. The application process will block eventually once it calls `acquire`.

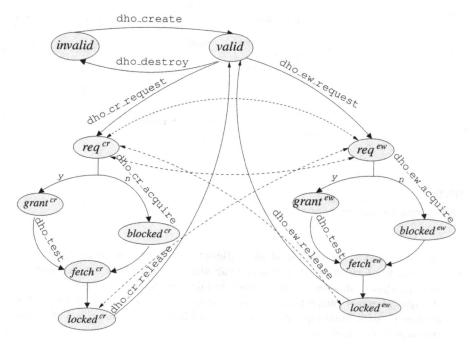

FIG. 10

Modeling: life cycle of requests-states of the *resource manager*.

5.3 OBSERVED DELAYS

In addition to the theoretical discussion, we aim to assess realistic delays that may be caused by the interaction between *peers*. The user asks for the control of a data resource and waits for a response. Aside from delays that are caused by the system, there are also some that are controlled by the user: the **DHO** cycle comprises two application dependent delays, namely T_{locked}, the application time spent inside the **critical section**, and $T_{Wblocked}$, the time that the application spends waiting before switching to the *blocked* state, ie, the call to one of the *acquire* functions.

We will vary them in our experiments to see the dependency of two other delays: T_{Wait}, the waiting time of request, ie, the time the application is blocked inside a call to an `acquire` function, and T_{DHO}, the entire cycle time of a given request.

$$T_{Wait} = T_{WaitGrant} \mid T_{Wblocked} + T_{grant} \mid T_{blocked} + T_{fetch} \qquad (1)$$

$$T_{DHO} = T_{WaitGrant} \mid T_{Wblocked} + T_{grant} \mid T_{blocked} + T_{fetch} + T_{locked} \qquad (2)$$

Table 1 List of Combined States

p	Idle		Req			Blocked	Locked
rm	valid	Unlock	req^{ew}	$grant^{ew}$	$fetch^{ew}$	$blocked^{ew}$	$locked^{ew}$
lm	blocked / Busy	blocked / Busy	Requesting / Busy	blocked / Busy	blocked / Busy	blocked / Busy	blocked / Busy

For readability, the Idle state of the lock manager is not represented.

p, peer; rm, resource manager; lm, lock manager.

5.4 CONNECTION AND DISCONNECTION AT APPLICATION LEVEL

We have shown that disconnecting from the system is subject to certain rules that are governed by the *lock manager*. However, the initiating event is explicitly triggered on the application level. It just needs to issue function calls to login or log-off the resource.

The `dho_destroy` function unlinks the **critical resource** from the *handle*. It represents the voluntary departure of the hosting *peer* and can be issued regardless of the currently assigned state. All functions that follow after `dho_destroy` are ignored since the *handle* is *invalid*.

Once the *resource manager* receives a departure request from the corresponding *peer*, it informs the corresponding *lock manager*. The *lock manager* carries out the departure as described for our extended algorithms (Section 3.2). First, the *lock manager* switches to **Exiting**. Then, it forwards the token to its **Next** or to one of its neighbors, while the corresponding *resource manager* invites that neighbor to map the data. At the end of the disconnection process the *resource manager* destroys the *handle* by assigning an *invalid* state. Finally, the *peer* enters the *Exit* state for the resource. All these stages may include the tree balancing (3.4)

5.5 DEVIATION FROM THE NORMAL DHO CYCLE

In addition to the above, **DHO** foresees all possible combinations of calls to its interfaces and acts accordingly: as a general policy, an application may choose not to respect the logical order of the calls to **DHO** functions as presented above without jeopardizing the consistency of the locks. If a **DHO** cycle is broken or canceled, the concerned *peer* will just loose its acquired FIFO position in the queue of requests.

Listing 1 shows an execution that deviates from the preferred order of execution. The effect of the `dho_ew_request`, eg, is that the *resource manager* is returned to the state of *valid* and that all priorities and a read-lock that eventually already had been acquired are lost. After that, the request is appended to the FIFO and has to wait for its term to regain the front position of the FIFO.

```
 1  char const* A;           // the name of the data resource
 2  dho_t *h;                // the handle
 3  double T_WBlocked;       // application dependent delays
 4  double T_Lock;
 5  dho_create(&h, &A);      // creating the handle, linking to A
 6      dho_cr_request(h);   // requesting a shared access
 7      sleep(T_WBlocked);   // sleeping or doing other
 8                           // computations ...
 9      dho_ew_request(h);   // aborting the previous request and
10                           // inserting a new exclusive request
11      request dho_test(h); // testing if the access has being
12                           // granted ...
```

```
13    dho_cr_release(h);        // ignored ...
14    dho_cr_acquire(&h);       // ignored ...
15    sleep(T_Lock);
16    dho_cr_release(h);        // ignored
17 dho_destroy(&h, &A);         // destroying the handle
```

LISTING 1

An example of an out of order DHO cycle

The dotted lines in Fig. 10 illustrate such behavior.

Also, all **DHO** functions that follow the call of `dho_destroy` will be ignored since the **critical resource** is not linked. The `dho_create` function must be called before any other **DHO** function can take effect, it makes the *handle valid*, again. The *peer* is connected to a given **Parent** according to the policy of our algorithms and according to the adopted balanced strategy (Section 3.5). From that point onward, the *resource manager* will be able to handle requests submitted by the user, whilst the *lock manager* will be ready to deal with those coming from **children** in the **Parent** tree.

6 EXPERIMENTAL RESULTS

This section encompasses some results for different combinations of requests. We used the *Grid Reality and Simulation environment* (GRAS), see Quinson (2006). GRAS is a socket-based API provided by the SimGrid toolkit, see Casanova et al. (2008) that allows the implementation of distributed programs. With GRAS, we can either simulate executions or deploy them on real platforms without even modifying or recompiling the code. We just have to re-link the program with the corresponding version of the support library. Under simulation mode, we exploited a description of a realistic platform, which is a subset of Grid'5000.[4] SimGrid provides XML tags for the definition of homogeneous clusters. Here is the description format of selected nodes belonging to two clusters used in our framework:

```
1 <?xml version='1.0'?>
2 <!DOCTYPE platform SYSTEM "http://simgrid.gforge.inria.fr/
     simgrid.dtd">
3 <platform version="3">
4    <cluster id="suno"
5      prefix="suno-" radical="0-25" suffix=".sophia.grid5000.fr"
6      power="1Gf" bw="125MBps" lat="50us"
7      bb_bw="2.25GBps" bb_lat="500us"/>
8    <cluster id="griffon"
9      prefix="griffon-" radical="0-25" suffix=".nancy.grid5000.
     fr"
```

---

[4]Grid'5000 is a large-scale and versatile testbed for experiment-driven research in all areas of computer science, with a focus on parallel and distributed computing including Cloud, HPC and Big Data.

```
10      power="1Gf"  bw="125MBps"  lat="50us"
11      bb_bw="2.25GBps"  bb_lat="500us"/>
12  </platform>
```

The above XML file reflects real physical features of the set of nodes that are interconnected through private links. Here, this selects 50 nodes as a whole, 25 in each cluster. We use such a platform description to launch benchmarks in simulation mode of GRAS before carrying them out directly on Grid'5000.

Two times, T_{Wblocked} and T_{Locked}, that are application dependent will be varied for our experiments. T_{Wblocked} is the time that the *peer* spends waiting until the call of dho_ew_acquire, while T_{Locked} is the *locking* time, that is the time the application spends inside the **critical section**.

T_{Idle} denotes the delay between two calls. It represents computational period of the application before inserting a new **DHO**. In addition to the **DHO** cycle time, we will analyze T_{Wait} and T_{Blocking} delays. T_{Wait} is the waiting time of a request, ie, the time between the request call and the return from fetching into the *locked* state.

T_{Blocking} is the time a *peer* is blocking before acquiring the resource, ie, the time between the call to acquire and the return from the fetching into state *locked*. They are respectively expressed by the following equalities, see Section 5.3 above for the different times:

$$T_{\text{Wait}} = T_{\text{WaitGrant}} \mid T_{\text{Wblocked}} + T_{\text{grant}} \mid T_{\text{blocked}} + T_{\text{fetch}} \tag{3}$$

$$T_{\text{Blocking}} = T_{\text{blocked}} + T_{\text{fetch}} \tag{4}$$

$$T_{\text{Dho}} = T_{\text{Idle}} + T_{\text{Wait}} + T_{\text{Locked}} \tag{5}$$

We assume that T_{Idle} is zero, so the *peers* insert a new request as soon as the previous cycle is achieved. *peers* carry out 100 cycles. Results refer to average values.

6.1 DHO CYCLE EVALUATION WITH ASYNCHRONOUS LOCKS

This series of experiments concerns a setting that uses *non-blocking* exclusive locks and that distinguishes a resource request and resource acquisition. Applications, as outlined above, with an expected T_{Wblocked} time of 0 s are strongly dependent on the resource, whilst those with a significant value of T_{Wblocked} may make progress, while acquiring the resource asynchronously.

Here, after an application dependent time T_{Wblocked}, the dho_test function returns to the state of the *handle*. If $grant^{ew}$ then dho_ew_acquire just acts as an intermediate phase for the $fetch^{ew}$ state before switching to that of $locked^{ew}$ (Listing 2).

```
1  char const* A;
2  int i;
3  dho_t h;
4  double DELAY, T_WBlocked, T_Lock;
5  ...
```

```
 6| dho_create(&h, A);      // link to the critical resource named by
   |    "A"
 7|                         // and create the handle
 8| do {
 9|    dho_ew_request(&h);  // request the data for writing
10|    sleep(T_WBlocked);   // wait a while or do some computations
11|    dho_test(&h);        // check if the lock has been granted
12|    dho_cr_acquire(&h);  // block and map the data in local memory
13|    ...
14|    sleep(T_Lock);       // keep the lock a while, for some
   |       modifications
15|    dho_cr_release(&h);  // release the lock
16| } while (i <100)
17| ...
18| dho_destroy(&h);        // destroy the handle
```

LISTING 2

Benchmark of exclusive locks

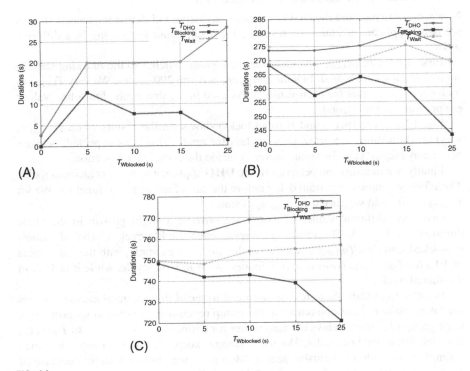

FIG. 11

Average duration of $\overline{T_{DHO}}$, $\overline{T_{Wait}}$ and $\overline{T_{Blocked}}$ by varying $T_{Wblocked}$.. (A) 0 s in **critical section**. (B) 5 s in **critical section**. (C) 15 s in **critical section**.

This series of benchmark is conducted with 50 *peers*. The data resource size is fixed to $50MiB$. Fig. 11 shows the observed delays (T_{DHO}, T_{Wait} and $T_{Blocking}$) with a set of experiences that fixes T_{locked} and vary $T_{Wblocked}$. With $T_{locked} = 0$ and $T_{Wblocked} = 0$ (Fig. 11A) *peers* then request the resource once the mapping is completed. In this case, it is clear that T_{DHO} corresponds to T_{Wait}, so the lines are superimposed.

Also, we note that T_{Wait} slightly increases in cases of non-zero values of $T_{Wblocked}$ (Fig. 11B and C), but this is not due to an extra latency for receiving the token. In fact, the *resource manager* assigns the *granted*[ew] state to the *handle* right after being informed by the *lock manager* that the token has been acquired. The growth of T_{Wait} rather reflects that the grant is taken a bit later (T_{grant}) because of the increased application delay $T_{Wblocked}$.

From Fig. 11B and C, we can conclude that if 5 s is taken for $T_{Wblocked}$, a good overlapping is provided for the application, specially between computation and data transferring.

6.2 SHARED AND EXCLUSIVE REQUESTS

Now we aim to measure the **DHO** cycle with exclusive and shared requests, so in this scenario, applications claim the resource for reading and for writing in a different order.

First, we fix $T_{Wblocked} = 0$ such that the handle switches to the *blocking* state as soon as requests are issued. In total, the *peers* perform 200 cycles. We vary T_{locked} in both cycles, such that for each value that is used in the first cycle, four other values are provided in the second.

Fig. 12A (write locks) and B (read locks) shows similar results when T_{locked} is varying. Both times are growing, a bit less for reads. This is as expected, because here many requests can be simultaneously inside the same critical section.

Finally, we measure the behavior of the **DHO** approach with asynchronous locks. Therefore, we impose a certain delay before the call of the `acquire` function. We set T_{locked} to 10 s and we vary the $T_{Wblocked}$ value.

Given the different values of T_{DHO}, we observe a slight growth in the cycle duration, see Fig. 13. The values are largest when the life cycle of shared request is blocked, and thus $T_{Wblocked}$ adds up to the time. For example, with the same value of 10 s for $T_{Wblocked}$, T_{DHO} is approximately $423s$ in write cycle, while it is $457s$ in the shared mode.

In order to explain these results, we need to recall that the *read manager* keeps the token while at least one reader in the group remains in the critical section. So, a large group of readers delays the next writer for a time that corresponds to $T_{Wblocked}$ from the first to the last reader. The *read manager* keeps the token for more time than a simple *peer* with an exclusive access. Moreover, we observe a slight decrease of T_{DHO} with a delay of $5s$ ($T_{Wblocked}$) before the call `dho_ew_acquire` function. Thus, a slight delay at application level provides a good overlap between computation and resource control.

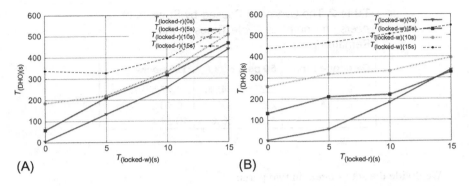

(A)   (B)

FIG. 12

Average durations for $\overline{T_{DHO}}$. For each value of T_{locked} in the first cycle, several other values are taken for the second cycle. The resource size is 50 MiB. (A) Variation of T_{locked} in write cycles. (B) Variation of T_{locked} in read cycles.

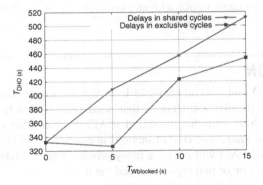

FIG. 13

Impact of the $T_{Wblocked}$ delay, in both cycles. T_{locked} is set to 10 s.

6.3 DHO CYCLE EVALUATION WITH MOBILITY OF PEERS

The last series of benchmarks concerns the mobility of *peers*. We aim to measure the overhead that is produced by removing *peers* from the remaining system. Once `dho_destroy` is issued, the *resource manager* destroys the *handle* that becomes *invalid* and then, all following **DHO** functions are ignored. Thus, the *lock manager* performs the **Exit strategy** of the **ELMP** algorithm.

Table 2 The Overhead Caused by Subsets of *peers* on Complete Cycle Times of the Remaining *peers*

Disconnection	50 *peers*	120 *peers*
25%	2.27 s 0.842%	4.27 s 0.725%
33%	2.65 s 0.98%	6.46 s 1.05%
50%	4.29 s 1.56%	10.34 s 1.68%

We divide the set of *peers* in two parts:

- *peers* in the first subset perform a complete cycle.
- In the second one, the *peers* interrupt their cycle by calling the `dho_destroy` function.

We only note the duration of uninterrupted DHO cycles for the first class, for the case that 25%, 33%, and 50% belong to the second class, respectively.

The overhead is approximately the same for both sizes (Table 2) and the additional latencies introduced by the departure of *peers* are negligible. However, we would expect an increase of these values with an even higher mobility frequency of *peers*.

7 DISCUSSION

The set of the **DHO** routines and the multi-level architecture provided in this chapter targets distributed parallel applications that need remote data resources for their computations. We have seen that through that API the user takes control of remote data, simply by inserting some **DHO** functions in existing code. Developers who are familiar with the MPI API will not have many problems to use **DHO** routines: **DHO** functions take only one or two arguments and the user dose not have to worry about technical details to access remote data resources.

Furthermore, access to data resources is requested by non-blocking functions. A set of *managers* handles asynchronous operations to allow the applications to continue doing computations after such a request has been registered. All negotiations for the data resource are transparently handled in the background during such a *non-blocking* phase, and the application can continue independently of the request. The user may also check through the `test` function whether access to the data has been granted in such a *non-blocking* section of the code. All of this allows computations to overlap with the internal processing of requests, which provides good performance for the total execution time.

Once the application process decides that it definitively needs the data resource it may acquire it by issuing a blocking function call. On return from that, the process has been granted the requested lock (exclusive-write or concurrent-read) and the data are mapped into its address space. There it is accessible through a `void*` or `void const*` pointer as long as the lock is held.

From a more technical point of view, our distributed system involves various processes that operate concurrently such that bottlenecks are avoided. The involved processes are mainly those from the same *peer* and from its "neighbors," that is other processes with which the *peer* interacted previously. For example, the mapping phase involves *resource managers* related to the *peer* and its **Predecessor**, that is the process that held the data resource previously and that is now transferring it to the *peer*. In the meantime, associated *lock managers* continue to deal with the arrival of new requests.

If the data resource is large, the bottleneck of a **DHO** system is necessarily the *fetch*^{ew} operation that transfers the data from one *peer* to the other. Obviously, such a phase is constrained by the overall bandwidth that is available to the application. The asynchronous operation of **DHO** warrants that this can remain the only constraint: latency constraints can be circumvented by overlapping data resource requests with computation.

8 CONCLUSION

In this chapter, we have presented a shared data system with two desirable properties from CAP: consistency and high availability. It also takes the need for transparency into account.

The proposed approach eases the development of resource-intensive applications that evolve in large-scale environments. The proposed design model is centered around a locking mechanism and data encapsulation. This is achieved by restricting the access to data through a *handle*, and by forcing data consistency across critical sections.

We proposed mutual exclusion algorithms based on a hierarchical tree structure. They are used to guarantee the consistency of accesses. They have been proven theoretically and experimentally to be scalable and flexible. *Safety* and *Liveness* properties of both algorithms have been demonstrated. We also studied two methods for keeping the tree structure balanced. This is necessary to keep the overall message complexity low, after a set of conversions of the tree structure have been triggered.

In a series of experiments we measured waiting times and the life time of requests. The experiments have shown that our system guarantees good performance.

We think that in the future a number of open issues should be explored. For example, it will be interesting to extend the capabilities of the system. According to Brewer (2012), consistency and availability should not necessarily be sacrificed when new partitions exist in the network. We may thus consider tolerating some partitions with a certain degree of consistency and/or of availability.

In addition, it would be interesting to extend **ELMP** to manage exclusive and inclusive access to *byte ranges* as, eg, for POSIX file locks. We will investigate the locking of ranges of the resource by different handles.

ACRONYMS

DHO	Data Handover
ELMP	Exclusive Locks with Mobile Processes
GRAS	Grid Reality and Simulation
p2p	*peer-to-peer*
RW-LMP	Read-Write Locks with Mobile Processes

GLOSSARY

DHO The Data Handover proposed interface is based on the abstract concept of the data and the local memory. By inserting the DHO function in the application code, the user claims a remote resource and then when available, maps that resource in local memory.

ELMP The Exclusive Locks with Mobile Processes algorithm extends the capabilities of the Naimi-Trehel algorithm with the scalability property.

GRAS The Grid Reality and Simulation API is a Socket-based library that provides a complete API to implement distributed applications on top of heterogeneous plateforms, either in simulation mode or in realistic environment.

Lock manager The lock manager negotiates remotely the lock with other managers according ELMP and RW-LMP algorithms. It interacts locally with the resource manager.

Read manager It handles the entry and the exit from the critical section by successive read processes. It is present in the RW-LMP algorithm solely.

Resource manager It forwards user's requests to the lock manager, achieves the mapping of the resource in local memory as soon as the lock is granted, and allows uploading the resource to a possible Next.

RW-LMP The Read Write Locks with Mobile Processes algorithm. This algorithm makes a second extension to the ELMP algorithm, by allowing both read and write requests to share the queuing (**Predecessor, Next**) list.

REFERENCES

Andersson, A., 1999. General balanced trees. J. Algorithms 30 (1), 1–18. http://dx.doi.org/10.1006/jagm.1998.0967.

Brewer, E., 2012. CAP twelve years later: how the "rules" have changed. Computer 45 (2), 23–29. ISSN 0018-9162. http://dx.doi.org/10.1109/MC.2012.37.

Brewer, E.A., 2000. Towards robust distributed systems (abstract). In: Proceedings of the Nineteenth Annual ACM Symposium on Principles of Distributed Computing, PODC '00. ACM, New York, NY, USA, pp. 7. http://dx.doi.org/10.1145/343477.343502.

Casanova, H., Legrand, A., Quinson, M., 2008. SimGrid: a generic framework for large-scale distributed experiments. In: 10th IEEE International Conference on Computer Modeling and Simulation—EUROSIM/UKSIM 2008. IEEE, Cambridge, UK, http://hal.inria.fr/inria-00260697/en/.

Courtois, P.J., Heymans, F., Parnas, D.L., 1971, October. Concurrent control with readers and writers. Commun. ACM 14 (10), 667–668. ISSN 0001-0782. http://dx.doi.org/10.1145/362759.362813.

Dijkstra, E.W., 1965. Solution of a problem in concurrent programming control. Commun. ACM 8 (9), 569. http://dx.doi.org/10.1145/365559.365617.

Fox, A., Brewer, E.A., 1999. Harvest, yield, and scalable tolerant systems. In: IN HOTOS-VII. Society Press, Los Alamitos, CA.

Galperin, I., Rivest, R.L., 1993. Scapegoat trees. In: Proceedings of the Fourth Annual ACM-SIAM Symposium on Discrete Algorithms, SODA '93. Society for Industrial and Applied Mathematics, Philadelphia, PA, USA, pp. 165–174, http://dl.acm.org/citation.cfm?id=313559.313676.

Gilbert, S., Lynch, N., 2002, June. Brewer's conjecture and the feasibility of consistent, available, partition-tolerant web services. SIGACT News 33 (2), 51–59. ISSN 0163-5700. http://dx.doi.org/10.1145/564585.564601.

Gustedt, J., 2006, Data handover: reconciling message passing and shared memory. In: Fiadeiro, J.L., Montanari, U., Wirsing, M. (Eds.), Foundations of Global Computing, Dagstuhl Seminar Proceedings, 05081, Dagstuhl, Germany, http://drops.dagstuhl.de/opus/volltexte/2006/297.

Hernane, S.L., Gustedt, J., Benyettou, M., 2011. Modeling and experimental validation of the data handover API. In: Riekki, J., Ylianttila, M., Guo, M. (Eds.), GPC, Lecture Notes in Computer Science, vol. 6646, pp. 117–126. Springer, Berlin.

Hernane, S.L., Gustedt, J., Benyettou, M., 2012. A dynamic distributed algorithm for read write locks. In: PDP, pp. 180–184.

Jagadish, H.V., Ooi, B.C., Vu, Q.H., 2005. Baton: a balanced tree structure for peer-to-peer networks. In: VLDB, pp. 661–672.

Jagadish, H.V., Ooi, B.C., Tan, K.L., Vu, Q.H., Zhang, R., 2006. Speeding up search in peer-to-peer networks with a multi-way tree structure. In: Proceedings of the 2006 ACM SIGMOD International Conference on Management of Data, SIGMOD '06. ACM, New York, NY, USA, pp. 1–12. http://dx.doi.org/10.1145/1142473.1142475.

Lamport, L., 1978, July. Ti clocks, and the ordering of events in a distributed system. Commun. ACM 21, 558–565. ISSN 0001-0782.

Lejeune, J., Arantes, L., Sopena, J., Sens, P., 2013. A prioritized distributed mutual exclusion algorithm balancing priority inversions and response time. In: 42nd International Conference on Parallel Processing, ICPP 2013, Lyon, France, October 1–4, 2013, IEEE Computer Society, Washington, DC, USA, pp. 290–299. http://dx.doi.org/10.1109/ICPP.2013.38.

Maekawa, M., 1985, May. An algorithm for mutual exclusion in decentralized systems. ACM Trans. Comput. Syst. 3, 145–159. ISSN 0734-2071.

mpi-2, 2016. Mpi-2: extensions to the message-passing interface. http://www.mpi-forum.org/docs/mpi-20-html/mpi2-report.html.

Naimi, M., Tréhel, M., 1988. How to detect a failure and regenerate the token in the $\log(N)$ distributed algorithm for mutual exclusion. In: Proceedings of the 2nd International Workshop on Distributed Algorithms. Springer-Verlag, London, UK, pp. 155–166.

Naimi, M., Tréhel, M., Arnold, A., 1996, April. A $\log(N)$ distributed mutual exclusion algorithm based on path reversal. J. Parallel Distrib. Comput. 34, 1–13. ISSN 0743-7315.

Quinson, M., 2006. GRAS: A Research and Development Framework for Grid Services. Rapport de recherche RR-5789. INRIA. http://hal.inria.fr/inria-00070232.

Quinson, M., Vernier, F., 2009. Byte-range asynchronous locking in distributed settings. In: 17th Euromicro International Conference on Parallel, Distributed and network-based Processing—PDP 2009, Weimar, Germany, http://hal.inria.fr/inria-00338189/en/.

Raymond, K., 1989. A tree-based algorithm for distributed mutual exclusion. ACM Trans. Comput. Syst. 7, 61–77.

Ricart, G., Agrawala, A.K., 1981, January. An optimal algorithm for mutual exclusion in computer networks. Commun. ACM 24, 9–17. ISSN 0001-0782.

Satyanarayanan, M., 2001. Pervasive computing: vision and challenges. IEEE Personal Commun. 8 (4), 10–17. http://dx.doi.org/10.1109/98.943998.

Sopena, J., Arantes, L.B., Bertier, M., Sens, P., 2005. A fault-tolerant token-based mutual exclusion algorithm using a dynamic tree. In: Euro-Par'05, pp. 654–663.

Wagner, C., Mueller, F., 2000. Token-based read/write-locks for distributed mutual exclusion. In: Proceedings from the 6th International Euro-Par Conference on Parallel Processing, Euro-Par '00. Springer-Verlag, London, UK, pp. 1185–1195.

Xhafa, F., Potlog, A.D., Spaho, E., Pop, F., Cristea, V., Barolli, L., 2015, March. Evaluation of intra-group optimistic data replication in p2p groupware systems. Concurr. Comput.: Pract. Exper. 27 (4), 870–881. ISSN 1532-0626. http://dx.doi.org/10.1002/cpe.2836.

Converged information-centric spaces based on wireless data hubs

7

M. Zhanikeev

Kyushu Institute of Technology, Iizuka, Fukuoka Prefecture, Japan

1 INTRODUCTION

Wireless standards have recently developed from 802.11g (IEEE Standard, 2003) to 802.11n (IEEE Standard, 2009) which offers higher throughput and can use multiple antennas (multiple-input multiple output, MIMO), making it possible to achieve rates up to 300 Mbps. The development continues with the 802.11ac standard with further improvements gradually entering practice. More details on the universe of wireless standards can be found in an excellent survey in Hiertz et al. (2010).

Dense wireless spaces is a separate topic in recent literature (Aerohive, 2013) and forms part of the overall guidelines for WLAN deployment (Bing, 2008) both in the form of high-density client devices and dense packing of multiple access points (APs). For example, the study in Yang and Rosdahl (2002) measured interferences in spaces with up to 50 APs and showed how interference depends on bulk size, among several other parameters. The topic of congestion is covered at length further on this chapter.

Wireless interference is also considered by research on *wireless beacons* (Chandra et al., 2007). The main advantage of beacons is that they can be used without an association between clients and APs, which adds more flexibility to multi-AP spaces. When frame rate of beacons is increased and a hack is used to allow data to be streamed continuously over multiple frames, interference also becomes a major problem. Beacons are also the obvious solution to the congestion problem as they naturally reduce interference—one beacon can broadcast to many devices where traditional networking would require individual devices to exchange traffic between each other in many pairwise unicast combinations.

All in all, wireless spaces are often congested, where *congestion* can take various practical forms, like, for example, physical signal interference, being unable to grab a channel or a time slot, etc. In this context, *opportunistic* and *cognitive* wireless networking are very popular topics in research. *Opportunistic* methods normally help

Pervasive Computing. http://dx.doi.org/10.1016/B978-0-12-803663-1.00007-3

devices to squeeze more bandwidth (channels, time slots) than would be considered *nominal*. *Cognitive* methods help in the discovery and creation of such opportunities on the fly. This chapter does not have room for an extended discussion on these two research topics, but will revisit them several times when discussing the general topic of *congestion*.

Note that these two problems are currently popular in *vehicular networks* (Akyildiz et al., 2008; Cheng et al., 2014), where cars *cognitively exploit opportunities* as they pass roadside infrastructures. This scenario is very similar to what this chapter will formulate for *wireless data hubs* (WDHs), which are, in a way, objects of infrastructure within a given wireless space—this chapter will mostly discuss a university campus but any finite space will do. However, the similarity ends there, while the technology discussed in this chapter defines the concept of virtual wireless networking and implements elements of *mobile clouds* (Fernando et al., 2013) such as *traffic offload*.

This chapter discusses the following kind of *converged infocentric space*. First, the wireless network is considered to be converged where users can use a mixture of *remote versus local* connectivities, changing the mixture on the fly. The wireless technologies in the mixture are *3G/LTE*, common/traditional *WiFi*, and *Peer-to-Peer (P2P) WiFi*. The term *WiFi* is preferred to the official *Wi-Fi* simply because the former is a much earlier type. The convergence of these technologies is implemented via the concept of *network virtualization*, specifically the *Group Connect* technology recently introduced in Zhanikeev (2013b). Note that the term *P2P* here does not refer to the well-known *P2P wireless networks* but rather to the networking stack inside wireless devices used for communication, initially in pairs of devices but ultimately in groups. For comparison between the concept of Group Connect discussed in this chapter and P2P wireless networking, see the early concept in Zhanikeev (2013b).

Information is at the center of the discussed wireless space and is hosted on the WDHs. As was mentioned above, the hubs run autonomously and have no wired or wireless connectivity, other than the short-term P2P WiFi connections to passing by wireless devices—students' smartphones in a university campus. These short sessions can therefore be considered as connections of the hub to the Internet—in fact, the virtualization formulation in this chapter allows for this way of viewing delegated connectivity. Autonomy is a major feature because such a box requires very little in way of installation and operational maintenance.

Another important side of the hub's operation is its *social sharing* feature. It is explained in the chapter that the P2P stack makes it possible to quickly reverse client-server roles in communicating pairs. In practice, this means that a user can download a file from the hub, and immediately *share* it with another user. To avoid confusion, all upload and download operations are viewed simply as *syncs*, where each sync is supposed to equalize content on both sides of the connection. Note that this feature takes root in the popular topic of *information dissemination* in social network analysis.

This chapter uses the following section split. Section 2 explains connectivity and congestion problems in existing wireless spaces and supports the argument for using commodity devices such as *wireless hard disks* (Western Digital Wireless HDD, n.d.) and TV dongles like Chromecast (Google Chromecast, n.d.). Section 3 resolves both problems via the Group Connect concept of wireless network virtualization as well as the *traffic offload* side effect of that core technology. Section 3 also has in-depth discussion of wireless stack found in commodity smartphones, specifically the traditional WiFi/3G/LTE stack versus the less-known P2P WiFi stack. Section 4 presents the core idea of the WDH, lists its objectives and operational parameters, and discusses its practical design and protocols. There is, in fact, already a prototype of WDH that runs on WiFi Direct and has been tested in a university campus. Section 5 models a university campus and analyzes performance of WDH compared to traditional and 4G+ technologies, where the two specific cases are *Group Connect versus 4G+* and *3G/LTE versus WDH with Group Connect*, with more details presented in said section. Section 6 summarizes the chapter.

2 CONNECTIVITY AND CONGESTION IN DENSE WIRELESS SPACES

Congestion problem is well recognized in wireless local access networks (WLANs) (Bing, 2008; Yang and Rosdahl, 2002). It is often referred to as *dense wireless networks* (Aerohive, 2013) hinting at the special treatment required for such networks to work efficiently. There is also research that studies practical dense wireless spaces, such as classrooms (Zhanikeev, 2013a).

Congestion is also recognized as a problem in 4G+ networks, where it is referred to as *interference problem*. It is not discussed in the mainstream literature on 4G and specifically the LTE-A standard (Zhang and Zhou, 2013; Dahlman et al., 2014), but can be found in some literature on the topic (Glisic, 2009).

However, the *connectivity problem* is completely ignored in the mainstream literature on WLANs, 4G+, and other modern wireless spaces, and has been raised for the first time in Zhanikeev (2016). This section discusses both the *congestion* and *connectivity* problems, as well as the connection between the two. A special method referred to as *time slot division* is presented at the end of this section as a solution to congestion in WLANs.

2.1 COMMON CONNECTIVITY PROBLEM

The connectivity problem is best presented via examples found in existing commodity devices. Two kinds of popular devices have this problem: *wireless hard disks* (Western Digital Wireless HDD, n.d.) and the various wireless TV dongles like *Chromecast* (Google Chromecast, n.d.). Note that the internals of the connectivity problem are discussed in the next section while this one discusses only the situations in which this problem reveals itself.

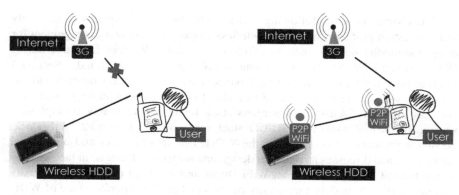

FIG. 1

A common connectivity problem that exists in commodity wireless devices and its simple solution places in the center of this chapter.

Fig. 1 explains the problem by comparing the current operation mode of the above devices to the new design offered as part of the solution in this chapter.

Let us first review what happens on the left side of the figure. First, the user starts up the device (wireless HDD or TV dongle) and waits for it to load. The user would then find and connect to the AP advertised by the device, thus, forming a direct network between the user's smartphone, for example, and the device. At this point, the Internet connection (3G or otherwise) would be lost. This, in a nutshell, is the *connectivity problem.*

Now, let us see how the problem can be resolved, using the method shown on the right side of Fig. 1. The user would *pair* with the device using a P2P WiFi technology—WiFi Direct (Zhanikeev, 2013b), Bluetooth, and NFC are the currently popular options. Once paired, the smartphone application can freely connect and exchange data with the device in the background. Connectivity problem here does not exist because the user's device can retain its current Internet connection. A longer discussion of this basic method is available in Zhanikeev (2013b).

Note that Chromecast and other popular commodity devices have recently come up with a partial solution to this problem. Further in this section, it will be shown that these solutions resolve the connectivity problem but create the congestion problem. This is the simple connection between the two problems.

2.2 EXAMPLE DEVICES AND OPERATION MODES

Having understood the basic connectivity problem, it is now helpful to expand the scope of the discussion and review several operation modes for commodity devices, namely the wireless HDD and TV dongles introduced above. Repeating an earlier statement, this section focuses on describing the problems while the next section will offer technical details on the internals of all the mentioned technologies. For example,

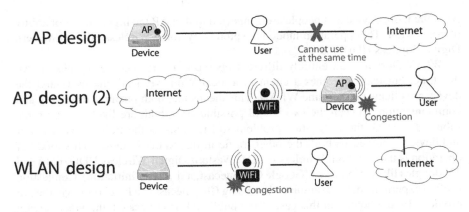

FIG. 2

Connectivity or congestion problems in the three popular designs found in commodity devices.

while this section talks about conventional versus P2P WiFi operation modes, the next section will discuss the technology hidden inside conventional versus P2P WiFi stacks in commodity devices.

Fig. 2 is basically a taxonomy for the various operation modes of wireless commodity devices. The rest of this section discusses each mode (referred to as design) separately.

AP Design is the default mode of both Wireless HDD and TV dongle devices introduced above. The device creates and expects users to use their own local AP, which, assuming that dual parallel connectivity is impossible, and it is in today's technology (Zhanikeev, 2013b), creates the connectivity problem, as was discussed in the previous section. Under the circumstances, users normally try to quickly finish their sessions with the devices so that they can abort the connection and switch back to and AP that provides the Internet connection. Note that the switching between APs is mostly manual, except for the cases when a user would turn off the device and wait for his or her own smartphone to revert back to the Internet-enabled AP. Even in this case, some manual work is required.

AP Design (2) is the second kind of AP mode developed specifically with the connectivity problem in mind. The core enabling technology here is simple and is commonly also found in modern WiFi Routers, where WiFi APs can work as *repeaters* for other APs in a multi-AP environment (Aerohive, 2013). Similarly, as Fig. 2 shows, the device gets its own Internet connection from another AP and retranslates it to its own wireless users via its own AP. While this does resolve the connectivity problem, by doing so this also creates the congestion problem. The obvious congested place is the device itself, which now has the added function of forwarding traffic between its own WLAN and the outside world. Although it is not marked in the figure, the other place of potential congestion is the public WiFi

AP—the more device and people are connected to that AP the higher the probability of congestion. This operation mode is exploited by some Wireless HDDs (Western Digital Wireless HDD, n.d.).

WLAN Design is an entirely different operation mode. The device has no AP this time, but itself becomes a client to a local WiFi AP. Both the users and the device are clients on the same WLAN. This means that both resource discovery and communication between the two is still possible since both are likely on the same subnet. However, the congestion problem still remains as the traffic between user and device is mixed with all the other traffic in that WLAN subnet. This mode of operation is used by both Wireless HDDs (Western Digital Wireless HDD, n.d.) and TV dongles like Chromecast (Google Chromecast, n.d.) (after initiation). Congestion is often experienced, for example, when using Chromecast in a hotel room via the AP provided by the hotel—in this case if the public AP is congested, the video stream sent from the user's smartphone/computer to Chromecast can be affected.

The *P2P solution* is not in the list of operation modes in Fig. 2, but the details of its operation are presented in great detail further on this chapter. When P2P WiFi is used, MultiConnect can be used (Zhanikeev, 2013b)—the technology that simply allows for two different modes of connectivity run in parallel—to allow for parallel connections from the user's smartphone to the device and separately to the Internet. This mode of operation is closest to the AP Design at the top of Fig. 2 but assuming that both connections are active and can be used in parallel. Congestion in this case is unlikely since one device would connect to a single user (smartphone) and that user would not have to compete for Internet access with the device. Congested Internet connection would only affect the user-Internet leg of the route and would have no effect on the device-user leg.

2.3 LITERATURE ON WIRELESS INTERFERENCE AND CONGESTION

Having established the basic properties of connectivity and congestion problems, this section can now review the literature on these topics. Specifically, literature on 4G+ and WiFi congestion are discussed. The topic of channel coding, namely the TDMA versus OFDMA discussion (Maodong et al., 2013), is left out of scope after the clear and simple statement that while OFDMA clearly has higher capacity, neither technology truly solves the congestion problem.

In 4G+ networks, LTE-A is currently considered as the soon-to-become standard suite of technologies (Zhang and Zhou, 2013; Dahlman et al., 2014). In the core of LTE-A is the concept of *small cells* (SCs) which are also known as *microcells*, *femtocells*, *eNB* (evolved node B), and others (Lopez-Perez et al., 2009; Weitzen et al., 2013)—the name of the technology is not important. The important part of LTE-A is the separation of backbone and access networks, where base stations (BSs) are elevated to the status of backbone nodes while SCs form the newly created layered of small-range (25–50 m) access nodes. Clearly, this technology, if not solving the congestion problem completely, manages to reduce congestion in the wireless backbone while localizing congestion at access level.

Congestion can still happen in LTE-A networks. When there are too many users, the congestion can happen in the backbone, not in the form of increased interference but as an inability of lend users to grab a free channel to communicate through the backbone. At access level, congestion can happen easily as each SC is contemplated to be similar to a WiFi router in overall capability and is assumed to be able to host between 5 and 10 users per SC. Again, all the users above that quota are likely to be refused a channel or time slot.

These problems are recognized in recent literature on 4G+ networks. Various social techniques are proposed (Glisic, 2009) that attempt to create a *cognitive*, *cooperative*, and *opportunistic* 4G+ network. For example, devices can use only a small portion of edge infrastructure for device-to-device (D2D) and machine-to-machine (M2M) communications (Jin et al., 2013). Other technologies along these lines are self-organized networks and cooperative multipoint (CoMP) (Glisic, 2009).

Research on congestion in local networks, namely WLANs, is also active. Since congestion and interference in WLANs are easier to measure, there are many studies that measure multi-AP and multidevice wireless spaces (Bing, 2008; Aerohive, 2013), both referred to as *dense wireless spaces*. Very good measurements based on number of APs and packet size are presented in Yang and Rosdahl (2002)— results reveal the physical limit of about 15 devices per AP. Measurements in a wireless classroom (Zhanikeev, 2013a) and a more recent trace at CRAWDAD (n.d.) offer additional insight into how congestion forms in dense wireless spaces. The latter two studies and the trace are used further in this chapter for modeling and analysis.

Since the infocentric space discussed in this chapter occupies roughly the same scope as WLANs, it is interesting to list all the distinct solutions for the congestion problem offered by WLANs-specific research.

Basic opportunistic/cognitive method is actively used in environments with high mobility, where vehicular networks are an excellent example. In vehicular networks, opportunistic/cognitive methods are solidified in the 802.11p standard (IEEE Standard, 2010; Jiang and Delgrossi, 2008). There is also active research on the various methods that allow for better throughput in settings when cars pass by roadside infrastructures at relatively high speeds (Akyildiz et al., 2008; Cheng et al., 2014). Apart for the speed-specific components, the same basic approach for the general wireless and 4G (Glisic, 2009) can be applied.

AP-dense wireless spaces (Aerohive, 2013) is a solution which has its downside. The manual in Aerohive (2013) performs many measurement studies in dense wireless spaces and gives solid advice on how to lower congestion by adding more APs to the space, yet not increasing the congestion by overstuffing the space with too many APs. In between these extremes, however, there is a state in which the congestion is much lower than it would be for a single-AP space.

Beacons are often discussed in literature as a good solution to the congestion problem (Chandra et al., 2007). Beacons are commonly used today for *ads* (message pushing) or as *Proof of Location* (coupons, etc.). However, Chandra et al. (2007) shows that beacons can also be used for streaming data—the method referred to as Beacon Stuffing (Chandra et al., 2007). In WLANs, beacons can help reduce congestion by having only one party broadcast at any given point in time while all the other devices would be set to receiving mode. While this method is the simplest, it also has the highest effect in terms of reducing congestion.

Positioning technology is also known under the name of *virtual coordinates*. The point of the technology is that two devices can define their relative distance to each other wirelessly (Banerjee et al., 2010) or by sound (Peng et al., 2007). A good overview of these technologies can be found in Liu et al. (2007). This research relates to the *dense wireless* technology above in that it has been shown that distance to AP directly affects the rate of wireless transmission (Aerohive, 2013). This connection is exploited further in the next section by showing that shorter high-throughput connections are better than all devices competing for bandwidth in a congested wireless space.

2.4 TIME SLOT DIVISION METHOD

First, it is important to establish that *infocentric space* does not imply the presence of *realtime communications*. In fact, the space can function normally under the delay tolerant network (DTN) paradigm as long as reasonable constraints are placed (Vasilakos et al., 2011). The main features of the infocentric space discussed in this chapter refer to the *content* itself. This chapter assumes content stored in WDHs is static for the most part. *Syncs* are necessary to upload a new file and possibly update a version of an existing file. All the other components in the technology presented further in this section exist mostly in order to provide efficient syncs between users and hubs and users and other users.

Time slot division multiple access (TSDMA) is not a brand new technology but is a useful term to refer to the proposed technology. The simple example illustrating the benefit of TSDMA is as follows. Let us assume we have two users that need to communicate through the same AP to download a large file. With Internet providing the perfect speed (and therefore, not being a bottleneck), if we measured the time it took the two users to download the file *in parallel* versus *in sequence*, we would find out that *sequential* access supports higher throughput and helps achieve shorter download times. Now, note that this example is trivial and serves only as an illustration to the TSDMA method, while the numeric results below are based on controlled experiments.

This basic premise is discussed in terms of the CoMP technology in 4G+ networks (Glisic, 2009). The main culprit here is the overhead it takes to support two parallel wireless connections. Most of the overhead does not come from software but is mostly physical and is spent on negotiating time slots, collision avoidance with packets from the other connection, etc.

A larger experiment for the same technology was conducted in a wireless class (Zhanikeev, 2013a). The recent trace from the experiment is available at CRAWDAD (n.d.). The experiment was conducted separately for a small number

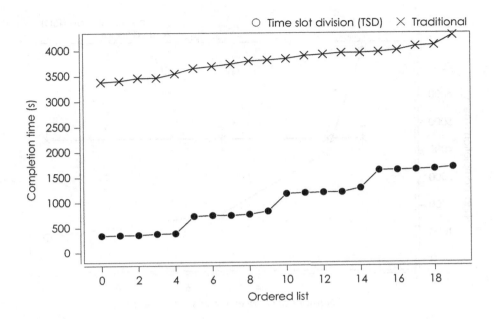

FIG. 3

Performance of TSDMA versus traditional wireless access.

of parallel connections versus the entire class of devices competing for the same AP. Apart from the number of devices, other parameters refer to the various qualities of traffic intensity such as *bulk size*, *gap* between requests, etc. As the outcome of the experiment, there is a trace that can be used to model a TSDMA environment.

Fig. 3 shows performance for downloading a single 100 Mb file by all 20 devices in a classroom. The comparison is between using the traditional all-parallel method versus careful scheduling of parallel batches using the TSDMA method. The specific case of TSD shown in the figure is the 5-per-batch mode—this is obvious from the ladder-like TSD curve. The outcome in the figure shows that it takes about 1500 s for the entire class to complete the downloads using the TSD method versus 4000+ s when all the devices compete in the wild. Note that both methods were supported by the trace which means that the results are near perfectly realistic. To obtain real results would require separate controlled experiments for all the possible batch sizes. As this research continues, such experiments will probably be conducted in the near future, but none are available at the time of writing.

Now, there are many reasons for the drastic gap in performance. As was explained in Zhanikeev (2013a), congestion (same as interference) in WLANs can cause several distinct problems:

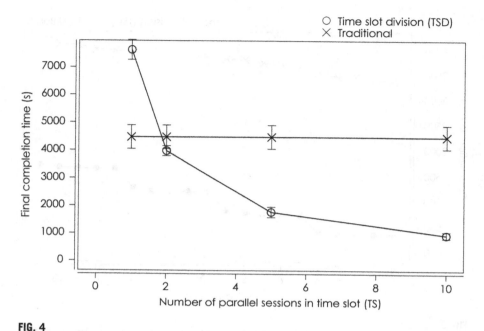

FIG. 4

Comparison of TSDMA with traditional wireless access for various batch sides.

- multiple retransmissions, prolonging the lifespan of a given connection;
- complete failure of connection, in which case HTTP requests would return empty results and would have to be resent—multiple repeats take up time and contribute to further delay.

In other words, *packet loss* in wireless domain has much higher effect than in wired networks.

Fig. 4 shows performance of the two above methods over a larger range of batch size. From 1 to 10-per-batch settings are tested, all the other conditions being the same. In fact, the traditional method has the same outcome in all cases because it has no dependence on batch size. From the figure we can see that the TSD method starts to outperform the traditional method at 2 parallel connections per batch. At 10-per-batch, total download time for the entire class can be brought down to 1000 s. Past these settings (larger batches), the interference starts to have its effect and it is likely that TSD will no longer be as efficient.

3 GROUP CONNECT AND WIRELESS TRAFFIC OFFLOAD

It is not common to view wireless devices in terms of their two separate wireless stacks. It is also rare to point out that the two stacks are capable of operating in parallel even if they use the same physical antenna (Zhanikeev, 2013b). However, these points are very important to a *converged wireless* space where two or more wireless technologies are expected to be used together seamlessly as part of the same wireless space. This section reviews the two wireless stacks—conventional versus P2P WiFi, and discusses the designs of networking mechanisms that puts the two stacks to work. As closely related topics, this section also introduces the basic idea of Group Connect (Zhanikeev, 2013b, 2016) and connects the technology to the concepts of *mobile clouds* (Fernando et al., 2013) and *traffic offload*.

3.1 TWO WIRELESS STACKS

Fig. 5 shows that the conventional (left) versus P2P (right) WiFi stacks presents in all commodity devices that support 3G/LTE/WiFi connectivity together with WiFi Direct (or Bluetooth, NFC, etc.). This section reviews the internal structure of these two stacks as well as the difference in their operation.

Conventional WiFi stack is built on top of MAC and IP layers. Here, the closely related problem is that of IP addresses, where IPv6 and its mobile version MIPv6 are expected to provide enough addresses for all devices in the world, but are yet to be deployed on a global scale.

On top of the IP layer, the conventional stack needs *WiFi AP* and *Web Server* to operate in the server mode, while the client mode can do without these two modules. The operation of this stack explains how Wireless HDDs (Western Digital Wireless HDD, n.d.) or Chromecast (Google Chromecast, n.d.) work on the inside—the

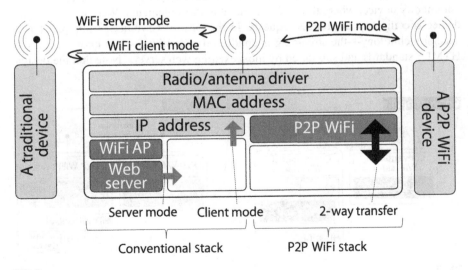

FIG. 5

The two wireless stacks available to all devices with P2P WiFi capability.

devices are implemented in the *server mode* while the client can follow a relatively simpler design. The conventional stack dictates the direction of connections—the client is always the one to initiate connections by sending web (HTTP) requests while the server is running continuously in the waiting mode, expecting connections from clients.

P2P WiFi stack on the right side of Fig. 5 is much simpler in design. There is only the *P2P WiFi* layer directly on top of MAC—this means that P2P WiFi communication does not require an IP address. There are many P2P WiFi platforms (layers) in practice, where WiFi Direct is commonly available on modern smartphones (Zhanikeev, 2014a, 2016).

The common process with the P2P WiFi stack is as follows. Both devices implement the same P2P WiFi stack (WiFi Direct, Bluetooth, MFC, etc.). The two devices first have to undergo the *pairing* process, which is a security precaution and normally requires entering and accepting the keys on both sides. Once paired, the two devices can initiate sessions with each other freely and in any direction.

Note that white/empty boxes in Fig. 5 stand for missing application logic. The missing spots are filled in by the respective applications further in this section.

3.2 CONVENTIONAL VERSUS P2P WiFi DESIGNS

Fig. 6 puts the two stacks into action. The two technologies powered by the two stacks are as follows.

Conventional is the same technology as was introduced above for Wireless HDDs (Western Digital Wireless HDD, n.d.) or Chromecast (Google Chromecast, n.d.). The technology assumes that a simpler client device connects to a more complex commodity device, where the latter should at least implement a Web Server and the device-specific app to process requests. In the case of Chromecast this part has a special technology—the streaming is conducted over *Web Sockets* known from the HTML5 standards and supported by most existing web servers. Note that the design

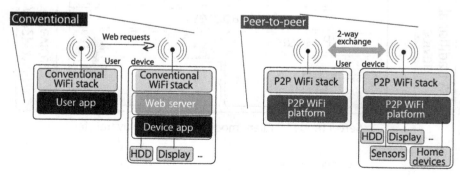

FIG. 6

Conventional versus P2P WiFi designs and operation logics.

makes no assumptions as to whether or not the commodity device implements a WiFi AP. In fact, this design is generic and works for all the connectivity designs discussed earlier in this chapter. Also note that *apps* are different between client and server, due to the uni-directional nature of web requests. This distinction is important because this problem is resolved in the P2P design below.

P2P technology on the right side of Fig. 6 immediately stands out by using the same *platform* for both user and commodity devices. The *apps* are absent and not important because the platforms can serve both as end apps for human operators as well as APIs for software at either end. The logic in this technology is also different and is based not on the direction of traffic but rather on the hardware functionality available at either end. Those devices that have HDD, display, sensor, and other hardware functions, are assumed to expose them via the P2P platform. In other words, the platform is expected to be flexible and generic in nature and be able to serve both receiving and sending modes of operation.

Let us examine several examples of using the P2P technology in practice. When used for *displays*, the user device would be sending and the commodity device would be receiving traffic. For a *sensor* device, the commodity device would normally initiate connections to push sensor data to one or many user devices within the communication range.

A minor note is due on the automation potential hidden behind the P2P technology. Normally, when one device pushes data to another, the receiving device would show an *accept/decline* alert that has to be attended to by humans. However, while developing the prototype presented further in this chapter, it was discovered that such alerts can be suppressed, thus, allowing for a high-level of automation of data exchange between devices. The WDH technology presented further in this chapter will heavily rely on this kind of automation.

3.3 BASIC IDEA OF GROUP CONNECT

Up to this moment, conventional versus P2P WiFi technologies and their stacks were considered as *rivals* by constantly comparing the features between the two. However, when the two stacks are merged into a single converged wireless technology, the resulting package opens up an array of brand new technologies. This section explains the basic concept behind such a merger, referred to as *Group Connect*.

Fig. 7 is a taxonomy of three distinct ways of connecting of *groups of users* to the Internet. This specific formulation is important—we are not trying to connect individual users to the Internet, or connect users within a group—the goal is to connect the entire group to the Internet, as efficiently as possible.

Single Connect in Fig. 7 is shown mostly for the sake of the argument. Each user in the group is connected to the Internet on an individual basis, each using its own available technology. Then, regardless of the fact that the group is local—that is, all the members are in the same geographical location—the only way members can communicate across each other is via the Internet. This sounds simple. In reality, users might be able to connect to each other, but given the *default connectivity*

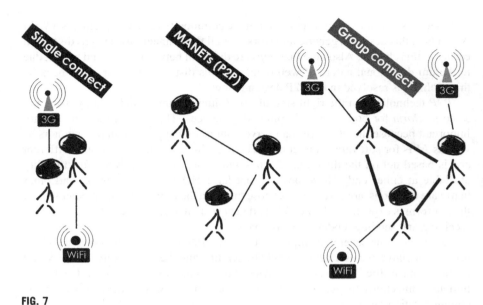

FIG. 7

Comparison of *SingleConnect*, *MANETS*, and *Group Connect* communication paradigms.

problem (Zhanikeev, 2013b) discussed above, each time the user has to choose between connecting to the Internet or connecting to another member of the group. In this model, it is assumed that P2P technology is not yet put to work (it will be in the last model).

MANETs are the case of pure-P2P networks and assume that members do not require individual Internet connections. However, since the Internet has to be provided within the objective, MANETs would normally define and share among members a single exit to the Internet. Note that this is not the same approach as is taken by *mobile clouds* (Fernando et al., 2013) discussed further in this chapter. In fact, mobile clouds solve precisely this problem in MANETs by moving closer in the direction of the Group Connect technology below.

Group Connect is the first time the two stacks—conventional versus P2P—are put together. Each member is assumed to have both the Internet (3G/LTE/WiFi) connection as well as the local P2P WiFi connection to all the members. Assuming the presence of parallel connectivity between the two—the research shows that it is possible in existing commodity devices (Zhanikeev, 2014a, 2016), the entire group can be considered as a whole entity. Further in this chapter it will be shown that *mobile clouds* share this concept of group as an entity and discriminate between *remote versus local* traffic. The Group Connect technology, however, has a completely different viewpoint, presented below.

Fig. 8 explains the basic concept of Group Connect. The left side (before) is the same as the Group Connect in Fig. 7, only after a minor redraw. The right side (after)

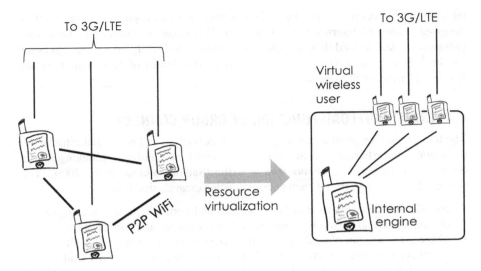

FIG. 8

Group Connect formulated as the virtualization technology for an arbitrary collection of wireless resources.

is the core premise of the technology, which assumes that the wireless networking resource of the entire group can be *virtualized* and treated as a single entity—referred to as *virtual wireless user* (VWU) by the figure.

The virtualization works as follows. All the internal connections among members of the group are hidden and are used by the VWU seamlessly and according to any logic defined by the application running in the group at the time. All the 3G/LTE connections are *pooled* and used by the VWU as a single connection, with the throughput being roughly the sum of throughputs on individual connections. Internal communications are truly near-seamless because the throughput on WiFi Direct (as an example of P2P WiFi) exceeds that of practical 3G/LTE rates by the factor of 10. The practical outcome in the VWU is the greatly boosted external throughput of the group.

Note that the Group Connect technology is helpful in many practical settings. For example, in vehicular clouds, groups of parked cards can be used as a single *cloud drive* (Zhanikeev, 2014b)—here, the technology also depends on the boosted throughput between the group of cars and the core cloud. The technology has also been used as a throughput booster at a university campus (Zhanikeev, 2014a). This latter technology is revisited later in this chapter when it is included as a complimentary technology to the WDHs.

It is important to remember that the WDHs themselves present a new viewpoint at the Group Connect concept. The hub becomes a member of multiple groups of wireless users, where all other members are human users with smartphones, tablets, etc. However, as will be shown further in this chapter, the hub itself is designed to have no Internet connection itself. This means that other members of its groups are asked to lend their Internet connections—indirectly, of course—in order for the hub to be able to download its content. The details of this technology are discussed further in this chapter.

3.4 TRAFFIC OFFLOAD FUNCTION OF GROUP CONNECT

The traditional viewpoint at the *traffic offload* technology is known under the name of *mobile clouds* (Fernando et al., 2013). This point is emphasized by making a clear distinction between *local versus remote* traffic (Satyanarayanan et al., 2009). The concept is similar to Group Connect but has some clear distinctions:

- Mobile clouds are not assumed to be groups and normally refer to sharing of computation load between a single mobile terminal and the core cloud.
- There is no concept of pooling and virtualizing network resources for all members of a group, if any—instead, it is more common in mobile cloud research to appoint a gate node on the border between local and remote, which is similar to what was done earlier in MANET research.

There is also minor confusion on the *direction* of the offload. Specifically, the two obvious directions are *device to cloud* versus *cloud to device*. Cuervo et al. (2010) platform specifically advocates the *device to cloud* mode, arguing that it is more efficient (faster) for smartphones to send computation jobs to the cloud and wait for the results than to attempt to complete the computation locally. In vehicular clouds, the other direction is also discussed, when groups of vehicles form a cloud drive which helps offload content from the core cloud to network edge (Zhanikeev, 2014b).

Mobile clouds often define the core problem as an *optimization problem* with the following main parameters:

- Battery efficiency (Amft and Lukowicz, 2009).
- Speed—faster to send to cloud and get results (Cuervo et al., 2010) or the other way around.
- Green clouds do the opposite thing by trying to offload computation and storage from the core to network edge, thus reducing power consumption of data centers.
- Sync volume—roughly stated as the tradeoff between syncing right now or waiting for some time to sync more efficiently at a later point in time.

There are many existing platforms that already support *mobile clouds* in practice (Huerta-Canepa and Lee, 2010; Cuervo et al., 2010).

Group Connect here offers an entirely different viewpoint at the offload technology by stating that one member of a group can *delegate* a part of his/her job to another group member. This basic concept is discussed in Zhanikeev (2014a) as part of a throughput boosting technology. Note that this statement adds another parameter to the optimization problem above.

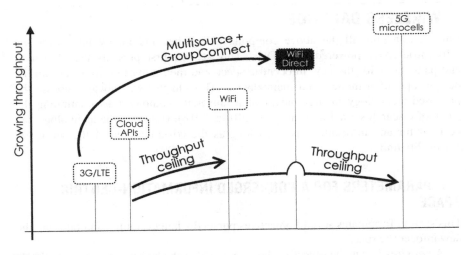

FIG. 9

The ladder of wireless technologies in the context of throughput ceilings and how they can be raised using Group Connect.

Fig. 9 provides the background for the popular technologies taking part in various kinds of offloads. We already know that 3G/LTE is very slow, which is proven by research in Zhanikeev (2013b) and a recent trace at CRAWDAD (n.d.). The trace shows that average throughput on 3G/LTE connections stays below 1 Mbps. This is mostly due to a growing number of customers and an inability of cellular providers to catch up with the greatly elevated levels of congestion.

The next slow technology is *cloud APIs*, which are not slow due to limited network capacity but rather because of restrictions on traffic as well as the various quotas imposed by cloud providers. At present, download/upload speeds to majority of popular cloud APIs is around 1–3 Mbps.

So, the problem here is that cloud APIs place a rough ceiling on throughput, invalidating all the improvements brought by Group Connect (WiFi Direct is the representative in the figure) or 4G+ technologies.

The solution is obvious—delegation of jobs to other members in the group. While each member is subjected to roughly the same limitations on their individual connections to cloud APIs, the limitation for the entire group, via delegation over Group Connect, can be increased to the sum of those for individual members. In other words, if individual data rates are at 2 Mbps for each member, the group of five members can pull content from the same cloud API at roughly 10 Mbps. The basic delegation method is based on sharing API tokens and downloading different parts of the same content, as is explained in Zhanikeev (2014a).

Note that this technique is similar to the *multisource content aggregation* method used in content delivery networks (CDNs) (Zhanikeev, 2016; Zhanikeev and Koide, 2013).

4 WIRELESS DATA HUB

This section puts all the above components together and finally introduces the infocentric space powered by WDHs. This section first presents the objectives and parameters for the new infocentric space and then moves on to describing its design, operation modes, and maintenance. This chapter will always discuss the proposed technology in the context of a university campus, thus continuing the chain of research started in Zhanikeev (2014a, 2016). However, the technology can be used for any infocentric space as long as the coverage area of the service is reasonably finite.

4.1 PARAMETERS FOR A CONVERGED INFORMATION-CENTRIC SPACE

This section formulates several objectives pursued when designing and building the new infocentric space.

A *no-wires box* is the objective that requires that the box that hosts each WDHs would have the minimum of wires connecting to it. Specifically, the requirement is that the box would have no 3G/LTE/4G+ connection it—otherwise, the presence of such a wireless resource would make the box roughly into an SC as was discussed for the 4G+ technologies above. The box is also not supposed to have the Ethernet connection/cable—in fact, such an operation mode would immediately complicate the design of the entire infocentric space. The box can only have a power cable but can be rid of that by running on batteries, if necessary.

P2P WiFi Only Mode is the natural second step after the *no-wires* objective above. Since the box has no other connections, it can only keep in touch with the outside world (content in case of this infocentric space) via the wireless users it briefly comes in contact with. Note that this is only a slightly different version of the basic Group Connect technology discussed above. In fact, including nonconnected members into the group can be considered as a kind of resource optimization problem in Zhanikeev (2016), where the nonconnected node can save power on remote connections and instead spend it on syncing content across all the members of the group. There are also similarities with DTN but not at depth (Vasilakos et al., 2011).

High Autonomy basically repeats the above objectives but also adds that the box should require very little maintenance. This mainly refers to the content hosted on the box. While it is not a major problem on one WDH, using multiple hubs across the campus can result in major differences in content depending on how popular a given location is. The autonomy here means that the infocentric space should be able to rectify the problem (ie, sync gap in content) with minimum effort and without resorting to having to connect the boxes wirelessly or with wires.

Flexibility of Use is the objective that the box can be used in a wide range of practical settings without changing the technology itself. The two distinct usecases considered further in this chapter are

- announcement boards scattered across the campus;
- a hub for sharing class materials—a sort of Lecture Management System for the entire campus.

These are the main objectives. Discussion further on this section will refer to this list when stressing the success in satisfying a given objective.

4.2 WIRELESS DATA HUB

Fig. 10 presents the overall idea of an infocentric space based on WDHs. The hub itself is simply a box mounted to a wall. As was discussed in the previous section, the box has no wires connected to it, other than, possibly, the power cable for uninterrupted power supply.

The inside of the box is also simple. It hosts

- a hard disk sufficient to store the content for the entire campus, given a given specific practical purpose; and
- a P2P WiFi interface to it, the interface being implemented in accordance with the detailed explanation given earlier in this chapter.

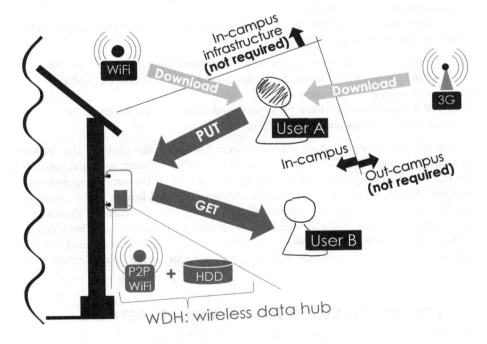

FIG. 10

The overall idea of the WDH.

Note that it is not difficult to implement such a box in practice using existing technology. Given the availability of WiFi Direct as the representative of the P2P WiFi technology, it was discovered that the easiest to build prototypes are the ones based on Android OS. Such boxes would be almost like smartphones connected to larger hard disks, with minimum effort spent on interfacing between these two parts.

Fig. 10 describes the basic usage patterns. For example, User A can put a file onto the WDH and User B can later retrieve the file from the box. However, the extended patterns are more interesting. The figure shows that User A can first download a file from the Internet using either WiFi or 3G/LTE connection and then upload the file to the box. Depending on which external connection is actually used, this can serve as a connection between either the global Internet or in-campus WiFi infrastructure, and the box. As was previously discussed, the box does not require the presence of external connectivity in real time, and is quite happy with secondary downloads from the wireless users passing by. The main strength of the box is in its ability to aggregate all the uploaded files and then share them with other users, thus disseminating the content across the campus. As was stated earlier, this part of the proposed technology is similar to the concept of *information dissemination* discussed in social network analysis. In fact, the WDH technology also has the sharing part discussed further in this chapter.

A major note is due on handling of the content itself. One would normally use the following two technologies:

- Indexing the entire filesystem to be able to calculate *filesystem diffs*—structures that can help quickly identify which files are to be synced between hubs and users or users and other users.
- *Version control* for individual files that would signal when a file has to be replaced with an updated version.

Put bluntly, these two technologies are out of scope in this chapter. The reader is redirected to the literature that focuses on this subject matter, as is the case of the P2P file sharing system in Zhanikeev and Koide (2013). The versioning problem is expected to be minor in the practical examples discussed further in this chapter, but for the sake of flexibility it cannot be ignored. The same research in Zhanikeev and Koide (2013) also discusses the versioning part of the technology. This chapter will simplify this part by assuming that there is only one file that needs to be disseminated across the campus, thus keeping the focus on the dissemination part of the technology.

4.3 WDH IN THE CENTER OF A SOCIAL WIRELESS NETWORK

The absence of networking across the multiple WDHs is a problem. In fact, one cannot saturate a given space with hubs at a reasonable cost—analysis further in this chapter will consider 5 and 25 hubs, which are clearly not enough to saturate the over 1000×1000 m area of the campus used for analysis. So, one has to make do with

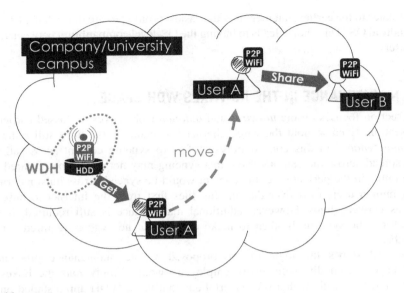

FIG. 11

Users playing the role of wireless data hubs when peer-communicating with other users.

a relatively small number of hubs installed at popular locations, plus rely on P2P sharing. These are the two main parts of the proposed infocentric space.

Fig. 11 shows a very simple method of dissemination based on the two simple operations. User A would first *GET* content from a WDH, then move to another location and *SHARE* it with another user.

The first assumption that helps embrace these actions within the same technology is based on the unified terminology. Instead of *put*, *get*, and *share* operations, both hubs and users always perform the *SYNC* operation. With a small discussion on filesystem indexing and file versioning above, the sync operation involves exchange of filesystem diffs in order to decide which files are to be synced and in which direction. Having identified that, the two devices can perform the sync by exchanging the files identified by the diff, thus bringing both filesystems to the same state.

The other assumption is that Group Connect is always used, meaning that data exchange always happens in groups, regardless of particular combinations of hubs and users. Some groups would have hubs as members while other would be comprised only of human users. The Group Connect is used at the full range of its capability by assuming that human users are connected to 3G/LTE networks.

Practical implementation of the above two assumptions is not difficult in practice. It was already mentioned that the technology based on the P2P WiFi stack leads to having the same platform at both ends of data exchange. This literally means that both the hub and smartphones of human users use the same platform.

This relates to the earlier statement that the easiest prototypes are those that are based on Android OS. This choice leads to having the OS-level compatibility between hubs and users.

4.4 MAINTENANCE IN THE No-WIRES WDH SPACE

This section focuses on the *no-wires* and *autonomy* objectives discussed earlier in this section. Even without the wires, the need to maintain the hubs still remains. The *maintenance* in this context mostly refers to syncing content across all the hubs spread across the campus. Note that syncing may not in fact be required for some hubs. In the perfect case, the content would be synced across hubs naturally, using human users to deliver the missing files first from the Internet to hubs as well as between hubs. However, additional maintenance is still required, if not to perform the sync itself, then to make certain that no sync is required across the hubs.

Fig. 12 shows the logic of the proposed simple maintenance procedure. A Manager—normally a university employee—would simply *tour* the boxes at regular intervals with his/her own smartphone that has a WDH app installed on it, that is, posing as a regular student device. At each box, the Manager would stop and wait for the sync to complete, if necessary.

Note that routing sequence and the overall design of this maintenance procedure is an interesting research problem. In the current prototype, the simple logic is to tour the hubs in the order from more popular to less popular hubs, making two rounds each time for resilience. However, other strategies are possible. For example, the Manager could ensure that his/her own device has the perfect state (all the content) before going on the maintenance tour, in which case the order is not important and only one round is sufficient to complete the procedure. Future work on the topic will look into other practical strategies in this part of the technology.

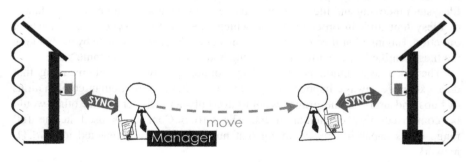

FIG. 12

Syncing content across WDH boxes using a Manager with a smartphone.

5 MODELING AND PERFORMANCE ANALYSIS

This section analyzes the performance of a university campus converted into an infocentric space power by WDHs. Several traces are used for modeling, some coming from different projects hosted on Crawdad public repository (CRAWDAD, n.d.), including traces for 3G/LTE throughput (CRAWDAD, n.d.), local data rates when using WiFi Direct for in-group communication (Zhanikeev, 2013b), and mobility traces for students in a university campus and its basic application method (Zhanikeev, 2014a). Analysis focuses on comparing performance of *3G with Group Connect versus 4G+* and *3G versus WDH with Group Connect* spaces.

5.1 MOBILITY TRACES AND THROUGHPUT DATASETS

The Crawdad repository hosts many publically available mobility traces (CRAWDAD, n.d.), of which those from the KAIST University campus are selected for analysis. The method used for processing and using the traces for analysis is described in Zhanikeev (2014a), and is only briefly repeated in this section.

Fig. 13 shows raw routes for 10 randomly selected students (ids plotted at end points of the routes). The plot is very messy, yet it reveals that some locations and routes across the campus are preferred to others. This is a natural feature and is to be found on most university campuses as well as other infocentric spaces.

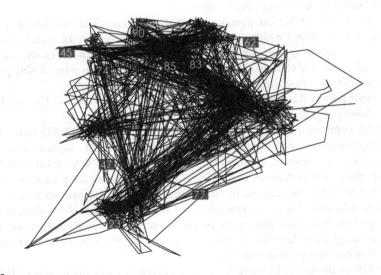

FIG. 13

Raw mobility routes that reveal popular locations within the campus.

It is necessary to process the raw routes into *hotspots*—locations on campus visited more frequently than others. The obvious ultimate goal of this search is to define locations where WDHs would be installed. The manual method would be to simply pick locations—for example, pick an accouchement board as the obvious location where students stop to check on the latest announcements. However, in order to support the multipurpose and generic nature of the proposed technology, the following statistical method is applied.

Processing starts from *raw routes* as in Fig. 13. Locations that form the routes are *quantified in coordinates* (to the nearest 10 m) to avoid noise from walking on a variety of surfaces, as well as the problem of small errors and deviations in GPS coordination (the trace is based on GPS). Routes are then *quantified in time* (in a manner of speaking) by removing quantified locations where a user has spent less than 30 s. Both quantization settings are selected arbitrarily but reflect the values found in practice as well as during testing of the prototypes.

The routes are then dispersed into individual locations and the *hotness* parameter is calculated for each location based on the number of times a given location is traversed, including the cases when the same user traversed the same location multiple times.

The last (but not least) processing step is to prune hotspots which are too close to other hotspots. To achieve this, the list of hotspots is walked in decreasing order of hotness removing for each hotspot all other hotspots further to the tail which are found to be within 100 m radius. The remaining hotspots are kept in the ordered list and are selected in decreasing order of hotness.

Fig. 14 shows 25 hottest places around the campus. The hotness is relative (absolute, not log scale) which explains the extreme difference in bullet size. It is clear that, if hotspots are selected in the decreasing order of hotness, they will be scattered all across the campus. This is good news because otherwise closely packed hubs would not be very efficient given the large size of the campus.

The other part of the modeling is based on the throughput traces. The two traces are as follows.

3G/LTE connections are modeled using the trace at CRAWDAD (n.d.) using the aggregation/processing method in Zhanikeev (2013b). Throughput values are aggregated for each hour of the day (only 1 day is used) and selected randomly for that hour based on the occurrence frequency. This means that each time a throughput has to be selected in simulation, the most probable value for that hour of the day is selected. The selection is random which means that less probable values are still picked but less frequently than more probable ones. In simulation, this section is performed using a weighted list of values, where the weight is based on the trace and used to alter the frequency of selection.

WiFi Direct throughput comes from the measurements in Zhanikeev (2013b)— the technology is known to be the fastest available P2P WiFi technology compared to Bluetooth, NFC, etc. The same basic selection approach is used except there is no dependence on hour of day—local connectivity is not affected by congestion in

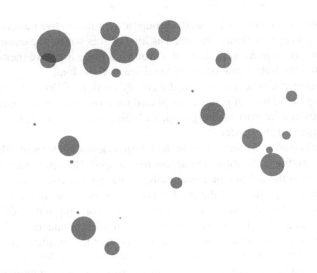

FIG. 14

Statistically defined 25 popular locations in the campus. Bullet size represents relative popularity.

the wireless backbone network. Instead, all the values are weighted based on their occurrence probability and are selected accordingly.

5.2 GROUP CONNECT AND WDH DEPLOYMENT MODELS

Analysis in this section is done in two combinations of technologies: *Group Connect versus 4G+* and *3G versus WDH with Group Connect*. Both have the Group Connect technology in them and both represent a practical way to build a converged infocentric space. This section describes all the specific models used in analysis. 3G and 4G+ models are straightforward because they are based on simple user-to-network connections—their respective settings are explained alongside with analysis results. On the other hand, Group Connect and WDH models are complex and require additional details offered in this section.

Data Hubs Only is a simple converged infocentric space that does not use the sharing feature implemented via Group Connect. Instead, each hub only syncs its content with passing by human users.

Hubs with Group Connect Paced is the *paced* version of the sharing feature added to the hubs. As was explained above, Group Connect simply views hubs as members of groups, making no technical distinction, but nevertheless benefiting automatically from the fact that hubs aggregate content from multiple users and are assumed to be much better members than humans.

Users are assumed to aggregate content from all the members via multiple substreams—details on the method can be found in Zhanikeev (2014a). The main distinction of the *paced* version is that the groups are limited to five members. If there is a hub in the group, it is always included as long as it is within the communication range. The range is 25 m for all groups. If a group has more than five members, then, except for within the hub, extra members are discarded randomly.

Hubs with Group Connect Greedy is the *greedy* version of Group Connect which is different only in the lack of restrictions placed on group size. Any member within the 25 m radius can be part of the group, including hubs. This explains the word *greedy* in the name of the model.

For simplicity and to avoid having to deal with indexes, filesystem diffs, and file versions, only one file is disseminated across the campus. However, various filesizes are tried to see how the volume of content affects the rate of dissemination.

Also note that, regardless of the model, human users are assumed to be always connected either to the Internet or in-campus network. For simplicity, 3G/LTE traces (described above) are used to model throughput on such connections. This means that hubs are not a strict requirement for a human user to complete the download. In other words, simulation results further in this section show how using hubs and Group Connect can help to improve download speeds for the total population of users on campus.

Finally, simulation is played in accordance with the following mobility logic. A random user is selected from trace and is denoted as the central node (the one that needs to download the content). An hour of the day is selected randomly and is used to define the current location of the user based on that user's mobility trace. The simulation for that user then starts and continues until the download has completed. All the nodes that are within a 25-m range at the same time are selected as group members. If hubs are in the range then the respective models would include hubs (or microcells in 4G+) as a group member.

In order to allow for continuity of content in hubs, simulation maintains the state for hubs and individual users across multiple single-user simulations. This means that, with time, hubs, and some users get filled with content and become more and more effective as members of groups. 100 batches each 1000 such rounds are simulated for each model. Results are aggregated and are presented as average values for each user.

5.3 GROUP CONNECT VERSUS 4G INFRASTRUCTURE

This section compares 4G+ infrastructure spread across the campus and the traditional 3G with the added Group Connect. 4G infrastructure nodes—the SCs are located at the hotspots calculated earlier in this section. Note that the locations are the same for SCs in 4G+ and hubs in the proposed technology. This is because such infrastructure does not depend on the technology but on the popularity of the locations. It is logical that nodes for any kind of infrastructure would be installed at locations with higher relative density.

Now, as was discussed earlier in this chapter, while, in accordance with current LTE-A standards, SCs should be able to provide up to 1 Gbps data rates, in practice it has been shown that such rates would not be possible. This analysis will make the same assumption that was discussed earlier in this chapter and will assume that the data rate on SCs (microcells) is limited by the rates allowed on cloud APIs.

The following setup is used. SCs (microcells) can provide at most 10 Mbps data rates—the limit is imposed by the cloud API deeper in network backbone. The range for SCs is 25 m. Analysis tested 5, 10, and 25 SCs located on the respective hotspots across the campus. By comparison, users that fail to connect to SCs as well as those that use the 3G/LTE infrastructure, are subjected to much lower throughputs (CRAWDAD, n.d.). However, this low throughput can be boosted by delegating download tasks and borrowing bandwidth from other users in the group—this is the part where Group Connect comes into play.

Fig. 15 focuses on throughput distribution (specifically the Mass Distribution Function) across the population of 100 users. The figure has four plots, each plot is considered in sequence in the rest of this section.

The *top-left* plot compares *traditional*, *4G+* (microcells), and *Group Connect* methods. The number of microcells in the 4G+ model is fixed at five. The traditional bullets (crosses) are almost nonvisible beyond the 1 Mbps point, which is true according to the respective trace. The best performance is for the 4G+ model, where approximately 10–15% of the population comes in contact with Microcells and experience higher throughput. However, this also means that the remaining 80% plus of population feel no benefit from the 4G+ infrastructure. The two Group Connect models are in between the two extremes, showing up to 3 Mbps throughputs—those

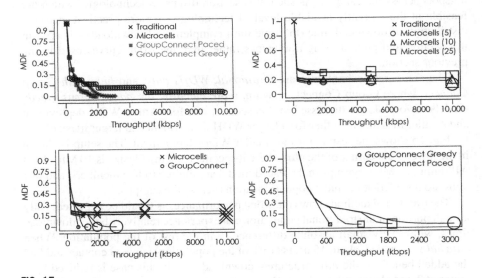

FIG. 15

Comparison of throughput in Group Connect versus LTE-A spaces. The wireless data hub is not yet employed.

are aggregate values for all the members in the group. Distributions are slightly less steep, showing that approximately 40% of the population can experience at least 1 Mbps of throughput, somewhat larger than offered by both the Traditional and 4G+ models.

The *top-right* plot focuses on traditional versus various sizes of 4G+ infrastructure. The same pattern as before is observed. The only difference is that we can now see how the size of the 4G+ infrastructure affects the throughput experienced to the benefit of the population. The plot shows that with 25 Microcells approximately 40% of the population can encounter at least one Microcell and benefit from its higher throughput.

The *bottom-left* plot is the comparison between all the three sizes of 4G+ infrastructure and all the Group Connect models, stressing the maximum throughputs experienced by each model. The best (greedy) Group Connect model can offer only about 3 Mbps to a very small number of users.

Finally, the *bottom-right* plot is the zoom-in into only the Group Connect models, making a distinction between Greedy and Paced models (3, 5, and 10 nodes allowed in groups) and showing more details about the distribution curves. As was mentioned before, the curves are not too steep and offer 1 Mbps and above throughputs to between 30% and 40% of the population.

5.4 WIRELESS DATA HUB VERSUS 3G/LTE SPACES

This section replaces 4G+ infrastructure nodes with hubs—both are installed at hotspots across the campus. As such, this section discusses technologies which are feasible at the currently available level of technology. A more practical metric—distribution of download time (the time until completion of download)—is used in this section and plotted using raw values rather than the MDF curves used in the previous section.

The compared technologies are *traditional*, *WDHs only*, and *hubs with Group Connect*, where Group Connect is, again, represented by the *paced* versus *greedy* models. Two plots are discussed in this section, one for a small WDH deployment and smaller files and the other for a larger WDH deployment and larger filesize.

Fig. 16 shows the results for the smaller WDH deployment. The setup is shown in the lower-right corner of the plot where it specifies that the filesize is 10 Mb, cloud API limit is 1 Mbps, groups in the Paced model are limited to five members, and five hubs are installed at the most popular locations across the campus.

The traditional method shows the worst performance, as would be expected. Only a small portion of the traditional population can experience relatively better download times, with a very small absolute difference from the rest of the population. When *data hubs* are added, about 15 users (15% of the population) come in contact and feel the added benefit of the infrastructure—download time in this case is reduced by a factor of 3 and above. When Group Connect feature are added on top of the hubs, the additional benefit is that an additional 30% of the population complete the download much sooner than the rest. The curve is on a slope but the average of the slope

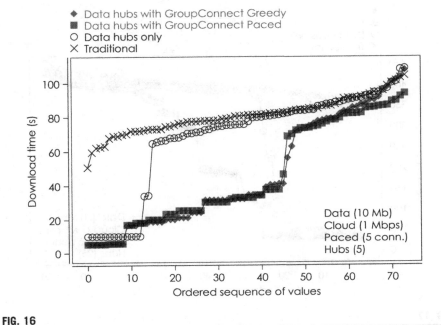

FIG. 16

Results for a relatively small space with five hubs and 10 Mb downloads for users.

between 20% and 50% points is around 30, which is an improvement at the factor of at least 2. Even past the 50% point, some of the remaining population manages to complete download somewhat faster than either the traditional of *data hub* cases. This shows that both hubs and Group Connect offer benefits which complement each other but can work individually if one is not activated for a given used.

Fig. 17 shows results for a larger WDH deployment—this time 25 hubs are used and users need to download 50 Mb files. The rest of the setup is the same. Note that the larger file size raises the average level in terms of the download time. However, for comparison it is sufficient to be able to compare between the methods using the relative difference.

The first major improvement from a larger WDH mesh is that about 20% of population can directly benefit, by coming in direct contact with a hub—this is a 5% improvement from the earlier case. This raises the potential issue of the tradeoff between increasing the size of WDH deployment and the added benefit such an increase would bring. In this case, the fivefold growth in size of the WDH mesh brought only 5% of improvement in terms of the number of encounters between users and hubs.

Group Connect offers yet additional benefit, roughly in the same way as it did in the first plot—the curve for about additional 40% of population benefits from the Group Connect directly or indirectly (through the dissemination effect). As in the

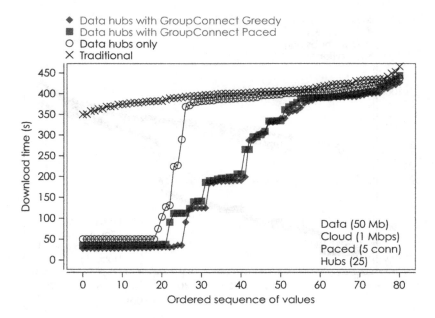

FIG. 17

Results for a larger space with 25 hubs and 50 Mb downloads.

first plot, the average level for this part of the population is about a twofold decrease in download time, distributed at a 45% angle roughly equally on both size from this point.

Comparing with the previous section where the sole use of Group Connect shows only a minor improvement, the results in this section are very encouraging in that they show that Group Connect can double the effect from the WDH mesh provided the two technologies are used together.

6 SUMMARY

This chapter presented a conceptually new information-centric space based on the concept of converged wireless networks and WDHs. The wireless networking inside the space is converged because it uses at least two connectivity modes—3G/LTE/WiFi and P2P WiFi. The hubs are relatively simple and use only the P2P WiFi functionality but the entire space strongly depends on the ability to use both connectivity modes in parallel.

The story of the new information-centric space starts with connectivity and congestion problems, to which this chapter dedicated an entire section. These two problems have a major effect on any information-centric space that depends on traditional networking. This includes the 4G+ wireless networks which, as this chapter shows, offer substantially higher data rates not a major increase in capacity in terms of the number of users. For example, the SCs at the newly created access layer in 4G+ networks are expected to accommodate only 5–10 subscribers. Such APs are bound to become quickly congested in dense spaces.

The density really has only one practical solution, which is outlined in this chapter—to allow users to disseminate data via user-user exchanges. In fact, the technology presented in this chapter does not make a distinction between hub-user and user-user data exchanges. Both operations are referred to as *syncs* which are generic operations and do not discriminate between parties or direction of exchange. The only factor taken into account is the difference in content. In practice, the technology behind syncs normally involves several well-known components, such as filesystem indexing, filesystem diffs, and file version control. This chapter places these technologies out of scope but does offer pointers to related literature.

For a truly efficient dissemination, it is important that users' devices (smartphones, tablets, etc.) can operate simultaneously in the two connectivity modes in the background. Before this is possible, the connectivity problem has to be resolved. In practice, each device can support only one Internet connection. The technology referred to as Group Connect gets around this problem by using the P2P WiFi stack for the second connectivity. The two modes are therefore the Internet connection plus a P2P WiFi connection directed at a nearby device, which can be another user or the newly proposed WDH. The resulting technology allows for seamless syncs which are executed in the background as a user passes by a hub.

The technology expands rapidly after this point. Each passing sync is accumulated by the hub. When many such syncs have been accumulated, the hub becomes a major player in content exchange as it has more files than any separate user. The syncing with passersby would probably change direction at this point, and the hub would supply passers by with the files they do not have. With no discernable difference between hubs and users in terms of logic and even software implementation, the same mechanism is true for users, where some active users can supply many less active ones with their up-to-date files. This, in a nutshell, creates an environment in which information can disseminate rapidly through the campus.

This chapter analyzed several infocentric spaces based on the various publically available mobility and throughput traces. Separate analysis was done comparing 4G with Group Connect and 3G with hubs and Group Connect. In the former case, Group Connect had only a minor effect on performance. In the latter case, the hubs alone greatly improved download speeds for up to 20% of the population, while adding the Group Connect functionality to hubs amounted to an additional 30% of the population improving their download performance at a lesser yet tangible rate.

The research in this chapter can be continued in various directions. First, it would be interesting to test the technology in a richer environment in terms of the content—many files with varying popularity rates (access frequency) could be tested to reveal how the efficiency of the proposed technology depends not only on the total volume of content but also on the distribution of popularity across individual files.

The basic prototype for the proposed technology has already been implemented. However, the automation part—the software running in hubs and user devices and ensuring that data exchanges between the two connectivity modes is done automatically and in the background—can be improved. For example, the pairing part at this time can only be done manually, but once paired, future connections (and delegation of partial downloads) can be done automatically. With a large number of students in a university campus, this is still a cumbersome procedure that students are asked to manually confirm for each new encounter. Automation of this part is the obvious future direction for the technology in this chapter.

ACRONYMS

AP   a wireless access point
D2D   the device-to-device mode of wireless communication under LTE-A
M2M   the machine-to-machine mode of communication under LTE-A
MANET   mobile ad-hoc network

GLOSSARY

AP design A client-device communication design in which the device implements a wireless AP to which the client connects; another form of the technology is when the device itself connects to other AP from which it can get access to the Internet and even extend it further to the client via its own AP.

CoMP Coordinated multipoint, a core technology in the LTE-A suite.

DTN Delay tolerant networks, the WDHs discussed in this chapter can be considered as static nodes in a DTN where client terminals are intermediaries in deliveries messages between them.

eNB Evolved node B, a common name to refer to the local wireless APs in LTE-A.

FDMA Frequency division multiple access, an alternative to TDMA, in which multiple channels are separated by frequency.

Group Connect A technology behind the WDHs discussed in this chapter, based on virtualization of wireless resources of a group.

LTE-A Long-term evolution advanced, a 4G+ wireless technology which is expected to replace the current LTE by 2020.

Maui A platform of Mobile Clouds, specifically balancing the load between client device and the cloud.

MIMO Multiple-input multiple output, a method for multichannel wireless communication using antenna arrays.

MIPv6 Mobile IP version 6, a wireless version of IPv6.

NFC Near field communication, another type of a P2P WiFi technology, in line with Bluetooth and WiFi Direct.

P2P Design
        Also referred to as the P2P Solution, is when the client uses a traditional WiFi stack for the Internet and P2P WiFi stack to communicate with the device, the main advantage of

this technology is that the two communication channels can operate in parallel with only minor interference.

SC Small Cell, another name for evolved-NodeB (eNB), MicroCells (MCs), femtocells, and others.

TDMA Time division multiple access, a wireless access technology based on separating channels into consecutive time slots.

VWU Virtual wireless user, an abstract construct used to describe a pool of wireless resources within a group of devices.

WDH Wireless data hub, the core technology discussed in this chapter, based on isolated wireless hubs spread within a limited area like a university campus.

WiFi Direct Is the most widespread P2P WiFi technology today, supported natively by Android OS since version 4.1, but also by many devices outside of Android OS.

WLAN Design A rival technology to the AP Design and P2P Design, where communication between the device and the client is done via a nearby AP.

REFERENCES

Aerohive, 2013. Aerohive Design and Configuration Guide: High-Density WiFi Networks. Aerohive Whitepaper.

Akyildiz, I., Lee, W., Vuran, M., Mohanty, S., 2008. A survey on spectrum management in cognitive radio networks. IEEE Commun. Mag. 40 (4), 40–48.

Amft, O., Lukowicz, P., 2009. From backpacks to smartphones: past, present, and future of wearable computers. IEEE Pervasive Comput. 8, 8–13.

Banerjee, N., Agarwal, S., Bahl, P., Chandra, R., Wolman, A., Corner, M., 2010. Virtual compass: relative positioning to sense mobile social interactions. In: 8th International Conference on Pervasive Computing, pp. 1–21.

Bing, B., 2008. Emerging Technologies in Wireless LANs: Theory, Design, and Deployment. Cambridge Press.

Chandra, R., Radhye, J., Ravindranath, L., Wolman, A., 2007. Beacon-stuffing: Wi-Fi without associations. In: 8th IEEE Workshop on Mobile Computing Systems and Applications (HotMobile), pp. 53–57.

Cheng, N., Zhang, N., Lu, N., Shen, X., Mark, W., Liu, F., 2014. Opportunistic spectrum access for CR-VANETs: a game-theoretic approach. IEEE Trans. Veh. Technol. 63 (1), 237–251.

CRAWDAD, n.d.a. CRAWDAD Dataset on Measurements of HTTP requests over 802.11 in dense wireless classrooms. http://crawdad.org/kyutech/interference (retrieved March 2016).

CRAWDAD, n.d.b. CRAWDAD Dataset on Measurements on real HTTP throughput via several 3G/LTE providers in Japan. http://crawdad.org/kyutech/throughput (retrieved March 2016).

CRAWDAD, n.d.c. CRAWDAD Repository of Mobility Traces. http://crawdad.cs.dartmouth.edu (retrieved March 2016).

Cuervo, E., Balasubramanian, A., Cho, D., Wolman, A., Saroiu, S., Chandra, R., Bahl, P., 2010. Maui: making smartphones last longer with code offload. In: 8th ACM International Conference on Mobile Systems, Applications, and Services (MobiSys), pp. 49–62.

Dahlman, E., Parkvall, S., Skold, J., 2014. 4G LTE/LTE-Advanced for Mobile Broadband. Academic Press.

Fernando, N., Loke, S., Rahayu, W., 2013. Mobile cloud computing: a survey. Futur. Gener. Comput. Syst. 29, 84–106.

Glisic, S., 2009. Advanced Wireless Networks: Cognitive, Cooperative and Opportunistic 4G Technology. Wiley.

Google Chromecast, n.d. https://www.google.ru/chrome/devices/chromecast (retrieved March 2016).

Hiertz, G., Denteneer, D., Stibor, L., Zang, Y., Costa, X., Walke, B., 2010. The IEEE 802.11 universe. IEEE Commun. Mag. 48 (1), 62–70.

Huerta-Canepa, G., Lee, D., 2010. A virtual cloud computing provider for mobile devices. In: 1st ACM Workshop on Mobile Cloud Computing and Services: Social Networks and Beyond (MCS), vol. 6, pp. 1–5.

IEEE Standard, 2003. Wireless LAN medium access control (MAC) and physical layer (PHY) specifications: further higher-speed physical layer extension in the 2.4 GHz band. IEEE Standard 802.11g, Supplement to Part 11.

IEEE Standard, 2009. Wireless LAN medium access control (MAC) and physical layer (PHY) specifications amendment 5: enhancements for higher throughput. IEEE Standard 802.11n.

IEEE Standard, 2010. Amendment 6: wireless access in vehicular environments. IEEE Standard 802.11p.

Jiang, D., Delgrossi, L., 2008. IEEE 802.11p: towards an international standard for wireless access in vehicular environments. In: IEEE Vehicular Technology Conference (VTC), pp. 2036–2040.

Jin, L., JuBin, S., Zhu, H., 2013. Network connectivity optimization for device-to-device wireless system with femtocells. IEEE Trans. Veh. Technol. 62 (7), 3098–3109.

Liu, H., Darabi, H., Banarjee, P., Liu, J., 2007. Survey of wireless indoor positioning techniques and systems. IEEE Trans. Syst. Man Cybern. 37 (6), 1067–1080.

Lopez-Perez, D., Valcarce, A., Roche, G., Zhang, J., 2009. OFDMA femtocells a roadmap on interference avoidance. IEEE Commun. Mag. 47 (9), 41–48.

Maodong, L., Zhenzhong, C., Yap-Peng, T., 2013. Scalable resource allocation for SVC video streaming over multiuser MIMO-OFDM networks. IEEE Trans. Multimedia 15 (7), 1519–1531.

Peng, C., Shen, G., Zhang, Y., Li, Y., Tan, K., 2007. Beepbeep: a high accuracy acoustic ranging system using cots mobile devices. In: 5th ACM International Conference on Embedded Networked Sensor Systems (SenSys), pp. 1–14.

Satyanarayanan, M., Bahl, P., Caceres, R., Davies, N., 2009. The case for VM-based cloudlets in mobile computing. IEEE Pervasive Comput. 8, 14–23.

Vasilakos, A., Zhang, Y., Spyropoulos, T., 2011. Delay Tolerant Networks: Protocols and Applications. CRC Press.

Weitzen, J., Mingzhe, L., Anderland, E., Eyuboglu, V., 2013. Large-scale deployment of residential small cells. IEEE Proc. 101 (11), 2367–2380.

Western Digital Wireless HDD, n.d. http://www.wdc.com/mypassportwireless (retrieved July 2015).

Yang, X., Rosdahl, J., 2002. Throughput and delay limits of IEEE 802.11. IEEE Commun. Lett. 6 (8), 355–357.

Zhang, X., Zhou, X., 2013. LTE-Advanced Air Interface Technology. CRC Press.

Zhanikeev, M., 2013a. Experiments on practical WLAN designs for digital classrooms. IEICE Commun. Express 2 (8), 352–358.

Zhanikeev, M., 2013b. Virtual wireless user: a practical design for parallel multiconnect using WiFi direct in group communication. In: 10th International Conference on Mobile and Ubiquitous Systems: Computing, Networking and Services (MobiQuitous).

Zhanikeev, M., 2014a. Group connect in a new wireless university campus. IEICE Tech. Rep. Smart Radio (SR) 114 (165), 27–30.

Zhanikeev, M., 2014b. The VOBILE CLOUD: cars are better for mobile clouds and group connect. IEICE Tech. Rep. Intell. Transport. Syst. 114 (369), 59–62.

Zhanikeev, M., 2016. Opportunistic multiconnect with P2P WiFi and cellular providers. In: Advances in Mobile Computing and Communications: 4G and Beyond (in print).

Zhanikeev, M., Koide, H., 2013. Yalms: a group drive API for cloud-based classrooms. In: IEICE Tech. Rep. Inform. Netw. 113 (303), 19–22.

CHAPTER

Data fusion for orientation sensing in wireless body area sensor networks using smart phones

8

D. Mahmood,[a], N. Javaid[a], M. Imran[b], U. Qasim[c], Z.A. Khan[d,e]

COMSATS Institute of Information Technology, Islamabad, Pakistan[a]
King Saud University, Almuzahmiah, Saudi Arabia[b]
Cameron Library, University of Alberta, Edmonton, AB, Canada[c]
Dalhousie University, Halifax, NS, Canada[d]
Higher Colleges of Technology, Fujairah, United Arab Emirates[e]

1 INTRODUCTION

Advancements in Information and Communication Technologies (ICT) has been revolutionary globally. In every aspect and field of life, things are changing; humans are seeking excellence day after day. The ICT outlined in this chapter is that involved in Smart Grids (the future of grids), in medical and bioinformatics, in computer science and many more. Sensor networks have proven their importance in almost every field of life. The Consideration of the potential of tiny nodes with little processing power, sensing and transmitting units has given birth to numerous sub domains in wireless personal area networks (WPANs). One of the most studied and useful domains is the Wireless Body Area Sensor Network (WBASN). These networks are mainly studied and applied as e-Health solutions. Considering healthcare, we can say that healthcare systems are in a transitional phase. Manual healthcare is being replaced by automated healthcare. It is transforming from centralized systems to distributed systems. If we fail to shift from centralization to distributed environments, our existing hospitals will be overwhelmed by the increasing population.

Besides there is more general awareness regarding healthcare. Now individuals are interested in observing their own physiology. Not only are sportsmen careful to monitor their health and fitness but also this type of technology can help in the prevention or control of diseases for individual from any background and with any medical history. Hence we can say that the coming era a shift from the hospital centric cure to the patient centric cure.

Pervasive Computing. http://dx.doi.org/10.1016/B978-0-12-803663-1.00008-5

2 WBASN AND E-HEALTH SYSTEMS

Considering present day era, we have reached a point where wireless communication is booming with numerous kinds of networks for numerous applications. There is a feeling that nothing we propose is outside the scope of the natural environment. One of emerging domains, ie, Body Area Network (BAN), has existed as long as any living being. We each have eyes that act as cameras seeing the environment, a nose that senses smell, a tongue that sense tastes and many sensors with in our skin that allow us to feel. All these sensors are connected to a hub known (the brain) and they send request/information and take orders. On sensing a smell, the sensor (nose) transmits a signal via a neuron to the brain and the brain gives orders regarding that specific environment. A variation on this concept is utilized in WBASNs. Sensors are deployed in/on a body through the underlying topology and they communicate with a central hub to give information/requests and take orders accordingly as depicted in Fig. 1.

Natural BANs are so perfect that there is no chance of collision amongst the various signals, and there is no energy issue, there is no malfunctioning in network behavior, until some unexpected event occurs. In comparison, the man-made BANs, on which researchers are working for the betterment of mankind, have countless issues. These cannot be as perfect as a natural BAN, though such artificial networks may help humans whose natural BAN is disturbed. A camera can be integrated that

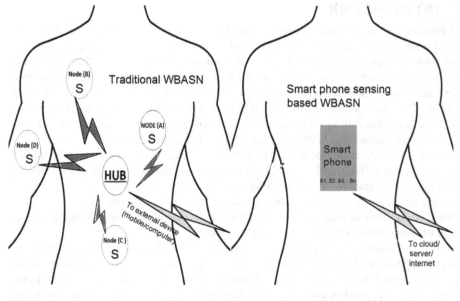

FIG. 1

WBASN for E-Health solutions.

may inform the brain regarding the environment it sees, or an ECG sensor may keep the doctor of a certain patient well informed regarding his heart condition. Besides medical issues, in today's digital era, why not exchange our digital profiles with each other by shaking hands or spend our leisure time playing motion games on a big screen and so on. We can use such networks for understanding the behavior of a targeted population regarding some predetermined subject. The application arena for a BAN is as wide as one can imagine. For any need applications sensor nodes need to be deployed on/in the body or in the vicinity of the body.

The sensor nodes generate sensed data and these data are used to investigate whatever it is intended to. At this point WBASNs present researchers with a challenge regarding the precise analysis and evaluation of data. The amount of data being sensed and transmitted continuously from the different sensors is enormous. Moreover, analyzing raw data can also be troublesome. The answer to these challenges is the Data Fusion Algorithm (DFA).

The concept of data fusion is not new. It is basically the procedure of gathering the data acquired from different sources and merging it to reveal a complete picture of an environment or state or any point of interest. If there is a large amount of information coming from different sources, using DFAs is a must for maintaining the quality and integrity of the data on which certain decisions are to be made. There are many algorithms and techniques for efficient data fusion (Majumder et al., 2001; Bar-Shalom and Li, 1995; Bar-Shalom et al., 1990; Raol, 2009; Zou and Sun, 2013; Cho et al., 2013). However, considering WBASNs, there are certain limitations; mainly with respect to power and computational constraints. The data fusion technique that has high computational cost with precision may not be applicable in certain scenarios where we have low computational power, and vice versa. These kinds of questions make researchers ponder not only on existing DFAs but also on the possibility of modifying or developing new algorithms for WBASNs.

2.1 DATA AGGREGATION AND DATA FUSION

In any sensor network, the amount of data generated for the sensed attribute/s of any sensor is enormous. Moreover, it is prone to corruption, as there might be interference. For example, interference due to pressure, temperature, EM waves, etc. This curried data cannot yield good results; in fact in WBASNs this can lead to disastrous decisions. Data Fusion is the answer to such failures or inaccuracies in the sensor readings. In the literature fusion is combined with many terms. We can find multiple terminologies that include fusion of data, ie, information fusion, data fusion, sensor fusion, data aggregation and sensor integration. All of these terms have been explicitly defined by their users and there is as yet no unified approach. Sensor Fusion normally relates with the fusion of data that sensors generate whereas, Information and data fusion are accepted as general terms with the same meaning (Abdelgawad and Bayoumi, 2012).

Joint Directors of Laboratories (JDL) (White, 1991) defines data fusion as "*multilevel, multifaceted process handling the automatic detection, association, correlation, estimation, and combination of data and information from several sources.*" Jayasimha (1994) states that data fusion is the "*Combination of data from multiple sensors to accomplish improved accuracy and more specific inferences that could be achieved by the use of single sensor alone*". In the same manner, multisensory fusion deals with the fusion of sensed data by different sensors and the orchestration of the data into one presentable format. Hence we can state that data fusion is the process of finding true values or reaching a correct decision by resolving conflicting sensed values via multiple sources.

Besides data fusion, there is another term that is widely used in the literature, data aggregation, mainly in the domain of Wireless Sensor Networks (WSN). Data aggregation refers to refining the voluminous raw data collected by a sensor. Simply stated, it is the summarization of the entire data. Fig. 2 illustrates the concept of multisensory data fusion, sensor data fusion, and sensor data aggregation. Data aggregation reduces the data and cannot be done for the applications where precision

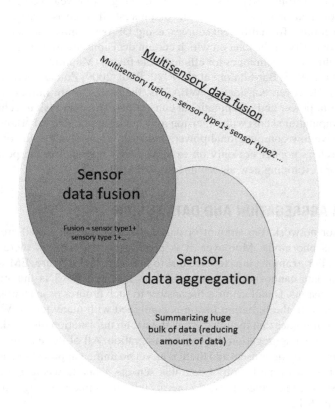

FIG. 2

Relationship amongst data aggregation and data fusion.

is demanded. Data aggregation may reduce the amount of data, but this may result in the elimination of an important set of data.

2.1.1 Data fusion algorithms

Data fusion is an important aspect in Computational Intelligence (CI). This results in making precise and accurate decisions. There is a huge application arena for DFAs. Anywhere we have to deal with data, or a large amount of data, and anywhere we need precision and data manipulation in a desired manner, DFAs provide the solution.

As shown in Fig. 3, DFAs can be grouped into four classes, ie, Inference, Estimation, Feature Maps and Reliable Abstract Sensing (Nakamura et al., 2007).

Inference algorithms are used when decisions rely upon the knowledge of perceived circumstances or situations or events. Inference means transition from one true state to another while the result is dependent on the previous result. Classical Inference algorithms are Baysian Inference (Box and Tiao, 2011), Dempster-Shafer Belief Accumulation Theory (Gordon and Shortliffe, 1984). Besides fuzzy logic (McNeill and Thro, 2014), Artificial Neural Networks (Mäkisara et al., 2014) and abductive reasoning (Walton, 2014) are major inference algorithms.

Feature Maps Algorithms intend to solve such problems where raw sensory data are not appropriate for use. Instead, certain features are selected amongst a whole set of sensed data. Normally Inference methods are used to extract a feature map.

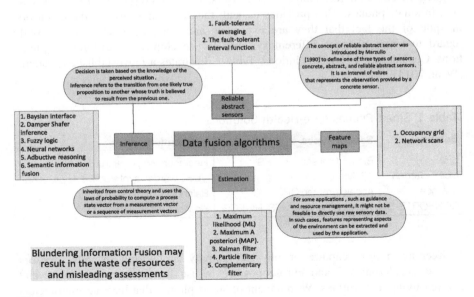

FIG. 3

Data fusion algorithms.

Occupancy Grid (Thrun, 2003) and Network Scans (Zhao et al., 2002) are two methods that lie in this class of algorithms.

Reliable abstract sensor methods are used in the context of time synchronization by maintaining lower and upper time boundaries (Marzullo, 1990). Fault Tolerant Averaging (Jayasimha, 1994) and Fault Tolerant Interval Function belong to Reliable Abstract Sensing group.

Estimation Algorithms are based upon control theory and are widely studied in different domains. The most prominent methods of this class are Maximum Likelihood (Kubo, 1992), Least Squares (Marquardt, 1963), Moving Average Filters (Sato, 2001), Kalman Filters (Srinivasan, 2015), Complementary Filters (Cockcroft et al., 2014), and Particle Filters (Gordon et al., 2004).

2.2 SMART PHONES FOR e-HEALTH MONITORING

The technology shift from mobile phones to smart phones is perhaps the fastest technology shift globally. Smart phones are penetrated deep into every ones lives. They have much more to offer than mobile phones. Today they have powerful processors, large memory, many built in sensors, along with multiple network interfaces. Discussing cellular technology, GSM is replaced with 3G and 4G networks offering high bandwidth that makes numerous applications feasible.

Confining ourselves only to sensory part, we can find accelerometers, gyroscopes, magnetometers, cameras, temperature sensors, GPS, microphones, ECG sensors, etc., in smart phones. This provides us with the opportunity to use these sensors in spite of the fact that they are expensive and complex sensory units. With regard to smart phones, different systems are developed for different applications. Considering e-Health solutions, Table 1 illustrates a few established systems (Want, 2014).

Table 1 Smart Phones for e-Health Solutions

Solution	Sensor Types	Application
SPA	Biomedical sensor, GPS	Heathcare suggestions
UbiFit Garden	3D Accelerometer	UbiFit Garden's Interactive Application
Balance	Accelerometer, GPS	Balancing
CONSORTS-S	Wireless Sensor, MESI RF-ECG	Healthcare Services

Keeping motion capture or physical activity monitoring in view, sensors such as accelerometers and gyroscopes are in use for different healthcare and assisted-living applications. With advent of smart phones that have accelerometers and gyroscope sensors research into their use for the said purpose has taken spotlight.

In this chapter, two sensor data fusion techniques (Kalman and Complementary) are analysed in context with WBASF anticipating WBASNs using smart phones. Simulations are conducted for comparison of these two estimation-based DFAs using comparative analysis. According to our results, considering human body movements, the Complimentary Data Fusion Algorithm (CDFA) is more appealing in comparison to the Kalman Data Fusion Algorithm (KDFA) due to its simplicity, and accuracy.

3 ORIENTATION SENSING

In WBASNs, activity monitoring and fall detection for the elderly is becoming a hot topic. Initially, we required a stationary-camera-based complex setup with very limited freedom of movement. This was replaced with Inertial Measurement Units (IMUs) for their improved mobility, wearability and ease of use (Bachmann et al., 2001; Zheng et al., 2005). These IMUs are now being replaced with smart phones that have built-in orientation sensors (Gyroscopes and Accelerometers). Moreover, they have high computational power and efficient transmitting modules making it more interesting for WBASF (Lane et al., 2010). The orientation sensors can track or monitor the activities of a human body precisely in accordance with its application and transmit the details directly to a programmed location.

As stated earlier, smart phones contain accelerometers and gyroscopes that can be related with motion capture systems in the form of IMUs. Pascu et al. (2012) proposed a medical application using smart phones for ambient health monitoring. The question of whether smart phones can take the place of IMUs is solved by Pascu et al. (2013). A motion capture facility if derived using kinematic models and displayed interpretable data on smart phone's screen. They used Kalman filtering for the data fusion of gyroscope, accelerometer and magnetometer sensory data. Besides Kalman filtering, Bayesian filtering, Central Limit Theorem and Dempster-Shafer are prominent.

3.1 SENSOR DATA FUSION: A LAYERED APPROACH

For Sensor data fusion, we have to iterate the whole procedure into three major steps as in Khaleghi et al. (2013) and illustrated in Fig. 4.

- Sensing phase: in which raw data is sensed by the sensor.
- Analysis phase: where decisions are to be made from sensed data.
- Dissemination phase: accurate information is handed over to user application.

At initial phase, ie, sensing phase, sensed data are processed to acquire different features, ie, mean, variance, min, max, etc. These features are submitted to the analysis phase. In the analysis phase, the required features are selected and fused

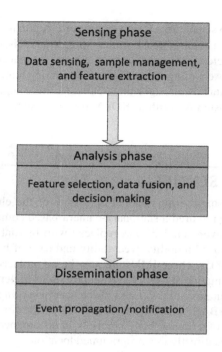

FIG. 4

Data fusion layers.

together to make a decision. That decision is fed to the dissemination phase from where this event is displayed on application modules.

To understand orientation sensing, we have to understand the basic functionality of the different sensors. The accelerometer and gyroscope are the most prominent ones besides magnetometer and inclinometer.

Accelerometers are meant to calculate G-force amongst the X, Y, and Z axes of any body. This sensor inevitably does not always work on the definition of acceleration as, *rate of change of velocity*. For simple motion-based sensing, these sensors are best to use. G-force embraces acceleration owing to gravity. If the sensor is placed facing up wards, the Z-axis reading of the accelerometer will be -1. Fig. 5 briefly describes calculations of an accelerometer.

Gyroscopes are meant to calculate angular velocities amongst X, Y, and Z axes. This sensor has no concern for orientation but takes care of rotation at different velocities. To accurately measure the orientation of a body, gyroscope and accelerometers have to consult each other to determine whether body is moving and in which direction. Fig. 5 explains the angular rotations that a gyroscope measures.

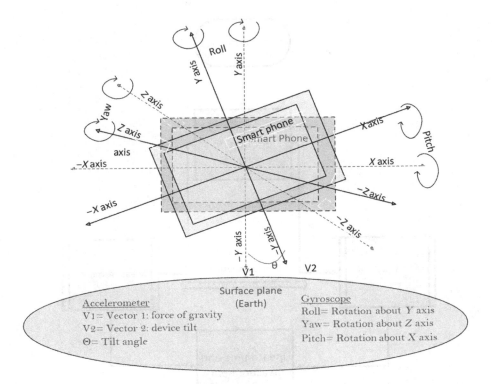

FIG. 5

Gyroscope accelerometer functioning.

The orientation of a body can be calculated with information gathered from the attached accelerometers and gyroscope articulated via quaternion and a rotation matrix to offer a precise calculation of the body's placement with respect to global coordinates.

4 ORIENTATION APPROXIMATION

The major objective of orientation approximation is to guess the rotation in relation to a coordinate frame of sensor and the rest of the world as precisely as possible. Three-dimensional IMUs typically use gyroscopes and accelerometers to measure the acceleration vector and rotational vector in a coordinate frame relative to global coordinates. Orientation approximation is conducted by fusing the above-mentioned vectors.

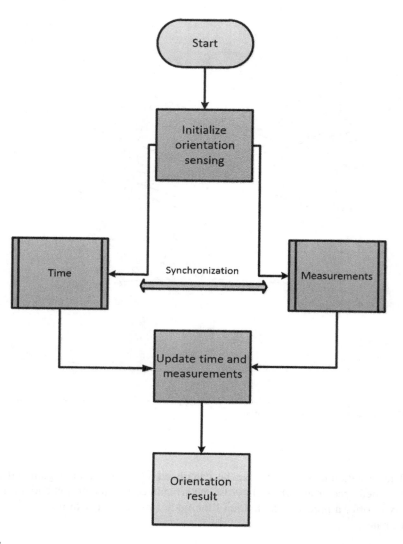

FIG. 6

Generalized orientation approximation algorithm.

4.1 GYROSCOPE ACCELEROMETER INTEGRATION

Gyroscope integration provides an approximation regarding relative rotation given that the initial rotation is known. This angular velocity, calculated by gyroscopes, is also directly integrated to deliver an accurate approximation even if the body is moving at high speed. A generalized orientation approximation algorithm is illustrated in Fig. 6. Authors in [32] presents gyroscope integration as in Eq. (1).

$$f_t = f_{t-1} + \frac{1}{2dt}(0, \vec{\omega}) \otimes \hat{f}_{t-1} \tag{1}$$

where

f_t = approximated orientation
dt = sample period
$\vec{\omega}$ = angular rate vector calculated in rad/s
$\otimes$ = quaternion multiplication operator.

Whenever any change in orientation occurs, approximated quaternion must also be normalized to omit or reduce angular errors that may persist. This integration presents two significant problems, ie,

- Any error in angular rate vector will increase cumulatively.
- Knowledge of the initial orientation of the body is a must to relate this to changes in positioning.

Vectors illustrate an approximation of the orientation that is related to the global coordinate frame. Combining these vectors and then comparing the result with the vectors for the initial position can provide us with details of the rotation that has occurred. Mathematically, this rotation "R" can be calculated as in Eq. (2).

$$R = \frac{v_i}{\vec{\omega}_i} \forall i \varepsilon (1, \ldots, n) \tag{2}$$

where

R = rotation
V_i = number of sensed vectors
$\vec{\omega}_i$ = reference vectors in global coordinates.

As depicted by Khaleghi et al. (2013) the qualms in sensory data rests not only due to inaccuracy and integration of noise in the sensed data, but wrong interpretations and inconsistencies also contribute in uncertainties regarding sensory data. The general algorithm used for orientation is defined as in Eqs. (3) and (4):

$$\vec{e} = \frac{\vec{a}}{||\vec{a}||} \tag{3}$$

$$R = [\vec{e}]^T \equiv \hat{f} \tag{4}$$

where $\vec{a}$ = acceleration vector.

Using vectors for approximation of orientation gives absolute values. On the other hand, if we discuss the accelerometer, it is polluted with noise due to the acceleration and gravity phenomenon that occurs in a moving body. Here we will discuss two of the most widely used DFAs, ie, Complementary filtering and Kalman filtering simultaneously.

4.2 COMPLEMENTARY FILTERING

CDFA is meant to derive one single output by combining two different measurements with different noise properties. Focussing on one case, accelerometer signal produces high frequency noise while the gyroscope results contain low frequency noise. These data fusion techniques apply both low and high pass filters as expressed in Eq. (5):

$$H_s = H_{LP(s)} + H_{HP(s)} = 1 \tag{5}$$

Using this approach of data fusion, we overcome the delay problem. Mathematically we can express CDFA equations as in Eqs. (6) and (7):

$$f_t = f_t + \frac{1}{k} f' \tag{6}$$

$$\hat{f}_t = \begin{cases} f_t' + \frac{1}{k}(f_t'' - f_t') & \text{for } |\|a\| - 1| < a_T \\ f_t' & \text{for } |\|a\| - 1| \geq a_T \end{cases} \tag{7}$$

where

f_t' = gyroscope integration
f_t'' = vector observation
k = filter co-efficient
a_T = threshold for attaining vector observation in linear accelerations.

The first part of the Eq. (7) maintains a high-frequency response while low-frequency noise is handled by the latter part of Eq. (7). The filter coefficient plays a vital role in drift cancelation rate control. As the values of drift cancelation coefficient increases, drift correction gets slower, however, more accuracy is guaranteed.

The complementary filter integrates the static truthfulness of the accelerometer and gyroscope within vibrant movements. In comparison with Kalman filter, it offers a constant gain.

4.3 KALMAN FILTER

For fusing multisensory data, Kalman filtering is one of the most widely accepted algorithm. Neil Armstrong, reached the moon on his spaceship Appollo, whose navigation computer followed *Kalman filtering*. Though recursive in nature, it shows its worth in the navigational systems of air crafts and in the field of robotics. Mainly this filter is well suited to the entire instrument trade and can be applied in any field requiring data fusion. KDFA gather the past knowledge of the dynamics for prediction of future states. Mathematically KDFA can be expressed as in Eq. (8) (Young, 2009).

$$\vec{x}_{k+1} = A\vec{x}_k + B\vec{u}_k + \vec{\omega}_k \tag{8}$$

where

$\vec{x}_k$ = state vector
A = transition matrix of prior states
B = state matrix of control inputs
ω = noise vector.
If $\vec{y}_k$ is a set of any measured state then it can be expressed as Eq. (9)

$$\vec{y}_k = C\vec{x}_k + \vec{\upsilon}_k \tag{9}$$

In Eq. (9), "C" is the matrix relating to the observed state while $\vec{\upsilon}_k$ is the noise vector.

Given the above-mentioned equations, the Kalman filter can be defined by Eqs. (10)–(12) as in Young (2009).

$$K_k = AP_kC^T(CP_kC^T + R_k)^{-1} \tag{10}$$

$$\hat{\vec{x}}_{k+1} = (A\hat{\vec{x}}_k + B\vec{u}_k) + k(\vec{y} + k + 1 - C\hat{\vec{x}}_k) \tag{11}$$

$$P_{k+1} = AP_kA^T + Q_k + AP_kC^TR_k^{-1} + CP_kA^T \tag{12}$$

where

K = Kalman gain
P = error covariance matrix
Q = uncertainty factor of the system
R_k = covariance matrix of noise vector $\vec{\upsilon}_k$

5 EXPERIMENTAL SETUP

The concept and the usability of data fusion in multiple fields of engineering and computer sciences is not a new thing. However, with emerging new technologies and applications, the said concept needs to be modeled in an efficient and progressive manner. Considering WBASNs, which are rapidly emerging as widely accepted technology, there are different sensors implanted or attached on a body. There are plenty of applications that need orientation sensors, ie, gyroscopes and accelerometers. Continuous sensing results in an enormous amount of data which needs to be analyzed precisely in order to get the desired and accurate results.

The smart phones today are equipped with numerous sensors, most commonly orientation sensors, gyroscopes and accelerometers. These sensors can play a vital role in fall detection and motion capture in relation to e-Health solutions. Sportsmen, often bowlers in cricket, often frequently suffer from backbone injury which can require them to visit a physiotherapist on a daily basis. To investigate improvements, sportsmen have to perform certain biological and motion tests that are expensive and time consuming. If a smart phone is attached to the patient's back that can continuously monitor its bend while walking, sitting or performing any activity this may be a better choice for monitoring the patient's rehabilitation.

In the same way an application is being developed on the basis of a gyroscope and accelerometer (built in sensors of smart phone) that continuously monitors and displays data on the smart phone as well as storing it on the phone's database.

This application is developed using two different data fusion techniques, ie, KDFA and CDFA, to compare results. KDFA comes with a high computational cost and brief history while CDFA is simple and easy to implement. The real-time fused data are collected and results are compared using MATLAB to verify which algorithm performs most efficiently in said scenario.

6 KALMAN AND COMPLEMENTARY FILTERING
6.1 ON TEST BASIS

Before getting real-time data, using Matlab we compared Kalman and Complementary filters to observe computational time, cost and complexity differences. Above all, the performance accuracy was also noted as shown in Fig. 7.

As one can easily see from the Fig. 7, the Kalman filtering results are not especially accurate in comparison with Complementary filtering. However, the Kalman filtering has a brief history in navigational systems, where drifts and angular velocities are easier to predict. In wireless body area sensor fusion (WBASF) it

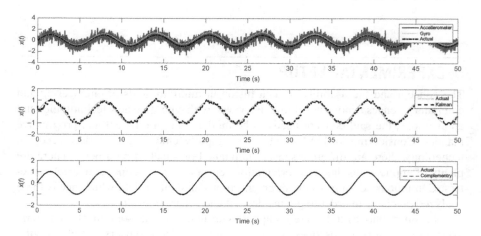

FIG. 7

CDFA and KDFA on test basis.

is relatively hard to predict both angular velocity and degree of movement. On the other hand, the Complementary filter has a constant gain that proves its worth in WBASF.

6.2 ON REAL-TIME DATA

Considering the results obtained in Fig. 7, an application is developed fusing the gyroscope and accelerometer data. The results obtained from the accelerometers are depicted in Fig. 8 considering X, Y, and Z axes. Whereas the roll rate, pitch rate and yaw rate of gyroscope are measured as in Fig. 9.

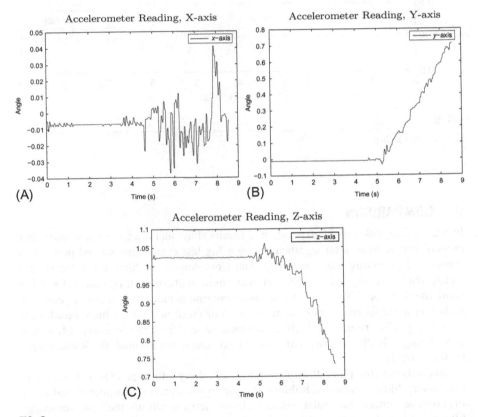

FIG. 8

Accelerometer readings. (A) Accelerometer reading, X-axis. (B) Accelerometer reading, Y-axis. (C) Accelerometer reading, Z-axis.

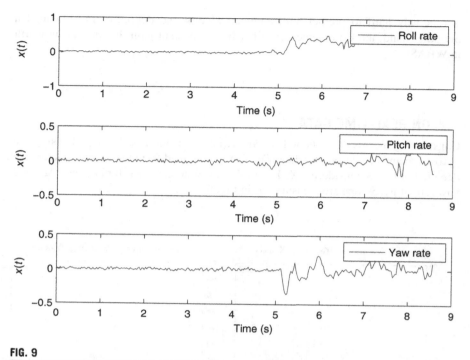

FIG. 9

Gyroscope reading.

6.3 COMPARISON

In accordance with Fig. 10 experimental results show that the Complementary filter outperforms Kalman filter significantly by using less computational and processing power and providing more accuracy. The Complementary filter for WBASF can be applied by having only vector and quaternion mathematical operators. On other hand, the traditional Kalman filter needs an enormous number of matrix operations, including multiplications and taking inverses of these matrices, which, besides the complexity, also results in high computational and processing costs. Moreover, considering WBASF, where prediction of next state is not optimal, the Kalman filter performs badly.

According to the plots illustrated in Fig. 10, along with Eqs. (8)–(12), the Complementary filter supersedes Kalman filtering in the aspect of computational costs. In simple arithmetic manipulations, and trigonometric notations, the Complementary filter bears less than 10% of the computational costs in comparison with the Kalman filter (Simon, 2010; Brückner et al., 2014). Table 2 depicts a comparative analysis of Kalman and Complementary filter techniques for WBASF.

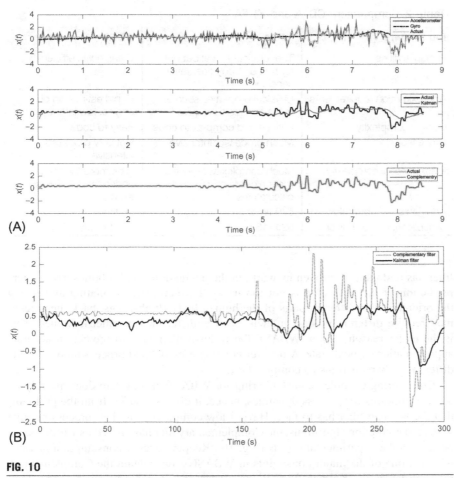

FIG. 10

KDFA vs CDFA as WBASF lgorithms. (A) Original vs KDFA vs CDFA. (B) KDFA vs CDFA.

7 DISCUSSION

What kind of help can a WBASN provide if the data collected are to complex to analyze and diagnose accurately? For this purpose efficient DFAs play a vital and very critical role. In our point of view, without efficient and accurate data fusion techniques WBASNs cannot work efficiently.

Our work is based on the abovementioned statement. Hence the Kalman and Complementary structures in relation to WBASF have been discussed and studied. Generally, the Kalman filtering is used more frequently due to its long history; however, it fails to provide efficient solutions in sensor fusion for BANs considering posture tracking for e-Health solutions. Besides human posture tracking, the Kalman

Table 2 Comparison: CDFA and KDFA

Parameters	KDFA	CDFA
Fusing abilities	Theocratically ideal but not for human body orientation sensing	Clear, noise efficient
Approximation requirements	Physical properties such as mass and inertia required	Rapid estimation of angles, low latency
Coding complexity	Difficult and complex to code	Easy to code
Processor	Much processor intensive	Not very processor intensive
Mathematical complexity	Much complexity, requires linear algebra and matrices calculations	A bit more theory to understand, however simpler
Addition and subtraction	579 times	36 times
Multiplication and division	524+46 times	39+1 times

filter has undoubtedly proven its worth in the navigational and robotics trade where prediction of the next state is not too tricky. Furthermore, calculating and fusing the orientation of different parts of the human body (limbs, legs, back, head, etc.) may require different process models, each with its own parametric values. This is the major reason why in WBASF the Kalman filter fails to predict an accurate approximation of next state. Moreover creating a predefined process model for the different body parts is also a complex task.

Considering Complementary filtering for WBASF, this system does not rely on any assumptions for process dynamics, hence, it does not suffer from the problems that the Kalman filter has to face. Having low complexity and less processing time with zero prediction algorithms, the Complementary filer has proved its worth, as can be seen in the experimental results (Fig. 10). Keeping energy consumption in view, which is one of the major constraints in WBASNs, once again the Complementary filter surpasses the Kalman filter as the processor is capable of much longer low-power sleep timings in comparison with the Kalman filter.

8 CONCLUSION AND FUTURE WORKS

WBASF is an emerging as well as challenging topic in research as well as medical/ instrumental industries. Advent of smart phones has taken spot light anticipating its utility as middleware due to its computational, storage and communication capabilities along with built in sensors. Reflecting orientation sensing, numerous DFAs are known and in this work, KDFA and CDFA are analysed considering smart phone as a middle ware. The Kalman data fusing technique has no doubt proven its metal in previous decades for calculating machine orientations. This technique predicts the future state in machines by using past knowledge (aircrafts and robots), although this is a less complex process in this arena. According to our study, work and experiments, when we analyze humans, the future prediction technique of the Kalman filter did not prove its worth. Moreover, its high complexity and computational costs forbid us from using it as a WBASF algorithm. The Complementary filter, in comparison with Kalman filter, shows better performance, with features such as simplicity and low processing, as discussed in Table 2.

In the future we are going to implement the Complementary filter for orientation-based data sensor fusion for patients that suffer back injuries and compare their results with those of the actual rehabilitation tests conducted by physiotherapists.

ACRONYMS

3G	3rd generation
4G	4rth generation
BAN	Body Area Network
CDFA	Complementary Data Fusion Algorithm
CI	Computational Intelligence
DFA	Data Fusion Algorithm
ECG	electrocardiogram
GSM	Global System for Mobile
ICT	Information and Communication Technology
IMU	Inertial Measurement Unit
JDL	Joint Directors of Laboratories
KDFA	Kalman Data Fusion Algorithm
WBASF	wireless body area sensor fusion
WBASN	wireless body area network
WPANs	wireless personal area network
WSN	wireless sensor network

GLOSSARY

Acceleration rate of change of velocity using the basic physics definition.

Accelerometers a sensor/instrument that calculates the velocity of any moving/vibrating body.

Activity monitoring monitoring any activity using any system. In this chapter, it refers to monitoring movement of the body using different sensors.

Angular velocities in classical physics it is the rate of change of angular position.

Assisted living offering a patient help in living with independence, dignity and care.

Body Area Networks a network of wearable/implanted inside body devices that are usually that sense sensing different attributes.

Computational constraints restrictions and limitations on the computing capability of a device, or power or any other.

Computational intelligence refers to the study of designing intelligent decision making devices regarding any specific problem.

Data aggregation summarizing a huge amount of data.

Data Fusion a process that integrates multiple data to provide one concrete, nearly accurate output.

Data Fusion Algorithms algorithms that perform data fusion.

e-Health healthcare practice supported electronically using ICT.

Gyroscopes a sensor that measure angular rotational velocity.

Information and Communication Technology is a parent terminology that includes any communication device integrated with any domain to attain specific results.

Inertial Measurement Unit an instrument composed of multiple sensors used to measure orientation of a body, normally used in aircrafts, spacecrafts, and the finding of any body movement disorders, etc.

Multisensor data fusion refers to fusing data collected from multiple types of sensors.

Orientation sensing states sensing or knowing velocity, acceleration and gravitational forces with respect to the outer world or any specific point.

Velocity in classical physics it is the rate of change in a position with respect to some point of reference.

Wireless body area sensor fusion refers to the fusion of data collected by sensors in a WBAN.

Wireless body area sensor network refers to the network of tiny sensors deployed on/in a body to sense different attributes as per need.

REFERENCES

Abdelgawad, A., Bayoumi, M., 2012. Data fusion in WSN. In: Resource-Aware Data Fusion Algorithms for Wireless Sensor Networks. Springer, Berlin, pp. 17–35.

Bachmann, E.R., McGhee, R.B., Yun, X., Zyda, M.J., 2001. Inertial and magnetic posture tracking for inserting humans into networked virtual environments. In: Proceedings of the ACM Symposium on Virtual Reality Software and Technology. ACM, New York, NY, pp. 9–16.

Bar-Shalom, Y., Fortmann, T.E., Cable, P.G., 1990. Tracking and data association. J. Acoust. Soc. Am. 87 (2), 918–919.

Bar-Shalom, Y., Li, X.R., 1995. Multitarget-Multisensor Tracking: Principles and Techniques, vol. 19. YBS Publishing, Storrs, CT.

Box, G.E., Tiao, G.C., 2011. Bayesian Inference in Statistical Analysis, vol. 40. John Wiley & Sons, New York.

Brückner, H.P., Krüger, B., Blume, H., 2014. Reliable orientation estimation for mobile motion capturing in medical rehabilitation sessions based on inertial measurement units. Microelectron. J. 45 (12), 1603–1611.

Cho, T., Lee, C., Choi, S., 2013. Multi-sensor fusion with interacting multiple model filter for improved aircraft position accuracy. Sensors 13 (4), 4122–4137.

Cockcroft, J., Muller, J., Scheffer, C., 2014. A complementary filter for tracking bicycle crank angles using inertial sensors, kinematic constraints and vertical acceleration updates. IEEE Sens. J. 15 (8), 4218–4225.

Gordon, J., Shortliffe, E.H., 1984. The dempster-shafer theory of evidence. In: Rule-Based Expert Systems: The MYCIN Experiments of the Stanford Heuristic Programming Project, vol. 3, pp. 832–838.

Gordon, N., Ristic, B., Arulampalam, S., 2004. Beyond the Kalman Filter: Particle Filters for Tracking Applications. Artech House, London.

Jayasimha, D., 1994. Fault tolerance in a multisensor environment. In: Proceedings of the 13th Symposium on Reliable Distributed Systems, 1994, IEEE, pp. 2–11.

Khaleghi, B., Khamis, A., Karray, F.O., Razavi, S.N., 2013. Multisensor data fusion: a review of the state-of-the-art. Inform. Fusion 14 (1), 28–44.

Kubo, H., 1992, January. Maximum likelihood sequence estimation apparatus. US Patent 5,081,651.

Lane, N.D., Miluzzo, E., Lu, H., Peebles, D., Choudhury, T., Campbell, A.T., 2010. A survey of mobile phone sensing. IEEE Commun. Mag. 48 (9), 140–150.

Majumder, S., Scheding, S., Durrant-Whyte, H.F., 2001. Multisensor data fusion for underwater navigation. Robot. Auton. Syst. 35 (2), 97–108.

Mäkisara, K., Simula, O., Kangas, J., Kohonen, T., 2014. Artificial Neural Networks, vol. 2. Elsevier, Amsterdam.

Marquardt, D.W., 1963. An algorithm for least-squares estimation of nonlinear parameters. J. Soc. Ind. Appl. Math. 11 (2), 431–441.

Marzullo, K., 1990. Tolerating failures of continuous-valued sensors. ACM Trans. Comput. Syst. 8 (4), 284–304.

McNeill, F.M., Thro, E., 2014. Fuzzy Logic: A Practical Approach. Academic Press, New York.

Nakamura, E.F., Loureiro, A.A., Frery, A.C., 2007. Information fusion for wireless sensor networks: methods, models, and classifications. ACM Comput. Surv. 39 (3), 9.

Pascu, T., White, M., Beloff, N., Patoli, Z., Barker, L., 2012. Ambient health monitoring: the smartphone as a body sensor network component. InImpact: J. Innov. Impact 6 (1), 62.

Pascu, T., White, M., Patoli, Z., 2013. Motion capture and activity tracking using smartphone-driven body sensor networks. In: Third International Conference on Innovative Computing Technology (INTECH), 2013, pp. 456–462.

Raol, J.R., 2009. Multi-Sensor Data Fusion With MATLAB®. CRC Press, Boca Raton.

Sato, H., 2001, October. Moving average filter. US Patent 6,304,133.

Simon, D., 2010. Kalman filtering with state constraints: a survey of linear and nonlinear algorithms. IET Control Theory Appl. 4 (8), 1303–1318.

Srinivasan, V., 2015. Sensor fusion techniques using extended kalman filter. Int. J. Adv. Eng. 1 (1), 18–22.

Thrun, S., 2003. Learning occupancy grid maps with forward sensor models. Auton. Robot. 15 (2), 111–127.

Walton, D., 2014. Abductive Reasoning. University of Alabama Press, Tuscaloosa, AL.

Want, R., 2014. The power of smartphones. IEEE Pervasive Comput. (3), 76–79.

White, F.E., 1991. Data fusion lexicon. Technical report. DTIC Document.

Young, A., 2009. Comparison of orientation filter algorithms for realtime wireless inertial posture tracking. In: Sixth International Workshop on Wearable and Implantable Body Sensor Networks, 2009. BSN 2009, pp. 59–64.

Zhao, Y., Govindan, R., Estrin, D., 2002. Residual Energy Scans for Monitoring Wireless Sensor Networks. Center for Embedded Network Sensing, UCLA.

Zheng, H., Black, N.D., Harris, N., 2005. Position-sensing technologies for movement analysis in stroke rehabilitation. Med. Biol. Eng. Comput. 43 (4), 413–420.

Zou, W., Sun, W., 2013. A multi-dimensional data association algorithm for multi-sensor fusion. In: Intelligent Science and Intelligent Data Engineering. Springer, Berlin, pp. 280–288.

Ubiquitous services independent of devices/platforms

Reuse of data from smart medical devices for quality control and evidence-based medicine

9

J. Sliwa

Bern University of Applied Sciences, Bern, Switzerland

1 INTRODUCTION

We are frequently confronted with brilliant visions of the wireless future of medicine, the classical one being the talk by Eric Topol[1] at TEDMED 2009. In this vision, vital parameters can be measured constantly and reliably. They are gathered on a common platform (a smartphone) and clearly visualized for the patient who is warned when an abnormal condition occurs. Likewise, all relevant information is transmitted to the hospital or to the practitioner who cares for the patient. It is there seamlessly integrated into the electronic health record (EHR) system. A competent doctor monitors the health state of the patient and takes actions if necessary. The costs are reimbursed by insurance according to the healthcare plan. Gathered data are used for advancing medical knowledge. The security and privacy of patient's data are assured. All this works for the maximal benefit of the patients and society as a whole.

However, the actual adoption of mobile medical devices into clinical practice lags far behind expectations. There are several reasons for this that we will discuss later. A major one is the necessary confidence in the quality of the devices, as they directly interact with humans and influence their health. This confidence can be gained by collecting and adequately analyzing the data generated during the process. This is the main subject of this chapter.

First, we outline the current state of the medical technology, showing the opportunities that arise from its rapid development. Then we name the obstacles that hinder its wide adoption. We take a closer look on the fact that such a device acts

---

[1] http://www.ted.com/talks/eric_topol_the_wireless_future_of_medicine (accessed June 14, 2015).

Pervasive Computing. http://dx.doi.org/10.1016/B978-0-12-803663-1.00009-7

as an element of a bigger Cyber-Physical System, changing in time, with humans in the loop, which makes the complete description and verification of the system impossible. Further on, designing and operating smart medical devices within a healthcare system requires a rare blend of skills. The cooperation of specialists having different backgrounds and mindsets is necessary.

We discuss in detail the primary use of data for direct health support and their reuse for quality assurance in medical research. We take a look at the involved stakeholders and their interests. Then we expose the arguments for the partly conflicting goals of privacy protection and high-quality research.

We quote some emerging platforms for data exchange and then propose a general architecture that combines organizational and technical elements and enables both support of the devices and a smooth data exchange.

We discuss selected technical problems and major challenges for data analytics. Finally, we stress the necessity of responsible handling of processed data and delivered results.

As getting a correct answer is impossible without posing a good question beforehand, we raise more questions than deliver answers and recipes. In this new field, defining research areas and exposing the complex, and nontechnical issues, is essential. We also express warnings and caveats, as in vital issues regarding human health is more important than speed.

2 STATE OF THE ART OF MEDICAL TECHNOLOGY

We observe a rapidly growing number of novel medical software applications and medical devices. Filippini (2012) and Maharatna and Bonfiglio (2013) give a current overview of the technology and its application in healthcare systems. First, the driving force is progress in the sensor and actuator technology. Especially as interfacing between the domains of electricity and chemistry becomes easier. More substances can be detected and, thanks to micro/nanotechnology substances, can be directly injected into the human body. There are portable devices to measure heart (ECG) and brain (EEG) signals. Connecting to smartphones makes local processing power available and permits communication with remote units (eg, hospitals). Novel devices can be fixed on the body, put on the skin as patches or woven into smart textiles. They also can be implanted. Smaller, low-power devices make the process simpler, also new methods of energy harvesting and inductive transfer of energy reduce the need for operational battery replacement. Personal devices on and in the body are connected via a body area network (BAN). Another setting is when the devices are placed in the local environment (home, apartment). We then talk about Ambient Assisted Living (AAL).

The main goal of such systems is to reduce the need for visiting the doctor in person and at the same time making frequent (or continuous) measurements possible. In this way, a patient with a chronic or acute condition can stay at home longer while receiving the same or better health care. Evidently, this will contribute to a reduction in (otherwise exploding) healthcare costs.

Some devices are intended for recreational use and aim to improve and control the physical performance of healthy individuals. Some are used for the regular monitoring of medical parameters (blood pressure, glucose level) in noncritical situations. Some are intended for life-saving functions, and in this case, elevated security standards have to be met. Low-risk devices can be sold on the open market without restrictions. Other devices require—depending on the risk level— either a premarket notification or a premarket approval. Many promising devices never overcome these regulatory hurdles, especially if developed by small start-up companies. At the component level, we see spectacular new sensors and actuators that connect the realms of biology, chemistry, physics, electronics, and information technology in ways unthinkable before. However, many of the new smart components stay at the level of the proof of concept and are not integrated into complete devices, fit for clinical use.

Applying a device for serious clinical use is connected with a significant health risk for the patient and a corresponding legal and financial risk for the producer. Reliability of the devices have to be improved and verified, and long-term operation has to be assured. If a device is to enter the healthcare system—to be recommended by a hospital and reimbursed by an insurance—its therapeutic effect has to be proven and be sufficient to justify its price. In this context we would like to distinguish between efficacy (therapeutic effect in laboratory), effectiveness (effect in the clinical practice), and efficiency (ratio of effect to price). Not all authors strictly follow these definitions. We will stick to the term effectiveness, because data in our framework are collected from actual deployed devices. Financial factors may also be applied if desired, but we will not expand on this subject.

In this chapter we concentrate on systems of implantable and wearable devices, connected via a BAN to a data aggregator, currently typically a smartphone (Fig. 1).

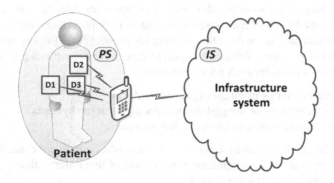

FIG. 1

Basic configuration.

This set is to be considered as a virtual multielement device, performing a common task in a coordinated way. Cavallari et al. (2014) present a survey on wireless BANs. Wac (2013) gives an overview of the use of the smartphone as a health informatics platform.

3 OBSTACLES TO THE ADOPTION OF SMART MEDICAL DEVICES IN THE PRACTICE

Although smart medical devices and telemedicine systems doubtlessly will shape the future of medicine, their actual adoption into clinical practice lags far behind expectations. There is an essential difference between a laboratory setting, with one test person and all specialists at hand, and a mass-produced device/system, distributed to remote places and installed and served by local doctors and nurses.

There are several major technical and organizational challenges to overcome:

- interoperability at all levels;
- configuration and deployment to the patients;
- servicing the deployed systems;
- ongoing quality control;
- engineering capabilities;
- understanding of the approval process; and
- proper business model.

Technically, one of the major problems is interoperability. Solving this is necessary if we want to flexibly configure the systems and select the best elements for every function from any producer. It has an economic background, as many producers prefer to protect their ecosystems with proprietary, undisclosed data formats and protocols. In consequence, the hospital and the patient may be prevented from including necessary devices because they are not supported by a chosen supplier. In the same way, if we want our devices to communicate directly with the hospital EHR system, the EHR system chosen will limit us to only certain suppliers.

An important case is the detection of complex events (Fig. 2) where synchronized measurements from many sources are used to detect, for example, a patient's urgent condition. Let us consider such measurements:

- D1 (accelerometer)—point event (tumbling down)
- D2 (ECG monitor)—prolonged abnormal waveform (arrhythmia)
- D3 (pulse meter)—limit value exceeded (fast pulse)

The combination of those measurements establishes a medical condition (eg, an emergency) with much better precision than each of them alone, thus significantly reducing the frequency of false alarms.

From the position of the system designer the necessity of an open, interoperable system is evident. If the best sensors of the classes D1, D2, and D3 are available from different producers, we want to be able to connect them into a closely coupled

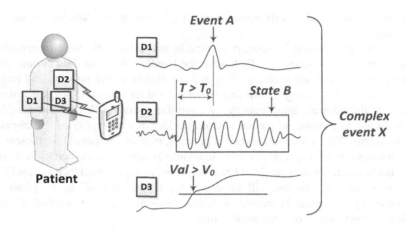

FIG. 2

Complex event.

system—with one communication device executing the event detection algorithm and with well synchronized clocks.

As far as possible, existing standards have to be respected. Currently we see a patchwork of partly overlapping initiatives backed by various organizations (St Cyr, 2013). Over time, the technology and market forces will determine the optimal solutions, whereas open standards will still coexist with the proprietary standards enforced by the major players. In the area of data exchange with medical devices, the predominant standard on the semantic level is HL7.[2] At the lower level the major standards are ISO/IEEE 11073[3] (Yao and Warren, 2005; Trigo et al., 2014) and ASTM F2671.[4] It is to be examined which competing standards will eventually predominate and to what extent they are applicable to low power micro/ nano sensors.

Distributing smart medical devices to the patients is a complex task. It is difficult from the medical point of view, especially when the device has to be implanted (Kramme, 2007; Fröhlig et al., 2013). Configuring a device like a defibrillator requires a special blend of medical and technical knowledge. This knowledge is today available in good hospitals. However, if a composite device has to be configured from individual sensors into a working BAN together with an application on a commercial smartphone, we enter a new domain. In order to set a wireless network, a good network supporter is necessary. Just trying to assign the tasks of installation and support to the clinical staff is unfeasible (Wagner et al., 2013). On the other hand,

---

[2]http://www.hl7.org/ (accessed July 18, 2015).
[3]http://www.continuaalliance.org/ (accessed July 18, 2015).
[4]http://www.astm.org/Standards/F2761 (accessed July 18, 2015).

working with frail and elderly patients is not a common skill among the network supporters.

Similarly, establishing a support service is not trivial. We have to remember that not only do the patients' calls have to be handled, but also data coming from the devices may indicate problems that are not visible to the patients and require an intervention. For example, missing or wrong values (outliers) suggest a wrong fixation of the device, empty battery, or a similar cause. In this case the medical personnel has to contact the patient, and depending of the severity of the disease it may be urgent. With a limited number of patients, normal personnel is sufficient, but above a certain limit a special organizational unit is necessary, especially with such cases that require, not only medical knowledge, but also profound technical skills.

Serious medical systems will be used only if "prescribed" by hospitals and reimbursed by insurance. Therefore, there is a necessity to provide a proof of safety, medical efficacy, and economic justification.

4 SMART MEDICAL DEVICES AS COMPLEX CYBER-PHYSICAL SYSTEMS

In the case of medical devices defining what the criteria are for a *good* device and for a *bad* one is complex. First, the device itself is composed of many elements or subsystems with many parameters that influence the quality of service. Second, it does not work on its own, but is part of an environment. Therefore, if we want to evaluate the net value of a device we have to take this environment into account (Fig. 3). We address here the subject of Cyber-Physical Systems (Suh et al., 2013) and the related field of Internet of Things (IoT) (DaCosta, 2013).

This environment consists of humans (Human in the Loop), technical systems, and the forces of nature.

As for humans, in the center there are the patients who want to receive the best treatment possible at a reasonable cost. We consider mostly telemedicine systems where the devices are delivered to the patients and are not directly supervised by health professionals. Therefore, the patients play a vital role in assuring the quality of the system. In the case of wearable devices they place them on their bodies. If a health monitoring system does not communicate automatically, data transmission has to be initiated by the patient. The devices may have batteries with various duty times, and the patients have to take care to recharge them when necessary. All these activities require certain manual and technical skills as well as concentration and an ordered lifestyle. We do not speak here of young people willing to improve their fitness but potentially of elderly patients with dementia, taking strong medication. All devices and their usage procedures have to be adapted to the capabilities of the patients.

Then we have various groups of helpers; people who want to deliver this treatment. The producers develop the devices. The doctors select the devices that will help their patients. Their skill level is an important factor for ensuring the success of

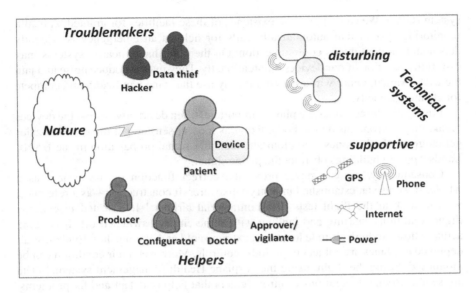

FIG. 3

Medical device and its environment.

the therapy. The doctors and clinics are the principal contacts for the patients and take on the final responsibility for the correct functioning of the delivered systems. The configurators are the people who combine separate devices into workable systems. They need a new, interdisciplinary set of skills. The controllers approve the devices for therapeutic use. After the introduction into the market they (as vigilantes) verify that those devices meet the requirements and have no adverse effects. Evidently, any of the people involved may have less than altruistic, though understandable, goals. The producers want to sell their devices, to protect their trade secrets, and to handle their errors discreetly. The doctors and clinics want to affirm their top professional positions, therefore in order to attract more patients, they may be prone to offer new (expensive) therapies beyond that which is necessity.

Software based, networked medical devices communicate electronically with the external world and are susceptible to attacks from hackers, who may carry out attacks for money or for fun (Hei and Du, 2013; La Polla et al., 2013; Fu and Blum, 2013). The patient data, stored, and transmitted by the devices are valuable to all sorts of data thieves. If a device having actuating elements is not properly secured, it may also be misused to directly damage the patient's health, for example, by activating the pacemaker's action. Software-based systems require occasional bug fixing—remote updates also provide a possible attack vector. Aside from the electronic attacks, the devices can be physically stolen or destroyed.

Networked devices depend on other technical systems. They need electrical power, phone signal, and Internet connection, possibly also global positioning system (GPS). We cannot take the existence of these facilities for granted. A health monitoring system that automatically calls for help in an emergency is critically dependent on continuous communication. On the other hand, nearby systems may distort the function of our devices unintentionally. They may introduce noise and jam the useful signal. Other wireless systems may use the same bandwidth and compete for channel capacity.

Finally, the forces of nature play an important, often destructive role—the devices break, they corrode inside the body, fixations loosen, sensors get dirty, and nozzles get clogged. Flesh, bones, and cloth attenuate the signal propagation in the BANs. Landscape and buildings obstruct the phone signal.

Consequently, we can never prove the correct function of the system as a whole. If we use an established industry—like aircraft construction—as a reference, we can look at the flight tests of a commercial airliner.[5] It is tested in extreme flight conditions, starting and landing with some engines switched off. It is being actually flown to high altitude locations, extreme cold and extreme hot. Evidently, all deployed airplanes are subject to periodic controls. Moreover, their condition can be monitored during the flight, using the Airplane Health Management system.[6] Data are sent to Boeing Operations Control Centers that help to detect and fix problems, assuring preventive, and predictive maintenance.

This example shows that high-responsibility systems, used in varying conditions, need constant monitoring. This is the main argument for the reuse of data for quality assurance and efficacy verification in the case of the medical grade medical devices.

5 INTERDISCIPLINARY APPROACH VERSUS MENTALITY MISMATCH

The field is new and skilled personnel are lacking. Designing, deploying, and servicing such devices require interdisciplinary skills (Fig. 4) in (at least) the following fields:

- sensorics
- applications for smartphones
- usability for various user groups
- computer security
- data management and privacy
- network configuration
- engineering a commercial product
- reliability

---

[5]http://www.bbc.com/future/story/20140319-stress-tests-for-safer-planes (accessed July 4, 2015).
[6]http://www.boeing.com/features/2013/07/bca-airplane-health-mgmt-07-30-13.page (accessed July 4, 2015); http://www.boeing.com/assets/pdf/commercial/aviationservices/brochures/AirplaneHealth Management.pdf (accessed July 4, 2015).

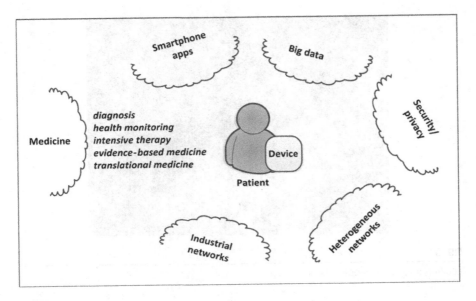

FIG. 4

Merging many worlds.

- medical case to be solved
- healthcare organization
- medical statistics
- Big Data (technical aspects)
- handling intellectual property
- approval process
- ensuring reimbursement
- reporting adverse reactions
- handling liability

Specialists in these fields come from different environments, have different backgrounds and mindsets, and do not communicate often. Evidently, a large producer has experience in gathering a multidisciplinary team. A project at a start-up company, however, typically begins around a single idea or invention, like a novel sensor or a medical smartphone app and then the missing elements are added.

This text is written from the perspective of an IT-specialists, therefore the suggestion for *looking into other people's books* regard mostly medical books. Fig. 5 deliberately stresses the size of some of these. As they are written for a different audience, extracting the relevant information is an art. We are not interested in all fine details, but it is important to notice where the possible problems lie. For example, the pacemaker leads (see Section 12.2) look just like input devices delivering some values. After a deeper inspection we notice that the reliability of these values is not

FIG. 5

Looking into other people's books.

so certain and the leads themselves need integrity and quality monitoring. A sample of the other important questions include

- How frequently has the value to be measured?
- What should be done if a value is missing?
- What needs to be done with an outlier?
- How will an emergency be detected?
- How reliable is the emergency detection algorithm—any false-positives?
- What is to be done in case of an emergency?
- In what time does the action have to take place?
- Are humans involved?
- What do the humans need to know?
- What can happen if no action is taken?
- How is the patient to be informed about the incident?, etc.

This means that from the IT point of view we are not so much interested in the medical semantics, but rather in the business process model.

Because the medicine specialists use their language and their mental framework, certain facts and dependencies are self-evident for them, but not for an IT specialist. Every field science uses its own set of acronyms, which are often large and sometimes ambiguous; therefore, a specialist in a different domain can miss some parts of the message altogether. The communication problem is important as one of the major reasons why projects fail, is because they are underspecified—some assumptions are made and vital problems are forgotten due to superficial domain knowledge. Also when replacing direct communication between humans with digital messaging, it is important to understand its subtleties, as not everything is directly visible to an external observer. Coiera (2015) devotes a whole chapter to the issue of unambiguous communication in the medical context. Wachter (2015) shows how the implementation of the EHRs reduces the informal communication between doctors and nurses and how formalizing it may lead to hiding the essential issues in the information noise.

Equally important, particularly in the data analysis phase, is good understanding of the statistical reasoning. Especially advisable are books that make the reader aware of common fallacies, like Wang (1993). They are sobering for those who aim for quick cutting-edge conclusions rather than for well-founded ones.

6 NECESSITY OF POSTMARKET SURVEILLANCE

For many reasons a one-time clinical study is not sufficient for a thorough evaluation of smart medical devices. The devices operate in a variable, undefined environment consisting of natural and technical conditions, as well as of humans who use and support them. A patient can be allergic to the used material, another one can misunderstand the instructions. During travel the phone signal can be missing or an insufficient roaming contract may inhibit the data transfer.

Furthermore, the devices change in time. Due to the detected problems the device may be updated—its mechanical part or software. The operating procedures may be changed or the personnel and the patients may be better instructed. In all such cases the compound (device + environment) is not the same, which invalidates the previous tests.

We want to know the long-term effects of the therapy, but the necessity of a long clinical trial collides with the pace of technical progress. Any change in the infrastructure, or deployment of new features (software and/or hardware) changes the system under test. If we require—correctly—that during the test all conditions remain *exactly* the same, the result will be of reduced value.

We, therefore, advocate the collection of data during the operation of the devices for continuous surveillance of installed devices in order to detect hidden flaws, rare defects, and results of material wearout and other forms of degradation. On one hand, we will obtain problem notifications regarding specific patients that require contacting them, that is, knowing their identities. On the other hand, we will have general results concerning the efficacy of therapy methods and quality of device classes and models. This information (with identities removed) will be analyzed by good statisticians and forwarded to the producers and to the approval authorities.

Those issues are well understood by the medical community. Sedrakyan et al. (2013) present the rationale for an international registry of cardiovascular devices, Kesselheim et al. (2014) even argue for compulsory postmarket research. Several organizations and initiatives are active in this field. In the United States we can name the Institute of Medicine (IOM), Patient-Centered Outcomes Research Institute (PCORI), FDA's (Food and Drug Administration) Sentinel Initiative, Medical Device

Epidemiology Network Initiative (MDEpiNet) or MedWatch, The FDA Safety Information and Adverse Event Reporting Program. Even if their number suggests overlapping competences, it shows also the growing importance of the issue.

Another important factor is the reimbursement of the therapies through insurance or from government authorities. There is a large market for consumer devices that are useful in prevention, for example, supporting a healthy lifestyle. The professional devices are, however, more expensive and their large-scale use is only possible if they are reimbursed. Therefore, the respective payers require a proof of their medical efficacy as well as of economic efficiency (what therapy improvement for what price). The new devices do not just induce costs—extensive use of medical devices may increase the possibilities of ambulant treatment and hence have a positive influence on the general costs of the system.

7 PRIMARY AND SECONDARY USE OF SMART MEDICAL DEVICES DATA

Data generated by smart medical devices can be (re)used for following main purposes:

- Health support (Fig. 6)
- Quality assurance (Fig. 7)
- Medical research (Fig. 8)

In all cases data have basically the same origin. However, for various usages different data extracts are needed. These data extracts are routed to different recipients. Their content has to ensure optimal usability and protect the privacy according to the context.

In the following, we will discuss in detail the named data flows.

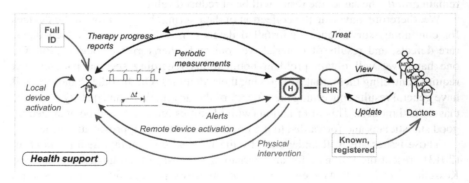

FIG. 6

Basic use of data: assuring direct patients care.

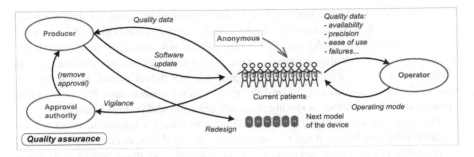

FIG. 7

Data reuse: quality assurance.

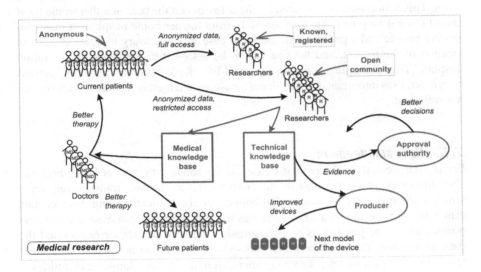

FIG. 8

Data reuse: medical research.

7.1 DATA FOR HEALTH SUPPORT

7.1.1 Data characteristics

The basic goal of smart medical devices is to provide health support to specific patients. In the reference configuration (Fig. 1) we have two levels of communication:

- Communication over the BAN between the sensors/actuators and the aggregator.
- Communication over the wide area network (phone) between the aggregator and the external institution (eg, hospital).

The delivered information can vary with respect to its quantity and temporal characteristics. It may consist of single values, signal waveforms, or images. A continuous waveform (ECG and EEG) typically is not necessary in its raw form. We have to extract features from it—calculate general properties (frequency and amplitude), assign to a category (healthy and risky) or detect events. As the sensors have limited resources, an optimized division of labor is necessary. We have to find a practical trade-off between storing data, computation and communication.

The aggregator can ensure a common timebase, which is important when precise temporal relations between the measurements sent by different cooperating sensors are required. In this way it can process signals coming from many sensors and detect combinations of them (complex events).

Sensor data may just periodically report the health parameters with no special action required. They may also detect emergencies—in this case an action has to be taken. This action may be executed by the actuators on the patient either in the local closed control loop or controlled remotely from his/her home hospital. It may also involve people and equipment. In the latter case it is necessary to know the actual location of the patient, and the task has to be assigned to the nearest cooperating hospital. This example shows us that real-life deployment of a health support system requires important organizational measures and merely technical solutions are not sufficient.

7.1.2 Data management

For regular treatments the patient's case can be handled by his/her home hospital. The difference in comparison to the traditional way is data transmission via a wireless channel and data storage that both occur automatically. Long-distance data transmission from the data aggregator has to be protected like any secure wireless transmission. The problem is the transmission between the sensors/actors and the data aggregator. These miniaturized, low-power devices cannot support the same level of security measures (like strong encryption) due to their limited capabilities.

When data reach the hospital, they are treated in a similar way as other data in a clinical information system and have to be protected accordingly. They are stored on disks accessible to the system operators and are visible to the medical personnel who are normally allowed to see them.

A different class of problems appears when an emergency service is needed in a remote location as in the example mentioned above. First, a network of cooperating institutions that agree to mutual assistance has to be defined. Then, procedures of the transfer of the patient's history are necessary. The intervening team has to know all relevant information, and have it available fast. When the case is closed, the home hospital needs to update the patient's record and the data held at the remote hospital must be removed as they are no longer necessary. The compensation for the service has to be set in advance, as well as the responsibility for the results, which may be especially difficult from a legal point of view in the case of an action need while the patient is abroad. Similar problems are being solved in the European e-Health Project epSOS.[7]

7.2 DATA FOR QUALITY ASSURANCE

7.2.1 Data characteristics

Data collected from smart medical devices can be used to evaluate the quality of the deployed equipment. Although the devices are thoroughly tested and formally approved, only the actual operation can give us information about long-term results, unforeseen adverse reactions, and rare incidents. If an unexpected event happens it may have various causes, just a few include: mechanical problem—fixture loosened, part broken; fluid sensor dirty, nozzle clogged; poor usability of the user interface—display unreadable, small keys, dialog unclear; battery depleted too fast; no phone signal available; external attack; etc.

Some faults can be diagnosed on the basis of the analysis of the sensor messages. In an optimal case, an intelligent device performs regular self-tests and informs about possible and actual problems, but often a problem analysis by a human is necessary. Industrial networks, like train control systems, periodically test their integrity. They have also well-defined real-time properties. In a similar way, a health supporting system has certain temporal requirements, depending on the severity of the treated disease.

The named problems can be fixed in very different ways, like upload of a corrected software version, device replacement, device redesign, or organizational changes. Therefore, in order to keep track of the quality problems and solutions a registry is necessary.

Medical software-based devices pose challenging problems to the statistical analysis. One of the problems is assuring a reasonable size of a statistical sample of comparable, uniform enough data. The products are often upgraded, therefore there are not so many identical devices deployed. Even when only a software bug on a device is being corrected, the device behaves differently, so strictly speaking, it is not the same device as before.

Moreover, a patient has not just one device, but a set of cooperating medical devices together with the specific model of a smartphone with specific phone applications loaded. Because of the interdependencies of the elements, any change of any element makes a different system, a different case to be evaluated. Because of this confused, dynamically evolving situation, the definition of the analysis processes requires the involvement of humans that understand the underlying problems.

7.2.2 Data management

The analysis of the data for quality assurance does not need personal information about the patients, therefore should be performed on anonymized data. This is

---

[7]http://www.epsos.eu/ (accessed July 16, 2015).

entirely true if we are interested in just the number of faults for a device model. If we want to find the cause of a problem, the procedure is more similar to an analysis of an airplane crash. Still, the name of the patient is not relevant, but we may need supplementary information; for example, What is his/her diet?, Does he/she do any physical exercises?, What is his/her age, gender, education level? If in case of an emergency no help came, or it came too late, it may have been caused by a software bug on the device, a loss of phone signal, inefficient information flow at the hospital or no free ambulance. Therefore, it may be necessary to perform an analysis of the case at a very detailed level, also with the access to the raw sensor data.

General statistical analysis is best performed by a team of independent researchers, trained in medicine and statistics, and who understand information and communication technology. For a precise analysis of a technical fault, representatives of the producers may have to be involved. The scenario outlined above shows that an interdisciplinary problem needs an interdisciplinary solution.

We see again how important, and how difficult it is, to define the rules of what data should be available, to whom and under what conditions.

7.3 DATA FOR MEDICAL RESEARCH

7.3.1 Data characteristics

Data collected by smart medical devices can finally be used for medical research. As the approval process for intelligent software-based devices is not as strict as for drugs (chemicals), it is important to evaluate the merits of the various devices in their actual application. Apart from comparing specific models, it is interesting to determine if a treatment method provides the expected results. In the case of drugs we expect healing or at least slowing of the progress of the disease. In the case of medical devices the effect may consist of enhancing the quality of life, reducing the costs and effort of routine measurements and consultations, improving the security, or delaying the transfer to a nursing home.

The information about the effectiveness of such systems is important for the hospitals applying them and having to choose the best one. It is also important for approval institution in order to reevaluate the deployed systems (postmarket surveillance) and to assess the costs, especially if they are covered by public funds. Furthermore, this information can serve the device developers and scientists in choosing the viable directions for further research.

7.3.2 Data management

In medical research the identity of the patient has no relevance, therefore anonymized data should be used. It is much more important to accumulate data from many medical institutions, related to systems of many producers. Also combining data from various sources is useful. For example, correlating medical data with data about lifestyle or social environment may give clues as to the causes of good or poor effectiveness of the systems. Of course, such correlated data permit to reidentify the patients if enough is known about their cases. It is, however, counterproductive to obfuscate the data used for scientific research. Bad data may lead to bad, harmful conclusions. It is, therefore, much more important to control the group of people allowed to access data, recording suspicious queries and limiting the size of detailed, nonaggregated data sets accessible to any single person.

It may be also useful—under certain conditions—to retrieve specific patients. Normally statistics is interested in the typical cases, not in the outliers. It may, however, happen, that some patients or some groups of them respond differently to a treatment. In the case of drugs, it could be a patient having an unexpected resistance to the disease. In such a case, a more profound analysis of previously not considered factors could help understanding of unknown aspects of the treatments.

8 STAKEHOLDERS AND THEIR INTERESTS

The proposed scheme is based on the cooperation of many partners. It will never function in real life if they are not sufficiently motivated to participate. Fig. 9 shows their interdependencies.

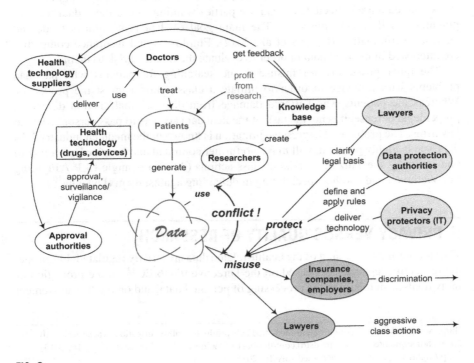

FIG. 9

Data management: stakeholders and their interests.

The *patients* want to receive the best treatment possible and the *hospitals* want to provide it. Both of them want to have the freedom to choose the therapies and devices and to avoid a vendor lock. With the registry, we propose a secondary use for patients' data, which is not aimed directly at supporting their own health. Ultimately the goal of collecting these data is to serve the patients better by optimizing the therapy and eliminating device faults. This approach corresponds to the trend toward predictive, personalized, preventive, participative (P4) medicine (Hood, 2013).

Strong, established *device producers* often prefer to protect their market share with proprietary standards. This is a winning strategy for the dominant players; as for the less strong ones it would limit the possible options for owning their products, which may reduce their chances of obtaining new customers. For small, innovative producers, participating in open standards is the only way to reach the market.

The producers may be reluctant to participate in the quality monitoring scheme, as it discloses the defects of their devices. On the other hand, speaking openly about the issues shows a producer as someone who plays fair and should eventually increase the patients' trust in them.

In many countries, there is growing pressure from the official bodies, for example, *approval authorities*, to be involved in the evaluation of medical effectiveness and financial efficiency. This pressure may be a decisive argument for participation.

As the data are collected, we can see parties wanting to use these data for own potentially self-serving purposes. The main goal of data protection is to defend against discrimination (Custers et al., 2012). Employers and insurance companies are interested in medical data in order to evaluate the financial risk to them.

The other possibility for misuse is the searching for patients who had had problems with a device in order to initiate a class action against the producers. Whereas the patients who suffered damage from devices' malfunction deserve a proper legal defense, it is not the task of medical data keepers to pass personal data to law firms. The problem of aggressive litigation is known in the medtech industry.[8] As the issue is highly political, will make no further comment and provide here a link to one company specializing in raising class actions (Alonso Krangle LLP[9]/"Fighting For Victims") and another specializing in defending against them (Dykema[10]).

9 PRIVACY VERSUS QUALITY OF RESEARCH

The storage and processing of the health-related data are strictly regulated. In Europe, the respective legislation is based on the Directive 95/46/EC[11] on the protection of individuals with regard to the processing of personal data, and on the free movement

[8]http://www.mddionline.com/article/trends-medtech-product-liability-litigation (accessed July 16, 2015); https://medtechboston.medstro.com/the-cost-of-doing-business/ (accessed July 16, 2015).
[9]http://fightforvictims.com/ (accessed July 16, 2015).
[10]http://www.dykema.com/services-practices-litigation.html (accessed July 16, 2015).
[11]http://eur-lex.europa.eu/legal-content/EN/TXT/?uri=CELEX:31995L0046 (accessed July 13, 2015).

of such data (Data Protection Directive) with various amendments and national implementations. It is soon to be replaced by the General Data Protection Regulation (GDPR), the draft[12] of which has been approved[13] on June 15, 2015.

In the United States, a similar regulation is in effect: Health Insurance Portability and Accountability Act (HIPAA[14]). The main goal of these acts of legislation is the protection of personal data. Every collection of data should have a well-defined purpose, rules of access and retention. It is explicitly prohibited to process personal data that outline: racial or ethnic origin, political opinions, religious or philosophical beliefs, trade-union membership, health or sex life. The technicalities of ensuring compliance with the privacy rules are well described in Robichau (2014). Various aspects, from privacy laws with regard to data reuse and technical solutions (privacy by design) are analyzed in-depth in Lane et al. (2014).

However, the legal rules are just the means to implement more general principles: having their source in the value system. A good introduction to such an approach can be found in Nissenbaum (2009). For some, the basic principle is the private ownership of any information related to a person. For others, the public good is predominant, therefore sharing information is socially valuable. Some argue that any information should be publicly available. Finally, some may think that anybody who has collected a dataset is free to reuse or sell it. The truth lies somewhere in the middle, is context-dependent, and may change in time.

There is dissent not only between the various views but also between the goals and the results that can result from an unforeseen situation. A spectacular example is the Germanwings Flight 9525 [15] on March 24, 2015. The crash was caused by the suicidal co-pilot who deliberately guided the plane onto the rocks. His state was known to the doctors but disclosing it to the employer is explicitly forbidden by the law. In this case breaking the rules would have saved 150 lives but changing them permanently would probably do more harm. On the Internet discussion forums a cultural cleavage could be seen—the American participants were shocked that lives had been lost due to secrecy and the Europeans, especially Germans, argued that effective privacy laws should be respected.

In the context of evidence-based medicine (EBM) there is a conflict between the desire to know everything possible about the patient's case and the privacy rules, as discussed in Sliwa and Benoist (2012a). In such research, one issue is how to connect the various aspects of the patient's case. Strictly speaking, data collection should have a well-defined purpose, contain only the necessary data and restrict connections to other collections. From the medical point of view it is an important restriction. Especially in elderly patients who may have many diseases (multimorbidity) and take many drugs that may possibly interact. They can also be using many medical devices.

---

[12]http://data.consilium.europa.eu/doc/document/ST-9565-2015-INIT/en/pdf (accessed July 13, 2015).
[13]http://www.dataprotectionreport.com/2015/06/european-council-approves-eu-general-data-protection-regulation-draft-final-approval-may-come-by-end-of-2015/ (accessed July 13, 2015).
[14]http://www.hhs.gov/ocr/privacy/ (accessed July 13, 2015).
[15]https://en.wikipedia.org/wiki/Germanwings_Flight_9525 (accessed July 10, 2015).

As we depart more and more from the mechanistic view of the human, we have to consider the interaction of lifestyle factors, etc., with the strictly medical ones. Even the emotional attitude of the patient toward the doctor and the therapy is important and is studied seriously, as in the Program in Placebo Studies & Therapeutic Encounter (PiPS)[16] at the Beth Israel Deaconess Medical Center/Harvard Medical School. An example of this approach is the Research Domain Criteria (RDoC) Project[17] (Insel and Cuthbert, 2015), which targets the precision medicine for mental disorders. The researchers want to improve the disorder classification by replacing the traditional symptom-based categories (like bipolar depression) with data-driven categories. For this goal, multidimensional data about the patients have to be analyzed, combining genetic, neurological, physiological, behavioral, and life experience (social, cultural, and environmental) factors, creating complex, and intertwined life stories. This is understandable, as mental disorders have many causes, and various internal states result in similar symptoms. In this way, however, the data collection process pushes the limits of the privacy laws.

The risk of connecting all patient's data lies in the fact that if the patient is reidentified on the basis of partial data, it is easier to obtain access to the rest. Evidently, the connection is done via the internal identifier, but the first step is done. The question is if the internal identifier is never visible, or it appears after all in the data are extracted. If it is visible, it should be properly encoded. The example of breaking the passenger privacy in the New York City taxicab dataset[18] shows how supplementary information (known format of original data) helps the attacker to crack the code. The deeper aspects of anonymization are presented in Raghunathan (2013).

A useful approach to improving privacy protection is the physical separation of personal and medical data. It has been field-tested for over 10 years in the implementation of a registry of orthopedic surgeries. The principle is described in Sliwa and Benoist (2012b). Personal data are stored on the server belonging to a partner institution, for example, a national medical association. Medical data are stored anonymously on the server of a research institute. Personal and medical data are connected only on the screen of a user (doctor and nurse) who works at the clinic that handles this patient and has corresponding access rights (Fig. 10). There is no access for the general public, all users are verified and registered. In this solution, if someone wants to download large datasets of patients with their medical histories, he/she has to bribe two system operators, both known personally. Besides hoping that they would respect their professional responsibility (Schneier, 2012), we know that the breach would mean the end of their professional careers.

---

[16]http://programinplacebostudies.org/ (accessed July 14, 2015).

[17]http://www.nimh.nih.gov/research-priorities/rdoc/index.shtml (accessed July 12, 2015).

[18]http://research.neustar.biz/2014/09/15/riding-with-the-stars-passenger-privacy-in-the-nyc-taxicab-dataset/ (accessed July 14, 2015).

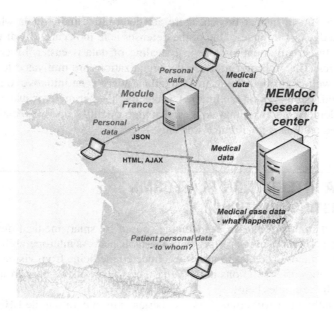

FIG. 10

Identity-related and clinical data are delivered from separate sources.

One of the general problems of data separation is that due to improving data mining algorithms the patient can be reidentified based on apparently irrelevant scraps of information. Moreover, we want to include on the medical side such parameters as height, weight, age, and gender, which are quite personal details. Recently there have been a number of efforts to use purely medical data as the electrocardiogram for biometrics (Silva et al., 2013). Evidently, genomic data, while being medical, can do more that just help to identify a person—they *are* his/her identifier.

Even the best design risks being outsmarted by an attacker, especially if the designers are biased by their *good guy* way of thinking. Therefore, the very existence of a data collection make a breach possible. Recently, we experienced attacks on the German Bundestag[19] and the French TV channel TV5.[20] Despite the unpleasant

---

[19]http://www.dw.com/en/german-media-cyber-attack-carried-out-on-bundestag/a-18452770 (accessed July 14, 2015).
[20]http://www.independent.co.uk/life-style/gadgets-and-tech/news/tv5monde-hack-staff-accidentally-show-passwords-in-report-about-huge-cyberattack-10168475.html (accessed July 14, 2015).

consequences of an insider breach, there are determined individuals who do it to gain knowledge or for money. One of the defenses is to look carefully at where data are stored. In certain countries physical stealing of data is easier, by criminals or by authorities. Therefore in Europe many organizations are motivated to store data on a local, well-controlled cloud. In Switzerland there is an initiative to construct a "Swiss cloud." However, on the Internet, protecting the perimeter is just a small part of the problem. Being *Swiss* may suggest that high-quality security specialists would be employed but this is no ultimate warranty.

10 DATA INTEGRATION PLATFORMS
10.1 EXISTING SOLUTIONS

Due to the disruptive changes in medicine caused by smart medical devices, new market niches attract many players, new and established. As interoperability and data exchange are major obstacles to moving connected medicine from vision to market, many companies offer solutions in this area. They have various backgrounds, as we will see in the examples below.

NantHealth[21] and AllScripts[22] have experience in integrating the EHRs systems and in interconnecting medical devices. Currently they have joined forces[23] to develop precision solutions at the point of care and introduce an integrated, evidence-based, personalized approach to healthcare solutions that includes actionable clinical data, enabling physicians to make informed decisions from complex genomic and proteomic analysis.

Cisco, a leader in computer networking, already having experience in IoT, will create the foundation for Connected Health[24] with Cisco Medical-Grade Network.

Samsung Simband[25] is intended as an open platform for integrating body sensors. In parallel, SAMI[26] will provide a secure cloud-based platform for collecting, storing, transforming, and exchanging data.

University of California San Diego hosts iDASH, one of the National Centers for Biomedical Computing. The goal of iDASH[27] is Integrating Data for Analysis, Anonymization and SHaring. A high performance infrastructure supports numerous data-rich medical projects. A special stress is put on privacy protection and consent management.

---

[21] http://nanthealth.com/ (accessed July 17, 2015).
[22] http://eu.allscripts.com/ (accessed July 17, 2015).
[23] http://nanthealth.com/press-releases/nanthealth-allscripts-join-forces-develop-precision-solutions-point-care-era-genomic-medicine/ (accessed July 17, 2015).
[24] http://www.ciscoconnectedhealth.com/ (accessed July 17, 2015).
[25] http://www.voiceofthebody.io/simband (accessed July 17, 2015).
[26] https://www.samsungsami.io/ (accessed July 17, 2015).
[27] https://idash.ucsd.edu/ (accessed July 17, 2015).

Finally, we mention two innovative companies, Vivametrica[28] and Pryv[29] that deliver health data analytics based mostly on wearable sensors.

10.2 PROPOSED ARCHITECTURE

10.2.1 General structure

In this section, we want to present an organizational and technical solution that supports the (re)use of data for health support, quality assurance, and medical research, as described in Section 7. We identify the organizational units needed to perform the necessary tasks. The information flow ensures a smooth functioning of the system and permits all participants to produce and receive the necessary data.

We consider here a health support system regarding a single medical problem, or a group of related problems, for example, cardiovascular diseases. It can be subdivided in following parts (Fig. 11):

- Patient's System: The set of devices delivered to the patient, the local network and installed software.
- Infrastructure System: hospitals and other supporting entities, communicating with the patients via wide area network and serving following purposes:
  o Direct Health Support
  o Quality Control and Evaluation (Medical Research)

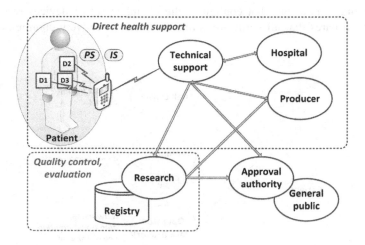

FIG. 11

Subsystems: patient (PS) and infrastructure (IS)—actors and data flows.

---

[28] http://vivametrica.com/ (accessed July 17, 2015).
[29] http://pryv.com/ (accessed July 17, 2015).

The Infrastructure System has to provide following functionality:

- Deployment and support
  - ○ Configuring and delivering to patients
  - ○ Network operation (connection with devices)
  - ○ Contacting patients
- Notifying producers, distributing updates
- Quality assurance and effectiveness evaluation
  - ○ Monitoring technical state
  - ○ Detecting failures
  - ○ Measuring medical effectiveness
- Extracting medical knowledge for better therapies

10.2.2 Technical support

A crucial unit, connecting all other elements, is the Technical Support (Fig. 12). It has to perform a number of functions that are necessary to ensure the operation of the system. These functions require special technical equipment and a novel set of skills that may exceed the current capacities of a typical hospital. They may be delivered by one or several organizations, depending on the necessary skills and equipment, and whether a direct contact with the patients and hospitals is needed.

Configurators

A configurator is a unit that configures the complete set of devices received by a patient. It cares that all hardware components can effectively communicate and

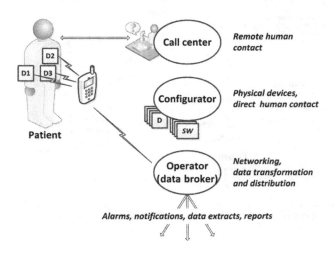

FIG. 12

Technical support—subunits.

that all software packages run on the data aggregator used by the patient. This aggregator may be a device (eg, a smartphone) owned by the patient or a special device preconfigured for this task. The configurator also performs the final delivery to the patient and gives him/her the necessary instruction. Having a supply of physical devices, the configurator will be contacted if a service or replacement is needed. The configurator acts on behalf of the hospital and provides the necessary technical expertise missing at the hospital. As the configurators interact with patients, they need to maintain local offices. In the case of implantable devices, the operation is performed at the hospital; this, however, seems not to require the presence of the configurator. Actual connection into a functioning BAN is done later, after the scar is healed. This geographical distribution permits various forms of organization—as separate, local companies or connected in one enterprise.

Operators (data brokers)

An operator is a unit that supports the continuous function of the system of distributed medical devices. In this respect we think mostly of assuring the network connection between the patients' aggregator devices and the hospital and other data destinations. The operator has to perform all transformations on data received from the patients and distribute them according to the predefined scheme. The operator has to know all communications partners. It also has to know the types and versions of all devices (sensors, actuators) used in the system and their producers in order to generate the status and malfunction notifications. Likewise, the information about the actual configuration of the device sets delivered to the patients is necessary for specific service functions, for example, status inquiries or software updates.

Call centers

The first function of a call center is to receive remarks, complaints, and service requests from the patients. Equally important is contact with the patient initiated by the service providers. The device set delivered to the patient may automatically provide information about a problem of which the patient is unaware. Sensor values that are systematically out of range suggest a wrong position or weak contact with the body. This again can be caused by dirt, humidity, or a loosened fixation. Signal from a device will be missing if its battery is drained or if the patient found the device to be uncomfortable and it has been removed. It also could be broken, lost, or stolen. The cause is unknown to the service providers. Therefore, the patient has to be personally contacted, otherwise his/her system will not work. The patient can correct the installation of the device, but if the problem is caused by a property of the installed devices—weight, size, or noise—this information can be a valuable input to the producers who could improve the design.

Evidently, if the contact has to be efficient, the patient has to be available and be in a position to concentrate on the problem. Therefore, a second call at another time of the day may be needed, and an additional follow-up call if the problem persists or reappears after a certain time. We see that the tasks of a call center are very similar to a customer relationship management (CRM) system. A 24 h/7 days operation is recommended. In addition to the technical and medical fundamentals, the personnel needs local language skills and the ability to interact with ill, elderly, uncertain, or angry people.

10.2.3 Research institute

Most elements in the presented structure are well-known partners, like hospitals, producers, etc. A special role is played by the vendor-independent research institute. Its main task is to support the registry that serves the continuous monitoring of the devices and therapies. The researchers have to define the logical structure of registry items that is a reasonable compromise between the diverging requirements: heterogeneity, variability, and a stable structure for comparison and research. The actual implementation and hosting may be provided by a partner with stronger IT skills. The researchers use this data collection to answer questions that could lead to better medical and economical decisions. They publish scientific papers and produce reports for cooperating medical societies and government offices or for the general public.

The researchers have to bring into play skills in the relevant medical fields and in statistics. The environment is very far from a clean randomized trial. The patients represent a known, but neither predefined nor balanced assortment of age, gender, lifestyle, and other properties. The device application is decided by the hospital, its elements are replaced, and its software is fixed and updated. This makes producing truthful statistics extremely challenging.

11 TECHNICAL CHALLENGES
11.1 STREAM PROCESSING

The values sent by a medical device come in the form of a data stream. There is also a growing literature regarding stream processing in the medical context: Aggarwal (2013), Andrade et al. (2014), Chakravarthy and Jiang (2009), and Gama and Gaber (2007). Those streams have a broad range of frequency values. At one end of the spectrum we have a series of daily measurements and at the other we have a continuous signal like an electrocardiogram (ECG). In the latter case the signal has to be preprocessed locally. Special states of the stream have to be detected and only the condensed information has to be transmitted. It may be a value going outside the expected range or a value peak (point event). It also may be a state of the signal of a certain duration, whereas the duration and other parameters (eg. grade of the arrhythmia) can be of relevance. Also the shape of the signal may be important. In the case of the ECG, an important indicator of an immediate health threat is a higher value (elevation) of the ST-segment of the periodic ECG waveform, so called STEMI (ST elevation myocardial infarction). [30] An important area of concern is the detection of complex events, as described in Section 3.

---

[30]http://www.learntheheart.com/cardiology-review/coronary-artery-disease-stemi/diagnosis/ (accessed July 11, 2015).

If we speak of temporal issues, reaction times to specific events may be crucial for the patient's health or life. In such a case first the message has to be immediately formed and transmitted, what is influenced by the quality and reliability of the communication link. Then, the message has to be received and dispatched to an automatic system or a human operator. If humans are involved, their skills and the structure of their organization are decisive.

11.2 STREAM DISTRIBUTION

In the structure proposed in Section 10.2 the central software module is the Operator. Its major task is distributing data to predefined recipients. The data extracts have to correspond to the access rules for the recipients. A data recipient corresponds to a real-world organization, like a hospital, producer, research institute, or other. Let us consider the data stream related to a patient as a sequence of items marked with a timestamp and a tag (Fig. 13). A recipient has access to certain types of items. For example, *yellow alarms* are useful for maintenance by the producer, but are considered his trade secret and are not to be disclosed. An item can be stripped of

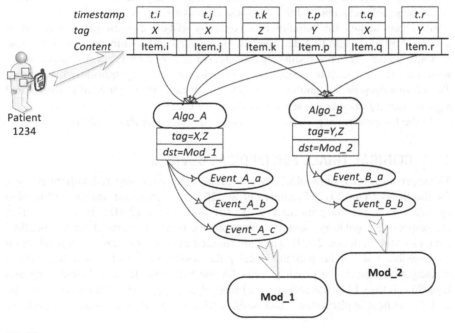

FIG. 13

Extracting multiple data streams.

patient's personal information, if it is directed to a research institute. Therefore the data extracts' definition—although configurable—has to be approved and cannot be loaded automatically.

The processing of the stream items is performed by externally provided algorithms, attached to the stream and corresponding to the data recipients. In addition to processing individual items, the algorithms can aggregate them or generate events based on them. Typically, an algorithm detecting special events in the data stream (cardiac arrhythmia, hypoglycemia, and sleep apnea) works with a rolling window over the data stream on which it performs a semantically meaningful computation. The core software of the operator is isolated from the semantics, it has only to distribute the items to the registered algorithms. Such decomposition will ensure the modular structure of the software.

In the example shown the source stream contains items tagged X, Y, or Z. There are two recipient modules: Mod_1 and Mod_2. The module Mod_1 has access to items of type X and Z that are processed by the algorithm Algo_1. This algorithm generates derived events: Event_A_a, Event_A_b, and Event_A_c.

12 CHALLENGES FOR DATA ANALYTICS

Evaluating smart medical devices and the therapies they are used for is a difficult task. The problem is new and the statistical models are not yet mature. We especially want to warn against the belief that data quantity will compensate for their uncertain quality. Any algorithm that does not divide by zero and terminates in a finite time will always deliver *some* results. If this algorithm is complex, cryptic, and evolves with data, it is difficult to verify. There is a risk of detecting spurious correlations. Therefore a deep understanding of the domain, critical attitude toward statistics, and a good quantity of common sense is certainly of use.

In the following, we present some major challenges for data analytics.

12.1 CLINICAL TRIALS FOR MEDICAL DEVICES

The approval process of medical devices is relatively new, compared with the process for the drugs (Yin, 2012; Friedman et al., 2010). A profound analysis, illustrated by many examples is presented in Becker and Whyte (2007). In every market the respective regulatory agency defines precise rules of approval for the medical devices (Abdel-Aleem, 2009). They are divided into several classes, depending on the possible risk to the patient. Usually the results of a well-controlled clinical investigation have to be provided only for the high-risk devices (Life-Saving and Life-Sustaining). FDA has recently (February 9, 2015) issued guidance regarding the mobile medical applications[31] that defines which apps are the focus of regulatory

---

[31] http://www.fda.gov/downloads/MedicalDevices/DeviceRegulationandGuidance/ GuidanceDocuments/UCM263366.pdf (accessed July 17, 2015).

oversight, which may meet the definition of medical device but are exempt from enforcement and which are not considered medical devices. Similarly, the European Commission is working on the update of its regulatory framework.[32] A good analysis from a technical and legal point of view can be found in Sorenson and Drummond (2014). As the process is highly dynamic, we will not comment on it here in detail.

In the design phase a risk analysis has to be performed (Gad, 2011). The main standards used in this context are ISO 14971:2007 (application of risk management to medical devices) and IEC 80001-1:2010 (application of risk management for IT-networks incorporating medical devices). The paper (Alemzadeh et al., 2013) provides an in-depth analysis of this process. A complex example of its application for hemodialysis devices is shown in Lodi et al. (2010). Pawar et al. (2012) discuss the quality evaluation of mobile patient monitoring systems and present a framework for their comparison. The results depend, however, on the actual assiduity of the people who perform the assessment, on their technical knowledge and capacity to imagine rare and novel risks.

A deep analysis of how to obtain knowledge from data is presented in Meulen et al. (2005), Djulbegovic et al. (2009), and Wyer and Silva (2009). The most trusted method is a randomized control trial (RCT). A double-blind experiment with medical devices is difficult to implement (Potapov et al., 2011; Lipton et al., 2010; Castro et al., 2010) as it is not easy to construct a fake device that it is not noticed by the patient. The paper by Zannad et al. (2014) presents an extensive analysis of the challenges facing the trials using the example of cardiovascular medical devices. The approval process is, however, far from perfect (Teow and Siegel, 2013) and risky devices may reach the market (Hauser, 2012).

12.2 PROBLEM COMPLEXITY—EXAMPLE

In order to better understand the complexity or the quality evaluation let us take regarding pacing leads as an example, ie, the wires that deliver energy to the heart muscle from a pacemaker or implantable cardioverter defibrillator (ICD). They also sense the heart parameters and send them back to the device. From the point of view of an IT specialist they are just input/output devices. This simple image will change if we look into a book addressed to health professionals (Fröhlig et al., 2013, p. 258). First, we see there are two basic types—unipolar and bipolar. Then, there are various materials and construction variants.

As for the quality differences between the unipolar and bipolar leads, the author quotes the data from the Danish registry. We see that the lifetime of the unipolar leads is significantly longer; however, some problems with the bipolar leads were caused by three models from two producers and when the faulty devices were

---

[32]http://ec.europa.eu/growth/sectors/medical-devices/index_en.htm (accessed July 17, 2015); http:// ec.europa.eu/growth/sectors/medical-devices/regulatory-framework/revision/index_en.htm (accessed July 17, 2015).

removed, the quality of both classes looked equal. Therefore, previous incidents with older devices should not pollute the results and should have no influence on future decisions.

To finalize, the authors give practical advice that the surgeon should use the type he/she has experience with, as changing to another model implies a learning curve with the potential for complications in the early stages. Due to the technical progress, the surgeon has to consider such decision.

Using this example we have seen that a nonintelligent and apparently insignificant element can have a crucial impact on the overall result. The simple statement "A is better than B" looks now much more complex and is really difficult to assess with statistics. Evidently, treating the issue without a deeper understanding of the underlying mechanism—according to the principle "let data speak for themselves"—is of little worth.

12.3 QUALITY OF A MEDICAL DEVICE—MULTIPLE ASPECTS

Until now we were speaking quite vaguely about the quality of the device. Formally, the device is either approved or denied. However, we cannot simply say the device is *good* or *bad*. The quality not only changes gradually, but it also has multiple aspects. For a smartphone we will look at its connectivity, screen, camera, performance, weight, price, and more. Most of those aspects have multiple criteria themselves.

In a similar way, we can assign smart medical devices into several classes according to their functions or subsystems. One device can belong to many classes. If we take the Medtronic Continuous Glucose Monitoring System (MiniMed® 530G with Enlite®—Fig. 14) as an example, we see that it is a (or has a):

- implantable device
- wearable device
- user-programmable device
- body area network
- wide area network (phone)

A class is related to a set of quality properties and to common possible problems or reasons for malfunction. Let us analyze the class *Wearable device*. All wearable devices are fixed to the patient's body. This poses a common set of problems: the fixation may be too tight (causing pain) or too loose (giving insufficient contact). They may be placed in the wrong position. The device may be obtrusive, heavy, and noisy. Consequently, the patient may remove the device, which will cause data loss and impair the treatment. Such an event should be detected remotely by the support team and prompt action.

In the following we list some examples of device classes. Some are defined by the location (wearable, implantable), some by networking function (wireless node, smartphone), and others by supplementary functionality (user programmable).

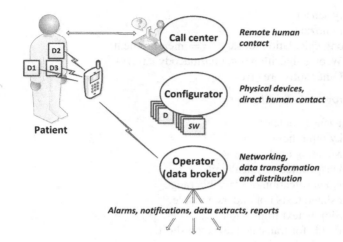

FIG. 14

Medtronic continuous glucose monitoring system.

Source: http://www.medgadget.com.

Equally we can identify common properties for devices according to their medical function, like pacemaker or insulin pump.

Wearable devices

- Obtrusive, heavy, and noisy
- Fixation:
    - o Too tight—causing pain, imprints, or eczema
    - o Too loose—insufficient/unstable contact to skin
    - o Loosens with time—bad contact, device slips off
- Visible, disclosing the disease, embarrassing

Implantable devices

- Interacts with body fluids:
    - o Erodes
    - o Releases harmful substances
- Short battery life
- Program update needs removing from body
- Software crashes require manual reset

Automatic drug distributors

- Wrong drug (side effects)
- Wrong dosage:

o Dirty sensor
o Dirty nozzle
o Wrong calculation: dosage $\Longleftarrow\Longrightarrow$ measurement:
  – Wrong algorithm (eg, pharmacodynamics)
  – Other software error

User-programmable devices

- User interface unclear:
  o Risky input fields:
    – Meaning unclear
    – Unspecified physical units
    – No verification of plausible range
  o Translated texts not understandable:
    – Sloppy text translation
    – Fields for translated texts too short:
  o Sequence of events/actions not intuitive

Wireless nodes

- Local wireless signal blocked by body/bones/clothing
- Different frequency range abroad
- Competing for bandwidth with neighboring devices
- Malicious human actions:
  o Eavesdropping
  o Triggering actions/reprogramming
  o Blocking by denial-of-service attacks
  o Battery depletion by (rejected) attacks

Smartphones and apps

- Depending on OS type and version
- Phone signal missing
- Roaming abroad
- Interacting with other applications:
  o Blocking resources, causing crashes
  o Malicious actions
- All attacks typical to this class of devices
- Data loss when not well protected and device stolen

12.4 MULTIPLE VARIANTS—SETTINGS OF A DEVICE

The function of a complex, software-based device depends on its settings. Therefore, for statistical evaluation it is not a uniform object. Again, it is useful to look into a medical book (Fröhlig et al., 2013, p. 324) treating the cardiac pacemaker therapy. We see a following list:

- Stimulation mode (DDD, VDD, D00, VVI, V00, AAI, AAT, A00, DVI, DAI, VAT, DDD + AT, DAT)

- Stimulation rate
- Stimulation amplitude
- AV-Delay
- Maximum Tracking Rate
- Sensitivity
- Refractory period, etc.

This list is followed by a long explanation of what modes and settings are to be used for different variants of cardiac insufficiency—neither do the patients form an uniform group. In this context the simple statement "The pacemaker X is good for treating heart failure" appears trivial. Our judgments have to be much more nuanced. It is evident that in the face of the number of combined possibilities obtaining statistically relevant results is a challenge. Additionally, rapidly evolving devices make quick assessment of the efficacy of long-term therapy difficult if not impossible.

12.5 VARIABILITY OF THE DEVICE—SOFTWARE UPDATES

Due to technical progress the devices change rapidly. Not only are new models developed, but also an already installed device—even an implanted one—can have its software modified, as a functional upgrade or a bug fixing. Strictly speaking after an upgrade it is not the same device, so the previous statistics should be invalidated. Restarting the evaluation would be wasteful, as we would lose a valuable set of data. The question is how to remove the abnormal states caused by the previous version's bugs that are now corrected. Let us assume that the basic medical algorithm is correct, but due to the bugs the software crashes from time to time (Fig. 15). Apart from some obvious problems caused by the bug, the rest remains unchanged.

These problematic effects may or may not be visible in the patient's state of health. It is possible that if we have a device that should send an alarm in the case of a cardiac failure, but it is not always ready because of occasional crashes, no harm may come to the patient if by chance no failure occurs during a crash. Such states should be detected by internal integrity checks, reported to the producer and corrected.

If on the other hand the software has a negative effect on the patient's health, we have to subtract it from the rest of our previous data, which is easier done than said. After the bug is corrected by the developers, the update has to be distributed to the deployed devices, which takes time and creates an intermediary period where some devices have the updated software and some do not. As a human body is a physical system with its own dynamics (Hargrove, 1998), its reaction time has to be taken into account. Moreover, previous experience with faulty therapy may leave traces.

Besides software modifications there are other issues where time plays a role. The device may wear out over time. The doctors and patients progress on their learning curve. The environment changes, for good or for bad. If our system depends on external services, their quality may improve but they also may be phased out as obsolete. The cyber attacks may get worse, the attackers use more sophisticated algorithms and their machines get stronger. The same is true for the data miners who

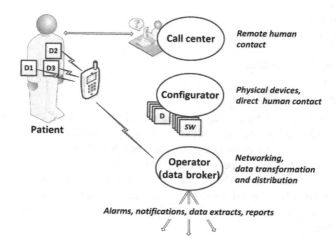

FIG. 15

Device versioning.

may try to reidentify the anonymous patients. Therefore, the quality of an unchanged software, without security patches, deteriorates with time.[33]

All these factors make it difficult to perform a proper clinical trial, especially if we want to assess the long-term effects of the therapy. This would require that during the trial all conditions were *exactly* the same, which is effectively impossible.

12.6 VARIOUS PATIENT GROUPS, UNBALANCED COHORT

Postmarket surveillance is an observational study with an unbalanced cohort. For high-risk devices the patients are selected according to a well-defined diagnosis, for example, a certain device is implanted only to patients with a specific condition and a defined survival probability. However, a device having a user interface will not only depend on the patient's biology but also on his/her behavior. User dialog designed for a *digital native* will not be usable for an elderly person, and a version designed for an old person may be boring to a young one. Sharples et al. (2012) study the consequences of the user-device interaction on the optimal medical device design. Lang et al. (2014) present a case study of the use of a cystic fibrosis physiotherapy device by adolescents. Speidel and Sridharan (2014) discuss crowdtesting as a method of quality assurance for mobile healthcare. Borsci et al. (2014) evaluate how many testers from various users groups are needed to assure the usability of medical devices.

---

[33]http://www.wired.com/2014/01/theres-no-good-way-to-patch-the-internet-of-things-and-thats-a-huge-problem/ (accessed July 12, 2015).

13 RESPONSIBILITY FOR PUBLISHED RESULTS

The perfect world is populated by noble researchers, honest leaders, and educated citizens. Noble researchers pursue the truth with the best methods possible. Honest leaders apply these results for the maximal benefit of educated citizens who are able to use the available information. The real world is different, but we have to strive for the ideal.

As a warning, we can quote Ioannidis (2005), stating brutally that "most published research findings are false." Young and Karr (2011) discuss more specifically the observational studies, where among many variables and with a little effort any type of correlation can be found, which leads to such "facts" like: "Women who eat breakfast cereal give birth to more boys." Finally, Nosek et al. (2012) criticize the desire to publish spectacular results as being detrimental to the search for truth.

If we use data to formulate general statements that influence human decisions, we have to be very careful. Having access to *Big Data*, it is tempting to present spectacular results that can look convincing, especially when suggestively visualized. Such overestimation of the deductive abilities of the computers, just because of their capacity, is not new. Already in 1963 the term GIGO (Garbage In, Garbage Out)[34] has been coined. An important *caveat* is the case of Google Flu Trends (GFT). The idea was that an algorithm based on the analysis of the social media should predict the influenza epidemics and the number of doctor visits better than the traditional methods. Some successes were noticed; however, the algorithms were quite unreliable, so it remained rather a curiosity than a serious tool. The details of this overhasty reasoning are presented in Lazer et al. (2014).

A philosophical introduction to the problem of information quality can be found in Floridi and Illari (2014). Sliwa and Benoist (2011) discuss more practical aspects of reusing information for science and in the decision process. Sliwa (2012) considers the use of pervasive monitoring not by a dictatorship, but by an overprotective *nanny state* that believes it is acting in the best interests of the population.

If scientific results are used to guide human actions, the scientists bear a high responsibility. An extreme case was the earthquake in L'Aquila, Italy, where the scientists who had not correctly predicted the event were convicted of manslaughter. In Nov. 2014 most of them were acquitted,[35] but the case is not yet closed.

Equally dangerous is spreading unnecessary fear. Therefore, care should be taken, for example, when informing about genetics, like in the online tests offered by 23andMe[36] and other companies. Generally, people are not good at evaluating the real risk. Sometimes spectacular but rare events trigger panic and an emotional, undeliberated counteraction is more harmful than its cause. Gigerenzer (2014), with

---

[34]https://en.wikipedia.org/wiki/Garbage_in,_garbage_out (accessed July 14, 2015).
[35]http://news.sciencemag.org/earth/2014/11/updated-appeals-court-overturns-manslaughter-convictions-six-earthquake-scientists (accessed July 16, 2015).
[36]https://www.23andme.com/ (accessed July 16, 2015).

many well-presented examples, is a good introduction to this subject. Among others, he discusses the utility and harms of breast cancer screening—a recent review on this question is in Independent UK Panel on Breast Cancer Screening (2012). The problem gained attention when Angelina Jolie, a famous actress, who after being diagnosed with a rare mutation of the BRCA1 gene, underwent a preventive double mastectomy and later had surgery to remove her ovaries. It is too early to decide if this decision was correct. An interesting question is in what way this case influenced the decisions in the greater public (Evans et al., 2014; Borzekowski et al., 2013).

Currently a much discussed problem is the (mis)use of *Big Data* for surveillance. Lyon (2014) gives a profound discussion of using this information to take decisions regarding people, especially in the fight against terror, where the consequences can be really hard. In this context let us mention the Congress on Privacy & Surveillance,[37] held on Sep. 30, 2013 at the EPFL in Lausanne. One of the speakers was Jacob Appelbaum.[38] When asked (by the author) if the NSA databases will not crumble under the weight of all the phone calls stored for 15 years, he answered: "it's not that they will be successful that we need to be worried about, what we need to worry about is they won't do a very good job but it will result in someone getting killed by a flying robot."

May this be a warning for us.

14 BACKGROUND/LITERATURE REVIEW/CONTEXT

As the field of smart medical devices is in constantly changing, it is important to access current information sources. Basic references, like books and scientific papers are quoted throughout this chapter where relevant. They provide background knowledge and in-depth analysis of selected issues.

More up-to-date information can be found at numerous conferences. The BIOSTEC[39] conference covers many aspects, from devices via analytics to system integration. BIOCAS[40] is a good source for sensorics. Health informatics is treated at BHI[41] and ICHI.[42] For a more practical approach, the HIMSS[43] conference can be recommended.

It is also necessary to follow Internet sources, like blogs, discussion groups, newsletters, press releases, and company websites. To give some examples, we can name the site of the Healthcare Information and Management Systems Society

---

[37] http://ic.epfl.ch/privacy-surveillance (accessed July 13, 2015).

[38] http://slideshot.epfl.ch/play/cops_appelbaum (accessed July 13, 2015).

[39] http://www.biostec.org/ (accessed July 4, 2015).

[40] http://biocas2015.org/ (accessed July 4, 2015).

[41] http://bhi.embs.org/ (accessed July 4, 2015).

[42] http://cs.utdallas.edu/ichi2015/ (accessed July 4, 2015).

[43] http://www.himssconference.org/ (accessed July 4, 2015).

(HIMSS),[44] the Journal of mHealth,[45] Nuviun,[46] Story of Digital Health,[47], or Connected Health Media.[48] On LinkedIn, there are many relevant discussion groups. It has to be said that as the market is booming, many try to enter it and establish their reputation, so the reader has to evaluate the quality him/herself. These sources are, however, essential for staying current with the developments.

15 CONCLUSION

We observe rapid progress in the domain of smart medical devices and telemedicine. First, regarding the devices themselves—novel sensors, miniaturization, and energy harvesting. They are better connected, on the physical level and thanks to smarter networking. New platforms for data integration, exchange, and analytics arise. Data analysis algorithms are improved.

However, the progress of integration of medical grade devices into actual clinical practice is slow, especially for multivendor, open systems. In our opinion, one of the reasons is the inherent risk associated with their use for serious medical cases. This issue can be alleviated with a vendor-independent, neutral system of quality monitoring. In this chapter we have presented basic organizational and architectural ideas that help to construct such a system.

It would be illusory to try to build a system to cover all connected cases for all patients. It seems reasonable to start with a well-defined medical case that would serve as a nucleus of crystallization. Main stakeholders and their interests have to be identified. A model of the medical case has to be developed:

- Which cases are to be treated?
- Which alternative therapies are to be considered?
- What medical devices are to be included?
- What device parameters are to be observed?
- What health parameters are to be considered?
- Who are the cooperating partners?
- How is the data stream to be divided?, etc.

Multiple variants of the devices and their variability in time call for novel statistical models. The system has to embrace change as a natural factor. After a certain amount of time a specific type of device is phased out, but we may consider what experience was gained and what is valid for future developments. Another issue is what demographic factors have to be included—to what extent the results for one patient group are transferable to another?

---

[44] http://www.himss.org/ (accessed July 4, 2015).
[45] http://www.thejournalofmhealth.com/ (accessed July 4, 2015).
[46] http://nuviun.com/ (accessed July 4, 2015).
[47] http://storyofdigitalhealth.com/about/ (accessed July 4, 2015).
[48] http://www.connectedhealthmedia.com/ (accessed July 4, 2015).

The success of such an effort requires a good level of skill in each of the individual fields and intensive interdisciplinary cooperation. A deep understanding of all factors is necessary, in addition to the apparently trivial ones. As the results will influence the choice of therapy, they have to be formulated cautiously, without the pressure to publish. The challenge lies in combining rapid development with scientific rigor.

The problem of reuse of medical data seems to be a field worth exploring for scientists, developers, and entrepreneurs in the years to come.

ACRONYMS

AAL   ambient assisted living
BAN   body area network
CRM   customer relationship management
EBM   evidence-based medicine
ECG   electrocardiography (recording of the electrical activity of the heart)
EEG   electroencephalography (recording of the electrical activity of the brain)
EHR   electronic health record
EPFL   Ecole Polytechnique Fdrale de Lausanne (Switzerland)
FDA   (US) Food and Drug Administration
GDPR   (European) General Data Protection Regulation
GIGO   Garbage In, Garbage Out
GPS   global positioning system
HIPAA   (US) Health Insurance Portability and AccountabilityAct
ICD   implantable cardioverter defibrillator
IoT   Internet of Things
IT   information technology
NSA   (US) National Security Agency
P4   medicine—predictive, personalized, preventive, participative medicine
RCT   randomized control trial
STEMI   ST elevation myocardial infarction (heart attack, visible on the ECG as the elevation of the ST segment)

GLOSSARY

Actuator A device acting directly on the patient's body, in contrast to the passive sensor.
Adverse reaction Negative reaction of the patient to the applied drug or therapy.
Ambient assisted living A system of devices (sensors) integrated into the house/apartment where the patient lives. Permits monitoring of his/her health and general condition in his/her known environment.
Anonymizing data Removing elements of data that permit the disclosure of the identity of the patient.
Big Data A collection of data, characterized by high volume, variety, velocity, and veracity (four V's).

Body area network A wireless network connecting wearable and implantable medical devices of a patient.

Cardiovascular Related to the heart and the blood vessels.

Clinical trial Formal experiment that tests a therapy method, with a clear goal and well-defined possible outcomes. Typically two balanced groups of patients are compared: one receiving the tested treatment and another one receiving no treatment (placebo) or a different one. The statistical evaluation of the results has a solid scientific base.

Cohort A group of patients participating in a trial.

Cyber-Physical(-Social) System a system containing computer infrastructure and physical elements, essentially dependent on the static properties and dynamical behavior of the physical part.

Defibrillator (implantable cardioverter-defibrillator—ICD) An active device, implantable inside the body, capable of correcting most life-threatening cardiac arrhythmias. The ICD is the first-line treatment and prophylactic therapy for patients at risk for sudden cardiac death.

Double blind trial A trial, where neither the patients nor the doctors know who is receiving the treatment and who belongs to the comparison group.

Effectiveness Therapeutic effect in the clinical practice.

Efficacy Therapeutic effect in laboratory.

Efficiency Ratio of the therapeutic effect to price.

Electronic Health Record Systematized collection of patient electronically stored health information in a digital format. These records can be shared across different healthcare settings, under the condition of interoperable data formats and communication protocols.

Energy harvesting Powering an implanted device with the energy of the body (warmth, movements). In this way, exchanging the battery is no longer necessary.

Engineering a product Transforming a laboratory model into a product that can be industrially produced and easily used.

Evidence-based medicine Medical practice based on the use of evidence from well-designed and conducted research.

Home hospital Hospital keeping the (major part of the) health record of a patient.

Human in the loop A human that is a vital element of the system. His/her skills are important to the function of the system. In the case of medicine and medical devices it may be a doctor, a nurse, a patient who has to install the device, or an operator of the phone network.

Inductive transfer of energy Contactless transfer of power to an implanted device from outside the body via electromagnetic induction. In this way, exchanging the battery is no longer necessary.

Internet of Things A network of physical objects (things) embedded with electronics, software, sensors, and network connectivity, which enables these objects to collect and exchange data. The number of elements can be large. As moving in the environment only with wireless connection, they will have special requirements on computing capacity and power.

Interoperability Capability of devices and systems to connect, interact, and exchange data.

Multimorbidity Having more than one disease.

Observational study A clinical study where the group of patients (cohort) is observed and the investigator does not influence the assignment of subjects into a treated group versus a control group.

Open standard A standard defined by a community, publicly discussed and fully disclosed. Enables the configuration of heterogeneous systems built with devices and computer systems delivered by various producers.

Open system A system based on open standards. Makes it easy to enter by a smaller startup company.

Pacemaker An active device which uses electrical impulses, delivered by electrodes contracting the heart muscles, to regulate the beating of the heart. The primary purpose of a pacemaker is to maintain an adequate heart rate, either because the heart's natural pacemaker is not fast enough, or because there is a block in the heart's electrical conduction system.

Postmarket surveillance Activities used to monitor the safety and effectiveness of medical devices once they are on the market. These activities are designed to generate information to quickly identify poorly performing devices and other safety problems, and accurately characterize real-world device performance and clinical outcomes.

Premarket approval Process of scientific and regulatory review to evaluate the safety and effectiveness of Class III medical devices. Class III devices are those that support or sustain human life, are of substantial importance in preventing impairment of human health, or which present a potential, unreasonable risk of illness or injury.

Premarket notification Submission made to the authority to demonstrate that the device to be marketed is at least as safe and effective, that is, substantially equivalent, to a legally marketed device that is not subject to premarket approval.

Proprietary standard A standard defined by a company, not publicly disclosed, or not with enough detail. Makes it difficult to connect devices or computer systems of other producers.

Randomized clinical trial A clinical trial where the patients' population (cohort) is randomly divided into the tested and the compared group.

Smart textiles Textiles, into which devices (sensors) are woven. They permit an unobtrusive long-term measurement, with good positioning of the sensors.

Spurious correlation An apparent correlation between two processes that are indeed not related (correlation does not imply causation).

Telemedicine Using telecommunications for medical purposes: consulting a doctor via a phone, automatic sending sensor values, etc. Allows for frequent contact or data exchange with lower costs and effort.

REFERENCES

Abdel-Aleem, S., 2009. Design, Execution, and Management of Medical Device Clinical Trials. John Wiley & Sons, Hoboken, New Jersey. ISBN-13: 978-0470474266; ISBN-10: 0470474262

Aggarwal, C.C., 2013. Managing and Mining Sensor Data. Springer Science & Business Media, Berlin, Germany.

Alemzadeh, H., Iyer, R.K., Kalbarczyk, Z., Raman, J., 2013. Analysis of safety-critical computer failures in medical devices. IEEE Secur. Priv. 11 (4), 14–26.

Andrade, H.C., Gedik, B., Turaga, D.S., 2014. Fundamentals of Stream Processing: Application Design, Systems, and Analytics. Cambridge University Press, Cambridge, United Kingdom.

Becker, K.M., Whyte, J.J., 2007. Clinical Evaluation of Medical Devices: Principles and Case Studies. Springer Science & Business Media, Berlin, Germany.

Borsci, S., Macredie, R.D., Martin, J.L., Young, T., 2014. How many testers are needed to assure the usability of medical devices? Expert Rev. Med. Devices 11 (5), 513–525.

Borzekowski, D.L., Guan, Y., Smith, K.C., Erby, L.H., Roter, D.L., 2013. The Angelina effect: immediate reach, grasp, and impact of going public. Genet. Med. 16 (7), 516–521.

Castro, M., Rubin, A.S., Laviolette, M., Fiterman, J., Lima, M.D.A., Shah, P.L., Fiss, E., Olivenstein, R., Thomson, N.C., Niven, R.M., et al., 2010. Effectiveness and safety of bronchial thermoplasty in the treatment of severe asthma: a multicenter, randomized, double-blind, sham-controlled clinical trial. Am. J. Respir. Crit. Care Med. 181 (2), 116.

Cavallari, R., Martelli, F., Rosini, R., Buratti, C., Verdone, R., 2014. A survey on wireless body area networks: technologies and design challenges. IEEE Commun. Surv. Tutorials 99, 1–23. doi:10.1109/SURV.2014.012214.00007.

Chakravarthy, S., Jiang, Q., 2009. Stream Data Processing: A Quality of Service Perspective: Modeling, Scheduling, Load Shedding, and Complex Event Processing, vol. 36. Springer Science & Business Media, Berlin, Germany.

Coiera, E., 2015. Guide to Health Informatics. CRC Press.

Custers, B., Calders, T., Schermer, B., Zarsky, T., 2012. Discrimination and Privacy in the Information Society: Data Mining and Profiling in Large Databases, vol. 3. Springer Science & Business Media, Berlin, Germany.

DaCosta, F., 2013. Rethinking the Internet of Things: A Scalable Approach to Connecting Everything. Apress.

Djulbegovic, B., Guyatt, G.H., Ashcroft, R.E., 2009. Epistemologic inquiries in evidence-based medicine. Cancer Control 16 (2), 158–168.

Evans, D., Barwell, J., Eccles, D.M., Collins, A., Izatt, L., Jacobs, C., Donaldson, A., Brady, A.F., Cuthbert, A., Harrison, R., et al., 2014. The Angelina Jolie effect: how high celebrity profile can have a major impact on provision of cancer related services. Breast Cancer Res. 16, 442.

Filippini, D., 2012. Autonomous Sensor Networks: Collective Sensing Strategies for Analytical Purposes. Springer Science & Business Media, Berlin, Germany.

Floridi, L., Illari, P., 2014. The Philosophy of Information Quality, vol. 358. Springer.

Friedman, L.M., Furberg, C., DeMets, D.L., et al., 2010. Fundamentals of Clinical Trials, vol. 4. Springer, Berlin, Germany.

Fröhlig, G., Carlsson, J., Jung, J., Koglek, W., Lemke, B., Markewitz, A., Neuzner, J., 2013. Herzschrittmacher-und Defibrillator-Therapie: Indikation-Programmierung-Nachsorge. Georg Thieme Verlag.

Fu, K., Blum, J., 2013. Controlling for cybersecurity risks of medical device software. Commun. ACM 56 (10), 35–37. doi:10.1145/2508701.

Gad, S.C., 2011. Safety Evaluation of Pharmaceuticals and Medical Devices: International Regulatory Guidelines. Springer, Berlin, Germany.

Gama, J., Gaber, M.M., 2007. Learning From Data Streams. Springer, Berlin, Germany.

Gigerenzer, G., 2014. Risk Savvy: How to Make Good Decisions. Penguin.

Hargrove, J.L., 1998. Dynamic Modeling in the Health Sciences. Springer Science & Business Media, Berlin, Germany.

Hauser, R.G., 2012. Here we go again another failure of postmarketing device surveillance. N. Engl. J. Med. 366 (10), 873–875.

Hei, X., Du, X., 2013. Security for Wireless Implantable Medical Devices. Springer, Berlin, Germany.

Hood, L., 2013. Systems biology and P4 medicine: past, present, and future. Rambam Maimonides Med. J. 4 (2). doi:10.5041/RMMJ.10112.

Independent UK Panel on Breast Cancer Screening, 2012. The benefits and harms of breast cancer screening: an independent review. Lancet 380 (9855), 1778–1786.

Insel, T.R., Cuthbert, B.N., 2015. Brain disorders? Precisely. Science 348 (6234), 499–500.

Ioannidis, J.P., 2005. Why most published research findings are false. Chance 18 (4), 40–47.

Kesselheim, A.S., Rajan, P.V., et al., 2014. Regulating incremental innovation in medical devices. BMJ 349, g5303.

Kramme, R., 2007. Medizintechnik: Verfahren, Systeme, Informationsverarbeitung; Mit 170 Tabellen. Springer, Berlin, Germany.

La Polla, M., Martinelli, F., Sgandurra, D., 2013. A survey on security for mobile devices. IEEE Commun. Surv. Tutorials 15 (1), 446–471.

Lane, J., Stodden, V., Bender, S., Nissenbaum, H., 2014. Privacy, Big Data, and the Public Good: Frameworks for Engagement. Cambridge University Press, Cambridge, United Kingdom.

Lang, A.R., Martin, J.L., Sharples, S., Crowe, J.A., 2014. Medical device design for adolescent adherence and developmental goals: a case study of a cystic fibrosis physiotherapy device. Patient Prefer. Adher. 8, 301.

Lazer, D., Kennedy, R., King, G., Vespignani, A., 2014. The parable of Google Flu: traps in big data analysis. Science 343 (14 March), 1203–1205.

Lipton, R.B., Dodick, D.W., Silberstein, S.D., Saper, J.R., Aurora, S.K., Pearlman, S.H., Fischell, R.E., Ruppel, P.L., Goadsby, P.J., 2010. Single-pulse transcranial magnetic stimulation for acute treatment of migraine with aura: a randomised, double-blind, parallel-group, sham-controlled trial. Lancet Neurol. 9 (4), 373–380.

Lodi, C.A., Vasta, A., Hegbrant, M.A., Bosch, J.P., Paolini, F., Garzotto, F., Ronco, C., 2010. Multidisciplinary evaluation for severity of hazards applied to hemodialysis devices: an original risk analysis method. Clin. J. Am. Soc. Nephrol. 5 (11), 2004–2017, http://dx.doi.org/10.2215/CJN.01740210, Article ID CJN-01740210.

Lyon, D., 2014. Surveillance, Snowden, and Big Data: capacities, consequences, critique. Big Data Soc. 1 (2). doi:http://dx.doi.org/10.1177/2053951714541861.

Maharatna, K., Bonfiglio, S., 2013. Systems Design for Remote Healthcare. Springer Science & Business Media, Berlin, Germany.

Meulen, R.H., ter Meulen, R., Biller-Andorno, N., Lenk, C., Lie, R., 2005. Evidence-Based Practice in Medicine and Health Care: A Discussion of the Ethical Issues. Springer, Berlin, Germany.

Nissenbaum, H., 2009. Privacy in Context: Technology, Policy, and the Integrity of Social Life. Stanford University Press, Palo Alto, California, United States.

Nosek, B.A., Spies, J.R., Motyl, M., 2012. Scientific utopia II. Restructuring incentives and practices to promote truth over publishability. Perspect. Psychol. Sci. 7 (6), 615–631.

Pawar, P., Jones, V., Van Beijnum, B.J.F., Hermens, H., 2012. A framework for the comparison of mobile patient monitoring systems. J. Biomed. Inform. 45 (3), 544–556.

Potapov, E., Meyer, D., Swaminathan, M., Ramsay, M., El-Banayosy, A., Diehl, C., Veynovich, B., Gregoric, I.D., Kukucka, M., Gromann, T.W., et al., 2011. Inhaled nitric oxide after left ventricular assist device implantation: a prospective, randomized, double-blind, multicenter, placebo-controlled trial. J. Heart Lung Transplant. 30 (8), 870–878.

Raghunathan, B., 2013. The Complete Book of Data Anonymization: From Planning to Implementation. CRC Press, USA.

Robichau, B.P., 2014. Healthcare Information Privacy and Security: Regulatory Compliance and Data Security in the Age of Electronic Health Records. Apress, New York, USA.

Schneier, B., 2012. Liars and Outliers: Enabling the Trust That Society Needs to Thrive. John Wiley & Sons, New Jersey, USA.

Sedrakyan, A., Marinac-Dabic, D., Holmes, D.R., 2013. The international registry infrastructure for cardiovascular device evaluation and surveillance. JAMA 310 (3), 257–259.

Sharples, S., Martin, J., Lang, A., Craven, M., O'Neill, S., Barnett, J., 2012. Medical device design in context: a model of user-device interaction and consequences. Displays 33 (4), 221–232.

Silva, H., Lourenço, A., Canento, F., Fred, A.L., Raposo, N., 2013. ECG biometrics: principles and applications. In: BIOSIGNALS, pp. 215–220.

Sliwa, J., 2012. Do we need a global brain? tripleC Cogn. Commun. Co-operation 11 (1), 107–116.

Sliwa, J., Benoist, E., 2011. Wireless sensor and actor networks: e-Health, e-Science, e-Decisions. In: 2011 International Conference on Selected Topics in Mobile and Wireless Networking (iCOST), pp. 1–6.

Sliwa, J., Benoist, E., 2012a. Medical evaluative research and privacy protection. In: Developments in E-Systems Engineering (DeSE).

Sliwa, J., Benoist, E., 2012b. A web architecture based on physical data separation supporting privacy protection in medical research. Int. J. Reliab. Qual. E-Healthc. 1 (4), 68–79.

Sorenson, C., Drummond, M., 2014. Improving medical device regulation: the United States and Europe in perspective. Milbank Q 92 (1), 114–150.

Speidel, D., Sridharan, M., 2014. Quality assurance in the age of mobile healthcare. J. mHealth 1 (2), 42–46. http://www.joomag.com/magazine/mag/0345100001397732888.

St Cyr, T.J., 2013. An overview of healthcare standards. In: 2013 Proceedings of IEEE, Southeastcon, pp. 1–5.

Suh, S.C., Tanik, U.J., Carbone, J.N., Eroglu, A., 2013. Applied Cyber-Physical Systems. Springer Science & Business Media, Berlin, Germany.

Teow, N., Siegel, S., 2013. FDA regulation of medical devices and medical device reporting. Pharmaceut. Reg. Affairs 2 (110), 2.

Trigo, J.D., Kohl, C., Eguzkiza, A., Martínez-Espronceda, M., Alesanco, A., Serrano, L., García, J., Knaup, P., 2014. On the seamless, harmonized use of ISO/IEEE11073 and openEHR. IEEE J. Biomed. Health Inform. 18 (3), 872–884.

Wac, K., 2013. Smartphone as a personal, pervasive health informatics services platform: literature review. ArXiv preprint arXiv:1310.7965.

Wachter, R., 2015. The Digital Doctor. McGraw-Hill Education, New York, USA.

Wagner, S., Hansen, F.O., Pedersen, C.F., Memon, M., Aysha, F., Mathissen, M., Nielsen, C., Wesby, O., 2013. CareStore platform for seamless deployment of ambient assisted living applications and devices. In: Proceedings of the 7th International Conference on Pervasive Computing Technologies for Healthcare, pp. 240–243.

Wang, C., 1993. Sense and Nonsense of Statistical Inference: Controversy: Misuse, and Subtlety. 176. Marcel Dekker, New York, ISBN-13: 978-0824787981; ISBN-10: 0824787986

Wyer, P.C., Silva, S.A., 2009. Where is the wisdom? I—A conceptual history of evidence-based medicine. J. Eval. Clin. Pract. 15 (6), 891–898.

Yao, J., Warren, S., 2005. Applying the ISO/IEEE 11073 standards to wearable home health monitoring systems. J. Clin. Monit. Comput. 19 (6), 427–436.

Yin, G., 2012. Clinical Trial Design: Bayesian and Frequentist Adaptive Methods, vol. 876. John Wiley & Sons, New Jersey, USA.

Young, S.S., Karr, A., 2011. Deming, data and observational studies. Significance 8 (3), 116–120.

Zannad, F., Stough, W.G., Pina, I.L., Mehran, R., Abraham, W.T., Anker, S.D., De Ferrari, G.M., Farb, A., Geller, N.L., Kieval, R.S., et al., 2014. Current challenges for clinical trials of cardiovascular medical devices. Int. J. Cardiol. 175(1), 30–37.

Measuring energy efficiency in data centers

10

M. Chinnici[a], A. Capozzoli[b], G. Serale[b]

ENEA, Rome, Italy[a]
Politecnico di Torino, Turin, Italy[b]

1 INTRODUCTION

The role of data centers (DCs) within society has lead to increasing interest in both information and communication technology (ICT) and the energy sector. The concept of energy efficiency is becoming a fundamental issue in DCs, both in the design and the operational stages, due to the increase in energy prices and policy pressures (Smith et al., 2009). Moreover, the expansion of large data sets (Big Data) and the related processing demands have led to an increase in power consumption, and electricity usage has become the most expensive portion of the costs in DCs (Tozer et al., 2013). In general, within a DC, approximately 80% of the total life cost is due to the energy consumption related to IT power and cooling demand, and only the remaining 20% of the investment is due to the infrastructure construction costs (Hill et al., 2009). In the last decade, the electricity consumption of DCs has grown by +11%/year, while the sum of all the sectors has increased by +3%/year (Koomey, 2011). This chapter discusses how to measure energy performance through appropriate metrics and proposes methodologies for their evaluation in DCs.

It is imperative that the electrical energy consumption and indoor environmental conditions (eg, temperature and relative humidity) are monitored in order to evaluate and measure the energy efficiency and the thermal management effectiveness of a DC. The energy performance evaluation of DCs should be based on globally accepted assessment strategies. These can be established in terms of common metrics to promote an improvement in energy saving strategies, the renovation and advance of infrastructures, and the management of procedures. In recent years, various metrics have been introduced for this purpose. Nevertheless, a complete regulatory framework, which provides standard methodologies for DCs in the field of energy metrics, is still not available (Capozzoli et al., 2015).

The existing metrics that have been developed to measure the energy efficiency and thermal performance of DCs are not always capable of tracking improvements at

Pervasive Computing. http://dx.doi.org/10.1016/B978-0-12-803663-1.00010-3

different levels of a DC. Furthermore, they can fail to estimate the impact of measures and strategies on DC energy performance. In general, these metrics are related to the energy or power consumption of the whole infrastructure (or a specific component or IT hardware), to the *useful work* of IT equipment or to thermal management. A new perspective is discussed in this chapter to connect thermal performance and energy efficiency metrics through a holistic approach. To this aim, both the state of the art and the future challenges and opportunities pertaining to the measurement of energy efficiency in DCs have been discussed. The following issues have been covered:

- A critical evaluation of the current energy consumption trends in DCs.
- A critical review of the most important metrics currently used in DCs.
- A discussion on the importance of matching thermal and energy requirements.
- A critical analysis of the impact of thermal management on the behavior of global energy consumption and on the reliability of IT equipment.
- A framework for the future development of energy performance metrics for DCs, and a proposal of a systematic approach that provides a unified framework for DC energy metrics.
- The most suitable emerging metrics in the context of Smart Cities.

This study highlights the importance of providing an exhaustive and unified framework for DCs, in terms of energy metrics. For this reason, a systematic approach has been used to harmonize the energy metrics scenario, which is often similar to the "Tower of Babel." The aim of the work was to provide a reliable methodology that could be used to categorize the energy metrics of DCs. This methodology could also offer a clear guide to DC managers on how to improve the efficiency of their facilities.

This chapter is arranged in seven sections. Section 2 provides an introduction to the basic problem of measuring energy efficiency in DCs and the challenges that this involves. Section 3 addresses the criteria and methodologies that can be considered to measure "energy efficiency" in DCs. This section also critically analyzes the current framework of metrics and where it falls short in regulating the development of energy efficiency metrics. Three different categories of metrics are analyzed in Sections 4–6: power/energy, thermal, and productivity metrics. Section 7 is devoted to a discussion on the future challenges, considering the mutual relation between energy efficiency metrics and the opportunity of introducing a framework for the measurement of energy efficiency in DCs.

2 PROBLEM STATEMENT

Information and communication technology (ICT) plays a leading role in the development and support of a number of activities in society. However, the role of ICT is ambivalent: on one hand, ICT is responsible for the energy consumption that is induced by ICT itself, but on the other hand it represents a potential opportunity of achieving energy efficiency across the economy. Hence, there is a growing perception that ICT can both reduce greenhouse gas emissions (environmental impacts) and help all economic sectors to become more energy efficient. In this context, ICT allows existing processes to be optimized and can enable technologies to reduce energy use. To date, while ICT contributes to a great extent toward the improvement in energy efficiency of a variety of industrial and service sectors, energy consumption by ICT itself is increasing. Hence, achieving energy efficiency within the ICT sector has become an important challenge.

DCs have become an important part of the ICT sector, where energy efficiency had been a secondary concern for a long time (Helal et al., 2005). More broadly speaking, inspiration for the energy efficiency of DCs can be drawn from any behavior that results in the use of less power (Uddin et al., 2014), which is achieved through the minimization of energy consumption using new products, architectures, and best practices. The concept of energy efficiency in DCs, which only a few years ago was restricted to enhancing IT equipment and their cooling systems, is today addressed to a variety of system-level technologies and associated services that will improve energy and environmental performances.

Overall, DCs have contributed to the increase in efficiency in society, improved convenience, and enhanced lifestyles. Since these achievements have been recognized, the demand for DCs has continued to increase, in both number and size, in order to accommodate the escalating user and application demands. However, DC owners and operators should take sufficient measures to cushion the risks associated with an increasing energy demand. At the same time, the need to invest in the energy efficiency of DCs is also becoming a priority. Urgent action is needed to control the greenhouse gas emissions that are indirectly introduced through the increasing usage of electricity by DCs, and many important initiatives have been put in place. Companies operating in DCs have launched research efforts to improve the energy efficiency of several components. Subsequently, different international initiatives (such as the EU-Code of Conduct for DCs, the Green Grid and the Energy Star Program) and energy efficiency criteria, benchmarks, best practice measures, and efficient product technologies have been proposed to support efficiency at both IT hardware and infrastructure levels (Schaeppi et al., 2012). These strategies have led to a slight reduction in the growth trend of electricity usage. For instance, in the past 5 years, the energy consumptions of DCs has only increased by about 50% of a scenario that had been predicted by Brill (2000). Guidelines are needed to investigate and propose ways of optimizing energy consumption in DCs. In the past, efficiency was incorrectly calculated by just adding together the efficiencies of the individual parts, as published by the manufacturers (Schaeppi et al., 2012).

Furthermore, attention was focused on the software running in the DC and the way that the workload was being processed. In fact, energy efficiency, from the computing perspective, has historically improved more slowly than performance or cost (Belady, 2016). Although technological progress has made it possible to take steps forward, in terms of energy consumption in DCs, efforts are still required and challenges still need to be faced in order to correctly measure energy efficiency.

The measurement of DC energy efficiency is therefore a complicated, inconstant problem that depends on the architecture, workload profiles, and environmental conditions. Its estimation has attracted a great deal of attention (Wang and Khan, 2011; Patterson et al., 2013; Schödwell et al., 2013). In order to compare the efficiency of different DCs, a set of measurements is needed. Therefore, DC operators and the related organizations have been motivated to develop energy performance metrics. They can be defined with an index or an indicator, which qualitatively or quantitatively evaluates the energy and/or environmental effects on a DC operation. Moreover, these metrics make it possible to establish a trend over time by means of the evaluation of their variations over different periods. They may also provide guidelines for the development of future DC technologies.

Different energy-efficiency metrics are typically used to benchmark the energy consumption of single products or product systems. The complexity of the "data center" product system is without doubt a challenging factor. It is therefore not surprising that a variety of metrics have recently been developed with the intention of quantifying specific aspects of DC energy performance.

Moreover, thermal management and air distribution performances are assuming a key role in achieving energy savings and IT equipment reliability for DCs (ASHRAE, 2011; Flucker and Tozer, 2012; Sullivan et al., 2006; Cho and Kim, 2011; Sharma et al., 2002; Tang et al., 2006b; Schmidt et al., 2005; Herrlin, 2005, 2007; Tozer et al., 2009). Hence, it is necessary to promote the extensive use of energy and thermal metrics to measure energy efficiency and to report the measured values (Capozzoli et al., 2014).

Metrics need to be generated so that an analysis can be performed: *are we doing the right things and doing things right?*. An analysis of metrics is necessary to be able to take appropriate action for the energy renovation of a DC.

One of the major aspects remains: *in what way is it possible to measure energy efficiency in DCs?* In fact, there is not a comprehensive answer to this question as, from the DC perspective, no standardized metrics have been introduced to determine the exact way of measuring its energy efficiency. Although several researchers are working on solutions in terms of energy metrics, their findings are still incomplete. Hence, the need to provide metrics and methods to measure energy efficiency in DCs is urgent. Metrics help and facilitate energy optimizations by defining energy efficiency techniques to implement green and energy efficient DCs (Schödwell et al., 2013).

The efficiency of energy use represents an important topic in the public policy agenda of many countries. However, as Patterson (1996) mentioned "Energy Efficiency is a generic term, and there is no one unequivocal quantitative measure of energy efficiency." The selected energy input and useful output depend on the nature of the analysis that has to be undertaken, but the following ratio, which is based on the first principle, is generally used to provide a definition of energy efficiency:

$$\text{Useful output of a process/Energy input into a process} \qquad (1)$$

Although this ratio is somewhat intuitive in the DC case, the measurement of energy efficiency can lead to difficulties and misunderstandings in the interpretation of the input/output indicators. De facto, metrics help to identify the areas in DCs that need to be improved in order to enhance energy efficiency. However, the problems of measuring energy efficiency remain clear, and even though metrics are available, there are no methodologies available that explain how, where, and when to use them. In general, the selected metrics rarely provide information about all the phenomena that affect the energy consumption in a DC. For example, power/energy metrics provide no information about thermal management phenomena. On the other hand, thermal metrics are of limited use because little information are obtained regarding the energy efficiency of a system (Shah et al., 2008). Hence, the existing types of metrics that have been developed to measure the energy efficiency and thermal performance of DCs are not capable (or are only in part capable) of tracking improvements and changes, and they fail to estimate the impact of these changes on DC performance. The metrics published in the literature can be related to the energy/power consumption of the whole infrastructure, to a specific component, to the IT hardware, to IT "useful work" or they can be connected to thermal aspects. Another important aspect that has to be analyzed is related to the "effectiveness" of measuring procedures. Effectiveness is defined as the capacity of metrics to provide data, in an appropriate way, in terms of "where", "what" and "on time".

It is well know that a DC is an integration of complex systems, and this complexity creates serious difficulties in setting up a methodology in terms of energy efficiency. In fact, many variables in DCs have to be taken into account. In Europe, there is a lack of a complete plan which can provide standard metrics and methodologies for DCs (Chinnici and Quintiliani, 2013). The evaluation of DCs should be based on globally accepted assessment systems, in terms of common metrics, that promote an improvement in energy savings, renovation and an improvement in infrastructures, management methods and so on (Capozzoli et al., 2015).

3 CRITERIA AND METHODOLOGY FOR THE METRICS SELECTION

This section is devoted to presenting the methodology used to categorize and organize all the existing DC metrics. The classification has been based on consistent criteria in order to provide a systematic approach to DC metrics.

The generalized framework reported in Table 1 is used for metric classification, taking into account the main features of all the indices. Furthermore, the most important applications, formulas, and details are dealt with in detail one at a time. A table based on the scheme in Table 1 is provided for each form of metrics. This table is useful to summarize the most important properties of each type of metric.

Table 1 General Metrics Framework

Metric	Formula	Scale	Assess	Introduced	Reference Range

The proposed framework that has been used to categorize the use of harmonized metrics in order to effectively achieve energy efficiency in DCs is organized around the typical attributes, as explained hereafter:

1. *Metric Name*: used to identify the metrics in the current scenario.
2. *Formula and Acronym*: used to express each type of metrics, in terms of mathematical formulation and its acronym. The symbols used in the formulas proposed in various papers have been unified to obtain a consistent nomenclature. In order to harmonize metric terminology, the following symbols are used: $\dot{W}$ [watts or kilowatts] for the instantaneous electrical power load/consumption; $\dot{W}^*$ [watts or kilowatts] for the installed electrical power capacity necessary to satisfy the peak consumption; W [watt-hours or kilowatt-hours] for the total energy consumption referring to a time period; $\dot{Q}$ [watts or kilowatts] for the thermal power exchanged; C [GbPS/cycles/Tb/OPS] for the computational/storage work of the IT equipment; C^* [GbPS/cycles/Tb] for the computational/storage peak capacity of the IT equipment; S [square meters] for the useful floor area of a DC; τ [hour] for the time interval; V [cubic meters] for volumes; V_W [liters] for the water usage; $\dot{V}$ [cubic feet meter per second] for the volumetric flow rate; T [kelvin or degree Celsius] for the temperature; $\dot{m}$ [kilograms per second] for the mass flow rate; c_p [joule per kilogram kelvin] for the specific heat of a material; $\dot{\Psi}$ [watts] for the exergy destruction; and n [$-$] for the quantity of a particular attribute. In some cases, it has not been possible to individuate a specific symbol to describe a physical quantity, and for these reason a longer expression (eg, a description in words) has been used. The subscript has always been expressed and abbreviations have been avoided in order to provide a unique interpretation. Furthermore, it is necessary to point out that many types of metrics can be expressed in both terms of power ratio and in terms of energy ratio. Moreover, certain formulas referring to different indices can seem to be almost identical, and when this has occurred, the volume of control, the data logging or the sampling frequency has been specified. For instance, in many cases the metrics take the form of a first law of efficiency (see Eq. 1), and as a consequence, the formulations can consider different control volumes for the useful work or for the energy input.
3. *Scale*: used to take into account both the nature of the variables that characterize each metrics and the system and/or components in which the metrics can be applied.

In order to deal with the second level of classification, information is introduced on the physical Infrastructure of a DC in which the metrics is applied. The metrics can be related to (Schödwell et al., 2013):

a. the whole physical infrastructure system of a DC;
b. a single subsystem (eg, whole air conditioning system, IT equipment, etc.);
c. a single component of a subsystems (eg, cooling chiller, evaporative tower, pumps and fans, UPS, server, etc.).

The site infrastructure includes all the items that support the IT equipment components such as: power delivery components (UPS, PDU, generators, batteries, switch gear, distribution losses external to the IT equipment), cooling system components (HVAC, chillers, cooling towers, CRACs, pumps, etc.), and other supporting components (lighting, access protection, video control, etc.). IT hardware systems are defined as the equipment that is used to manage, process, store, or route data within the raised floor space in the DC. It includes components associated with all of the IT equipment, such as computing equipment (server machines, clients, network, storage, etc.), supplementary equipment (monitors, workstations/laptops used to monitor or control the DC).

4. *Assess*: used to underline the main objectives and to provide the targets of each metric. In this context, the *target* label provides information on the possible outcomes of a given metric. Besides the aforementioned high-level objectives (see point 3) related to the whole infrastructure system level, or to the component level, additional objectives and hence classification criteria have been considered.

5. *Introduced by*: used to indicate the author(s) who first introduced the metrics and/or its application in literature.

6. *Reference Range*: used to show the typical or recommended values of the metrics (when applicable).

According to the proposed framework, which provides common metrics criteria, the metrics are described in the following sections pertaining to the covering of certain areas considering their measurement capability (Power/Energy, Thermal, and Productivity Metrics), facility power utilization and system space used within the DC.

Power/energy metrics
The variables are related to energy consumption (kilowatt-hour) or power demand (kilowatt) at different levels. This category includes the cluster of indices used to assess the energy efficiency of a DC and its subsystems. These metrics can refer to the whole DC structure or to a particular component (eg, a part of the HVAC system, an operational auxiliary, etc.). In general, these indices are dimensionless and are defined in a similar way to the energy efficiency structure (see Eq. 1), which is represented by the ratio of net useful work obtained to the total demand required as input. The definition of what useful work is and what the required power is can vary for each metric.

Thermal metrics
The variables are related to the temperature or mass flow rate. This category generally includes indices related to airflow performance and thermal management. These metrics are used to assess the thermal efficiency of a DC and to detect any anomalous behavior (eg, hot spots), which could influence the temperature fields and, consequently, the reliability of the IT equipment.

Productivity metrics
The variables are related to data transfer, the computing process or storage. This category includes indices related to the quantity of the useful work within a DC from an IT perspective. Hence, these indices should lead to questions such as What is the useful work of a DC? and How does one calculate the useful work of a DC?

4 POWER/ENERGY METRICS

This cluster of metrics provides information on the efficiency of a DC in terms of global energy consumption, which is connected directly to the consumption of its single subsystems. In fact, the overall energy consumption of a DC is related to the associated energy demand for each unit. It can generally be observed that the main causes of energy consumption in a DC are due to the *IT equipment* and *HVAC system* (HVAC, chillers, cooling towers, CRACs, pumps, etc.) that are used to control the environmental conditions of the DC. A third category of energy consumption is related to the *support system* which is composed of the UPS and its batteries, the lighting system, the system delivering electricity, and the auxiliaries for the security. According to Yuventi and Mehdizadeh (2013), Dumitru et al. (2011), and Pelley et al. (2009), the energy consumption related to IT equipment ranges from 30% to 60%; the HVAC consumption from 33% to 55%; while the support system consumption ranges from 6% to 18%. Fig. 1 offers a schematic description of the energy power fluxes from the main components of a DC (power cooling system and computing system); a typical layout of the infrastructure system and its subsystems is highlighted. Once the most useful systems of a DC have been presented, different partitions of energy consuming subsystems have been given. Furthermore, according to the work of Pelley et al. (2009), five distinct subsystems that account for most DC power draws can be identified. However, if the aforementioned categories are opportunely merged, it could be possible to reduce them to the previously listed categories: servers and storage systems (IT equipment); cooling and humidification systems (HVAC system); networking, delivery components, switch gear, generators, PDUs, batteries, and UPS (support system); and other auxiliaries, such as that used for lighting or physical security (support system).

Several indices are available in the literature concerning the scheme presented in Fig. 1, related to the whole DC infrastructure and the single subsystems serving a facility. For this reason, the authors decided not to list all the metrics belonging to this cluster in a single table, but to use a list of subtables related to different aspects that can be assessed through different metrics.

An innovative classification has been proposed by the authors with the aim of providing a clear framework for the selection of the most appropriate metrics, considering the role of the different actors involved in a DC and the purpose of the analysis.

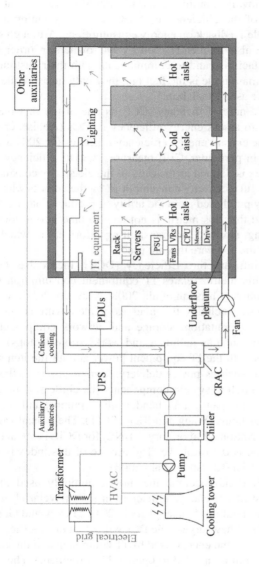

FIG. 1

Schematic description of the layout of a DC with the electrical, refrigerant, chilled water, and air fluxes highlighted.

The key to reading the tables on power/energy metrics is based on both the "scale" dimension (whole DC, subsystem, etc.) and the "assessment" (target) of each index.

The first set of metrics is presented in Table 2. The set refers to the whole DC structure. The metrics involved in this set has the aim of providing—at a stakeholder level—the awareness of the efficiency of a DC, and of obtaining a single index capable of giving simple feedback on energy consumptions. Although some of these metrics (eg, PUE) are also frequently used by DC owners in order to assess the sustainability of their facilities and to communicate with their customers on "How green is a DC?"—the main issue is the fact that they only measure the efficiency of the whole infrastructure as a "black box."

The Coefficient of Energy Efficiency (CEE) is one of the first metrics to have been proposed (2004) to assess energy efficiency in DCs (Aebischer et al., 2004). Reference values of the current energy efficiency practices for 2004 are available in Eubank et al. (2004). In particular, CEE measures the DC efficiency of electricity consumption. The index is defined as the ratio of the electricity consumed by the IT equipment (called "useful electricity consumption" by the authors who proposed the index) to the electricity purchased from the utility or produced on site. However, the same proponents stated that this metric is not able to take into account the energy efficiency of processing, storing, and transmitting information, which depends on both the hardware and the software that are used.

The Data Center infrastructure Efficiency (DCiE) metric has been accepted widely in industry. This metric relates IT equipment consumption to the whole infrastructure consumption (Christian et al., 2008; Azevedo, 2008). In the formula, the IT equipment power includes the load associated with all components of the IT equipment (ie, computation, storage and network equipment, along with supplemental equipment such as monitors and workstations/laptops), and the total facility power includes both the IT equipment power and all the items that support the IT equipment load, such as power delivery components (ie, UPS, generators, PDUs, batteries, etc.), cooling system components (ie, chillers, computer room air conditioning units, direct expansion air handler units, pumps, and cooling towers), and other miscellaneous items (Wang and Khan, 2011). The typical value suggested by Lawrence Berkeley National Laboratory (LBNL) for DCiE is about 0.5. However, the most common value is 0.7 or above. The inverse of this index is called Power Usage Effectiveness (PUE) (Christian et al., 2008).

In recent years, PUE has become the most commonly used metric for the measurement of infrastructure energy efficiency in DCs (Avelar et al., 2012), due to its simplicity of interpretation (Schaeppi et al., 2012). Pettey and Goasduff (2010) reported that about 80% of new large-scale DCs will adopt this metrics in 2015. PUE shows the relation between the energy used by IT equipment and the energy used by other facilities (ie, the cooling needed to operate IT equipment). The value of PUE can range between 1 and 3. Therefore, a PUE value of 2 indicates that for every watt required by the IT power, an additional watt is consumed to cool and distribute power to the IT equipment. Hence, the ideal value of this metric is 1, which means that all

Table 2 Power/Energy Metrics Related to the Whole DC Infrastructure

	Metrics	Formula	Scale	Assess	Introduced	Reference Range
1	Coefficient of Energy Efficiency	$CEE = \dfrac{\dot{W}_{Useful}}{\dot{W}_{Total}}$	DC	Electricity consumption efficiency	Aebischer et al. (2004)	1.54–1.97 (Eubank et al., 2004)
2	Data Center infrastructure Efficiency	$DCiE = \dfrac{\dot{W}_{ITequipment}}{\dot{W}_{Facility}}$	DC	Electricity consumption efficiency	Christian et al. (2008) and Azevedo (2008)	0.80–0.27 (Shiino, 2010) 0.78–0.28 (Koomey, 2011)
3	Power Usage Effectiveness	$PUE = \dfrac{\dot{W}_{Facility}}{\dot{W}_{ITequipment}}$ $PUE = \dfrac{1}{DCiE}$ $PUE = 1 + PLF + CLF$	DC	Electricity consumption efficiency	Christian et al. (2008)	1.25–3.75 (Shiino, 2010) 1.30–3.60 (Koomey, 2011)
4	Key Performance Indicator of Task Efficiency	$KPI_{TE} = \dfrac{W_{DC}}{W_{ITequipment}}$	DC	Electricity consumption efficiency	ETSI (2013)	–

the power required by the DC is used for the IT equipment (Thegreengrid.org, 2011), Benchmark values ranging from 1.25 to 3.75 were suggested by Shiino (2010), while Koomey found a range between 1.30 and 3.60 (mean value 1.92) comparing 61 DCs.

DCiE and PUE were proposed by the Green Grid, which then discussed them in great detail in several technical reports (Christian et al., 2008; Azevedo, 2008; Avelar et al., 2012; Pettey and Goasduff, 2010; Thegreengrid.org, 2011; Haas and Froedge, 2009). Both types of metrics are based on the same measurement values, but DCiE is easier to read as it has a percentage scale; higher values signal a higher efficiency of the DC. The European Telecommunications Standards Institute (ETSI) introduced an index to calculate the energy efficiency of a DC (Aebischer et al., 2004), that is, the Key Performance Indicator of Task Efficiency (KPI_{TE}) (ETSI, 2013), which refers to the consumption over a year of activity. Although the latter index is similar to PUE, as far as the mathematical formulation is concerned, the way the various terms included in the index are calculated is quite different. In fact, the power absorbed by the IT equipment is considered the useful work of a DC (further information about useful work is provided in the section on productivity metrics), while the power consumption of other uses represents an energy waste. The power consumption of the total facility is the sum of the power load due to IT equipment and the power loads due to other auxiliary uses (lighting, distribution, cooling, safety, UPS, etc.).

There are a number of known shortcomings in the measurement and use of DCiE and PUE for the calculation of DC energy efficiency. The practical weaknesses are related to the measurement of IT power consumption. In other words, they are related to the point at which the energy used by IT equipment is measured. The measured value can in fact vary according to where it is measured. Moreover, PUE always requires the continuous measurement of the energy consumption instead of a single snapshot measurement to make the outcome meaningful, because it is influenced by several time dependent factors (Schaeppi et al., 2012). Access to measured data is frequently almost impossible to obtain. Apart from these practical issues, the main problem is that PUE does not account for the power distribution or cooling losses inside IT equipment (Patterson, 2008). In fact, any efficiency measure that addresses IT equipment will probably cause a PUE increase. In addition, the PUE metrics does not consider the useful work done by a DC, as introduced by Patterson et al. (2013).

In order to overcome the weaknesses of the PUE metric and to provide practical guidelines, new versions of PUE were proposed. The Green Grid proposed the partial PUE (pPUE) and the scalability PUE (sPUE) for a comprehensive examination of the PUE metrics; the first one provides a definition of PUE for partitions in a DC (i.e., a container of IT equipment, a modular portion of a DC), while the scalability PUE was introduced to show how well a DC's total energy consumption scales with changes in its IT equipment loads.

Apart from the aforementioned high-level metrics concerning the whole DC infrastructure, there are also metrics based on the efficiency of systems (such as the Power Load Factor [PLF] and the Cooling Load Factor [CLF]), and on single components in a DC, as introduced in Table 3. Indeed, Table 3 reports the power/energy metrics that can be used to break down the whole DC into smaller subassemblies, including a single system. Table 3 focuses on indices referring to auxiliaries' subsystems that can be used or for converting and managing electrical energy or for guaranteeing the necessary services to DC operations (such as lights). The submetrics related to HVAC system components are listed in Table 4.

Unlike high-level metrics, Tables 3 and 4 offer detailed information on single systems, but they have to be combined to obtain a view of the whole DC environment. In particular, the PUE (see Eq. 3 in Table 2) is defined as the sum of two subindices (Table 3): the CLF and the PLF. The CLF is defined as the total power consumed by an HVAC system divided by the IT Load while the PLF is defined as the total power dissipated by the switch gear, UPSs, PDUs, etc., divided by the IT loads. Hence, the PUE metric can also be evaluated by adopting a further division into two other subindices (Christian et al., 2008; The Green Grid Technical Committee, 2007).

The Other Load Factor (OLF) coefficient was introduced by Schödwell et al. (2013). This is another coefficient that should be considered in the procedure of breaking down the DC into the various parts. OLF is used to take into account the energy overheads of a DC system that do not belong to an HVAC system or which are dissipated toward electrical energy transformations (energy system losses), such as lights. The latter are investigated in more detail by means of the Lighting Power Density (LPD), which accounts for DC lighting energy efficiency (Mathew et al., 2010). This coefficient measures the power required to light each square meter and it is expressed in watts per square meter (or watts per square foot). As lighting is a secondary use for a DC, a lower value of this metric corresponds to better energy efficiency. In particular, values between 0 and 10 W/m^2 are considered for a low lighting density, while values over 16 W/m^2 are considered for a high lighting density.

In the same paper, Schödwell et al. (2013) introduced indicators to evaluate the efficiency of the single components for energy storage, energy distribution and energy conversion that were previously classified by Azevedo and Rawson (2008). These coefficients are labeled as energy Storage Efficiency (eSE), energy Distribution Efficiency (eDE), and energy Conversion Efficiency (eCE), respectively. They represent a further subdivision of the PLF into smaller subsystems. However, indices capable of assessing the efficiency and the right capacity design of UPS systems are necessary. The UPS Load Factor (UPS-LF) and UPS System Efficiency (UPS-SE) metrics were introduced in Azevedo and Rawson (2008) to satisfy these aims.

As previously mentioned, another table has been necessary for the HVAC system components. Table 4 summarizes several metrics for various components of the HVAC system. Metrics related to the air/water economizer have been reported in this subset, even though economizers can be considered components that affect the whole DC scale.

Table 3 Power/Energy Metrics Related to a DC Broken Down Into Sub-assemblies

	Metrics	Formula	Scale	Assess	Introduced	Reference Values
5	Power Load Factor	$PLF = \dfrac{\dot{W}_{Electrical\_system}}{\dot{W}_{ITequipment}}$	Electrical auxiliaries	Electricity consumption efficiency	Christian et al. (2008) and The Green Grid Technical Committee (2007)	–
6	Cooling Load Factor	$CLF = \dfrac{\dot{W}_{HVACsystem}}{\dot{W}_{ITequipment}}$	HVAC	Electricity consumption efficiency	Christian et al. (2008) and The Green Grid Technical Committee (2007)	–
7	Other Load Factor	$OLF = \dfrac{\dot{W}_{Other\_uses}}{\dot{W}_{ITequipment}}$	Auxiliaries	Electricity consumption efficiency	Schödwell et al. (2013)	–
8	energy Storage Efficiency	$eSE = \dfrac{W_{Storage\_output}}{W_{Storage\_input}}$	Electrical auxiliaries	Electricity consumption efficiency	Schödwell et al. (2013) and Azevedo and Rawson (2008)	–
9	energy Distribution Efficiency	$eDE = \dfrac{W_{Distribution\_output}}{W_{Distribution\_input}}$	Electrical auxiliaries	Electricity consumption efficiency	Schödwell et al. (2013) and Azevedo and Rawson (2008)	
10	energy Conversion Efficiency	$eCE = \dfrac{W_{Conversion\_output}}{W_{Conversion\_input}}$	Electrical auxiliaries	Electricity consumption efficiency	Schödwell et al. (2013) and Azevedo and Rawson (2008)	–
11	Lighting Power Density	$LPD = \dfrac{\dot{W}_{Lighting}}{S_{DC}}$	Auxiliaries	Lighting performance	Mathew et al. (2010)	0–40 W/m² (Mathew et al., 2010)
12	UPS Load Factor	$UPS\text{-}LF = \dfrac{\dot{W}_{UPS\_output}}{\dot{W}^{*}_{UPS\_output}}$	Electrical auxiliaries	Electricity consumption efficiency	Mathew et al. (2010)	0.4–0.9 (Mathew et al., 2010)
13	UPS System Efficiency	$UPS\text{-}SE = \dfrac{\dot{W}_{UPS\_output}}{\dot{W}_{UPS\_input}}$	Electrical auxiliaries	Electricity consumption efficiency	Mathew et al. (2010)	85–95% (Mathew et al., 2010)

Table 4 Power/Energy Metrics Regarding the Single Components of the HVAC System

	Metrics	Formula	Scale	Assess	Introduced	Reference Values
14	Coefficient Of Performance	$COP = \dfrac{\dot{Q}_{cooling\_produced}}{W_{absorbed}}$	HVAC	Component energy performance	–	2–5
15	Cooling System Efficiency	$CSE = \dfrac{\bar{\dot{Q}}_{HVAC}}{\bar{\dot{Q}}_{Load}}$	HVAC	Component energy performance	Mathew et al. (2010)	1–0.5 kW/ton (Mathew et al., 2010)
16	Cooling system Sizing Factor	$CSS = \dfrac{\dot{Q}^{*}_{Chiller}}{\dot{Q}^{*}_{Load}}$	HVAC	Component energy performance	Mathew et al. (2010)	1–2.75 (Mathew et al., 2010)
17	Cooling system Capacity Factor	$CCF = \dfrac{\dot{Q}^{*}_{Cooling}}{1.1 \times UPS_{output}}$	HVAC	Component energy performance	Strong and Brill (2013)	1–over 3 (Strong and Brill, 2013)
18	Airflow Efficiency	$AE = \dfrac{\sum_{i=1}^{n} \dot{W}_{i,fan}}{\sum \dot{V}_{air}} \cdot 100$	HVAC	Component energy performance	Mathew et al. (2010)	> 1 W/cfm (standard); <1 W/cfm (good) (Mathew et al., 2010)
19	HVAC System Effectiveness	$HVAC_{SE} = \dfrac{W_{ITequipment}}{W_{HVAC} + W_{(fuel+steam+chilled)} \times 293}$	HVAC	Component energy performance	Wang and Khan (2011) and Mathew et al. (2009)	0.5–3.5 (Mathew et al., 2009)
20	Chiller Efficiency	$Ch\text{-}E = \dfrac{W_{absorbed}}{\dot{Q}_{cooling\_produced}}$ $Ch\text{-}E = \dfrac{1}{COP}$	HVAC	Component energy performance	Greenberg et al. (2006)	–
21	Tower Efficiency	$To\text{-}E = \dfrac{W_{cooling\ tower}}{\dot{Q}_{cooling\_produced}}$	HVAC	Component energy performance	Greenberg et al. (2006)	–
22	Water Pump Efficiency	$WP\text{-}E = \dfrac{W_{water\ pump}}{\dot{Q}_{cold\_transported}}$	HVAC	Component energy performance	Greenberg et al. (2006)	–
23	Air Economizer Utilization	$AEU = \dfrac{\tau_{Air\ economizer}}{24 \cdot 365}$	DC-HVAC	Economizer performance	Mathew et al. (2010)	Depends on the external climate
24	Water Economizer Utilization	$WEU = \dfrac{\tau_{Water\ economizer}}{24 \cdot 365}$	DC-HVAC	Economizer performance	Mathew et al. (2010)	Depends on the external climate

The Coefficient Of Performance (COP) is a widely used metric in the HVAC and refrigeration sectors. It represents the ratio of cooling (or heating) power provided to electrical energy consumed by a chiller (or a heat pump) (ASHRAE, 2001). The higher the COP value, the lower the operating costs of the refrigerating machine. An extension of COP is represented by the Cooling System Efficiency (CSE) of a DC (Mathew et al., 2010). This metric also considers the auxiliaries (eg, pumps and cooling towers) and characterizes the overall efficiency of the cooling system, in terms of energy input per unit of cooling output. The index is expressed in kilowatts per refrigeration tons and in Mathew et al. (2010) values over 1 kW/ton were indicated as standard performance, while values below 0.5 kW/ton were considered good performance (the lower, the better).

The cooling system sizing (CSS) factor is defined as the ratio of the installed cooling capacity to the peak cooling load (Mathew et al., 2010). This index measures the percentage of working hours of a cooling system at part-load conditions. The cooling system usually has different efficiencies between partial and full loads (generally the highest efficiency is around 80% of the load). A high CSS value suggests a good potential and scalability of the cooling system (Wang and Khan, 2011).

Airflow Efficiency (AE) measures the overall AE and it is defined as the ratio of the total fan power required to the unit of airflow (Mathew et al., 2010). It is expressed as joules per cubic meter of air flowing in the HVAC system. This index provides an overall measure of the efficiency of the airflow moving through a DC. Moreover, the metric evaluates pressure drops as well as fan system efficiency: the higher the AE value, the better the fan efficiency, and pressure drop distribution. Although it can be very important for the design of the air distribution, only a few reference values are available in the literature on this index.

HVAC System Effectiveness ($HVAC_{SE}$) could be calculated to evaluate the overall efficiency potential of the cooling system. This metric was described in Mathew et al. (2009), as the fraction of the IT equipment energy to the sum of all the electrical energy voices of HVAC auxiliaries (chiller, fan movement, pumps, evaporative towers, chilled water, and other auxiliaries). A higher value of this metric, compared to the peers, means a higher potential to reduce HVAC energy use (Wang and Khan, 2011). Lower values of HVAC system effectiveness may indicate that the server systems are far more optimized and efficient than the HVAC system.

Greenberg et al. (2006) introduced metrics to evaluate the efficiency of the single components of an HVAC system in depth. Chiller Efficiency (Ch-E) refers to the chiller and it is the inverse of the COP. Cooling Tower Efficiency (To-E) evaluates the efficiency of the evaporative tower circuit, while Water Pump Efficiency (WP-E) measures the pumping efficiency of the system. Pumping efficiency can vary to a great extent, depending on the configuration of the system. Lintner et al. (2011) provided general guidelines for the optimization of the pumping efficiency for DCs of any configuration.

The Cooling Capacity Factor (CCF) individuated by Upsite Technologies (Strong and Brill, 2013) is completely different from the previous metrics. The aim of this index is to find a way of solving overheating problems. The metric is calculated by dividing the sum of all the running cooling unit capacities (kilowatts) by 110% of the UPS output of the room, which is equal to the IT critical load (kilowatts). When the CCF of a computer room is calculated, an excess cooling capacity and opportunity for improvements in order to avoid hot spot problems emerges (Strong, 2012).

AEU and WEU metrics are related to the possibility of using external air or water to directly (or indirectly) cool a DC (Zhang et al., 2014). Air Economizer Utilization (AEU) is a metric that is related to the airflow economizer system. The airflow economizer is a component of the cooling system which allows it to work in a *free cooling* condition, and controls the environmental temperature directly in comparison to the colder outdoor air (Niemann et al., 2011; Kaiser et al., 2011; Chen et al., 2012). A consistent energy saving can be obtained from air-side *free cooling*, especially in cold climates, where the outdoor air is colder than the indoor condition for a long period of time (Harvey et al., 2011). For this reason, the possibility of free cooling is closely related to the location in which the DC is installed (Depoorter et al., 2015; Malkamäki and Ovaska, 2012). AEU is defined as the percentage of hours per year in which the economizer system can work in either full or complete operation mode (Mathew et al., 2010). It could be used in the design stage of a DC to select a location that maximizes the theoretical number of hours of air-side economizer usability. Furthermore, during the operational stage, AEU measures the potential for increasing energy savings through the use of an air-side economizer system (Wang and Khan, 2011). Water Economizer Utilization (WEU) is an index that describes the water-side economizer system. In this case, it utilizes a natural cold source through a cooling water infrastructure and the free cooling process can therefore be introduced without compromising the internal environment (Zhang et al., 2014). Moreover, it could be separated into three further types: direct water-cooled system (Clidaras et al., 2009), cooling tower system, and air-cooled system (Niemann et al., 2011; Potts, 2011). Like AEU, WEU is also defined as the percentage of hours per year in which the economizer system can work in either full or complete operation mode (Mathew et al., 2010).

The efficiency of a single subsystem is not the only element that conditions DC sustainability. In fact, it is also necessary to take into account the presence of Renewable Energy Sources (RES) on-site and the recovery of some energy wastes. An excellent review by Oró et al. (2015) describes the state of the art of these energy efficiency strategies. For example, two different DCs with the same PUE could show different levels of integration with RES and connections to smart grids (Malkamäki and Ovaska, 2012; Stewart and Shen, 2009; Goiri et al., 2013; Arlitt et al., 2012). DCs that are combined with RES may partially schedule their workloads, according to the availability of such energies (Li et al., 2010). Indices have been necessary to measure the potential energy and cost saving achieved through these energy efficiency strategies (Table 5).

Table 5 Power/Energy Metrics Used to Assess the Renewable Energy Share and the Smart Grid Integration of a DC

	Metrics	Formula	Scale	Assess	Introduced	Reference Values
25	Energy Reuse Factor	$ERF = \dfrac{W_{Reuse}}{W_{Total\_facility}}$	DC	Renewable energy share	Global Taskforce Reaches Agreement on Measurement Protocols for GEC, ERF, and CUE (2012)	0–1
26	Green Energy Coefficient	$GEC = \dfrac{W_{Renewable}}{W_{Total\_facility}}$	DC	Renewable energy share	Global Taskforce Reaches Agreement on Measurement Protocols for GEC, ERF, and CUE (2012)	0–1
27	Energy Reuse Effectiveness	$ERE = (1 - ERF) \cdot (1 - GEC) \cdot PUE$	DC	Renewable energy share	Patterson et al. (2010)	The lower the better
28	KPI of energy reuse	$KPI_{Reuse} = \dfrac{W_{Reuse}}{W_{DC}}$	DC	Renewable energy share	ETSI (2013)	0–1
29	KPI of renewable energy	$KPI_{Ren} = \dfrac{W_{Renewable}}{W_{DC}}$	DC	Renewable energy share	ETSI (2013)	0–1
30	Data Center Performance	$DC_P = KPI_{TE} \cdot (1 - W_{Reuse} \cdot KPI_{Reuse}) \cdot (1 - W_{Ren} \cdot KPI_{Ren})$	DC	Renewable energy share	ETSI (2013)	The lower the better
31	On-site Generation Efficiency	$OGE = \dfrac{\sum a_{Fuel} \cdot W_{fuel}}{W_{Total\_facility}}$	DC	Renewable energy share	GreenIT (2011)	–
32	Electricity Production Rate	$EPR = \dfrac{W_{Generated}}{W_{Sources}}$	DC	Renewable energy share	Schödwell et al. (2013)	–

The Green Grid introduced the Energy Reuse Factor (ERF) and the Green Energy Coefficient (GEC). The ERF takes into account the potential recovery of some energy wastes (Ward et al., 2012; Brunschwiler et al., 2009, 2010) outside the DC, for example, the energy from the DC reused in other parts of the facility or campus with beneficial results. Other examples of reusing energy for different utilities have been reviewed by Ebrahimi et al. (2014). The GEC calculates the percent of energy that is *green* (Global Taskforce Reaches Agreement on Measurement Protocols for GEC, ERF, and CUE, 2012). The maximum value of this index is 1, which indicates that 100% of the total energy is *green* energy. For the definition of *green energy*, the metric recommends referring to regional and local definitions. Combining ERF and GEC with the PUE results in the energy reuse effectiveness (ERE) index (Patterson et al., 2010). For the same reasons, ETSI proposed the Key Performance Indicator of energy Reuse (KPI_{Reuse}) and Key Performance Indicator of Renewable energy (KPI_{Ren}), which, combined with the KPI_{TE}, result in the Data Center Performance (DCP) metrics (Shiino, 2010). The On-site Generation Efficiency (OGE) metric (GreenIT, 2011) attempts to include the effects of using on-site Combined Heat and Power (CHP) plants in a single index (Darrow and Hedman, 2009; Guizzi and Manno, 2012); these effects had previously been neglected in the GEC. OGE takes into account the simultaneous presence of different power carriers. It is possible to multiply the various energy consumptions by the energy conversion coefficient of the used energy carrier (which is 0 for renewable energies but assumes different values for other carriers according to the national standards). The Electricity Production Rate (EPR) (Schödwell et al., 2013) assesses the share of electricity generated on site through CHPs, relative to the source energy used.

Another group of metrics recognizes the need to consider aspects other than just the simple energy use for energy sustainability. Examples of other aspects concerning the environmental impact of a DC are the consumption of natural resources (such as water), the emission of pollutants (such as carbon footprint) and the necessity of disposing of the materials at the end of their life (waste production). The metrics related to these aspects are summarized in Table 6.

The Carbon Emission Factor (CEF) (Belady et al., 2010) is an auxiliary metric that is similar to other indices existing in the literature and which is not specific for DCs (Eia.gov, 2013). It is defined as the equivalent kilograms of CO_2 per unit of energy expressed in kilowatt-hour. Carbon Usage Effectiveness (CUE) addresses the specific carbon emissions of DCs (Belady et al., 2010). It is a natural extension of the PUE that enables DC operators to quickly assess the relative sustainability of their facilities and to determine whether any sustainable energy improvements need to be made through a comparison of the results with similar structures. A similar concept is the basis of the Energy Carbon Intensity (ECI) metric (GreenIT, 2011). Like OGE, ECI also takes into account the different possible power carriers supplied in a DC. Each different carrier is weighted with its own carbon intensity factor, CI_{Fuel}.

The Water Usage Effectiveness (WUE) index was introduced by the Green Grid to address water usage in DCs (Eia.gov, 2013). This index includes water used for humidification and water evaporated on site for energy production and cooling of the

Table 6 Power/Energy Metrics Used to Assess Pollutant and Waste Emissions and Natural Resource Consumption

	Metrics	Formula	Scale	Assess	Introduced	Reference Values
33	Carbon Emission Factor	$CEF = \dfrac{CO_2\text{emitted}}{W}$	DC	Carbon emissions	Belady et al. (2010)	Eia.gov (2015)
34	Carbon Usage Effectiveness	$CUE = \dfrac{CO_2\text{emitted}}{\dot{W}_{ITequipment}}$ $CUE = CEF \times PUE$	DC	Carbon emissions	Belady et al. (2010)	0 ideal (Belady et al., 2010)
35	Energy Carbon Intensity	$ECI = \dfrac{\sum CI_{Fuel} \cdot W_{Fuel}}{W_{Facility}}$	DC	Carbon emissions	GreenIT (2011)	–
36	Water Usage Effectiveness	$WUE = \dfrac{V_{W\_Annual}}{\dot{W}_{ITequipment}}$	DC	Water waste	Patterson et al. (2011)	0 ideal (Patterson et al., 2011)
37	Energy Water Intensity Factor	Water used for generating energy	DC	Water waste	Patterson et al. (2011)	0 hydro, PV, wind; 0.8 natural gas; 2.2 coal; 3.3 nuclear, solar concentrated
38	Water Usage Effectiveness source	$WUE_{Source} = WUE + EWIF \times PUE$	DC	Water waste	Patterson et al. (2011)	0 ideal (Patterson et al., 2011)
39	Electronics Disposal Efficiency	$EDE = \dfrac{\text{Responsibly disposed materials}}{\text{Disposed materials}}$	DC	Material recycling	Brown (2012)	Always ≤1 (Brown, 2012)
40	Material Recycling Ratio	$MRR = \dfrac{\text{Recycled materials}}{\text{Disposed materials}}$	DC	Material recycling-	Schödwell et al. (2013)	–
41	IT Recycling Metric	$IT\text{-}RM = \dfrac{\text{Weight Responsibly Disposed}}{\text{Weight Disposed}}$	IT equipment	Measures resource efficiency in terms of sustainable disposal of IT assets- Minimizes emiss	Brown (2012)	Always ≤1 (Brown, 2012)

DC and its support systems. Nevertheless, it is only representative of the water used for DC on-site operations. For this reason, the Water Usage Effectiveness source (WUESource) metric was introduced (Eia.gov, 2015). This metric also considers off-site water consumption due to energy production and power generation. In order to estimate the water used for energy production, the auxiliary Energy Water Intensity Factor (EWIF) index, which is expressed in Liters per kilowatt-hour, was introduced (Brown, 2012). This is a particular coefficient that depends on the type of thermoelectric generation that is adopted and which needs specific local and regional boundary conditions to be calculated. Torcellini et al. (2003) established that the national US average value was 1.8 l/kWh in 2003, even though solar, wind, and hydro power generation was taken as 0.

Nowadays, the complete Life Cycle Assessment (LCA) of a DC and its components assumes more and more importance than in the past (Hannemann et al., 2008; Uddin and Rahman, 2012). In order to address continuous improvements in the computing capacity of a server, IT equipment is very often substituted. A white paper produced by the Green Grid (Wang et al., 2015) provides a framework to identify and describe the elements necessary to assess the complete LCA of DC, taking all the relevant environmental impacts into consideration. Electronics disposal efficiency (EDE) is a metric that was introduced by the Green Grid (Brown, 2012) to evaluate the IT recycling of DCs. This metric measures the percentage of the *responsibly disposed* IT equipment on the total amount of IT equipment. Third-party certification is necessary to evaluate *responsible disposal*. A definition of *responsible disposal* is given in Brown (2012), which states that the disposal must adhere to standards that minimize the possible environmental and human impact of IT equipment disposal and seek to maximize the recovery of usable components and embedded materials. The Material Recycling Ratio (MRR) is a work in progress index which can measure the ratio of recycled material (Schödwell et al., 2013).

Table 7 shows the last set of power/energy metrics. It is a particular group of metrics that was developed with the aim of improving the earnings of companies and stakeholders related to DCs. These indices are somehow also involved in energy efficiency aspects, because any resource waste represents an inefficiency that reduces the capability of a DC.

The Corporate Average Datacenter Efficiency (CADE) index is a metric that was proposed by the analysts of the Uptime Institute and McKinsey (Kaplan et al., 2008). It is used to measure the individual and combined energy efficiency of corporate, public sector, and third part hosted in DCs. It is not related to a single infrastructure, but it evaluates the efficiency across the entire corporate footprint. A ranking of the efficiency CADE level is given to stakeholders in order to make them aware of their DC energy efficiency. Level 1, with $0 < CADE > 5\%$, represents the actual value for a DC in 2008, while Level 5, with $CADE > 40\%$, indicates the expected value for future DCs. Detailed suggestions on how to reduce the CADE index through several facility improvements were given in Wang et al. (2015).

CADE depends on other indices hidden within this metric. Indeed, CADE depends on the Facility Efficiency (FE) index—which extends the DCiE concept, considering that a partial use of a DC represents a source of waste for a company—which

Table 7 Power/Energy Metrics Related to Business Purposes

	Metrics	Formula	Scale	Assess	Introduced	Reference Values
42	Corporate Average Datacenter Efficiency	$CADE = FE \times ITAE$	DCs	Energy efficiency of the whole DC of a company	Kaplan et al. (2008)	0–5% (2008 Level) 5–20% (2012 level) > 20% (expected improvements)
43	Facility Efficiency	$FE = FU \times DCiE$	DC	Energy and exploitation efficiency	Kaplan et al. (2008)	–
44	Facility Utilization	$FU = \dfrac{\dot{W}_{ITactual}}{\dot{W}_{ITcapacity}}$	DC	Exploitation efficiency	Kaplan et al. (2008)	–
45	Space Usage Effectiveness	$SD = \dfrac{n_{racks}}{S}$ $RPD = \dfrac{\dot{W}}{rack}$	DC	Exploitation efficiency	Wang et al. (2015)	Difficult to introduce improvements if $SD = 1.9$–2.8 Rack/m^2

in turn depends on the Facility Utilization (FU). FU index was introduced to evaluate the ratio of the actual IT equipment power in use and the total IT equipment power capacity of a DC. It measures the resource efficiency, in terms of the maximum utilization of the available IT power. Average values could be calculated, referring to a period of time using energy consumptions. Each DC is measured independently with a weighted average value that is based on the installed computational capacity.

Another useful index for energy managers and DC stakeholders, which was introduced with the aim of measuring the effective use of resources, is the Space Usage Effectiveness (SpUE) index (Wang et al., 2015). This is a new index that was introduced in 2014 by the Green Grid. This metric is used to address one of the most important challenges that DC owners face: the optimization of space usage in DCs. It was proposed in order to solve the problem of floor space mismanagement in DCs. In fact, significant amounts of space could be freed in many DCs through a spatial re-organization and optimization, thereby delaying unnecessary additional investments linked to the construction of new infrastructures. The SpUE index is evaluated through a comparison of two subindices: Space Density (SD), which assesses the number of racks per square meter, and Rack Power Density (RPD), which considers the IT equipment power installed (measured in kilowatts) per each rack.

Finally, a broad spectrum of different IT power/energy metrics was introduced for DCs. The most common ones are listed in Table 8. These metrics reflect the power required by IT systems (ie, for servers, storage, networks, etc.). The "Reference Values" column is not present in Table 8, because these metrics have not yet been supported by reference values.

In general, the metrics shown in Table 8 focus on the power/energy consumption of server systems, or storage systems connected to networks or other server components. These metrics deliver detailed information on single systems, but they have to be combined to obtain a view of the whole IT environment. Space, Watts and Performance (SWaP) proposed by SUN Microsystems, and Data Center computed efficiency (DCcE) are examples of this kind of metrics. The latter is not in itself a productivity metric because it does not show how much work is being done by the DC. The Green Grid has provided two other metrics, which are similar to DCcE: Data Center storage Efficiency (DCsE) and Data Center network Efficiency (DCnE). The former can be used to assign the efficiency of storage and the latter for the network system (Blackburn et al., 2010).

5 THERMAL METRICS

The most common design structure in a DC is characterized by a raised floor with the racks arranged in a hot/cold aisle layout. In computer room air conditioning (CRAC), the hot exhaust air from the racks is cooled and it is usually supplied chilled through an under-floor plenum, while the exhaust air returns to the CRAC from the ceiling. Fig. 2 shows this typical air distribution layout in a DC.

Table 8 IT Level Power/Energy Metrics

	Metrics	Formula	Scale	Assess	Introduced
46	Server computed Efficiency	$ScE = \sum_{i=1}^{n} \dfrac{\text{Primary services server } i}{\text{Total services server } i}$	IT equipment	Measures the share of primary services related to secondary IT services (virtualization, backup, etc.)	Blackburn et al. (2010)
47	DC computed Efficiency	$DCcE = \sum_{i=1}^{n} ScE_i$	IT services	Measures the share of primary services related to secondary IT services (virtualization, backup, etc.)	Blackburn et al. (2010)
48	Space, Watts and Performance	$SWaP = \dfrac{\text{Performance}}{S \cdot \dot{W}_{IT}}$	IT equipment	Gives a comprehensive assessment of the server's efficiency	Rivoire et al. (2007)
49	IT Hardware Energy Overhead Multiplier	$H\text{-}EOM = \dfrac{W_{IT}}{W_{\text{computing components}}}$	IT equipment	Characterizes the energy overheads induced by the internal power and cooling components of the IT system Minimizes energy use	Stanley et al. (2007)
50	Deployed Hardware Utilization Ratio	$DH\text{-}UR_{\text{Server}} = \dfrac{\text{Servers running live application}}{\text{Servers deployed}}$ $DH\text{-}UR_{\text{Storage}} = \dfrac{\text{Amount of frequently accessed data}}{\text{Amount of storage deployed}}$	IT equipment	Measures the fraction of servers that is running productive applications and the fraction of storage that is holding active data Scalable	Stanley et al. (2007)

51	Deployed Hardware Utilization Efficiency	$DH\text{-}UE_{Server} = \dfrac{\text{Servers necessary to handle peak load}}{\text{Servers deployed}}$	IT equipment	Determines the efficiency of server capacity planning scalable	Stanley et al. (2007)
52	Server Utilization	$Server\text{-}U = \dfrac{C_{CPU}}{C * CPU}$	IT equipment	Determines the minimum utilization of the CPU, memory bandwidth/space, IO/space on the disks and NIC/HBA bandwidth scalable	Belady and Patterson (2008)
53	Storage Utilization	$Storage\text{-}U = \dfrac{C_{storage}}{C*_{storage}}$	IT equipment	Determines the used storage space relative to the storage space capacity scalable	Belady and Patterson (2008)
54	Network Utilization	$Network\text{-}U = \dfrac{C_{bandwith}}{C*_{bandwith\ capacity}}$	IT equipment	Determines the percentage of bandwidth used relative to the bandwidth capacity	Belady and Patterson (2008)
55	Computed Load Density	$CLD = \dfrac{\dot{W}_{IT}}{S}$	IT equipment	Measures the resource efficiency in terms of area usage Minimizes energy use	Mathew et al. (2010)

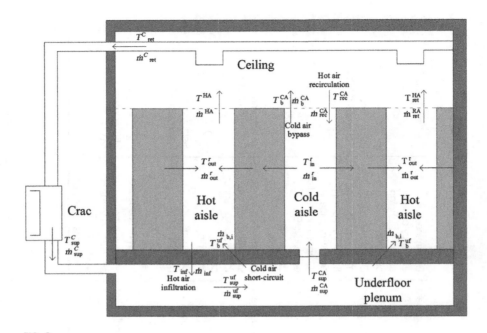

FIG. 2

Schematic of the most important thermal phenomena that occur in a DC.

The thermal management of a DC is very important to ensure the reliability of the IT equipment and a reduction in the risk of failure (ASHRAE, 2011). For this reason, it is mandatory to take into account the heat and airflow exchanges that occur within a DC environment. Some air management problems have been observed by several researchers for the hot/cold aisle layout.

Two main problems in particular have been identified: *air by-pass*, and *air recirculation*. In the first case, a fraction of inlet cold air does not contribute to the cooling of the IT equipment (because the flow rate is too high or the air leaks through cable cutouts). Moreover, a higher amount of cold air results in excess fan energy and reduced return air temperatures. In the second case, the cold air intake into the IT equipment is not sufficient (because of by-pass problems or an incorrect air distribution system design) and, as a consequence, a fraction of air from the hot aisle is recirculated, thus resulting in a higher equipment inlet temperature. The same effect of recirculation can be related to the incomplete rack slot occupation of the IT equipment. Finally, some authors identified a further air management problem related to hot air drawn into the under-floor plenum due to a negative pressure phenomenon.

Phenomena such as hot air recirculation, cold air infiltration, or cold air short-circuiting could cause local hot spots that represent a possible risk for DC thermal management, and therefore its reliability.

In order to offset hotspots, CRAC units are often set up to supply air at a lower supply temperature, with consequent higher energy consumption. This requires an oversized design of the cooling system to deal with these instantaneous phenomena of required overcooling. Air management problems lower the cooling efficiency and lead to a vicious cycle of a rising local temperature. In this context, it becomes important to investigate the supply airflow efficiency and the thermal field in the DC environment.

In general, the previously introduced power/energy metrics are not necessarily capable of detecting hotspots, which can be local phenomena whose influence on the global energy consumption could be negligible. This is due to the fact that a few racks in a DC could be suffering from local air management problems and, as a consequence, the global energy indicators might not vary significantly.

In order to take into account the local and the global thermal management of a DC, several thermal metrics have been introduced. Most of these metrics can be calculated through experimental or numerical data. Thermal metrics are used to evaluate the DC airflow performance and thermal management at both the design and the operational stages. The main heat transfer phenomena that occur in a DC and the physical quantities that have to be measured for metric assessment are reported in Fig. 2.

A review of the most important existing thermal metric is presented in this section. Furthermore, an innovative classification of these metrics has also been introduced by the authors. Thermal metrics are classified as global or local. Global metrics provide average thermal or airflow efficiency information, while local metrics are able to give information on the punctual and specific thermal fields within a DC. Most of the following thermal indices were proposed for large-scale DCs. Furthermore, since racks and vent tiles are standardized, the thermal indices can be applied to any DC at a server, rack, row, or room level.

Table 9 reports the thermal metrics that can be used to investigate the global thermal management of a DC. In general, they are based on the average air temperature of a DC room and can be used to investigate the global thermal behavior.

Sharma et al. (2002) proposed two dimensionless parameters to evaluate the thermal design and performance of large-scale DCs: the Supply Heat Index (SHI) and the Return Heat Index (RHI). These metrics allow the incidence of cold and hot air mixing, related to the racks and to the CRAC unit, to be evaluated. These metrics are based on the enthalpy increase due to hot air recirculation phenomena, but they can also refer to average temperature differences through different elements of the DC (cold aisle, hot aisle, CRAC unit). For this reason, they are somewhat easy to calculate and measure (Tang et al., 2006b). A value of 0 for SHI and 1 for RHI means that there is no recirculation of hot air, and the air inlet temperature of the racks is equal to the air supply temperature from the CRAC unit.

These metrics are scalable and potentially applicable at a rack, row, or whole DC level. In general, they are used at the DC level. In this case, these dimensionless parameters constitute limits to the description or prediction of the local conditions, such as hot spot phenomena. The average temperature values considered by these

Table 9 Thermal Metrics Used to Investigate the Global Thermal Management of a DC

	Metrics	Formula	Scale	Assess	Introduced	Reference Values
56	Supply Heat Index	$SHI = \dfrac{\Delta \dot{Q}^{CA}}{\dot{Q}^r + \Delta \dot{Q}^{CA}}$ $SHI = \dfrac{\sum_i \sum_j \left(T^r_{in_{i,j}} - T^C_{sup}\right)}{\sum_i \sum_j \left(T^r_{out_{i,j}} - T^C_{sup}\right)}$	Global, local	Warm air infiltration inside cold aisle	Sharma et al. (2002)	Target: 0 Good < 0.2
57	Return Heat Index	$RHI = \dfrac{\Delta \dot{Q}^C}{\dot{Q}^r + \Delta \dot{Q}^C}$ $RHI = \dfrac{\sum_k \dot{m}^C_{sup_k} \cdot c_p \cdot \left(T^C_{ret_k} - T^C_{sup}\right)}{\sum_i \sum_j \dot{m}^f_{out_{i,j}} \cdot c_p \cdot \left(T^r_{out_{i,j}} - T^C_{sup}\right)}$ $RHI = 1 - SHI$	Global, local	Return heat at CRAC units after recirculation	Sharma et al. (2002)	Target: 0 Good > 0.8
58	Negative Pressure ratio	$NP = \dfrac{\dot{m}_{inf}}{\dot{m}^C_{sup}}$ $NP = \dfrac{T^{uf}_{sup} - T^C_{sup}}{T^C_{ret} - T^{uf}_{sup}}$	Global	Warm air infiltration inside air-supply plenum due to negative pressure	Tozer (2006) and Tozer et al. (2009)	—
59	By-Pass ratio	$BP = \dfrac{\dot{m}^{uf}_b + \dot{m}^C_b}{\dot{m}^{uf}_{sup}}$ $BP = \dfrac{T^s_{out} - T^C_{ret}}{T^{uf}_{out} - T^{uf}_{sup}}$	Global	Mass flow rate that returns to CRAC units without heat power exchange	Tozer (2006) and Tozer et al. (2009)	Target:0 Good: 0 ÷ 0.05 Acceptable 0.05 ÷ 0.2
60	Recirculation ratio	$R = \dfrac{\dot{m}^C_{rec}}{\dot{m}^s_{in}} \qquad R = \dfrac{T^s_{in} - T^{uf}_{sup}}{T^s_{out} - T^{uf}_{sup}}$	Global	Mix between cold air supply and exhaust air from hot aisle	Tozer (2006) and Tozer et al. (2009)	Target: 0 Good < 0.2
61	BALance	$BAL = \dfrac{\dot{m}^C_{sup}}{\dot{m}^s_{in}} \qquad BAL = \dfrac{T^s_{out} - T^s_{in}}{T^C_{ret} - T^C_{sup}}$ $BAL = \dfrac{1 - R}{(1 - BP) \cdot (1 + NP)}$	Global	Balance between airflow to CRAC unit and across IT equipment	Tozer (2006) and Tozer et al. (2009)	
62	Return Temperature Index	$RTI = \dfrac{\sum_i \dot{m}^f_{in_i}}{\sum_k \dot{m}^C_{sup_k}} \cdot 100$ $RTI = \dfrac{T^C_{ret} - T^C_{sup}}{T^r_{out} - T^r_{in}} \cdot 100$	Global	Balance between airflow across IT equipment and to CRAC unit	Herrlin (2007)	Target: 100%; Good: 95 ÷ 105%; Poor: < 70% ∧ >130%

indices are not able to identify fast temperature increases due to local hot spots. A DC with a favorable global profile can in fact still be affected by local hotspots. Moreover, RHI and SHI do not take into account the by-pass effect on the recirculation phenomenon. Several researchers have demonstrated that these indices lead to a macro evaluation of the recirculation phenomena, but they fail (even when they are calculated at a rack level), especially when the rack intake temperatures need to be evaluated considering IT equipment reliability. The poor ability of these indices to reliably evaluate the climatic operating conditions of IT equipment has been dealt with by several researchers (Cho and Kim, 2011; Schmidt et al., 2005; Srinarayana et al., 2014).

The temperature of the air supplied to the cold aisle is the most important parameter for airflow efficiency. However, the SHI and RHI indices do not change sensibly when the temperature value is modified. In fact, these thermal metrics are mainly related to temperature differences and not to a local or single temperature value, as previously mentioned. Metrics that are classified as local, which are described hereafter, are instead sensitive to this important design parameter.

Tozer introduced a group of metrics to evaluate the different phenomena that could occur in DCs (Tozer et al., 2009; Tozer, 2006). These metrics are based on the mass flow rate and energy balance in a DC and can be applied at a rack, row, or whole DC level. In the first three indices—Recirculation (R), By-Pass (BP), and Negative Pressure (NP)—phenomena are studied. NP takes into account the effect of ambient air infiltration into the under-floor plenum in proximity of the CRAC unit, caused by negative pressures due to a high airflow speed.

All these indices are expressed as ratios of the flow rates or of the average temperature differences. Considering only the sensible load, recirculation becomes equal to SHI. BALance (BAL) measures the difference between cold air produced by the cooling plant and the servers' request. It represents the balance between the airflow rate produced by the CRAC and the server request (Tozer and Salim, 2010) and it can be expressed as a function of both the by-pass and the recirculation ratio. In different case studies, it has been noticed that the considered average temperatures cause acceptable errors (Matley and Herrlin, 2010). In this way, it is very easy to make measurements with punctual values. Only the infiltration due to negative pressure is difficult to measure directly and it should be calculated by a Computational Fluid Dynamics (CFD) model. However, the group of metrics gives information on by-pass and recirculation phenomena, which can occur simultaneously: a large by-pass rate could cause a recirculation effect, because of less airflow availability.

The Return Temperature Index (RTI) was introduced into the literature by Herrlin (2007). The index gives information on the recirculation or by-pass in a DC, and it is based on the percentage ratio of the total airflow mass rate at a rack inlet to the total airflow rate produced by the CRAC unit. Furthermore, RTI can be defined as the percentage ratio of the return and supply temperature difference at the CRAC unit on the temperature difference across the IT equipment. If RTI assumes a value of 100%, a perfect balance between the airflow requested by the rack and that supplied by the CRAC is reached. Values below 100% mean that the airflow has bypassed the IT equipment and the airflow produced by the CRAC is higher than the IT equipment request. On the other hand, values above 100% mean that recirculation occurs, and the IT equipment has ingested hot air from the surrounding environment. The index could be coupled to rack cooling index (RCI; below described) to obtain more detailed information on the thermal behavior of a DC: RCI provides the rack health cooling conditions, and RTI becomes a tool to investigate airflow efficiency (Herrlin, 2007).

The second subset of thermal metrics is reported in Table 10. This category includes local thermal metrics based on the punctual air temperatures or mass flow rates of a rack. They are used to investigate the airflow and thermal exchanges at the server or rack level, and are also able to highlight the temperature distribution over the rack height.

The RCI was proposed by Herrlin (2005, 2007). The aim of this metric is to provide a tool that can be used to evaluate rack intake temperatures and to compare them with the allowable and recommended temperatures in DCs, telecom central offices, and mission-critical facilities in general. The threshold values can be found in ASHRAE guidelines (eg, T.C. 9.9 (ASHRAE, 2011)) or can be imposed by the thermal manager. RCI assumes two expressions, in relation to high and low temperature limitations. For the lowest and the highest limits, RCI considers both the allowable and the recommended temperature values. If no rack intake temperature exceeds either the recommended or the allowable values, the RCI is equal to 100%, while it is lower if one or more temperatures exceed the recommended range. Since the aim of cooling is to guarantee a healthy condition of the IT equipment, RCI is the most important metric to evaluate thermal behavior of the equipment situated in the racks. However, the effect of temperature variation could also be analyzed using the standard deviation of the rack intake temperatures (Tang et al., 2006a). In addition, several guidelines consider the evaluation of these metrics for thermal effectiveness (ASHRAE, 2011; Mathew et al., 2010; Lintner et al., 2011). RCI is a valid index to diagnose IT equipment problems. However, it does not give information about the sources of the problem. The parallel evaluation of other global metrics is necessary for this purpose (Herrlin and Khankari, 2006).

The β index was defined by Schmidt et al. (2005) to compare the local and average temperature values. The aim is to evaluate the increase in temperature of a local rack. This index has also been introduced to overcome some intrinsic limitations of SHI and RHI: they cannot provide a good evaluation of local-level problems, which could result in a dangerous cooling condition of the IT equipment. A value of 0 for this metric means the absence of recirculation, while a value above 1 indicates the presence of complete self-heating.

VanGilder (2011) tried to model airflow recirculation with an index called Recirculation Index (RI), which was based on the mass flow rate balance. The Capture Index (CI) represents the evolution of RI (VanGilder and Shrivastava, 2007). CI allows the airflow ingested by a local component to be evaluated. It is measured in a cold aisle or hot aisle, for rack or local extractor units, respectively. A CI value

Table 10 Thermal Metrics Used to Investigate Local Phenomena

	Metrics	Formula	Scale	Assess	Introduced	Reference Values
63	Rack Cooling Index—low	$RCI_{LO} = \left[1 - \dfrac{\sum_{i=1}^{n}\left(T_{LO-rec} - T_{in_i}^r\right)}{n \cdot (T_{LO-rec} - T_{LO-allow})} \right] \cdot 100$	Local	Rack cooling efficiency considering a lower threshold value	Herrlin (2005, 2007)	Ideal: 100%; Good ≥ 96%; Acceptable 91 ÷ 95%; Poor: ≤ 90%
64	Return Heat Index—high	$RCI_{HI} = \left[1 - \dfrac{\sum_{i=1}^{n}\left(T_{in_i}^r - T_{HI-rec}\right)}{n \cdot (T_{HI-allow} - T_{HI-rec})} \right] \cdot 100$	Local	Rack cooling efficiency considering an upper threshold value	Herrlin (2005, 2007)	Ideal: 100%; Good ≥ 96%; Acceptable 91 ÷ 95%; Poor: ≤ 90%
65	β Index	$\beta = \dfrac{T_{in}^r(z) - T_{sup}^C}{T_{out}^r - T_{in}^r}$	Local	Local increase in air temperatures along the rack	Schmidt et al. (2005)	Target: 0
66	Capture Index—cold aisle	$CI_{CA} = \dfrac{\dot{m}_{in_i}^C}{\dot{m}_{sup_i}^C}$	Local	Cold airflow ingested by a rack	VanGilder and Shrivastava (2007)	–
67	Capture Index—hot aisle	$CI_{HA} = \sum_{j=1}^{N} \dfrac{C_{ret_j}^C \cdot \dot{m}_{ret_j}^C}{\dot{m}_{out_i}^r}$	Local	Warm airflow captured by a local extractor or cooler	VanGilder and Shrivastava (2007)	–

of 100% indicates good cooling performance, while 0% indicates a bad cooling condition. Although these indices only give information on the mass flow rate, a value of 0% does not necessarily imply that the local air temperatures overpass the threshold values (Burkhard and Nurnus, 2011). Since both indices are based on airflow rates, sufficiently good results can be obtained by means of CFD analysis. In loco measurements only provide rough results with nonnegligible errors. For this reason, CI is generally computed at the design stage in order to improve the design parameters, and it is associated with a temperature difference between a threshold value and the airflow temperature ingested by a rack (Dcimsupport.apc.com, 2014).

In order to achieve a better thermal management of a DC, the overall and local phenomena should be investigated at the same time. It is in fact interesting to be aware of the thermal distribution at all levels in a DC to ensure IT equipment reliability, to assess the absence of over-cooling to ensure energy savings, to investigate the presence of by-pass or recirculation phenomena, and to obtain information on the overall AE. This kind of approach could be defined *glocal*, in this way underlining the fact that it considers both global and local thermal metrics for the evaluation of the thermal management in a DC. The simplest way of fulfilling this purpose is to couple the so-far proposed metrics in an appropriate way. They can in fact all be used as single indices to investigate a single phenomenon or coupled to each other for a more detailed analysis. An example of this application was suggested by Cho and Kim (2011), who proposed the Overall Airflow Efficiency Evaluation Standard. This standard represents a parameter that somehow summarizes the knowledge acquirable from several of the metrics that have been dealt with in this Section 5. Moreover, the authors provided the scale of the relative importance of the various metrics. Considering benchmark values for each metric, an overall evaluation was proposed with a rating varying from poor to very good. Whenever IT equipment reliability is the main aim of air-conditioning, RCI_{HI} is the first metric that has to be evaluated. RCI_{LO} is then calculated to assess the absence of over-cooling, which could lead to wasted energy. RTI provides information on the occurrence of bypass or recirculation, while SHI and RHI offer information on the airflow energy efficiency.

Overall, air management efficiency should be evaluated taking into account, at the same time, different air management metrics proposed in literature. In particular, the thermal metrics at a local level (eg, RCI and/or β) should be assessed. An analysis on the other global thermal indices (eg, RTI, SHI, and RHI) should then be conducted, in which it is important to characterize the airflow behavior and the energy saving opportunities.

A further extension of the *glocal* approach includes the application of metrics that consider the global functioning of a DC through the mutual interrelationship between the different pieces of equipment and the components of a DC. The four metrics that belong to this approach are listed in Table 11.

Cross Interference Coefficients and Thermal Influence Indices represent similar indicators that can be used to evaluate the interrelationship between different DC components. Both of them are based on mass flow rate models, and good results can be achieved with the CFD method. The main difference between the two metrics is

Table 11 Thermal Metrics Used to Investigate "Glocal" Aspects

	Metrics	Formula	Scale	Assess	Introduced	Reference Values
68	Cross Interference Coefficients	$A = \begin{bmatrix} \alpha_{11} & \cdots & \alpha_{1n} \\ \vdots & \ddots & \\ \alpha_{n1} & & \alpha_{nn} \end{bmatrix}$ $K \cdot \vec{T}^s_{out} =$ $K \cdot \vec{T}^C_{sup} - A' \cdot K \cdot \vec{T}^C_{sup} + A' \cdot K \cdot \vec{T}^s_{out} + \vec{P}$	Glocal	Thermal management	Tang et al. (2006b)	–
69	Thermal Influence Indices	Calculate the influence of one element to another	Glocal	Thermal management	Bhagwat et al. (2012)	0–1
70	Exergy	$\dot{\psi}_{DC} = \dot{\psi}_{racks} + \dot{\psi}_{CRAC} + \dot{\psi}_{airspace}$	Glocal	Energy consumption and thermal management	Shah et al. (2008)	–
71	Power Density Efficiency	$PDE = \dfrac{\frac{\dot{W}_{IT}}{V_{racks}}}{\left(\frac{\dot{W}_{IT}}{V_{racks}} + \frac{\dot{W}_{facility}}{V_{ITequipment}} \right)}$ $PDE = \left[1 + \frac{V_{racks}}{V_{ITequipment}} \cdot \left(\frac{\dot{W}_{facility}}{\dot{W}_{IT}} \right) \right]^{-1}$	Glocal	Energy consumption and thermal management	Lajevardi et al. (2014)	65% (Lajevardi et al., 2014)

the component on which they are focused. While the Cross Interference Coefficients method only considers IT equipment, the Thermal Influence Indices indicator also involves the CRAC unit. In the latter case, the field of knowledge becomes a little larger.

Cross Interference Coefficients are based on the abstract heat flow model of DCs proposed by Tang et al. (2006b). The heat power algorithm is modeled within the DC environment, considering thermal interference among different pieces of IT equipment, or nodes, caused by recirculation. Cross Interference Coefficients are parameters that can provide information on the self-interference of a node, or cross interference between one node and another. Each coefficient is obtained as the percentage of heat power exiting from a node and entering another one. The whole Cross Interference Coefficients Matrix (CICM) represents the total interference between nodes in a DC. By considering the influence of the power consumption of different pieces of equipment stable, a DC can be represented by a system that is based on the CICM and some column vectors (eg, the outlet temperature, server power consumption, and air supply temperature). From local behavior to a global DC, this system provides sufficiently good information to analyze both the cooling condition of the IT equipment and the global effect of recirculation.

In a similar way, the Thermal Influence Indices proposed in Bhagwat et al. (2012) are metrics that can be used to measure the casual relationship between heat sources and sinks. The IT equipment and the CRACs are considered to be thermal components with the same influence. The concept is similar to the previously described CICM. The thermal influence indices represent the ratio between the heat power at the inlet component coming from a source and the total heat power at the inlet component.

Both these metrics can be used during the design stage and during the operation time of a DC. Once the casual relationships between components have been defined, the indices can be used to maximize the heat load (in the design stage) or to optimize the airflow supply temperatures (in the operation stage). They play a very important role during the operational stage. These indices could represent the structure of a task scheduling algorithm with thermal awareness (Tang et al., 2006a, 2008) that links the problem of server functioning to the thermal environment. When these algorithms are used, it is possible to schedule the computational load of a DC and optimize the energy consumption and integration in a smart grid (Tian and Zhao, 2015; Cupertino et al., 2015).

Power/energy metrics and thermal metrics are generally used together to asses both thermal manageability and energy efficiency of a DC at the same time. For instance, SHI and RTI are usually used to detect the recirculation and by-pass, while PUE is used to attest the global energy consumption. The fact that the analysis requires three different indicators shows that there is a poor relationship between the metrics.

In order to overcome this kind of problem, the exergy-based approach was proposed by Shah et al. (2008). This is a second law analysis that considers both global thermal management and local phenomena (such as recirculation or by-pass) as irreversible process sources of exergy losses. The authors evaluated three elements that participate in the exergy loss balance: air space, rack space, and CRAC units. Moreover, three further subelements were defined concerning the airspace: aisles (hot and cold) airspace, rack unit airspace, and CRAC unit airspace. The whole DC was divided into a structure composed of small volume elements, each of which includes the different exergy loss sources. An exergy balance was calculated for each finite volume, considering a further element as the sum of the exergy of the elements, that is, potential recoverable exergy. A map of the DC that highlights the exergy losses in the various subelements can provide information on the occurrence of different local phenomena. Furthermore, the sum of the different exergy losses provides a metrics for the overall DC. An application of this method was provided in the paper and a CFD analysis was applied to a case study to show how this metric is more sensitive to recirculation phenomena than traditional temperature-based thermal metrics. Moreover, the exergy approach can be used not only for thermal manageability, but also to evaluate the energy efficiency of a DC. In fact, the global share of recoverable exergy represents an energy waste for the DC, and it can identify a possible improvement for decreases in energy consumption.

A similar holistic approach is the one that has recently been introduced with the Power Density Efficiency (PDE) index (Lajevardi et al., 2014). The aim of this metric is to capture both the energy efficiency and the thermal assessment of a DC at the same time, and it can thus be used as a support for DC designers and operators. The formulation of PDE is similar to PUE concept, but each power/energy term is weighted on the control volume, which it refers to. Authors state that in this way PDE can be used to evaluate any possible changes in a DC layout and configuration, and to evaluate the possible causes of bad air flow management due to higher volumes not occupied by servers.

From the discussion presented in this section, it can be inferred that energy and thermal metrics accomplish different tasks, that is, energy assessment and real-time diagnostics, respectively. These tasks should always be coupled for a comprehensive DC performance analysis.

6 PRODUCTIVITY METRICS

In the previous sections, a clear picture of the existing metrics to assess the energy efficiency in DC was presented. Moreover a proposal of a unified framework for DC energy efficiency metrics was discussed in detail. Unfortunately, until now in the DC metrics scenario a limited attention has been given to the development of metrics aimed at clearly defining the useful work, that is, metrics aimed to gauge the *real computing* (e.g., workload-related metrics) carried out by a DC. Generally, the useful work of a DC is represented by the computing activity of an IT (computing, storing, and transferring data—IT services), while all the other categories are only auxiliaries for this purpose.

Recently, an increasing interest on productivity metrics in Cloud Computing (CC) has been observed; indeed, CC supports a large number of users coming from different organizations and for this reason characterization of workloads in terms of energy is needed.

So far, none of the current metrics gives a practical measure of the useful work in a DC. De facto, the actual opportunity of calculating the useful work in a mathematical form remains particularly complicated. In other words, energy efficiency is only assessed indirectly, for instance as in PUE, in which the portion of energy actually employed for computing, is measured. In the PUE definition, no mention is made of where the energy goes, or how it is employed; PUE only provides information on the utilization of power in IT equipment and infrastructures. Since the issue related to quantifying useful work in a DC energy efficiency assessment is relevant, this chapter can help in gaining a better understanding of the use of the metrics that cover this research area. The approach used to evaluate the productivity of a DC is based on the energy efficiency, which is defined as the ratio of the useful work output (server utilization) to the total energy expanded to support the corresponding computational work. The productivity metrics can facilitate the evaluation of the energy and they can be used as indicators to rank and classify IT systems and DCs, regardless of their size, capacity or physical location. The variables that have to be taken into account to use productivity metrics are related to data transfer, the computing process and storage.

Energy efficiency metrics, introduced to focus on computing power/energy demands in relation to the useful work, are summarized in Table 12. Productivity metrics differ from other metrics in their approach to how they assess useful work. However, they all have a subjective component, as the productivity outcomes (eg, order of the processes in terms of time) of DC applications must be defined by humans. Thus, an application of such a metric is complex and unique for each DC (Schlitt et al., 2015). Unlike the previous tables, Table 12 does not provide *Reference Values*, because no values are available for these kinds of metrics.

Several attempts have been made to define the productivity metrics for DCs. The most significant is the Data Center energy Productivity (DCeP) metric, which was introduced by the Green Grid (2009) (Cupertino et al., 2015). This metric relates the produced useful work to the total energy consumed in a DC; DCeP is related to both the site infrastructure and the IT equipment. This metric in a mathematical form can be defined as follows:

$$DCeP = \frac{C}{W_{DC}} = \frac{\sum_i^n [V_i \cdot U_i(T,t) \cdot T_i]}{W_{DC}}. \tag{2}$$

The term "useful work" describes the number of tasks executed by a DC, and W_{DC} represents the power or energy, respectively, consumed to complete the tasks. In the above formulation, n is the number of tasks initiated during the assessment window, V_i is a normalization factor that allows the tasks to be summed, U_i is a time-based utility function for each task, t is the elapsed time from the initiation to the completion of the task, t_i is the absolute time of completion of the task. The term $t_i = 1$ when the task is completed during the assessment window, and is 0 otherwise (DC4Cities, 2014). The assessment windows must be defined in such a way to allow

Table 12 Productivity Metrics

	Metrics	Formula	Scale	Assess	Introduced
72	Data Center energy Productivity	$DCeP = \dfrac{C}{W_{DC}}$	DC	Characterizes the energy requested to produce useful computational work in a DC	Belady and Patterson (2008) and Anderson et al. (2008)
73	Data Center Performance Efficiency	$DCPE = \dfrac{C}{\dot{W}_{DC}}$	DC	Explains the efficiency of a DC in terms of power (expansion of PUE and DCE)	The Green Grid Technical Committee (2007)
74	Data Center Performance per Watt	$DCPpW = \dfrac{C}{\dot{W}_{DC}}$	DC	Defines the number of operations completed per joule	Tian and Zhao (2015)
75	Data Center IT Utilization	$DCIU = \dfrac{C}{C^*}$	DC	Represents how much of the IT equipment of the DC is currently being utilized	Belady and Malone (2007)
76	IT Equipment Utilization	$ITEU = \dfrac{C}{C^*}$	IT equipment	Measures IT equipment utilization	Kaplan et al. (2008) and Belady and Patterson (2008)
77	IT-power Usage Effectiveness	$ITUE = \dfrac{W_{IT}}{W_{computing\ components}}$	IT equipment	Represents the total energy consumed by the IT–computer components (CPU, memory, fabric)	Patterson et al. (2013)
78	Total power Usage Effectiveness	$TUE = PUE \cdot ITUE$	DC	Combines PUE and ITUE	Patterson et al. (2013)

(Continued)

Table 12 Productivity Metrics—Cont'd

	Metrics	Formula	Scale	Assess	Introduced
79	Computed Power Efficiency	$CPE = \dfrac{ITEU}{PUE}$	DC	Estimates the energy efficiency and IT resource of the infrastructure system	Belady and Malone (2007)
80	IT Productivity per Embedded Watt	$IT\text{-}PEW = \dfrac{C[\text{Trans, IO, Cycles}]}{W_{IT}}$	IT equipment	Measures the IT energy productivity, work defined as network transaction storage or computing cycles	Brill (2007)
81	IT energy Productivity	$ITeP = \dfrac{C}{W_{IT}}$	IT equipment	Computes IT productivity as the sum of the completed tasks relative to IT energy use	Anderson et al. (2008)
82	IT Equipment Efficiency	$ITEE = \dfrac{C[\text{OPS, IOPS, GbPS}]}{W_{IT}}$	DC	Computes the IT equipment energy efficiency	Kaplan et al. (2008) and GITPC (2012)
83	IT Asset Efficiency	$ITAE = ITEE \cdot ITEU$	DC	Computes the energy productivity and resource efficiency of the IT systems	Kaplan et al. (2008) and GITPC (2012)

the DC variations over time to be captured. The DCeP factor gives an estimate of the performance of the DC and it is known to be accurate due to its relativity.

Owing to the aforementioned definition problem of useful work, there is no practical way of solving the DCeP formula. However, eight proxy measures, which can be used instead of useful work, are given in a paper by Green Grid (Tang et al., 2008). These proxies basically reduce the useful work to productivity, performance, and utilization. In a recent study (Tang et al., 2008), the authors drew some conclusions and indicated that useful work refers to the operational utilization of IT equipment, and they left it up to the user to evaluate and assess the level of usefulness of the IT work-output for their business.

An alternative and practical solution to calculate useful work was proposed within the DC4 Cities Project 1 (EU FP7 Program), in which a methodology on the use of artificial workloads, such as benchmarks was developed. In particular, the useful work and the corresponding energy consumption of a set of applications/services running in a DC were calculated using several benchmarks. Since it is difficult to compare applications (web server, DB server, mail server, etc.), the procedure tries to extrapolate the normalization factor (see factor V_i in Eq. (2)) and to establish the amount of energy consumed in terms of operations.

The Green Grid has proposed the Data Center Performance Efficiency (DCPE) metric, which explains the efficiency of a DC in terms of power consumption, when the specific level of work (or service) is given. DCPE is basically an expansion of PUE and DCE.

Other examples of productivity metrics are those of the Data Center Performance per Watt (DCPpW) and data center IT utilization (DCIU) introduced by Dell (Pflueger, 2008). In the DCIU formula, the total useful work represents the aggregate computation performed in the DC, while the total computational peak capacity represents the potential amount of computation available if all the computed resources are being utilized to their full potential. DCPpW differs from DCeP because it provides a generic measurement only related to the year in which a server was purchased. Hence, DCIU provides information on how well IT equipment is being utilized while DCPpW deals with the overall productivity of a DC.

IT Equipment Utilization (ITEU) is a metric that can be used to define the energy saving level of IT equipment. The metric can be useful when the improvement in the utilization ratio is being considered. The "IT" value in the PUE formula represents the IT equipment or all the items inside the server or cluster, while it represents only the computational components (CPU, memory, fabric), but not the cooling, power supplies, or voltage regulators, that otherwise is considered in the IT-power Usage Effectiveness (ITUE) equation. Hence, ITUE takes into account the energy inside the IT. At a DC level, combining ITUE and PUE, it is possible to obtain TUE.

Computed Power Efficiency (CPE) seeks to identify the overall efficiency of a DC, while taking into account the fact that not all the electrical power delivered to the IT equipment is transformed by that equipment into a useful work product. The IT Equipment Efficiency (ITEE) metric can be compared to its equivalent DCeP metrics, defined by the Green Grid, and IT Asset Efficiency (ITAE) represents a combination of ITEE and ITEU. In particular, ITEE is the metric that can be used to express the relationship between the potential capacities of IT equipment in a DC and the energy consumption. ITEE can be used to establish the average efficiency of all the IT equipment installed in a DC.

7 CHALLENGES IN DATA CENTER ENERGY EFFICIENCY METRICS

Energy efficiency metrics are important tools for the monitoring of energy use and environmental conditions at a DC scale. These metrics make it possible to quantify the performance of a DC and compare different technologies and strategies. De facto, a highly efficient DC is valuable in terms of owners and operators and appeal to customers. Moreover, the need to invest in energy efficiency is becoming a priority in the Smart Cities context.

An exhaustive framework of the actual situation has been obtained from the previous review of DC metrics. On one hand, it is clear that the higher number of components and processes present in a DC requires an equally large number of metrics in order to be capable of understanding all the phenomena that occur. On the other hand, a great number of these metrics are actually very seldom used. For instance, according to Schödwell et al. (2013), only a few metrics are currently considered in DCs and many DC stakeholders do not know of their existence. This is due to the fact that they are based on difficult-to-measure quantities, or are only capable of pinpointing phenomena that are considered marginal and not comparable with reference/benchmark values.

Despite the development of various metrics for the evaluation of the energy efficiency of DCs, no metrics have been proposed to simultaneously evaluate the impact of different systems within a DC and to capture and merge several phenomena (eg, thermal and computing processing). Owing to the limitations of the existing energy efficiency metrics, an overall strategy is needed to promote the use of harmonized metrics in order to effectively achieve energy efficiency in DCs.

For this purpose, this chapter has provided both a critical analysis of the most important energy efficiency metrics currently used for DCs and has carried out a "pruning" and simplification process with the aim of suggesting an appropriate consultation. This work in fact began with a look at the variables and physical models on which metrics are based, and in the meantime an innovative classification was provided. Finally, considerations have been made, in terms of productivity and thermal management (local-global). Moreover the discussed interlink between the metrics represents an important challenge for the implementation of a methodological framework, in terms of both practical use and energy efficiency policies and requirements. Furthermore, the lack of metrics to cover certain aspects has also been dealt with.

The presented holistic framework helps the reader to simultaneously take into account the effects of different metrics. For example, in a given DC, the improvement in a specific efficiency metrics could result in another metric looking worse (Global

Taskforce Reaches Agreement on Measurement Protocols for GEC, ERF, and CUE, 2012). Hence, it could be useful to adopt a holistic approach based on a vector of efficiency metrics to evaluate the whole DC without overemphasizing or overlooking any systems. In order to understand the interactions between metrics and the exact DC consumption situation, several aspects should be considered. For example, in Global Taskforce Reaches Agreement on Measurement Protocols for GEC, ERF, and CUE (2012), the authors identified three important aspects:

- *IT*—Measures the potential IT work output compared to the expected energy consumption and measures the operational utilization of IT equipment.
- *Data center facility and infrastructure*—Measures the DC infrastructure and efficiency.
- *Renewable energy impact*—Measures renewable energy technologies and the re-use of energy to reduce carbon.

A practical way of representing several metrics in a holistic framework is to use a spider or radar chart. In a spider chart, the metrics of all the desired outcomes are distributed on its axes to evaluate the total energy efficiency of a DC. However, it is imperative to establish a pivot metric for each aspect that should be taken into account according to the classification introduced in this chapter.

The number of metrics may vary, depending on the choice of metrics made by the DC operator. Once the metrics have been selected, the operator will also need to identify a start and end point for each axis. In some cases, no theoretical maximum and minimum values or benchmark values are available. Therefore, the ends of the axis will have to be established on the basis of target values or other estimates. The selection of metrics and of the axis end points indicates the need for implicit weighting of the metrics, and care should therefore be taken during this process. A representative metric for each of the subsystems in a DC needs to be selected in this process.

A schematic of the workflow in a DC that influences the metrics is shown in Fig. 3. Four different layers can be observed according to a top-down approach. The top layer characterizes the boundary conditions of the system. These are the IT demands required by the DC, the indoor environmental conditions set by the DC managers (ASHRAE, 2011) and the outdoor environmental conditions that influence the various HVAC subsystems. The first two inputs can be controlled by the operators through an appropriate scheduling of the workload or a modification of the indoor environmental sets. The second layer represents the core of the system. The green box in the middle of the scheme of Fig. 3 symbolizes the DC facility with its subsystems: HVAC system, IT equipment, and support system. The performance of the components of the subsystems is influenced by the performance included in the previously described top layer. The physical power input of the infrastructure is on the right of the DC. It is divided between the on-site production and the electricity delivered by the grid. The on-site production could be further split into RES or non-RES productions. The second layer on the left represents the physical outputs flowing out of the system. It is composed of environmental emissions, waste

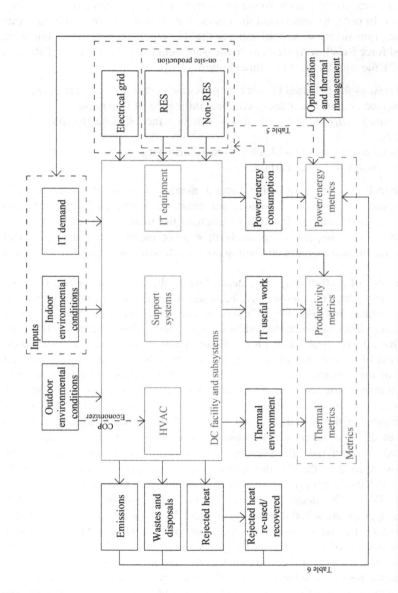

FIG. 3

Scheme of links among systems within a DC.

production, the disposal of components, and heat rejection. A part of this heat can be recovered and re-used in the infrastructure. The third layer of the scheme is composed of the output parameters that influence the DC efficiency: indoor thermal environment, IT useful work, and power/energy consumption. Power consumption in particular influences the energy required by the infrastructure, and for this reason it is connected to the electrical grid and to the on-site production boxes. All the metrics are included in the dashed red line box representing the fourth layer of the scheme. They represent a simple interpretation of the processes that occur in the upper layers. The double-headed arrows represent the interactions between the metrics. Moreover, in modern and future DCs, metrics could be used as inputs for an optimization process. An iterative process is required for this purpose. The steps of this procedure are: metrics measurements based on the actual conditions, a comparison between the actual values and reference values of an efficient DC, an evaluation of the possible improvements, modification of the IT work schedule or the thermal management of the infrastructure, repetition of the steps since no optimization is required. This procedure is becoming popular in the setting up of modern DC management procedures. Several optimization and workload scheduling proposals are available in the literature (Tang et al., 2006a, 2008; Moore and Chase, 2005). However, in most existing DCs, the monitoring of the parameters for the evaluation of metrics is not an easy task. In fact, there is a lack of measurement points in these infrastructures due to the limited installation of monitoring systems in old-concept infrastructures. For this reason, new, noninvasive measurement systems that are capable of being incorporated into existing infrastructures are strongly recommended. For instance, systems based on infrared technologies could be an interesting solution for the in-field monitoring of environmental parameters at a large scale (Favoino et al., 2014).

In conclusion, the challenge of measuring energy efficiency in a DC is to capture the emerging requirements of the DC that have to be integrated into a complex system and their interaction with renewable energies. Moreover, this work highlights the importance of the adoption of productivity metrics related to useful work. Their inclusion in a holistic framework represents an essential challenge to complete the energy metrics scenario of a DC.

Efforts to harness energy metrics as a means of achieving common policies and regulatory strategies for energy efficiency in DCs have been focused on European projects, in particular projects funded under the Smart Cities Call 2013 (iDC4Cities, Dolfin, Genic, Green Data Net, GEYSER, RenewIT). The DC4Cities project has led to the Smart City Cluster[1] collaboration, a European Commission initiative to establish collaboration among researchers in research projects that have similar objectives. The Smart City Cluster collaboration is at the moment composed of seven groups working on projects that are mostly funded by the EU FP7 Program (CoolEmALL and All4Green). The main objectives of the Cluster are to ensure

---

[1] https://ec.europa.eu/digital-agenda/en/news/cluster-fp7-projects-proposes-new-environmental-efficiency-metrics-data-centres.

Table 13 Metrics Proposed by the Smart Cities Cluster Collaboration

Parameter	Metrics
Flexibility mechanisms in DCs: • Demand shifting: workloads are shifted from a time period to another, but always within the same DC; • Demand being federated: shifting the workloads to other DCs.	• **Adaptability Power Curve (APC)** • **Data Center Adapt (DCA$_{dapt}$)** • **Adaptability Power Curve at renewable energies (APC$_{ren}$)** • Flexible Energy Rate (FER) Managed Energy Rate (MER) • Managed flexible energy index Federated Energy Weight (FEW) • Federated COP • Federated RES
Economic impact	• **Energy Expenses Savings (EES)**
Environmental impact	• **CO_2 emissions savings (CO_2 savings)** • **Primary Energy savings (PE savings)**
Renewable integration: • Energy produced locally and renewables usage • Energy recovered: Heat recovered • Grid interaction indicators	• Renewable usage: Ren Percent • Renewable usage: RenEPPercent • Renewable usage: RenThermPercent • Renewable usage: RenEPThermPercent • Renewable usage: TotalEPPercent • Energy recovered: ReusePercent • Load cover factor • Supply cover factor • **Grid Utilization Factor—GUF**

that all the projects are able to use common key performance indicators (KPIs) to characterize the energy, environmental and economic behavior of their DCs, thus enabling a comparison to be made between different projects, and to collaborate with DC standardization organizations. The metrics and methodologies that are listed in Table 13 are some of the results that have been obtained at Cluster level (European Commission, 2015). However, the methodology has been developed only for some of them (the metrics highlighted in bold type).

Another important open research challenge is related to the energy efficiency metrics of CC DCs. CC is a popular computing paradigm enabled by the large number of DCs and by the advantages of virtualization.

In this scenario assessing the energy performance is important for understanding the operation of existing DCs and crucial for the design and construction of next generation systems for CC (Fiandrino et al., 2015). Currently, most of the available metrics are unable to differentiate between the individual IT subsystems;

for example, it is not possible to distinguish the efficiency of DC communication systems from the efficiency of the computing servers; unfortunately, both metrics remain considered under the common umbrella of IT equipment (Kliazovich et al., 2015). Ideally, the power consumption of computing servers should be proportional to the workload, in reality that is not true. Indeed, it can seen that computing servers' power consumption becomes more proportional to the workload and effective at low utilization levels, while network power consumption remains a concern. Hence, it is necessary to calculate the relative energy costs for server workload and to assess the degree of energy proportionality for network devices for CC. Current research by Fiandrino et al. (2015) presents an interesting overview of metrics (communication and power-related) for CC DCs.

ACKNOWLEDGMENTS

The authors would like to acknowledge the contribution in the framework of the energy metrics achieved into DC4Cities project (FP7-SMARTCITIES-2013, ICT-2013.6.2) and Smart Cities Cluster activities.

ACRONYMS

CC	cloud computing
CFD	computational fluid dynamics
CHP	combined heat and power plant
CRAC	computer room air conditioning
DC	data center
HVAC	heating ventilation and air conditioning
ICT	information and communications technology
IT	information technology
KPI	key performance indicator
LCA	life circle assessment
PDU	power distribution unit
PSU	power supply unit
RES	renewable energy source
UPS	uninterruptible power supply

SYMBOLS

C	computational/storage work of IT equipment (GbPS/cycles/Tb/OPS)
C^*	computational/storage peak capacity of IT equipment (GbPS/cycles/Tb)
c_p	specific heat of a material (J/kg K)
$\dot{m}$	mass flow rate (kg/s)
n	quantity of a particular attribute (−)

$\dot{Q}$ exchanged thermal power (W or kW)

S useful floor area of a DC (m^2)

T temperature (°C or K)

V volume (m^3)

V_W water volume usage (L)

$\dot{V}$ volumetric flow rate (m^3/s)

W total energy consumption referring to a time period (Wh or kWh)

$\dot{W}$ instantaneous electrical power load/consumption (W or kW)

$\dot{W}^*$ installed electrical power capacity necessary to satisfy the peak consumption (W or kW)

τ time interval (h)

$\dot{\Psi}$ exergy destruction (W)

TECHNICAL WORDS

Air management
Batteries
Chiller
Cloud computing
Data center
Energy metrics
Exergy
Free-cooling
Power metrics
Productivity metrics
Rack
Scalability
Smart cities
Storage
Thermal management
Thermal metrics
Useful work
Workload

REFERENCES

Aebischer, B., Eubank, H., Tschudi, W., 2004. Energy efficiency indicators for data centers. In: Int. Conf. Improv. Energy Effic. Commer. Build., Frankfurt, pp. 1–17.

Anderson, D., Cader, T., Darby, T., Gruendler, N., Hairiharan, R., Holler, A., et al., 2008. Technical report. A framework for data center energy productivity. White paper #13. The Green Grid, Beaverton, OR.

Arlitt, M., Bash, C., Blagodurov, S., Chen, Y., Christian, T., Gmach, D., et al., 2012. Towards the design and operation of net-zero energy data centers. In: Proc. IEEE 13th Annu. Intersoc. Conf. Therm. Thermomechanical Phenom. Electr. Syst., San Diego.

ASHRAE, 2001. ASHRAE Handbook: Fundamentals. American Society of Heating, Refrigerating and Air Conditioning Engineers, Atlanta, GA.

ASHRAE, 2011. Thermal Guidelines for Data Processing Environments—Expanded Data Center Classes and Usage Guidance. American Society of Heating, Refrigerating and Air Conditioning Engineers, Atlanta, GA.

Avelar, V., Azavedo, D., French, A. 2012. Technical report. PUE: a comprehensive examination of the metric. White Paper #49. The Green Grid, Beaverton, OR.

Azevedo, D., 2008. The Green Grid metrics: data center infrastructure efficiency (DCIE) detailed analysis. Green Grid White Pap. 14, 1–16.

Azevedo, D., Rawson, A., 2008. Measuring data center productivity. The Green Grid, Beaverton, OR.

Belady, C., 2016. In the data center, power and cooling costs more than the IT equipment it supports. In: Electronics Cooling Magazine—Focused on Thermal Management, TIMs, Fans, Heat Sinks, CFD Software, LEDs/Lighting. [online] Electronics-cooling.com. Available at: http://www.electronics-cooling.com/2007/02/in-the-data-center-power-and-cooling-costs-more-than-the-it-equipment-it-supports/ (accessed 25.02.16).

Belady, C., Malone, C., 2007. Metrics and an infrastructure model to evaluate data center efficiency. In: ASME 2007 InterPACK Conf., vol. 1, pp. 751–755.

Belady, C., Patterson, M., 2008. Technical report. The green grid productivity indicator. White Paper #15. The Green Grid, Beaverton, OR.

Belady, C., Azevedo, D., Patterson, M., Pouchet, J., Tipley, R., 2010. Technical report. Carbon usage effectiveness (CUE): a Green Grid data center sustainability metric. White Paper #32. The Green Grid, Beaverton, OR.

Bhagwat, H., Singh, A., Vasan, A., Sivasubramaniam, A., 2012. Thermal influence indices: causality metrics for efficient exploration of data center cooling. In: 2012 Int. Green Comput. Conf. (IGCC), San Jose, CA. IEEE, pp. 1–10.

Blackburn, M., Azevedo, D., Hawkins, A., Ortiz, Z., Tipley, R., Van Den Berghe, S., 2010. The Green Grid data center compute efficiency metric: DCcE. 1–15.

Brill, K., 2007. Technical report. Data Center Energy Efficiency and Productivity. Site Infrastructure White Paper. Santa Fe (NM): The Uptime Institute.

Brill, K.G., 2000. 2005-2010 Heat Density Trends in Data Processing Computer, Systems, and Telecommunications Equipment. In: Site Infrastructure White Paper. The Uptime Institute, Santa Fe, NM.

Brown, E., 2012. Technical report. Electronics disposal efficiency (EDE): an IT recycling metric for enterprises and data centers. White Paper #53. The Green Grid, Beaverton, OR.

Brown, R., Masanet, E., Nordman, B., Tschudi, B., Shehabi, A., Stanley, J., et al., 2007. Report to congress on server and data center energy efficiency. Public Law 109-431. Ernest Orlando Lawrence Berkley National Laboratory, Berkeley, CA.

Brunschwiler, T., Smith, B., Ruetsche, E., Michel, B., 2009. Toward zero-emission data centers through direct reuse of thermal energy. IBM J. Res. Dev. 53 (3), 11:1–11:13. doi:10.1147/JRD.2009.5429024.

Brunschwiler, T., Meijer, G., Paredes, S., Escher, W., Michel, B., 2010. Direct waste heat utilisation from liquid-cooled supercomputers. In: Proc. 14th Int. Heat Transf. Conf., Washington, DC, pp. 1–12.

Burkhard, H., Nurnus, J., 2011. Thin film thermoelectrics today and tomorrow. In: Electronics Cooling Magazine—Focused on Thermal Management, TIMs, Fans, Heat Sinks, CFD Software, LEDs/Lighting. [online] Electronics-cooling.com. Available at: http://www.electronics-cooling.com/2011/09/thin-film-thermoelectrics-today-and-tomorrow/ (accessed 25.02.16).

Capozzoli, A., Serale, G., Liuzzo, L., Chinnici, M., 2014. Thermal metrics for data centers: a critical review. Energy Procedia 62, 391–400.

Capozzoli, A., Chinnici, M., Perino, M., Serale, G., 2015. Review on performance metrics for energy efficiency in data center: the role of thermal management. Lect. Notes Comput. Sci. 8945, 135–151.

Chen, Y., Zhang, Y., Meng, Q., 2012. Study of ventilation cooling technology for telecommunication base stations: control strategy and application strategy. Energy Build. 50, 212–218.

Chinnici, M., Quintiliani, A., 2013. An example of methodology to assess energy efficiency improvements in datacenters. In: IEEE Third Int. Conf. Cloud Green Comput., Karlsruhe, pp. 459–463.

Cho, J., Kim, B., 2011. Evaluation of air management system's thermal performance for superior cooling efficiency in high-density data centers. Energy Build. 43, 2145–2155.

Christian, B., Rawson, A., Pfleuger, J., Cader, T., 2008. Green grid data center power efficiency metrics: PUE and DCIE. 1–9.

Clidaras, J., Stiver, D., Hamburgen, W., 2009. Water-based data center. U.S. Patent No. 7,525,207. Washington, DC: U.S. Patent and Trademark Office.

Cupertino, L., Da Costa, G., Oleksiak, A., Piatek, W., Pierson, J.M., Salom, J., et al., 2015. Energy-efficient, thermal-aware modeling and simulation of data centers: the CoolEmAll approach and evaluation results. Ad Hoc Netw. 25, 535–553.

Darrow, K., Hedman, B., 2009. Technical report. Opportunities for combined heat and power in data centers. ICF international. Arlington (VA): Oak Ridge National Laboratory for US Dept. of Energy.

Dcimsupport.apc.com, 2014. Working with Capture Index—User Assistance for StruxureWare Data Center Operation 7.2—StruxureWare for Data Centers Support. [online] Available at: http://dcimsupport.apc.com/display/public/UAOps72/Working+with+Capture+Index;jsessionid=9E5C6D8B373D3BF87AC84943AAB2 (accessed 25.02.16).

DC4Cities, 2014. Deliverable D7.1. Description of energy metrics for datacentres. FP7-SmartCities 2013 (ICT), Project N. 609304. European Commission, Europe.

Depoorter, V., Oró, E., Salom, J., 2015. The location as an energy efficiency and renewable energy supply measure for data centres in Europe. Appl. Energy 140, 338–349.

Dumitru, I., Fagarasan, I., Iliescu, S., Said, Y., Ploix, S., 2011. Increasing energy efficiency in data centers using energy management. In: IEEE/ACM Int. Conf. Green Comput. Commun., vol. 2011, pp. 159–165.

Ebrahimi, K., Jones, G., Fleischer, A., 2014. A review of data center cooling technology, operating conditions and the corresponding low-grade waste heat recovery opportunities. Renew. Sustain. Energy Rev. 31, 622–638.

Eia.gov, 2013. How much carbon dioxide is produced per kilowatthour when generating electricity with fossil fuels?—FAQ—U.S. Energy Information Administration (EIA). [online] Available at: http://www.eia.gov/tools/faqs/faq.cfm?id=74&t=11 (accessed 25.02.16).

Eia.gov, 2015. How much carbon dioxide is produced per kilowatthour when generating electricity with fossil fuels?—FAQ—U.S. Energy Information Administration (EIA). [online] Available at: http://www.eia.gov/tools/faqs/faq.cfm?id=74&t=11 (accessed 25.02.16).

ETSI, 2013. Operational energy efficiency for users (OEU): global KPI for data centres. 1.

Eubank, H., Aebischer, B., Lewis, M., Jon, K., Tschudi, W., Peter, R., et al., 2004. High performance data centers. In: Int. Conf. Improv. Energy Effic. Commer. Build., Frankfurt, pp. 1–10.

European Commission, 2015. New Report Released on Methodologies for Measuring Environmental Efficiency Metrics for Data Centres. Digital Single Market. [online] Available at: https://ec.europa.eu/digital-agenda/en/news/new-report-released-methodologies-measuring-environmental-efficiency-metrics-data-centres (accessed 29.02.16).

Favoino, F., Capozzoli, A., Perino, M., 2014. Temperature field real-time diagnosis by means of infrared imaging in data elaboration center. In: Proc. 8th Int. Symp. Heating, Vent. Air Cond. Lect. Notes Electr. Eng., vol. 263, pp. 455–463.

Fiandrino, C., Kliazovich, D., Bouvry, P., Zomaya, A., 2015. Performance metrics for data center communication systems. In: 2015 IEEE 8th Int. Conf. Cloud Comput., pp. 98–105.

Flucker, S., Tozer, R., 2012. Data centre energy efficiency analysis to minimize total cost of ownership. Build. Serv. Eng. Res. Technol. 34, 103–117.

GITPC, 2012. Technical report. DPPE: holistic framework for data center energy efficiency–KPIs for infrastructure, IT equipment, operation (and renewable energy). Tokyo (Japan): Japan National Body/Green IT Promotion Council.

Global Taskforce Reaches Agreement on Measurement Protocols for GEC, ERF, and CUE, 2012. Harmonizing global metrics for data center energy efficiency. [online] Thegreengrid.org. Available at: http://www.thegreengrid.org/~/media/WhitePapers/Harmonizing%20Global%20Metrics%20for%20Data%20Center%20Energy%20Efficiency%202012-10-02.pdf?lang=en (accessed 25.02.16).

Goiri, I., Katsak, W., Le, K., Nguyen, T., Bianchini, R., 2013. Parasol and GreenSwitch: managing datacenters powered by renewable energy. In: Proc. 18th Int. Conf. Archit. Support Program. Languages Oper. Syst., Houston, p. 13.

Greenberg, S., Tschudi, W., Weale, J., 2006. Technical report. Self Benchmarking Guide for Data Center Energy Performance. Berkeley (CA): Ernest Orlando Lawrence Berkley National Laboratory.

GreenIT, 2011. Proposal of OGE (on-site generation efficiency metric) and ECI (energy carbon intensity metric) Tokyo (Japan): Green IT Promotion Council (GIPC).

Guizzi, G., Manno, M., 2012. Fuel cell-based cogeneration system covering data centers' energy needs. Energy 41, 56–64.

Haas, J., Froedge, J., 2009. Usage and public reporting guidelines for the Green Grid's infrastructure metrics PUE/DCiE. Green Grid White Pap. 22, 1–15.

Hannemann, C., Carey, V., Shah, A., Patel, C., 2008. Lifetime exergy consumption of an enterprise server. In: ASME 2008 2nd Int. Conf. Energy Sustain. Collocated With Heat Transf. Fluid Eng. 3rd Energy Nanotechnol. Conf., Jacksonville (Florida), pp. 35–42.

Harvey, T., Patterson, M., Bean, J., 2011. Technical report. Updated air side free cooling maps: the impact of ASHRAE 2011 allowable ranges. White Paper #46. The Green Grid, Beaverton, OR.

Helal, S., Mann, W., King, J., Kaddoura, Y., Jansen, E., 2005. The gator tech smart house: A programmable pervasive space. Computer 38 (3), 50–60.

Herrlin, M., 2005. Rack cooling effectiveness in data centers and telecom central offices: the rack cooling index (RCI). ASHRAE Trans. 111, 1–11.

Herrlin, M., 2007. Airflow and cooling performance of data centers: two performance metrics. Digit. Power Forum 114, 10–12.

Herrlin, M., Khankari, K., 2006. Method for optimizing equipment cooling effectiveness and HVAC cooling costs in telecom and data centers. ASHRAE Trans. 114, 1–9.

Hill, D., Barroso, A., Holzle, U., Kaxiras, S., Martonosi, M., Olukotun, K., 2009. The datacenter as a computer. An introduction to the design of warehouse-scale machines. In: Synth. Lect. Comput. Archit., vol. 1, pp. 1–108.

Kaiser, J., Bean, J., Harvey, T., Patterson, M., Winiecki, J., 2011. Technical report. Survey results: data center economizer use. White Paper #41. The Green Grid, Beaverton, OR.

Kaplan, J., Forrest, W., Kidler, N., 2008. Technical report. Revolutionizing data center energy efficiency. New York (NY): McKinsey & Company.

Kliazovich, D., Bouvry, P., Granelli, F., da Fonseca, N., 2015. Energy consumption optimization in cloud data centers. In: da Fonseca, N., Boutaba, R. (Eds.), Cloud Serv. Networking, Manag. Wiley-IEEE Press, pp. 1–33.

Koomey, J., 2011. Technical report. Growth in data center electricity use 2005 to 2010. Burlingame (CA): Analytics Press.

Lajevardi, B., Haapala, K., Junker, J., 2014. An energy efficiency metric for data center assessment. In IIE Annual Conference Proceedings. Institute of Industrial Engineers-Publisher, pp. 1715–1722.

Li, C., Zhou, R., Li, T., 2010. Enabling distributed generation powered sustainable high-performance data center. In: Proceedings 14th Int. Heat Transf. Conf., Washington, pp. 35–46.

Lintner, W., Tschudi, B., Otto, V., 2011. Technical Report. Best Practices Guide for Energy-Efficient Data Center Design. National Renewable Energy Laboratory (NREL) of US Dept. of Energy.

Malkamäki, T., Ovaska, S., 2012. Solar energy and free cooling potential in European data centers. Procedia Comput. Sci. 10, 1004–1009.

Mathew, P., Ganguly, S., Greenberg, S., Sartor, D., 2009. Self-Benchmarking Guide for Data Centers: Metrics, Benchmarks, Actions, New York (NY): Lawrence Berkeley National Laboratory (LBLN) and New York State Energy Research and Development Authority (NYSERDA).

Mathew, P., Greenberg, S., Sartor, D., Bruschi, J., Chu, L., 2010. Self-Benchmarking Guide for Data Center Infrastructure: Metrics, Benchmarks, Actions. New York (NY): Lawrence Berkeley National Laboratory (LBLN) and New York State Energy Research and Development Authority (NYSERDA).

Matley, R., Herrlin, M., 2010. Technical report. Data center air management research. California: Emerging Technologies Coordinating Council and Pacific Gas and Electric.

Moore, J., Chase, J., 2005. Making scheduling "Cool": temperature-aware workload placement in data centers. In: USENIX Annu. Tech. Conf., pp. 61–74.

Niemann, J., Bean, J., Avelar, V., 2011. Technical report. Economizer modes of data center cooling systems. White Paper #132. Rueil-Malmaison (France): APC and Shneider-Electric—Data Center Science Center.

Oró, E., Depoorter, V., Garcia, A., Salom, J., 2015. Energy efficiency and renewable energy integration in data centres. Renew. Sustain. Energy Rev. 42, 429–445. doi:10.1016/j.rser.2014.10.035.

Patterson, M., 1996. What is energy efficiency? Concepts, indicators and methodological issues. Energy Policy 24, 377–390.

Patterson, M., 2008. The effect of data center temperature on energy efficiency PUE = total power. In: Therm. Thermomechanical Proc. 11th Intersoc. Conf. Phenom. Electron. Syst. 2006, ITHERM, pp. 1167–1174.

Patterson, M., Tschudi, B., Otto, V., Cooley, J., Azavedo, D., 2010. Technical report. ERE: a metric for measuring the benefit of reuse energy from a data center. White paper #29. The Green Grid, Beaverton, OR.

Patterson, M., Azevedo, D., Belady, C., Pouchet, J., 2011. Technical report. Water usage effectiveness (WUE): a Green Grid data center sustainability metric. White paper #35. The Green Grid, Beaverton, OR.

Patterson, M., Poole, S., Hsu, C., Maxwell, D., Tschudi, W., Coles, H., et al., 2013. TUE, a new energy-efficiency metric applied at ORNL's Jaguar. Lect. Notes Comput. Sci. (including Subser Lect Notes Artif Intell Lect Notes Bioinformatics) 7905, 372–382. LNCS.

Pelley, S., Meisner, D., Wenisch, T., VanGilder, J., 2009. Understanding and abstracting total data center power. In Workshop on Energy-Efficient Design during 2009 International Symposium on Computer Architecture. Austin (TX).

Pettey, C., Goasduff, L., 2010. Gartner says energy: related costs account for approximately 12 percent of overall data center expenditures. http://www.gartner.com/newsroom/id/1442113.

Pflueger, J., 2008. Technical report. Re-defining the "Green" Data Center. A Dell Technical White Paper. Round Rock (TX): Dell.

Potts, Z., 2011. Technical report. Free cooling technologies in data centre applications. Manchester (UK): Sudlows.

Rivoire, S., Shah, M., Ranganathan, P., Kozyrakis, C., Meza, J., 2007. Models and metrics to enable energy-efficiency optimizations. Computer (Long Beach Calif.) 40, 39–48.

Schaeppi, B., Bogner, T., Schloesser, A., Stobbe, L., de Asuncao, M., Bogneri, T., et al., 2012. Metrics for energy efficiency assessment in data centers and server rooms. In Conference: Electronics Goes Green 2012 (EGG), Berlin (Germany).

Schlitt, D., Schomaker, G., Nebel, W., 2015. Gain more from PUE: assessing data center infrastructure power adaptability. In: 3rd Int. Work Energy-Efficient Data Centres, vol. 8945, pp. 152–166.

Schmidt, R., Cruz, E., Iyengar, M., 2005. Challenges of data center thermal management. IBM J. Res. Dev. 49, 709–723.

Schödwell, B., Erek, K., Zarnekow, R., 2013. Data center green performance measurement: state of the art and open research challenges. Association for Information Systems (AIS), Atlanta (GA).

Shah, A., Carey, V., Bash, C., Patel, C., 2008. Exergy analysis of data center thermal management systems. J. Heat Transf. 130. Article ID 021401.

Sharma, R., Bash, C., Patel, C., 2002. Dimensionless parameters for evaluation of thermal design and performance of large-scale data centers. In: 8th AIAA/ASME Jt. Thermophys. Heat Transf. Conf., Reston, Virginia. American Institute of Aeronautics and Astronautics, pp. 1–11.

Shiino, T., 2010. Japan's approach to reducing greenhouse gas emissions from data centers. Nomura. Res. Inst. Pap. 1–19.

Smith, V., Ellis, R., Van Der Perre, D., Latreche, A., Hearnden, J., Gajic, L., et al., 2009. The green grid energy policy research for data centres. TheGreenGrid, France, The Netherlands and the United Kingdom. White paper #25. The Green Grid, Beaverton, OR.

Srinarayana, N., Fakhim, B., Behnia, M., Armfield, S., 2014. Thermal performance of an air-cooled data center with raised-floor and non-raised-floor configurations. Heat Transf. Eng. 35, 384–397.

Stanley, J., Brill, K., Koomey, J., 2007. Technical report. Four metrics define data center "Greenness". White paper. Santa Fe (NM): The Uptime Institute.

Stewart, C., Shen, K., 2009. Some joules are more precious than others: managing renewable energy in the datacenter. In: Proc. Hot Power.

Strong, L., 2012. Connecting the dots between cooling capacity, it load and airflow management. Data Center J. [online]. Available at: http://www.datacenterjournal.com/connecting-dots-cooling-capacity-load-airflow-management-3/ (accessed 25.02.16).

Strong, L., Brill, K., 2013. Technical report. Cooling capacity factor (CCF) reveals stranded capacity and data center cost savings. Albuquerque (NM): Upsite Technologies.

Sullivan, R., Strong, L., Brill, K., 2006. Technical report. Reducing bypass airflow is essential for eliminating computer room hot spots. Site Infrastructure White paper. Santa Fe (NM): The Uptime Institute.

Tang, Q., Gupta, S., Varsamopoulos, G., 2008. Energy-efficient thermal-aware task scheduling for homogeneous high-performance computing data centers: a cyber-physical approach. IEEE Trans. Parallel Distrib. Syst. 19, 1458–1472.

Tang, Q., Gupta, S., Stanzione, D., Cayton, P., 2006a. Thermal-aware task scheduling to minimize energy usage of blade server based datacenters. In: IEEE Dependable, Auton. Secur. Comput. 2nd IEEE Int. Symp., Indianapolis, pp. 1–8.

Tang, Q., Mukherjee, T., Gupta, S., Cayton, P., 2006b. Sensor-based fast thermal evaluation model for energy efficient high-performance datacenters. In: IEEE Fourth Int. Conf. Intell. Sens. Inf. Process. ICISIP, pp. 203–208.

The Green Grid Technical Committee, 2007. Green grid metrics: describing datacenter power efficiency. Technical Committee White Paper. The Green Grid, Beaverton, OR.

Thegreengrid.org, 2011. Reccomandation for measuring and reporting overall data center efficiency measuring PUE for data centers. [online] Available at: http://www.thegreengrid.org/~/media/WhitePapers/RecommendationsforMeasuringandReportingOverallData CenterEfficiency2010-07-15.ashx?lang=en (accessed 25.02.16).

Tian, W., Zhao, Y., 2015. Load balance scheduling for cloud data centers. In: Optim. Cloud Resour. Manag. Sched., pp. 65–114.

Torcellini, P., Long, N., Judkoff, R., 2003. Consumptive water use for U.S. power production, Golden.

Tozer, R., 2006. Data Centre Energy Saving: Air Management Metrics. Datacenter Dynamics. [online] Available at: http://archive.datacenterdynamics.com/focus/archive/2006/12/data-centre-energy-saving-air-management-metrics (accessed 25.02.16).

Tozer, R., Salim, M., 2010. Data center air management metrics—practical approach. In: IEEE Therm. Thermomechanical Phenom. Electron. Syst., pp. 1–8.

Tozer, R., Salim, M., Kurkjian, C., 2009. Air management metrics in data centres. ASHRAE Trans. 2009, 115.

Tozer, R., Flucker, S., Romano, A., 2013. Scalable data centre efficiency. In: CIBSE Tech. Symp, Liverpool, pp. 11–12.

Uddin, M., Rahman, A., 2012. Energy efficiency and low carbon enabler green IT framework for data centers considering green metrics. Renew. Sustain. Energy Rev. 16, 4078–4094.

Uddin, M., Shah, A., Rehman, A., 2014. Metrics for computing performance of data center for instigating energy efficient data centers. J. Sci. Ind. Res. 73, 11–15.

VanGilder, J., 2011. Real-time data center cooling analysis. In: Electronics Cooling Magazine—Focused on Thermal Management, TIMs, Fans, Heat Sinks, CFD Software, LEDs/Lighting. [online] Electronics-cooling.com. Available at: http://www.electronics-cooling.com/2011/09/real-time-data-center-cooling-analysis/ (accessed 25.02.16).

VanGilder, J., Shrivastava, S., 2007. Capture index: an airflow-based rack cooling performance metric. ASHRAE Trans. 113, 126–136.

Wang, D., Cao, B., Chang, T., Baohong, H., Jie, L., Xiongwei, L., et al., 2015. Space usage effectiveness (SPUE^{TM}). Tokyo (Japan): The Green Grid.

Wang, L., Khan, S., 2011. Review of performance metrics for green data centers: a taxonomy study. J. Supercomput. 63, 639–656.

Ward, E., Goedke, M., Brenner, P., Go, D., 2012. A simplified thermodynamic model for waste heat utilization from a containerized data center experimental platform. In: 13th IEEE ITHERM Conf. Therm. Thermomechanical Phenom. Electron. Syst., San Diego, CA, pp. 521–529.

Yuventi, J., Mehdizadeh, R., 2013. A critical analysis of power usage effectiveness and its use in communicating data center energy consumption. Energy Build. 64, 90–94.

Zhang, H., Shao, S., Xu, H., Zou, H., Tian, C., 2014. Free cooling of data centers: a review. Renew. Sustain. Energy Rev. 35, 171–182.

Enhancing energy efficiency in buildings through innovative data analytics technologies[a]

11

A. Capozzoli, T. Cerquitelli, M.S. Piscitelli

Politecnico di Torino, Turin, Italy

1 INTRODUCTION

In the last few years, much research has been attracted to building data computing issues, with specific attention being drawn to energy consumption and energy efficiency.

Energy efficiency is a growing policy priority for many countries around the world, as governments seek to reduce wasteful energy consumption and encourage the use of renewable sources. The International Energy Agency (IEA) has estimated that in terms of primary energy consumption, buildings represent roughly 40%.

In the last decade building energy modeling was mainly based on engineering methods and on the use of dedicated building energy simulation tools. This approach gave the designer the opportunity to accurately estimate the performance of buildings in terms of energy use. However, this direct modeling approach can often be time-consuming and requires remarkable technical expertise, as well as detailed building physics information provided by the user. Therefore, in practice more and more researchers rely on data-driven tools based on machine learning and intelligent methods. In fact, there has been an increase in an unconventional approach in the building physics to improve energy performance due to the growing availability of building-related data and platforms that can manage them.

Buildings have always been rich sources of data and these data can lead to several revenue opportunities in terms of energy saving. Consequently, there is an increasing need to collect a great amount of heterogeneous data and information.

---

[a]The authors, Alfonso Capozzoli, Tania Cerquitelli, and Marco Savino Piscitelli, confirm that the images included in this chapter are original and created by the authors.

Pervasive Computing. http://dx.doi.org/10.1016/B978-0-12-803663-1.00011-5

Thanks to the adoption of information and communication technologies in buildings, a growing number of complex databases is becoming available. Continuous advancements in electronics and digital systems has further reduced the cost of both smart meters and communication and data collection facilities. Thanks to innovative instrumentation, communication and data handling, an advanced metering infrastructure can perform real-time data acquisition from consumers, and transmit and store the data. Moreover, sensors can be tailored on the needs and wishes of users and system designers, according to cost and functionality.

The proliferation of sensor networks for monitoring energy, indoor and outdoor environmental parameters has made huge archives of measurements with temporal and spatial references available to facility managers. In recent years many multi-utility companies operating in the sectors of electricity, thermal energy for district heating, gas, management of integrated water services, and waste collection and disposal have deployed wireless sensor networks based on sensors and smart meters to remotely control the services provided. Thus, the monitoring system needs to manage several million measurements per day. Due to the large volume of energy-related data being collected, different approaches exploit innovative technologies for Big Data management. Advancement in Big Data and analytics technologies has opened the prospect of new possibilities.

Innovative management systems should be designed to continuously monitor a smart city environment and provide all final users (citizens, governments, stake holders) with the tools to improve energy efficiency.

Specifically, important research activities have been carried out to use database management systems, exploratory data mining techniques, and statistical tools in the field of storage and analysis of energy data to evaluate the efficiency of buildings.

To characterize energy consumption different analytics methods have been proposed in the literature both by energy scientists and professionals. The use of machine learning techniques in the field of building energy performance provides high levels of accuracy, processing times which are faster than simulations and information not readily extractable from building-related data. Building-related data potentially contain knowledge about the interactions between building energy consumption and the factors that influence it. Therefore, energy data can provide information about building operation modes, making it possible to improve management and reduce energy demand. Retrieving the hidden knowledge that can be extracted from these data is highly desirable in order to improve building energy performance. However, exploring such data and understanding the underlying energy patterns is a complex issue. Hence, in this chapter the authors aim to give a comprehensive overview of the possible building-related applications which researchers have been investigating over the past few years in the field of data analytics technologies.

Research on these large data volumes has been carried out on the following areas: (i) supporting data visualization and warning notification (Wijayasekara et al., 2014); (ii) efficient storing and retrieval operations based on NoSQL databases (Van der Veen et al., 2012); (iii) characterizing consumption profiles among different users (Ardakanian et al., 2014; Depuru et al., 2011); and (iv) identifying the main factors that increase energy consumption (eg, floors and room orientation (Filippn and Larsen, 2009), location (Depuru et al., 2011)).

Intelligent data analysis is also carried out in building applications to identify typical load profiles of consumers and to develop a set of rules for automatic classification. Data analytics has also been performed to derive energy benchmarks that enable the categorization of buildings based on operational energy use. Other studies, have investigated the opportunity of analyzing large data sets in building automation systems with the aim of improving building operational performance.

In Fig. 1 a list of several applications where data analytics methods (eg, data mining, machine learning) are extremely useful is shown. These applications concern energy demand estimation/prediction, fault detection and diagnosis (FDD), energy benchmarking, occupant behavior and energy profiling. These techniques are used for building engineering applications and expertise in building physics is necessary in order to: select the attributes related to the demand objectives, choose the most suitable methodology to adopt and interpret the extracted knowledge for practical uses. In the proposed methodological process, the analyst also has a key role in the post-mining phase. This is due to the fact that the knowledge extracted from the data cannot be translated directly into energy efficiency strategies: it needs to be interpreted and driven by a domain expert.

In a building physics context, the different applications are closely linked to the available data. Each dataset has its own characteristics that determine the quantity and quality of knowledge extractable through intelligent processes. In the case of building-related data, some of the most important attributes are listed below:

- Spatial scale (group of buildings, building, representative building space)
- Energy services (heating, cooling, domestic hot water, ventilation, lighting, electrical appliances)
- Data features (minimum, maximum, mean, standard deviation)

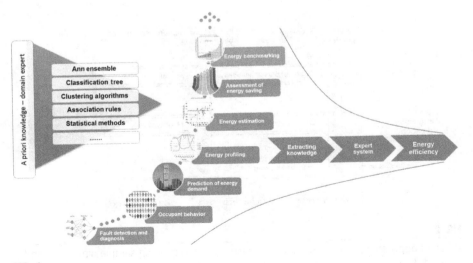

FIG. 1

Different applications in building physics of data analytics technologies.

- Measurement accuracy (sensor tolerance)
- Timestamp accuracy
- Sampling frequency (annual, monthly, daily, hourly, sub-hourly, etc.)
- Recording period length (year, season, etc.)
- Data source (sensor, web platform, simulation, etc.)

Depending on the quantity and quality of available data, different in-depth energy analyses from a single building to large building stock can be performed (Corgnati et al., 2013). Fig. 2 shows the relationship between possible applications and building sample dimension with the corresponding most suitable reference time range. In addition, the authors believe that sampling frequency can be considered one of the most important constraints in the evaluation of the expected objectives. Various targeted analyses can be addressed according to the sampling frequency, ranging from annual to sub-hourly data, such as energy performance characterization of a specific building or a general overview of the energy-profile tendencies of a country.

Regardless of the type of application, adequate and good-quality data (representative of the most influencing factors) are the cornerstone of detailed energy and performance analysis to pinpoint potential operation issues in buildings and identify energy-saving strategies. Furthermore, since building-related data often consist in time series data, the dynamic nature of the building operations is another important factor to take into account. For this reason, new temporal data mining techniques that aim to capture relationships in a dataset over time are necessary.

This chapter discusses a wide range of interesting analyses of energy-related data with different applications in building physics and highlights the great potential of the knowledge discovery process in relation to energy data to define the future strategies for energy efficiency.

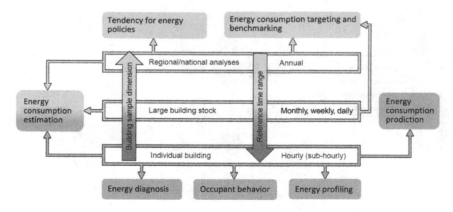

FIG. 2

Different applications in building physics according to the building sample dimension and detail of data.

2 BUILDING ENERGY MODELING APPROACHES

Energy performance in buildings is influenced by many factors, such as indoor micro-climatic and weather conditions, building envelope characteristics, the operation and efficiency of HVAC system, equipment, occupants and their behavior. Defining the intended purpose of a given building energy analysis is a crucial step in the selection of the most suitable building modeling approach to be adopted. The approach should be able to address the analysis requirements with an acceptable level of accuracy. The requirements of building energy analysis may include design optimization, energy management, energy audit, energy certification, energy diagnosis and so on. Different classifications have been proposed in the literature.

ASHRAE (ASHRAE, 2009) proposed general categorization considering two different approaches (Fig. 3): the forward (direct) approach and the data-driven (inverse) approach.

In the first case, the evaluation of building energy use is based on the application of a thermal/engineering model with known system structure and envelope propri-eties as well as forcing variables and boundary conditions (forward approach). This approach requires a high level of building physics expertise and it can be more or less complex depending on the expected accuracy, its dynamic or steady state nature and output time frequency. This kind of analysis requires a detailed description of the properties to model physical phenomena affecting the building behavior and operation. ESP-r, BLAST, DOE-2, TRNSYS, and Energy Plus are the most popular simulation codes based on forward simulation models.

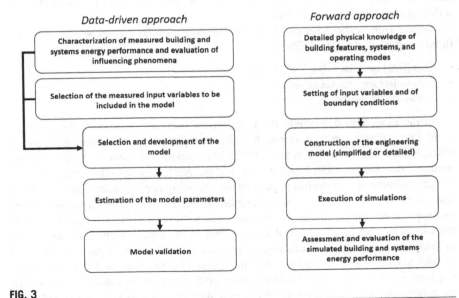

FIG. 3

Forward approach and data-driven approach.

In the data-driven approach, the input (influencing variables) and output (building energy use) are known and measured and the objective is to estimate by means of statistical analyses the system parameters and to describe the mathematical model. Using a data driven approach the model parameters are estimated considering the actual working conditions, and it is possible to evaluate the as-built system performance.

Data-driven modeling, based on the application of statistical and intelligent methods is useful in evaluating demand-side management (DSM) strategies, identifying energy conservation measures in existing buildings and for the development of baseline models in energy conservation measurement and verification projects. Through a data driven approach, it is possible to evaluate the causes of incongruities (dependent by occupant behaviour or uncorrect building operation) of actual consumption compared with design predictions or to isolate the energy savings due to a specific retrofit action.

Moreover, two primary types of inverse models are classified in the literature: steady-state inverse models and dynamic inverse models. In the steady-state models the transient effect of variables is not considered and the analyses are more appropriate considering sampling frequency of variables equal to or greater than 1 day. The dynamic models are instead able to capture the effects related to the thermal mass of the envelope or from setback thermostat strategies. They are more complex in comparison to the steady-state models and need more detailed measurements for the training of the model.

Typical single and multiple linear regressions (MLRs) fall under the "black box" steady-state models. Dynamic inverse models include equivalent thermal network analysis, ARMA models, Fourier series models, machine learning methods, and artificial neural networks (ANNs).

Data-driven methods for energy-use evaluation in buildings can be classified into three categories (ASHRAE, 2009):

- Empirical or "black-box" approach,
- Calibrated simulation approach,
- "Gray-box" approach.

In the **empirical approach**, the most typical techniques use linear or change-point linear regression to correlate building energy use with weather data and/or other influencing variables related to building operation (input). Single variate, multivariate, change point, Fourier series and the ANN belong to this category.

The **calibrated simulation approach** uses building performance simulation tools and calibrates the physical input variables in such a way that measured energy use approaches that predicted by the simulation. Several difficulties are related to the use of this approach. Typical issues concern the arrangement and preparation of weather data used by simulation programs, the selection of the methods and metrics to calibrate the model and the uncertainty to measure some input parameters required for simulation (e.g. building mass, infiltration coefficients, etc.). However, the calibrated simulation approach requires a high level of user skill and knowledge.

The **gray-box approach** first uses a model to represent physical structure of the building or air conditioning system, and then the representative parameters are estimated using measured data by statistical analysis. This approach can be considered as a trade-off between physical and inverse based methods. This kind of method is useful mainly in existing buildings when a building physical model is available but is incomplete or not detailed.

A further interesting classification was proposed by Pedersen. In Pedersen (2007) three methodologies to categorize load and energy estimations are defined:

Statistical approaches/regression analyses: these approaches are based on linear or multivariate regression analyses. Statistical regression models correlate the energy consumption with the influencing variables. These kinds of models have been used to (i) predict the energy performance considering simplified variables (eg, weather parameters), (ii) predict some useful energy indices, (iii) estimate important parameters of building, such as total heat loss coefficient, total heat capacity and gain factor.

In some simplified engineering models, the regression is used to obtain an energy signature.

Energy simulation programs: these programs uses weather data and detailed building and systems characteristics to simulate the building energy request for different energy uses.

Intelligent computer systems: these systems are based on machine learning algorithms that are capable of discovering hidden patterns and correlations based on the analysis of measured performance data.

The dynamic forward models can be very elaborate and can be applicable for accurate calculations. In contrast, by adopting some simplified engineering methods in some cases a good accuracy can be obtained. A drawback of detailed engineering model concerns the high complexity and the high uncertainty of some input information. The statistical models are relatively easy to implement but often are affected by inaccuracy and low versatility. Artificial neural networks and support vector machine models are very useful in non-linear problems and they have been applied with success in building energy prediction. The disadvantages of these two types of models are that they require sufficient historical performance data for the training and can be very complex.

3 ENERGY DATA MANAGEMENT AND MINING SYSTEMS

An Energy data Management and Mining System is a set of tools able to collect different kinds of energy data (eg, measurements collected through a district heating system), enrich them with open source information (eg, meteorological data provided by web services), and efficiently store and manage the sensor data and enriched information. Integrated data are then elaborated to compute interesting key performing indicators (KPI) and/or mined with complex data mining algorithms to discover previous unknown and interesting knowledge. The general architecture of this kind of system is shown in Fig. 4. Four different layers can be identified. The first one, named source layer, includes objects providing different kinds of data to the system. This layer includes all the objects that provide source data to the system such as smart meters, wireless sensor network and web services that continuously provide

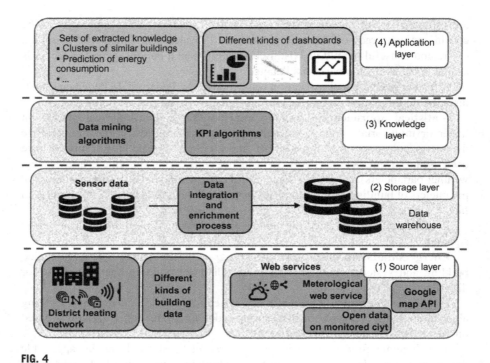

FIG. 4

A general architecture to collect, store and analyze energy-related data.

data that is of interest. For example, collected data may include energy consumption logs provided by thermal smart meters, indoor climate conditions monitored through indoor temperature sensors or open data on meteorological information provided by a web service. The data layer stores sensor data in a relational database, including information on the main features characterizing each building (eg, address and volume), the list of sensors located in each building, the main characteristics for each sensor (eg, unit of measure, description, sensor type and model), and the collected measurements for all sensors. On average, one data frame is received from each building every 5 min.

Sensor data are integrated and enriched with open source information that is interesting for the analysis. For example, since meteorological information represents an important issue in the energy efficiency domain, it has been widely integrated with sensor energy-related data. For instance, historical meteorological data are available through the Weather Underground web service, which gathers data from personal weather stations (PWS) registered by users. For a large number of cities, at least 20 PWS are distributed throughout the territory. This service provides meteorological data with high accuracy modeling showing the real conditions registered in a city neighborhood. Enriched data are usually stored in a data warehouse, where data are de-normalized and represented by means of a document structure. Redundant information is added to each record (document) to speedup read performance and yield fast querying and KPI computation. The model design is aimed at providing a human-readable document format.

The knowledge layer includes a wide range of data mining algorithms and KPIs to discover interesting knowledge. Different analytics algorithms can be exploited for discovering interesting correlations among data, define user profiling models, and identify groups of similar energy-efficient buildings. For example, association rules, a powerful exploratory data mining approach, can be easily exploited to discover correlations between energy consumption patterns, indoor climate conditions and meteorological conditions.

The last layer, named the application layer, provides knowledge discovered regarding different kinds of users, such as energy manager (responsible for the energy services provided), energy analyst (expert in energy consumption), consumer (building condos administrators or the public administration), and users living in the building. In the latter layer, informative dashboards may be generated based on a selection of KPIs to produce useful feedback for different users and suggest ready-to-implement energy efficient actions or strategies. Different types of charts or maps can be exploited to display extracted knowledge to end users in an informative and user-friendly way.

A wide range of different technologies can be exploited in the design and development of each layer of the energy data management and mining systems. In the next section different proposed approaches for the source layer are presented while the remaining layers are analyzed in depth in Sections 5 and 6.

4 COLLECTING AND STORING ENERGY DATA

Building energy-related data can be categorized according to three main strategies based on how data are generated or collected, ie, measurement, survey, and simulation (Babaei et al., 2015). Therefore, the available data source influences the dataset's level of detail and the corresponding targeted analyses. In Fig. 5, different

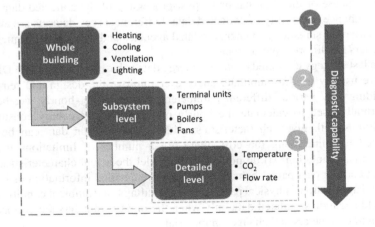

FIG. 5

Different levels of detail for collecting and storing energy data.

levels of detail for collecting and storing energy data are shown. Specifically, the level of detail (data granularity) depends on the complexity of the implemented hardware/software systems deployed to collect the data samples. Detailed data are usually collected by deploying a large-scale sensor network to monitor energy consumption by using either a smart device to measure energy usage for the entire building, or an extensive network with a large number of sensors to record each appliance's energy usage.

In order to continuously monitor energy consumption, different gateway boxes can be installed in buildings. Specifically, a large number of sensors, in charge of the each gateway, can be deployed in buildings to monitor thermal energy under different aspects, such as instantaneous power, cumulative energy consumption, water flow and corresponding temperatures. The frequency of relevant events (eg, sampling, processing, and communicating) is set according to the type and nature of a deployed sensor. Sensors periodically transmit their status and gathered measurements. Power consumption reducing strategies are also exploited to extend battery life. Furthermore, sensor devices are able to transfer gathered measurements to a gateway box through a short-range and low-power wireless network. Remote communications, between gateway boxes and the energy provider management systems, are established via wired and wireless telephone networks.

Survey data are acquired by interviewing people (companies or consumers) through ad hoc questionnaires defined with the help of professional surveyors. Web-based portals are usually exploited to reach a large number of individuals and collect data. Collected responses are analyzed and pre-processed to generate the corresponding datasets. Survey datasets are usually mined in order to characterize consumers' energy consumption profiles and behaviors, demographic characteristics, building characteristics, and consumer feedback on indoor comfort. Although survey datasets are much smaller than measurement datasets, survey strategy is still exploited to reach consumers spread over a wide geographical area. A key issue to address when carrying out extensive surveys is the minimizing of possible inaccuracies in the recorded data. The employment of professional interviewers during the data collection phase or the exploitation of post-processing of the collected data can be used to enhance the quality of collected data. Different survey datasets are available at the bureau of statistics and energy-related agencies and they can be requested by researchers for different research purposes.

The last strategy exploited to collect energy data is based on simulation. Different tools are usually used to simulate, analyze or improve the design and retrofitting of buildings, by various different parameters. For example, hourly weather data are normally used to calculate the hourly performance and energy consumption of buildings with given characteristics. Although simulation data can be easily generated by minimizing the cost, there are a number of limitations involved. Specifically, simulations (i) do not correctly model the actual characteristics of the building and the occupants' behaviors; (ii) require detailed information as building types and applications, physical parameters of buildings, and ambient conditions; and (iii) yield accurate simulated data only when the input parameters are correctly set, as ambient parameters and changes in material.

To store the above energy-related data different database technologies can be exploited. Data collected through smart meters are fixed and constant, thus relational databases (DBMS—database management system) can be exploited to efficiently store and manage them. A DBMS is a software system able to manage large, shared collections of data that are persistent, by ensuring their reliability and privacy. A DBMS guarantees that users and application programs, which utilize a database, can ignore the designing details used in the construction of the database. The most widespread data model is the relational data model. The latter defines the relationship builder, which organizes the data into sets of homogeneous (fixed structure) records. The relationships are represented as tables.

Moreover building data can be both structured and unstructured. Operational data of building systems is often structured, but maintenance information is much more unstructured. Traditional technologies were unable to adequately make use of the rich unstructured data in buildings, since they require normalization for any kind of analytics. Current Big Data technologies make it possible to use static textual data like maintenance documents, system specifications, drawings and similar materials.

When collected data are more variable and heterogeneous as survey data, a document-oriented distributed data-warehouse technology is usually exploited. Data-warehouse technology supports periodic loading of collected data. This database technology is also used when collected energy data are enriched with user feedback on indoor climate conditions as well as with meteorological data. A document-oriented distributed data warehouse, such as MongoDB (Chodorow and Dirolf, 2010), provides rich queries, full indexing, data replication, horizontal scalability and a flexible aggregation framework, including a distributed map-reduce engine to efficiently manage large data collections.

In a number of smart cities today, extensive smart metering grids, involving thousands of buildings, are usually deployed. Since a large volume of data are collected, innovative database storage based on cloud technology are used for storing and processing all monitored data. As shown in Fig. 6 the gateways, installed in buildings, send the data frame to the cloud architecture, where data packets are first authenticated and then assigned to one of four dispatchers to guarantee system reliability. Each dispatcher delivers the frame to a computer cluster, including different processing servers where data are stored in a distributed file system (ie, HDFS). When the process server has stored the frame correctly, the dispatcher sends the ACK to the gateway which can send the next data frame. Each processing server works through the received data and stores the results in a relational and distributed or parallel database. In a distributed database system, data are physically stored across several sites, and each site is typically managed by a DBMS that is capable of running independently. Data storage and the degree of autonomy of individual sites have a great impact on all aspects of the system, including query execution, query optimization, concurrency control and recovery. A parallel database system seeks to improve performance through parallelization of various operations, such as loading data and query execution. Although data may be stored in a distributed fashion, the distribution is used to improve system performance.

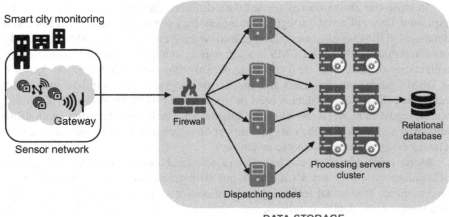

Smart city monitoring

Gateway

Sensor network

Firewall

Dispatching nodes

Processing servers
cluster

Relational
database

DATA STORAGE

FIG. 6

A cloud architecture to collect energy data in a smart city environment.

5 KNOWLEDGE DISCOVERY PROCESS ON BUILDING ENERGY DATA

Fig. 7 presents a framework of the knowledge discovery process in energy data which mainly includes four phases (Fan et al., 2015). Data pre-processing includes two tasks, i.e., data preparation and data visualization. These steps are fundamental in improving the quality of a given dataset and transforming the data into appropriate formats for the application of data analytics methods. The visualization step is necessary in order to have an outline of the preliminary knowledge about the macro-proprieties of data. Data segmentation is aimed at identifying typical homogenous patterns through the segmentation of the dataset into several subsets. Knowledge discovery deals with the application of different DM techniques, to discover hidden knowledge. The purpose of knowledge exploitation is to select, understand, and use the knowledge discovered. The learning process can be adopted in specific forms of application including building performance evaluation, fault detection and diagnosis and system control optimization.

5.1 DATA PRE-PROCESSING

The two tasks of data pre-processing phase are: data preparation and data characterization. Data preparation consists of three sub-tasks including data cleaning, data transformation and data reduction.

Several studies have demonstrated that the process of data preparation is usually time consuming and can account for 80% of the total data mining process (Xiao

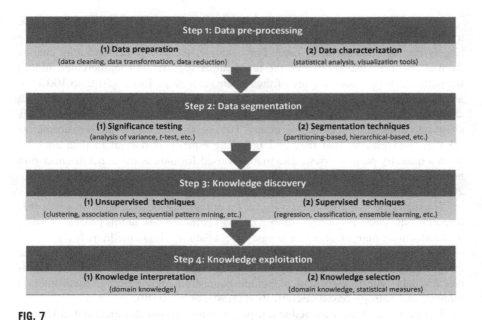

FIG. 7

Framework of the knowledge discovery process in building energy data.

and Fan, 2014). Moreover, this phase is also crucial considering that the accuracy and reliability of the results in the model-based methods are largely dependent on the data quality. Data quality in the building management system could be low for different reasons such as measurement noise, uncertainties, data transmission, improper maintenance, sensor faults, and insufficient calibration. Typical problems in data sets are related to missing values and outliers, which may negatively affect the knowledge discovery process.

The purpose of the data cleaning process is to manage missing values, resolve inconsistencies, and detect and remove outliers. Missing values can be filled in using the global constant, moving average, imputation or inference-based models (Xiao and Fan, 2014). Inconsistencies in a data set are related to the differences in the data scales or units and they can be solved using data fusion schemes or physical redundancy (Xiao and Fan, 2014).

Outliers are records that appear to deviate significantly from other elements in the sample in which they occur. Outlier can be also defined as an observation (or subset of observations) that appears to be inconsistent with the remainder of that set of data. The outliers can be detected using statistical methods, unsupervised clustering and supervised classification methods. When a time series is analyzed, the outliers can be classified into two different types: punctual outliers and anomalous data subsequences. In the data pre-processing phase, the identification of the first type of outliers is needed, whenever infrequent sequential patterns could be detected through further investigation at a later stage.

The process of data transformation consists of scaling data and data type transformation. In a typical building related data set the scale of variables can vary largely due to different units used. For example, the power demand may change from 0 kW to thousands of kW, the temperature (eg, outdoor temperature, indoor temperature, supply temperature of the system) can range from −20°C to 100°C or a typical signal of a fan can range from 0 to 1. Since the performance of some data analytics methods (e.g., support vector machine) can be negatively affected by this situation, data scaling becomes necessary. The purpose of data scaling is to normalize the data variables so that they end up being equally important in data analysis from a quantity point of view. The methods used for data scaling include max-min normalization, Z-score normalization, and decimal point normalization (Hastie et al., 2009).

The data type transformation is useful for organizing the data set in an applicable format for the data mining algorithm. The most common task in this process consists in transforming numerical data into categorical data (eg, high, medium, low).

For example, conventional association rule mining algorithms can only manage categorical data while the majority of building-related variables are numeric. Methods for data type transformation include equal-frequency binning, equal-interval binning, and entropy-based discretization (Hastie et al., 2009).

The purpose of the data reduction phase is to improve computation efficiency through the reduction of data dimensions. Sampling techniques are commonly used for the reduction of the observation sampled at a specific time frequency related to each variable.

The reduction of variables of interests and significance, can be done through domain knowledge or data reconstruction methods (such as the principal component analysis) or using heuristic methods (such as the step-wise forward selection and backward elimination methods).

Finally, visualization tools play an essential role in the first stage of a mining process. This phase makes it possible to have an initial understanding of the data, considering it is a challenge to visualize multidimensional data in a comprehensive way. For instance, box plots, carpet plot and histograms are efficient in displaying data distribution and evolution, as well as for performing a frequency analysis; scatter plots are useful in discovering correlations, descriptive statistics for understanding limits and the distribution of data to be analyzed.

5.2 DATA SEGMENTATION

Data segmentation is an important phase considering that the values of the variables, their influence on energy consumption and their mutual correlation can largely vary with different boundary conditions. The opportunity to find more homogenous sub-datasets according to their own typical pattern through a partitioning analysis, helps improve knowledge acquisition (Fan et al., 2015). The distance among the objects within each sub-dataset decreases, allowing a more effective analysis of hidden patterns and correlations. Methods for the segmentation of a dataset can differ.

A high domain expertise is needed in order to determine the segmentation criteria to be adopted. A significance test also can be adopted with the aim of finding the variables affecting the intrinsic characteristics of the data set. Moreover, clustering analysis is recommended for the partitioning of the dataset. A common process of segmentation consists in using ANOVA method to analyze the significance of time variables (month, day of the week, hour) and then a cluster analysis for the partitioning according to the significant variables. In this way, typical sub-datasets are obtained according to the day of the week (eg, weekdays, weekends) or the hour of the day (eg, working hours, non-working hours).

5.3 KNOWLEDGE DISCOVERY

The knowledge discovery phase represents the actual mining process. A number of data mining (DM) techniques can be used and new methods are emerging. The selection of the most appropriate DM technique depends on the problem under consideration, the level and quality of available data and the degree of domain expertise.

A wide range of data mining algorithms have been proposed in the literature to find patterns representing knowledge not directly mined from massive data repositories. Data mining activities include studying correlations among data, extracting information for prediction, grouping data with similar properties. Furthermore, different data mining techniques can be coupled to mine building-related data, such as cluster analysis and data classification, or cluster analysis and Association Rule Mining (ARM). Our belief is that data mining algorithms could play an important role in discovering interesting knowledge for energy efficiency in buildings.

The potential applications in building physics are related to the development of predictive models and optimization strategies, detection and diagnosis of abnormalities, the evaluation of effects of influencing factors on building energy consumption. A brief description of exploited data mining algorithms in the energy research field is given below.

5.3.1 Clustering algorithms

Cluster analysis is an exploratory data mining technique exploited in different application domains including energy field. Cluster analysis aims at grouping a data object collection into subsets (clusters) based on object properties, without the support of additional a priori knowledge (in contrast with classification algorithms using class label information). The goal is that objects in the same cluster are very similar to one another and different from the objects in other clusters (Pang-Ning et al., 2006).

Clustering algorithms can be classified into two main categories: prototype- and density-based algorithms. In prototype-based algorithms (eg, K-means (Juang and Rabiner, 1990), K-medoids (Kaufman and Rousseeuw, 1990)), a cluster contains data objects which are closer (more similar) to the prototype that defines the cluster than to the prototype of any other cluster. The prototype is either the most representative point (K-medoids) or the mean point (K-means) in the cluster. These algorithms tend to find well-separated spherical-shaped clusters, but they are sensitive to outliers. In density-based algorithms (eg, DBSCAN (Ester et al., 1996)), a cluster is a dense area of data objects surrounded by an area of low density. These algorithms are less sensitive to outliers, and can identify non-spherical-shaped clusters. In the following, we give a brief overview of the main characteristics of the K-means and DBSCAN algorithms.

The K-means clustering algorithm (Juang and Rabiner, 1990) finds k clusters represented by their centroids. k is a user-specified parameter and centroid is the mean value of the objects in the clusters. K-means is based on an iterative procedure, preceded by a set-up phase where k objects of the dataset are randomly chosen as the initial centroids. Each iteration performs two steps. In the first step, each object is assigned to the cluster whose centroid is the nearest to that object. In the second step, centroids are relocated by computing the mean of the objects within each cluster. Iterations continue until the k centroids do not change.

The K-means algorithm is effective for spherical-shaped clusters. Nevertheless, it may have problems due to the random initialization of centroids and a single execution of the procedure may not guarantee the homogeneity of the discovered clusters. K-means is also sensitive to outliers, cluster size, densities of data points, non-globular shapes of clusters and outliers. K-means also requires the a-priori knowledge of the number of clusters. Despite of all these limitations, K-means could be computationally faster and produce tighter clusters (especially if clusters are globular).

In the DBSCAN algorithm (Ester et al., 1996), density is evaluated based on the user-specified parameters Eps and MinPts. A dense region in the data space is an n-dimensional sphere with radius Eps and containing at least MinPts objects. DBSCAN iterates over the data objects in the collection by analyzing their neighborhood. It classifies objects as being (i) in the interior of a dense region (a core point), (ii) on the edge of a dense region (a border point), or (iii) in a sparsely occupied region (a noise or outlier point). Any two core points that are close enough (within an Eps' distance of one another) are put in the same cluster. Any border point close enough to a core point is put in the same cluster as the core point. Outlier points (ie, points far from any core point) are isolated. In contrast the K-means algorithm, DBSCAN can effectively discover clusters of arbitrary shape and filter out outliers, thus increasing cluster homogeneity. The number of expected clusters is not required, but the user should specify the Eps and MinPts parameters.

5.3.2 Classification algorithms

Classification is the task of creating a model, which assigns objects to one of several predefined categories, to analyze the properties of classes and to automatically classify a new object. A classification model is typically used (i) to predict the class label for a new unlabeled data object, (ii) to provide a descriptive model explaining what features characterize objects in each class. Classification methods include various techniques such as the decision tree, rule-based, naive Bayes, neural networks, and support vector machines (SVM) classifiers. Each technique employs different learning algorithms to build models with good generalization capability, ie, models that accurately predict the class labels of previously unknown records. Generally, the construction of the classification model is performed by dividing the available dataset into a *training set*, which is to be used in the construction phase of the classifier, and a *test set* for validation.

Decision tree classifiers provide a readable classification model that is potentially accurate in many different application contexts, including energy-based applications. The decision tree classifier (Pang-Ning et al., 2006) creates the classification model by building a decision tree. Each node in the tree specifies a test on an attribute, each branch descending from that node corresponds to one of the possible values for that attribute. Each leaf represents class labels associated with the instance. Instances in the training set are classified by navigating them from the root of the tree down to a leaf, according to the outcome of the tests along the path. Starting from the root node of the tree, each node splits the instance space into two or more sub-spaces according to an attribute test condition. Then moving down the tree branch corresponding to the value of the attribute, a new node is created. This process is then repeated for the subtree rooted at the new node, until all records in the training set have been classified. The decision tree construction process usually works in a top-down manner, by choosing an attribute test condition at each step that best splits the records. There are many measures that can be used to determine the best way to split the records. The Gini index impurity-based criterion for growing the tree (Pang-Ning et al., 2006) is often exploited. It measures how often a randomly chosen instance from the set would be incorrectly labeled if it were randomly labeled according to the distribution of labels in the subset.

SVMs (Pang-Ning et al., 2006) were first proposed in statistical learning theory. SVM is able to deal with high-dimensional data and it generates a quite comprehensive (geometric) model. An SVM predictor is based on a kernel function K that defines a particular type of similarity measure between data objects. Examples of kernel functions are linear, RBF (radial basis function), polynomial, or sigmoid kernel. The SVM learning problem can be formulated as a convex optimization problem, in which different algorithms can be exploited to find the global minimum of the objective function.

ANNs (Pang-Ning et al., 2006) simulate biological neural systems. The network consists of an input layer, n hidden layers, and an output layer. Each layer is made up of nodes. Each node in a layer takes as input a weighted sum of the outputs of all the nodes in the previous layer, and it applies a nonlinear activation function to the weighted input. The network is trained with back propagation and learns by iteratively processing the set of training data objects. For each training data object, the network predicts the target value. Then, weights in the network nodes are modified to minimize the mean squared prediction error. These modifications are made in a backwards direction, that is, from the output layer through each hidden layer down to the first hidden layer.

5.3.3 Association rules

ARM is a data mining method for identifying all associations and correlations between attribute values. The output is a set of association rules that are used to represent patterns of attributes that are frequently associated together (ie, frequent patterns).

Let D be a dataset whose generic record r is a set of features. Each feature, also called *item*, is a couple (attribute, value). Since we are interested in analyzing energy building features, each feature models a specific characteristic of a building (eg, energy performance index, transparent surface).

An *itemset* is a set of features. The *support count* of an itemset I is the number of records containing I. The support $s(I)$ of an itemset I is the percentage of records containing I. An itemset is frequent when its support is greater than, or equal to, a minimum support threshold MinSup. Association rules identify collections of itemsets (ie, set of features) that are statistically related (ie, frequent) in the underlying dataset.

Association rules (Pang-Ning et al., 2006) are usually represented in the form $X \rightarrow Y$, where X (also called rule antecedent) and Y (also called rule consequent) are disjoint itemsets (ie, disjoint conjunctions of features). Rule quality is usually measured by rule support and confidence. *Rule support* is the percentage of records containing both X and Y. It represents the prior probability of $X \cup Y$ (ie, its observed frequency) in the dataset. *Rule confidence* is the conditional probability of finding Y given X. It describes the strength of the implication and is given by $c(X \rightarrow Y) = s(X \rightarrow Y)/s(X)$.

Given a dataset D, a support threshold MinSup, and a confidence threshold MinConf, the mining process discovers all association rules with support and confidence greater than, or equal to, MinSup and MinConf, respectively.

Furthermore, to rank the most interesting rules, the lift index is also used to measure the (symmetric) correlation between antecedent and consequent of the extracted rules. The lift of an association rule lift $(X \rightarrow Y) = c(X \rightarrow Y)\}/s(Y) = s(X \rightarrow Y)/s(X)s(Y)$, where $s(X \rightarrow Y)$ and $c(X \rightarrow Y)$ are respectively the rule support and confidence, and $s(X)$ and $s(Y)$ are the supports of the rule antecedent and consequent. If lift $(X, Y) = 1$, itemsets X and Y are not correlated, i.e., they are statistically independent. Lift values below 1 show a negative correlation between itemsets X and Y, while values above 1 indicate a positive correlation. The interest of rules having a lift value close to 1 may be marginal.

5.4 KNOWLEDGE EXPLOITATION

The purpose of knowledge exploitation is to analyse, interpret and use the knowledge discovered (Fan et al., 2015). Different approaches are proposed in the literature to discover useful hidden rules and to analyse the patterns. The interpretation of the results of mining process requires domain expertise in order to support the knowledge discovered by means of data analytics. The final scope is to convert knowledge discovered into practical actions aimed at enhancing the building's energy performance.

Knowledge extracted from energy-related data is presented to different users according to their operational role to gain insights into the available data. Extracted knowledge should be informative and, at the same time, easy to understand and to exploit in decision making. Four operational roles of the energy miner system can be identified: (i) the Energy Manager is responsible for the energy services provided. He/she needs to access summary and high-level information in order to grasp the overall picture of the energy situation of the city district under observation. He/she requires dashboards showing knowledge at a higher level of granularity (eg, city district). (ii) The Energy Analyst is an expert in energy consumption. He/she is interested in analyzing the complete streams of collected data to observe and understand the phenomenon, analyze the different components and identify possible causes. He/she needs to inspect a significant volume of data to work out the position of the anomaly. (iii) The Consumer represents the condominium administrator, who is interested in assessing the efficiency of the heating system, as well as in establishing best practices that should/could lead to energy savings while maintaining the desired level of indoor comfort. He/she only needs to visualize a few indicators, possibly presented in a clear and intuitive way. (iv) The Users living in the building are interested in maintaining indoor wellness and understanding how their behaviors affect energy consumption so that they can achieve a significant reduction in their energy expenditure.

6 ENHANCING ENERGY EFFICIENCY THROUGH DATA ANALYTICS: APPLICATIONS IN ENERGY AND BUILDINGS

As mentioned above, the quantity and quality of building-related data are strictly connected with the feasibility of specific analyses. Useful information hidden in building data should be extracted for the purpose of energy saving. This information can be extracted from the measured building-related data. The information can then be translated into useful knowledge to be used in daily building operations. Note that the real data of a building contains the actual information of the building operations and thus can reflect the building's performance accurately. Moreover, vast amounts of data on building operations and management have been collected and stored, since building automation systems is becoming a part of building design. In general, building-related data includes climatic data, physical parameters, operational data, user-related data and time variables. In Fig. 8 the main factors used in a building energy consumption analysis are listed. Clearly the information to be collected are complex due their heterogeneity. Therefore, for such a complex system it is legitimate to use the term big data.

Big data are available from different sources at a very high speed, volume and level of heterogeneity. To extract useful information from Big Data, optimal methodological process, analytics capabilities and competences are needed. Today, different questions on building operational performance improvement need to be answered.

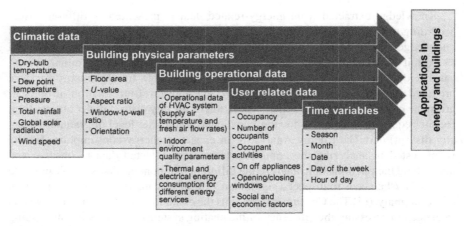

FIG. 8

Building-related data according to different categories of influencing factors.

- How can a prediction model of building energy consumption be developed that is easy to interpret and has few explanatory variables?
- How can recommendations be made to change some occupant behaviors in order to save energy?
- How can behaviors that should be changed be identified?
- How can useful information from building operational data be acquire din order to better understand building behavior and develop methodology to reduce its energy consumption?

Considering the limitations of the statistical analysis, analytics technologies to process measured building-related data can be adopted. Data mining techniques lead to the automatic analysis of huge amounts of data. They can be used to extract interesting, useful, and previously unknown knowledge from data, and therefore they fit well with the purpose of this study.

The next sections show some building physics fields in which, awareness of the potential of data analytics is developing.

6.1 THE PREDICTION OF BUILDING ENERGY CONSUMPTION

One of the most well-developed applications following a data-driven approach is the prediction of building energy consumption. The prediction of building energy demand is an application that requires a high level of data detail and also an adequate number of input variables. Nowadays, the prediction of building energy consumption plays a significant role in building performance assessment, optimization of building at the operational level, evaluation of DSM strategies and FDD. Moreover, building energy prediction also plays a key role in decision-making to reach achievable energy saving.

On the other hand, the great potential of energy prediction is thwarted by the complexity of the systems inside buildings. This is due to the growing variety of multi-energy plant systems, type of loads and occupation demand. These are the distinctive characteristics of a building. Together with external climatic conditions, indoor comfort and electrical appliances or devices, they make the prediction a difficult issue. For prediction, it is important to take into account the factors that both directly and indirectly influence building energy consumption.

After collection, data cannot be used directly in the construction of a predictive model because they could contain redundant information, seasonal effects (linked to the different uses of the system plant during the year), abnormal values and multicollinearity. At a higher level, one of the problems characterizing building-related data concerns the monitoring system installed. Often meters and sensors lack maintenance and calibration, are installed incorrectly, or have low resolution and quality due to cost considerations. Therefore, the construction of prediction models based on available data must follow a rigorous methodological process to maximize accuracy and robustness.

Another aspect linked to the accuracy of building energy prediction is the reference time range. For this reason, in prediction analysis it is possible to identify three different macro-categories known as: short-term load forecasting (STLF), medium-term load forecasting (MTLF), and long-term load forecasting (LTLF). Each of these categories has a different time range, which is typically between 24 h (STLF) and 1 year (LTLF) and different possible applications (Ahmad et al., 2014). The focus is currently on short-term prediction given its close linkage to the day-to-day operations.

Nowadays, there are many prediction models developed by combining several methods, in order to solve prediction difficulties and find the best accuracy in prediction. There are several popular methods used for predicting building energy consumption (Zhao and Magoulès, 2012), which can be grouped into three categories: engineering method, statistical method and artificial intelligence method (Lazos et al., 2014).

MLR is a statistical model, that has been successfully used to predict peak electricity load, hourly air conditioning load, and hourly total building energy consumption (Yiu and Wang, 2007). Aranda et al. (2012) developed three MLR models for predicting annual energy consumption in the Spanish Banking sector. The three models can be used to estimate the annual energy consumption in different climatic boundary conditions. While MLR models have been widely used in several building physics applications, machine learning techniques can be considered innovative in this research field.

The decision tree belongs to the machine learning supervised algorithms. This method was recently used for predicting building energy consumption. Yu et al. (2010) used the decision tree to predict and classify the building the energy use intensity (EUI) of Japanese residential buildings. According to Mikučionienė et al.

(2014) the decision tree method is suitable for improving the criteria of energy efficiency measures in building renovation. The opinion of the authors is that this algorithm can provide useful information that allows designers to easily understand a building's energy consumption pattern. Furthermore, the selection of the influencing variables to be used as predictors in CART is supervised.

Capozzoli et al. (2015a) developed two different models for estimating annual heating energy consumption in 80 schools in the province of Turin. The models used are a MLR and a CART. The accuracy of the two models proved quite satisfactory. The authors think that the greatest advantages in using the CART method are the easy model setting, and the form of the model output. Indeed, practical and easy-to-use decision rules can be extracted from the classification tree in order to be used by energy managers. The authors believe MLR and CART are complementary, not antagonistic. Moreover, future research should investigate the possibility of coupling the two models in order to achieve better accuracy in estimation. Model ensembling could be useful when the leaf nodes of CART have large confidence intervals. In this case, the development of an MRL model in each final node may better explain the dataset variance. However, the clusterwise regression method (Hsu, 2015) integrates cluster analysis and regression. This method is based on the minimization of an objective function finding simultaneously the optimal parameters for both clustering and regression. In this way, the mixture model achieves better accuracy in prediction than the approach based on two steps in series (first cluster analysis then prediction model).

One of the most important problems linked to the development of prediction models is the uncertainty of input parameters. For this reason, in some cases it is useful to use methods allowing the analyst to quantify the uncertainty of the prediction. In Heo and Zavala (2012) and Manfren et al. (2013) Gaussian process regression (GPR) has been proposed for building energy estimation. According to Heo and Zavala (2012) GPR is more suitable than MLR in characterizing the complex phenomenon of building energy consumption.

In different applications, support vector regression (SVR) has proved useful for prediction purposes. In Dong et al. (2005), good accuracy in cooling load and monthly utility bill prediction was observed. In four commercial buildings located in Singapore Dong et al. applied SVR to predict monthly utility bills. The prediction was based on weather data (ambient temperature, relative humidity and global solar radiation) collected for each building. The accuracy achieved was close to 96% (Dong et al., 2005).

ANN and SVM are artificial intelligence methods widely used in several applications due to their remarkable flexibility. ANN has been used for predicting building energy consumption as a whole, as well as disaggregate loads. In thermal and electrical energy prediction, ANN was tested with different objectives. In thermal energy prediction, numerous researchers have predicted space cooling load (Li and Huang, 2013; Li et al., 2009), space heating load (Aydinalp et al., 2004; Mihalakakou et al., 2002), and hot-water heating load (Aydinalp et al., 2004). Moreover, According to Capozzoli et al. ANN is a useful method for the detection of faults in lighting electrical consumption (Capozzoli et al., 2015b).

Fan et al. (2014) proposed a data mining approach for predicting next-day energy demand and peak power demand of the tallest building in Hong Kong. This novel methodology can be summarized in three steps: pre-processing, variable selection, and prediction model construction. The first step was to identify abnormal daily energy consumption profiles. The outlier detection was performed through the merge of feature extraction techniques, clustering analysis, and the generalized extreme studentized deviate (GESD) method. The second step was to select the optimal inputs to develop eight predictive models (MLR, autoregressive integrated moving average (ARIMA), SVR, random forests (RF), multi-layer perceptron (MLP), boosting tree (BT), multivariate adaptive regression splines (MARS), and k-nearest neighbors (kNN)). The parameters of each model were then obtained through leave-group-out cross validation (LGOCV). Finally, a genetic algorithm (GA) was used to optimize the weight of each model. The main objective is to achieve accuracy of prediction better than those of base models through data-driven model ensembling. The results show that the methodology is robust and avoids over fitting problems.

6.2 ENERGY PROFILING IN BUILDINGS

Energy profiling can provide information on the pattern of both the whole building's total energy use and each end-use, based on different time scales. Besides this, it can help building managers to investigate the discrepancies of energy use characteristics between different seasons, working day and non-working day, day and night, peak and base, etc.

Energy profiling is developed from the application of data mining techniques and pattern recognition on historical energy consumption data. There are two expected goals to achieve and these can be summarized as follows:

- Detection of users' typical load profiles;
- Identification of anomalous trends.

In Ramos et al. (2015) a data-mining-based methodology to characterize typical load profiles of MV customers in Portugal, was proposed. The representative electrical load profiles were obtained through cluster analysis. After data partitioning, a classification model was applied to include a new customer in one of the four clusters obtained. Typical load profiles allow the energy supplier to set automatic classification rules for new customers. For distribution companies, as for customers, knowledge of typical profiles can bring many advantages in terms of applicable tariff plan in the day-ahead energy market.

In the past decade, the growing availability of monitored temporal data, such as time series data, produced a renewed interest in the field of data mining. Time series represent the most important class of sequential data, in which records are indexed by time.

Time series data are characterized by high dimensionality and continuous updating. On the other hand, the potential research direction in time series area attracts more and more experts due to their complexity. The nature of time series data introduces a new concept of similarity between samples. The similarity based on exact match is replaced by the approximation-based approach. One of the most important objectives of temporal data mining (eg, on energy consumption time series) is finding similar profiles in a time series through the subsequent search of *motifs*. Unlike search and retrieval applications, in the pattern discovery approach there is no specific query to search in a database. The aim is simply to exploit all patterns of interest.

This requires dimensionality reduction and data segmentation. Keogh and Pazzani (2000) proposed a method for time series representation, aimed at reducing the dimension of original data. This method called piecewise aggregate approximation (PAA), is based on a temporal segmentation in which the mean value of each segment represents the set of data points included in that segment. Moreover, Lin et al. (2007) proposed a method called Symbolic Aggregate approXimation (SAX) in order to convert the output of PAA into a symbolic string. In this method, considering a standardized time series (previously reduced with PAA), it is possible to obtain equally probable areas under the standard Gaussian curve that are represented by a symbol (eg, alphabetic letter). The symbols subsequence establishes a symbolic string that is consistent with the time series. The more frequent patterns are defined as *motif* while the infrequent patterns are categorized as *discord*.

It is clear that the opportunity to identify typical load profiles (in terms of a symbolic string) makes it possible to detect abnormal (infrequent) profiles. In energy profiling applications, the detection of anomalies should take place at the single values level as well as at trend energy level. In Miller et al. (2015) an automated daily pattern filtering of building energy performance data was developed. SAX, motif and discord extraction, and cluster analysis were applied in two different case studies with different end-use and weather conditions (international school campus in a tropical climate, an office building from a temperate European climate). For the first case study anomalous daily profiles, due to cooling system faults, were found. Moreover, for both case studies reference profiles that may be used in modeling calibration were produced.

Therefore, pattern recognition and clustering techniques can detect an anomalous consumption profile and are particularly suitable for FDD purpose. In our opinion, data mining may be the most suitable approach for intelligent load profiling analysis of smart buildings.

Moreover, as in any other field of research, the extractable knowledge from data is directly proportional to the awareness of the domain expert that provides the analysis.

6.3 FAULT DETECTION AND DIAGNOSIS

In Section 6.1 several prediction models were presented that are also useful tools in the detection of anomalies in building energy consumption. For example, a residual analysis between predicted and measured data can be used as an intelligent real-time system for fault detection. For this purpose, the premises are the absence of anomalies in the training dataset of a prediction model and a high level of accuracy and robustness. Nowadays, there is an increasing awareness of the fact that, during operations, buildings do not meet designers' expectations. According to Wu and Sun (2011), around 20% of energy consumption in buildings is attributable to incorrect system configurations and inappropriate operating procedures. For example, in commercial buildings inefficient system plants waste an estimated 15–30% of energy used (Schein et al., 2006; Katipamula and Brambley, 2005). The growing availability of building-related data (eg, energy consumption) collected and stored through energy management and control systems offers analysts the possibility of evaluating the occurrence, location and cause of the fault (Isermann, 2005).

Therefore, powerful robust and efficient methodologies are required to transform a huge amount of data into useful knowledge. In the literature, it is possible to identify two different fundamental approaches to FDD in buildings (Seem, 2007): a component level approach and a whole building approach. The bottom-up approach (component level) refers to the system equipment faults. The top-down approach (whole building level) focuses on the total building energy consumption (cooling, heating and electrical demand).

In the last few years, several studies have been conducted on both approaches. In Khan et al. (2013), a data mining based methodology was proposed to analyze real-time hourly measured energy and power consumption data for lighting in an office building. Statistical-based, distance-based, deviation-based and density-based methods were used in order to analyze abnormal energy consumption. For this purpose, classification of data is the first step before detecting potential outliers. CART, K-Means and DBSCAN algorithms respectively have been used. The GESD algorithm was used to find outlier values in each class and cluster resulting from CART and K-Means outcomes. The DBSCAN is able to directly identify the outliers, grouping them in an isolated cluster, automatically. Finally, a comparison of methods has been carried out. Results show that the proposed approach is robust and minimizes time for fault detection.

ARM was utilized with the aim of examining all associations and correlations among building operational data and to discover useful knowledge about energy conservation (Yu et al., 2013). The procedure was able to identify energy waste in the air-conditioning system, detect equipment faults (eg, if fans in a fresh air handling unit have a fault) and propose low/no cost strategies for saving energy in system operation.

Seem (2007) provided a method for deducing information on weekly energy consumption changes by grouping days with similar power consumption. This method was used to evaluate abnormal energy demand through comparison with previous energy consumption.

Lauro et al. (2014) developed a hybrid statistical and inferential methodology for FDD at component level. Firstly, fault detection was performed on fan coils' energy-consumption monitored data using peak detection and density-based clustering methods. A modified Z-score index was used in order to quantify the severity of abnormal values identified. Secondly, fuzzy sets and fuzzy logic were implemented for the purpose of fault diagnosis. Fuzzy logic represents an extension of Boolean logic, which uses a set of rules to define the causal interaction between input and output variables.

Dodier and Kreider (1999) presented a method suitable for detecting faults in energy consumption at both whole building (total thermal energy) and component (eg, chiller electric consumption) level. To determine abnormal energy consumption they used an energy consumption index (ECI). The ECI is the ratio of real energy consumption to predicted energy consumption using neural network. If the ratio is between a fixed lower limit (eg, 0.875) and upper limit (eg, 1.125) the system works normally.

Energy indicators are useful tools, which help energy managers identify significant variations in building energy consumption. Energy indicators are also widely used in benchmarking applications, for example to determine if a building is more efficient than other similar buildings.

6.4 BENCHMARKING

The main goal of a benchmarking system is to evaluate the divergence between the energy consumption of a building and a reference value. To achieve this, a benchmarking system should be able to obtain a reference building from a sample of similar buildings. Hence, in these kinds of analysis it is important to take into account the various factors that can generate different energy performance in buildings such as: abnormal weather conditions, building physical characteristics, occupant behavior, and system malfunctioning.

Depending on the application of the benchmarking system, it is possible to develop different methods for public benchmarking (previous performance of similar buildings, current performance of similar buildings) and internal benchmarking (previous performance of the same building, and intended performance of the same building). In public authorities and institutions in order to achieve energy efficiency in their buildings, the first two benchmarking systems are used. The other methods are applied internally for continuous energy commissioning.

According to the literature, benchmarking methods can be categorized as follows: simple normalization, ordinary least square (OLS), data envelopment analysis (DEA), stochastic frontier analysis (SFA), the model-based method (simulation), and ANN (Chung, 2011).

Simple normalization provides performance indicators, like kWh/m^2 or MJ/m^2, which represent energy-use reference values, which are useful for building users.

Authors in Acquaviva et al. (2015) proposed two KPI indicators based on the energy signature computed through a Big Data methodology. The energy signature of a building is obtained by a linear regression of the power used for heating on the difference between the internal temperature and the external temperature. This method is used to estimate the total heat loss coefficient of a building, which is considered a key envelope indicator. Specifically the energy signature analysis (ESA) system, presented in Acquaviva et al. (2015), provides scalable and distributed analytics services in near real-time to compute different KPIs. The most interesting ones are the following:

- The intra-building KPI compares latest observations with past energy demand in the same conditions, for example in a similar outdoor temperature and indoor temperature.
- The inter-building KPI ranks the overall building performance with respect to nearby and similarly characterized buildings by considering spatial co-location, building size, usage patterns (eg, residential, office, public building).
  A simple KPI is represented by the average energy consumption per unit of volume.
- Building KPI: calculated for single buildings. It can also be normalized according to the degree-days and the known indoor temperature.
- Neighborhood KPI: calculated for buildings in the same neighborhood.
- Building-type KPI: calculated on buildings of the same type and in the same neighborhood.
- Climate KPI: calculated on all buildings of the same type and in the same neighborhood, considering only consumption during specific outdoor conditions (temperature range).

Moreover, regression-based systems have a better capacity for taking into account factors that can affect energy performance in buildings. Sharp (1995) developed a stepwise linear regression model in order to evaluate the influencers of EUIs for office buildings. The main factors taken into account were: building size, number of workers, number of computers, occupancy, operating schedule, presence of an economizer and presence of a chiller. Regression residuals were used as measures of energy inefficiency. The main problem for regression-based benchmarking systems is to avoid multicollinearity risk, especially in the case of a large dataset, which may compromise the estimations' robustness. As mentioned above, another advanced method is the ANN. Wong et al. (2010) used an ANN model in the evaluation of the energy performance of office buildings located in Hong Kong. The results show that the ANN model achieves more accuracy in the prediction of electricity use for periods in which the energy end-use is evident (ie, summer cooling and winter heating). Starting from this assumption the multi-criteria approach (Lee and Lin, 2011), based on the different energy end-uses (eg, heating, cooling, lighting, appliances) is more suitable than the single-angle benchmarking (eg, total energy consumption). According to this Wang (2015) derived seven quantitative efficiency indicators for a comprehensive multi-criteria benchmarking. Considering different indicators at the same time reduces the level of similarity required between the buildings to be compared. On the other hand, there is an increase in the detail of information to be collected from each building.

The authors think that energy benchmarks facilitate the allocation of necessary funds for building energy retrofit in the public or private sector. In this context, prediction models need to be highly accurate and robust. Moreover, it is important for these models to be easily understood by all those involved in energy planning from single building to large building stock.

6.5 OCCUPANT BEHAVIOR

Among the various factors influencing building energy consumption, occupant behavior plays an essential role. Occupant behavior is associated with various activities that have a direct or indirect impact upon building energy consumption.

According to D'Oca and Hong (2014) it is possible to group all the factors that influence the occupant actions into five main categories. These typological factors called "drivers" contain external and individual parameters:

- Physical driver: the internal and external environment, such as temperature, wind speed, humidity, illumination, odor;
- Contextual driver: the building characteristics, such as dimensions, insulation, type of heating system;
- Psychological driver: the drive to satisfy needs;
- Physiological driver: age, activity level and health;
- Social driver: interaction between occupants.

The stochastic nature of the phenomena related to occupant behavior makes a forward approach particularly complicated. For this reason, there recently has been growing interest in the study of occupant behavior to evaluate possible energy saving that may be achievable through a data-driven approach.

For example, the usage of certain electrical devices in buildings can be inferred from the total daily (or monthly, annual) energy consumption. Different studies have been carried out in residential buildings in particular. Ouyang and Hokao (2009) investigated achievable energy-saving by improving user behavior in 124 households in China. In this study, these houses were divided into two groups: in the first group occupants received energy-saving education while in the other group, the occupants' behavior remained unchanged. The results show how, in energy consumption, the sociological aspect of occupants is a factor that is as important as it is uncertain.

From the comparisons between the monthly household electricity usage for both groups, it was found that energy-conscious behavior could reduce household electricity consumption by more than 10%.

An in-depth study of occupant behavior can be useful in fine-tuning energy simulations in order to get more realistic results in terms of the potential energy saving that can be achieved.

Al-Mumin et al. (2003) simulated occupant behavior improvement by using the energy simulation program ENERWIN. The first step was to collect data and information on occupancy patterns and operation schedules of electrical devices in 30 residences in Kuwait. The second step was to simulate occupant behavior by using ENERWIN with default values and modified values after data collection. The results show that this approach is more suitable for estimating annual electricity consumption reduction.

Also in Yu et al. (2011) a methodology for identifying and improving occupant behavior in residential buildings was developed. End-use loads of various electrical devices were used to deduce user activities indirectly. The first step was to divide these end-use loads into two levels (main and sub-category) that referred to two-level activities. A building with the most comprehensive household appliances was identified and used as a case building. The remaining buildings were grouped into four clusters by using a K-means clustering algorithm. The typical occupant behavior was characterized within each cluster. Finally, the case building was compared with the other buildings in order to detect possible energy inefficiency linked to occupant behavior. A rules set was used in order to discover associations between different user activities.

The methodology allows designers to identify the behavior that should be modified, and to provide occupants with recommendations. For example, the results in Yu et al. (2013) have demonstrated that the use of a TV (in the master bedroom on the second floor of the considered apartment) would quite possibly lead to the use of a lamp on the second floor. The reason for this may have been that the building's occupants always turned the lights on when they were watching TV. An effective way of reducing energy consumption in this building is to watch TV with a dim light. In D'Oca and Hong (2014) a data mining based approach is proposed to identify useful patterns of window opening and closing scenarios in an office building naturally ventilated, located in Germany. A three step process was developed. Firstly, a logistic regression was applied to the collective data on window opening behavior. The main objective was to identify and characterize the most important influencing factors. Secondly, a cluster analysis was applied to obtain different behavioral patterns. Finally, through an associations rule set, the occupants were split into different user profiles. The results show that occupants in naturally ventilated buildings accept a wide range of temperatures.

Moreover, in D'Oca and Hong (2015) a data set of 16 offices (differently exposed to the solar radiation) using 10 min' interval occupancy data is mined over a 2-year period. The K-means algorithm was used to disaggregate the occupants in four occupancy clusters. The results show that real working profiles may vary significantly during the course of the week and can be broadly different from the default profiles suggested in building energy modeling programs, like EnergyPlus or IDA-ICE. The calibrated models (eg, on occupancy) have the task of reproducing properties of behavioral patterns to be checked during model validation. Clearly, this kind of calibration represents a complex issue.

In these aforementioned works, it is clear that in occupant behavior applications, both forward and data-driven approaches are useful in identifying and quantifying potential energy saving in buildings.

7 LESSONS LEARNED

The application of data analytics algorithms represents a powerful opportunity to extract useful information from the building-related data to enhance energy efficiency. Moreover, data warehouse technology can be effectively exploited to store a large volume of heterogeneous energy-related data and support the decision-making process.

The applications discussed in the previous section demonstrate the usefulness of data analytics technologies in building engineering. The prediction of building energy consumption is a fundamental tool for the evaluation of building performance, for the optimization of a building's operation, for the detection and diagnosis of faults and for demand side management. The ensembling of different methods can provide better accuracy than base models. In particular, an ensemble approach can improve fault detection by minimizing false anomalies and identifying types of faults. The authors believe that an automated approach in this kind of application will support the Building Energy Management System (BEMS) in real-time maintenance tasks by monitoring and detecting outliers in the energy consumption time series. Moreover, automating the process will help energy managers avoid manual detection of faults.

The planning of ordinary management activities and strategic planning, which target energy efficiency improvements, require robust estimation models. The measures that a public authority adopt in order to accomplish energy savings in the building sector can be based on an actions list that takes into account the priority in the renovation of single buildings grouped in the same stock. For this purpose, it is extremely important to quickly and reliably estimate energy consumption in buildings.

Moreover, knowledge of the typical load profiles can provide many advantages for different actors. In the electrical energy market it may enable the establishment of business contracts between distributers and suppliers in the liberalized market.

Regarding occupant behavior, the classification tree and rule models can be used to understand repetitive occupancy patterns in order to optimize operation, maintenance and energy performance both at the single office and at the office building level. Extracted knowledge can effectively enhance user awareness of their energy and thermal consumption and encourage them to pursue energy saving strategies. Knowledge extracted from energy-related data produces useful feedback for users and suggests ready-to-implement energy efficient actions.

Although, data analytics technologies can process massive data effectively, its application in buildings remains a great challenge.

A plethora of both general purpose and tailored algorithms are available for each data mining technique, and in most cases no algorithm is universally superior. Several issues determine which algorithm performs best, including input data cardinality, data distribution and the analysis end-goal. The selection of an optimal algorithm, as well as the tuning of its parameters, has to be manually performed by an experienced computer scientist, seeking a good trade-off between execution time and accuracy. Finally, to extract meaningful and interesting knowledge items, while keeping the number of extracted results within manageable limits, a large number of experiments should be performed and the results manually evaluated by a domain expert. The whole process requires a considerable amount of expertise and effort. Thus, new scalable approaches capable of self-configuring to automatically extract actionable knowledge from massive energy-related data repositories will fuel the next generation of miner system.

8 CONCLUSIONS AND EMERGING TRENDS IN DATA ANALYTICS TECHNOLOGIES

In today's world large volumes of energy-related data have continuously been generated in Smart Cities environment at an unprecedented rate, to such an extent that the volume of energy data is rapidly scaling towards "Big Data." Hence, analyzing energy datasets often becomes computationally prohibitive. To efficiently analyze Big Data collection, a promising research direction is the design and development of distributed solutions.

The interest in Big Data solutions and innovation is continuously growing both in the industrial and research domains. Industries are attracted by the business opportunities arising from the design and implementation of hardware technologies and applications to effectively support all the crucial aspects of Big-Data management. Researchers, instead, are interested in the challenging issues coming from the application of innovative data management and mining techniques to new and more complex fields (eg, energy-related data) as well as the design of innovative systems able to continuously monitor a wide geographical area and collect a large volume of heterogeneous and rich data. When dealing with Big Data collections, such as energy-related datasets, the computational cost of the data mining process (and in some cases the feasibility of the process itself) can potentially become a critical bottleneck in data analysis. To date, parallel and distributed approaches have been adopted to increase efficiency and scalability. The current trend explored by cloud providers, such as Windows Azure, is that OS offering an increasingly heterogeneous portfolio of online services in the cloud, spanning traditional IaaS (Infrastructure-as-a-Service) and PaaS (Platform-as-a-Service) as well as business analytics-oriented cloud-based tools. Different research has also focused on designing and implementing systems based on Big-Data technologies to provide different cloud-based analytics services.

Proposed solutions are general purpose (Zulkernine et al., 2013) or tailored to a given application domain, such as thermal energy consumption (Anjos et al., 2014), residential energy use (Wang et al., 2009), renewable energy (Lu et al., 2013), air pollution levels (Rios and Diguerez, 2014). Authors in Zulkernine et al. (2013) highlight the key features that should be included in an analytics cloud service.

Thereafter, the conceptual architecture of a Big Data analytics service provisioning platform in the cloud (CLAaaS) is presented. The platform will provide on-demand data storage and analytics services through customized user interfaces and will apply Service Level Agreements (SLAs) to provide controlled access to software and data resources. The components of the proposed platform are grouped into three functional categories: service management, workflow management, and data management.

The EDEN system (Acquaviva, 2015) a digital platform for energy data engagement, connects sensors, buildings, people, and providers. EDEN exploits data coming from sensors that monitor district heating networks and from public web services to: (i) provide enriched energy information, (ii) suggest energy-saving strategies, (iii) enhance users' energy awareness, and (iv) reduce building energy consumption. Specifically, EDEN monitors and analyses the thermal energy consumption of building heating systems, it engages people by collecting feedback and making them aware of their energy and thermal consumption and encourages users to pursue energy-saving strategies, thus stimulating sustainable behaviors to optimize energy consumption.

A parallel effort has focused on the design and implementation of a distributed system, named ESA (Acquaviva et al., 2015), to constantly inform users about their energy consumption and building performance. ESA exploits a Big-Data approach to perform a scalable and distributed computation of the building energy signature in terms of the computation of the total heat loss coefficient estimation, whose aim is twofold: to evaluate and rank building efficiency/performance over time, and to forecast the power demand.

Both EDEN and ESA have been designed and developed as a cloud-based service on top of a MongoDB distributed cluster. The MapReduce jobs of all energy consumption KPIs (in EDEN) as well as the estimation of the total heat loss coefficient (in ESA) were developed through custom JavaScript functions, and executed using the MongoDB Map Reduce framework.

As researchers in energy-related applications and technologies we believe that data mining and machine learning techniques provide great potential when applied to building energy applications. Furthermore, energy data analysis has to deal with massive datasets, typical examples of Big Data. Less effort has been spent in this direction, as witnessed by the scientific literature. The Apache Hadoop platform, together with its extensions, such as Apache Spark, being the current de-facto standard in the big data environment, is currently considered the most promising foundation for building an effective data analytics framework for energy data. Being able not only to collect but also to analyze Big Data collections will be of huge value from both an economic and a social point of view. In the data mining domain, most of the technologies involved in Big-Data analytics have to be redesigned and adapted to the main features of energy data.

ACRONYMS

ANN	artificial neural network
ANOVA	analysis of variance
ARIMA	autoregressive integrated moving average
ARM	association rule mining
ASHRAE	American Society of Heating, Refrigerating, and Air-Conditioning Engineers
BEMS	Building Energy Management System
BT	boosting tree
CART	classification and regression tree
DBMS	database management system
DEA	data envelopment analysis
DM	data mining
DSM	demand-side management
ECI	energy consumption index
ESA	energy signature analysis
EUI	energy use intensity
FDD	fault detection and diagnosis
GA	genetic algorithm
GESD	generalized extreme studentized deviate
HDFS	Hadoop distributed file system
IEA	International Energy Agency
kNN	k-nearest neighbors
KPI	key performing indicators
LGOCV	leave-group-out cross validation
LTLF	long-term load forecasting
MARS	multivariate adaptive regression splines
M&V	measurement and verification
MLP	multi-layer perceptron
MLR	multiple linear regression
MTLF	medium-term load forecasting
MV	medium voltage
NoSQL	not only structured query language
OLS	ordinary least square
PAA	piecewise aggregate approximation
PWS	personal weather stations
RF	random forests
SAX	symbolic aggregate approximation
SFA	stochastic frontier analysis
STLF	short-term load forecasting
SVM	support vector machines
SVR	support vector regression

GLOSSARY

Apache Hadoop platform an open-source software to efficiently support reliable, scalable, and distributed computing. It supports simple programming models for the distributed processing large data collections across clusters of computers.

Energy data management and mining system a set of tools able to efficiently store, manage and analyze different kinds of energy data.

Key performance indicator (KPI) a type of performance measurement computed over the time to compactly represent the performance of the object under analysis.

Model ensembling ensemble methods use multiple learning algorithms in order to achieve better predictive performance than it could be obtained from any of the constituent single algorithms.

Personal weather station (PWS) a private device including different weather measuring instruments/sensors. Each sensor is able to measure a kind of meteorological data such as temperature, relative humidity, pressure, rain fall, wind speed and direction.

TECHNICAL WORDS

Association rules
Classification algorithms
Classification tree
Artificial neural network
Support vector machine
Cluster analysis
DBSCAN algorithm
K-means algorithm
Key performance indicator
Apache Hadoop platform
Benchmarking
Fault detection
Multiple linear regression

REFERENCES

Acquaviva, A., 2015. Enhancing energy awareness through the analysis of thermal energy consumption. In: Proceedings of the Workshops of the EDBT/ICDT, vol. 1330, pp. 64–71.

Acquaviva, A., et al., 2015. Energy signature analysis: knowledge at your fingertips. In: IEEE International Congress on Big Data, pp. 543–550.

Ahmad, A.S., Hassan, M.Y., Abdullah, M.P., Rahman, H.A., Hussinm, F., Abdullah, H., 2014. A review on applications of ANN and SVM for building electrical energy consumption forecasting. Renew. Sust. Energy Rev. 33, 102–109.

Al-Mumin, A., Khattab, O., Sridhar, G., 2003. Occupants' behavior and activity patterns influencing the energy consumption in the Kuwaiti residences. Energy Build. 35, 549–559.

Anjos, D., Carreira, P., Francisco, A.P., 2014. Real-time integration of building energy data. In: IEEE International Congress on Big Data, pp. 250–257.

Aranda, A., Ferreira, G., Mainar-Toledo, M.D., Scarpellini, S., Sastresa, E.L., 2012. Multiple regression models to predict the annual energy consumption in the Spanish banking sector. Energy Build. 49, 380–387.

Ardakanian, O., Koochakzadeh, N., Singh, R.P., Golab, L., Keshav, S., 2014. Computing electricity consumption profiles from household smart meter data. In: EDBT/ICDT Workshops'14, pp. 140–147.

ASHRAE, 2009. Energy estimating and modeling methods. Chapter 19.

Aydinalp, M., Ugursal, V.I., Fung, A.S., 2004. Modeling of the space and domestic hot-water heating energy-consumption in the residential sector using neural networks. Appl. Energy 79, 159–178.

Babaei, T., Abdi, H., Lim, C.P., Nahavandi, S., 2015. A study and a directory of energy consumption data sets of buildings. Energy Build. 94, 91–99.

Capozzoli, A., Grassi, D., Causone, F., 2015a. Estimation models of heating energy consumption in schools for local authorities planning. Energy Build. 105 (January 2006), 302–313.

Capozzoli, A., Lauro, F., Khan, I., 2015b. Fault detection analysis using data mining techniques for a cluster of smart office buildings. Expert Syst. Appl. 42, 4324–4338.

Chodorow, K., Dirolf, M., 2010. MongoDB: The Definitive Guide. O'Reilly Media, Sebastopol, CA.

Chung, W., 2011. Review of building energy-use performance benchmarking methodologies. Appl. Energy 88 (5), 1470–1479.

Corgnati, S.P., Bednar, T., Jang, Y., Yoshino, H., Filippi, M., Danov, S., Nord, N., Schweiker, M., Ghiaus C., Capozzoli, A., Talà, N., Fabi, V., 2013. Total energy use in buildings. Analysis and evaluation methods. Final report Annex 53. Statistical analysis and prediction methods. Institute for Building Environment and Energy Conservation, pp. 1–246.

Depuru, S., Wang, L.D.V., Nelapati, P., 2011. A hybrid neural network model and encoding technique for enhanced classification of energy consumption data. In: Power and Energy Society General Meeting, pp. 1–8.

D'Oca, S., Hong, T., 2014. A data-mining approach to discover patterns of window opening and closing behavior in offices. Build. Environ. 82, 726–739.

D'Oca, S., Hong, T., 2015. Occupancy schedules learning process through a data mining framework. Energy Build. 88, 395–408.

Dodier, R.F., Kreider, J.F., 1999. Detecting whole building energy problems. ASHRAE Trans. 105 (1), 579–589.

Dong, B., Cao, C., Lee, S.E., 2005. Applying support vector machines to predict building energy consumption in tropical region. Energy Build. 37, 545–553.

Ester, M., Kriegel, H.P., Sander, J., Xu, X., 1996. A density-based algorithm for discovering clusters in large spatial databases with noise. Knowl. Discov. Data Min., 226–231.

Fan, C., Xiao, F., Wang, S., 2014. Development of prediction models for next-day building energy consumption and peak power demand using data mining techniques. Appl. Energy 127, 1–10.

Fan, C., Xiao, F., Yan, C., 2015. A framework for knowledge discovery in massive building automation data and its application in building diagnostics. Autom. Constr. 50, 81–90.

Filippn, C., Larsen, S.F., 2009. Analysis of energy consumption patterns in multi-family housing in a moderate cold climate. Energy Policy 37 (9), 3489–3501.

Hastie, T., Tibshirani, R., Friedman, J., 2009. The Elements of Statistical Learning: DataMining, Inference and Prediction. Springer Series in Statistics, New York.

Heo, Y., Zavala, V.M., 2012. Gaussian process modeling for measurement and verification of building energy savings. Energy Build. 53, 7–18.

Hsu, D., 2015. Comparison of integrated clustering methods for accurate and stable prediction of building energy consumption data. Appl. Energy. 160, 153–63.

Isermann, R., 2005. Fault Diagnosis Systems. An Introduction From Fault Detection to Fault Tolerance. Springer, Berlin.

Juang, B.H., Rabiner, L., 1990. The segmental k-means algorithm for estimating parameters of hidden markov models. IEEE Trans. Acoust. Speech Signal Process. 38 (9), 1639–1641.

Katipamula, S., Brambley, M., 2005. Review article: methods for fault detection, diagnostics, and prognostics for building systems—a review. part II. HVAC&R Res. 11 (1), 169–187.

Kaufman, L., Rousseeuw, P.J., 1990. Finding Groups in Data: An Introduction to Cluster Analysis. Wiley, New York.

Keogh, E., Pazzani, M., 2000. A simple dimensionality reduction technique for fast similarity search in large time series databases. In: Proceedings of the 4th Pacific-Asia Conference on Knowledge Discovery and Data Mining, Current Issues and New Applications, 122–133.

Khan, I., Capozzoli, A., Corgnati, S.P., Cerquitelli, T., 2013. Fault detection analysis of building energy consumption using data mining techniques. Energy Procedia 42, 557–566.

Lauro, F., Moretti, F., Capozzoli, A., Khan, I., Pizzuti, S., Macas, M., 2014. Building fan coil electric consumption analysis with fuzzy approaches for fault detection and diagnosis. Energy Procedia 62, 411–420.

Lazos, D., Sproul, A.B., Kay, M., 2014. Optimisation of energy management in commercial buildings with weather forecasting inputs: a review. Renew. Sust. Energy Rev. 39, 587–603.

Lee, W., Lin, Y., 2011. Evaluating and ranking energy performance of office buildings using grey relational analysis. Energy 36 (5), 2551–2556.

Li, Q., Meng, Q., Cai, J., Yoshino, H., Mochida, A., 2009. Predicting hourly cooling load in the building: a comparison of support vector machine and different artificial neural networks. Energy Convers. Manag. 50 (1), 90–96.

Li, Z., Huang, G., 2013. Re-evaluation of building cooling load prediction models for use in humid subtropical area. Energy Build. 62, 442–449.

Lin, J., Keogh, E., Wei, L., Lonardi, S., 2007. Experiencing SAX: a novel symbolic representation of time series. Data Min. Knowl. Discov. 15, 107–144.

Lu, S., Liu, Y., Meng, D., 2013. Towards a collaborative simulation platform for renewable energy systems. IEEE Ninth World Congress on Services, SERVICES 2013, Santa Clara, CA, USA, June 28–July 3, 2013, pp. 9–12.

Manfren, M., Aste, N., Moshksar, R., 2013. Calibration and uncertainty analysis for computer models–a meta-model based approach for integrated building energy simulation. Appl. Energy 103, 627–641.

Mihalakakou, G., Santamouris, M., Tsangrassoulis, A., 2002. On the energy consumption in residential buildings. Energy Build. 34, 727–736.

Mikučionienė, R., Martinaitis, V., Keras, E., 2014. Evaluation of energy efficiency measures sustainability by decision tree method. Energy Build. 76, 64–71.

Miller, C., Nagy, Z., Schlueter, A., 2015. Automation in construction automated daily pattern filtering of measured building performance data. Autom. Constr. 49, 1–17.

Ouyang, J., Hokao, K., 2009. Energy-saving potential by improving occupants' behavior in urban residential sector in Hangzhou City, China. Energy Build. 41, 711–720.

Pang-Ning, T., Steinbach, M., Kumar, V., 2006. Introduction to Data Mining. Addison-Wesley.

Pedersen, L., 2007. Use of different methodologies for thermal load and energy estimations in buildings including meteorological and sociological input parameters. 11 (1364), 998–1007.

Ramos, S., Duarte, J.M., Duarte, F.J., Vale, Z., 2015. A data-mining-based methodology to support MV electricity customers' characterization. Energy Build. 91, 16–25.

Rios, L.G., Diguerez, J.A.I., 2014. Big data infrastructure for analyzing data generated by wireless sensor networks. In: IEEE International Congress on Big Data, pp. 816–823.

Schein, J., Bushby, S.T., Castro, N.S., House, J.M., 2006. A rule-based fault detection method for air handling units. Energy Build. 38, 1485–1492.

Seem, J., 2007. Using intelligent data analysis to detect abnormal energy consumption in buildings. Energy Build. 39, 52–58.

Sharp, T., 1995. Energy benchmarking in commercial office buildings. In: ACEEE Summer Study on Energy Efficiency in Buildings, vol. 4, pp. 321–329.

Van der Veen, J., van der Waaij, B., Meijer, R., 2012. Sensor data storage performance: SQL or NoSQL, physical or virtual. In: IEEE 5th International Conference on Cloud Computing (CLOUD), 2012, pp. 431–438.

Wang, C., de Groot, M., Marendy, P., 2009. A service-oriented system for optimizing residential energy use. IEEE International Conference on Web Services, ICWS, vol. 2009, pp. 735–742.

Wang, E., 2015. Benchmarking whole-building energy performance with multi-criteria technique for order preference by similarity to ideal solution using a selective objective-weighting approach. Appl. Energy 146, 92–103.

Wijayasekara, D., Linda, O., Manic, M., Rieger, C., 2014. Mining building energy management system data using fuzzy anomaly detection and linguistic descriptions. IEEE Trans. Ind. Inform. 10 (3), 1829–1840.

Wong, S.L., Wan, K.K.W., Lam, T.N.T., 2010. Artificial neural networks for energy analysis of office buildings with daylighting. Appl. Energy 87 (2), 551–557.

Wu, S., Sun, J.Q., 2011. Cross-level fault detection and diagnosis of building HVAC systems. Build. Environ. 46 (8), 1558–1566.

Xiao, F., Fan, C., 2014. Data mining in building automation system for improving building operational performance. Energy Build. 75, 109–118.

Yiu, J.C.M., Wang, S., 2007. Multiple ARMAX modeling scheme for forecasting air conditioning system performance. Energy Convers. Manag. 48, 2276–2285.

Yu, Z., Fung, B.C.M., Haghighat, F., 2013. Extracting knowledge from building-related data–a data mining framework. Build. Simul. 6, 207–222.

Yu, Z., Haghighat, F., Fung, B.C.M., Yoshino, H., 2010. A decision tree method for building energy demand modeling. Energy Build. 42 (10), 1637–1646.

Yu, Z.J., Haghighat, F., Fung, B.C.M., Morofsky, E., Yoshino, H., 2011. A methodology for identifying and improving occupant behavior in residential buildings. Energy 36 (11), 6596–6608.

Zhao, H.X., Magoulès, F., 2012. A review on the prediction of building energy consumption. Renew. Sust. Energy Rev. 16 (6), 3586–3592.

Zulkernine, F.H., Martin, P., Zou, Y., Bauer, M., Gwadry-Sridhar, F., Aboulnaga, A., 2013. Towards cloud-based analytics-as-a-service (claaas) for big data analytics in the cloud. In: IEEE International Congress on Big Data, BigData Congress, pp. 62–69.

Pervasive computing and applications

A failure detector based on processes' relevance and the confidence degree in the system for self-healing in ubiquitous environments

12

A.G.d.M. Rossetto[a], C.O. Rolim[b], V. Leithardt[b], G.A. Borges[b], C.F.R. Geyer[b], L. Arantes[c], P. Sens[c]

Federal Institute of Rio Grande do Sul (IFSUL), Passo Fundo, RS, Brazil[a]
Institute of Informatics, Federal University of Rio Grande do Sul, Porto Alegre, RS, Brazil[b]
Sorbonne Universités, UPMC Univ Paris 06, CNRS, INRIA, LIP6, Paris, France[c]

1 INTRODUCTION

Ubiquitous computing has its origins in the visionary work of Marc Weiser who, at the beginning of the 1990s, predicted the existence of environments saturated with computing devices and communication capabilities, highly integrated with human users (Weiser, 1991). The aim of ubiquitous computing is to make the devices as much as possible "invisible." They should operate with minimum user intervention and their functions must be transparent to users. However, due to the nature of ubiquitous systems, nodes (eg, sensors) are frequently prone to failure. These systems must, thus, present autonomic computing capabilities which render them more autonomous, to some extent, in the presence of failures so as not to depend on human intervention for preventing undesirable consequences (Sterritt, 2005) induced by the failures.

One of the properties of autonomic computing is self-healing. A system designed with this feature automatically discovers, diagnoses, and reacts to disruptions (Ganek and Corbi, 2003). The system must then be able to detect failures and make the necessary adjustments to prevent them from having an undesirable impact on the application which should keep active and available. Hence, a failure detection service which delivers monitory information about the functioning of the system nodes is a crucial feature for self-healing systems. In order to meet such a requirement, this work proposes a new unreliable failure detector (FD), denoted *Impact Failure Detector*.

Pervasive Computing. http://dx.doi.org/10.1016/B978-0-12-803663-1.00012-7

In our approach, we consider that the Impact FD is one of the components of a Self-healing Module (Rossetto et al., 2014). The latter aims to cater for the needs of ubiquitous systems which must manage applications that are distributed and adaptive to the changing requirements of the environment. Hence, a Self-healing Module should be available anywhere and at any time, deal with failures at run time and, whenever a failure is detected, it has to make the necessary adjustments to avoid error propagation which can result in major damage to the application. Notice that the self-healing module can be incorporated in any ubiquitous system, regardless of its architecture. Basically, it has two components: the FD and adaptation manager (AM), as shown in Fig. 2. The former consists of an adaptive unreliable FD that is responsible for detecting crash failures of different entities (nodes, sensor, etc.) that need to be monitored in the system. The AM provides suitable adaptation strategies, aiming at reducing the impact of the detected failure on the application. We emphasize that the focus of the current work is not the AM but to propose a suitable FD for service.

Contrary to traditional unreliable FDs (Chen et al., 2002; Bertier et al., 2003) that output the set of nodes suspected of having failed, the Impact FD outputs a *trust level* and a *status* (trusted or not trusted) concerning a given system S. The output can be considered as the degree of confidence in the system. To this end, an *impact factor*, defined by the user, is assigned to each node and the *trust level* is equal to the sum of the impact factor of trusted nodes, ie, those not suspected of failure. Furthermore, an input *threshold* parameter defines a trust level limit value, over which the confidence degree on S is not affected. Hence, by comparing the trust level with the *threshold*, the system is considered trusted or not. If it is not the case, the AM decides if some measures must be taken (urgently or not, with regard to the trust level output). In other words, when the FD informs, by *status* output, that S is not trusted, the AM analyzes the *trust level* output and make a decision about the recovery strategy and/or system reconfiguration.

In Hayashibara et al. (2004), the authors propose the Accrual ϕ FD which, similarly to our approach, outputs a suspicion level on a continuous scale. However, the ϕ FD does not analyze the output but just replays it to the application.

We should point out that both the *impact factor* and the *threshold* render the estimation of the confidence of S more flexible. For instance, it might happen that some processes in S are faulty or suspected of being faulty but S is still considered to be trusted. Consequently, the AM will be less requested, since there is some flexibility for nodes failure. Furthermore, the Impact FD is easily configurable and adaptive according to the needs of the application or system requirements that can dynamically change. For instance, the application may require a stricter monitoring of nodes during the night than during the day. For such an adaptation, it is only necessary to adjust the *threshold*.

This chapter is structured as follows. In Section 2 we provide a background regarding the self-healing property and unreliable FDs. In Section 3, some application scenarios are presented. In Section 4, the self-healing module is described and Section 5 presents the Impact FD. Section 6 presents some of the preliminary evaluation results obtained from experiments conducted with real traces on Planet-Lab (PlanetLab, 2014). Section 7 discusses some existing related studies. Finally, Section 8 concludes the paper and outlines some of our planned future research.

2 BACKGROUND

This section gives some background to self-healing and unreliable FDs . Firstly, we present some basic concepts about self-healing and discuss the challenges they raise for research. Then, we outline some principles about unreliable FDs and their implementation.

2.1 SELF-HEALING PROPERTY

According to Ghosh et al. (2007), self-healing can be defined as the property that enables a system to detect that it is not operating correctly and, without (or with) human intervention, make the necessary adjustments to restore itself to normalcy. The self-healing property has emerged from the autonomic computing paradigm introduced by IBM (Kephart and Chess, 2003) which states that the system must provide self-management. As the authors point out, the management of systems poses a real challenge since evolution of systems brings increasing total ownership costs. Hence, systems should be autonomous, to some extent, so as not to depend on human intervention when carrying out basic management tasks. Autonomic computing is designed to address the current concerns of complexity and total cost of ownership, since it is able to meet the needs of pervasive and ubiquitous computing as well as communication (Sterritt, 2005). In Kephart and Chess (2003), the authors divide the essential features of autonomic computing into four self properties which self-management systems must possess:

- *Self-configuring*: Readjust itself on-the fly;
- *Self-healing*: Discover, diagnose, and react to disruptions;
- *Self-optimization*: Maximize resource utilization to meet the needs of end-user;
- *Self-protection*: Anticipate, detect, identify, and protect itself from attacks.

In Sterritt (2005), the author argues that a system designed to have self-healing properties should be able to discover when its behavior deviates from its correct operation and automatically reconfigure itself in order to tolerate the deviation. This property provides an effective and automatic recovery service when faults are detected, since it not only masks the failures, but also identifies the problem and how to repair it, without any interruption to the service and a minimum external intervention. Its goal is to reduce the number of faults so that applications are kept active and available at all times.

As stated in Psaier and Dustdar (2011), a loop covering three stages (detecting, diagnosing, recovery) should be executed to achieve self-healing goals:

- Detecting: in this stage, any suspicious information received from reports or samples is filtered so that malicious information or attacks can be detected;
- Diagnosing: on the basis of any discovered attacks or threats, an analysis of the root cause is conducted and then an appropriate recovery plan is put into effect in accordance with the predefined policies;
- Recovery: the planned adaptations are then carefully applied to the system so that the system's constraints are taken into account and any unpredictable side effects are avoided.

The authors point out that in the self-healing concept, it is not trivial to make a distinction between the systems intentional states and its degraded or unacceptable ones. To tackle such a problem, it is thus necessary to define for a system the criteria considered to be "healthy" as well as thresholds that detect the system's "unhealthiness" and then launch a self-healing process (Ghosh et al., 2007) to restore the system to normalcy. Note that these criteria dynamically change whenever the use of the system is revised by the users or there are variations in the conditions under which the system operates. Therefore, there are fuzzy zones, ie, degraded states, which separate the acceptable from unacceptable behaviors of a system, which depend on the user choices and environmental changes. In our proposal (see Section 5), such a transition is tuned with a threshold parameter which defines a trust level limit value, over which the confidence degree in system is not affected.

Different strategies can be used to check or maintain the normal functionality of the system, ie, its health. They must be able to detect fuzzy zones and distinguish "healthy" states from "unhealthy" ones. The definition of what strategies will be adopted in the design of a self-healing system depends on the kind of the system and user requirements. In addition, contemporary large-scale networked systems have become highly distributed and allow new levels and structures of management and organization (Psaier and Dustdar, 2011). For instance, in Big Data stream systems, which need to implement security threat detection and prediction mechanisms that allow the processing of log data in real time for detecting rare events or unexpected online user behavior, traditionally this has been done by the off-line processing of log data (Xhafa et al., 2015). This brings up new challenges to the design of self-healing systems, which should find a satisfying trade-off between the vision of a perfectly functioning environment and the real requirements of an adaptive but at times not-fully operational runtime.

2.2 UNRELIABLE FAILURE DETECTORS

In the following of this article, we consider that there is one process by node (site) or sensor. Therefore, the word process can mean a node, sensor or site.

A *correct* process is a process that never fails during the whole execution; otherwise it is *faulty*.

In synchronous systems, message-transmission delays and process speed are bounded and known, such that a simple timeout mechanism can be used to surely assert if a node has failed or not. On the other hand, in asynchronous distributed systems there are no bounds on process speed neither are there on message delay. Therefore, no mechanism can ensure the failure of a remote process since it is impossible to know whether the latter has actually crashed or whether its message transmissions are delayed for some reason (Arantes et al., 2010).

An important abstraction for the development of fault-tolerant distributed systems is the unreliable FDs (Chandra and Toueg, 1996). Their aim is to encapsulate the uncertainty of the communication delay between two distributed nodes.

An unreliable FD can be seen as an oracle that gives information, not always correct, about processes failures and it is based on the state notion of process's (trusted or suspected). It thus usually provides a list of processes suspected of having crashed. According to Hayashibara et al. (2003), an unreliable FD module can make mistakes (1) by erroneously suspecting some correct process (false suspicion), or (2) by not suspecting a process that has actually crashed. If later, the FD detects its mistake, it corrects the mistake. For instance, FD can stop suspecting at time $t + 1$ some process that it suspected at time t. Unreliable FDs are characterized by two properties, *completeness* and *accuracy*, as defined in Chandra and Toueg (1996). The completeness is related to the FD capability of suspecting every faulty process permanently, while accuracy concerns the capability of not suspecting correct processes. FDs are then classified according to two completeness proprieties and four accuracy properties (Chandra and Toueg, 1996):

- Strong (resp. weak) completeness: Eventually every process that crashes is permanently suspected by every (resp. some) correct process.
- Strong (resp. weak) accuracy: No (resp. some) process is suspected before it crashes.
- Eventual strong (resp. weak) accuracy: There is a time after which correct processes (resp. some correct process) are (is) never suspected by any correct process.

Notice that the type of accuracy depends on the synchronism or stability of the network. For instance, a strong accuracy requires a synchronous system while an eventual strong one relies on a partially synchronous system, which eventually ensures a bound for message transmission delays and processes speed.

The combination of the above properties yields eight classes of FDs as shown in Table 1.

Table 1 Failure Detectors Classification

Completeness	Accuracy			
	Strong	Weak	Eventual strong	Eventual weak
Strong	P	S	$\Diamond P$	$\Diamond S$
Weak	Q	W	$\Diamond Q$	$\Diamond W$

Source: Based on Chandra, T.D., Toueg, S., 1996. Unreliable failure detectors for reliable distributed systems. J. ACM 43 (2), 225–267.

2.2.1 Implementation of failure detectors

The literature has several proposals for implementing unreliable FDs, which usually exploit either a *timer-based* or a *message-pattern* approach.

In the *timer-based* strategy, FD implementations make use of timers to detect failures in processes. Every process q periodically sends a control message (*heartbeat*) to process p that is responsible for monitoring q. If p does not receive such a message from q after the expiration of a timer, it adds q to its list of suspected processes. The use of *timeouts* assumes that the system is either synchronous or partially synchronous.

The *message-pattern* strategy does not use any mechanism of timeout. In Mostefaoui et al. (2003), the authors propose an implementation that uses a request-response mechanism. A process p sends a *QUERY* message to n nodes that it monitors and then waits for responses (*RESPONSE* message) from α processes ($\alpha \leq n$, traditionally $\alpha = n - f$, where f is the maximum number of failures). A query issued by p ends when it has received α responses. The other responses, if any, are discarded and the respective processes are suspected of having failed. A process sends *QUERY* messages repeatedly if it has not failed. If, on the next request-response, p receives a response from a suspected process q, then p removes q from its list of suspects. This approach considers the relative order for the receiving of messages that always (or after a time) allows some nodes to communicate faster than the others.

2.2.2 Estimation of heartbeat arrivals

Aiming at reducing both the number of false suspicions and the time to detect a failure, Chen et al. (2002) propose an approach to estimate the arrival of the next heartbeat which is based on the history of heartbeat arrival times and a safety margin (α). The timer is then set according to this estimation.

The estimation algorithm is the following: process p takes into account the n most recent heartbeat messages received from q, denoted by $m_1, m_2, \ldots, m_n$; $A_1, A_2, \ldots, A_n$ are their actual receipt times according to p's local clock. When at least n messages have been received, the theoretical arrival time $EA_{(k+1)}$ for a heartbeat from q is estimated by:

$$EA_{(k+1)} = \frac{1}{n} \sum_{i=k-n}^{k} (A_i - \Delta_i * i) + (k+1)\Delta_i$$

where Δ_i is the interval between the sending of two q's heartbeats. The next timeout value which will be set in p's timer and will expire at the next freshness point $\tau_{(k+1)}$, is then composed by $EA_{(k+1)}$ and the constant safety margin α:

$$\tau_{(k+1)} = \alpha + EA_{(k+1)}$$

Bertier et al. (2003) have extended Chen's approach by proposing an estimation function which combines Chen's with Jacobson's 1988 estimation. However, their approach is more suitable for LAN environments.

3 MOTIVATION SCENARIOS

The Impact FD can be applied to different distributed scenarios and it is flexible enough to meet different needs. It is quite suitable for environments where there is node redundancy or nodes with different capabilities. The following examples illustrate scenarios where the module can be used.

A system in the area of healthcare requires the use of several sensors to measure different kinds of information about the health status of a person, such as, vital signs, location, falls, gait patterns, and acceleration. From this perspective, this scenario is critical since faults in the components can risk the patient's life. For instance, let us consider a scenario with four sensors: q_1—*body temperature;* q_2—*pulse;* q_3—*electrocardiogram(ECG)*; and q_4—*galvanic skin* as well as node p, which is responsible for collecting information from these sensors and taking appropriate action based on the output of the Impact FD. In this example, some sensors are not considered to be critical, such as the sensor q_1 which measures the temperature. On the other hand, q_3, the ECG sensor, is crucial. Therefore, the impact factor assigned to q_3 should be higher than q_1's. Furthermore, q_3 collects data about both the heartbeats and electrical activity of the heart while q_2 is a type of sensor that also collects data about the heartbeats. Hence, there is redundancy of information, ie, the failure of the q_2 sensor is not critical enough to make the system vulnerable and endanger the life of the monitored person. We could then define a threshold that equals the sum of the impact factor of all the sensors minus q_2's impact factor since, the failure of q_2 does not jeopardize the trustworthiness of the system.

Another important scenario that motivates our proposal is Ubiquitous Wireless Sensor Networks (WSNs). These kinds of networks are deployed to monitor physical conditions in various places such as geographical regions, agricultural land, battlefields, etc. In WSNs, there are a variety of sensor nodes with different battery resources and communication or computation capabilities (Ishibashi and Yano, 2005). However, these sensors are prone to failures (eg, battery failure, process failure, transceiver failure, etc.) (Geeta et al., 2013). The Ubiquitous WSNs are usually used either in hostile or highly dynamic conditions, where human interference in the WSNs is very rare (Gaber and Hassanien, 2014). Hence, it is necessary to provide failure detection and adaptation strategies in order to ensure, as much as possible, that the failure of sensor nodes does not affect the overall task of the network. Redundant use of sensor nodes, reorganization of sensor network, and overlapped sensing regions are some of the techniques used to increase the fault tolerance and reliability of the network (Abbasi et al., 2014).

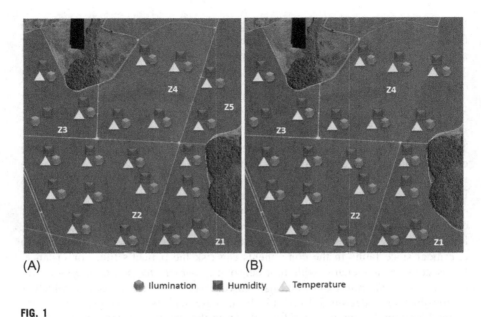

(A) (B)

● Ilumination ■ Humidity ▲ Temperature

FIG. 1

Ubiquitous WSN in a vineyard.

Let us take as an example a Ubiquitous WSN that collects environmental data within a vineyard (Fig. 1A), which is grouped into management zones (Z1–Z5) according to different characteristics (eg, soil properties). Each zone is composed of sensors of different types (eg, humidity control sensors, temperature control sensors, etc.) and the density of sensors in each zone depends on the characteristics of the latter. That is, the number of sensors can be different for each type of sensor within a given zone. Furthermore, sensors' redundancy ensures both area coverage and connectivity in case of failure. We can thus consider each management zone as a single set whose sensors of the same type are grouped into subsets. This type of grouping approach enables the definition of a threshold, which is equal to the minimum number of sensors that each subset must have in order to keep connectivity and the application functioning all time. Moreover, in some situations there might be a need to dynamically reconfigure the density of the zones (Fig. 1B). In this case, the *threshold* value would change.

4 SELF-HEALING MODULE

Fig. 2 presents the Self-Healing Module which can be incorporated in a ubiquitous system, regardless of the architecture of the latter. It has two components: the *FD* and

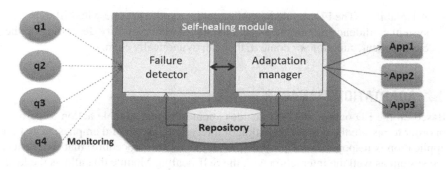

FIG. 2

Self-healing module.

the *AM*. The former consists of an adaptive FD that is responsible for detecting crash failures of the different entities (nodes, sensors, etc.) that need to be monitored in the system. The AM makes decisions in order to adopt suitable adaptation strategies, aiming at reducing the impact of the detected failure. According to Bracewell et al. (2003), in the event of a failure, real-time decisions must be made as to whether the system or application should seek to perform its mission during fault recovery by operating out of spec with regard to meeting real-time deadlines or with regard to maintaining replica consistency. In this context, we can say that the FD is done in real-time, however, the failure recovery process depends on the strategy to be adopted.

4.1 FAILURE DETECTOR

In order to fulfill the requirements of ubiquitous environments, an FD should present the following features:

- Strong completeness : The FD oracle of a correct process should eventually detect all failures.
- Grouping: The user of the FD, in our case the AM, is interested in knowing if the system is trusted or not. Therefore, the FD output should express the confidence about the system as a whole (set of nodes) and not about each node individually. Moreover, it must provide the possibility of organizing nodes with some common characteristics in groups, ie, subsets (see Section 3).
- Flexibility: Nodes can be of different relevance or have different roles in the system. Consequently, their respective failures may have different impact on the proper functioning of the system. The FD must take into account such an heterogeneity. Furthermore, some systems tolerate a margin of failures (eg, systems with redundant nodes) which the FD should also consider.

- Adaptability: The FD should be configurable in order to cope with different system confidence requirements, ie, the fault margin may vary depending on the environment, situation, or context, that can dynamically change.

4.2 ADAPTATION MANAGER

Based on the FD output, the AM decides about the most suitable action to perform in order to restore the correct operation of the system. We should emphasize that the application is responsible for providing both the action (procedure) that will restore the system as well the interaction with the Self-healing Module that allows the latter to trigger the execution of the corresponding procedure. Therefore, there exists an interaction protocol between the Self-healing Module and the application.

The Self-healing Module allows the user to previously configure the data required for self-healing. Such a configuration is stored in the Repository (see Fig. 2). Fig. 3 shows the class model that defines data for the Self-healing Module.

A *node* is a hardware entity that is part of the ubiquitous system. A node can be a *detector* or not. A detector node can monitor a single node or a set of nodes

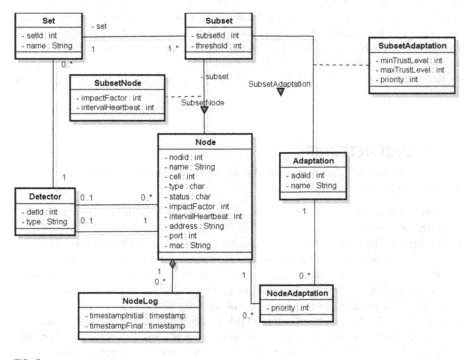

FIG. 3

Class model of self-healing module.

(*set*) while a set can be composed by only one subset or several ones. Adaptations (*Adaptation*) can be configured to nodes and sets, including more than one in each case, with priority levels.

Whenever requested, the FD informs if the system is trusted or not. If it is not, the AM takes a decision about the need for an adaptation. If the latter is necessary, it chooses a reconfiguration strategy and communicates it to the application which will activate it. We highlight once again that the AM is not the focus of this work.

5 IMPACT FAILURE DETECTOR

We consider a distributed system which consists of a finite set[1] of processes $\Pi = \{q_1, \ldots, q_n\}$ with $|\Pi| = n$. Failures are only classified as crashes. Other types of failures (eg, misbehavior, transient, etc.) are the object of a study that will be carried out in the near future. A crashed process never recovers. We assume the existence of some global time denoted T. A failure pattern is a function $F : T \to 2^{\Pi}$, where $F(t)$ is the set of processes that have failed before or at time t. The function $correct(F)$ denotes the set of correct processes, ie, those that have never belonged to a failure pattern (F), while $faulty(F)$ denotes the set of faulty processes, ie, the complement of $correct(F)$ with respect to Π.

The Impact FD can be defined as an unreliable FD that provides an output related to the trust level with regard to a set of processes. If the trust level provided by the detector is equal to or greater than a given threshold value defined by the user, the confidence in the set of processes is ensured. We can thus say that the system is trusted. We denote FD $(I_p{}^S)$ the Impact FD module of process p and S is a set of processes of Π. When invoked in p, the Impact FD $(I_p{}^S)$ returns the $trust\_level_p{}^S$ and $status_p{}^S$ (trusted/not trusted) values. The $trust\_level_p{}^S$ is a set that contains the trust level of each subset, ie, it expresses the confidence that p has in the set S. The $status_p{}^S$ informs whether the system is *trusted* or *not trusted* according to the analysis of the *threshold*.

Each process $q \in S$ has an *impact factor* value $(I_q | I_q > 0 : I_q \in \mathbb{R})$. Furthermore, the set S can be partitioned into m disjoint subsets. Notice that the grouping feature of the Impact FD allows the process of S to be partitioned into disjoint subsets, in accordance with a particular criterion. For instance, in a scenario where there are different types of sensors, those of the same type can be gathered in the same subset, as in the example of the ubiquitous WSN of Section 3. Let then define $S^* = \{S_1^*, S_2^*, \ldots, S_m^*\}$ as the set S partitioned into m disjoint subsets where each S_i^* is a set composed of the tuple $\langle id, impact \rangle$, where id is a process identifier and *impact* is the value of the impact factor of the process in question.

---

[1] In this work, "set" and "multiset" are used interchangeably. Unlike a set, an element of a multiset can appear more than once. This allows different processes to have the same identity.

$S^* = \{S_1^*, S_2^*, \ldots, S_m^*\}$ is a set of processes of such that $\forall i, j, i \neq j, S_i^* \cap S_j^* = \emptyset$ and $\bigcup\{q| \langle q, \_\rangle \in S_i^*; 1 \leq i \leq m\} = S$.

We denote $trusted_p^S(t) = \{trusted_1(t), \ldots, trusted_m(t)\}$, where each $trusted_i$ $(1 \leq i \leq m)$ contains the processes of S_i^* that are not considered faulty by p at $t \in T$. Similarly to S_i^*, each $trusted_i$ is composed of the tuple $\langle id, impact \rangle$.

The *trust level* at $t \in T$ of processes $p \notin F(t)$ of S is the denoted $trust\_level_p^S$ such that $trust\_level_p^S(t) = \{trust\_level_i | trust\_level_i = sum(trusted_i(t)); 1 \leq i \leq m\}$ where the function *sum(subset)* returns the sum of the impact factor of all the elements of *subset*. In other words, the $trust\_level_p^S$ is a set that contains the trust level of each subset of S^* expressing the confidence that p has in the set S.

An acceptable margin of failure, denoted as the $threshold^S$, characterizes the acceptable degree of failure flexibility in relation to set S^*. The $threshold^S$ is adjusted to the minimum trust level required for each subset, ie, it is defined as a set which contains the respective threshold of each subset of S^*: $threshold^S = \{threshold_1, \ldots, threshold_m\}$.

The $status_p^S$ is generated at t based on the comparison of the $threshold^S$ with $trust\_level_p^S(t)$. If, for each subset of S^*, the $trust\_level_i(t) \geq threshold_i$, S is considered to be *trusted* at t by p, ie, the confidence of p in S has not been compromised; otherwise S is considered *not trusted* by p at t.

Table 2 shows several examples of sets and their respective threshold. In the first example (a) there is just one subset with three processes. Each process has an impact factor equal to 1 and the *threshold* defines that the sum of the impact factors of non-faulty processes must be at least equal to 2, ie, the system is considered trusted whenever there are two or more correct processes. The example (b) shows a configuration where the processes must be monitored individually. Each process is in a subset and the threshold defines that if any of the processes fails, the system is not trusted anymore. In the next example (c), S has two sets with three processes each. The *threshold* requires at least two correct processes in each subset. The last example (d) has a single subset with five processes with different impact factor values and *threshold*. The latter defines that the set is trusted whenever the sum of the impact factors of correct processes is at least equal to seven.

In Table 3, we consider a set S, where S^* is composed by three subsets: S_1, S_2, and S_3 ($S^* = \{\{\langle q_1, 1 \rangle, \langle q_2, 1 \rangle\}, \{\langle q_3, 3 \rangle\}, \{\langle q_4, 4 \rangle, \langle q_5, 4 \rangle, \langle q_6, 4 \rangle\}\}$). The values of $threshold^S$ define that the subsets S_1 and S_2 (resp. S_3) must have at least one (resp. 2)

Table 2 Examples of Sets and Threshold

	S^*	$threshold^S$
a	$\{\{\langle q_1, 1 \rangle, \langle q_2, 1 \rangle, \langle q_3, 1 \rangle\}\}$	$\{2\}$
b	$\{\{\langle q_1, 1 \rangle\}, \{\langle q_2, 1 \rangle\}, \{\langle q_3, 1 \rangle\}\}$	$\{1, 1, 1\}$
c	$\{\{\langle q_1, 1 \rangle, \langle q_2, 1 \rangle, \langle q_3, 1 \rangle\}, \{\langle q_4, 2 \rangle, \langle q_5, 2 \rangle, \langle q_6, 2 \rangle\}\}$	$\{2, 4\}$
d	$\{\{\langle q_1, 1 \rangle, \langle q_2, 1 \rangle, \langle q_3, 1 \rangle, \langle q_4, 5 \rangle, \langle q_5, 5 \rangle\}\}$	$\{7\}$

Table 3 Example of FD ($I_p{}^S$) Output: S^* Has Three Uniform Subsets

t	F(t)	trusted$_p{}^S$(t)	trust_level$_p{}^S$	Status
1	$\{\{(q_2,1)\},\{\},\{\}\}$	$\{\{(q_1,1)\},\{(q_3,3)\},$ $\{(q_4,4),(q_5,4),(q_6,4)\}\}$	$\{1,3,12\}$	Trusted
2	$\{\{(q_2,1)\},\{\},$ $\{(q_5,4),(q_6,4)\}\}$	$\{\{(q_1,1)\},\{(q_3,3)\},$ $\{(q_4,4),(q_5,4)\}\}$	$\{1,3,8\}$	Trusted
3	$\{\{(q_2,1)\},\{\},$ $\{(q_6,4)\}\}$	$\{\{(q_1,1)\},\{(q_3,3)\},$ $\{(q_4,4)\}\}$	$\{1,3,4\}$	Not trusted
4	$\{\{(q_2,1)\},\{(q_3,3)\},$ $\{(q_5,4),(q_6,4)\}\}$	$\{\{(q_1,1)\},\{\},$ $\{(q_4,4)\}\}$	$\{1,0,4\}$	Not trusted

$S^* = \{\{(q_1,1),(q_2,1)\},\{(q_3,3)\},\{(q_4,4),(q_5,4),(q_6,4)\}\}$.
$threshold^S = \{1,3,8\}$.

correct process(es). The table shows several possible outputs for FD ($I_p{}^S$): the set S is considered trusted whenever, for each subset S_i^*, $trust\_level_i(t) \geq threshold_i$.

We should point out that both the *impact factor* and the *threshold^S* render the estimation of the confidence of S flexible. For instance, it might happen that some processes in S are faulty or suspected of being faulty but S is still considered to be trusted. Furthermore, the *threshold^S* increases the tolerance S to false suspicions, thus reducing wrong decisions by the AM.

It is also worth noting that the Impact FD is easily configurable according to the needs of the environment. The *threshold^S* can be tuned in order to provide a more restrict or softer monitoring. Such an adaptability, as mentioned in the previous section, is essential in dynamic environments such as ubiquitous ones. Notice that the Impact FD can also be applied when the application needs individual information about each process of S. In this case, each process must be defined as a subset (see example (b) of Table 2).

6 PERFORMANCE EVALUATION

In this section, we first describe the environment in which the experiments were conducted and the QoS metrics which were used. Following this, we analyze some evaluation results with different configurations of node sets with regard to both the impact factor and the threshold as well as making a comparison with the results of Chen FD (Chen et al., 2002), whose output is a list of suspect processes.

6.1 ENVIRONMENT

We used realistic trace files collected from ten nodes of PlanetLab (PlanetLab, 2014), as summarized in Table 4. The experiment started on July 16, 2014 at 15:06 UTC, and finished one full week later. Each site sent heartbeat messages to other sites at a rate

Table 4 Sites of Experiments

ID	Site	Local
0	ple4.ipv6.lip6.fr	France
1	planetlab1.jhu.edu	USA East Coast
2	planetlab2.csuohio.edu	USA, Ohio
3	75-130-96-12.static.oxfr.ma.charter.com	USA, Massachusetts
4	planetlab1.cnis.nyit.edu	USA, New York
5	saturn.planetlab.carleton.ca	Canada, Ontario
6	PlanetLab-03.cs.princeton.edu	USA, New Jersey
7	prata.mimuw.edu.pl	Poland
8	planetlab3.upc.es	Spain
9	pl1.eng.monash.edu.au	Australia

Table 5 Sites and Heartbeat Sampling

Site	Messages	Mean (ms)	Min (ms)	Max (ms)	Stand. Dev. (ms)
0	5,424,326	100.058	0.025	26,494.168	19.525
2	1,759,989	100.415	0.031	509.093	9.275
3	5,426,843	100.012	0.027	1227.349	1.709
4	5,414,122	100.247	0.003	1193.276	18.595
5	5,413,542	100.258	0.006	657,900.226	310.958
6	5,426,700	100.015	0.003	3787.643	2.557
7	5,424,117	100.062	0.006	59,603.188	31.229
8	5,424,560	100.054	0.027	11,443.359	100.714
9	5,422,043	100.100	0.004	30,600.076	18.798

of one heartbeat every 100 ms (the sending interval). Table 5 shows information about the heartbeat messages received by site number *1* (the monitor node). We observe that the mean inter-arrival times of received heartbeats is very close to 100 ms. However, in some sites, the standard deviation is very high, for example in site *5*, for which the standard deviation is 310.958 ms with a minimum of 0.006 ms, and a maximum of 657,900.226 ms. Such values inform that, for a certain time interval during execution, the site stopped sending heartbeats and then started again afterwards. Note also that site *2* stopped sending messages after approximately 48 h and, therefore, there are just 1,759,990 received messages. Finally, we observe that sites *3* and *6* (resp. *5* and *8*) are the most stable (resp. unstable) sites.

The implementation of Impact FD for the evaluation was based on Algorithm 1 presented in Rossetto et al. (2015). This algorithm employs the timer-based approach which uses Chen's heartbeat estimation. Moreover, we consider an asynchronous system with message losses.

It should be pointed out that, despite the "large-scale" system and the high latency among the nodes, these traces of PlanetLab contain a large amount of data concerning the sending and reception of heartbeats, including unstable periods of links and message loss which induce false suspicions. Therefore, such traces can characterize any distributed system that uses FDs based on heartbeats, including self-healing ones. Furthermore, since our experiments were conducted using the PlanetLab traces, all of them reproduce exactly the same scenarios of sending and reception of heartbeats by the processes.

6.2 QoS METRICS

In order to evaluate the Impact FD, we use three of the QoS metrics proposed by Chen et al. (2002): detection time, average mistake rate, and query accuracy probability. Considering two processes q and p where p monitors q, the QoS of the FD at p can be determined from the transitions between the "trusted" and "not trusted" states with respect to q.

- Detection time (T_D): is the time that elapses from the moment that process q crashes until the FD at p starts suspecting q permanently.
- Average mistake rate (λ_R): represents the number of mistakes that FD makes in a unit time, ie, the rate at each an FD makes mistakes.
- Query accuracy probability (P_A): is the probability that the FD output is correct at a random time.

For the estimation of the arrival time of the next heartbeat we have applied Chen's approach (Chen et al., 2002), described in Section 2.2. The authors suggest that the safety margin α should range from 0 to 2500 ms. We set the window size for all experiments to 100 samples, which means that the FD relies only on the last 100 heartbeat message samples in order to compute the estimation of the next heartbeat arrival time.

6.3 SET CONFIGURATION

We defined a set composed of sites 0, 2, 3, 4, 5, 6, 7, 8, and 9 ($S = \{\{0, 2, 3, 4, 5, 6, 7, 8, 9\}\}$). Site *1* was the monitor node (p). Table 6 shows the five configurations with regard to impact factor values that we have considered for S in the experiments. For all configurations, the sum of impact factor of processes is 27.

6.4 EXPERIMENTS

6.4.1 Experiment 1—query accuracy probability

The aim of this experiment is to evaluate the query accuracy probability (P_A) with different threshold values (18, 20, 21, 22, 23, 24, and 25) and different impact factor configurations (Table 6). We considered the fault margin as being $\alpha = 400$ ms.

Table 6 Set Configurations

Config	Impact Factor of Each Site
Set 0	$I_0 = 2$; $I_2 = 1$; $I_3 = 6$; $I_4 = 6$; $I_5 = 1$; $I_6 = 6$; $I_7 = 1$; $I_8 = 2$; $I_9 = 2$;
Set 1	$I_0 = 1$; $I_2 = 2$; $I_3 = 6$; $I_4 = 6$; $I_5 = 2$; $I_6 = 6$; $I_7 = 2$; $I_8 = 1$; $I_9 = 1$;
Set 2	$I_0 = 6$; $I_2 = 2$; $I_3 = 1$; $I_4 = 1$; $I_5 = 2$; $I_6 = 1$; $I_7 = 2$; $I_8 = 6$; $I_9 = 6$;
Set 3	$I_0 = 2$; $I_2 = 6$; $I_3 = 1$; $I_4 = 1$; $I_5 = 2$; $I_6 = 1$; $I_7 = 2$; $I_8 = 6$; $I_9 = 6$;
Set 4	$I_0 = 2$; $I_2 = 1$; $I_3 = 6$; $I_4 = 6$; $I_5 = 1$; $I_6 = 6$; $I_7 = 2$; $I_8 = 2$; $I_9 = 1$;
Set 5	$I_0 = 3$; $I_2 = 3$; $I_3 = 3$; $I_4 = 3$; $I_5 = 3$; $I_6 = 3$; $I_7 = 3$; $I_8 = 3$; $I_9 = 3$;

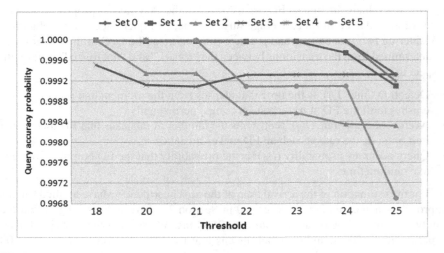

FIG. 4

PA vs. threshold with different set configurations.

Fig. 4 shows that the P_A decreases when the threshold increases. It is important to remember that the *threshold* is a limit value defined by the user and if the FD trust level output value is equal to, or greater than, the threshold, the confidence in the set of processes is ensured. Hence, the results confirm that when the threshold is more flexible, the query accuracy probability is greater.

On the one hand, *"Set 0"* configuration has the highest P_A for all *thresholds* due to the assignment of high (resp. low) impact factors for the most stable (resp. unstable) sites. On the other hand, *"Set 2"* and *"Set 3"* have the lowest P_A since the unstable sites have high impact factor values in these sets. For instance, for site *8*, the mean of the inter-arrival times for the received heartbeats is 100.05 ms, but the standard deviation is 100.71 ms. The impact factor assignment thus has an impact on the P_A performance.

"Set 5" presents an abrupt decrease when the *threshold* = 25. Such a behavior can be explained since, in this set configuration, all sites have the same impact factor (3). Therefore, every false suspicion leads the *trust_level* to be smaller than the *threshold* (25), which increases the mistake duration and, as a result, the P_A decreases.

Notice that site *2* failed after approximately 48 h. Thus, after its crash, the FD output, which indicates *status* = *not trusted*, is not a mistake, ie, it is not a false suspicion. Hence, in *"Set 3"*, whose impact factor of site *2* is 6 (high), the *PA* is constant for a *threshold* greater than, or equal to, 22: after the crash of site *2*, the FD output *state* is always "not trusted" and false suspicions related to other sites do not modify it. The average mistake duration in the experiment is thus smaller after the crash, which improves the P_A.

In order to further compare the P_A of Impact FD with an approach that monitors the processes individually, we monitored each site using the same Chen algorithm and parameters ($WS = 100; \alpha = 400\,ms$). The mean P_A obtained was 0.979788. Such a result shows that, independently of the set configuration, Impact FD presents higher P_A than Chen FD since the former has enough flexibility to tolerate failures, ie, the mistake duration only starts to be computed when the Impact FD output *state* informs that the system is "not trusted," contrarily to individual monitoring, as Chen FD, where every false suspicion increases the mistake duration.

The results of this experiment highlight the fact that the assignment of heterogeneous impact factors to nodes can degrade the performance of the FD, especially when unstable sites have a high impact factor.

6.4.2 Experiment 2—detection time

In the second experiment, we evaluated the average query accuracy probability (P_A) regarding the average detection time (T_D). To this end, we varied the safety margin (Chen's estimation) to get different values for the detection time. It was varied with intervals of 100 ms, starting at 100 ms. In this experiment the *"Set 0"* configuration was employed and different thresholds defined. We chose this set because it had the best P_A for all thresholds in Experiment 1. We also evaluated the P_A and T_D for Chen's algorithm, which outputs the set of suspected nodes.

Fig. 5 shows that for high threshold and detection time close to 200 ms, the P_A of the Impact FD is smaller, independently of the threshold, because the safety margin (used to compute the expected arrival times) is, in this case, equal to 100 ms, which increases both the number of failure suspicion and mistake duration. However, when T_D is greater than 230 ms, the P_A of Impact FD is considerably higher than that of Chen. After a detection time of approximately 400 ms, the P_A of Impact FD becomes constant regardless of the detection time and threshold, and gets close to 1. Such a behavior can be explained since the higher the safety margin, the smaller the number of false suspicions, and the shorter the mistake duration which confirms that when the timeout is short, failures are detected faster but the probability of having false detections increases (Satzger et al., 2007).

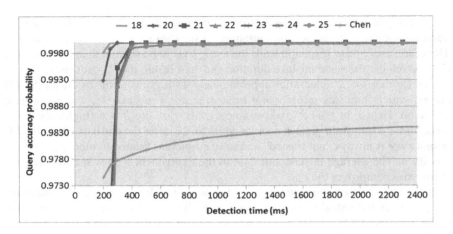

FIG. 5

P_A vs. T_D with different thresholds.

6.4.3 Experiment 3—average mistake rate

In this experiment, we have evaluated the average detection time versus the mistake rate (mistakes per second). We considered the *"Set 0"* configuration and the mistake rate is expressed in a logarithmic scale. It can be observed in Fig. 6 that the mistake rate of the Impact FD is higher when the detection time is low (smaller than 400 ms)

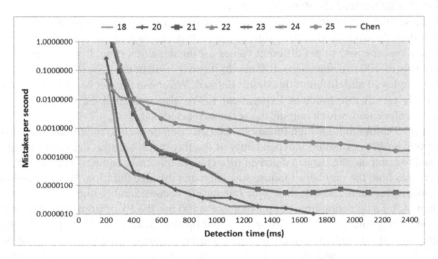

FIG. 6

λ_R vs. T_D with different thresholds.

and the threshold is high (from 23 to 25). Such a result is in accordance with Experiment 2: whenever the safety margin is small and the *threshold* tolerates fewer failures, the Impact FD makes mistakes more frequently. In other words, the mistake rate decreases when the threshold is more flexible or the time detection increases.

7 RELATED WORK

Related studies can be divided into two groups: (1) ubiquitous systems with failure handling and (2) FDs respectively.

In the first group, we find middlewares like Gaia, SAFTM, or MARKS. Gaia provides fault tolerance based on fail-stop model. Only devices (eg, laptops, portable devices, etc.) can host applications (Chetan et al., 2005). Whenever the middleware detects a lack of heartbeat messages, it infers a contextually appropriate surrogate device where the application can be restarted (rollback). The fault tolerant self-adaptive SAFTM middleware (Cai et al., 2012) detects failures by continuous monitoring of the state of the components (eg, CPU, memory, OS, I/O, network operations, etc.) and dynamically building the self-adaptive mechanism in accordance with the various types of failures. The MARKS (ad hoc) middleware has a unit called ETS (efficient, transparent, and secure), which is self-healing (Sharmin et al., 2006). By predicting failures, it conducts an analysis of the changing rate of the status of each device (eg, memory, energy, communication signal, etc.). With regard to fault containment, it isolates the faulty device and assigns the service to a provider of alternative resources. Bourdenas et al. (2010) proposed the Starfish, a self-healing framework for pervasive systems, that follows the Self-Managed Cell (SMC) architectural paradigm. Starfish was an instantiation of a SMC for wireless sensor networks. It supports adaptation on nodes thereby allowing deployment of new strategies at run-time. However, it only provides recovering from sensor failures and does not consider other type of failures of pervasive computing.

We observe in the above works that there exist some limitations with regard to adaptation: in presence of failures, most of them use a fixed criterion for adaptation. Moreover, they do not provide an FD tailored for the features of a ubiquitous environment, such as grouping, flexibility, or adaptability, like that proposed in the current work.

In the second group, there are some important studies that address FDs. Most of the unreliable fault detectors in the literature are based on a binary model and provide as output a set of process identifiers, which usually reveals the number of processes currently suspected of having failed (Chandra and Toueg, 1996; Bertier et al., 2003). However, in some detectors, such as class Σ (resp., Ω) (Delporte-Gallet et al., 2004), the output is the set of processes (resp., one process) that are (resp., is) not suspected of being faulty, ie, *trusted*.

FD of class Σ (Sigma or quorum) outputs, for any failure pattern, any time τ, and any process p_i, a set of processes that are said to be *trusted* by p_i at time τ, such that the two following properties are satisfied: (1) the two sets of trusted processes intersect; (2) eventually every trusted process is correct (Delporte-Gallet et al., 2003). Upon invocation by a process, an FD of class Ω outputs the identity of a process. In addition, there is a time after which such an identity always concerns the same correct process for all correct processes that invoke the FD (Delporte-Gallet et al., 2004).

The ϕ Accrual FD (Hayashibara et al., 2004) proposes an approach where the output is a suspicion level on a continuous scale, instead of providing information of a binary nature (trust or suspect). It is based on an estimation of inter-arrival times assuming that inter-arrivals follow a normal distribution. The suspicion level captures the degree of confidence with which a given process is believed to have crashed. If the process actually crashes, the value is guaranteed to accrue over time and tends toward infinity. In Satzger et al. (2007), the authors extended the Accrual FD by exploiting histogram density estimation. Taking into account the sampled inter-arrival times and the time of the last received heartbeat, the algorithm estimates the probability that no further heartbeat messages arrive from a given process, ie, the latter has failed. Accrual FDs aim to decouple monitoring from interpretation. Lavinia et al. (2010) present an FD system to fulfill the requirements of large-scale distributed systems. The solution is based on clustering, the use of a gossip-based algorithm for detection at local level and the use of a hierarchical structure among clusters of detectors along which traffic is channeled. Its architecture allows applications to specify different QoS detection levels and the FD consists of monitoring processes and stations throughout the systems and detecting errors in the shortest time.

Starting from the premise that applications should have information about failures to take specific and suitable recovery actions, the work in Leners et al. (2013) proposes a service to report faults to applications. The latter also encapsulates uncertainty which allows applications to proceed safely in the presence of doubt. The service provides status reports related to fault detection with an abstraction that describes the degree of uncertainty.

Considering that each node has a probability of being byzantine, a voting node redundancy approach is presented in Brun et al. (2011) in order to improve the reliability of distributed systems. Based on such probability values, the authors estimate the minimum number of machines that the system should have in order to provide a degree of reliability that is equal to or greater than a threshold value.

With respect to the above works, none of them deal with the subsets' nor processes' relevance and are not easily configurable to the needs of the system. Furthermore, among them, only Accrual and Adaptive Accrual have the output as a suspicion level. However, they do not analyze the output but just replay it to the application, in contrast to the Impact FD, which compares the trust level output with the threshold defined by the user.

8 CONCLUSION AND FUTURE WORK

Towards a solution for a self-healing module in ubiquitous environments, we have presented a new unreliable FD, denoted the Impact FD, which provides an output related to a set of processes and not just to each one individually. Both its *impact factor* and the *threshold* offer a degree of flexibility since they enable the user to tune the Impact FD in accordance with the specific needs and acceptable margin of failure of the application. In some scenarios, the failure of low impact or redundant nodes does not jeopardize the confidence in the system, while the crash of a high impact factor one may seriously affect it. Either softer or stricter monitoring is thus possible. Furthermore, they also might weaken the rate of false responses when compared with traditional unreliable FDs. The performance evaluation results show that the assignment of a high (resp. low) impact factor to more stable (resp. unstable) nodes increases the query accuracy probability of the FD.

As a future work, we intend to extend the Impact FD so that it addresses the question of misbehavior failures. Another direction of our research is the dynamic adaptation of nodes' impact factor values according to their respective stability. A third aim is to conduct other experiments on different networks such as WiFi or LAN and thus be able to compare the Impact FD with other well-known FDs. Finally, we look forward to evaluating the self-healing module in ubiquitous scenarios.

ACRONYMS

P_A	query accuracy probability
T_D	detection time
λ_R	average mistake rate
AM	adaptation manager
CPU	central processing unit
ECG	electrocardiogram
ETS	efficient, transparent, and secure
FD	failure detector
I/O	input/output
IBM	International Business Machines
LAN	local area network
MARKS	middleware adaptability for resource discovery, knowledge usability and self-healing
ms	millisecond
OS	operating system
QoS	quality of service
resp.	respective
SAFTM	self-adaptive fault-tolerant middleware
SMC	self-managed cell
UTC	universal time coordinated
WS	window size
WSN	wireless sensor network

GLOSSARY

Asynchronous distributed systems A distributed system is asynchronous if there is no bound on message transmission delay, clock drift, or the time to execute a processing step.

Average mistake rate Represents the number of mistakes that a failure detector makes in a unit time, ie, the rate at each a failure detector makes mistakes.

Detection time The time that elapses from the moment that process q crashes until the failure detector at p starts suspecting q permanently.

Heartbeat strategy An implementation of FD where every process q periodically sends an "I am alive" message to the processes in charge of detecting its failure. If a process p does not receive such a message from q after the expiration of a timeout, it adds q to its list of suspected processes.

Query accuracy probability The probability that the failure detector output is correct at a random time.

Synchronous distributed systems A distributed system is synchronous if there are bounds on transmission delay, clock drift and processing time and these bounds are known.

Unreliable failure detector An oracle that provides information about process failures. An FD is unreliable in the sense that it can make mistakes, that is, it may not suspect a crashed process or suspect a correct one.

REFERENCES

Abbasi, A.Z., Islam, N., Shaikh, Z.A., et al., 2014. A review of wireless sensors and networks' applications in agriculture. Comput. Stand. Interfaces 36 (2), 263–270.

Arantes, L., Greve, F., Sens, P., 2010. Unreliable failure detectors for mobile ad hoc networks. In: Handbook of Research on Mobility and Computing: Evolving Technologies and Ubiquitous Impacts. IGI Global, Pennsylvania, USA, p. 20.

Bertier, M., Marin, O., Sens, P., et al., 2003. Performance analysis of a hierarchical failure detector. In: DSN, vol. 3, pp. 635–644.

Bourdenas, T., Sloman, M., Lupu, E.C., 2010. Self-healing for pervasive computing systems. In: Architecting Dependable Systems VII. Springer, Berlin, pp. 1–25.

Bracewell, T., Narasimhan, P., Raytheon, I., 2003. A middleware for dependable distributed real-time systems. In: Joint Systems and Software Engineering Symposium, Falls Church, VA.

Brun, Y., Edwards, G., Bang, J.Y., Medvidovic, N., 2011. Smart redundancy for distributed computation. In: 31st International Conference on Distributed Computing Systems (ICDCS), 2011. IEEE, pp. 665–676.

Cai, H., Peng, C., Jiang, L., Zhang, Y., 2012. A novel self-adaptive fault-tolerant mechanism and its application for a dynamic pervasive computing environment. In: 15th IEEE International Symposium on Object/Component/Service-Oriented Real-Time Distributed Computing Workshops (ISORCW), 2012. IEEE, pp. 48–52.

Chandra, T.D., Toueg, S., 1996. Unreliable failure detectors for reliable distributed systems. J. ACM 43 (2), 225–267.

Chen, W., Toueg, S., Aguilera, M.K., 2002. On the quality of service of failure detectors. IEEE Trans. Comput. 51 (5), 561–580.

Chetan, S., Ranganathan, A., Campbell, R., 2005. Towards fault tolerance pervasive computing. IEEE Technol. Soc. Mag. 24 (1), 38–44.

Delporte-Gallet, C., Fauconnier, H., Guerraoui, R., 2003. Shared memory vs message passing. Technical Report, 77.

Delporte-Gallet, C., Fauconnier, H., Guerraoui, R., Hadzilacos, V., Kouznetsov, P., Toueg, S., 2004. The weakest failure detectors to solve certain fundamental problems in distributed computing. In: Proceedings of the Twenty-Third Annual ACM Symposium on Principles of Distributed Computing. ACM, New York, NY, pp. 338–346.

Gaber, T., Hassanien, A.E., 2014. An overview of self-protection and self-healing in wireless sensor networks. In: Bio-inspiring Cyber Security and Cloud Services: Trends and Innovations. Springer, Berlin, pp. 185–202.

Ganek, A.G., Corbi, T.A., 2003. The dawning of the autonomic computing era. IBM Syst. J. 42 (1), 5–18.

Geeta, D., Nalini, N., Biradar, R.C., 2013. Fault tolerance in wireless sensor network using hand-off and dynamic power adjustment approach. J. Netw. Comput. Appl. 36 (4), 1174–1185.

Ghosh, D., Sharman, R., Rao, H.R., Upadhyaya, S., 2007. Self-healing systems survey and synthesis. Decis. Support Syst. 42 (4), 2164–2185.

Hayashibara, N., Défago, X., Katayama, T., 2003. Two-ways adaptive failure detection with the ϕ-failure detector. In: Workshop on Adaptive Distributed Systems (WADiS03). Citeseer, pp. 22–27.

Hayashibara, N., Defago, X., Yared, R., Katayama, T., 2004. The φ accrual failure detector. In: Proceedings of the 23rd IEEE International Symposium on Reliable Distributed Systems, 2004. IEEE, pp. 66–78.

Ishibashi, K., Yano, M., 2005. A proposal of forwarding method for urgent messages on an ubiquitous wireless sensor network. In: 6th Asia-Pacific Symposium on Information and Telecommunication Technologies, 2005. APSITT 2005 Proceedings. IEEE, pp. 293–298.

Jacobson, V., 1988. Congestion avoidance and control. In: ACM SIGCOMM Computer Communication Review, vol. 18. ACM, New York, NY, pp. 314–329.

Kephart, J.O., Chess, D.M., 2003. The vision of autonomic computing. Computer 36 (1), 41–50.

Lavinia, A., Dobre, C., Pop, F., Cristea, V., 2010. A failure detection system for large scale distributed systems. In: International Conference on Complex, Intelligent and Software Intensive Systems (CISIS), 2010. IEEE, pp. 482–489.

Leners, J.B., Gupta, T., Aguilera, M.K., Walfish, M., 2013. Improving availability in distributed systems with failure informers. In: Proc. of NSDI.

Mostefaoui, A., Mourgaya, E., Raynal, M., 2003. Asynchronous implementation of failure detectors. In: 43rd Annual IEEE/IFIP International Conference on Dependable Systems and Networks (DSN), 2013. IEEE Computer Society, pp. 351–351.

PlanetLab, 2014. Planetlab. http://www.planet-lab.org.

Psaier, H., Dustdar, S., 2011. A survey on self-healing systems: approaches and systems. Computing 91 (1), 43–73.

Rossetto, A., Rolim, C., Leithardt, V., Geyer, C.F., Arantes, L., 2014. An architecture for resilient ubiquitous systems. In: International Conference on Health Informatics.

Rossetto, A.G., Geyer, C.F., Arantes, L., Sens, P., 2015. Impact: an unreliable failure detector based on processes relevance and the confidence degree in the system. Tech. rep. https://hal.inria.fr/hal-01136595.

Satzger, B., Pietzowski, A., Trumler, W., Ungerer, T., 2007. A new adaptive accrual failure detector for dependable distributed systems. In: Proceedings of the 2007 ACM Symposium on Applied Computing. ACM, New York, NY, pp. 551–555.

Sharmin, M., Ahmed, S., Ahamed, S.I., 2006. Marks (middleware adaptability for resource discovery, knowledge usability and self-healing) for mobile devices of pervasive computing environments. In: Third International Conference on Information Technology: New Generations, 2006. ITNG 2006. IEEE, pp. 306–313.

Sterritt, R., 2005. Autonomic computing. Innov. Syst. Softw. Eng. 1 (1), 79–88.

Weiser, M., 1991. The computer for the 21st century. Sci. Am. 265 (3), 94–104.

Xhafa, F., Naranjo, V., Caballe, S., Barolli, L., 2015. A software chain approach to big data stream processing and analytics. In: Ninth International Conference on Complex, Intelligent, and Software Intensive Systems (CISIS), 2015. IEEE, pp. 179–186.

Video streaming: Overview and challenges in the internet of things

13

R. Pereira[a], E.G. Pereira[b]

Liverpool John Moores University, Liverpool, United Kingdom[a]
Edge Hill University, Ormskirtk, United Kingdom[b]

1 INTRODUCTION

Video streaming has received much attention for some time now, and its popularity has grown manifold in the last decade, particularly with the deployment of widely known video streaming services, such as YouTube, Netflix, Hulu, Daily Motion, and others. Video streaming now accounts for a large share of the total traffic the Internet, and as such the transmission mechanisms used by video servers have an impact not only on the quality of the video presentation to the clients, but also on the total traffic impact on the network.

Developments in the 1980s in the field of video compression, alongside the first steps in the popularization of the Internet in the early 1990s, created the natural motivation for video data to be transmitted over the Internet. Due to the voluminous nature of video data, the concept of streaming quickly grew in popularity as it enabled viewers of a video to view the data without having to first fully download the whole video. Since then, the technologies that impact on video processing and streaming (networking, computing, compression, storage, etc.) have evolved continually at a high pace.

As a result, many new techniques for video streaming have developed. Moreover, with the continual expansion of computing, now encompassing everyday objects, the concepts of ubiquitous and pervasive computing describe a world in which the boundaries between the virtual and real world have been blurred. Wireless networks and mobile computing now feature in most distributed applications, leading to a substantially new challenge for video streaming: the computing/memory/energy capabilities of small mobile devices, and the low-quality channels interconnecting them and linking them to the Internet, impose limitations on the quality of videos that can be streamed. It also suggests the need for multiple encoding levels for each title, so that devices and networks of different characteristics can be supported.

Pervasive Computing. http://dx.doi.org/10.1016/B978-0-12-803663-1.00013-9

In this chapter, we review a range of relevant aspects associated with streaming: in Section 2, the main architectures are discussed; Section 3 considers in some detail the streaming mechanisms that use the HTTP protocol at the application level; Section 4 provides an overview of the structure and organization of content delivery networks (CDNs); Section 5 presents a discussion of mobile peer-to-peer streaming; Section 6 focuses on compression/encoding schemes and their relationship to streaming mechanisms, followed by Cloud Based Encoding and Transcoding in Section 7. We then discuss the Internet of Things (IoT) and applications related to video streaming. Concluding remarks are presented in Section 10.

2 ARCHITECTURES

The early days of video streaming, in the 1990s, saw the development of streaming protocols for the main distributed computing paradigm of the period, the Client-Server model (C/S). The dominant multimedia streaming protocols of that period were the RTP/RTCP protocols, as well as the RTSP for user input. These will be discussed briefly in this section, with HTTP streaming presented in more detail in Section 3. Regarding the early C/S streaming model over the Internet, the existing transport protocols, TCP and UDP, were not suitable or sufficient for video streaming. The UDP being the bare bones, as a streamlining protocol based on the transmission of independent datagrams, provided no specific support for multimedia streams. On the other hand, the TCP protocol provides features that can be detrimental to the real-time nature of video streaming, such as congestion control, and the associated reduction of the data transmission rate following packet losses due to the assumption of congestion in the network. Moreover, in such a scenario, the retransmission of lost packets would be wasteful, as they are likely to arrive too late to be presented to the client.

The real-time transport protocol (RTP) was designed and implemented to provide the missing ingredient: a supplement to the UDP protocol that incorporated functionalities suitable and necessary for streaming real-time data. In the protocol stack, the RTP sits atop the UDP layer, between the transport and the application layers. The use of the UDP as transport protocol benefits from UDP's opportunistic nature, in the sense that the server can send packets to the maximum link bandwidth, and also that UDP is streamlined, with a smaller protocol header and no retransmission overheads. The RTP protocol is used for carrying the video data from client to server, and to include information that helps with intra-stream synchronization via a timestamp, data encoding identification and packet numbering. A control dialogue between the server and the client, in parallel with the video data transmitted, is supported by using another protocol, the real-time control protocol (RTCP). With the RTCP, clients and servers maintain a communications channel for sending each other control information about the related RTP stream, which enables some management of the quality of service (QoS) achieved. User input for VCR like functionality is transmitted to the server by means of yet another related protocol, the real-time streaming protocol (RTSP), an example of a session control protocol, which plays an important role in managing active sessions.

Despite the existence of end systems control protocols such as RTCP, the Internet is in most parts based on best effort delivery, leading to packet losses as well as variable delay. Packet losses can have some impact on the quality of the video stream presentation, particularly as congestion builds up and congestion avoidance mechanisms such as random early detection (RED) drop packets to try and reduce the sending rate of TCP entities. In order to reduce the impact of packet losses on the perceptual quality of the video presentation, some *error control mechanisms* have been proposed and designed. One important type of error control mechanism is *Forward Error Correction*: this mechanism is based on the concept of sending redundant data early, interleaved with timely data, so when a data packet fails to arrive at the client, the missing data has already been partially included in earlier packets, thus enabling the reconstruction of the missing packet data. There are a number of other techniques that are used to try and reduce the impact of missing data, some of which are based on the specific encoding mechanism used, and interpolation of the existing data to attempt the recreation of the missing video frames (Li et al., 2013).

Peer-to-peer (P2P) streaming mechanisms developed later as a scalable solution to the growing popularity of video streaming. The client server model, in its initial version, placed an excessive burden on the server, and, although some of the problems were mitigated by the adoption of multicast protocols, the central source of video still became a limitation to scalability. With P2P, the peers consume resources *and* supply resources to other peers. In this manner, there is an inherent scalability in the system, since each new peer shares the burden in transmitting video data using their upload bandwidth. For P2P streaming to work well, and considering most peers have limited upload bandwidth due to the nature of most subscriber's access being asymmetric (greater download bandwidth than upload bandwidth), P2P schemes are based on dividing the full video into chunks, or segments, that can be downloaded from different peers. There are a number of important aspects about how peers are connected logically with each other, and also how peers can identify the peers that hold the data segments they need.

A common arrangement is for each peer to have information about a limited number of peers, which are known as *neighbors*. This limited mesh overlay is used for peers to communicate with each other and find information about peers that have the various segments of the video to be downloaded. Unlike static files where all chunks can be requested in parallel, video streaming uses the concept of a sliding window of video segments. The sliding window keeps moving forward, and as it does so new segments are requested. An important issue to be resolved in a P2P network is the location of the resources: whereas in a Client-Server interaction the servers are well known and can be easily contacted by the clients, in a P2P network with thousands or millions of peers, it is not a trivial issue for each peer to know which of the other peers hold the specific segments of the video. One alternative is for there to be a central server for the provision of a lookup service. However, the adoption of a centralized service would still lead to scalability issues, as well as being a central point of failure. A more distributed solution is to put resource identifiers through a hash function, and locate the hashed results with a corresponding peer, based on the identity of the peer. This is a dynamic arrangement, as peers need to continually consider the location of the resource as peers continually join and leave the overlay. The distributed hash works in conjunction with the mesh of neighbors in the following way: when a peer identifies a segment that it needs to download, the hash of the segment is calculated and passed to the neighbor whose ID is the nearest to the hash obtained. This neighbor then repeats the process until the actual peer holding the resource is found, which can then send the resource directly to the peer requesting it.

Despite the benefits of scalability and some well-developed techniques for establishing neighbors and resource placement and discovery, P2P can be some inconvenient for the users as they require specific software as well as having to keep ports open past firewalls and NAT. The most widely used application protocol in the Internet is the HTTP due to the popularity of the Web. Moreover, the HTTP port poses no filtering issues with firewalls, for instance. From the perspective of users and resource managers, a client server solution based on HTTP would make sense. On the negative side, the following issues needed to be overcome: First, the fact that HTTP uses the TCP protocol. As discussed earlier, the TCP is not the most suitable transport protocol for a real-time streaming application. One way to mimic streaming is to use a progressive HTTP download: the client requests the file to be viewed via an HTTP get request. The only difference with normal HTTP requests is that with video data the media player starts displaying the data from the buffer, rather than waiting for the full download to complete. Unlike with RTP streaming, with progressive download the video data are not sent at the consumption bit rate, and normally the clients buffers substantially more data than with RTP, in advance of viewing the data. Also, the video is fully downloaded to the client's hard disk. The scalability problem with the client server approach has been mitigated by the establishment of CDNs that replicate content geographically and distribute the load between the various servers in the CDN. To account for variable channel quality (particularly associated with wireless networks) as well as variability in device capabilities, dynamic adaptive streaming over HTTP was proposed and many implementations are now available (Li et al., 2013; Stockhammer, 2011). The main idea of adaptive streaming is that for each video, many streams of different quality are encoded. As a result, depending on the availability of bandwidth between client and server, the client can change, dynamically, between various alternative streams. When there is more bandwidth available, the client requests segments of higher quality, conversely when congestion builds up and there is less available bandwidth, the client requests lower quality, and therefore lower bit rate, streams.

3 STREAMING MECHANISMS WITH HTTP

The transmission mechanism used by the video streaming server can involve a transmission schedule based on the presentation bit rate of the compressed video.

In such cases, the server sends each client data at the rate of consumption by the client. Alternatively, data-smoothing algorithms may be applied to the video data in order to reduce the variability of the data rate typical of compressed video data (Pereira et al., 2007; Bewick et al., 2005; Salehi et al., 1998; Rao and Raghavan, 1999; Hadar and Cohen, 2001). It has been shown that YouTube adopts a different strategy, although there are variations depending on the container (eg, Flash, HTML5) as well as the browser used by the client, a common mechanism is for YouTube servers to send data in 2 phases. The buffering phase, in which a certain amount of data are sent at a high rate from the server to the client, and then the steady-state phase, where the server oscillates between on and off states, sending blocks of data at a high rate during the on state, followed by no data transmitted during the off state.

Web Servers use HTTP as the main communication protocol at the application layer. The existing web infrastructure, and the fact that the port number 80 used by HTTP is allowed normally past firewalls, has created strong arguments for adopting HTTP as the communication protocol for video data, rather than those described above in traditional streaming. Progressive HTTP download was then adopted by most video servers, such as YouTube, whereby the HTTP requests by the client is serviced by the server and the client media player presents the data contained in the file while the file is being downloaded (Rao et al., 2011; Adhikari et al., 2012b; Summers et al., 2012). With progressive downloading, rather like with streaming, the client does not need to download the whole file before viewing parts of it. Some of the specific behavior, however, is quite different: if a viewer pauses the media player, progressive downloads will continue downloading the file until it is completed, and upon the viewer resuming play, the presentation will continue. With traditional RTSP-based streaming, pausing would send a message to the server to stop sending the data. In the case that the viewer chooses not to resume download, the HTTP mechanism would clearly waste bandwidth.

The most common way a user accesses videos in the YouTube system is by visiting the YouTube website. The web browser normally includes an Adobe Flash Player plug-in, which is the default container used with YouTube when videos are accessed from a PC. Another container, HTML5, does not require any proprietary plug-in and is the default container for mobile devices with native applications for Android and iOS.

We will describe, in some detail, the streaming mechanism that has been reported in the literature (Rao et al., 2011; Adhikari et al., 2012b; Summers et al., 2012) for Flash container. The data transmission by the server can be seen as having two distinct stages: buffering and the on-off cycles, that follow the buffering stage. The buffering stage has the purpose of delivering sufficient data to the client in order to ensure smooth playback without interruptions that would be due to the variable delay (Jitter) in the network. In the buffering stage, the server transmits a certain predefined amount of data continually, at the available bandwidth. The client starts reading from the buffer, and as the client reads and removes data from the buffer at the consumption rate, the server moves onto the next stage, where data are sent one block at a time at the available bandwidth, followed by a period of no transmission, then another block is transmitted followed by no transmission, and so on. Block sizes can vary, but various experiments have indicated that multiples of 64KB seem to be prevalent.

The amount of data buffered in the buffering stage may vary, depending on the system and the browser being used. Values may be determined by the size of data, or by an equivalent playback time. During the on-off steady state transfer cycles, in addition to the size of the block transmitted, which can be variable, the effective data rate of the full cycle can also be adjusted to be slightly, or somewhat, above the mean data consumption rate, thus approaching the buffer it typically becomes fuller at the end of each cycle. The ratio between the data rate averaged over a cycle and the mean consumption rate is called the accumulation rate, and this should be greater than or equal to 1.

In recent years, some information about the workings of YouTube and its data transmission mechanisms have come to light following experimental research, and we will now summarize some of the recent work in this topic, that is, available from the literature.

Rao et al. (2011) present measurements that help determine the profile of video streaming traffic: the streaming strategies used by YouTube and Netflix are presented for different browsers, including mobile devices running Android or iOS native applications. The characteristics of data-transfer phases are presented, and the streaming strategies are classified as to whether the on-off cycles are short, long, or non-existent.

Adhikari et al. (2012b) present their work following measurements to reveal the internal mechanisms used by YouTube to deliver their video streams. They report the use of flat video id space by YouTube, multiple DNS namespaces, the logical organization of video servers and the cache hierarchy used.

A specific investigation was carried out by Summers et al. (2012) regarding the benefits or otherwise of dividing video files into chunks that contain portions of the video. They showed that there is little difference in performance between these approaches, except when aggressive pre-fetching techniques are used, in which case storing the video as a single file appeared to be beneficial.

Plissoneau and Biersack (2012) considered streaming from an ISP perspective focusing their attention on YouTube and DailyMotion sites, and investigated the Autonomous Systems (AS) selected to serve each request, and it was found that the choice of AS selected had a considerable impact on the video reception quality. They also considered the link between reception quality and user behavior, and found that most videos are not fully downloaded with users abandoning the viewing part way through.

The authors in Ghobadi et al. (2016) present a mechanism for limiting the transmission rate used by YouTube servers during streaming. As observed above, the normal mode of transmission is quite bursty, placing a great deal of stress on router queues and causing congestion-related problems, such as packet drops and forcing TCP's congestion control algorithms to reduce the rate considerably. They show that by limiting the TCP transmission rate by placing an upper limit on the congestion window, the rate of retransmissions and packet losses can be greatly reduced.

There are clear disadvantages, from the point of view of the network load, in sending bursty traffic as YouTube does. It is well known that the less variable and bursty the traffic profile of a stream, the less it is likely to cause congestion and, consequently, packet losses and high delays. In this work, however, we do not extend the analysis to network performance implications, which will be the subject of future work. The focus is on the buffering requirements on the clients and also on the amount of data transmitted and discarded, ie, wasted bandwidth, when a client aborts a stream part way through.

Another consideration which is left out of this paper is the server buffering requirements, which arise from the need to harmonize different rates of data retrieval from secondary storage and rates of transmission. In previous work, the authors considered video streaming server buffering requirements for consumption rate transmission and for smoothed video streams. In the future, we will also consider server buffering requirements for YouTube type transmission mechanisms.

With video streaming servers, due to the timing requirements of each frame in the sequence, data smoothing is normally restricted to sending data ahead of schedule, or work-ahead smoothing (Bewick et al., 2005; Salehi et al., 1998; Rao and Raghavan, 1999). A typical trace of compressed video is presented below in Fig. 1, where the variability in the data rate is evident.

Both the RTSP and HTTP progressive downloading streaming mechanisms, however, are based on the transmission of a given video file from the server to the client. The client may be able to select from a number of files for the same video, each of a different video quality and thus different bit rate. There is a great deal of

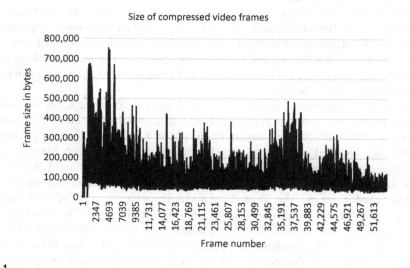

FIG. 1

Profile of a compressed video, showing the variable bit rate that results from constant quality.

variability from client to client with regards to the bandwidth available to them. Also, different devices may have different capabilities in processing and display resolution. However, this is a static selection that is made before transmission starts, and once started the same file is used until the end. In addition to the variability from client to client, which dictates the need for different encoding qualities and thus bit rates, there is also variability over the lifetime of a streaming session for each client: this may be caused by network load fluctuations, and also, in the case of mobile users, due to handover from one cell to another. Dynamic adaptation to network conditions is, therefore, an interesting way forward, whereby the server can switch from one video quality to another. The clear benefits from this concept include: support for uninterrupted streaming under less favorable connection conditions, as the client monitors the connection and estimates the bandwidth availability (by monitoring packet delays and/dropped packets) and adapts to them by requesting segments of the video that can be delivered with the bandwidth available in real time; scalability, as the servers are not saddled with the task of monitoring the networking conditions for each client, rather, each client is responsible for monitoring the state of the connection and making the decision as to when to switch to a different quality level; and seamless transition between quality levels—this can be achieved, as will be described in the next sessions, by having all quality files for the same video having the same GOP start points, so transitions can take place at the beginning of segments that are time-aligned with the equivalent segment in each of the other files of different quality level.

One can view DASH as a form of hybrid scheme, as it has elements from both traditional streaming and progressive download. It uses the HTTP as the transport protocol, but it does not perform a progressive download of the complete file. Rather, the client media player requests, sequentially, byte range downloads that correspond to small chunks of the video file (Stockhammer, 2011; Zambelli, 2009; De Cicco and Mascolo, 2010). The whole file is logically seen as being composed of segments of a few seconds' duration, typically one or a few GOPS, which are then requested one after the other. When the original file is compressed, eg, with an MPEG4 encoder, different files are prepared to support different bit rates. A typical arrangement is for six levels of quality to be used.

There are a number of implementations of the DASH concept, all with small variations. We will consider here the Microsoft approach: IIS Smooth Streaming (Zambelli, 2009). IIS Smooth Streaming uses MP4 file format. There is a different file for each encoded quality and, therefore, different bit rate. Each file is divided into small chunks a few seconds long, normally 2 seconds. These chunks are referred to as fragments, and the fragments of each file are stored contiguously on disk, to facilitate random access (Fig. 2). A client makes requests via an HTTP GET method that specifies the starting position of the first frame in the GOP. The information a client needs for accessing the various fragments of a file is described in an XML file that is referred to as the *manifest* file. Specifically, it contains the available bit rates of each file for that video, the resolution of each file, and the duration of every fragment of the video. In each GET request, the client then will specify the quality level and the starting time of the fragment.

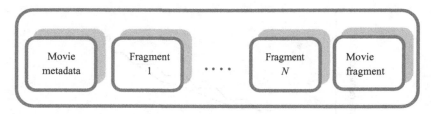

FIG. 2

Structure of a smooth streaming file with N fragments.

The file format used for smooth streaming files follows the overall organization of MP4 files, whose basic units are called "boxes". The file starts with file-level metadata, followed by the movie fragments. The last box facilitates the seeking of various fragments in the file.

Although the rationale for DASH appears persuasive, there is an argument for the simplicity of the progressive download, which has the advantage of lower complexity and processing by client and server. One point in question is, considering for, instance, the specific transmission mechanism adopted by YouTube, that given the amount of buffering performed at the beginning of the streaming, it may be unnecessary to adjust to a variable available bandwidth, at what level of bandwidth deterioration, ie, how small would the bandwidth need to be, and for how long, to force the stream to break due to underflow of the buffer?

On the other hand, as a progressive download relies to a large extent on having a sufficient amount of data in the buffer prior to starting the media presentation at the client (for instance, YouTube applies pretty aggressive buffering, typically enforcing a 40s buffer occupancy level prior to commencing the presentation), this may lead, potentially, to a considerable initial delay, if the available bandwidth during the initial stages is too low. This would be a marked advantage for DASH over progressive downloading, as DASH is less reliant on buffering and seems to apply the initial buffering in parallel with the data presentation (Fig. 3).

These pros and cons in performance need to be set in the right context, which would also include the fact that, with DASH, the client is forced to, at times, rely on low-quality video, as opposed to relying on more buffering. At this stage, comparisons become subjective to some extent, and can be measured with qualitative research on Quality of Experience (QoE).

4 CONTENT DELIVERY NETWORKS

With the explosive growth of Internet traffic that followed the expansion of the Web, social networks, online games, video streaming, video telephony, mobile technology and software download, the Internet ecosystem has become very complex, with a variety of specialist services that depend and interact with each other. As some

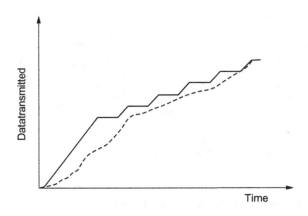

FIG. 3

Transmission mechanism with YouTube Flash (*continuous line*) and with a consumption rate transmission mechanism (*dashed line*).

companies specialized in providing digital content and services typically over the Web, others supplied the physical infrastructure for housing the digital content in an effective and efficient way. The latter service also became quite specialized and more important given the scale of the Internet, both in terms of the number of users and in terms of geographical spread. CDNs thus evolved, investing heavily on server network infrastructure, and the optimized mechanisms for serving users globally.

This separation enabled digital content providers to focus on their product and not have to worry about the set-up of servers, their location, connections to ISPs or core backbones of the Internet, and so forth. This is especially true for the smaller companies. Larger content providers are more likely to be able to afford their own content distribution network. In some cases, major players on the Internet such as Google have acquired content sharing companies such as the video sharing service YouTube. In any case, the concept of a CDN is an important one which encompasses a range of strategies and mechanisms that support the delivery of multimedia content in an effective way. Clearly, this is not a trivial problem, the solution to which requires careful analysis of Internet traffic patterns, cost-effective deployment of servers, mechanisms for efficient load sharing, QoS requirements for different types of media, caching mechanisms, routing and costs of traversing other networks. Poor performance by a video streaming delivery service is likely to leave a negative impression of the provider. There are a number of services that require customer subscription for online video content delivery, such as Netflix and Hulu, and high-quality video delivery is expected. To overcome the limitations of the Internet in terms of QoS provision, very careful planning is necessary to promote high-quality video streaming. There are some big challenges that need to be overcome in order to ensure smooth and timely delivery of data by CDNs. For instance, for Web content, many sites adopt complex dynamic logic that cannot be cached closer to users;

another pressing issue is the fact that users of mobile devices may be requesting, increasingly, content that has not been optimized for mobile devices, which also are often quite far away from the any servers.

As mentioned above, some of the large video content providers have their own CDN. In the US, the dominant video content providers online are Netflix and Hulu. Both offer content from the major TV and movie studios, to subscribers who pay for mostly online delivery, although Hulu also offers DVD postage service. Netflix initially employed the services of commercial CDNs, such as Akamai and Limelight, responsible for over 30% of Internet traffic in the US. In June 2012, Netflix announced it was rolling out its own CDN to deliver its own content. The announcement suggested that the commercial DDNs would still be used for some time, but eventually all Netflix content would be delivered by its own CDN, Open Connect. The statement by Netflix read (Netflix, 2012):

> Now, in addition to these general-purpose commercial CDNs, we are enabling ISPs to get Netflix video data from Open Connect, a single-purpose Netflix content delivery network we've established. The world's other major Internet video provider, YouTube, has long had its own content delivery network. Given our size and growth, it now makes economic sense for Netflix to have one as well. We'll continue to work with our commercial CDN partners for the next few years, but eventually most of our data will be served by Open Connect.

Hulu's content initially was distributed by Akamai. Since 2010, Hulu has been using a multi-provider strategy by having its content distributed also by Limelight and Level3. The work presented in Adhikari et al. (2012a) conducts a series of measurements to try and establish Hulu's mechanism for selecting the CDN for delivering each video upon user request. It concludes, amongst other things, that:

> (1) Hulu CDN selection is done on Hulu's control servers and are communicated to the clients through the manifest files. The preferred CDNs are randomly assigned based on pre-determined probabilities, which are independent of location, video and time. (2) The preferred CDN is also independent of instantaneous available bandwidth observed at the client, although the client can adapt to network congestions by first lowering rate and then switching to different CDNs.

The other leading Internet video provider, YouTube, uses its own CDN for distributing its videos worldwide. As YouTube is the leading video sharing site with a worldwide reach, the organization of its CDN is a truly enormous task of very high complexity. Since 2006, YouTube has been part of Google, and since then YouTube content has been delivered via its own infrastructure, although before then YouTube used third party CDNs. The Google CDN now used to distribute YouTube videos consists of hundreds of edge-nodes throughout the Internet, where each edge-node contains hundreds of video servers, or caches (Giordano et al., 2015). To give an idea of the scale of the operation, there are estimated to be around one billion YouTube users in the world, and approximately 6 billion hours of videos are watched worldwide each month (Giordano et al., 2015). Although Google does not divulge the infrastructure of the Google CDN, there have been a number of experimental studies conducted in order to try and understand it. In Adhikari et al. (2012b), a distributed active measurement system was setup to identify the working of the YouTube video delivery system. They have concluded that the system consists of three major components: the video id space, a three tier cache hierarchy, and a multi-layered DNS namespace. These are described in detail in the referenced paper. In Giordano et al. (2015), a technique is presented to monitor the YouTube delivery system in order to identify changes in its structure. Another piece of work Casas et al. (2014) discusses the characteristics of YouTube traffic accessed through mobile and fixed-line networks. Specifically, the analysis covers YouTube content provisioning, considering the main attributes of the hosting servers as seen from both types of networks. It was shown that YouTube's use of caching in mobile networks greatly benefits the quality of the delivery to mobile devices.

5 MOBILE P2P STREAMING

With the dramatic growth of the mobile device usage many multimedia service providers have started utilizing the mobile peer-to-peer (P2P) streaming option as an alternative to the multimedia CDNs. Research shows that with the mobile devices getting smarter, equipped with longer battery life and more processing power, the mobile P2P video streaming approaches as opposed to client-server model is gaining considerable attention amongst both academic and commercial communities (Kim and Park, 2014; Eittenberger et al., 2012). In this model distributed/end-nodes known as "peers" can communicate with each other as equal parties. In other words they can serve as both clients and servers, which is an opposite model to the client server approach where the end-nodes can only receive and consume services.

In the not-too-distant past, the P2P model was most well-known for file sharing and its ability to provide faster music sharing facilities between the users (peers). In some cases (PPStream, Xunlei, SopCast) supported video streaming too, but mostly over the traditional "wired" networks with PCs or other none-battery-operated devices deploying the services. Most recently, with the advances in mobile communications, wireless networks and cellular networks, P2P promises to provide traffic and load balancing solution with lower costs and higher scalability (Li et al., 2013). The cost-effectiveness is guaranteed by its design nature of not requiring underlying network infrastructure. Another advantage of the P2P model is that a peer is not only downloading a video stream but also sending requests for the video streams to other peers, which helps with the scalability issue (Li et al., 2013).

Large video content providers, such as YouTube, Netflix and others have at different times reported that they have been considering moving from CDN to mobile P2P streaming, but nothing has been officially documented regarding this change. What can be observed in the current academic literature, however, is that interest in using P2P mobile video streaming is growing in both academic and non-academic communities. As a result, there is an ongoing effort to address a number of related issues, such as: bandwidth limitation, security, battery life limitation, load balancing and QoS (Wichtlhuber et al., 2012; Jin and Kwok, 2010). Furthermore, P2P media streaming has been demonstrated to be an effective approach not only in the entertainment domain, but also in other areas such as assisted living, healthcare, and surveillance.

6 ENCODING

One of the fundamental enabling technologies for digital video is compression: the voluminous nature of video data requires efficient compression mechanisms that can substantially reduce the volume of the data whilst at the same time preserving a high-quality experience. In its original form, smooth video with high resolution and color depth generates many hundreds of Mbps. Storing full videos, and transmitting them in real time would take current technology beyond breaking point for CDNs and the Internet. It is of paramount importance that we are able to compress such data to much more tractable data rates and file sizes. Rates of hundreds of Kbps or a few Mbps are typical for most encoders, and moreover lower-quality videos in the region of tens of Kbps are achievable.

All compression techniques exploit some form of redundancy of the data. In the case of video data, there are two main types of redundancy: spatial redundancy and temporal redundancy. Spatial redundancy is present in all still images, and temporal redundancy is present in the sequence of still images that forms a video stream. Video encoders exploit both forms of redundancy. Most encoders apply motion estimation and compensation, as well as the discrete co-sine transform (DCT). Without loss of generality, we describe the main aspects of the MPEG4, H.264/5 video encoding standards, and how these standards can be used in conjunction with video streaming techniques.

The overall arrangement adopted by MPEG4 and H.264/5 standards is to subdivide the whole sequence of still images that forms a video stream into smaller sub-sequences, known as group of pictures (GOP). A typical GOP size is about 10 still images or *frames*. The temporal redundancy is exploited within each GOP in the following way: as frame rates are typically higher than 25 frames per second in the original sequence, each frame being compressed, the *target frame*, tends to be similar to other frames nearby in the sequence, the *reference frames*. Motion estimation and compensation are used to find similar regions (pixel macroblocks) in the reference frames, to calculate the relative displacement, and compute the difference between the target macroblock and the reference macroblocks. Three types of frames are defined: the I frames (Intraframe) that start each GOP, the P frames (Predicted) that reference only previous frames, and the B frames (Bi-directional) that reference both previous and future frames in a GOP. This being the basic structure of compressed video, there are many specific techniques for deriving the I, B, and P frames, and the reader is referred to Seeling and Reisslein (2014) for in-depth treatment of the specific techniques. For live streaming, the timing dependencies associated with the encoding of B frames may in some situations prove a limiting factor. For instance, with MPEG4, the classical B frame encoding used imposes low delay. On the other hand, the H.264 and H.265 adopt a more complex, hierarchical multilevel B encoding which incurs extra delays. For live interactive streams, this may lead to an excessive delay.

We discuss in the remainder of this section some aspects of these standards that have specific relevance to video streaming. One important aspect of any video CODEC when dealing with commercial online streaming is the *Rate-Distortion* (RD) characteristic of the encoder. The RD curve is the plot of distortion (normally the Peak Signal to Noise Ration (PSNR) video quality) as a function of average video bitrate. It dictates the amount of compression achieved as a function of the quality of the compressed video compared to the original. For instance, the H.265 encoder has an RD efficiency twice as high as H.264; in other words, it achieves twice the compression for the same compressed video quality. This is of very high relevance for commercial video distributors as compression rate and encoded quality have high impact on the transmission costs and the satisfaction of the customers. On the other hand, H.265 algorithms are substantially more processing intensive, which makes it less amenable for smaller mobile devices than for the more mature H.264 and MPEG4 codecs.

Another important aspect is whether the encoder produces non-scalable or scalable streams. The MPEG4 and H.264 standard (Seeling and Reisslein, 2014; ITU, 2016; Baccichet et al., 2007) provide a variety of encoding mechanisms, including the Advanced Video Coding AVC for non-scalable coding, and the scalable coding is provided by both MPEG4 and H.264 SVC. Scalable coding consists of a base layer with sufficient content at lower quality, supplemented, when appropriate, by layers of higher quality that can be added to the base layer to improve the quality of the presentation. We now briefly describe the main forms of scalability and discuss some of the implications for streaming.

Temporal scalability:

- With temporal scalability, the base layer consists of only some of the frames in each GOP (regular subsets of the frames that compose a whole video) being displayed. Higher layers are added by including more frames in each GOP;

Spatial scalability:

- The base layer has a lower resolution than the original picture and higher layers of better quality can be achieved by adding more pixels to the base layer;

Quality (SNR) scalability:

- The base layer is encoded with a lower quality (coarse quantization with high quantization parameter value) with higher quality layers being available via successively finer quantization.

H.264 provides an extra, novel SNR quantization scalability mechanism known as H.264 SVC Medium Grain Scalability (MGS) Encoding, which splits a given SNR quality enhancement layer into up to 16 MGS layers. This promotes a much more flexible and RD efficient stream adaptation.

7 CLOUD BASED ENCODING AND TRANSCODING

Cloud computing will play a major role in the Future Internet. Clouds provide on-demand access to applications, platforms and infrastructure. Moreover, the elastic provision associated with clouds brings benefits in terms of costs and utilization of the cloud infrastructure. Cloud computing has the following characteristics: on-demand service; network access; resource pooling; elasticity; resource usage measurement. Cloud computing provides an appropriate model for handling resource intensive computation as well as scalable data storage (Armbrust, 2009).

One of the most widely used cloud based models for processing the type of data normally referred to as Big Data is the MapReduce model: with MapReduce, the tasks associated with a specific analytics job are planned for execution on a computer cluster. There are a number of implementations of MapReduce model, Hadoop being one of the most widely used ones. The Hadoop distributed file system (HDFS) replicates datasets over many nodes, in order to impose some locality on the analytics tasks generated (Dittrich and Quiane-Ruiz, 2012).

As the framework associated with managing and deploying resource intensive computation on the cloud has been successfully deployed, typically using Hadoop, an interesting development has been the utilization of this framework in order to carry out video encoding and transcoding (Xu et al., 2014; Kim et al., 2013; Garcia Kunzel et al., 2010). Video data in a wide variety of formats generated by different sources can only be viewed by some devices, a situation that becomes more critical with the heterogeneity of the devices in the Future Internet. Moreover, some video sources may generate raw, uncompressed video which would need to be compressed and encoded prior to distribution. Video Transcoding Systems take video files with a variety of formats as input and generate as output videos in a given standard format.

Video encoding and transcoding are resource intensive applications, as the complex search associated with matching regions (macroblocks) across different video frames is very time consuming. Hadoop platform is used to split a video sequence into a number of chunks, which can be deployed in parallel to the available servers in the cloud. The resulting reduction in encoding time is very substantial and a wide range of speed up values have been reported in Pereira et al. (2010).

Overall, this is a promising arrangement, and one where naturally some challenges still remain. But the continual growth of mobile device usage coupled with higher-quality communication networks, media streaming devices and increased popularity of video content, video transcoding techniques on the cloud will facilitate the delivery of ever larger amounts of video to heterogeneous devices.

8 INTERNET OF THINGS

We have witnessed, over the last two decades, a continuous shift in the computing paradigm, in which distributed systems have evolved to encompass ever more devices and objects that were, traditionally, not within the scope of computing. The convergence of the networking-computing-telecommunications domains was the precursor of a much wider expansion of the computing world to include real-life objects, thus blurring the boundaries between *real world things* and computers. This is the scenario we are currently starting to experience, and for which many challenges and opportunities are becoming apparent. The concept of the IoT has therefore evolved, drawing from advances in mobile computing and the solid foundations in distributed computing (Fig. 4).

As can be expected from a relatively recent concept that encompasses a wide range of disciplines, the IoT is open to alternative definitions. The IoT is defined by Cluster of European Research projects on the IoT (CERP-IoT) as "*a dynamic global network infrastructure with self capabilities based on standard and interoperable communications protocols where physical and virtual things have identities, physical attributes, virtual personalities and use intelligent interfaces, and are seamlessly integrated into the information network*" (Jain et al., September 2009). In the IoT, "things" are expected to become active participants in business, information and social processes where they interact among themselves and with the environment. Data and information is "sensed" about the environment, and objects react autonomously to the "real/physical world" events as well as influence it (Sundmaeker et al., 2010).

The now widespread availability of devices with computing and communication capabilities, and the technology that enables communications between devices over ad hoc wireless channels, has modified the way people conduct their social/work/

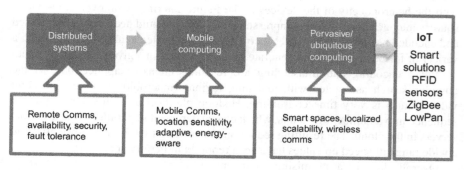

FIG. 4

Evolution of internet technology.

From Pereira, R., Pereira, E., 2015. Video encoding and streaming mechanisms in IoT Low Power Networks. In: FICloud 2015, August 24–26, 2015, Rome.

financial interactions, with an increasing fraction of such communications now taking place digitally. An important aspect of such communications is that they can take place as much as possible in a natural, intuitive manner, as in the case of video and voice communications. Audio and video streaming now accounts for over 50% of Internet traffic by most estimates. It is also expected that this ratio is likely to increase, as increasing sections of the population worldwide interact socially and professionally over the Internet.

8.1 INTERNET OF THINGS APPLICATIONS

IoT has the potential to impact on several application domains. There are a number of taxonomies of the application areas in the literature based on various metrics such as usage areas, network type, availability, heterogeneity and others (Gubbi et al., 2013; Gluhak et al., 2011; Vermesan et al., 2010; Akyildiz et al., 2006). However, for the purpose of the work presented in this chapter, we have looked at application domains where IoT will generate and use multimedia data supported by wireless networks. Guillemin et al. in their early paper on the IoT vision (Guillemin et al., 2010) have identified several IoT application areas spreading from aerospace and aviation to recycling. In the more resent work done by J. Gubbi et al. the application areas were classified into personal and health, enterprise, utilities and mobile categories (Gubbi et al., 2013). We have aligned these categories with the Smart Cities agenda (Fig. 5) and established application areas where video streaming could be potentially used.

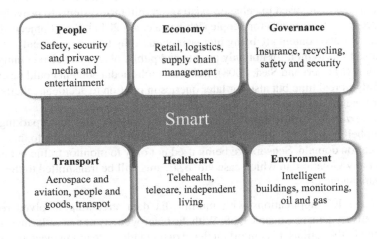

FIG. 5

IoT applications in Smart Cities.

The vision of interconnected smart objects "things" enabling a smart and safer way of living for humans is not a distinct future and many of the application areas of the IoT will rely on multimedia networks and the use of video streaming. Media and entertainment being the most obvious examples, other areas include the safety, security, surveillance, telehealth and independent living, to named just as few, all extensively using real-time video streaming and multimedia sensor networks. Indeed, in their paper on IoT vision Guillemin et al. (2010) describe the vision of Future Internet based on *"Standard communication protocols considering the merging of computer networks, Internet of Media (IoM), Internet of Services (IoS), and Internet of Things (IoT), into a common global IT platform of seamless networks and networked 'things'"*. The IoM will play a crucial role in fulfilling the vision of IoT and is expected to overcome the challenges in scalable video coding and processing, being able to dynamically adapt to heterogeneous networks (Stockhammer, 2011). Recent developments in Wireless Sensor Networks (WSN) mean that sensors can now collect visual and audio data from heterogeneous sources, and provide real time storage and processing for multimedia data. All the areas depicted in Fig. 4 will benefit from such developments.

- *Healthcare*—telecare technology relies on WNS and smart "things" gathering health data from patients which enables ubiquitous delivery of healthcare services. Video and audio sensors can be used for delivering enhanced monitoring and diagnosis services remotely. Monitoring the elderly, or those with conditions such as dementia or epilepsy could benefit from systems that enable real-time video processing and infer emergency situations (Jara et al., 2013; Fernandez and Pallis, 2014).
- *Surveillance, safety and security*—video and audio sensors and interconnected cameras are being used to enhance existing surveillance systems to provide safer and secure environments for people (Ishikawa et al., 2011). Smart objects that generate video content are being increasingly used by law enforcement organizations to monitor not only private and public places, but also country boarders (Merneri and Sasi, 2008). Relevant multimedia content could be crucial not only in real time but also for later queries in relation to accidents, thefts or other type of violation.
- *Transportation*—traffic monitoring, congestion evidence and smart parking (Campbell et al., 2005) are a few of those areas that IoT is bringing to this application domain. Sensors are being used not only to monitor traffic but also to detect any violation, in which case video streams will be transmitted to the relevant agencies.

Some of the IoT applications with multimedia data streaming involved require content delivery with reasonable QoS. With the heterogeneity of networks involved in most of the IoT solutions it is important that existing video streaming mechanisms are carefully considered and evaluated against the communication networks supporting the smart IoT-based solutions.

9 LOW POWER PERSONAL AREA NETWORKS

The realization of the IoT will require the incorporation of wireless networks of low power devices. The limitations associated with these networks are mainly that: such devices have, typically, limited power, computation and storage capabilities; the wireless channels used for communications between such devices or to a base station are likely to be low quality, short range and to use low bit rate channels. Moreover, with regards to the devices themselves, they can be classed as either reduced function devices (RFD) or full function devices (FFD). RFD are likely to contribute the majority of the devices in the IoT, thus designing communications and computing algorithms and mechanisms for RFD is the appropriate approach (IETF, 2015).

Given the variable nature of the devices and networks to be expected in the IoT scenario, it was important that the associated technology, protocols, and related mechanisms for communications between these devices were subjected to standardization efforts, to ensure interoperability between the devices, as well as adequate IP networking with the traditional Internet. A number of challenges ensue when IP connectivity is included: the low quality of the wireless channels dictate low bandwidth and high error rate, and the low processing/storage capability of the devices further requires that the transmission packets are small. Low-power wireless personal area networks (LoWPAN) have been specifically designed to serve mostly so-called RFDs but also to accommodate FFDs in small numbers (IETF, 2015). Both types of devices are short range, low bit rate, low power and low cost. RFDs being very limited in their computational power, memory and energy availability are normally supported by the FFDs, which provide basic functions such as network coordination, packet forwarding, interfacing with other networks, etc.

One of the obvious issues with connecting the LowPANs to the overall Internet is the proliferation of addresses required for identifying such a large number of devices. As a consequence, incorporating IPv6 as the network layer protocol is necessary, as it has a large enough address space for this scenario. The standard put forward is the 6LoWPANs, which assumes, among other constraints and characteristics, the following:

– Small packet size. Since the maximum physical layer packet is 127 bytes (based on the IEEE802.15.4), 81 octets for data packets are available after consideration of low layer header overheads;
– Low bandwidth. Data rates of 250 kbps, 40 kbps, and 20 kbps for different physical layers defined.

Due to the limited packet size, headers have to be compressed, the routing protocol must have low or no overheads on data packets and should be balanced with topology changes and power conservation. Moreover, the routing protocol should also consider the low cost and power taking in account the maintenance and storage of large routing tables is not achievable for high performance.

With applications that comprise video streaming, the above assumptions and limitations associated with LoWPANs severely restrict the type of encoding that can be adopted. Many of the encoding schemes and data presentation mechanisms on the client side rely on a fair amount of computation and memory. Next we consider a number of encoding formats associated with the H.264 standard and assess them against the requirements and limitations imposed by LoWPANs (Martinez-Julia et al., 2013).

9.1 EVALUATION OF H.264 FOR LowPANS

In order to consider the suitability of H.264 encoding mechanisms to LoWPANs, which may have a combination of FFDs and RFDs communicating over low-quality wireless channels, we consider a variety of statistics available from a library of H.264 encoded video traces, encoded with different parameters. For instance, we consider scalable and non-scalable encoding—also known as "single layer" encoding, as well as a variety of quantization and resolution parameters. The library used is available at http://trace.eas.asu.edu/tracemain.html and includes other encoding standards as well, such as H.265 and MPEG4 video traces. For detailed descriptions of the traces, and guidance for using them in performance evaluation studies, please consult (Seeling et al., 2004; Van der Auwera et al., 2008).

Firstly we consider a set of traces with CIF format, non-scalable encoding with different quantization levels and GOP structure, each of which, therefore, leads to different qualities. The video characteristics are presented in Table 1 (Pereira and Pereira, 2015). We now briefly explain some of the parameters that are presented in Table 1.

GOP refers to the structure of the sequence. As these can be arranged in different ways, each trace is based on a specific GOP structure. The scheme used to describe the GOP in the table below is GxBy, where x is the total number of frames in a GOP, and y is the number of B frames between 2 reference frames.

We first discuss the results in Table 1, which presents results for the non-scalable encoding version of H.264. We note that different GOP patterns lead to differences in achieved bit rates, although this difference is relatively minor. Different quantization levels, however, lead to very substantial differences in bit rates after compression. For the mean bit rates, going from low to medium quantization level reduces the bit rate approximately by a factor of 10. A similar reduction factor occurs when going from medium to high quantization level. We further notice that, for all the GOP patterns considered, only when a high quantization level was used were all the mean and peak rates within the 250 Kbps data rate associated with LoWPANs. For the medium quantization level, two out of three videos had mean bit rates too high for LoWPANs channels.

The statistics available from the scalable encoding schemes only allowed us to calculate the mean bit rates for the base layers, which are presented in Table 2. Moreover, for spatial scalability, only the G16B3 GOP pattern was available in the library. We only considered the medium quantization level for the following reason:

Table 1 Mean and Peak Bit Rates for Three Videos—H.264 Non-Scalable Encoding

Bit Rate (BR)	GOP: G16B1			GOP: G16B7			GOP: G16B15		
	Low Q	Med Q	High Q	Low Q	Med Q	High Q	Low Q	Med Q	High Q
Video A									
Mean BR	4.1 Mbps	389 Kbps	35 Kbps	3.8 Mbps	362 Kbps	39 Kbps	3.9 Mbps	362 Kbps	41 Kbps
Peak BR	9.9 Mbps	2.6 Mbps	227 Kbps	9.6 Mbps	2.3 Kbps	210 Kbps	9.7 Mbps	2.3 Mbps	208 Kbps
Video B									
Mean BR	2.5 Mbps	185 Kbps	19 Kbps	2.1 Mbps	185 Kbps	21 Kbps	2.2 Mbps	187 Kbps	23 Kbps
Peak BR	9.8 Mbps	2.4 Mbps	192 Kbps	9.6 Mbps	2.2 Mbps	186 Kbps	9.8 Mbps	2.3 Mbps	188 Kbps
Video C									
Mean BR	7.8 Mbps	609 Kbps	48 Kbps	7.2 Mbps	557 Kbps	55 Kbps	7.3 Mbps	551 Kbps	58 Kbps
Peak BR	12.4 Mbps	2.3 Mbps	238 Kbps	12.1 Mbps	2.1 Mbps	243 Kbps	12.2 Mbps	2.1 Mbps	233 Kbps

Table 2 Mean Bit Rates of Base Layers for Three Videos—H.264 SVC, Temporal and Spatial Scalable Encoding

Mean Bit Rate (BR)	GOP:G16B1 Medium Q	GOP:G16B3 Medium Q	GOP:G16B7 Medium Q	GOP:G16B15 Medium Q
Video A				
Temporal Base Layer	340 Kbps	284 Kbps	197 Kbps	145 Kbps
Spatial Base Layer		129 Kbps		
Video B				
Temporal Base Layer	165 Kbps	153 Kbps	121 Kbps	104 Kbps
Spatial Base Layer		61 Kbps		
Video C				
Temporal Base Layer	522 Kbps	440 Kbps	314 Kbps	240 Kbps
Spatial Base Layer		147 Kbps		

it was clear that for low quantization level, the bit rate would be too high. Also, we know from the non-scalable table that for high quantization level the mean bit rates would be sufficiently low for the LoWPAN channels. We, therefore, only needed to further investigate the bit rates for medium quantization levels.

For temporal scalability, we observed from Table 2 that medium quantization may produce acceptable bit rates for some videos for some of the GOP patterns, but the only GOP pattern that had bit rates below 250 Kbps for all videos considered was G16B15. It is not hard to see why: this GOP has 15 B frames out of 16, therefore the base layer has a very low frame rate of I frames only. It does not present smooth movement, as typically less than 10 fps appear progressively jittery.

For spatial scalability, the QCIF format is used for the base layer. We note that all videos achieve bit rates below 250 Kbps, thus being suitable for LoWPANs. It is also to be noted that, given the devices in question, QCIF format may be appropriate, particularly for low-resolution displays, which may be the case for low-power devices.

10 CONCLUSIONS

Developments in a wide range of related technologies—processing, storage, networking, compression and mobile computing—and the continual popularization of the Web, have led to huge changes with an enormous socio-economic impact, with the widespread adoption of a different way of life based on technology-mediated communication. This has impacted on how people live their lives: work, entertainment, leisure, education, social interaction, commercial transactions and even healthcare are progressively being conducted via digital devices across the Internet. Media rich networked and mobile applications support this shift in the global lifestyle.

Video appears, in this scenario, as one of the most widely used types of media: movie and TV streaming, videoconferencing, education, video telephony, gaming, video sharing in social networks, remote medical diagnoses all rely heavily on video streaming in some form. This poses a number of interesting and difficult challenges which are driving innovation in a variety of technological areas.

We have discussed the nature of video data and its voluminous characteristics. From that perspective, compression is a fundamental concept of paramount importance for the facilitation of video storage and distribution. Compression is an area of continual evolution, supported by the development of novel algorithms as well as the increasing processing and memory capacity of devices, which enable the adoption of ever more complex algorithms to achieve better RD efficiency, improving the quality of compressed videos at lower bit rates, thus enhancing the cost effectiveness of video service infrastructure. In this respect, we have discussed the emergence of specialist CDN providers: the complexity and scale of the current Internet has led to the need for ever more efficient content delivery infrastructures, of worldwide scope. As CDNs promote their services based on their ability to deliver QoS adequate to the requirements of video streaming, it is fundamental that their network of servers is of a large scale, but also cost effective. The principle of locality to the consumer of a stream in order to achieve low delays and error rates, informs the need for efficient caching mechanisms and cooperation with ISPs.

We presented a discussion of the evolution of the video streaming architecture, from the early days of client-server delivery and the scalability issues that surfaced with the popularization of video streaming, via the emergence of P2P solutions with their inherent scalability of the paradigm, as each consumer of resources also offers their own resources to other consumers. We discussed some aspects of P2P networking, the organization of the overlay and the location of resources in the network. The drawbacks of P2P solutions were also raised, mostly in terms of user friendliness and also some networking limitations. This led to the Web-based model, in which CDNs provide highly scalable support for digital content creators.

There are a variety of streaming mechanisms that can be adopted, and from the early days, specialized protocols for streaming were developed. The RTP/RTCP protocols were designed as solutions to the lack of specific multimedia transport protocols, and the apparent lack of suitability of either the UDP or the TCP protocols. The supplementary transport functionality provided by the RTP protocol was designed to support multimedia data networking, on top of the basic UDP protocol. Although this was a technically sound solution, the already widespread existence of Web servers based on the HTTP protocol made a strong case for using the HTTP protocol as the application level protocol for streaming. The initial solution was based on progressive download, which is, strictly speaking, not a form of streaming, but one that mimicks streaming behavior. Later, dynamic adaptive streaming over HTTP, DASH, based on repeated requests by the client for consecutive segments of the video stream, was popularized via a number of implementations. The dynamic nature of the Internet and fluctuations in available resources provided a motivation for DASH: the client can request, for each segment, a different quality level based on the assessment of the available bandwidth presently on the path from server to client.

We discussed also the challenges proposed by the developments associated with smart objects and the Internet of Things. These objects of varying computing, memory and energy capacity are connected to each other and via base stations to the Internet by means of low-quality, variable channels. This, in some respects, will drive the technology in video streaming and the miniaturization of computing. There has never been a more exciting time for developments in computing, and video streaming technologies are certain to provide some of the most interesting developments in the new computing frontier.

ACRONYMS

6LoWPAN	IPv6 over low power wireless personal area networks
CIF	common intermediate format
CDN	content delivery networks
C/S	client-server
DASH	dynamic adaptive streaming
DCT	discrete co-sine transform
FFD	full function devices
GOP	group of pictures
HDFS	Hadoop distributed file system
HTML	hyper text markup language
HTTP	hypertext transfer protocol
IoT	Internet of Things
LowPANs	low power personal area networks
P2P	peer-to-peer
MPEG	moving picture experts group
QCIF	quarter common intermediate format
QoS	quality of service
RD	rate distortion
RED	random early detection
RFD	reduced function devices
RTP	real-time transport protocol
RTCP	RTP control protocol
RTSP	real-time streaming protocol
SVE	scalable video encoding
TCP	transmission control protocol
UDP	user datagram protocol

GLOSSARY

6LowPANs A standard for using IPv6 over low power personal area networks.

Cloud computing Generic model for delivery of hosted services over the Internet.

Compression The process reformatting data to reduce its size.

Content delivery networks Networks that specialize in hosting content (usually from client organizations) for delivery to clients.

Hadoop An open-source software framework for scalable, distributed computing of large data sets.

Internet of Things A network of physical objects with computing and communications capabilities.

MapReduce A model for processing large data sets using parallel algorithms to explore clusters of servers.

Mobile P2P The concept of peer nodes collaborating over wireless channels.

Netflix A large commercial provider of video-on-demand for streaming over the Internet.

Peer-to-peer/P2P A distributed computing paradigm based on collaboration and sharing resources between peer nodes, as opposed to the Client Server paradigm.

Progressive download A technique that enables content to be displayed by a web browser during download.

Protocols The sets of rules for correct communication of data across communication channels and networks.

Scalable video encoding A type of video encoding based on a low quality base layer to which high quality layers can be added.

Transcoding The process of converting from one encoding format to another.

Video encoding The specific data format resulting from the compression process.

Video frames The still images that compose a video sequence.

Video streaming The technique that enables video data to be presented by the media player as the data arrives at the client, thus not having to fully download the file prior to display.

YouTube A video sharing, web based service that allow users to upload, download and share videos using MPEG4/H.264 formats.

REFERENCES

Adhikari, V., Guo, Y., Hao, F., Hilt, V., Zhang, Z.L., 2012a, A tale of three CDNs: an active measurement study of Hulu and its CDNs. In: Proceedings of the Infocom.

Adhikari, V.K., Jain, S., Chen, Y., Zhang, Z.L., 2012b, Vivisecting YouTube: an active measurement study. In: Proceedings of INFOCOM.

Akyildiz, I.F., Melodia, T., Chowdhury, K.R., 2006. A survey on wireless multimedia sensor networks. Comput. Netw. 51 (4), 921–960.

Armbrust, M., 2009. Above the Clouds, A Berkeley View of Cloud Computing. Technical Report UCB/EECS-2009-28, February [online].

Baccichet, P., Rane, S., Chimienti, A., Girod, B., 2007. Robust low-delay video transmission using H.264/AVC redundant slices and flexible macroblock ordering. In: IEEE International Conference on Image Processing, ICIP 2007.

Bewick, C., Pereira, R., Merabti, M., 2005. Admission control and routing of smoothed video streams. Int. J. Simul. Syst. Sci. Technol. 6 (3–4), 61–68.

Campbell, J., Gibbons, P.B., Nath, S., Pillai, P., Seshan, S., Sukthankar, R., 2005. IrisNet: an Internet-scale architecture for multimedia sensors. In: Proceedings of the ACM Multimedia Conference.

Casas, P., Fiadino, P., Bar, A., D'Alconzo, A., 2014. YouTube all around: characterizing YouTube from mobile and fixed-line network vantage points. In: 2014 European Conference on Networks and Communications, EuCNC 2014, Bologna, IT, June 23, 2014.

De Cicco, L., Mascolo, S., 2010. An experimental investigation of the Akamai adaptive video streaming. In: Proc. of USAB WIMA.

Dittrich, J., Quiane-Ruiz, J., 2012. Efficient big data processing in Hadoop MapReduce. In: Proceedings of the VLDB Endowment, August 27–31, 2012, vol. 5, 12, Istambul.

Eittenberger, P.M., Herbst, M., Krieger, U.R., 2012. RapidStream: P2P streaming on Android. In: Proceedings of IEEE 19th International Packet Video Workshop, May 10–11, 2012, Germany, Munich.

Fernandez, F., Pallis, G.C., 2014. Opportunities and challenges of the Internet of Things for Healthcare. In: Proceedings of the International Conference on Wireless Mobile Communications and Healthcare, MobiHealth'14, Athens.

Garcia Kunzel, A., Kalva, H., Fuhrt, B., 2010. A study of transcoding on cloud environments for video content delivery. In: 3rd ACM Workshop on Mobile Cloud Media Computing, MCMC'10, October 29, 2010, Firenze, Italy.

Ghobadi, M., Cheng, Y., Jain, A., Mathis, M., 2016. Trickle: rate limiting YouTube video streaming. In: Proceedings of USE.

Giordano, D., Traverso, S., Grimaudo, L., Mellia, M., 2015. YouLigther: an unsupervised methodology to unveil YouTube CDN changes. In: 27th International Teletraffic Congress (ITC 27), September 8–10, Ghent, Belgium.

Gluhak, A., Krco, S., Nati, M., Pfisterer, D., Mitton, N., Razafindralambo, T., 2011. A survey on facilities for experimental Internet of Things research. IEEE Commun. Mag. 49, 58–67.

Gubbi, J., Buyya, R., Marusic, S., Palaniswami, M., 2013. Internet of Things (IoT): a vision, architectural elements, and future directions. Futur. Gener. Comput. Syst. 29, 1645–1660.

Guillemin, P., Vermesan, O., Harrison, M., Vogt, H., Kalaboukas, K., Tomasella, M., Wouters, K., Gusmeroli, S., Haller, S., 2010. Vision and challenges for realising the Internet of Things. In: CERP-IoT: Cluster of European Research Projects on the Internet of Things.

Hadar, O., Cohen, R., 2001. PCRTT enhancement for off-line video smoothing. J. Real Time Imaging 7 (3), 301–314.

IETF, 2015. IPv6 Over Low-Power Wireless Personal Area Networks (6LoWPANs): Overview, Assumptions, Problem Statement, and Goals RFC 4919. https://datatracker.ietf.org/doc/rfc4919/?include_text=1.

Ishikawa, N., Kato, T., Osano, T., 2011. High-definition surveillance camera control system from mobile phones. In: Inproceedings of the 8th Annual IEEE Consumer Communications and Networking Conference–Pecial Session Ecological Home Network, Las Vegas, USA.

ITU, 2016. Recommendation ITU-T H.264. http://www.itu.int/en/ITUT/publications/Pages/recs.aspx.

Jain, A.K., Hong, L., Pankanti, S., September 2009. Internet of Things–Strategic Research Roadmap. Technical report, Cluster of European Research projects on the Internet of Things.

Jara, A.J., Zamora-Izquierdo, M.A., Skarmeta, A.F., 2013. Interconnected framework for mHealth and remote monitoring based on the Internet of Things. IEEE J. Sel. Areas Commun./Suppl. 31 (9).

Jin, X., Kwok, Y., 2010. Cloud assisted P2P media streaming for bandwidth constrained mobile subscribers. In: Proceedings of the 16th IEEE International Conference on Parallel and Distributed Systems, December 8–10, 2010, Shanghai, China.

Kim, J., Park, S., 2014. Resource analysis for mobile P2P live video streaming. In: Ubiquitous Information Technology and Applications, Lecture Notes in Electrical Engineering, vol. 280.

Kim, M., Cui, Y., Han, S., Lee, H., 2013. Towards efficient design and implementation of a Hadoop-based distributed video transcoding system in cloud computing environment. Int. J. Multimedia Ubiquit. Eng. 8 (2).

Li, B., Wang, Z., Liu, J., Zhu, W., 2013. Two decades of Internet video streaming: a retrospective view. Trans. Multimed. Comput. Appl. 2 (3).

Martinez-Julia, P., Garcia, E., Murillo, J., Skarmetta, A., 2013. Evaluating video streaming in network architectures for the Internet of Things. In: 7th International Conference on Innovative Mobile and Internet Services in Ubiquitous Computing.

Merneri, K., Sasi, S., 2008. Automated surveillance of intruders as US boarders. In: Novel Algorithms and Techniques in Telecommunication, Automation and Industrial Electronics. Springer, Berlin.

Netflix, 2012. Announcing the Netflix Open Connect Network. http://blog.netflix.com/2012/06/announcing-netflix-open-connect-network.html.

Pereira, R., Azambuja, M., Breitman, K., Endler, M., 2010. An architecture for distributed high performance video processing in the cloud. In: IEEE 3rd International Conference on Cloud Computing, July 5–10, 2010.

Pereira, R., Grishikashvili, E., Ajeyi, O., 2007. Efficient real-time packet scheduling for smoothed video streams. Int. J. Simul. 8 (3), 47–60.

Pereira, R., Pereira, E., 2015. Video encoding and streaming mechanisms in IoT Low Power Networks. In: FICloud 2015, August 24–26, 2015, Rome.

Plissoneau, L., Biersack, E., 2012. A longitudinal view of HTTP video streaming performance. In: Proceedings of the 3rd Multimedia Systems Conference, MMSys'12.

Rao, A., Lim, Y.S., Barakat, C., Legout, A., Towsley, D., Dabbous, W., 2011. Network characteristics of video streaming traffic. In: ACM CoNEXT.

Rao, S.G., Raghavan, S.V., 1999. Fast techniques for the optimal smoothing of stored video. Multimedia Syst. 7 (3), 222–233.

Salehi, J., Zhang, Z., Kurose, J., Towsley, D., 1998. Supporting stored video: reducing rate variability and end-to-end resource requirements through optimal smoothing. IEEE/ACM Trans. Networking 6 (4), 397–410.

Seeling, P., Reisslein, M., 2014. Video traffic characteristics of modern encoding standards: H.264/AVC with SVC and MVC extensions and H.265/HEVC. Sci. World J. 2014.

Seeling, P., Reisslein, M., Kulapala, B., 2004. Network performance evaluation with frame size and quality traces of single-layer and two-layer video: a tutorial. IEEE Commun. Surv. Tutorials 6 (3) 58–78.

Stockhammer, T., 2011. Dynamic adaptive streaming over HTTP–standards and design principles. In: ACM Multimedia Systems, vols. 133–143.

Summers, J., Brecht, T., Eager, D., Wong, B., 2012. To chunk or not to chunk: implications for HTTP streaming video server performance. In: Proceedings of NOSSDAV'12.

Sundmaeker, H., Guillemin, P., Friess, P., Woelfflé, S., 2010. Vision and challenges for realising the Internet of Things. In: Cluster of European Research Projects on the Internet of Things–CERP IoT.

Van der Auwera, G., David, P.T., Reisslein, M., 2008. Traffic and quality characterization of single-layer video streams encoded with H.264/MPEG-4 advanced video coding standard and scalable video coding extension. IEEE Trans. Broadcast. 54 (3) 698–718.

Vermesan, O., Harrison, M., Vogt, H., Kalaboukas, K., Tomasella, M., Wouters, K., Gusmeroli, S., Haller, S., 2010. Vision and challenges for realising the Internet of Things. In: CERP-IoT: Cluster of European Research Projects on the Internet of Things.

Wichtlhuber, M., Ruckert, J., Stingl, D., Schulz, M., Hausher, D., 2012. Energy-efficient mobile P2P video streaming. In: Proceedings of IEEE 12th International Conference on Peer-to-Peer Computing (P2P), September 3–5, 2012, Tarragona, Spain.

Xu, H., Wang, L., Xie, J., 2014. Design and experiment analysis of a Hadoop-based video transcoding system for next generation wireless sensor networks. Int. J. Distrib. Sens. Netw. 2014.

Zambelli, A., 2009. IIS Smooth Streaming Technical Overview. Microsoft Corporation.

Extending cloud-based applications with mobile opportunistic networks: Security issues and privacy challenges

14

S. Pal[a], W. Moreira[b,c]

School of Computer Science, University of St Andrews, St Andrews, United Kingdom[a]
COPELABS, University Lusofona, Lisbon, Portugal[b]
PPGMO, Federal University of Goiás, Goiás, Brazil[c]

1 INTRODUCTION

With the tremendous growth in the number of mobile devices in recent years, people are looking for more advanced platforms in order to use their computational applications more quickly and in a more convenient way. These mobile devices are some of the most popular platforms to access the Internet, and the frequency of usage of cloud-based solutions through these devices has increased remarkably (Nguyen et al., 2011). The term "cloud" (Armbrust et al., 2010) refers to the hosted service (eg, processing, storage), which is a fast-growing technology in today's busy technological world. Users can avail themselves of the cloud services anywhere at any time with the help of the Internet. Unlike other traditional services, the cloud uses the "pay-as-you-go" scheme, which makes this technology more flexible to its users.

Mobile users are able to connect cloud-based applications into their mobile devices like other traditional desktop or workstation computers with the help of the available network connections. Therefore, the advent of cloud-based applications and the advanced techniques of wireless communications, along with the evolved smart mobile devices, enable mobile-cloud technology (Giurgiu et al., 2009), which is becoming an integral part of our daily lives by providing a new, straightforward means for information sharing in today's digital society. In mobile-cloud technology either the cloud computing applications are running on the mobile devices or the devices are using cloud-based applications with the help of a mobile

Pervasive Computing. http://dx.doi.org/10.1016/B978-0-12-803663-1.00014-0

445

application (Khan et al., 2014). This mobile-cloud integration allows resource-constrained devices to experience the advantages of cloud-based applications, which in turn improve the computational capabilities, storage size, battery power as well as contextual awareness of these devices (Bahl et al., 2012).

However, while the use of mobile-cloud technology improves the opportunity to use cloud-based applications through resource-constrained mobile devices, one of the major constraints of using this technology is that it needs a continuous network connection for communication with its users. This is difficult in places without a readily available infrastructure (eg, in sparse) rural areas but also in places with infrastructure (eg, in high density) urban areas with restricted access (due to security reasons) and suffering from high levels of interference.

In such situations, mobile opportunistic networks (Lakkakorpi et al., 2010) enable users to access available network connections depending upon the different contact opportunities with other users (ie, considering human interactions), and whether they are willing to store and forward information on behalf of others until such information is delivered to its intended destinations (cf. interaction in the "user's mobile devices" layer of Fig. 1). Mobility and interactions are important parts in this type of network. There is no fixed communication path available and the delivery of messages depends upon sporadic contacts among the users within the network. This type of communication can be established by creating a network in which locally available users utilize their mobile devices for information exchange with their peers in a proximal distance (Pelusi et al., 2006). The fundamental motivation of such a network is to enable communication over a shorter range, where a user can contact others located at a fairly close distance.

Thus, as shown in Fig. 1, the envisioned mobile opportunistic/cloud-based network relies upon the contact opportunities available among different users' devices to access cloud-based applications. That is, users help one another by storing, carrying, and forwarding data according to their available resources and communication networks, allowing the extension of cloud-based applications to areas where access to information is desired, but connectivity is rather poor or may not even be available. For example, a tourist, exploring a rural area, would like to share his photos using his cloud-assisted online photo sharing account (eg, flicker[1]). Since the Internet connection is not easily found in such area, he can rely upon our envisioned mobile opportunistic/cloud-based network: his device could exploit the contact opportunities with devices of nearby local users, which would allow him to access a cloud-assisted platform to share his photos with his online friends. This is highly influenced by the local user's social collaborations and willingness to actively take part in the communication. This is a decentralized environment which is able to adopt heterogeneity of the networks and mobile devices. Users (eg, tourists) can find a local user (eg, local people) who may be able to help them to access to a cloud-based application.

---

[1] https://www.flickr.com/.

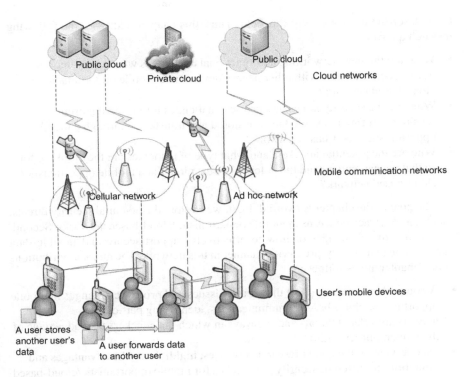

Public cloud

Private cloud

Public cloud

Cloud networks

Mobile communication networks

Cellular network

Ad hoc network

User's mobile devices

A user stores
another user's
data

A user forwards data
to another user

FIG. 1

Vision toward a comprehensive and collaborative opportunistic mobile/cloud-based
network, where users can seamlessly integrate their mobile devices and cloud-based
applications in a challenged environment.

Therefore, the emergence of a mobile opportunistic/cloud-based network is
promising for communication in such challenged environments. In short, this new
networking trend fuses efficient user collaborations and interactions with the help
of mobile opportunistic networks to avail the users of cloud-based applications.
However, it introduces new security issues and privacy challenges due in part to
the network's heterogeneity, user's mobility, device's limited resources (eg, battery,
storage) as well as the sharing of the user's location and personal information
(Rosado et al., 2012).

Most of the recent research has been focused on the development of opportunistic networks and mobile-cloud technology, along with their issues and challenges (Fernando et al., 2013; Helgason et al., 2010; Conti and Kumar, 2010), but
exactly how mobile opportunistic networks can be employed to provide a secure
and improved quality-based service in challenged environments is an area that is
lacking in present research. We envision future research on this issue and try to collate

the state-of-the-art research in this field. Thus, this chapter addresses the following research questions:

- What are the new networking and functional challenges when users' mobile devices communicate with other nearby devices in a mobile opportunistic/ cloud-based network?
- What are the security issues and privacy challenges for protecting users' sensitive information while they are stored and transferred through a mobile opportunistic/cloud-based network?
- Who are the potential attackers and what type of resources are they looking for so that we can understand the potential threat model in a mobile opportunistic/ cloud-based network?

The goal of the chapter is twofold. First, we explore the potential security threats, attacks, and privacy concerns in mobile opportunistic/cloud-based networks. Second, we identify the challenges of how to effectively support secure and flexible data transmission in a privacy-preserving manner in this network. The major contributions of this chapter are as follows:

- A comprehensive analysis of the security issues and privacy challenges in mobile opportunistic/cloud-based communications, identifying particular networking-related threats and the ways in which the attackers take advantage of the vulnerabilities within the system.
- An overview of the recent research advances, highlighting the advantages and limitations to different security approaches for mobile opportunistic/cloud-based networks.
- A detailed analysis of the existing vulnerabilities and threats within these security approaches of mobile opportunistic/cloud-based networks, identifying what type of service models are vulnerable to attacks and how these models are affected by threats and security challenges.
- A mapping of the relationships between vulnerability and threats as well as the possible countermeasures to solve or address these issues by exploring the existing security and privacy-aware solutions to help defeat the threats that may compromise the system.
- An original set of future research challenges, with the intent to bring attention to motivate further research on enabling privacy-assured data transmission and securing data storage in mobile opportunistic/cloud-based networks.

The rest of the chapter is organized as follows. Section 2 describes the security and privacy issues related to networking and functional challenges in mobile opportunistic/cloud-based networks and their possible defenses. Section 3 explores the security and privacy issues related to data storage and resource management challenges in such networks along with possible countermeasures. Finally, we discuss the future research directions in Section 4, and present our concluding remarks in Section 5.

2 NETWORKING AND FUNCTIONAL CHALLENGES

In this section, we discuss four major networking and functional challenges concerning the use of mobile opportunistic/cloud-based networks through users' mobile devices, and the resulting security and privacy issues that arise from these challenges. These are related to the nodes' mobility, heterogeneity of networks, constraints related to the mobile devices, and users' behavior.

2.1 HIGH MOBILITY OF THE NODES

Users' mobility patterns play a significant part in the transferral of information in a real-life scenario (Karamshuk et al., 2011). In the mobile opportunistic/cloud-based scenario that we envision, nodes (ie, the users in real-life) expect to send and retrieve information while they carry on their daily routines (Alberti et al., 2015). Thus, nodes are highly dynamic in nature and the devices in the network may rely on sporadic connections with other nearby mobile devices as an opportunity for data forwarding, regardless of the availability of network connectivity and of the surrounding set of neighboring devices (Moreira and Mendes, 2015a,b).

An important feature of a mobile opportunistic/cloud-based network is that it shall not keep track of the current network topology. So, the data-forwarding decision is made exclusively based on knowledge available locally (Pelusi et al., 2006). A routing path between the source and destination may not exist and a node forwards packet to intermediate nodes until the intended destination is found. Therefore, it is impractical to establish end-to-end secure routing strategies for this communication.

Consequently, mobile opportunistic/cloud-based communications require highly dynamic security and privacy solutions that do not depend of a predefined path, and that should take place at every hop.

With that in mind, security schemes could exploit mechanisms analogous to the custody transfer found in delay-tolerant networking (DTN) (Fall, 2003). In this case, the current node sending the message shall guarantee a secure delivery to a next hop: by employing trust mechanisms, which characterize how reliable the next hop may be (Ballester Lafuente et al., 2014).

As privacy leakage is inherent to this hop-based scenario (ie, attackers explicitly target an individual or a group of individual's data stored in a cloud database), relational privacy could be employed while storing and sharing data in a mobile opportunistic/cloud-based network. Strong relational privacy (eg, a friendship or contractual association) can mitigate data leakage by keeping a trusted relationship between the users participating in data forwarding (Wang, 2010).

In the context of mobile opportunistic/cloud-based networks, a node should share data with other nodes following a reliable relation between them. A node should use secure encryption techniques for storing data in a cloud data center. The information provenance mechanism for cloud-based networks that identifies fault identification and security violations by using the dynamic nature of the network could be an alternative. This solution is able to maintain the integrity of electronic data in storage and archival services while transferring them from one user to another by dynamic encryption mechanisms (Sakka et al., 2010).

Another alternative to improve hop-based security could be the utilization of a key management framework that enables the bootstrapping of local security associations between a node and its neighbors along with the discovery of the neighborhood topology (Shikfa et al., 2010). In mobile opportunistic/cloud-based networks, this framework could prevent "sybil attacks" (Douceur, 2002), where a node's reliability is affected by the foreign-attacked nodes.

It is imperative that, when addressing the privacy and security issues concerning the use of cloud-based solutions through different mobile opportunistic contacts, new solutions consider dynamic mechanisms that could mitigate these emerging security threats and attacks, resulting from how users move within the system.

2.2 HETEROGENEITY OF NETWORKS

Heterogeneity here refers to the use of different connectivity means to access data. In a mobile opportunistic/cloud-based network, mobile devices do not use a unique type of connectivity all the time (Stuedi et al., 2010).

This connectivity is limited (eg, user's 3G plan) and may vary from place to place (eg, home, on the bus). Such a connection can be provided from a wired network, that has high bandwidth; from wireless local (school) and/or wide (municipality) area networks with limited bandwidth; through wireless private area network by means of Bluetooth; or from the user's cellular network (Lei et al., 2013).

Additionally, communication in mobile opportunistic/cloud-based networks depends upon the node's mobility and their interactions, and the availability of networks to which users connect (Sanaei et al., 2014). In the absence of a global infrastructure, users roam between and/or connect to different types of networks, constantly searching for available connections in order to share information with one another. Needless to say users may end up as victims of other malicious users offering "free" connectivity.

There are strategies to deal with security and privacy issues resulting from this network heterogeneity. The "Intelligent Radio Network Access" architecture seamlessly integrates the device's dynamics and heterogeneity of the available networks based on the user's application requirements (Mannweiler et al., 2009). This architecture uses a uniform resource identifier (URI), provided by the service broker in the network. URI is a unique user's identification that provides a context-aware service management to that user in a specific network.

Within the mobile opportunistic/cloud-based network, this URI gives a unique user identification for seamless communication using different connectivity and networks. This in turn may result in a decrease in the number of unauthorized users accessing the network.

Another alternative helps user's mobile devices to get an alternative connection to avail a seamless cloud-based application during a connection failure, while traveling though a heterogeneous network (Huerta-Canepa and Lee, 2010). This architecture depends upon the nearby user who may be able to provide a stable connection for communication. Therefore, this architecture may help users to communicate with one another to avail themselves of a network connection in a challenged environment.

The lack of a global infrastructure opens up the possibility of a threat as users rely on different networks for communication, which may be insecure. For instance, an attacker creates vulnerabilities by decrypting a hash that is not strongly protected by encryptions. This adds a new level of complexity for security systems to these kinds of networks on which the mobile users easily rely.

Therefore, nodes in a mobile opportunistic/cloud-based network need seamless integration between the different connectivity means to which they normally resort. Nodes accessing data via different network connections should be provided with trusted connectivity and supported by dynamic routing protocols that follow the node's trusted encounters for controlling data exchange at runtime.

2.3 DEVICE CONSTRAINTS

Mobile devices are limited in various ways, for example, battery lifetime, available storage or processing power (Giurgiu et al., 2009). In mobile opportunistic/cloud-based networks, these limitations are the major constraints to providing a seamless service to its users.

Due to the limitations of battery lifetime in these devices, it is not possible to run them all the time in challenged environment, for example, for a tourist who is traveling in a rural place. Therefore, depending upon the user's choice, a device may be configured to shutdown wireless cards to spare battery, thus affecting its communication capabilities.

Moreover, keeping track of contact opportunities tends to be more expensive in terms of energy usage than maintaining existing connections. To address this battery-related constraint, a context-aware battery management system for mobile devices may be employed (Ravi et al., 2008). This context-aware battery management system warns the user when it detects a power limitation. The usefulness of this system is that it considers the current set of running applications and predicts the one most important to the user. This system can also distinguish between the important and nonimportant calls depending upon the previous applications and uses.

Therefore, in a challenged environment this system can save battery power by choosing intermediate devices that could improve the user's access to cloud space. However, it is difficult to predict the patterns all the time due to a user's mobility, interactions, present locations, and various calling patterns.

Similarly, storage and device processing power may be already committed locally to the user's own applications, which at times can make it hard to share with other users. As this constant search for the resources can introduce vulnerabilities inside the system (eg, malicious nodes may offer their resources to get access to user's information), users must be provided with alternatives to get access to different resources that guarantee a secured data exchange (Hung et al., 2012).

This type of issue can be solved through a cryptography-based security architecture for accessing stored data in a cloud-based infrastructure (Sedayao et al., 2009). With this architecture, users have exclusive control of the private key for accessing their data. In mobile opportunistic/cloud-based networks, this architecture can prevent unwanted data access from other users in the system. However, it does not support data integrity if the system is compromised by the attackers.

Future research needs to focus on the faster discovery of nearby users' devices from the perspective of an external user (eg, a tourist) locating a safer path that connects to a group of target users with similar interests (eg, users interested in sports, literature, food) in a challenged environment. Consequently, this will help to mitigate the battery-related issues in such communications as only relevant intermediate users are selected in the communication path.

Additionally, the present mobile opportunistic/cloud-based networks require a strict security architecture that supports secure/privacy-aware computation offloading mechanisms and being optimized in terms of device's heterogeneity. Based on this, strong data encryption techniques can be enforced to secure communication between users from intruders who may hack the network during data offloading (Meng et al., 2015).

This further ensures that the user's privacy remains protected with trust management and private data isolation from unwanted user access to the device and data loss from lost or stolen devices. The former issue (ie, data isolation from unwanted user's access) can be dealt with using a thin client like antimalware/antivirus or a strong system password may be installed which must be updated frequently to monitor malware.

Further, the latter issue (ie, lost or stolen devices) can be addressed by employing a secure data processing framework (Huang et al., 2011). In this framework, the end users have full control of the data stored in a cloud database (ie, virtual hard drive). Each mobile device is virtualized and processes data using a trust-based mechanism. Therefore, in the context of a mobile opportunistic/cloud-based network, if a user's mobile device is lost or stolen, the data can easily be retrieved or transferred securely into another system.

2.4 UNPREDICTABLE USER BEHAVIOR

In mobile opportunistic/cloud-based networks, resources need to be shared among mobile nodes that act as relay entities for this type of communication. As the mobile devices belong to the users, the users' interactions and willingness to share the information/resources with each other is vital in this respect, and this may vary from region to region, with cultural and language barriers, and differences in human behavior (Karim and Mahmoud, 2013).

In a real-life environment the exact behavior of a user is unpredictable. A node (ie, a user in real-life) can enter or leave the network at will, they can turn on and off their mobile devices at their preferences. These are situations in which contact opportunities for storing and forwarding information at runtime are easily lost. Furthermore, these situations introduce security issues, as users may find themselves in an unknown area (once they turn their devices back on) and the available contact opportunities may be toward malicious nodes.

The altruism can also cause uncertainty in many ways for social-based communication. However, in a real-life application scenario, selfish behavior is more general and difficult to avoid. Proper incentive mechanisms can help users to perform accordingly to actively participate in communication (Wang et al., 2012).

Based on this principle, mechanisms for detecting selfish behavior and encouraging cooperative behavior are imperative (Ciobanu et al., 2014). By employing social knowledge when detecting selfish nodes in the system, data exchange can easily take place among trusted nodes, mitigating security issues that arise from uncooperative behavior.

Moreover, incentives may be extended in terms of the social reputation, where users gain a higher position in the social community based on their satisfactory behavior. This helps to encourage other users to engage in the data exchange process, and reduces the chances of interaction with malicious users (Scekic et al., 2013).

User behavior inference and incentive mechanisms can help mitigate the effects of unpredictability and a lack of cooperative behavior. Therefore, secure exchange can be guaranteed, as data can travel only between those who are available at the given moment and that trust one another.

In addition, several social-aware (ie, utilizing levels of social relationships besides the physical contact) and social-oblivious (ie, focusing solely on the physical contact among users) mechanisms exist that focus on the importance of message forwarding in a mobile opportunistic/cloud-based network (Moreira and Mendes, 2013). These mechanisms establish the baseline for the implementation of novel routing mechanisms that will be able to forward messages even considering the unpredictable behavior of users by looking at trust and social similarities between these users.

Consequently, research is needed to investigate local users' social interactions and group-based community structures for sharing information to improve the message delivery performance (eg, for the tourists) in a challenged environment. It would be helpful to combine content knowledge (eg, content type, content interest) with user social proximity within the mobile opportunistic/cloud-based network. This would, in turn, bring benefits to the users in the form of faster and better message delivery performance, overcoming lack of trust and cooperative behavior that can easily be found in such challenged networks.

2.5 SUMMARY

In this section, we have discussed relevant *networking and functional challenges* from the security and privacy perspectives in the context of mobile opportunistic/cloud-based networks.

We have learned that security and privacy issues are the bottleneck to the system and also considered the mobility of nodes, heterogeneity of networks, device constraints and the unpredictability of users' behavior.

From the security perspective, it is important to take into consideration strong encryption-based techniques to secure the exchange of users' data over the network. On the other hand, from a privacy viewpoint, it is necessary to take proper safeguards to ensure that the users' private data are protected at data storage from unauthorized user access.

Regarding *security issues*, there are a number of concerns that need to be addressed in a mobile opportunistic/cloud-based network and these depend upon the node's service provision and various network-communication means. Some of these security issues are new to the network (eg, security issues due to the lack of dynamic resource management or device's battery power) and some of them are the same as those for the traditional service provision models (eg, sybil attacks or nontrusted user's access to the system).

Security threats and associated risks can be caused by the unwanted data access by malicious nodes in the network, which is difficult to predict due to the dynamic behavior and high mobility of the nodes. These security risks are related to the application, middleware, and the wireless physical layers' perspectives. Moreover, the lack of a standardized communication protocol between and within the mobile opportunistic/cloud-based networks, makes it difficult to apply a requirement-specific security model to the system. The device's constraints related to battery power or available storage also pose an increased risk compared to traditional desktop applications and may introduce vulnerability to the system in the form of intruders in a malicious wireless network environment offering an easy access to resources.

Concerning *privacy issues*, mobile opportunistic/cloud-based networks pose an inherent challenge to data privacy because data in such networks are being stored in numerous intermediate nodes, some of which may not be trusted. The major privacy issues are related to leakage of a user's private data and unauthorized secondary access of a user's personal-identifiable-information (PII).

Opportunistic/cloud-based networks in the context of the aforementioned networking and functional challenges, these privacy threats differ according to the type of application scenario and communication technology. More generally, the dynamic nature of such networks raises great privacy concerns due to the lack of a standard privacy-aware security framework. This is a consequence of the absence of network topological information and the lack of a fixed end-to-end communication path between the nodes.

These privacy issues may also rise due to the lack of a user's control over the network, unauthorized data access during the communication, or the complexity of access through different networks and communications means. However, in a mobile opportunistic/cloud-based network, it is impractical to use centralized control systems as the node's high mobility and the user's unpredictable behavior make it difficult to establish an end-to-end, secured path between the communicating nodes.

Table 1 Security and Privacy Issues due to Networking and Functional Challenges in Mobile Opportunistic/Cloud-Based Networks

Challenges	Security/Privacy Issues	Measures
High mobility of the nodes	Can cause "sybil attacks", where a node's reliability is affected by the foreign-attacked nodes	Requires highly dynamic security solutions that do not depend over a predefined path
Heterogeneity of networks	Data leakage risks in part due to the nontrusted data communication in different networks	Requires strong data encryption mechanisms to protect sensitive information
Device constraints	Limited resources may lead users to rely on the "goodness" of malicious users	Requires secure context-aware service management systems
Unpredictable user's behavior	User's selfish behavior can affect the overall data communication and may damage user's privacy	Requires proper incentive mechanisms for users to perform accordingly to reduce altruism in the communication

Therefore, strict dynamic security and privacy-aware mechanisms are needed for stronger user access control over the data while are being forwarded through the network. Thus, from the data processing point of view, guarantees of where the user's data are located and what is being done with them must be ensured. This in turn will help to locate the present position of the data in the network and, furthermore, it may assist a node in finding another closely related one (eg, node with a similar interest) to assist in forwarding the message.

Table 1 highlights the resulting security and privacy issues and potential countermeasures that stem from the identified networking and functional challenges in mobile opportunistic/cloud-based networks.

The *high mobility of nodes* creates different security risks for the users through the possible disclosure of a user's private information to the attackers. To address this issue, we can use a dynamic privacy-aware framework, which can mitigate data leakage in the system by using the user's relation-privacy (Wang, 2010). This framework is useful for application in mobile opportunistic/cloud-based networks, as it relies on a dynamic privacy-aware solution by keeping the trusted relationship between the users while considering node's high mobility.

Moreover, a dynamic security management approach is required for maintaining data integrity at storage as well as when transferring these data between the users (Sakka et al., 2010). This encryption-based security mechanism is important in the context of mobile opportunistic/cloud-based networks as it addresses data security issues both in storage and runtime, and takes into consideration the node's high mobility during the process of data forwarding.

Another security framework can be used in mobile opportunistic/cloud-based networks to prevent "sybil attack" (ie, node's reliability is affected by the foreign-attacked nodes) by using the discovery of the neighborhood topology

(Shikfa et al., 2010). This framework is relevant to use in mobile opportunistic/cloud-based networks as the data forwarding fully relies on the neighboring nodes in such networks.

In addition to mobility, the *heterogeneity of networks* creates possible security and privacy challenges due to the part of such networks that may not be trusted for a secure communication. Additionally, when locally available network communication is used for routing in mobile opportunistic/cloud-based networks, another factor that needs to be considered is the trust relationship between the users themselves.

These issues can be mitigated by a security architecture that helps users' mobile devices to get a secure alternative network connection to avail a seamless cloud-based application in the time of a connection failure (Huerta-Canepa and Lee, 2010). The heterogeneity of networks is taken into consideration by exploiting collaboration among the users within the network: the architecture depends upon the locally available users' interactions who are willing to take part in this communication.

Therefore, in mobile opportunistic/cloud-based networks, this architecture is feasible for use in accessing an available network connection and securing the communication in challenged environments (eg, rural areas or with restricted/full of interference access networks) that may lack a fixed network infrastructure for communication.

Furthermore, *device constraints* must be accounted for when attempting to solve security and privacy issues. For instance, the limited battery power is a large constraint for mobile devices regarding communication in such challenged environments. In such environments, it is not feasible for a user to search for a nearby user in a constant state of neighbor discovery mechanisms as this will reduce the device's battery lifetime and lead to the loss of required bandwidth for other communications.

To address this issue in mobile opportunistic/cloud-based networks, a context-aware mobile battery management system may be employed (Ravi et al., 2008). Such a system may help identify the users communication needs and patterns in a mobile opportunistic/cloud-based network, restricting the unnecessary use of the mobile device according to its present battery capacity.

On the other hand, this battery limitation can introduce new security threats due to the certain change in data integration. This includes the perseverance of data quality that can be compromised by the malicious nodes (McMorran et al., 2014). Based upon this, a cryptography-based security solution may be employed for protecting data at storage where users have exclusive control over the private key (Sedayao et al., 2009). In mobile opportunistic/cloud-based networks, securing data integrity is a desired feature when data are being transferred through different networking means, as to keep the encrypted private key exclusive to the user.

Finally, collaborations and active participation are important to overcome the issues related to *unpredictable user behavior* in a mobile opportunistic/cloud-based network. But in real-life, the behavior of users is difficult to predict in a system as it varies from place to place.

Notwithstanding, to reduce users' selfish behavior in refusing to take an active part in communication, incentive-based social reputation mechanisms can be used within the routing protocols (Wang et al., 2012; Scekic et al., 2013). These solutions may help to improve message delivery performance in such communications and encourage other users to actively take part in data forwarding.

Furthermore, these incentives can be made in terms of monetary support or assigning a social rank (ie, there are some nodes that are very active in data forwarding and are treated as good data forwarders) to overcome or control this unpredictability of user behavior.

3 DATA STORAGE AND RESOURCE MANAGEMENT CHALLENGES

In this section, we identify the security and privacy issues associated with data storage and resource management in a mobile opportunistic/cloud-based network. We outline different existing solutions and the possible countermeasures toward the development of a privacy-aware/secure mobile opportunistic/cloud-based network, and explore how to overcome problems that may arise from users' authorization and authentication, users' identities, application-level security, data storage protection, multitenancy risks and resource-related challenges, data confidentiality and location-related privacy issues during such communications.

3.1 USERS' AUTHORIZATION AND AUTHENTICATION

Mobile opportunistic/cloud-based networks help users to avail themselves of cloud-based solutions in challenged environments, for example, in high access networking zones, or even in the areas with a high roaming cost. In such cloud-based services, the cloud service provider (CSP) maintains the monitoring of the non-trusted cloud service user (CSU) that may introduce potential threats to the system (Li et al., 2015a).

In a private cloud (ie, a cloud computing platform dedicated to a specific organization), proper safeguards can be used, as this type of cloud is fully maintained and operated by a specific organization according to their policies and requirements. But in the case of a public cloud environment (ie, a cloud computing platform available to the common people), proper security measures (eg, enforcing strong data encryption mechanisms or implementing security "firewalls") must be considered in order to ensure users' authorization and authentication (Fernandes et al., 2014). Sometimes, the basic requirement for a user who accesses multiple cloud-based services is a single-sign-on technique (ie, user authentication for multiple user accounts/applications across different systems) (Za et al., 2011).

But from the security and privacy point of view, if an attacker gets access to a user's access credentials to enter into the system, it is easy to compromise all the other systems relying on such single-sign-on session. Therefore, in addition to applying safeguards to cloud domains, systems relying on single-sign-on session should be protected against vulnerabilities, for example, unauthorized access to the system and diversion of the traffic from the original destination or even data eavesdropping while it is being transferred between different cloud domains (Zissis and Lekkas, 2012). In relation to the mobile opportunistic/cloud-based networks, this issue can be addressed by using a unitary token-based authorization and authentication mechanism (Chang and Lee, 2012). With this unitary token, a user can access multiple accounts or is capable of assessing several applications seamlessly.

In physical domains, users' collaborations and social interactions are important when storing, carrying, and forwarding data through a mobile opportunistic/cloud-based network that depends upon a ubiquitous mobile and wireless network system for communication between its peers.

Thus, in such open and disconnected mobile communication environments, security issues are significant for data dissemination and this needs to be addressed properly in terms of authorization and authentication to protect users' data.

In addition to the secure mechanisms for ensuring users' authorization and authentication, we should enforce mechanisms for data processing that are able to dynamically support concurrent access controls to disseminate data to their intended destinations (Feldman et al., 2010).

Along similar lines, cloud-based services not only provide abstractions for users concerning service aggregation, underlying software-platform abstraction or application programming interface (API) abstraction, but they also offer third-party web-based service components (eg, mashups to the users), which in general is the process where several services are combined into a single integrated unit (Minhas et al., 2012). But, from the security and privacy point of view, it is important to control access to underlying databases by ensuring that the combined resources held by mashups are not compromised by the malicious users (De Ryck et al., 2012).

In mobile opportunistic/cloud-based networks, these types of services can introduce security risks from the third-party relationship with the service providers. To address this, security policies should be employed using users' authentication by exchanging only authorized information (Hobel et al., 2013). Therefore, supporting authorization and authentication of these services is necessary in mashups, and needs to be enhanced to prevent attacks, and to provide a secure message delivery in such networks.

3.2 USER IDENTITY

Mobile opportunistic/cloud-based networks may help improve the accessibility and availability of information using co-located user network connections to relay information instead of relying on a fixed infrastructure for communication.

From the accessibility point of view, there is a trend toward enabling mobile users to audit the data and grant access to other users who can "operate" (eg, read/write/modify) the data according to their preferences (Ahmed et al., 2015). But from the availability point of view, the major challenge is to get an available cloud-based application that can allow these types of data-enabling mechanisms with higher bandwidth utilization to the mobile devices in a challenged environment (Huang et al., 2011).

For instance, in such challenged environments connections may be available with the help of a nearby user, but from the user's privacy point of view whether to trust (eg, ensuring user's identity) the nearby user for use in communication must be considered (Mont et al., 2003). Additionally, from the security point of view, in a malicious wireless network environment it is possible to create a fake relationship with other users by manipulating numerous encounters (Czeskis et al., 2012). This can easily immobilize the operation of the whole network.

In a mobile opportunistic/cloud-based network, these issues may take place when one device generates and shares redundant encountering records with another nearby device by unauthorized data manipulations, which in turn creates a "black-hole attack" to derange the entire data forwarding performance of the system (Al-Shurman et al., 2004). In this attack, the router becomes compromised by the foreign-attacked nodes that drop packets for a particular network destination.

Therefore, the user's identity is important to secure reliable relations for the participants in data forwarding (Mishra et al., 2013). Therefore, we can use trusted identity management mechanisms that deal with identifying individuals or any domain in a system (Park et al., 2013). This may be done at different levels, for example, a region, a network, an individual, or even within an organization.

In the context of a mobile opportunistic/cloud-based network, proper identity management and access control must be enforced for mitigating the potential threats and attacks. Moreover, placing restrictions within the system by establishing credible identities to allow user access to the resources is also necessary.

3.3 APPLICATION-LEVEL SECURITY

The use of cloud-based applications normally requires a web-based interface in which users access their cloud services. Looking from a security point of view, this can be a potential place for attackers to enter into the system through the victim's profile. Weak credentials (eg, a weak password), nonverification of an unauthorized access, or even the insufficient data validation can make the system vulnerable.

In a mobile opportunistic/cloud-based network, if an attacker gains access to a user's credentials, it is possible to perform malicious activities, for example, accessing user's sensitive information, manipulation of private data, or even redirecting unwanted transaction in the system (Zhang et al., 2009).

Therefore, in a scenario where content also may be transported by unknown/untrustworthy users, potential countermeasures would play an important role to avoid these types of risks and exploitation of infrastructure-less communication.

In consideration of this, users should select a strong password while registering themselves to the system and change or update it frequently. Moreover, a promising approach in this direction is to employ mechanisms to create dynamic credentials for protecting data in the system (Xiao and Gong, 2010). These dynamic credentials change in value once a user changes location or when he/she has exchanged a certain number of data packets with others.

Such a mechanism is useful in mobile opportunistic/cloud-based networks, as this makes it difficult for attackers to find the correct credential at a specific location to hack a user's account in order to gain entry into the system.

3.4 DATA STORAGE PROTECTION

In a traditional on-premise application deployment model, sensitive information is stored within a secure boundary based on an organization/company's policy, fixed security measures, and protocols. In mobile opportunistic/cloud-based networks, there is no fixed infrastructure for communication. Users must somewhat overcome the inherent uncertainty of an available contact opportunity, making them rely upon locally available infrastructures while hoping for the secure handling of their data (Li et al., 2015b). Therefore, how to efficiently protect user's data inside such decentralized environments is especially challenging while storing that data locally on a device.

To address this, traditional encryption-based security mechanisms can be employed but the growing concern in the use of mobile-cloud networks is regarding the level of control required over a CSP and in what ways a cloud provider can prove itself trustworthy to its client's encrypted data at storage, when the service provider itself holds the corresponding encryption keys (Grobauer et al., 2011). Therefore, it must be ensured that the cloud-managed user data are protected from vulnerable service providers via encryption in the data storage (Van Dijk et al., 2012).

Moreover, support for dynamically concurrent access control must be provided given the user's high mobility (users access information in different locations from different devices). To address this, a mechanism that supports dynamic access control and employs fault-tolerant and data integrity schemes to guarantee proper handling of the user data should be implemented (Bowers et al., 2011).

An alternative mechanism for ensuring data integrity in data transmissions in a mobile opportunistic/cloud-based network can be achieved by employing a third-party auditor (TPA), which checks the integrity of stored data in an online storage (Wang et al., 2009). The use of a TPA eliminates the direct involvement of clients in the system, which is important for achieving the economic and performance advantages of cloud-based solutions. This solution also allows the support of data dynamics via most general forms of data operations, for example, block modification, insertion and deletion, which further ensures user privacy by fastening data integrity.

Along similar lines, the privacy-preserving data mining mechanisms can be used for securing sensitive data (Verykios et al., 2004). The major purpose of this data mining technique is to selectively identify the patterns for making predictions of stored data in a data center.

However, within the context of mobile opportunistic/cloud-based networks, it is difficult to structure a pattern for stored data due to the lack of a fixed infrastructure or routing protocol for data storage or data forwarding. These networks face challenges of mining a user's PII, which has various privacy concerns that create potential security risks to the system. To this end, an anonymization algorithm for privacy-preserving data mining based on the generalization technique can be employed (Mohammed et al., 2011). This noninteractive anonymization algorithm provides a better classification analysis of stored data in a privacy-preserving manner.

On the other hand, a growing concern in mobile opportunistic/cloud-based networks is the ability of processing large amounts of data (ie, Big Data (Che et al., 2013)) by using the resource-constrained mobile devices (Qi and Zong, 2012). The Big Data mining extended the data mining techniques to allow emerging innovative approaches on a large scale that keep in mind the increased value of the user's PII. When the volume of data increases in such networks, the concerns is the availability of networks for communications to satisfy the required bandwidth for data processing, which may introduce security and privacy issues to the system (Xu et al., 2014).

From the security point of view, a malicious insider can extract a user's private information and use this information to violate data integrity using unwanted applications (eg, modification in certain part of data). Moreover, in Big Data mining this problem increases with the large volume and velocity of the data streams (Michael and Miller, 2013). Focusing on these issues in a mobile opportunistic/cloud-based network, a major security challenge is how to protect and conduct integrity assessments in such large scaled data, when a seamless network communication may not always be available. The security-monitoring management scheme may be employed to track, log and record such malicious activity (Marchal et al., 2014). By detecting unwanted data manipulation, this scheme allows prevention of further data loss by mitigating potential damage in the network.

Additionally, in the context of data mining, from the privacy point of view, risks (eg, user's private data disclosure or distortion of sensitive information) may arise with the possible exposure of a user's PII to a malicious network environment while data are being collected, stored, and analyzed by such a data mining process (Sagiroglu and Sinanc, 2013). In mobile opportunistic/cloud-based networks, this privacy issue may emerge from the potential risk of losing a user's personal information during storage and manipulation of such data through this data mining process. Secure multiparty computation techniques can be employed (Hongbing et al., 2015), helping to filter malicious users during data communication by mapping the various data elements' authenticity.

Another concern relates to the privacy and security risks that arise due to data leakage. To address such data leakage, a technique that breaks down sensitive data into insignificant fragments can be employed (Anjum and Umar, 2000). This ensures that a fragment will not contain all of the significant information by itself. By redundantly separating such fragments across various distributed systems, this will mitigate the data leakage problem.

Data leakage may result from the way data flows through these networks. This can be solved through the use of strong network traffic encryption techniques related to secure socket layer (SSL) and the transport layer security (TLS)

(Ordean and Giurgiu, 2010). Furthermore, security mechanisms based on distributed cryptography, for example, high-availability and integrity layer (HAIL) (Bowers et al., 2009), can further prevent data leakage by allowing a set of servers to prove to a client that a stored file is intact and retrievable. In mobile opportunistic/cloud-based networks, HAIL can also prevent data leakage while managing file integrity and availability across a collection of independent storage services.

Moreover, from the data storage point of view, data backup is a critical aspect in order to facilitate recovery in the case of connection failures. For example, new privacy issues may arise in the network, for example, potential data loss from data backup in a third-party user within a malicious wireless network environment (Subashini and Kavitha, 2011). It is challenging to manage a privacy-aware data backup mechanisms for users in a mobile opportunistic/cloud-based network, because there are no contemporary paths available between any pair of nodes at a given time. Defense mechanisms like strong security schemes at data storage are therefore needed. Such mechanisms may use attribute-based encryption techniques to protect a user's data as a way to mitigate data backup issues (Zhou and Huang, 2013). Within the context of mobile opportunistic/cloud-based networks, this feature allows data backup, preventing potential disclosure of a user's sensitive information.

3.5 RISKS IN MULTITENANCY AND RESOURCE-RELATED CHALLENGES

Scalability, configurability via metadata and multitenancy introduce security and privacy concerns in a mobile-cloud network. In such networks, cloud-based solutions provide massive scalability where customers have multiple copies of customized instances of the software in the system (Grobauer et al., 2011). In the configurability via metadata process, vendors provide different instances of the applications for each customer. Customers can change these instances according to their choices. In the case of multitenancy, vendors provide a single instance for all customers in the system where a user's data resides at the same location.

Intrusion of malicious data in such systems can be done either by hacking through loopholes in the application or by injecting a client's code into the system (Kieyzun et al., 2009). A hacker can write a masked code and inject it into the application and when this code is executed without verification, there is a high potential of intrusion into the user's data. This multitenancy approach leads to an efficient utilization of resources, but at the same time the risk of data leakage between the tenants (ie, users) is high. To this end, cloud-assisted storage systems should be employed to ensure a distinct boundary for each user's data in its multitenant system. The boundary must be ensured not only at the physical level, but also at the application level. Such applications should be intelligent enough to segregate the data from the different users (Jasti et al., 2010).

Furthermore, the virtualized cloud-based environments are vulnerable as they add more points of entry as well as more interconnection complexity. Attacks against the administrative domain (eg, the virtual machine monitors [VMMs]) can compromise a client's security and privacy.

From the security point of view, risks may arise due to the lack of efficient managing and partitioning of resource-intensive components in different virtualized layers. This may cause potential vulnerability to attackers, who may manipulate malicious codes into the system or breach the security layers. This can result in a "botnet attack" in which attackers gain control over the service provider's resources (Lombardi and Pietro, 2011). From the privacy point of view, risks may emerge while offloading mobile applications to a virtualized remote cloud server for data execution. In such situations, a user's private information is obtained by a "sniffing attack" where the attackers change sensitive data by gaining unauthorized access control over the service user (Ohlman et al., 2009).

A new self-service cloud (SSC) model can be used to address these types of security and privacy shortcomings of cloud virtualizations (Butt et al., 2012). The SSC allows clients to administer their own virtual machines (VMs), while disallowing the cloud's administrative domain from inspecting a client's VM state. In addition, by modifying the Xen hypervisor,[2] this model enables providers and clients to establish mutually trusted services that can check regulatory compliance while preserving a client's privacy.

In mobile cloud-based networks, proper data isolation, therefore, allows access of VMs to each user (Aminzadeh et al., 2015). It is also possible that running two applications that use high memory and network bandwidth degrades the overall performance for the users. This poses a challenge to construct hypervisors or processors that will better isolate users' applications from each other.

When introducing this data isolation process to a public cloud domain, interference encountered between VMs introduces a new class of attacks named resource-freeing attacks (RFAs) (Varadarajan et al., 2012). The RFA attack occurs when a new VM suffers due to performance interference, it can affect the workload of other VMs on the same physical server in a way that improves its own performance while degrading others. To address such issues, the architecture that eliminates the hypervisor attack surface can be employed (Szefer et al., 2011). This type of architecture removes the need for VMs to constantly interact with the hypervisor during a task execution. The advantages of this architecture are that it is able to scale and manage VMs concurrently in mobile-cloud infrastructures and it is flexible with today's commodity hardware.

However, from the data management's perspective, it is difficult to scale and manage the conventional VMs over different administrative domains. This is in part due to the distance between the user (ie, service requester) and these administrative domains, which may be located far away from each other. This uniform distribution of resources sometimes causes a high communication overhead in message communication (Van Cleeff et al., 2009). This issue can be addressed by replicating and

---

[2]http://www.xenproject.org/.

distributing the VM's components nearer to the users (or the devices), in the form of Cloudlets (Verbelen et al., 2012). The Cloudlets are the clusters of computers that improves the network performance through high speed and low latency utilization. But from the security and privacy point of view, data integrity, users' trust, and identity are major issues in Cloudlet deployments (Satyanarayanan et al., 2009).

To address this challenge, "stealthmem," a system-level protection mechanism against cache-based side channel attacks, could be employed (Kim et al., 2012). In this mechanism hypervisor or the operating system provides each user (VM or application) with a small amount of memory that is largely free from cache-based side channels. Unlike the existing state-of-the-art mitigation methods, stealthmem works with existing commodity hardware and does not require intense changes to application software.

In addition, it is also important to ensure efficient dynamic resource management to adjust congested conditions at runtime to reflect situational changes to the users within the network. But in the case of the denial of service (DoS) attacks (Bicakci and Tavli, 2009), attackers make the resources unavailable to the intended users and flood the network, which creates congestion and high traffic within the system. If the system becomes congested, the entire network functionality may collapse. To address these attacks, flooding attack prevention (FAP) mechanisms can be employed in the system (Yi et al., 2005). In this mechanism, when an attacker node broadcasts exceeding packets by flooding the network, its immediate neighbor node determines the high traffic rate and consequently reduces the corresponding priority with that node.

In mobile opportunistic/cloud-based networks, an efficient and effective mechanism is therefore required to control this traffic congestion accordingly with more realistic scenarios to mitigate "DoS" attacks (Peng et al., 2007). Defense mechanisms based on secure network monitoring can be used to in part address such attacks (Tartakovsky et al., 2006). This mechanism uses various network loads and usage patterns to identify and detect the attacker-node that may lead to change in network traffic within the system. Therefore, proper countermeasures need to be built to ensure that the data forwarding in mobile opportunistic/cloud-based networks is secure and meets its performance requirements. Additionally, new techniques to leverage users' social influence and secure interactions to reduce traffic congestion at runtime can also be employed.

3.6 DATA CONFIDENTIALITY

Mobile opportunistic/cloud-based networks may deliver flexible services in many ways, for example, managing an online personal health record or even managing sites which directly or indirectly relate to users' personal information and identification. In such networks, the user's entire content may be stored on a locally available device that inherits several confidentiality issues. Moreover, the location of data in storage may also introduce significant risks toward the confidentiality of the stored data, since it lacks effective and common processes for protecting these stored data in different locations.

To address such issues, a framework can be used to determine the security risks associated with cloud-assisted online platforms (Saripalli and Walters, 2010). Here, "risk" is defined as a combination of the probability of a security threat event and its behavior. This iterative convergence approach allows a comparative resource to assess service provider's relative robustness in different domains, which mitigates the confidentiality issues by assessing security risks for the user's data.

Furthermore, in mobile opportunistic/cloud-based networks, from the communication point of view, the major obstacle is to get continuous streaming while the devices are changing the networks and connections frequently. Communications in these networks take place over several other networks.

In such open wireless networking environments, confidentiality risk comes from man in the middle (MITM) attacks (Guha et al., 2007) where the attackers secretly create a fake communication between the users by manipulating numerous encounters and generate potential threats toward their data confidentially. In such attacks, malicious nodes create a fake communication path between the two nodes and secretly control the communication, while these two nodes believe that they are directly connected for communication with each other. To address this issue, a potential security mechanism that blocks malicious users can be used. This is able to mitigate the MITM attack on a third-party software (Knockel, 2012).

3.7 LOCATION-RELATED PRIVACY ISSUES

In mobile opportunistic/cloud-based networks, issues related to location privacy are fundamentally different from those affecting the traditional infrastructure-based mobile communication networks (Consolvo et al., 2005).

The location can be easily obtained simply by keeping track of how users interact with each other. For instance, during data transmission a node can track an other node's information. In such cases node's contact histories or social relationship (eg, friendship network) can be revealed, exposing the specific location of a target node for deploying an attack.

Thus, solutions that take into consideration a user's mobility contacts and social graph to secure privacy by keeping trusted relationships between the users can be employed (Hossmann et al., 2010). This prevents the user's location from being easily inferred from how the user interacts in mobile opportunistic/cloud-based networks.

On the other hand, from the storage point of view, in mobile-cloud networks users may want to control the location where their virtual resources are stored and make sure that they are processed in a secure place of their own choice. From the security and privacy point of view, this is to make sure that the location information is given to the right parties, under the right circumstances to protect the user's identity. In this case, a cryptography-based secure access control framework can be employed (Zhu et al., 2013), which helps protect a user's privacy by using location-based authentication.

Also, a mechanism for verifying the geographic location of a virtual resource in a cloud-based environment can be used (Krauß and Fusenig, 2013). This mechanism identifies physical machines by a trusted platform module (TPM) and a trusted authority verifies the actual location of the resource in the physical machines. The TPM can detect the geographic location of a virtual resource and can control it to prevent the movement of virtual resources to an undesired location by the service provider.

This mechanism not only moves the resources into the user's desired choice of location but ensures the integrity of the stored data. The mechanism consists of two phases: initialization and verification. In the initialization phase, a new machine is registered by the service provider in its location and in the verification phase, users verify their VM's location into the system. Therefore, in mobile opportunistic/cloud-based networks the use of this mechanism is promising, as it ensures the secure location of data and maintains data integrity in the system (Zakhary et al., 2014).

3.8 SUMMARY

In this section we have discussed relevant security and privacy issues associated with *data storage and resource management challenges* in mobile opportunistic/cloud-based networks.

We have comprehended that such issues may be due to the lack of proper security mechanisms for data encryption as well as improper resource management with the nontrusted users in a malicious wireless network environment.

In mobile opportunistic/cloud-based networks, the technological and user's behavioral issues increase the privacy risks while storing, carrying, and forwarding data within the network. Therefore, proper management procedures (eg, strong encryption mechanisms) should be taken in order to diminish user data privacy in the system. On the other hand, the stored data should be kept private from other users while storing or forwarding it to the next hop.

However, similar to the networking and functional challenges (in Section 2), we have found that it is difficult to enforce a standard privacy-aware/security model for mobile opportunistic/cloud-based networks as these networks do not have any fixed infrastructure for an end-to-end communication or due to the lack of a centralized control system.

Nevertheless, we observed that the potential of using social reputation-based incentive mechanisms may be introduced in such networks to further motivate users to take part in trusted communication. This in turn will help to improve users' social interactions and increase other contact opportunities while collaborating with their peers. In Table 2, we present a quick overview of the security models/solutions, highlighting their mechanisms and addressed issues.

In general, within the context of data storage and resource management, we outlined that the *privacy issues* in mobile opportunistic/cloud-based networks are different from the traditional solutions used in other wireless networking systems.

Table 2 Different Security-Related Models/Solutions, Their Mechanisms, and the Potential Issues They Have Addressed in the Context of Mobile Opportunistic/Cloud-Based Networks

Security Model/Solutions	Security Mechanism	Issues Addressed
SPORC (Feldman et al., 2010)	EnCy	User's authentication
Hourglass (Van Dijk et al., 2012)	EnCy	Insecure data flow
Knockel (Knockel, 2012)	EnCy	MITM attack
HAIL (Bowers et al., 2009)	EnCy	Storage security
Stealthmem (Kim et al., 2012)	EnCy	Side channel attack
Xiao and Gong (2010)	AuAc	Dynamic data access
QUIRC (Saripalli and Walters, 2010)	AuAc	User's authentication
Bicakci and Tavli (2009)	AuAc	DoS attack
NoHype (Szefer et al., 2011)	AuAc	Hypervisor attack
SSC (Butt et al., 2012)	AuAc	Data security
Anjum and Umar (2000)	AuAc	Data security
Bowers et al. (2011)	TrSe	Data storage failures
Wang et al. (2009)	TrSe	Data integrity
Krauß and Fusenig (2013)	TrSe	Data leakage

EnCy, encryption-based mechanism; AuAc, authorized user access control; TrSe, trust-based security mechanism

Moreover, several issues, for example, authorization and authentication, user's identity issues, data storage as well as unwanted data leakage within the network, makes the system vulnerable due to the lack of proper safeguards to mitigate the privacy-related threats and attacks. But we have noticed that it is difficult to enforce bulletproof protection mechanisms in a mobile opportunistic/cloud-based network as communication in this network relies upon several intermediate nodes that may not be trusted. Therefore, there is a need for dynamic privacy-aware mechanisms for protecting user's data in the system.

On the other hand, from a *security point of view*, a mobile opportunistic/cloud-based network can be more at risk from the malicious behavior of the users (eg, a potential identity threat) during the data transmission between the nodes. In such networks, data exchange may take longer due to high traffic/data-congestion in the network, and such longer data exchanges may be affected by potential attackers that get enough time to hack the data.

There is, therefore, more potential for implementing encryption-based data security mechanisms to protect data during transmissions. However, we have found that the dynamic nature of mobile opportunistic/cloud-based networks make it impractical for establishing a standard security framework in such networks. This in turn encourages reliance upon the traditional security mechanisms with best practices according to the user's/system's requirement.

Table 3 Security and Privacy Issues in Mobile Opportunistic/Cloud-Based Networks Resulting From User's Authorization and Authentication, Identity, Data Confidentiality, and Location-Related Privacy Issues

Challenges	Security/Privacy Issues	Measures
User's authorization and authentication	Security risks may arise from the third-party relationship with the service provider	Employ unitary token-based authorization and authentication mechanisms
User's identity	Redundant encountering records with another nearby device by unauthorized data manipulations	Enforce trusted identity management mechanisms which deal with identifying individuals or any domain in a system
Data confidentiality	The user's privacy and confidentiality risks depend upon the terms and conditions of the service providers	Data management policy should be enforced for ensuring user's privacy in data forwarding
Location-related privacy issues	Location can be easily obtained simply by keeping track of how user interact with other	Secure user's relation privacy by keeping trusted relationship between the users

Table 3 highlights the resulting security and privacy issues and potential countermeasures that stem from the identified storage and resource management challenges in mobile opportunistic/cloud-based networks, based on the user's authorization and authentication, user's identity, data confidentiality, and location-related privacy issues.

User's authorization and authentication are important to secure trusted communication and efficiently manage resources between the users within the network. To this end, in a mobile opportunistic/cloud-based network, proper safeguards must be taken in cloud domains as well as in the physical domains. Moreover, systems relying on single-sign-on sessions must be kept protected from intruders.

In this case, in a cloud domain, unitary token-based authorization and authentication mechanisms can be employed (Chang and Lee, 2012). This unitary token is a one time password which is difficult for the attacker to overcome due to its time limitation (ie, valid for a limited time). On the other hand, in a physical domain, security policies should be enforced using the user's authentication by exchanging only authorized information (Hobel et al., 2013). This in turn will ensure a secure message delivery in the network while preserving user's privacy.

The understanding of issues related to the *user's identity* is important as this helps to improve the accessibility and availability of resources through a secure and trusted communication. But from the security and privacy point of view, a major challenge is to find a trusted user (eg, ensuring user's identity) for data exchange. Additionally, in a malicious wireless network environment, it is also possible to create a "black-hole attack" using a fake relationship with other users by manipulating numerous encounters.

Trusted identity management mechanisms, therefore, must be employed that deal with identifying an individual/organization or any domain/region in a system (Park et al., 2013). This improves the overall message delivery performance by keeping routers safe from the foreign-attacked nodes.

Overlooking the *user's data confidentiality* may introduce security and privacy risks to the system. If a system becomes compromised, security and privacy risks may arise from a possible MITM attack, in which attackers create a fake communication by manipulating numerous encounters between the users participating in data forwarding. Then, attackers secretly control the communication, which degrades the overall network performance.

In this case, a risk management framework can be employed to address an active attack on user's confidentiality (Saripalli and Walters, 2010). Based on the quantitative confidentiality assessment, this framework helps to mitigate security risks associated with cloud-assisted online platforms. The mitigation, however, depends upon the assumptions specific to communication issues (eg, decision-making context of a specific group) and application-specific requirements (eg, a long password that gives the user permission to access an account).

In a mobile opportunistic/cloud-based network, communication depends upon several intermediate nodes, of which some may be nontrustworthy. In such communications, the location of user/resource can be easily obtained simply by tracking users' interactions with each other. This may lead to an attack on a specific user/resource being deployed. Therefore, the identified *location-related privacy issues* help us understand how to enhance a secure data communication while preserving user's privacy.

For that, a location-based security architecture can be employed (Krauß and Fusenig, 2013), which encompasses a secure data protection technique that verifies the geographic location of resources in a cloud-based environment. Moreover, this helps to protect user's privacy and maintain data integrity by using trusted relationship between the users when transferring data through different network platforms.

Regarding the application-level security, data storage protection, and multitenancy and resource management challenges, Table 4 highlights the resulting security and privacy issues and potential countermeasures that stem from the storage and resource management approaches in mobile opportunistic/cloud-based networks.

Application-level security is important as an application platform (eg, a web-browser) can be a potential place for attackers to enter into the system. Strong user access credentials (eg, passwords to enter into a system/application) can be used to secure the system. To this end, encryption-based dynamic data protection mechanism can be employed for protecting data in a mobile opportunistic/cloud-based network (Xiao and Gong, 2010).

Such a mechanism presents an algorithm to create dynamic credentials, which helps protect data in the system from changes in the user's location. These dynamic

Table 4 Security and Privacy Issues in Mobile Opportunistic/Cloud-Based Networks Resulting From Application-Level Security, Data Storage Protection, and Multitenancy and Resource Management Challenges

Challenges	Security/Privacy Issues	Measures
Application-level security	Accessing user's sensitive information and manipulation of private data	Users should select strong credentials (eg, password) and change/update it frequently
Data storage protection	Protect encrypted data at storage from service providers, when the service provider themselves holds the corresponding encryption keys	Strong encryption-based security mechanisms must be employed in data storage
Risks in multitenancy and resource-related challenges	Data manipulation by hacking or by injecting malicious codes into the system	Enforce a strong boundary of user's stored data both in physical and application level

credentials change the value once a user changes location or when he/she has exchanged a certain number of data packets with others (ie, after some transactions). In this way, this mechanism makes it difficult for attackers to get into the system by finding the correct user credentials at a specific location.

The *protection of data storage* is important in any system. But in a mobile opportunistic/cloud-based network, how to efficiently protect user's data inside a decentralized and distributed environment is especially challenging due to the absence of a centralized control system.

If data storage becomes compromised, potential security and privacy risks may arise from the unwanted data manipulation or sudden change in the data integration process, where the attackers modify some parts of the data.

Additionally, in a malicious wireless network environment potential security and privacy threats may come by the potential data loss from data backup in a third-party user. This creates the potential for disclosure of a user's sensitive information to the attackers.

To address the potential loss of a user's private information and secure data storage, encryption-based security architecture can be employed (Van Dijk et al., 2012), ensuring that the cloud-managed client's data are protected via encryption during data transmission, as well as inside a data storage.

Furthermore, an architecture for ensuring data integrity during data transmission can also be employed (Wang et al., 2009). This architecture uses a TPA to monitor data streams and preserve the data integrity while eliminating malicious users. Thus, in a mobile opportunistic/cloud-based network, it helps to maintain the system's performance during data forwarding by keeping the user's privacy.

In a malicious network environment, the attackers try to gain control over the resources by hacking through the loopholes in the application or by injecting a malicious code into the system. Thus, in the context of security and privacy, the major *risks in multitenancy and resource-related challenges* are how to protect user's privacy and establish a distinct boundary for each user's data in a multitenant system for a secure data manipulation.

To this end, potential security and privacy threats may come from a "botnet attack" in which the attackers gain control over the service provider's resources. Then, the attackers flood the network with unwanted data streams or drop a significant amount of data packets directed to a particular destination node. This may causes high levels of data congestion and further immobilize the data forwarding operation within the network.

To mitigate such issues, a privacy-aware, data-intensive security technique can be employed (Butt et al., 2012). Such techniques automatically partition a computing job according to the security levels required for the data residing in multiple domains. Furthermore, placing restrictions for the users within the system by establishing a secure and reliable relation by monitoring and controlling data packets during high traffic, is also necessary (Tartakovsky et al., 2006).

4 FUTURE RESEARCH QUESTIONS

In this chapter, we have assessed some of the fundamental security and privacy issues involved in extending cloud-based applications with the help of mobile opportunistic networks. In this section, we outline some of the issues and open questions related to the future research directions to this end.

Given the fact that the nodes on a mobile opportunistic/cloud-based network rely on the sporadic contact with the other nodes in the network, these intermediate nodes may present malicious behavior that can introduce security and privacy issues to the system. Therefore, the exchange of user's data is not always safe.

The mobility of nodes and different network connections make it more insecure in terms of authentication issues while storing or sharing data with a newly encountered node. Present research needs to be improved in this area where a user's reliable relations with others can be used for data exchange or forwarding.

Our current study identified the challenges to building a scalable and loosely coupled solution to find nearby users for information exchange in a mobile opportunistic/cloud-based network.

Thus, a major concern, *how to secure communications in a privacy-preserving manner* for a node traveling over a heterogeneous mobile opportunistic/cloud-based network? To this end, based on what we have studied in this chapter, this issue can be mitigated by potential applications employing privacy-aware access-control mechanisms (Shikfa et al., 2010; Klein et al., 2010).

Network heterogeneity and the high mobility of nodes make it impractical to have an end-to-end communication protocol in a mobile opportunistic/cloud-based network. The node's mobility for data forwarding fully depends upon the opportunity for instigating an encounter with another node when both of them are broadcasting messages within a specific range of communications (eg, Wi-Fi or Bluetooth communication ranges).

Therefore, our present study indicates the future research question, *how do protocols relying on locally available connections* in a mobile opportunistic/cloud-based network need to be improved when end-to-end key agreements prove impractical between the nodes?

Still what remains unsolved is the lack of end-to-end key agreements that can be generated and uniformly distributed in the network. The major reason for this is the lack of a centralized system to control such network communications. But it is difficult when implementing this in a real-life mobile opportunistic/cloud-based network scenario, as this is greatly influenced by the unpredictability of user's behavior. However, what we have learned is that the problems related to protocols and available network connections can be improved by employing privacy-preserving document extraction techniques (Wang, 2010; Sakka et al., 2010).

Our study summarized the security risks, attacks, and related concerns to the user's privacy/security in a mobile opportunistic/cloud-based network (Table 2). We outlined the models and architectures that can mitigate these issues in the network. It is difficult to predict what data an attacker could possibly be looking for in order to make the system vulnerable or inject a malicious code into the system.

However, the proper safeguards should be used for protecting the user's data in the system. Based on what we have learned, we raise this next future research question: *what types of confidential information are attackers attempting* to breach, thus making a mobile opportunistic/cloud-based network vulnerable? To this end, secure dynamic identity-based credential mechanisms can be used to mitigate these risks in a mobile opportunistic/cloud-based network (Xiao and Gong, 2010).

Concerning users' collaborations and social interactions, these issues are important in order to store, carry, and forward messages from source to destination. However, a node may be willing to cooperate only after getting specific information about the peer to be helped. From the privacy point of view of the prospective helper node, this is relevant as it may not want to share its mobile device and network with strangers.

Therefore, in this case another research question is: how could the helper node find information about the peer in order to trust it? In Sections 2 and 3, we analyzed the relationship between the security and privacy in a system and found that the major future research directions can be made based on the following research question: *what types of personal information can be shared* during the collaboration of message forwarding with the other unknown users in a mobile opportunistic/cloud-based network?

This is important as the user's unpredictable behavior can introduce potential risks into the system. We observed that, future research needs to be improved regarding trusted users' communications in data forwarding. Based on the lessons learned, these issues and challenges can be addressed by employing trusted agent-based intrusion tolerance mechanisms (Anjum and Umar, 2000).

Furthermore, for protecting the system and securing a communication from malicious users and nontrusted service providers, a risk assessment framework may be employed to determine the authorized users and trusted service providers within the system during the data transmission (Saripalli and Walters, 2010).

However, the current state-of-the-art research in mobile opportunistic/cloud-based networks should consider the following open research question: *how are the user's personal information and their social relationships helping attackers to generate threats and potential risks within the system?*

5 CONCLUSION

In this chapter, we address the security and privacy issues in mobile opportunistic/cloud-based networks. First, we discuss different security and privacy issues related to networking and functional challenges along with their possible countermeasures. Then, we explore the security and privacy issues associated with data storage and resource management challenges with detailed discussions.

We overview the present state-of-the-art research advances in these fields by highlighting the advantages and limitations to each of the approaches for mobile opportunistic/cloud-based networks. We analyze the existing vulnerabilities and threats within the security system in such networks. Further, we map the relationships between vulnerability and threats as well as outline the possible countermeasures to solve/mitigate these issues. Finally, we derived a set of future challenges, to address security and privacy issues by enabling privacy-assured data transmission and securing data storage in a mobile opportunistic/cloud-based network.

We find that the potential threats and attacks are significant while users access cloud-based solutions via their devices in a mobile opportunistic/cloud-based network. Moreover, in the context of networking and functional challenges, the high mobility of the nodes, heterogeneity of networks, device constraints, and unpredictable user behavior introduce new security and privacy issues into the system. Clearly, this results in unwanted data access by malicious nodes to the network, affecting the user's privacy. A dynamic privacy-aware solution preserving trusted relationship between the users is a promising direction to secure the system.

On the other hand, in the context of data storage and resource management challenges, the user's authorization and authentication, identity, application-level security, data storage protection, risks in multitenancy, resource-related challenges, data confidentiality, and location-related privacy issues introduce new security and privacy concerns in the system.

These may result in a flooding attack within the network where the attackers make the resources unavailable to the intended users by dropping packets, or overflow the network by generating enormous number of unwanted data packets, which creates congestion and high levels of traffic within the system. We observed that, in a mobile opportunistic/cloud-based network, proper safeguards are necessary to mitigate these security- and privacy-related threats and attacks. To this end, secure network monitoring management mechanisms can be employed.

More generally, we understand that, the absence of a centralized control mechanism as well as the lack of an end-to-end communication protocol make it difficult to implement a privacy-aware security framework in such networks. Therefore, during message exchange, a user must rely upon the trusted relationship with its peers. To this end, our current study gives a detailed view of the state-of-the-art research in mobile opportunistic/cloud-based networks with the input of the most recent research works available in these areas.

We also plan for more comprehensive experiments with real-life data targeting the issues raised in this chapter, which in turn shall help us to understand and propose the necessary improvements to be made in the performance of message exchange in secure, real-world deployments of mobile opportunistic/cloud-based networks.

ACRONYMS

3G	third generation
API	application programming interface
CSP	cloud service provider
CSU	cloud service user
DoS	denial of service
DTN	delay tolerant networking
FAP	flooding attack prevention
HAIL	high-availability and integrity layer
MITM	man in the middle
P2P network	peer-to-peer network
PDA	personal digital assistant
PII	personal-identifiable-information
QUIRC	quantitative risk and impact assessment framework
RAF	resource-freeing attack
SSC	self-service cloud
SSL	secure socket layer
TLS	transport layer security
TPA	third-party auditor
TPM	trusted platform module
URI	uniform resource identifier
VMMs	virtual machine monitors
VMs	virtual Machines

GLOSSARY

Challenged environments Sparse or rural areas that lack a proper infrastructure, and in high density, urban areas with restricted/full of interference access networks where connectivity cannot be assumed available.

Cloud A hosted service over the Internet. Users can use such services using a pay-as-you-go scheme, anytime and anywhere with the help of an available Internet connection.

Mobile cloud Refers to the service that combines mobile computing and cloud-based services. In this service, either a mobile application runs on the remote cloud server or a cloud-based application runs inside a user's mobile device.

Opportunistic networks An advanced form of mobile ad-hoc networks (MANETs) that supports delay-tolerant networking. In an opportunistic network, user's data are forwarded with the help of other users within the network. There is no end-to-end communication path available in such networks. User's social interactions and collaborations greatly influence the overall message delivery performance.

ACKNOWLEDGMENTS

The first author would like to acknowledge the Scottish Informatics and Computer Science Alliance (SICSA) and the University of St Andrews. The second author would like to acknowledge Fundação de Amparo à Pesquisa do Estado de Goiás (FAPEG), PNPD/CAPES, and Prof. Dr. Marcos Aurélio Batista.

REFERENCES

Ahmed, E., Gani, A., Sookhak, M., Hamid, S.H.A., Xia, F., 2015. Application optimization in mobile cloud computing: motivation, taxonomies, and open challenges. J. Netw. Comput. Appl. 52, 52–68. ISSN 1084-8045.

Al-Shurman, M., Yoo, S.M., Park, S., 2004. Black hole attack in mobile ad hoc networks. In: Proceedings of the 42nd Annual Southeast Regional Conference. ACM, Huntsville, Alabama, pp. 96–97.

Alberti, A.M., Moreira, W., da Rosa Righi, R., Neto, F.J.P., Dobre, C., Singh, D., 2015. Towards an opportunistic, socially-driven, self-organizing, cloud networking architecture with novagenesis. In: Proc. 2nd International Workshop on Emerging Software as a Service and Analytics, pp. 27–36.

Aminzadeh, N., Sanaei, Z., Ab-Hamid, S.H., 2015. Mobile storage augmentation in mobile cloud computing: taxonomy, approaches, and open issues. Simul. Model. Pract. Theory 50, 96–108.

Anjum, F., Umar, A., 2000. Agent based intrusion tolerance using fragmentation-redundancy-scattering technique. In: Wireless Communications and Networking Conference, WCNC, vol. 3. IEEE, pp. 1101–1106.

Armbrust, M., Fox, A., Griffith, R., Joseph, A.D., Katz, R., Konwinski, A., Lee, G., Patterson, D., Rabkin, A., Stoica, I., Zaharia, M., 2010. A view of cloud computing. Commun. ACM 53 (4), 50–58. ISSN 0001-0782.

Bahl, P., Han, R.Y., Li, L.E., Satyanarayanan, M., 2012. Advancing the state of mobile cloud computing. In: Proc. 3rd Workshop on Mobile Cloud Computing and Services. ACM, Low Wood Bay, Lake District, UK, pp. 21–28.

Ballester Lafuente, C., Seigneur, J.M., Sofia, R., Silva, C., Moreira, W., 2014. Trust management in uloop. In: Aldini, A., Bogliolo, A. (Eds.), User-Centric Networking, Lecture Notes in Social Networks. Springer International Publishing, pp. 107–119.

Bicakci, K., Tavli, B., 2009. Denial-of-service attacks and countermeasures in IEEE 802.11 wireless networks. Comput. Stand. Interfaces 31 (5), 931–941. ISSN 0920-5489.

Bowers, K.D., Juels, A., Oprea, A., 2009. HAIL: a high-availability and integrity layer for cloud storage. In: Proc. 16th Conference on Computer and Communications Security. ACM, New York, USA, pp. 187–198.

Bowers, K.D., van Dijk, M., Juels, A., Oprea, A., Rivest, R.L., 2011. How to tell if your cloud files are vulnerable to drive crashes. In: Proc. 18th Conference on Computer and Communications Security. ACM, Chicago, IL, USA, pp. 501–514.

Butt, S., Cavilla, A.L., Srivastava, A., Ganapathy, V., 2012. Self-service cloud computing. In: Proc. Conference on Computer and Communications Security. ACM, New York, USA, pp. 253–264.

Chang, C.C., Lee, C.Y., 2012. A secure single sign-on mechanism for distributed computer networks. IEEE Trans. Ind. Electron. 59 (1), 629–637. ISSN 0278-0046.

Che, D., Safran, M., Peng, Z., 2013. From big data to big data mining: challenges, issues, and opportunities. In: Hong, B., Meng, X., Chen, L., Winiwarter, W., Song, W. (Eds.), Database Systems for Advanced Applications, Lecture Notes in Computer Science, vol. 7827. Springer, Berlin, Heidelberg, pp. 1–15.

Ciobanu, R.I., Dobre, C., Dascălu, M., Trăuşan-Matu, S., Cristea, V., 2014. Sense: a collaborative selfish node detection and incentive mechanism for opportunistic networks. J. Netw. Comput. Appl. 41, 240–249. ISSN 1084-8045.

Consolvo, S., Smith, I.E., Matthews, T., LaMarca, A., Tabert, J., Powledge, P., 2005. Location disclosure to social relations: why, when, & what people want to share. In: Proc. SIGCHI Conference on Human Factors in Computing Systems, CHI. ACM, Portland, Oregon, USA, pp. 81–90.

Conti, M., Kumar, M., 2010. Opportunities in opportunistic computing. Computer 43 (1), 42–50. ISSN 0018-9162.

Czeskis, A., Dietz, M., Kohno, T., Wallach, D., Balfanz, D., 2012. Strengthening user authentication through opportunistic cryptographic identity assertions. In: Proc. Conference on Computer and Communications Security. ACM, New York, USA, pp. 404–414.

De Ryck, P., Decat, M., Desmet, L., Piessens, F., Joosen, W., 2012. Security of web mashups: a survey. In: Tuomas, A., Jrvinen, K., Nyberg, K. (Eds.), Information Security Technology for Applications, Lecture Notes in Computer Science, vol. 7127. Springer, Berlin, Heidelberg, pp. 223–238.

Douceur, J.R., 2002. The sybil attack. In: Revised Papers from the First International Workshop on Peer-to-Peer Systems. Springer-Verlag, London, UK, pp. 251–260.

Fall, K., 2003. A delay-tolerant network architecture for challenged internets. In: Proc. Conference on Applications, Technologies, Architectures, and Protocols for Computer Communications: SIGCOMM '03. ACM, Karlsruhe, Germany, pp. 27–34.

Feldman, A.J., Zeller, W.P., Freedman, M.J., Felten, E.W., 2010. SPORC: group collaboration using untrusted cloud resources. In: Proc. 9th USENIX Conference on Operating Systems Design and Implementation. USENIX Association, Berkeley, CA, USA, pp. 337–350.

Fernandes, D.A., Soares, L.F., Gomes, J.A.V., Freire, M.M., Inácio, P.R., 2014. Security issues in cloud environments: a survey. Int. J. Inf. Secur. 13 (2), 113–170. ISSN 1615-5262.

Fernando, N., Loke, S.W., Rahayu, W., 2013. Mobile cloud computing: a survey. Futur. Gener. Comput. Syst. 29 (1), 84–106. ISSN 0167739X.

Giurgiu, I., Riva, O., Juric, D., Krivulev, I., Alonso, G., 2009. Calling the cloud: enabling mobile phones as interfaces to cloud applications. In: Proc. ACM/IFIP/USENIX 10th International Conference on Middleware. Springer-Verlag, Urbana, IL, USA, pp. 83–102.

Grobauer, B., Walloschek, T., Stocker, E., 2011. Understanding cloud computing vulnerabilities. IEEE Secur. Priv. 9 (2), 50–57. ISSN 1540-7993.

Guha, R.K., Furqan, Z., Muhammad, S., 2007. Discovering man-in-the-middle attacks in authentication protocols. In: Military Communications Conference, MILCOM'07. IEEE, pp. 1–7.

Helgason, O.R., Yavuz, E.A., Kouyoumdjieva, S.T., Pajevic, L., Karlsson, G., 2010. A mobile peer-to-peer system for opportunistic content-centric networking. In: Proc. 2nd SIGCOMM Workshop on Networking, Systems, and Applications on Mobile Handhelds. ACM, New Delhi, India, pp. 21–26.

Hobel, H., Heurix, J., Anjomshoaa, A., Weippl, E., 2013. Towards security-enhanced and privacy-preserving mashup compositions. In: Janczewski, L., Wolfe, H., Shenoi, S. (Eds.), Security and Privacy Protection in Information Processing Systems, IFIP Advances in Information and Communication Technology, vol. 405. Springer, Berlin, Heidelberg, pp. 286–299.

Hongbing, C., Chunming, R., Kai, H., Weihong, W., Yanyan, L., 2015. Secure big data storage and sharing scheme for cloud tenants. IEEE Commun. China 12 (6), 106–115. ISSN 1673-5447.

Hossmann, T., Spyropoulos, T., Legendre, F., 2010. Know thy neighbor: towards optimal mapping of contacts to social graphs for DTN routing. In: Proc. 29th Conference on Information Communications, INFOCOM. IEEE Press, San Diego, CA, USA, pp. 866–874.

Huang, D., Zhou, Z., Xu, L., Xing, T., Zhong, Y., 2011. Secure data processing framework for mobile cloud computing. In: IEEE Conference on Computer Communications Workshops, pp. 614–618.

Huerta-Canepa, G., Lee, D., 2010. A virtual cloud computing provider for mobile devices. In: Proc. 1st Workshop on Mobile Cloud Computing; Services: Social Networks and Beyond. ACM, San Francisco, CA, pp. 61–65.

Hung, S.H., Shih, C.S., Shieh, J.P., Lee, C.P., Huang, Y.H., 2012. Executing mobile applications on the cloud: framework and issues. Comput. Math. Appl. 63 (2), 573–587. ISSN 0898-1221.

Jasti, A., Shah, P., Nagaraj, R., Pendse, R., 2010. Security in multi-tenancy cloud. In: IEEE International Carnahan Conference on Security Technology (ICCST). IEEE, pp. 35–41.

Knockel, J.R.J., 2012. Protecting free and open communications on the Internet against man-in-the-middle attacks on third-party software: We're FOCI'd.

Karamshuk, D., Boldrini, C., Conti, M., Passarella, A., 2011. Human mobility models for opportunistic networks. IEEE Commun. Mag. 49 (12), 157–165. ISSN 0163-6804.

Karim, L., Mahmoud, Q., 2013. A hybrid mobility model based on social, cultural and language diversity. In: Proc. 9th International Conference on Collaborative Computing: Networking, Applications and Worksharing (Collaboratecom). IEEE, pp. 197–204.

Khan, A., Othman, M., Madani, S., Khan, S., 2014. A survey of mobile cloud computing application models. IEEE Commun. Surv. Tutorials 16 (1), 393–413.

Kieyzun, A., Guo, P.J., Jayaraman, K., Ernst, M.D., 2009. Automatic creation of SQL injection and cross-site scripting attacks. In: Proc. 31st International Conference on Software Engineering. IEEE Computer Society, Washington, DC, USA, pp. 199–209.

Kim, T., Peinado, M., Ruiz, G.M., 2012. Stealthmen: system-level protection against cache-based side channel attacks in the cloud. In: Proc. 21st USENIX Conference on Security Symposium: Security '12. USENIX Association, Berkeley, CA, USA, pp. 189–204.

Klein, A., Mannweiler, C., Schneider, J., Schotten, H.D., 2010. Access schemes for mobile cloud computing. In: Proc. 11th International Conference on Mobile Data Management (MDM). IEEE, Washington, DC, USA, pp. 387–392.

Krauß, C., Fusenig, V., 2013. Using trusted platform modules for location assurance in cloud networking. In: Lopez, J., Huang, X., Sandhu, R. (Eds.), Network and System Security, Lecture Notes in Computer Science, vol. 7873. Springer, Berlin, Heidelberg, pp. 109–121.

Lakkakorpi, J., Pitkänen, M., Ott, J., 2010. Adaptive routing in mobile opportunistic networks. In: Proc. 13th International Conference on Modeling, Analysis, and Simulation of Wireless and Mobile Systems. ACM, Bodrum, Turkey, pp. 101–109.

Lei, L., Zhong, Z., Zheng, K., Chen, J., Meng, H., 2013. Challenges on wireless heterogeneous networks for mobile cloud computing. IEEE Wirel. Commun. 20 (3), 34–44. ISSN 1536–1284.

Li, J., Liu, Z., Chen, X., Xhafa, F., Tan, X., Wong, D.S., 2015a. L-ENCDB: a lightweight framework for privacy-preserving data queries in cloud computing. IEEE Trans. Cloud Comput. 79, 18–26.

Li, J., Tan, X., Chen, X., Wong, D., Xhafa, F., 2015b. OPOR: enabling proof of retrievability in cloud computing with resource-constrained devices. IEEE Trans. Cloud Comput. 3 (2), 195–205.

Lombardi, F., Pietro, R.D., 2011. Secure virtualization for cloud computing. J. Netw. Comput. Appl. 34 (4), 1113–1122. ISSN 1084-8045.

Mannweiler, C., Klein, A., Schneider, J., Schotten, H., 2009. Exploiting user and network context for intelligent radio network access. In: Proc. International Conference on Ultra Modern Telecommunications Workshops, pp. 1–6.

Marchal, S., Jiang, X., State, R., Engel, T., 2014. A big data architecture for large scale security monitoring. In: 2014 IEEE International Congress on Big Data (BigData Congress), pp. 56–63.

McMorran, A., Rudd, S., Shand, C., Simmins, J., McCollough, N., Stewart, E., 2014. Data integration challenges for standards-compliant mobile applications. In: Proc. T D Conference and Exposition, IEEE PES, pp. 1–5.

Meng, T., Wang, Q., Wolter, K., 2015. Model-based quantitative security analysis of mobile offloading systems under timing attacks. In: Gribaudo, M., Manini, D., Remke, A. (Eds.), Analytical and Stochastic Modelling Techniques and Applications, Lecture Notes in Computer Science, vol. 9081. Springer International Publishing, pp. 143–157.

Michael, K., Miller, K., 2013. Big data: new opportunities and new challenges. IEEE Comput. 46 (6), 22–24. ISSN 0018-9162.

Minhas, S.S., Sampaio, P., Mehandjiev, N., 2012. A framework for the evaluation of Mashup tools. In: Proc. 9th International Conference on Services Computing (SCC). IEEE, pp. 431–438.

Mishra, D., Kumar, V., Mukhopadhyay, S., 2013. A pairing-free identity based authentication framework for cloud computing. In: Lopez, J., Huang, X., Sandhu, R. (Eds.), Network and System Security, Lecture Notes in Computer Science, vol. 7873. Springer, Berlin, Heidelberg, pp. 721–727.

Mohammed, N., Chen, R., Fung, B.C., Yu, P.S., 2011. Differentially private data release for data mining. In: Proc. 17th SIGKDD International Conference on Knowledge Discovery and Data Mining. ACM, San Diego, CA, USA, pp. 493–501.

Mont, M., Pearson, S., Bramhall, P., 2003. Towards accountable management of identity and privacy: sticky policies and enforceable tracing services. In: Proc. 14th International Workshop on Database and Expert Systems Applications, pp. 377–382.

Moreira, W., Mendes, P., 2013. Social-aware opportunistic routing: the new trend. In: Woungang, I., Dhurandher, S.K., Anpalagan, A., Vasilakos, A.V. (Eds.), Routing in Opportunistic Networks. Springer, New York, pp. 27–68.

Moreira, W., Mendes, P., 2015a. Dynamics of social-aware pervasive networks. In: Proc. IEEE PERCOM Workshop (PerMoby), St. Louis, USA, pp. 463–468.

Moreira, W., Mendes, P., 2015b. Impact of human behavior on social opportunistic forwarding. Ad Hoc Netw. 25, 293–302. ISSN 15708705.

Nguyen, A.D., Senac, P., Ramiro, V., 2011. How mobility increases mobile cloud computing processing capacity. In: proc. 1st International Symposium on Network Cloud Computing and Applications (NCCA). IEEE, pp. 50–55.

Ohlman, B., Eriksson, A., Rembarz, R., 2009. What networking of information can do for cloud computing. In: The 8th IEEE International Workshops on Enabling Technologies: Infrastructures for Collaborative Enterprises, pp. 78–83.

Ordean, M., Giurgiu, M., 2010. Implementation of a security layer for the SSL/TLS protocol. In: Proc. 9th International Symposium on Electronics and Telecommunications (ISETC), pp. 209–212.

Park, I.S., Lee, Y.D., Jeong, J., 2013. Improved identity management protocol for secure mobile cloud computing. In: Proc. 46th Hawaii International Conference on System Sciences (HICSS), pp. 4958–4965.

Pelusi, L., Passarella, A., Conti, M., 2006. Opportunistic networking: data forwarding in disconnected mobile ad hoc networks. IEEE Commun. Mag. 44 (11), 134–141. ISSN 0163-6804.

Peng, T., Leckie, C., Ramamohanarao, K., 2007. Survey of network-based defense mechanisms countering the dos and ddos problems. ACM Comput. Surv. 39 (1), 1–42. ISSN 0360-0300.

Qi, X., Zong, M., 2012. An overview of privacy preserving data mining. Procedia Environ. Sci. 12, Part B, 1341–1347. ISSN 1878-0296.

Ravi, N., Scott, J., Han, L., Iftode, L., 2008. Context-aware battery management for mobile phones. In: Proc. IEEE PERCOM '08. IEEE Computer Society, Washington, DC, USA, pp. 224–233.

Rosado, D.G., Gómez, R., Mellado, D., Fernández-Medina, E., 2012. Security analysis in the migration to cloud environments. Future Internet 4 (2), 469–487. ISSN 1999-5903.

Sagiroglu, S., Sinanc, D., 2013. Big data: a review. In: The International Conference on Collaboration Technologies and Systems, pp. 42–47.

Sakka, M., Defude, B., Tellez, J., 2010. Document provenance in the cloud: constraints and challenges. In: Aagesen, F., Knapskog, S. (Eds.), Networked Services and Applications—Engineering, Control and Management, Lecture Notes in Computer Science, vol. 6164. Springer, Berlin, Heidelberg, pp. 107–117.

Sanaei, Z., Abolfazli, S., Gani, A., Buyya, R., 2014. Heterogeneity in mobile cloud computing: taxonomy and open challenges. IEEE Commun. Surv. Tutorials 16 (1), 369–392. ISSN 1553-877X.

Saripalli, P., Walters, B., 2010. QUIRC: a quantitative impact and risk assessment framework for cloud security. In: Proc. 3rd International Conference on Cloud Computing. IEEE, Florida, USA, pp. 280–288.

Satyanarayanan, M., Bahl, P., Caceres, R., Davies, N., 2009. The case for vm-based cloudlets in mobile computing. IEEE Pers. Commun. 8 (4), 14–23. ISSN 1536-1268.

Scekic, O., Truong, H.L., Dustdar, S., 2013. Incentives and rewarding in social computing. Commun. ACM 56 (6), 72–82. ISSN 0001-0782.

Sedayao, J., Su, S., Ma, X., Jiang, M., Miao, K., 2009. A simple technique for securing data at rest stored in a computing cloud. In: Jaatun, M., Zhao, G., Rong, C. (Eds.), Cloud Computing, Lecture Notes in Computer Science, vol. 5931. Springer, Berlin, Heidelberg, pp. 553–558.

Shikfa, A., Onen, M., Molva, R., 2010. Bootstrapping security associations in opportunistic networks. In: Proc. IEEE PERCOM Workshops. IEEE, Mannheim, Germany, pp. 147–152.

Stuedi, P., Mohomed, I., Terry, D., 2010. Wherestore: location-based data storage for mobile devices interacting with the cloud. In: Proc. 1st Workshop on Mobile Cloud Computing and Services: Social Networks and Beyond. ACM, San Francisco, CA, pp. 1–8.

Subashini, S., Kavitha, V., 2011. Review: a survey on security issues in service delivery models of cloud computing. J. Netw. Comput. Appl. 34 (1), 1–11. ISSN 1084-8045.

Szefer, J., Keller, E., Lee, R.B., Rexford, J., 2011. Eliminating the hypervisor attack surface for a more secure cloud. In: Proc. 18th Conference on Computer and Communications Security, CCS '11. ACM, New York, USA, pp. 401–412.

Tartakovsky, A., Rozovskii, B., Blazek, R., Kim, H., 2006. A novel approach to detection of intrusions in computer networks via adaptive sequential and batch-sequential change-point detection methods. Trans. Sig. Proc. 54 (9), 3372–3382. ISSN 1053-587X.

Van Cleeff, A., Pieters, W., Wieringa, R.J., 2009. Security implications of virtualization: a literature study. In: Proc. International Conference on Computational Science and Engineering—Volume 03. IEEE Computer Society, Washington, DC, USA, pp. 353–358.

Van Dijk, M., Juels, A., Oprea, A., Rivest, R.L., Stefanov, E., Triandopoulos, N., 2012. Hourglass schemes: how to prove that cloud files are encrypted. In: Proc. Conference on Computer and Communications Security. ACM, New York, USA, pp. 265–280.

Varadarajan, V., Kooburat, T., Farley, B., Ristenpart, T., Swift, M.M., 2012. Resource-freeing attacks: improve your cloud performance (at your neighbor's expense). In: Proc. Conference on Computer and Communications Security. ACM, New York, USA, pp. 281–292.

Verbelen, T., Simoens, P., De Turck, F., Dhoedt, B., 2012. Cloudlets: bringing the cloud to the mobile user. In: Proc. 3rd Workshop on Mobile Cloud Computing and Services. ACM, Low Wood Bay, Lake District, UK, pp. 29–36.

Verykios, V.S., Bertino, E., Fovino, I.N., Provenza, L.P., Saygin, Y., Theodoridis, Y., 2004. State-of-the-art in privacy preserving data mining. SIGMOD Rec. 33 (1), 50–57. ISSN 0163-5808.

Wang, H., 2010. Privacy-preserving data sharing in cloud computing. J. Comput. Sci. Technol. 25 (3), 401–414. ISSN 1000-9000.

Wang, Q., Wang, C., Li, J., Ren, K., Lou, W., 2009. Enabling public verifiability and data dynamics for storage security in cloud computing. In: Proc. 14th European Conference on Research in Computer Security, ESORICS'09. Springer-Verlag, Heidelberg, pp. 355–370.

Wang, Y., Chuah, M.C., Chen, Y., 2012. Incentive driven information sharing in delay tolerant mobile networks. In: IEEE GLOBECOM. IEEE, Anaheim, CA, USA, pp. 5279–5284.

Xiao, S., Gong, W., 2010. Mobility can help: protect user identity with dynamic credential. In: Proc. 11th International Conference on Mobile Data Management (MDM). IEEE, Washington, DC, USA, pp. 378–380.

Xu, L., Jiang, C., Wang, J., Yuan, J., Ren, Y., 2014. Information security in big data: privacy and data mining. IEEE Access 2, 1149–1176. ISSN 2169-3536.

Yi, P., Dai, Z., Zhong, Y., Zhang, S., 2005. Resisting flooding attacks in ad hoc networks. In: Proc. International Conference on Information Technology: Coding and Computing (ITCC'05)—Volume 02. IEEE Computer Society, Washington, DC, USA, pp. 657–662.

Za, S., D'Atri, E., Resca, A., 2011. Single sign-on in cloud computing scenarios: a research proposal. In: D'Atri, A., Ferrara, M., George, J.F., Spagnoletti, P. (Eds.), Information Technology and Innovation Trends in Organizations. Physica-Verlag HD, pp. 45–52.

Zakhary, S., Radenkovic, M., Benslimane, A., 2014. Efficient location privacy-aware forwarding in opportunistic mobile networks. IEEE Trans. Veh. Technol. 63 (2), 893–906. ISSN 0018-9545.

Zhang, X., Schiffman, J., Gibbs, S., Kunjithapatham, A., Jeong, S., 2009. Securing elastic applications on mobile devices for cloud computing. In: Proc. Workshop on Cloud Computing Security. ACM, Chicago, IL, USA, pp. 127–134.

Zhou, Z., Huang, D., 2013. Efficient and secure data storage operations for mobile cloud computing. In: Proc. 8th International Conference on Net. and Ser. Management, Las Vegas, Nevada, pp. 37–45.

Zhu, Y., Ma, D., Huang, D., Hu, C., 2013. Enabling secure location-based services in mobile cloud computing. In: Proc. 2nd SIGCOMM Workshop on Mobile Cloud Computing. ACM, Hong Kong, China, pp. 27–32.

Zissis, D., Lekkas, D., 2012. Addressing cloud computing security issues. Future Gener. Comput. Syst. 28 (3), 583–592. ISSN 0167-739X.

Glossary

6LowPANs A standard for using IPv6 over low power personal area networks.

Acceleration Rate of change of velocity by basic physics definition.

Accelerometer A sensor/instrument that calculates velocity of any moving/vibrating body activity monitoring any activity using any system. Throughout the book, it can refer to the monitoring of the movement of the body using different sensors.

Actuator Device that receives data and subsequently acts properly on a mechanism or system.

Ad hoc solution Solution designed for a specific task and it is nongeneralizable or adaptable to other purposes.

Adverse reaction Negative reaction of the patient to the applied drug or therapy.

Altruism The act of favoring others instead of oneself.

Ambient assisted living A system of devices (sensors) integrated into the house-/apartment where the patient lives. Such a system permits the monitoring of his/her health and general condition in his/her known environment.

Angular velocities By classical physics, it is rate of change of angular position.

Anonymizing data Removing elements of data that permit to disclose the identity of the patient.

AP A wireless access point.

AP design A client-device communication design in which the device implements a wireless AP to which the client connects; another form of the technology is when the device itself connects to another AP from which it can get access to the Internet and even extend it further to the client via its own AP.

Apache Hadoop platform An open-source software to efficiently support reliable, scalable, and distributed computing. It supports simple programming models for the distributed processing of large data collections across clusters of computers.

Assisted living Relates to offering a patient independence, dignity, and care.

Asynchronous distributed systems A distributed system is asynchronous if there is no bound on message transmission delay, clock drift, or the time to execute a processing step.

Availability Measures the capability of an entity to provide data when information about a region is needed.

Average mistake rate Represents the number of mistakes that a failure detector makes in a unit time, ie, the rate at which a failure detector makes mistakes.

Big Data A collection of data, characterized by high volume, variety, velocity, and veracity (4Vs).

Body area network A network of wearable/implanted inside body devices that usually are sensors sensing different attributes.

Business logic Set of events and actions that models the functionalities that a system provides.

CAN provider (CANP) A business entity, actually being an enhanced NP (the additional CAN functions are performed by network nodes and therefore they are executed by the Network Provider). It offers content-aware network services to the upper layer entities.

Cardiovascular Related to the heart and the blood vessels.

Challenged environments Challenged environments refer to sparse or rural areas that lack proper infrastructure, and in high density, urban areas with restricted/-full of interference access networks where connectivity cannot be assumed to be available.

City image Technique that provides a visual summary of the city dynamics based on the movements of people.

Clinical trial Formal experiment that tests a therapy method, with a clear goal and well-defined possible outcomes. Typically two balanced groups of patients are compared: one receiving the tested treatment and another one receiving no treatment (placebo) or a different one. The statistical evaluation of the results has a solid scientific base.

Cloud Cloud refers to a hosted service over the Internet users can employ the pay-as-you-go scheme, anytime and anywhere with the help of an available Internet connection.

Cloud computing Generic model for delivery of hosted services over the Internet.

Cohort A group of patients participating in a trial.

Coordinated multi-point (CoMP) A core technology in the LTE-A suite.

Compression The process of reformatting data to reduce its size.

Computational constraints Restrictions and limitations on computing that may be the capability of a device, or power or any other.

Computational intelligence Refers to the study of designing intelligent decision making devices regarding any specific problem.

Content aware network (CAN) An emerging concept but is currently not sufficiently developed neither in terms of architectural complete specifications nor in real deployment.

Content consumer (CC) or end-user (U) An entity (human plus a terminal or a process), which establishes a contract with a service provider for service/content delivery. These users are the final target recipients of services.

Content delivery networks Networks that specialize in hosting content (usually from client organizations) for delivery to clients.

Content provider (CP) Gathers/creates, maintains, and distributes digital information. The CP owns/operates network hosts that are the source of downloadable content but it might not own any networking infrastructure to deliver the content.

Context awareness A property of mobile devices that is defined complementarily to location awareness. Whereas location may determine how certain processes in a device operate, context may be applied more flexibly to mobile users, especially with users of smart phones.

Cooperation Occurs when an individual devotes an effort that implies a cost in some collective activity expecting some benefit.

Currency Represents the temporal utility of the data, from the moment it is created until it becomes worthless.

Cyber-physical(-social) system A system containing computer infrastructure and physical elements, essentially dependent on the static properties and dynamical behavior of the physical part.

D2D The device-to-device mode of wireless communication under LTE-A.

Data aggregation Summarizing huge bulk of data.

Data fusion Process that integrates multiple data to provide one concrete, near to accurate output.

Data fusion algorithms Algorithms that perform data fusion.

Decoupling The separation of previously linked systems so that they may operate independently.

Defibrillator (implantable cardioverter-defibrillator—ICD) An active device, implantable inside the body, capable of correcting most life-threatening cardiac arrhythmias. The ICD is the first-line treatment and prophylactic therapy for patients at risk for sudden cardiac death.

Design pattern General reusable solution to a commonly occurring problem within a given context in software design.

Detection time The time that elapses from the moment that process q crashes until the failure detector at p starts suspecting q permanently.

DHO The data handover proposed interface is based on the abstract concept of the data and the local memory. By inserting the DHO function in the application code, the user claims a remote resource and then when available, maps that resource in local memory.

Double blind trial A trial, where neither the patients nor the doctors know who is receiving the tested treatment and who belongs to the compared group.

Delay Tolerant Networks (DTNs) The wireless data hubs discussed in this chapter can be considered as static nodes in a DTN where client terminals are intermediaries in deliveries messages between them.

E-health Healthcare practice supported electronically using ICT.

Ecosystem Platform defined by more components that can interact together.

Effectiveness Therapeutic effect in the clinical practice.

Efficacy Therapeutic effect in laboratory.

Efficiency Ratio of the therapeutic effect to price.

Electronic health record Systematized collection of patient electronically stored health information in a digital format. These records can be shared across different healthcare settings, under the condition of interoperable data formats and communication protocols.

ELMP The exclusive locks with mobile processes algorithm extends the capabilities of the Naimi-Trehel algorithm with the scalability property.

Energy data management and mining system A set of tools able to efficiently store, manage, and analyze different kinds of energy data.

Energy harvesting Powering an implanted device with the energy of the body (warmth, movements). In this way, exchanging the battery with an operation is no more necessary.

Engineering a product Transforming a laboratory model into a product that can be industrially produced and easily used.

Entity Component that interact with a system.

Evidence-based medicine Medical practice based on the use of evidence from well-designed and conducted research.

Evolved node B (eNB) A common name to refer to the local wireless APs in LTE-A.

Framework Abstraction in which software providing generic functionality can be selectively changed by an additional user-written code, thus providing application-specific software.

Frequency division multiple access (FDMA) An alternative to TDMA, in which multiple channels are separated by frequency.

Gamification The use of game features as incentive mechanisms to perform tasks.

GRAS The grid reality and simulation API is a socket-based library that provides a complete API to implement distributed applications on top of heterogeneous platforms, either in simulation mode or in realistic environment.

GroupConnect A technology behind the wireless data hubs discussed in this chapter, based on virtualization of wireless resources of a group.

Gyroscope A sensor that measure angular rotational velocity.

Hadoop An open-source software framework for scalable, distributed computing of large data sets.

Heartbeat strategy An implementation of a failure detector where every process q periodically sends an "I am alive" message to the processes in charge of detecting its failure. If a process p does not receive such a message from q after the expiration of a timeout, it adds q to its list of suspected processes.

Home-Box (HB) A business entity, which can be partially managed by the SP, the NP, and the end-user. The HBs can cooperate with SPs in order to distribute multimedia services (eg, IPTV) in different modes (eg, P2P).

Home hospital Hospital keeping the (major part of the) health record of a patient.

Hops The number of steps needed for a look-up to be successful.

Human in the loop A human that is a vital element of the system. His/her skills are important to the function of the system. In the case of medicine and medical devices it may be a doctor, a nurse, a patient who has to install the device, but also an operator of the phone network.

Inductive transfer of energy Contactless transfer of power to an implanted device from outside the body via electromagnetic induction. In this way, exchanging the battery with an operation is no longer necessary.

Inertial measurement unit An instrument composed of multiple sensors used to measure orientation of a body normally used in aircrafts, spacecrafts, finding any body movement disorders, etc.

Information and communication technology Is a parent terminology that includes any communication device integrated with any domain to attain specific results.

Information system Organized system for the collection, organization, storage, and communication of information.

Internet of things A network of physical objects (things) embedded with electronics, software, sensors, and network connectivity, which enables these objects to collect and exchange data. The number of elements can be large. As moving in the environment only with wireless connection, they will have special requirements for computing capacity and power. Or, the network of physical objects or "things" embedded with electronics, software, sensors, and network connectivity, which enables these objects to collect and exchange data.

Interoperability Capability of devices and systems to connect, interact, and exchange data.

Joining an overlay The process of becoming a new member in the overlay network.

Key performing indicator (KPI) A type of performance measurement computed over time to compactly represent the performance of the object under analysis.

Latency Time interval between the stimulation and response.

Leaving an overlay The process in which a node becomes unavailable in the overlay network.

Lock manager The lock manager negotiates remotely the lock with other managers according ELMP and RW-LMP algorithms. It interacts locally with the resource manager.

Look-up The process for searching for a certain resource.

Long-term evolution advanced (LTE-A) A 4G+ wireless technology which is expected to replace the current LTE by 2020.

M2M The machine-to-machine mode of communication under LTE-A.

Mainstream technology Technology belonging to various categories subjected to large usage.

MANET Mobile ad hoc network.

MapReduce A model for processing large data sets using parallel algorithms to explore clusters of servers.

Maui A platform of mobile clouds, specifically balancing the load between client device and the cloud.

Middleware Computer software that provides services to software applications beyond those available from the operating system.

MIPv6 Mobile IP version 6, a wireless version of IPv6.

Mobile cloud Mobile cloud refers to the service that combines mobile computing and cloud-based services. In this service, either a mobile application runs on the remote cloud server or a cloud-based application runs inside a user's mobile device.

Mobile P2P The concept of peer nodes collaborating over wireless channels.

Model ensembling Ensemble methods use multiple learning algorithms in order to achieve better predictive performance than could be obtained from any of the constituent single algorithms.

Multimorbidity Having more than one disease.

Multiple-input multiple output (MIMO) A method for multi-channel wireless communication using antenna arrays.

Multisensor data fusion Refers to fusing data collected from multiple types of sensors.

Near field communication (NFC) Another type of a P2P WiFi technology, in line with Bluetooth and WiFi Direct.

Netflix A large commercial provider of video-on-demand for streaming over the Internet.

Network provider (NP) Traditionally offers connectivity providing reachability between network domains/hosts. NPs own and administer IP connectivity infrastructures. They interact with each other for the purpose of expanding the geographical span of the offered connectivity services.

Observational study A clinical study where the group of patients (cohort) is observed and the investigator does not influence the assignment of subjects into a treated group versus a control group.

Open standard A standard defined by a community, publicly discussed, and fully disclosed. Enables the configuration of heterogeneous systems built with devices and computer systems delivered by various producers.

Open system A system based on open standards. Makes it easy to enter by a smaller startup company.

Opportunistic networks Opportunistic networks are an advanced form of mobile ad hoc networks (MANETs) that supports delay-tolerant networking. In an opportunistic network, users' data are forwarded with the help of other users within the network. There is no end-to-end communication path available in such networks. Users' social interactions and collaborations greatly influence the overall message delivery performance.

Orientation sensing States sensing or knowing velocity, acceleration, and gravitational forces with respect of outer world or any specific point.

P2P design Also referred to as the P2P solution, is when client uses traditional WiFi stack for the Internet and P2P WiFi stack to communicate with the device, the main advantage of this technology is that the two communication channels can operate in parallel with only minor interference.

Pacemaker An active device which uses electrical impulses, delivered by electrodes contracting the heart muscles, to regulate the beating of the heart. The primary purpose of a pacemaker is to maintain an adequate heart rate, either because the heart's natural pacemaker is not fast enough, or because there is a block in the heart's electrical conduction system.

Paradigm Distinct set of concepts or thought patterns, including theories, research methods, postulates, and standards for what constitutes legitimate contributions to a field.

Peer-to-peer (P2P) A distributed application architecture that partitions tasks or workloads between peers. Peers are equally privileged, equipotent participants in the application. They are said to form a peer-to-peer network of nodes.

Personal weather station (PWS) A private device including different weather measuring instruments/sensors. Each sensor is able to measure a kind of meteorological data such as temperature, relative humidity, pressure, rain fall, and wind speed and direction.

Point-to-point connection Dedicated connection link between two systems or processes that directly connects two systems.

Postmarket surveillance Activities used to monitor the safety and effectiveness of medical devices once they are on the market. These activities are designed to generate information to quickly identify poorly performing devices and other safety problems, and accurately characterize real-world device performance and clinical outcomes.

Precision Defines how well certain data reflects the current state of a specific phenomenon or locality.

Premarket approval Process of scientific and regulatory review to evaluate the safety and effectiveness of Class III medical devices. Class III devices are those that support or sustain human life, are of substantial importance in preventing impairment of human health, or which present a potential, unreasonable risk of illness or injury.

Premarket notification Submission made to the authority to demonstrate that the device to be marketed is at least as safe and effective, that is, substantially equivalent, to a legally marketed device that is not subject to premarket approval.

Probability of correctness Denotes the probability that a given data are correct.

Progressive download A technique that enables content to be displayed by a web browser during download.

Proprietary standard A standard defined by a company, not publicly disclosed, or not with enough detail. Makes it difficult to connect devices or computer systems of other producers.

Protocols Sets of rules for correct communication of data across communication channels and networks.

PSN Participatory sensor network relying on the idea of participatory sensing, which can be defined as a system that supports a distributed process of gathering data about personal daily experiences and various aspects of the city. Such a process requires the active participation of people using portable devices to voluntarily share contextual information and/or make their sensed data available, ie, the users manually determine how, when, what, and where to share the sensed data. Thus, through PSNs we can monitor different conditions of cities, as well as the collective behavior of people connected to the Internet in (almost) real time.

QoC Any information that describes the quality of the inferred context, which is consistent with our needs.

QoD Any information about the technical properties and capabilities of a given device.

QoS Any information that describes how well a service operates.

Query accuracy probability The probability that the failure detector output is correct at a random time.

Randomized clinical trial A clinical trial where the patients' population (cohort) is randomly divided into the tested and the compared group.

Read manager Handles the entry and the exit from the critical section by successive read processes. It is present in the RW-LMP algorithm solely.

Real-time system System that must process information and produce a response within a specified time, else risk severe consequences, including failure.

Requirements specification Description of a software system to be developed, laying out functional and nonfunctional requirements.

Resolution Denotes the granularity of the information.

Resource manager Forwards user's requests to the lock manager, achieves the mapping of the resource in local memory as soon as the lock is granted, and allows uploading the resource to a possible Next.

RW-LMP The read write locks with mobile processes algorithm. This algorithm makes a second extension to the ELMP algorithm, by allowing both read and write requests to share the queuing (Predecessor, Next) list.

Scalability Capability of a system to handle a growing amount of work, or its potential to be enlarged in order to accommodate that growth.

Scalable video encoding A type of video encoding based on a low quality base layer to which high-quality layers can be added.

Scenario The set of interactions that take part in accomplishing a task.

Selfishness The act of benefiting oneself instead of another.

Sensing layer Represents data, with its attributes, from a particular data source, for example, a particular PSN.

Sensor Device that detects events and sends data about the events to a system.

Service environment (SE) In charge of assuring the composition of services and the delivery of content to end-users throughout the network.

Service provider (SP) Delivers services and aggregates content from multiple CPs for offering/delivering it to CCs. SPs may not necessarily own a transport infrastructure, but rely on the connectivity services offered by Network Providers (NPs).

SLA/SLS Important concepts helping to control the business actors and/or layers commitments in satisfying requests of other entities. SLA/SLS definitions and usage especially in a dynamic environment by using negotiation protocols is still an open issue. SLA/SLS have been insufficiently studied and used in a P2P context.

Small cell (SC) Another name for Evolved Node B (eNB), MicroCells (MCs), femtocells, and others.

Smart textiles Textiles, into which devices (sensors) are woven. They permit an unobtrusive long-term measurement, with good positioning of the sensors.

Spurious correlation An apparent correlation between two processes that are, indeed, not related (correlation does not imply causation).

Synchronous distributed systems A distributed system is synchronous if there are bounds on transmission delay, clock drift, and processing time and these bounds are known.

Telemedicine (using telecommunications for medical purposes) Consulting a doctor via a phone, automatic sending sensor values, etc. Allows for frequent contact or data exchange with lower costs and effort.

Time division multiple access (TDMA) A wireless access technology based on separating channels into consecutive time slots.

Transcoding Process of converting from one encoding format to another.

Trust-worthiness Similar to the probability of correctness, but it is used to classify the quality of the user that generated the data.

Tweets Personal updates in texts up to 140 characters shared on Twitter.

Unreliable failure detector An oracle that provides information about process failures. An FD is unreliable in the sense that it can make mistakes, that is, it may not suspect a crashed process or suspect a correct one.

Up-to-dateness Describes the age of the data.

User environment (UE) In direct relation with the end-user knowing his characteristics and interacting with the Service Environment for an efficient service provision.

User profile A collection of data that characterizes both the user and his operational context, thus both static and dynamic information.

User/service interface A graphical user interface of the services accessible to the end-user.

Validity A set of rules that can be used to validate the generated data, according to previous knowledge about the type of the data and the behavioral pattern of the users.

Velocity In terms of classical physics, it is the rate of change of position with respect to some point of reference.

Video encoding The specific data format resulting from the compression process.

Video frames The still images that compose a video sequence.

Video streaming The technique that enables video data to be presented by the media player as the data arrives at the client, thus not having to fully download the file prior to display.

Virtual content-aware network (VCAN) Support for a layer, offering enhanced support for packet payload inspection, and processing and caching in the network equipment. It improves data delivery via classifying and controlling messages in terms of content, application, and individual subscribers, assure QoS and improve network security via content-based monitoring and filtering.

Virtual wireless user (VWU) An abstract construct used to describe a pool of wireless resources within a group of devices.

WiFi Direct Is the most widespread P2P WiFi technology today, supported natively by Android OS since version 4.1, but also by many devices outside of Android OS.

Wireless body area sensor fusion Refers to the fusion of data collected by sensors in a WBAN.

Wireless body area sensor network Refers to the network of tiny sensors deployed on/in a body to sense different attributes as per need.

Wireless data hub (WDH) The core technology discussed in this chapter, based on isolated wireless hubs spread within a limited area like a university campus.

WLAN design A rival technology to the AP design and P2P design, where communication between the device and the client is done via a nearby AP.

YouTube A video sharing, web-based service that allows users to upload, download and share videos using MPEG4/H.264 formats.

Acronyms

3G	3rd generation
4G	4th generation
6LoWPAN	IPv6 over low power wireless personal area networks
AAL	ambient assisted living
AES	advanced encryption standard
AM	adaptation manager
ANN	artificial neural network
ANOVA	analysis of variance
AP	access point
API	application programming interface
ARIMA	autoregressive integrated moving average
ARM	association rule mining
ASHRAE	American Society of Heating, Refrigerating, and Air-Conditioning Engineers
BAN	body area network
BANBody	area network
BAS	building automation system
BEMS	building energy management system
BT	boosting tree
C/S	client/server
CA	certification authority
CAN	content addressable network
CART	classification and regression tree
CATI	content-aware transport information
CC	cloud computing
CCDF	complementary cumulative distribution function
CDF	cumulative distribution function
CDFA	complementary data fusion algorithm
CDN	content delivery networks or content distribution network (depending on context of use)
CFD	computational fluid dynamics
CI	computational intelligence
CIF	common intermediate format
CM	connection manager
CoAP	constrained application protocol
CoMP	coordinated multipoint
CP	content provider
CPU	central processing unit
CRAC	computer room air conditioning
CRM	customer relationship management

CSP	cloud service provider
CSU	cloud service user
D2D	device-to-device
DASH	dynamic adaptive streaming over HTTP
DBMS	database management system
DC	data center
DCT	discrete cosine transform
DDS	data-distribution service for real-time systems
DEA	data envelopment analysis
DFA	data fusion algorithm
DHO	data handover
DHT	distributed hash tables
DM	data mining
DoS	denial of service
DSM	demand-side management
DTN	delay tolerant networks
E	entity
EBM	evidence based medicine
ECG	electrocardiogram or electrocardiography (recording of the electrical activity of the heart)
ECI	energy consumption index
EEG	electroencephalography (recording of the electrical activity of the brain)
EHR	electronic health record
ELMP	exclusive locks with mobile processes
eNB	evolved node B
EPFL	Ecole Polytechnique Fdrale de Lausanne (Switzerland)
ESA	energy signature analysis
ETS	efficient, transparent, and secure
EU	depending on context, if means end-user or European Union
EUI	energy use intensity
EUT	end-user terminal
FAP	flooding attack prevention
FD	failure detector
FDA	(US) Food and Drug Administration
FDD	fault detection and diagnosis
FDMA	frequency division multiple access
FFD	full function devices
GA	genetic algorithm
GDPR	(European) General Data Protection Regulation
GESD	generalized extreme studentized deviate
GFS	Google file system
GIGO	garbage in, garbage out
GOP	group of pictures

GPS	Global Positioning System
GSM	Global System for Mobile
HAIL	high-availability and integrity layer
HB	home-box
HDFS	Hadoop distributed file system
HIPAA	(US) Health Insurance Portability and Accountability Act
HTML	Hyper Text Markup Language
HTTP	Hyper Text Transfer Protocol
HTTPS	Hyper Text Transfer Protocol Secure
HVAC	heating ventilation and air conditioning
I/O	input/output
IaaS	infrastructure as a service
IBM	International Business Machines
ICD	implantable cardioverter defibrillator
ICT	information and communication technology
IEA	International Energy Agency
IMU	inertial measurement unit
IoT	Internet of Things
IoT6	researching IPv6 potential for the Internet of Things
IP	Internet protocol
IPTV	Internet protocol television
IPv6	Internet protocol version 6
IT	information technology
JDL	Joint Directors of Laboratories
JSON	JavaScript object notation
KDFA	Kalman data fusion algorithm
kNN	k-nearest neighbors
KPI	key performance indicator
LAN	local area network
LCA	life cycle assessment
LGOCV	leave-group-out cross validation
LowPANs	low power personal area networks
LTE-A	long-term evolution advanced
LTFF	long-term traffic flow forecasting
LTLF	long-term load forecasting
M&V	measurement and verification
M2M	machine-to-machine communication
MANET	mobile ad hoc network
MARKS	middleware adaptability for resource discovery, knowledge usability and self-healing
MARS	multivariate adaptive regression splines
MIMO	multiple-input multiple output
MIPv6	mobile IP version 6
MITM	man in the middle

MLP	multilayer perceptron
MLR	multiple linear regression
MM	message manager
MPEG	moving picture experts group
MQTT	MQ telemetry transport
ms	millisecond
MTLF	medium-term load forecasting
MV	medium voltage
NFC	near field communication
NoSQL	not only structured query language
NP	network provider
NSA	(US) National Security Agency
oBIX	open building information xchange
OLS	ordinary least square
OS	operating system
P/S	publish/subscribe
P2P	peer-to-peer
P2PBA	peer-to-peer bee algorithm
P2P network	peer-to-peer network
P4 medicine	predictive, personalized, preventive, participative medicine
PA	query accuracy probability
PAA	piecewise aggregate approximation
PaaS	platform as a service
PC	principal component
PDA	personal digital assistant
PDU	power distribution unit
PII	personal-identifiable-information
PKI	public key infrastructure
PnP	IPSec plug and play IP security
PoI	point of interest
PSNs	participatory sensor networks
PSU	power supply unit
PWS	personal weather stations
QCIF	quarter common intermediate format
QoC	quality of context
QoD	quality of device
QoE	quality of experience
QoS	quality of service
QUIRC	quantitative risk and impact assessment framework
R	average mistake rate
RAF	resource-freeing attack
RCT	randomized control trial
RD	rate distortion
RED	random early detection

RES	renewable energy source
resp.	respective
RESTful	representational state transfer
RF	random forests
RFD	reduced function devices
RTCP	RTP control protocol
RTP	real time transport protocol
RTSP	real time streaming protocol
RW-LMP	read-write locks with mobile processes
SaaS	software as a service
SAFTM	self-adaptive fault-tolerant middleware
SARIMA	seasonal autoregressive integrated moving average
SAX	symbolic aggregate approximation
SC	small cell
SDP	session description protocol
SFA	stochastic frontier analysis
SIP	session initiation protocol
SMC	self-managed cell
SP	service provider
SR	service registry
SSC	self-service cloud
SSL	secure socket layer
STB	set-top box
STEMI	ST elevation myocardial infarction (heart attack, visible on the ECG as the elevation of the ST segment)
STFF	short-term traffic flow forecasting
STLF	short-term load forecasting
SVC	scalable video coding
SVE	scalable video encoding
SVM	support vector machines
SvPDD	self-validated public data distribution
SVR	support vector regression
T	translator
TCP	transmission control protocol
TD	detection time
TDMA	time division multiple access
TLS	transport layer security
TOR	the onion router
TPA	third party auditor
TPM	trusted platform module
UC	use case
UDP	user datagram protocol
UGC	user-generated content
UMM	unstructured multisource multicast

UP	user profile
UPS	uninterruptible power supply
URI	uniform resource identifier
URL	uniform resource locator
UTC	universal time coordinated
VANETs	vehicular networks
VMMs	virtual machine monitors
VMs	virtual machines
VoD	video on demand
VWU	virtual wireless user
WBASF	wireless body area sensor fusion
WBASN	wireless body area network
WDH	wireless data hub
WPAN	wireless personal area network
WS	web service or window size (depending on context of use)
WSN	wireless sensor network

Index

Note: Page numbers followed by *f* indicate figures and *t* indicate tables.

Printed in the United States
By Bookmasters